VOICES OF PRINCIPLE AND PROMISE

Voices of Principle and Promise features are first-hand accounts that bring real-life voices to the forefront—voices of teachers, other educators, and students. You'll hear how education has affected their lives in light of the discussion of the chapter.

VOICES OF PRINCIPLE AND PROMISE

Mary Antin, a Russian Immigrant in School

Mary Antin, a poet and novelist, was born in Polotsk, Russia, in 1881 to a Jewish family. Victims of several pogroms—violent attacks on Jewish communities—her family emigrated to America, settling in Boston in 1894. There, Mary attended Boston's Girls' Latin School and wrote poetry. The following piece describes the difficulties she faced in school.

It is not worth while to refer to voluminous school statistics to see just how many "green" pupils entered school last September, not knowing the days of the week in English, who next February will be declaiming patriotic verses in honor of George Washington and Abraham Lincoln, with a foreign accent, indeed, but with plenty of enthusiasm. It is enough to know that this hundred-fold miracle is common to the schools in every part of the United States where immigrants are received (Antin, 1912, p. 206).

Mary Antin had had some education in Russia and had a proud and supportive family to cheer her on. She also had caring teachers, who worked overtime to ease her way:

> Whenever the teachers did anything special to help me over my private difficulties, my gratitude went out to them, silently. It meant so much to me that they halted the lesson to give me a lift, that I needs must love them for it. Dear Miss Carrol, of the second grade, would be amazed to hear what small things I remember, all because I was so impressed at the time with her readiness and sweetness in taking notice of my difficulties. Says Miss Carrol, looking straight at me: "If Johnnie has three marbles, and Charlie has twice as many, how many marbles has Charlie?" I raise my hand for permission

www.

Questions to Consider

1. In what ways did Mary Antin feel different?
2. How did she cope with these differences?
3. What were some factors in her background, her family life, her new environment, and within herself that helped her succeed as a student and a future citizen?

APPLYING WHAT YOU'VE LEARNED

End-of-chapter *Applying What You've Learned* activities engage individuals, small groups, and whole classes in tasks that will bring to life the concepts and issues presented in the text and associated primary source readings. At least one of these activities is marked with an icon that directs you to the book's website, where you can find the material to complete the activity.

APPLYING WHAT YOU'VE LEARNED

1. www. The textbook website includes resources from the Library of Congress on Indian boarding schools. Read some of the memoirs and letters home written by boarding school children and record your thoughts in response to their experiences. Find information on an Indian-run reservation school of today to see how attitudes toward native culture and curriculum have changed.
2. Watch a video depicting the traumatic experience of school desegregation in the American South and, later, in the North. Suggestions are *Common Ground;* the PBS documentary, "Eyes on the Prize" or a segment of its video series on the history of education, *School* (see Websites to Explore). Record your impressions.
3. Find out what percentage of school principals, curriculum directors, and school superintendents in your area are women.
4. Assemblyman Benjamin Franklin argued for English as the language of instruction in the schools of colonial Pennsylvania. Two hundred and fifty years later, the question of "English-only" classrooms is still argued. Research current laws in your state regarding the education of English language learner (ELL) children. Do these children receive bilingual education, which provides first-language instruction in the content areas—math, science, social studies—while they learn English, so they do not fall behind their English-speaking age-mates? Or are they "immersed" in English-only classrooms? Search sources such as *Education Week* and newspaper articles to find arguments for both positions.

TEACHING ON PRINCIPLE AND PROMISE
The Foundations of Education

Mary-Lou Breitborde
Salem State College

Louise Boyle Swiniarski
Salem State College

Houghton Mifflin Company Boston New York

To my family. Thanks for your strength and your love.
—M. L. B.

To Joe, for your encouragement, your empathy and your belief in me.
—L. B. S.

Publisher: Patricia Coryell
Senior Sponsoring Editor: Sue Pulvermacher-Alt
Senior Development Editor: Lisa Mafrici
Development Editor: Julia Casson
Senior Project Editor: Jane Lee
Editorial Assistant: Kristen Truncellito
Senior Art and Design Coordinator: Jill Haber
Senior Photo Editor: Jennifer Meyer Dare
Senior Composition Buyer: Sarah Ambrose
Manufacturing Coordinator: Chuck Dutton
Marketing Manager: Laura McGinn
Marketing Assistant: Erin Lane

Cover Image: Front cover (from left to right): © Getty Images; © Stockbyte; © Getty Images; © Amos Morgan/Getty Images; © Ryan McVay/Getty Images. Spine: © Ryan McVay/Getty Images

ACKNOWLEDGMENTS:
Chapter Opener Photos Chapter 1: © Michael J. Doolittle/The Image Works; Chapter 2: © Jim West/The Image Works; Chapter 3: © Elizabeth Crews; Chapter 4: © Elizabeth Crews; Chapter 5: © Elizabeth Crews; Chapter 6: © Michael Zide; Chapter 7: © Bettmann/CORBIS; Chapter 8: Photo by H. Knadle, courtesy of Cheyenne Settler's Heritage Society; Chapter 9: © Tony Freeman/PhotoEdit; Chapter 10: © David Young-Wolff/PhotoEdit; Chapter 11: © Michael Newman/PhotoEdit; Chapter 12: © Sean Cayton/The Image Works

All other photo credits appear with the photo captions. Text credits appear on page 548 at the end of the book.

Printed in the U.S.A.

Library of Congress Control Number: 2003109859

ISBN: 0-618-25147-2

123456789-DOW-09 08 07 06 05

CONTENTS

PREFACE

This book examines the philosophical, historical, and sociological roots of basic questions and answers in the field of education and, specifically, in American public education.

Who Should Read This Book and Why?

This book is written for you—an aspiring or growing teacher taking a Foundations in Education course. As an educator, you will be entrusted with the education of generations of Americans. We believe that you need to consider deep questions about purpose and effect in education—What are schools for? What do they actually accomplish? How do they serve society?—Addressing these critical questions will help you to understand the public school system, to evaluate its successes and problems, and to make sound decisions about educational practice. It is our hope that this book will help you develop a set of beliefs about what constitutes a good education so that you can advocate for your own practice and for the children in your charge. We want to support you in articulating those beliefs to colleagues, administrators, parents, and to the children themselves. After reading this book, we hope you feel confident about how to translate those beliefs into your work.

Writing this book helped us to frame what we see as the difficult problems and choices facing schools today and to examine the roots of those problems and choices. It gave us a vehicle for articulating our own principles and describing what we believe are the ongoing promises and possibilities for public education.

American education is at a crossroads. Changes happening in our schools are also happening in education worldwide. Schools are social institutions in every nation of the world, in what many call the global village. Events in one corner of the globe affect schools in another. This book examines the international as well as the national factors that influence educational change at home and abroad. We agree with the United Nations Commission on the Rights of the Child that all children have the right to an education that will help them to lead healthy and productive lives. Toward that end, we hope to help you chart a professional course that will help you to develop challenging curriculum, to implement principled teaching practices, and to provide safe school environments in which all children can learn.

What's Different About This Book?

Our goal in this text is to present a variety of perspectives on five essential questions: Who is the educated person? What is worth knowing? What is learning? What is good teaching? What is the role of school in society? We address these questions as past and present seminal educational thinkers have addressed them in order to provide new perspectives on the nature, purpose, and outcomes of education, and to encourage you to come to your own conclusions.

We include two chapters on philosophy of education, because we believe that it is important to understand the underpinnings of philosophy before tackling specific issues and concerns of public education. A central and wonderful feature of life in the United States is the rich diversity of its people. Our two history chapters integrate the educational experience of the many groups that make up the American portrait. Unique to this text is a final chapter that champions the idea of unity within diversity by focusing on the goal of creating community in the public schools.

In this text you will find that primary sources are abundant in the excerpts used throughout the narrative, in the Directly from the Source feature in each chapter, and in the end-of-chapter Critical Readings section. We cannot emphasize enough the importance of reading the central works in education from their primary source. This is a means to obtain basic knowledge, to obtain the foundations of education, and to read the original words of people important to the history and development of education. Each chapter poses questions for you to think about as you reflect on what you have learned, and each chapter contains activities designed to help you apply what you have learned to your observations and experiences outside of the college classroom. The book's companion website offers connections to activities in the text as well as complete primary source documents for pieces that are excerpted in the text. The website icon www identifies excerpts that can be found in full on the website.

What Is Our Point of View?

Our views on education are grounded in the belief that the context and goals of education are ultimately social but affect individuals in ways we cannot predict. Life in schools is embedded with values, politics, and ideologies—sometimes written down and sometimes tacitly informing the curriculum, instructional approaches, and relationships inside their walls. What students make of their school experience, however, is unpredictable and idiosyncratic, based on the ability of all humans to construct their own meaning of things. We believe that the natural gap between teaching and learning is a good thing. It allows for the emergence of a greater "knowledge" or "truth" through a mutually respectful exchange of experiences and perspectives. This is not to say that schools should be without clear goals. We unequivocally assert that these goals should focus on improving life for all people.

We come to these beliefs from years of experience as classroom teachers and professors of education. Our beliefs are influenced by the times in which we have lived and worked, the values conveyed to us by our families of origin, the content of our cultural backgrounds, and our own schooling. We recognize that we have been influenced as well by our own students, from the preschoolers to the elementary and high school students to the undergraduate and graduate students we have taught.

Organization of the Book

The chapters of this text are framed within five essential questions, with each chapter addressing one of these essential questions:

- Who is the educated person?

- What is worth knowing?
- What is learning?
- What is good teaching?
- What is the role of school in society?

Chapter 1, "The Educated Person," examines multiple perspectives on what it means to be educated. **Chapter 2,** "Philosophical Roots of Education," offers the basics of the philosophical roots of education, and **Chapter 3,** "Philosophies of Education," delves into the specific philosophies of education. **Chapter 4,** "Decisions about Curriculum," and **Chapter 5,** "Thinking About Learning," move forward from this philosophical base and look at how educators make decisions about school curricula based on their assumptions about how children learn.

Chapter 6, "The Nature of the Teaching Profession," looks at the nature of the teaching profession and presents some models and images of schoolteachers of yesterday and today. **Chapter 7,** "School and Society in American History: The First Hundred Years," and **Chapter 8,** "Movement and Change in School and Society: The Second Hundred Years," provide a thorough discussion of the history of American education. These chapters examine many populations including men and women, Native Americans, immigrants, African Americans, Latinos, and Asians. Woven chronologically into the history of American education, we see the experiences of each of these groups in U.S. public education and also include the voices of prominent individuals.

Chapter 9, "The Problem of Equity," is dedicated to the problem of equity in education. While the United States can be proud of its tradition of free and available schooling, there have been vast differences in the quantity and quality of education based on socioeconomic status, race, gender, and geography. This chapter describes the effect of this inequality on those groups who may have been underserved and considers multiple perspectives on the issues.

Chapter 10, "Social and Moral Education," looks at the moral and social education of children. What social lessons do children learn in school? How do schools prepare them for citizenship in adult society? What values are they exposed to in schools? **Chapter 11,** "Educational Reform," provides insight into educational reform and several successful models of education reform. **Chapter 12,** "Creating Educational Communities," extends the discussion on educational reform by offering a rationale and suggestions for creating educational communities. Within each chapter we pose multiple points of view on the issues under discussion, provide you with abundant primary sources, and offer examples of how educational theory and research apply to teaching practices and classroom life.

Features of the Book

We developed several features to enhance your experience with this text. The features provide in-depth views of complex topics in education. They allow you to hear the voices of those close to the heart of education. We ask you to use these features as opportunities for critical thinking and analysis, as well as aids for study.

- Each chapter begins with an **advance organizer** to provide you with an overview of the topics in the chapter. This is followed by an **opening vignette** that provides a real life picture of the central ideas in the chapter.

- **Primary Source Excerpts.** As you read each chapter, you'll find many excerpts from important contemporary and historical documents in education.
- **Directly from the Source** features offer a primary source document that allows readers to take a closer look at a topic that is central to the chapter discussion. You'll have the opportunity to think through issues and concepts with "A Closer Look at the Issues" questions at the end of the feature.
- **Voices of Principle and Promise** features are firsthand accounts that bring real-life voices to the forefront—voices of teachers, other educators, and students. You'll hear how education has affected their lives in light of the discussion of the chapter.
- **Summary.** Each chapter ends with a Summary, which captures the major points of discussion.
- End-of-chapter **Questions for Reflection** ask the reader to extend, apply, and synthesize the concepts and information in the chapter, and to develop their own questions as a result of the reading. These can be used as study guides for the chapter.
- **Applying What You Learned.** These activities engage individuals, small groups, and whole classes in tasks that will bring to life the concepts and issues presented in the text and associated primary source readings; for example, staged debates, focused classroom observations, and position papers. These activities provide opportunities to apply what you have learned and to develop as a future teacher. At least one of these activities is marked with an icon that directs you to the book's website. www. To complete the activity, you'll need to view the visual presentation on the website.
- **Websites to Explore.** Here you will find online sources related to chapter content as well as organizations carrying out related work.
- **Critical Readings.** Each chapter concludes with a section of readings from primary sources. These documents represent seminal works in education. "A Closer Look at the Issues" questions encourage serious thought about these readings.
- The **References** section contains sources cited in the chapter. We have carefully chosen sources that represent important work by theorists and researchers in education; we hope you will refer to these readings as you prepare your class work and keep them close at hand as you continue your education. We urge you to look for the readings in educational journals and libraries. Many are sources you will want as you build your professional library.

Ancillaries

The accompanying **Instructor's Resource Manual** provides outlines for each chapter, sample syllabi to help build your course, additional assignments, lecture ideas, small group and in-class activities, and test questions.

The Companion Website offers important opportunities to read the words of the philosophers and education writers cited in the excerpts throughout the text.

Rather than leave you only with our analysis of their ideas, we want to provide you with primary sources so that you can evaluate the writer's point of view and its impact. In addition, the website offers questions and activities which instructors and readers can use to extend and apply the primary readings, and it presents a vehicle for online discussion and collaborative work. The book's website includes resources for the application activities included in the end-of-chapter section called "Applying What You Learned," as well as the complete primary documents referred to as excerpts in the chapter. You'll also find suggestions for in-class and follow-up activities related to those documents.

Houghton Mifflin Video Cases are available online and organized by topic. Each "case" is a three- to five-minute module consisting of video and audio files presenting actual classroom scenarios that depict the complex problems and opportunities teachers face every day. The video and audio clips are accompanied by "artifacts" to provide background information and allow pre-service teachers to experience true classroom dilemmas in their multiple dimensions.

To access the password-protected Primary Source Documents and Video Cases on the Companion Website, use the following username and password:

username: primary sources
password: sources

Acknowledgments

In the preparation of a book such as this one, which covers so much ground in the field of education, many contribute to the effort. We appreciate the various helpful suggestions made by reviewers of the first and second drafts of this manuscript. These reviewers include:

Mary Frances Agnello, University of Texas, San Antonio
Leslie Bolt, James Madison University
Theresa J. Canada, Western Connecticut State University
Ronnie Casella, Central Connecticut University
David M. Dees, Gannon University
Martin Eigenberger, University of Wisconsin, Parkside
Robert V. Farrell, Florida International University
Michael Hayes, Washington State University
Sharon F. Hobbs, Montana State University, Billings
Justen Infinito, Ball State University
William R. Martin, George Mason University
Thad Maxwell, Nazareth College
Martha Whitaker, Utah State University

We would also like to acknowledge the help of editors and designers at Houghton Mifflin for their guidance. We thank Sue Pulvermacher-Alt, Senior Sponsoring Editor; Lisa Mafrici, Senior Development Editor; Julia Casson, Development Editor; Jane Lee, Senior Project Editor; Peggy Flanagan, copyeditor; Ann Schroeder, photo researcher; and Henry Rachlin, book designer. Very special thanks to Ann Greenberger, our development editor, who worked with us closely throughout the project. We are grateful for her excellent suggestions, her thorough reading and research, and her consummate patience.

Together, we would like to thank Salem State College for its support, especially the faculty and staff of the School of Education and the Graduate School, and Tracy Drysdale, our helpful and cheerful graduate assistant. Many people contributed their recollections of their own schooling and teaching and are exemplars of educational principle and promise. Among them were Roda Amaria, Diana Beck, Linda Connell, Claire Crane, Beverly Gerson, Mary Ann Grassia, Donna Graham Harris, Xavier Romano, and Nikki Miller.

In addition to her colleagues and students at Salem State College, Dr. Breitborde would like to thank the faculty and staff at Knox College in Galesburg, Illinois, who offered time, space, and resources in the fall of 2003 when she served as a Visiting Professor and carried out some of the research for this book. Special thanks to Lawrence Breitborde, Sandy and Phoebe, for sharing their home and office and the former teachers and alumnae/alumni of one-room schoolhouses in Illinois who contributed their memories and their time. Finally, she would like to thank her family and friends for their continued support and Bob Scheier, for his writing help and his cheerleading.

Dr. Swiniarski owes a great debt to her many students for their input into this book as well as her friends and colleagues for their sustaining interest. She wishes to give special acknowledgment to her husband, Joseph Swiniarski, for the continued encouragement and assistance he gave throughout the writing of this book.

We invite you to journey through these pages to explore the foundations of public education in America—its history, its philosophy, its societal place and social effects, the organization of its subject matter content, and its approaches to instruction. As we will argue throughout the book, American public schools have been a great experiment from their birth, established with the promise that they will prepare everyone—regardless of background—as members of a just, effective, and thriving democracy and as citizens of the world.

The Educated Person

1

I believe that education is the fundamental method of social progress and reform. . . . I believe that the community's duty to education is, therefore, its paramount moral duty. By law and punishment, by social agitation and discussion, society can regulate and form itself in a more or less haphazard and chance way. But through education society can formulate its own purposes, can organize its own means and resources, and thus shape itself with definiteness and economy in the direction in which it wishes to move. John Dewey, "My Pedagogic Creed," 1897.

In 1983 the former Soviet Union and the United States were engaged in a cold war, stumbling toward an accord aimed at preventing nuclear holocaust, but deeply entrenched in two very different systems of beliefs about human motivation, the nature of freedom, and the role of government. During this time, one of us traveled to the former Soviet Union. A researcher from a Soviet academic institute, whose longtime area of study was U.S. politics and policies, guided the tour. "What I will never understand," he wondered aloud to us, "is how your country can have allowed so much dissension, so many differences of opinion, and have survived. How can that be?" (Breitborde, 1983).

The answer to his question lies at the heart of the great experiment that is American democracy. It lies in the assumption that human beings are capable of, and responsible for, making decisions about their own lives and their common well-being, no matter how diverse their backgrounds, their experiences, or their beliefs. But the quality of these decisions—and the ultimate success of the democracy—depends on their being made by people knowledgeable about important issues and educated to think about them in clear and critical ways. The democratic system of government in the United States involves endless discussions, debates, trials, and tribulations concerning laws and policies that will affect all of us. It rests on the hope that individual citizens will consider how their actions and personal advantages affect their neighbors and look beyond their own special interests to the welfare of the nation and the world. John Dewey said that "a democracy is more than a form of government; it is primarily a mode of associated living, of conjoint communicated experience."

Thus, defining a system of education that will support and improve the democracy must be part of the debate. As citizens of a democracy we have both the right and the responsibility to decide how our schools will educate new generations of democratic citizens—what information, skills, and dispositions young people will need to become full and effective participants in the democracy, and how to ensure that all young people have the opportunity to gain them. Public schools can, as Dewey says in the opening quotation, formulate our societal purposes and steer our nation in the direction we choose. But in a nation as culturally, regionally, economically, and religiously diverse as the United States, debate about public schools is active and often contentious. To help frame this debate, we offer a set of fundamental questions that will be revisited throughout this book. These questions have no right and wrong answers, but are designed to stimulate discussion and help you think about educational issues as your understanding of them grows. As we address the many issues about the content, form, and results of public education, we invite you to think through your own beliefs about these essential questions:

- Who is the educated person?
- What is worth knowing?
- What is learning?
- What is good teaching?
- What is the role of school in society?

American Ideals and the Value of Education

In setting down the rationale for America's independence from England, Thomas Jefferson borrowed from John Locke the principle that the God-given ability to reason entitled human beings to determine how we were to be governed, by

Thomas Jefferson argued that the "publick happiness" and the preservation of the rights and liberties of all citizens would be ensured by educating everyone for at least three years, longer for those endowed with "genius and virtue," at the "common expence of all."
Source: © Bettmann/CORBIS

whom, and to what extent (Locke, 1692). However, Jefferson predicted that the inborn power to reason would not be sufficient to ensure the success of the American experiment in democracy. That success would depend on a well-informed and broad-minded voting public; in short, decisions should be made by "educated persons" who understood what laws, policies, and structures were necessary for their own and others' welfare. In "A Bill for the More General Diffusion of Knowledge," Jefferson wrote,

> . . . whence it becomes expedient for promoting the publick happiness that those persons, whom nature hath endowed with genius and virtue, should be rendered by liberal education worthy to receive, and able to guard the sacred deposit of the rights and liberties of their fellow citizens, and that they should be called to that charge without regard to wealth, birth or other accidental condition or circumstance; but the indigence of the greater number disabling them from so educating, at their own expence, those of their children whom nature hath fitly formed and disposed to become useful instruments for the public, it is better that such should be sought for and educated at the common expence of all, than that the happiness of all should be confided to the weak or wicked (in Boyd et al., 1950).

Free Education Is a State Decision

Although his bill, introduced to the Virginia legislature in 1779, did not pass, it demonstrated Jefferson's commitment to a system of free public education for those children, excluding slaves, "whom nature hath fitly formed and disposed" to ensure the rights and responsibilities of their fellow citizens. Despite his belief that a working democracy would depend on an educated public, the Constitution—which Jefferson helped create to maintain the principles contained in the Declaration of Independence—made no mention of education. It included no mandate to the federal government to establish schools. Instead, the Tenth Amendment provided that "[t]he powers not delegated to the United States by the Constitution, nor prohibited by it to the states, are reserved to the states respectively, or to the people." To protect the people against an oppressive central government such as the one they had just won independence from, the Constitution limited federal intervention in matters the people could be expected to handle themselves.

While Jefferson would work tirelessly to establish a system of schooling in his native state of Virginia, with varying degrees of success and some failure, it was not until the middle of the nineteenth century, under the leadership of Horace Mann, Massachusetts's first Secretary of Education, the first U.S. Commissioner of Education, and the father of the movement to establish free public "common" schools, that the nation as a whole would presume that "the powers not delegated" to the federal government should include free and accessible schools funded out of the public tax coffers. But it was left to local and state governments to establish schools, develop curricula, and set the requirements for graduation. One result of this local and state control is that there have been great differences in the quantity and quality of education offered to particular groups in particular locations at particular times in the history of the nation. The education of women, children of color, children with disabilities, and the rural and urban poor has been compromised by prejudices embodied in the laws and practices of many states and localities. In recent years the federal Department of Education, originally established in 1867 to help the states carry out their responsibility for public education, along with Congress and the federal courts, have taken an increasingly active role in attempting to provide more access and a more equitable and standardized education for all children.

The Debate About Education Begins

From the beginning of our nation, then, the matter of whether to establish schools at all, never mind what should go on inside them or what should be the result, has been a subject of debate and controversy. Perhaps no other American institution is so subject to public scrutiny and criticism, so hotly argued about, as our public schools. Throughout our nation's history, and continuing today, serious questions have been asked about what should be taught in schools, how to teach it, how best to measure whether students learn it, even who should decide. Currently, federal and state governments advocate granting **vouchers** to parents so they can choose which schools their children should attend. They fund **charter schools,** special public schools that are established by groups of parents and/or educators, funded with local monies, but exempt from many existing rules and regulations. The "charter" is granted based on an approach to education that is different from what the regular public schools offer. These schools compete with the regular local public schools. Federal and state governments mandate annual testing to hold schools accountable for the specific knowledge and skills expected of the educated person.

Old assumptions about the place of religious belief and the relationship between church and state have been questioned and requestioned. Although the characteristics of the educated person once included being "God-fearing," a belief reflected in Bible-based reading texts and mandated morning recitations of the Lord's Prayer, reforms of the 1960s abolished school prayer. Thirty years later, the

What should be taught in schools? Students in class saying the Pledge of Allegiance.
Source: © Bob Daemmrich/The ImageWorks

federal court revisited the question and decided to allow voluntary prayer meetings and meditations on school grounds.

In the 1970s and 1980s most curriculum theorists and policymakers believed that the process of learning was more important than any particular set of facts. This stance has since been reversed by the current insistence that students master a standard stock of knowledge. And the question of whether there should be "standards" at all is continually debated: Should curriculum and instruction be the same for everyone, or should they be tailored to the special learning needs and backgrounds of children of different neighborhoods and geographical areas? In this pluralistic nation, what adaptations, if any, should be made for children of different cultures and native languages? Should children who have not yet learned English be taught in their native language so as not to fall behind in their knowledge of mathematics, science, and social studies? Should children learn the history of their local communities? Or is it more important to emphasize the history of the whole nation, where all American children reside?

In the 150 or more years of national public schooling, there have been ongoing arguments about whether more or less is better: Are larger schools with a greater number and variety of resources better than smaller schools with their potential for more personal relationships between students and staff? Is it better to acquaint students with a broad range of information about many subjects or to have them study a few topics in greater depth?

Our cultural diversity has sparked arguments about school policies and procedures that govern everything from the school calendar to what students are allowed to wear. Communities with large populations of students of particular religions may schedule the calendar to include their holidays—for example, Good Friday and Passover. The fact that many Puerto Rican and Dominican children return to their island homelands with their families to observe the several weeks of their Christmas season may cause significant disruption; some communities allow for the absence by requiring alternative work assignments, while in others the lengthy absence has severe consequences. In France, the principle of secularism—separation of church and state—has resulted in a law that forbids public school students to wear head coverings and other conspicuous articles of clothing that have religious significance—for example, Islamic head scarves, Jewish skullcaps, and large Christian crosses. In America, where the separation of church and state is similarly written into the Constitution, no such laws governing religious apparel exist.

And the ultimate social purpose of public schooling is debated as well: Should schools turn out graduates who are equipped for jobs in the current economy and life in contemporary times? Should we teach them computer skills? Media literacy? How to write a check, keep a budget, fill out an application, have "safe sex"? Or should we prepare students more generally to face an always uncertain future, equipping them with the skills of planning, decision making, collaboration, critical reading and writing, and a stock of knowledge that transcends particular times and places? Should we lead students to understand the roots of pervasive problems that need new solutions by new generations? Should the curriculum address the causes and consequences of the racism that sickens society, the inequities that divide the haves from the have-nots, the violence that threatens us personally and globally, the environmental drain on essential resources? Do schools serve the public interest by responding to today's needs, or is it their responsibility to lead initiatives for social change?

Voices of Principle and Promise in Education

In a pluralistic nation bent on governing itself in ways that protect individual freedoms and preserve a common welfare, debates about the purpose, practice, and outcome of public education are to be expected and welcomed. Having long ago decided to forego the authority, and perhaps security, of a monarchy, a state-established church, or even an official national language, Americans took on the responsibility of creating and re-creating governing policies based only on the rule of law embodied in the Constitution. Everyone has a right to a vote and an opinion on the issues that affect their lives, including public education. As history changes, as our population changes, we try hard to hold on to the basic principles that underlie our nation while at the same time responding to changing needs and realities. We learn about the mistakes we've made as a nation, mistakes that have limited the educational and economic prospects of individuals and groups and that have sometimes cost lives. And we argue about how to correct those mistakes. At different times in the history of American public education, different voices predominate. We have called those voices conservative and liberal, traditional and progressive, idealistic and realistic, individualist and collectivist, teacher-centered, curriculum-centered, child-centered. Amid the arguments, however, are factors that make American education distinguishable from schooling in other places. These factors inhere in the basic ideology that grounds the nation and the particular characteristics of our people. We are, as the Soviet tour guide observed, a nation of dissenters somehow committed to a common cause. In the wake of the September 11 (2001) attack on America, two bumper stickers emerged: One says, "United We Stand"; the other, "Divided We Stand." The sentiments on these two bumper stickers are not mutually exclusive.

The Essential Questions in Education

Throughout this book, we frame debate and dissension concerning the nature and value of education and the role of the schools around the five essential questions mentioned at the beginning of this chapter: Who is the educated person? What is worth knowing? What is learning? What is good teaching? What is the role of the school in society? The answers to these questions are not simple, nor are they absolute. Our definition of an educated person, for example, may depend on what we think an individual needs to know or be able to do in a particular period in history or a particular place on the earth. Definitions of what it means to be educated vary across cultures, with some valuing book learning and others skilled artisanship and still others the kind of wisdom that comes from deep reflection on life experience. As you read through this section, think about and write down your initial responses to each of the five essential questions and consider the factors that influenced your answers. Were they based on your own experiences? On your understanding of what's needed for twenty-first-century life? On a set of fundamental beliefs? Would your answers be different if you lived in different circumstances? What do you need to know in order to come to clearer and more satisfying conclusions? We suggest that after reading the other chapters in the book (where we address these five questions in much more depth) you respond to the questions again, and look not only at whether your answers have changed or been reinforced, but also at the information and ideas that you considered as you formulated them.

Who Is the Educated Person?

Is the educated person a well-rounded individual, or someone who knows a few things very well? Does she have well-developed "life skills" that allow her to function in the world or does she have a wealth of coherent and creative ideas—or some of both? Is the educated person familiar with a traditional stock of knowledge that includes classic literature, music, social and political theory, scientific principles, geography, and history? Is a person educated if he or she has a working knowledge of what it takes to survive and contribute to the American economy and society? Are these goals compatible? Is a person educated if he thinks clearly about issues but confines himself to thought—a Monday morning quarterback, or an armchair critic? Or, to be educated, must he do something with his ideas, take some action? Is the educated person necessarily an ethical person? Can you be educated and not be "good"?

Historic Ideas About the Educated Person Historically, conceptions about the educated person were restricted to particular kinds of school experiences for particular groups in society. The educated person was probably a man whose family background and income provided him with access to what was considered to be the finest schooling available. Women were not expected to aspire to becoming educated; in some cases, they were not expected even to learn to read or write. Others excluded from general assumptions about who might become educated were people of color—for example, African Americans, Native Americans, and Mexican Americans; nineteenth century immigrants from Ireland, China, and elsewhere; the working class and the poor; and people with disabilities—among them, the deaf and the blind. Since the mid-twentieth century, conceptions of the educated person have broadened. It is still true, however, that many people mark an educated person as someone who looks, speaks, and acts in ways that reflect the dominant social group, even though these characteristics may have little to do with the quality of his or her education or with notions of what an educated person knows and is able to do.

You will learn in Chapter 2 that Plato thought that having great knowledge meant also having great virtue; if you have discovered the truth of things, you have therein also discovered the highest good. Cardinal John Henry Newman, in his treatise on the value of a university education (1854, 1910), described the educated person as being well read and familiar with a wide range of literature, philosophy, and science. To Newman, such a person would be a great conversational companion, confident in society and curious about learning. In *The Idea of a University*, excerpted in this chapter, he says that the educated person is never bored. Thomas Jefferson also assumed that the educated person had a wide, or "liberal," knowledge of many things, as he himself had.

On the other hand, John Locke (1692) was far less concerned that the educated person had academic knowledge. He was more concerned that this person display good "breeding" and wisdom in conducting the everyday affairs of his life. Locke believed that a good education developed a person's morality along with the faculty of reason. The ability to get along with other people, participate in the life of a community, and have a good command over one's own affairs were characteristic of Locke's educated person.

Not content with the idea that the ability to get along with people marked the educated person, John Dewey (1915, 1933) insisted that the individual living in

Directly from the Source

Description of Thomas More *by Desiderius Erasmus*

Source: Life and Writings of Blessed Thomas More by T. E. Bridgett, 1913. London: Burns Oates & Washbourne. http://pw2.netcom.com/~rjs474/thomasmore/1519lett.html. Accessed March 6, 2004.

The following is taken from a letter from Desiderius Erasmus to Ulrich von Hutten in 1519, in which Erasmus describes his good friend Thomas More:

You ask me to paint you a full-length portrait of More as in a picture. Would that I could do it as perfectly as you eagerly desire it. At least I will try to give a sketch of the man, as well as from my long familiarity with him I have either observed or can now recall. . . . His countenance is in harmony with his character, being always expressive of an amiable joyousness, and even an incipient laughter, and, to speak candidly, it is better framed for gladness than for gravity and dignity, though without any approach to folly or buffoonery. The right shoulder is a little higher than the left, especially when he walks. This is not a defect of birth, but the result of habit, such as we often contract. In the rest of his person there is nothing to offend. His hands are the least refined part of his body.

He was from his boyhood always most careless about whatever concerned his body. His youthful beauty may be guessed from what still remains, though I knew him when he was not more than three-and-twenty. Even now he is not much over forty. He has good health, though not robust; able to endure all honourable toil, and subject to very few diseases. He seems to promise a long life, as his father still survives in a wonderfully green old age. . . .

He speaks with great clearness and perfect articulation, without rapidity or hesitation. He likes a simple dress, using neither silk nor purple nor gold chain, except when it may not be omitted. It is wonderful how negligent he is as regards all the ceremonious forms in which most men make politeness to consist. He does not require them from others, nor is he anxious to use them himself, at interviews or banquets, though he is not unacquainted with them when necessary. But he thinks it unmanly to spend much time in such trifles. Formerly he was most averse to the frequentation of the court, for he has a great hatred of constraint (tyrannis) and loves equality. Not without much trouble he was drawn into the court of Henry VIII, though nothing more gentle and modest than that prince can be desired. By nature More is chary of his liberty and of ease, yet, though he enjoys ease, no one is more alert or patient when duty requires it.

He seems born and framed for friendship, and is a most faithful and enduring friend. He is easy of access to all; but if he chances to get familiar with one

society be able to think critically about it, exhibiting a kind of "social intelligence." In modern times Nel Noddings (1992) defines this social intelligence as the ability to care, while Paulo Freire (1970) sees it as an understanding of the political and economic conditions that affect one's own life and one's own community.

To the "humanist" philosopher Desiderius Erasmus (1519), what marked an educated person was his or her moral character. Erasmus's description of his friend the author and statesman Sir Thomas More, excerpted in this chapter, pays homage to a man who is a "perfect friend" as well as an intellectual.

To the eighteenth-century philosopher Jean-Jacques Rousseau, further discussed in Chapter 2, the educated person was a self-reliant and independent-minded man, who understood the difference between needs and desires and learned from direct experience how to satisfy his needs. (Rousseau thought women's aspirations should be confined to supporting their husbands and children.) Rousseau's educated person had good judgment and common sense and a self-esteem borne of the knowledge that he could take care of himself and his family. This is Rousseau's description of Emile, his model student:

whose vices admit no correction, he manages to loosen and let go the intimacy rather than to break it off suddenly. When he finds any sincere and according to his heart, he so delights in their society and conversation as to place in it the principal charm of life. He abhors games of tennis, dice, cards, and the like, by which most gentlemen kill time. Though he is rather too negligent of his own interests, no one is more diligent in those of his friends. In a word, if you want a perfect model of friendship, you will find it in no one better than in More. In society he is so polite, so sweet-mannered, that no one is of so melancholy a disposition as not to be cheered by him, and there is no misfortune that he does not alleviate. Since his boyhood he has so delighted in merriment, that it seems to be part of his nature; yet he does not carry it to buffoonery, nor did he ever like biting pleasantries. When a youth he both wrote and acted some small comedies. If a retort is made against himself, even without ground, he likes it from the pleasure he finds in witty repartees. Hence he amused himself with composing epigrams when a young man, and enjoyed Lucian above all writers. Indeed, it was he who pushed me to write the "Praise of Folly," that is to say, he made a camel frisk.

In human affairs there is nothing from which he does not extract enjoyment, even from things that are most serious. If he converses with the learned and judicious, he delights in their talent; if with the ignorant and foolish, he enjoys their stupidity. He is not even offended by professional jesters. With a wonderful dexterity he accommodates himself to every disposition. As a rule, in talking with women, even with his own wife, he is full of jokes and banter. No one is less led by the opinions of the crowd, yet no one departs less from common sense. One of his great delights is to consider the forms, the habits, and the instincts of different kinds of animals. There is hardly a species of bird that he does not keep in his house, and rare animals such as monkeys, foxes, ferrets, weasels and the like. If he meets with anything foreign, or in any way remarkable, he eagerly buys it, so that his house is full of such things, and at every turn they attract the eye of visitors, and his own pleasure is renewed whenever he sees others pleased.

A Closer Look at the Issues

1. What personal characteristics or values does Erasmus infer from More's physical appearance? Do you agree that personal appearance and habits are indicative of an educated person?
2. Erasmus says about his friend Thomas More that "no one is less led by the opinions of the crowd," yet he says More is "a most faithful and enduring friend," able to get along with everyone. How can both character traits be true?
3. Based on his flattering portrait of his friend, how do you think Erasmus would define the "educated person"?

> [Emile's] ideas are limited but distinct. If he knows nothing by heart, he knows much by experience. If he reads less well in our books than does another child, he reads better in the book of nature. His mind is not in his tongue but in his head. He has less memory than judgment. He knows how to speak only one language, but he understands what he says. . . . He never follows a formula, does not give way before authority or example, and acts and speaks only as it suits him. . . . Emile has little knowledge, but what he has is truly his own. . . . Emile has a mind that is universal not by its learning but by its faculty to acquire learning; a mind that is open, intelligent, ready for everything. . . . It is enough for me that he knows how to find the "what's it good for?" in everything he does and the "why?" in everything he believes (1762, pp. 159, 207).

A Contemporary View Building on Rousseau's conception of the educated person, and extending it to women, the existentialist-feminist contemporary philosopher Maxine Greene (1982) believes that the hallmark of an educated person is the ability to be open to experience and to consider multiple points of view.

Greene's educated person is "wide awake" to life, open to many ways of thinking, willing to engage in dialogue, and a co-creator of culture. He or she searches for personal meaning in experience and for a shared "intersubjective agreement" that includes the rich and varied meanings that a diverse, democratic society offers. The educated person constructs himself or herself through open-minded learning and reflection, and shares with others in constructing the world. Greene's educated person uses the arts—literature, visual art, music—as vehicles for understanding the human experience, including the experiences of those whose lives are different.

> For us, education signifies an initiation into new ways of seeing, hearing, feeling, moving. It signifies the nurture of a special kind of reflectiveness and expressiveness, a reaching out for meanings, a learning to learn. . . . I hope you think about what happens to you when it becomes possible to abandon one-dimensional viewing, to look from many vantage points and, in doing so, construct meanings scarcely suspected before. . . . Our object . . . where young people are concerned, is to provide increasing numbers of opportunities for tapping into long unheard frequencies, for opening new perspectives on a world increasingly shared (Greene, 1999, pp. 7, 89).

For some educators, the characteristics of an educated person depend on the needs and conditions of the times. In the early twentieth century in the United States, for example, Booker T. Washington and W. E. B. Du Bois argued over what definition of the educated person was most helpful to the future of the black population. To Washington, educated African Americans had academic knowledge, but more importantly, they had learned a skill or trade that would make them economically valuable to both the black and the white society. Du Bois, on the other hand, argued that the definition of an educated African American was no different from the definition of an educated white American at the time, which included having acquired broad and deep information, excellent speaking and writing skills, and a critical mind.

In succeeding chapters, the central question, "Who is the educated person?" will be framed within traditional, modern, and evolving philosophies of education and changes in the historical conditions of public education in the United States. We will also use this question to analyze educators' various decisions about curriculum, instruction, and school organization. Next, let's turn to our second essential question, about what knowledge educated people possess.

What Is Worth Knowing?

The educated person knows something. Questions about what the educated person should know are questions about **curriculum,** the subject matter of education. For example, how important is it to know our roots in the important ideas and events of western civilization versus the ideas and events of the many other civilizations in the world? Should the content of the curriculum change as the population of children in America's schools changes? Should schools make time to teach keyboarding skills, conflict resolution, and health education? Should the curriculum include exposing children to a variety of career possibilities? What is the place of the arts in American schools? Is it important to know the difference between Michelangelo and Modigliani, or to be able to express oneself in the way these artists did? Or should schools encourage children to explore different media in order to express themselves in unique and personal ways?

As the world evolves and techniques for communication and research abound, the amount of available information expands and the need to set priorities increases. The simple fact is that there is far too much information to include in twelve or thirteen years of six-and-a-half-hour school days. The essential question for educators seems to be not, What should we include? but, What can we leave out? Here is an example from Dr. Breitborde's teaching career:

> In 1975, I had a job as a fifth grade teacher. I taught reading/language arts and social studies. I knew that the topic of study for fifth grade social studies was American history, but there were no specific guidelines for what to teach within that broad topic. So, drawing on my own memories of fifth grade, and on my own interests, I developed my own curriculum plan. I would start with Native Americans, a group that had not yet been regularly included in typical fifth grade social studies curricula, and a group that had successfully gained the attention of the American public in the heady political protests of the 1960s and early 1970s. I also decided to do a unit on African American history (called "black history" at the time) because I had had a college course in it and had done some work with an African American history museum. Since I was adding two new units of study to the 180-day school year, something had to go. I decided that would be the traditional unit on "the explorers." Although I could reel off dates and routes for the voyages of Ferdinand Magellan, Amerigo Vespucci, Ponce de Leon, Hernando de Soto, and the rest (I even knew that John Cabot was actually Giovanni Caboto), it seemed to me that this information was pretty useless. So, out went the explorers.
>
> Ten years later, in 1985, after I became a professor of education, I was working with a local school district on ways to make their social studies curriculum more meaningful to their multicultural student population. Immigrants from the Caribbean and from Central and South America had entered the community and its schools in great numbers, speaking Spanish, Portuguese, and Haitian Creole. As a specialist in multicultural education and teaching to diverse populations, I was called on to help them relate subject matter to the experiences and backgrounds of the newcomers. American history was still taught in the fifth grade. Among my suggestions: "Emphasize that the people of their heritage made great contributions to American history." Back went the explorers.

Unfortunately, American schools frequently face tight budgets that limit the number of teachers that can be hired and the number of subjects that can be taught. Too often school administrators and school committees have to decide what to cut. A principal may be faced with the difficult decision of whether to drop the physical education teacher or the music teacher, the computer teacher or the world languages teacher. Though the cuts are budget driven, the decisions are based on philosophical beliefs about what's worth knowing.

Professional organizations and governments influence decisions about what to teach in schools. There are national groups that guide the teaching of each subject area. These groups include, for example, the National Council of Teachers of English, the National Council of Teachers of Mathematics, the National Science Teachers Association, the National Council for the Social Studies, and the International Society for Technology in Education. Each of them periodically issues guidelines for teachers in these subject areas. Currently, the voices of these groups have been eclipsed by federal and state governments who have mandated high-stakes tests in a few subject areas in an attempt to ensure that all children know the same things. The federal Department of Education under President Bush's No Child Left Behind Act is requiring annual tests in reading, mathematics, and science, to be followed later by tests in other areas. Because of these tests, and the requirement that schools publish the results, teachers are focusing on these three subject areas far more than the subject areas not tested. At the present time, many teachers don't get the chance to consider what they believe is worth knowing.

What Is Learning?

What does it mean to say we've "learned"? To Plato, learning meant being able to think and debate logically and critically. To Aristotle, learning meant being able to apply what we know to real-life activities. To John Dewey, learning was the ability to reflect on experience, to make sense of what came our way, and to grow personally and socially as a result. To Arthur Bestor and E. D. Hirsch, an essential component of learning is mastering information. To philosopher Maxine Greene, learning opens our minds to new realities. To Paolo Freire, learning improves our understanding of politics and our ability to improve our social conditions. So, even the definition of what it means to learn varies.

The question of how we learn is also a matter of debate: Some would say we learn best by being exposed to the well-articulated ideas of the highest authorities, the great writers and thinkers, those whose words have stood the test of time and become "classic." Others say learning happens only through direct contact: We learn only what we experience ourselves. To these people, learning involves action: manipulating things, experimenting, observing, and doing something with the thing to be learned. Scientists claim they learn by observing and testing. Clerics refer to divine revelation as the source of their learning. The artists and therapists among us speak of "intuition" and "insight" as the way they learn.

In the past twenty years there has been much research into the various ways that people learn. You may be someone who learns best by sitting alone in a room with a book, accompanied only by the peace and quiet of your own thoughts and responses. Or you're someone who needs to talk things through with a friend or a study group to understand what it is you're supposed to be learning. The process of learning may be affected by our biological and cultural differences, in the various ways our brains work, or in the habits of mind we learned at home.

The process of learning may also be affected by the media we use to learn. It is possible that if we're always presented with information printed in books and articles in an outlined, sequential format, we may learn to learn in that linear, orderly way. We may develop habits of mind based on the way information is formatted. The explosion of new technologies as tools for researching and presenting information has provided us with new organizational formats. Terms such as *random access* and *streaming video* say much about the ways we perceive information, take it into our brains, and use it. Technology has had a significant impact on the way children learn; it may also have affected, and changed, habits of learning.

Our beliefs about how people learn affect not only how we learn ourselves, but also the decisions we make as educators about how we will teach.

"I don't have an answer, but you've sure given me a lot to think about."

Source: ©The New Yorker Collection 1997 Bernard Schoenbaum from cartoonbank.com. All rights reserved.

What Is Good Teaching?

Serious attention has only recently been paid to the question of how to teach. In colonial America, "good teaching" was construed as the ability to discipline students. Teachers were rehired if they were successful at keeping a classroom of multi-aged students focused on their work and well behaved, usually by means of the "hickory stick." Even in the late-nineteenth century, programs that prepared new teachers assumed that teacher training meant an introduction or review of the subject matter to be taught in school. The original one-year curriculum at Salem Normal School, founded in 1854 as the forerunner of Salem State College (where both authors work today), included literary studies, mathematics, physical sciences, and a category labeled "the decoratives," comprised of drawing and foreign languages, with a course on school law and another on "the theory and practice of teaching." It was a curriculum that mirrored that of the better high schools in the region (Maloney, 1990). As late as the mid-twentieth century, the requirement for a license to teach in the one-room schoolhouses of rural Illinois was a subject matter test designed and administered by the county superintendent (Breitborde, 2003b). The assumption at that time was that if one mastered subject matter content, one would be able to teach it.

Gradually, the idea that good teaching meant the ability to present an articulate lecture or demonstration of a subject that the teacher knew well gave way to a complex and substantial **pedagogy,** or the art and science of teaching. A plethora of

Voices of Principle and Promise

My Pedagogic Creed
by John Dewey

I believe that the school is primarily a social institution. Education being a social process, the school is simply that form of community life in which all those agencies are concentrated that will be most effective in bringing the child to share in the inherited resources of the race, and to use his own powers for social end.

I believe that education, therefore, is a process of living and not a preparation for future living.

I believe that the school must represent present life—life as real and vital to the child as that which he carries on in the home, in the neighborhood, or on the playground.... [E]ducation which does not occur through forms of life, or that are worth living for their own sake, is always a poor substitute for the genuine reality and tends to cramp and to deaden.

I believe that the school, as an institution, should simplify existing social life; should reduce it, as it were, to an embryonic form ... believe that, as such simplified social life, the school life should grow gradually out of the home life; that it should take up and continue the activities with which the child is already familiar in the home.... It is the business of the school to deepen and extend his sense of the values bound up in his home life.

I believe that much of present education fails because it neglects this fundamental principle of the school as a form of community life. It conceives the school as a place where certain information is to be given, where certain lessons are to be learned, or where certain habits are to be formed. The value of these is conceived as lying largely in the remote future; the child must do these things for the sake of something else he is to do; they are mere preparation. As a result they do not become a part of life experience of the child and so are not truly educative.

I believe that the moral education centers around this conception of the school as a mode of social life, that the best and deepest moral training is precisely

textbooks on teaching methodology followed. Today, pedagogy, or "best practices," is carefully delineated in the teaching standards required by state teacher licensure boards. Many states require a master's degree and documented years of successful classroom experience for full professional licensure. The National Board of Professional Teaching Standards (2002) conveys master teacher status on teachers who choose to apply by preparing portfolios, videotapes, references, and written statements that attest to their excellence.

Despite changes in the formal preparation of teachers and the requirements for a teaching license, there have always been good teachers. While the license indicates serious preparation, it may be a necessary but insufficient condition for good teaching. In the pages of this book you will find examples of good teachers who were graduated from the finest teacher education institutions in the country. You will find others whose race or gender or time in history prevented their completing any such program; still others who never intended to teach but became teachers through serendipity.

The question remains whether *good teaching* refers to a set of well-defined behaviors applicable to all teaching situations, or a set of adaptive behaviors effective with particular students at particular grade levels and subject areas. Is there room in a definition of good teaching for both the interesting lecturer and the teacher whose students choose their own subjects of research? As you think back to your own schooling, what good teachers come to mind? Did they have similar teaching styles? Were they good for the same reasons? Did all your friends agree on who was a good teacher and who was a poor one? Or do children of particular backgrounds, interests, and learning needs require teachers with particular teaching styles? Parker Palmer (1995) would argue that good teaching is not defined by a specific that which one gets through having to enter into proper relations with others in a unity of work and thought.

I believe that the child should be stimulated and controlled in his work through the life of the community.... [U]nder existing conditions far too much of the stimulus and control proceeds from the teacher, because of neglect of the idea of the school as a form of social life.

I believe that ... the teacher is not in the school to impose certain ideas or to form certain habits in the child, but is there as a member of the community to select the influences which shall affect the child and to assist him in properly responding to these influences....

I believe that education is the fundamental method of social progress and reform.... I believe that education is a regulation of the process of coming to share in the social consciousness; and that the adjustment of individual activity on the basis of this social consciousness is the only sure method of social reconstruction....

I believe, finally, that the teacher is engaged, not simply in the training of individuals, but in the formation of the proper social life.... [E]very teacher should realize the dignity of his calling; that he is a social servant set apart for the maintenance of social order and the securing of the right social growth.

Source: The School Journal, 54 (3), pp. 77–80.

Questions to Consider

1. When Dewey says that the "present education" neglects the principle of the school as a form of community life, that schools are places where others dictate the particular information and habits that children should learn, he was talking about schools at the turn of the twentieth century. In your opinion, is this statement still true?
2. Dewey calls on schools to create embryonic forms of community by "simplify[ing] existing social life." In what ways can teachers create in their classrooms a microcosm of the larger society?

set of behaviors or strategies, but that good teaching comes from a teacher's sense of his own identity, and from his ability to teach in accordance with that identity—to teach, in Palmer's terms, with integrity.

Good teaching prepares students for their roles as citizens in the American democracy and the larger world. Good teachers do their work in schools that have broad-reaching social goals. We now turn to the question of the nature of those goals.

What Is the Role of the School in Society?

Everyday life in classrooms requires that teachers' primary concerns be the needs of the children in front of them and the responsibility to present the curriculum in meaningful and understandable ways. Ultimately, however, the work of teachers is part of the mission of public schools to respond to the needs and demands of the society that creates them. A central question guiding the social mission of schools is whether they should aim to prepare students for society as it exists with its current needs and demands—a **transmissive** role—or whether their end goal should be **transformative,** to improve society, and foster social change. Is it the schools' responsibility to transmit to a new generation what previous generations have known and accomplished, to provide students with the knowledge and skills necessary to converse with each other and keep existing institutions functioning and productive? Or is it the schools' responsibility to transform, to enlighten students to new possibilities for themselves, their country, and the world?

John Dewey, whose long life spanned times of great change in the United States, from the industrial revolution to the Korean War, believed that public schools could be models of democratic society and could also transform society in ways that supported peace and social justice. To Dewey, schools were social institutions, and students and teachers were equal participants in a community of living and learning. In *My Pedagogic Creed* (see Voices of Principle and Promise), Dewey explains the beliefs that ground his vision of schools as essential instruments of social progress and social change.

Dewey's ideas about the promise of public schools as vehicles for improving society arose from his awareness of the injustices and inequities that existed in the nation. It took several decades for the general public to reach the same conclusion. In the 1960s, following two decades of fierce nationalism, white middle- and upper-class Americans came to realize that the way of life they were enjoying was not shared by all. Michael Harrington's book *The Other America* (1962) woke the public and policymakers to the fact that there were vast differences in the quality of life led by people in different regions and of different races, social classes, and genders. America, it turned out, was both a land of opportunity and a land of oppression, depending on your color, your class, your relative wealth, and where you lived. Knowledge of racism and its effects, of poverty, and of the public schools' role in perpetuating injustice and inequity (Kozol, 1992) reoriented our vision of the social role of schools. The original academic mission of public schools expanded to include **compensatory education,** which was an effort to correct old inequities by providing special services to those whose life conditions compromised their academic and economic success. Initiatives such as President Johnson's War on Poverty, including Head Start, Title I, and affirmative action programs attempted to equalize education for all groups. Ensuing decades brought new curricula in peace education, environmental education, global education, and community service learning to draw students' attention to their responsibilities as citizens of the world. Today's schools are charged with the responsibility of teaching children how to keep themselves healthy and safe, how to manage their anger, and how to get along with people of different faiths and backgrounds, in addition to their academic subject matter.

Many schools encourage students to work collectively on activities based on particular social issues such as peace, sustaining the environment, or community service, in order for students to develop an awareness of such issues.
Source: © Steve Skjold/PhotoEdit

E. D. Hirsch, whose work is excerpted at the end of this chapter, would have the schools help children achieve **cultural literacy** (1987); that is, be familiar with the stock of knowledge and literary traditions of a particular culture that enables its members to communicate with each other. Recalling the purpose of education in early America (see Chapter 7), Hirsch looks to the schools to ensure that a diverse population can participate in a common culture, thus preserving social order. Many disagree with his assumption that there is one cultural tradition in the United States that all children should learn. These critics hope the schools will teach children to be aware of and respect different cultural traditions and knowledge bases and be able to work together toward a better future for everyone despite, or perhaps because of, those differences.

Guiding Principles on the Nature and Purpose of Education

Each chapter in this book presents a variety of answers to the preceding questions. We will draw on the ideas of philosophers and educational thinkers of yesterday and today, as well as research and practice in teaching and learning. However, the book is grounded in a point of view on the nature, purpose, and outcomes of education that represents our own philosophy and experience in the field of education. We believe that education is a project that is ultimately social but whose effects on individuals and on society cannot be predicted. While values, ideologies, and politics affect life in schools, through both clearly stated curriculum goals and also hidden messages in the way teachers teach and schools are organized, students and teachers construct their own meanings of the things that happen during the school day. What students and teachers make of their school experience is unpredictable and idiosyncratic. We believe that the natural gap between what is intended and what is actually learned and practiced is a good thing. The gap between teaching and learning means that knowledge, or truth, is created through the interchange of ideas in a community of teachers and students; the pursuit of truth is greater than the sum of its parts. But despite the unpredictability of the process and the outcomes, educators need to have clear goals. We believe those goals should be focused on improving life on earth for all people.

We encourage you to develop your own principles about education that you will adhere to when you begin teaching. Your guiding principles will help you to become a reflective educator with a sense of who you are as a teacher and what you believe. They will keep you focused on your goals for your own work and for your students, and provide you with a rationale for the decisions you will be making in the classroom. We hope you will begin to develop these principles as you read through the issues addressed in this book, as you listen to and discuss issues with teachers, mentors, and fellow students, and as you observe life in schools and classrooms. We hope your list of guiding principles will be your own, culled from all these experiences and perhaps informed a bit by a critical consideration of the point of view we offer here. The following is a list of the principles that guide our work as teachers and teacher educators:

1. *Education is a moral enterprise.* It is never value free. Acts of teaching, such as the way we organize students in our schools and classrooms, the subject matter we choose to adopt, the norms and rules of behavior we impose on our students, the quality of our interactions with them and with our colleagues, the achievements we celebrate and the ones we do not, carry messages about what we think is right and good (Dewey, 1935).

2. *Education is a political enterprise.* The relationships between teachers and students, the manner in which education resources are distributed across communities and within schools and classrooms, the allocation of decision- making responsibility for the curriculum, for funding, for teacher licensure and evaluation, are matters of power (Anyon, 1998; Freire, 1970). Assumptions and allocations of power change with historical progress and demographic shifts that result from waves of immigration, for example. We believe that all children in America have the right to a free public education appropriate to their needs and that "equity" does not necessarily mean "sameness."

3. *Public schools are linked to the social, cultural, and economic conditions of the societies and communities in which they find themselves.* These conditions include, for example, the social mores and assumptions of the times, the relative ability of a community to generate taxes to support schools, the academic and career expectations its families hold for their children, the norms and values in the prevailing culture, the educational background of parents and their sense of their own power with regard to schools. What we might call "family and social capital" affect the availability of resources, the needs of students, the involvement of their families, the school curriculum, perhaps even the instructional strategies teachers use. Children's academic success relies in great part on the support they receive from their families and communities, though parent involvement can take various forms. For some children and some communities, schools need help from other social institutions to accomplish their academic mission (Dryfoos, 1994; Breitborde, 2003a). We believe that because public schools are central to the functioning and growth of our democracy, they should be provided with whatever resources they need to accomplish their work.

4. *The ultimate aim of public education is the improvement of life on earth for all its people.* We are all—teachers and students and their families—citizens of the world. The health and welfare of America's population is inextricably linked to the health and welfare of people in other parts of the world. Education has the power to endow new generations with the knowledge and skills to maintain a sustainable physical environment, to distribute adequate material resources to everyone, to provide good health care, and to find peaceful ways of resolving conflicts. Based on our nation's commitment to democratic equality and human rights, American schools can have an important role in promoting the basic rights articulated by the United Nations (UNICEF, 1999; United Nations, 1989).

5. *American schoolchildren benefit from the increasingly rich cultural and linguistic variety of their classrooms.* Because of our place in history as an open door to immigrants and refugees, American public education has a special mission: to welcome new students and families and to help them adapt to life in their new home while respecting their unique contribution to the evolving "American" culture. We believe that this diversity provides students with important new information and perspectives that expand their minds, open their hearts, and prepare them better for global citizenship.

6. *Knowledge is socially constructed* (Mills, 1959, 1976; Vygotsky, 1978). Our human ability to perceive and understand is bound by our own needs, interests, and personal histories. As these needs, interests, and histories change, as local

An example of a one-room schoolhouse in rural Brazil.
Source: Courtesy of Cleti Cervoni

and global events occur, as new information surfaces and new theories and research techniques evolve, we change our conceptions of what is true, real, and appropriate. What we "knew" in 1492 is not what we "know" now nor what we will "know" in years to come. Knowledge is not static, but develops through dialogue and the exchange of human experiences and multiple perspectives. Essential to the development of knowledge, therefore, are open-mindedness, curiosity, and respectful communication.

7. *Teaching and learning are reciprocal and interdependent processes.* The developing nature of knowledge means that teachers are always learners, and learners potentially teachers. Authority in education should be anthropological (Benne, 1970); that is, it should be inherent in the knowledge that the teacher or the student has at the moment. There is much our students can learn from us, and much we can learn from our students. We must assume that our students know something and look for ways they can express that knowledge. If we do not make time to listen to them or invite them to share with us what they know, we limit our own understanding and denigrate theirs.

8. *Teaching and learning are also independent processes.* What we teach is not necessarily what our students learn. Human beings are active meaning-makers (Fosnot, 1996). They take in experiences in different ways, and take away from those experiences what they will, or need. They have wonderful ideas, which may be different from our own, and which we might not anticipate (Duckworth, 1987). The gap between teaching and learning is a creative one. It makes room for the very diversity of thought and talent that is essential not only to human activity but also to the development of knowledge. The fact that teaching and learning do not perfectly correspond means that teachers

must use a variety of strategies and materials to convey the same or similar information, and that student learning should be assessed in multiple ways, in multiple contexts. While we ought to have minimum (though high) standards of knowledge and performance for children, we need to leave room for the variety of ways in which students obtain information, follow their interests, apply their talents, and express what they have learned (see, for example, Gardner, 1983; Guild and Garger, 1998).

9. *Teaching strategies and materials are less important to good teaching than the teacher himself or herself,* the beliefs that ground how he or she interacts with students, and the messages conveyed to students about information, learning, values, and human nature. Good teaching comes in many forms, and the *who* is more important than the *what* or the *how.* It is essential, therefore, that teachers understand their own values and assumptions, the limitations to what they know and understand, and the particular strengths they bring to their work. Good teachers are reflective and honest with themselves. They have a strong sense of identity and a commitment to teach with integrity (Palmer, 1995).

10. *The hidden curriculum is as much, if not more, important to children's futures as the stated, or written, curriculum.* The **hidden curriculum** includes the knowledge, values, attitudes, norms of behavior, and beliefs that students acquire in schools that are not part of the formal written curriculum objectives; messages that have moral and social meaning. Children's "lived experiences" of school are holistic and sensory and social, as well as academic. When we urge them to do their own work or to be good citizens, when we ask them to raise their hands or line up for recess, when we trust them to deliver messages to the office, when we assign research topics or allow them to choose their own, when we reward them with gold stars or pizza parties or the chance to have their story published in the school paper, we teach them about work, citizenship, motivation, freedom, and talent. In classroom life, there are crowds, praise, and power (Jackson, 1990). Children must find their social place among their classmates, within an institution more concerned with categorical performances than personal identities (Dreeben, 1968). Teachers may vary in the academic performance they expect from different students; children may be labeled as gifted, slow, difficult. In school, along with reading, writing, and arithmetic, children learn how to get along in the world, and what the world expects of them.

11. *Teachers are agents of personal and social change.* We have the power to transform lives. This transformative power is both micro and macro. It inheres in specific acts; we recall Jonathan Kozol's opinion that teaching someone to read can be a radical act (Kozol, 1972). It can enlarge children's visions for themselves, "wake them up," as Maxine Greene (1982) says, to new ways of seeing and new possibilities for existing. It can arm students with a set of skills and information that will allow them to rise above troubled family situations and offer them opportunities for further education and meaningful work. Teaching can also transform whole populations. International health and welfare agencies report that educating women in developing nations significantly impacts their children's survival (Swiniarski and Breitborde, 2003). School integration, affirmative action, and federal special education laws have changed the futures of whole groups of underserved populations in America. Thousands of

immigrants flock to the shores of this country each year in search of a free education for their children, which they trust will lead them to a better way of life.

12. *Teaching is the noblest of professions and should be treated with the highest respect.* As moral and intellectual exemplars, teachers should be held to high professional standards. Following the dictates of the sociological definition of professionalism (Etzioni, 1969), those standards, however, should be developed by teachers themselves. In determining the standards of their profession, public school teachers need to listen to and collaborate with the public that employs them as well as the students in their charge. Teachers need to do a better job at articulating their special knowledge and their myriad responsibilities. On behalf of themselves and their students, teachers' voices should be principled and loud.

Defining Terms in Education

Before we leave this introductory chapter we want to clarify the meaning of four words frequently used in our field. *Training, learning, education,* and *schooling* are terms used interchangeably in everyday discourse, but their meanings differ in important ways. Because we ask you to consider deep issues and come to your own conclusions based on careful and precise thought, we think the language used to consider those issues ought to convey precise meanings.

Training

From childhood we have been taught to do many things. When we were toddlers, someone taught us to hold a spoon to lift food to our mouths, to say "please" and "thank you," and to use the "potty." In elementary school, we were probably taught to bounce a ball, to take turns, and to raise our hands when we had a question or an answer. Outside school, we may have been taught to make a bed using hospital corners, to ride a bike, to execute a swan dive, to stop the car at red lights, to operate a cash register, to type, or to enter data into a computer. These behaviors are called *training* because they share some characteristics: they are automatic, they are rote responses, they are acquired through practice, they become habitual, they are specific to particular circumstances and/or equipment, and they do not require much thought. In fact, in some cases, too much thinking gets in the way of our performing them; for example, if we stop and think before we stop at a red light, we might cause an accident. If we fall out of practice, perhaps because our circumstances change, or if the equipment used in our original training becomes obsolete, we may lose the ability to perform these behaviors. They are temporal. They are examples of *training*.

Learning

Learning implies much more than training. Learning requires thought and reflection. It is permanent in that it changes the person doing the learning in some fundamental way, large or small. Learning implies growth; it may lead us to new understandings, new ways of behaving, even a change of values. It is idiosyncratic; that is, unique to the individual. Our seventh and eighth principles described previously portray the learner as an active maker of meaning who incorporates new

Table 1.1 Characteristics of Training and Learning

Training	Learning
Automatic, Mechanical, Unthinking	Deep, Thoughtful, Reflective
Intentional	Intentional or Unplanned
Repeated, Recurring, Habitual	Spontaneous, New, Incidental
Achieved through practice	Achieved through understanding
Standard for the task	Idiosyncratic and contextual
Outcome is new behavior	Outcome is personal growth

learning experiences into her already existing knowledge. The learner selectively perceives and organizes information in ways that are unique to her because of her past experiences, her current situation, or, perhaps, her learning style.

Learning can be intended, or it can be incidental or accidental. You might, for example, decide you want to learn how to write science fiction and succeed in writing a good story, an example of purposeful learning. As you ride the city bus to class each week, you may learn much that you did not intend—that there are many more ethnic groups living in the city than you had thought, that people will strike up a conversation if you say hello to them, that you enjoy the variety of architecture that characterizes the neighborhoods on the bus route. Learning often impels more learning; it can make the learner curious to learn more. Your learning about the styles of architecture in different parts of the city may spur you to find out why certain materials were used, or what the styles are called. Table 1.1 shows a comparison of the characteristics of training and learning.

Education

By *education* we mean a planned and directed course of study. Your science fiction class may be part of a college major in creative writing or literature. That literature major may be part of the liberal arts education that you have chosen. Perhaps your secondary education was vocational, one that prepared you for a specific career. *Education* is a program of directed learning that has a goal. The goal might be set by someone or by a body such as a state board of education or a local school committee. Or it might be set by the person being educated. You might decide, for example, to educate yourself in the classics of literature, either by enrolling in a formal program of study or by completing your classics education at home with books borrowed from the local library.

Schooling

Finally, *schooling* refers to the institutions that offer us an education. We are "schooled" in our local public school systems, in private academies, or in religion-based parochial schools. We may even be "home schooled." In all these cases, the term *schooling* relates to a structure or organizational system whose purpose is to

KEY TERMS

charter schools, p. 4
compensatory education, p. 16
cultural literacy, p. 17
curriculum, p. 10
hidden curriculum, p. 20
pedagogy, p. 13
transmissive vs. transformative functions of school, p. 15
vouchers, p. 4

WEBSITES TO EXPLORE

http://www.who.int. The World Health Organization's clearinghouse of data on health and physical conditions around the world. The site includes references to research on the link between education and children's health in developing countries.

http://www.nbpts.org/standards/standards.html. The National Board of Professional Teaching Standards offers national criteria for teaching excellence and awards "national certification" to teachers who submit multimedia portfolios attesting to their having met the standards.

http://www.unicef.org/crc/crc.htm. United Nations Convention on the Rights of the Child (1989). Accessed July 29, 2002. The convention establishes a set of physical, social, legal, and educational conditions that children deserve no matter where they live in the world. The United States has yet to ratify the document.

http://www.unicef.org. UNICEF.

http://www.ed.gov/Speeches/08-1995/religion.html. United States Department of Education, Guidelines on Religion in the Schools. Accessed March 6, 2004. Richard Riley, former U.S. Secretary of Education, issued a statement to educators providing information on what is appropriate and legal with respect to religious expression or information in public schools. These guidelines address, for example, the difference between teaching about religion and religious practice, and limitations on prayer.

CRITICAL READINGS

What Every American Needs to Know

BY E. D. HIRSCH

My son John, who recently taught Latin in high school and eighth grade . . . mentioned to his students that Latin, the language they were studying, is a dead language that is no longer spoken. After his pupils had struggled for several weeks with Latin grammar and vocabulary, this news was hard for some of them to accept. One girl raised her hand to challenge my son's claim. "What do they speak in Latin America?" she demanded.

At least she had heard of Latin America. Another day my son asked his Latin class if they knew the name of an epic poem by Homer. One pupil shot up his hand and eagerly said, "The Alamo!" Was it just a slip for *The Iliad?* No, he didn't know what the Alamo was, either. To judge from other stories about information gaps in the young, many American school children are less well informed than this pupil. The following, by Benjamin J. Stein, is an excerpt from one of the most evocative recent accounts of youthful ignorance.

> I spend a lot of time with teenagers. Besides employing three of them part-time, I frequently conduct focus groups at Los Angeles area high schools to learn about teenagers' attitudes towards movies or television shows or nuclear arms or politicians. . . . I have not yet found one single student in Los Angeles, in either college or high school, who could tell me the years when World War II was fought. Nor have I found one who could tell me the years when World War I was fought. Nor have I found one who knew when the American Civil War was fought. . . . A few have known how many U.S. senators California has, but none has known how many Nevada or Oregon has. ("Really? Even though they're so small?") . . . Only two could even approximately identify Thomas Jefferson. Only one could place the date of the Declaration of Independence. None could name even one of the first ten amendments to the Constitution or connect them with the Bill of Rights. . . .
>
> On and on it went. On and on it goes. I have mixed up episodes of ignorance of facts with ignorance of concepts because it seems to me that there is a connection. . . . The kids I saw (and there may be lots of others who are different) are not mentally prepared to continue the society because they basically do not understand the society well enough to value it.

My son assures me that his pupils are not ignorant. They know a great deal. Like every other human group they share a tremendous amount of knowledge among themselves, much of it learned in school. The trouble is that, from the standpoint of their literacy and their ability to communicate with others in our culture, what they know is ephemeral and narrowly confined to their own generation. Many young people strikingly lack the information that writers of American books and newspapers have traditionally taken for granted among their readers from all generations. For reasons explained in this book, our children's lack of intergenerational information is a serious problem for the nation. The decline of literacy and the decline of shared knowledge are closely related, interdependent facts. . . .

We have ignored cultural literacy in thinking about education—certainly I as a researcher also ignored it until recently—precisely because it was something we have been able to take for granted. We ignore the air we breathe until it is thin or foul. Cultural literacy is the oxygen of social intercourse. Only when we run into cultural illiteracy are we shocked into recognizing the importance of the information that we had unconsciously assumed.

To be sure, a minimal level of information is possessed by any normal person who lives in the United States and speaks elementary English. Almost everybody knows what is meant by dollar and that cars must travel on the right-hand side of the road. But this elementary level of information is not sufficient for a modern democracy. It isn't sufficient to allow us to read newspapers (a sin against Jeffersonian democracy), and it isn't sufficient to achieve economic fairness and high productivity. Cultural literacy lies above the every-day levels of knowledge that everyone possesses and below the expert level known only to specialists. It is that middle ground of cultural knowledge possessed by the "common reader." It includes information that we have traditionally expected our children to receive in school, but which they no longer do.

During recent decades Americans have hesitated to make a decision about the specific knowledge that children need to learn in school. Our elementary schools are not only dominated by the content-neutral ideas of Rousseau and Dewey, they are also governed by approximately sixteen thousand independent school districts. We have viewed this dispersion of educational authority as an insurmountable obstacle to altering the fragmentation of the school curriculum even when we have questioned that fragmentation. We have permitted school policies that have shrunk the body of information that Americans share, and these policies have caused our national literacy to decline. . . .

Just how fragmented the American public school curriculum has become is described in "The Shopping Mall High School," a report on five years of firsthand study inside public and private secondary schools. The authors report that our high schools offer courses of so many kinds that "the word 'curriculum' does not do justice to this astonishing variety." The offerings include not only academic courses of great diversity, but also courses in sports and hobbies and a "services curriculum" addressing emotional or social problems. All these courses are deemed "educationally valid" and carry course credit. Moreover, among academic offerings are numerous versions of each subject, corresponding to different levels of student interest and ability. Needless to say, the material covered in these "content area" courses is highly varied.

Cafeteria-style education, combined with the unwillingness of our schools to place demands on students, has resulted in a steady diminishment of commonly shared information between generations and between young people themselves. Those who graduate from the same school have often studied different subjects, and those who graduate from different schools have often studied different material even when their courses have carried the same titles. The inevitable consequence of the shopping mall high school is a lack of shared knowledge across and within schools. It would be hard to invent a more effective recipe for cultural fragmentation.

The formalistic educational theory behind the shopping mall school (the theory that any suitable content will inculcate reading, writing, and thinking skills) has had certain political advantages for school administrators. It has allowed them to stay scrupulously neutral with regard to content. Educational formalism enables them to regard the indiscriminate variety of school offerings as a positive virtue, on the grounds that such variety can accommodate the different interests and abilities of different students. Educational formalism has also conveniently allowed school administrators to meet objections to the traditional literate materials that used to be taught in the schools. Objectors have said that traditional materials are class-bound, white, Anglo-Saxon, and Protestant, not to mention racist, sexist, and excessively Western. Our schools have tried to offer enough diversity to meet these objections from liberals and enough Shakespeare to satisfy conservatives. Caught between ideological parties, the schools have been attracted irresistibly to a quantitative and formal approach to curriculum making rather than one based on sound judgments about what should be taught.

Some have objected that teaching the traditional literate culture means teaching conservative material. Orlando Patterson answered that objection when he pointed out that mainstream culture is not the province of any single social group and is constantly changing by assimilating new elements and expelling old ones. Although mainstream culture is tied to the written word and may therefore seem more formal and elitist than other elements of culture, that is an illusion. Literate culture is the most democratic culture in our land: it excludes nobody; it cuts across generations and social groups and classes; it is not usually one's first culture, but it should be everyone's second, existing as it does beyond the narrow spheres of family, neighborhood, and region.

As the universal second culture, literate culture has become the common currency for social and economic exchange in our democracy, and the only available ticket to full citizenship. Getting one's membership card is not tied to class or race. Membership is automatic if one learns the background information and the linguistic conventions that are needed to read, write, and speak effectively. Although everyone is literate in some local, regional, or ethnic culture, the connection between mainstream culture and the national written language justifies calling mainstream culture the basic culture of the nation.

Source: E. D. Hirsch, *Cultural Literacy: What Every American Needs to Know.* (1987). Accessed at http://www.msu.edu-jdowell/Illiteracy.html on March 6, 2004.

A Closer Look at the Issues

1. Do you agree with Hirsch that there is a definable "mainstream culture" in America that everyone needs to know?
2. Is it more important that children learn the kind of information that Hirsch laments many of them don't know, or that they learn how to think clearly?

Literacy for What?

BY MAXINE GREENE

[L]iteracy ought to be conceived as an opening, a becoming, never a fixed end. I believe, with Dewey and Gibert Ryle, that fundamental skills are only the foundation, the first level, and that learning does not actually begin until people begin teaching themselves. . . . Ryle says that teaching ought to open gates, not close them. . . . And teaching, too, includes enabling persons to perceive alternative realities, or desirable orders of things. Only when they can see things as if they could be otherwise, are they free in any meaningful sense. . . .

This view of teaching is very much at odds with the approach taken in many classrooms today. . . . Teachers are schooled to think of students as reactive creatures, behaving organisms. Over-affected by the technical ethos, they are likely to focus on measurable or observable performance or to function according to what Ryle calls a "crude, semi-surgical picture of teaching as the forcible insertion into the pupil's memory of strings of officially approved propositions. . . . " When the reward system of a school is geared toward guaranteeing certain predefined performances or the mastery of discrete skills, teachers too often become trainers—drilling, imposing, inserting, testing, and controlling. They are too distanced from their students to talk with them or to them. Instead, they talk *at* them, work *on* them very often, but not *with* them.

One of the important contributions to be made to the initiation into . . . literacy, is the overcoming of [a] sense of powerlessness. . . . We must do all we can to enable the young to articulate, to express what they see and hear. They need to be empowered to give voice to what horrifies them, what dulls and deadens them—by telling their stories aloud, writing logs, keeping journals, inventing fictions, creating poetry, editing newsletters, or even rendering what they perceive through paint or gesture or sound. To speak through one of these several languages is not only a way of overcoming passivity; it is a way of being free along with others, because to speak or to express is to give public form to private awareness, to communicate what is known. It is to develop the power Virginia Woolf talks about: the power against nonbeing and loneliness—the "nondescript cotton wool" that obscures so much of life.

. . . The teacher of literacy, to be authentic and effective, must be inquirer, discoverer, critic, sometimes loved one. He or she must be someone who cares, someone who is ready to engage a subject matter or a created form as an always open possibility. The true teacher of literacy is not the kind who comes to class having "done" *Romeo and Juliet* or the history of the Civil War or the science of genetics—with all questions answered and the subject turned into an object ready to be consumed. Rather, he or she must be prepared to think critically, giving good reasons for the claims made and even the demands, encouraging students to look critically upon the performances in which they are asked to engage, participating in discussions with the students, making explicit the norms that govern their being together, keeping the enterprise open, allowing for possibility. . . .

Our task is to move young people to be able to educate themselves and to create the kinds of classroom situations that stimulate them to do just that. Doing so, they may find themselves in a position to discover and use certain of the concepts that enable literate human beings to impose order and meaning on inchoate experience. Concepts are perspectives of a sort; they are clusters of meaning. They empower persons to organize experience in order to interpret it, to have some power over it, to see and, yes, to say. To achieve literacy is, in part, to learn how to think conceptually, to structure experience, to look through wider and more diverse perspectives at the lived world.

Obviously, in many schools the public emphasis is on literacy, basic skills, and test results, and there are administrators throughout the U.S. who care mainly about numbers and what is finally quantifiable. And there are abstracted faces in classrooms, young people for whom school is far less important than television or pop music or life on the streets. . . . It seems evident that, if the school's primary function is to countervail against all of this, the literacy it attempts to make possible must be linked to critical reflectiveness, to wide-awakeness. Indeed, I insist that no other institution or agency in society has that particular responsibility. If we in education do not succeed in accomplishing this mission, we shall . . . leave a population passive, stunned, and literally thoughtless in front of television or with miniature speakers in their ears. . . . Horror, despair, passivity, and nondescript cotton wool. We have only to offer the power that comes with the ability to explain, to locate, to conceptualize, to perceive possibilities. That, as I see it, signifies literacy.

Let me conclude with a section from Niozake Shange's choreodrama, *For Colored Girls Who Have Considered Suicide When the Rainbow is Enuf*, because it deals with the theme of this article and because it suggests so very much.

de library waz right down from de trolly tracks
cross from de laundry-mat
thru de big shinin floors & granite pillars
ol' st. louis is famous for
I found toussaint
but not til after months uv
cajun Katie/pippi longstockin
christopher robin/eddie heyward and a pooh bear
in the children's room
only pioneer girls & magic rabbits
& big city white boys
i knew i wasn't sposedta
  but i ran into the ADULT READING ROOM
    & came across
      TOUSSAINT
        my first blk man
    (i never counted george washington carver
      cuz I didn't like peanuts)
        still
Toussaint waz a blk man a Negro like my mama
  say
who refused to be a slave
& he spoke French
& didn't low no white man to tell him nothing
  not napolean
  not maximillien
  not robespierre
TOUSSAINT L'OUVERTURE
waz the beginning uv reality for me
in the summer contest for
who colored child can read
15 books in three weeks
i won and raved abt TOUSSAINT L'OUVERTURE
at the afternoon ceremony
waz disqualified
  cuz Toussaint
    belonged in the ADULT READING ROOM

It did not matter. She loved Toussaint. She took him home, and he became her imaginary friend. And she walked with him and explored with him and talked to him, until finally she met a boy named Toussaint Jones who turned out to be not too different from her Toussaint; but this one spoke English and ate apples and was all right with her: "no telling what all spirits we cd move down by the river." And the section ends, "hey wait."

Would such a person *not* master the basics, with the Adult Reading Room in sight? I ask myself how we can create situations that might release persons to take the kind of leap that girl took—away from the magic rabbits of the children's room to the Adult Reading Room. No one could have predicted that that child would find Toussaint; but I want to believe that there is always a Toussaint waiting there ahead, if we dare to think in terms of beginnings, to see from the vantage point of the beginner, the seeker—instead of seeing from the vantage point of the system or the bureaucracy or the framework. What supervisor, principal, testmaker . . . could possibly predict a little girl's making that run in to the Adult Reading Room and finding the beginning of her reality that way . . . ? And when she says, "hey wait," we know she has that sense of incompleteness that will impel her on, and we know no measurement scale can grasp that either.

Source: Maxine Greene, "Literacy for What?" *Phi Delta Kappan* (January, 1982), pp. 326–329.

A Closer Look at the Issues

1. What does Greene mean by "literacy ought to be conceived as an opening, a becoming, never a fixed end"?
2. While Greene's conception of cultural literacy is very different from E. D. Hirsch's, he might point out that throughout her article Greene makes reference to writers she hopes all her readers are familiar with; thus, that she is culturally literate by his definition. In their beliefs about literacy, or cultural literacy, where do the two part company?

3. How is literacy related to power? How is this connection evident in the excerpt about the Adult Reading Room from Shange's play?

4. A central goal of education for Greene is to help students become "wide awake" to life. By her definitions and standards, are you wide awake? Are you literate?

REFERENCES

Anyon, J. (1998). Social class and the hidden curriculum of work. In Shapiro, H. S. and S. B. Harden, eds., *The Institution of education.* Needham Heights, MA: Simon & Schuster.

Benne, K. (1970). Authority in education. *Harvard Educational Review,* 70 (3): pp. 385–410.

Boyd, J. P. et al., eds. (1950). *The papers of Thomas Jefferson.* Princeton, NJ: Princeton University Press.

Breitborde, M. L. (1983). Personal interview, Moscow, former U.S.S.R.

Breitborde, M. L. (2003a). Lessons learned in an urban school: Preparing teachers for the educational village. *The Teacher Educator,* 38 (2).

Breitborde, M. L. (2003b). One-room schools of Illinois in the twentieth century: An oral history. Unpublished research. Available from the author.

Bridgett, T. E. (1913). *Life and writings of blessed Thomas More.* London: Burns Oates & Washbourne. http://pw2.netcom.com/~rjs474/thomasmore/1519lett.html Accessed March 6, 2004.

Dewey, J. (1897). My pedagogic creed. *The School Journal,* 54 (3), pp. 77–80.

Dewey, J. (1915). *The school and society.* Chicago: University of Chicago Press.

Dewey, J. (1933). *How we think.* Boston: D.C. Heath.

Dewey, J. (1935). The teacher and his world. *The Social Frontier,* 1 (1), p. 7.

Dreeben, R. (1968). *On what is learned in school.* Reading, MA: Addison-Wesley.

Dryfoos, J. (1994). *Full-service schools: A revolution in health and social services for children, youth, and families.* San Francisco: Jossey-Bass.

Duckworth, E. (1987). *The having of wonderful ideas and other essays on teaching and learning.* New York: Teachers College Press.

Erasmus, D. Letter to Ulrich von Hutten (1519). In Bridgett, T. E. (1913). *Life and Writings of Blessed Thomas More.* London: Burns Oates & Washbourne.

Etzioni, A., ed., (1969). *The semi-professions and their organization: Teachers, nurses, social workers.* New York: Free Press.

Fosnot, C. (1996). Constructivism: A psychological theory of learning. In C. Fosnot, ed., *Constructivism: Theory, perspectives, and practice.* New York: Teachers College Press.

Freire, P. (1970). *Pedagogy of the oppressed.* New York: The Seabury Press.

Gardner, H. (1983). *Frames of mind: The theory of multiple intelligences.* New York: Basic Books.

Greene, M. (1982). Literacy for what? *Phi Delta Kappan* (January) pp. 326–329.

Greene, M. (1999). *Variations on a blue guitar.* New York: Teachers College Press.

Guild, P. B. and S. Garger (1998). *Marching to different drummers.* Alexandria, VA: Association for Supervision and Curriculum Development.

Hirsch, E. D. (1987). *Cultural literacy: What every American needs to know.* Boston: Houghton Mifflin.

Harrington, M. (1962). *The other America: Poverty in the United States.* New York: Macmillan.

Jackson, P. (1990). *Life in classrooms.* New York: Teachers College Press.

Kozol, J. (1972). *Free schools.* Boston: Houghton Mifflin.

Kozol, J (1992). *Savage inequalities: Children in America's schools.* New York: HarperPerennial Publishers.

Locke, J. (1692). *Second treatise of government.* Edited by C. B. Macpherson. Reprint, Indianapolis: Hackett Publishing, 1980.

Locke, J. (1692). *Some thoughts concerning education.* Harvard Classics, 1909–14, Vol. 37, Part I. New York: P. F. Collier & Son.

Maloney, J. M. (1990). *Salem Normal School 1854–1905: A tradition of excellence.* Acton, MA: Tapestry Press.

Mills, C. W. (1959, 1976). *The sociological imagination.* New York: Oxford University Press.

National Board of Professional Teaching Standards. Arlington, VA: Author. http://www.nbpts.org/ standards/standards.html. Accessed July 29, 2002.

Newman, J. H. (1854, 1910). *The idea of a university: Essays, English and American, with introductions notes and illustrations.* New York: P. F. Collier & Son (1910). Harvard classics, no. XXVIII.

Noddings, N. (1992). *The Challenge to care in schools.* New York: Teachers College Press.

Palmer, P. (1995). *The courage to teach.* San Francisco: Jossey-Bass.

Rousseau, J.-J. (1762). *Emile.* Translated by A. Bloom. New York: Basic Books, 1979.

Swiniarski, L. B. and M.-L. Breitborde (2003). *Educating the global village: Including the child in the world.* Upper Saddle River, NJ: Merrill Prentice Hall.

UNICEF (1999). *Human rights for children and women: How UNICEF helps make them a reality.* NY: Author. United Nations (1989). Convention on the Rights of the Child. http://www.unicef.org/crc/crc.htm. Accessed July 29, 2002.

Vygotsky, L. S. (1978). *Mind in society.* Cambridge, MA: Harvard University Press.

2 Philosophical Roots of Education

ESSENTIAL QUESTION

Who is the educated person?

On September 12, 2001, Ms. Graham walked into her sixth grade classroom in a middle school in Washington, D.C., with fear and trepidation. No teaching strategies textbook had prepared her for the task she was about to undertake. It was the day after a disaster that had shaken the country and the rest of the world. Her students would want to talk about it. Some of them might know someone who had died. The night before she had learned that the friend of a colleague had died in the attack on the Pentagon.

A veteran teacher with a confidence borne of thirty years of classroom experience, Ms. Graham was afraid today; afraid of the subject matter of the discussion she was about to have with her students, afraid she wouldn't be able to handle their feelings about the tragedy, afraid of her own feelings. On this critical day, she would have to call on her deepest beliefs about her responsibility to her students and about how to help them reach a true understanding of the traumatic event. What did the students need to know about this tragedy? What did she want them to learn? What was the best way to teach this? What was the role of the school, if any, in addressing the events of this day? ■

How Is Philosophy Important to Education?

In schools across America on September 12, 2001, principals and teachers made decisions about how to deal with the attacks on the World Trade Center and the Pentagon the day before. Some principals brought the entire school together for a large group presentation and discussion. In New York City, counselors were brought in to help teachers and students cope with their grief, their fears, and their anger. In many classrooms, teachers set aside the lesson plan book and discussed the events with their classes, believing that it was their professional responsibility to address children's feelings as well as their academic lives. Some teachers considered the discussion to be a valuable learning experience, what the philosopher John Dewey would call a "teachable moment." To these teachers, important current events are essential elements in a curriculum; the subject matter of school should be relevant to life outside the building. Others chose not to undertake the responsibility, perhaps believing that it was the role of families and religious institutions, or perhaps believing that school should be a haven from society, a place whose business is purely the pursuit of academic knowledge. The decisions that educators made that day were based on their philosophies of education: on the appropriate role of schools and teachers, the nature of knowledge, and what and how children are capable of learning at different ages. Teachers who had thought through their philosophies and knew how to implement them in the classroom were better prepared for this task than those who had not.

Behind the decisions teachers make about what they should teach, to whom, and how, are conceptions they hold about reality, human nature, and learning. In other words, decisions about what to teach will come from your beliefs, or philosophy, about the world and how it works. For this reason, it is important to closely examine your beliefs, and to understand what underlies your decisions. What is your philosophy of life? Of education? In this chapter and the next we examine these questions. Let's start with some of the basic philosophical questions that we explore in this chapter:

- On what basis do we distinguish between the important information and ideas we want to present to our students and the information that is unimportant? In other words, how do we determine, What is worth knowing?
- How do we know that what we are teaching is true? In other words, how do we determine, What is good teaching?
- By what means do we assume students will understand what we teach? In other words, how do we determine, What is learning?
- How can education help move us toward our vision of the "good society"? In other words, how do we determine, What is the role of the school in society?

On the surface, these appear to be basic decisions about curriculum and instruction, but they are based on answers to some deep philosophical questions that have been debated for thousands of years. We believe that before educators can fashion a picture of the ideally educated person, they must first examine their fundamental beliefs about reality, truth, value, power, and authority. Once educators formulate these beliefs, they can make school and classroom decisions that are coherent—that fit together logically—and consistent. Such decisions are stable and predictable and ground all actions. Coherence and consistency in teaching is important in two ways: First, children understand information better if it fits together in a meaningful way with other information they've received previously. Second, as Principle 10 in Chapter 1 states, the hidden curriculum—the way we relate to children, how we organize the classroom, how we tell them they should behave—is as powerful a learning message as the stated, or written, curriculum. Underlying their discussions on September 12, 2001, teachers conveyed messages to children about how power is distributed in the world and in this country, about what is of value to people, and about what is real and true.

Parker Palmer, whose most famous work is the book *The Courage to Teach* (1995), says that good teachers teach with integrity. Their work reflects a set of beliefs that guides their lives. If we are to teach with integrity, we must first know what we believe. The questions asked in this introduction are contained in the branches of philosophy called metaphysics, epistemology, axiology, and politics. The following sections of this chapter discuss the metaphysical, epistemological, axiological, and political questions related to subject matter and the practice of education.

Branches of Philosophy and Their Application to Education

At the root of philosophy is the study of what exists. If the primary work of teachers is to guide students in understanding the world, they need first to examine what it is. Metaphysics is the branch of philosophy that addresses the nature of existence, the nature of what is true. Related to metaphysics is epistemology, which is the study of knowledge about reality. Teachers guide students not only to think about the world but also to make judgments about what is good and bad, right and wrong; the branch of philosophy called axiology is concerned with how to make those judgments. Sub-branches of axiology are aesthetics, the study of what is beautiful to our sensory experience, and ethics, the study of moral choices. Related to ethics is politics, or the study of just behavior and how power and resources are distributed in a society. We will now discuss these branches of philosophy and explain how they influence education and classroom life.

Metaphysics: What Is Real? What Is Worth Knowing?

The branch of philosophy known as **metaphysics** asks, What is real? The word *metaphysics* is Greek in origin; *physics* means "nature" and *meta* means "over" or "beyond." In attempting to distinguish between what is real and not real, metaphysicians ask whether reality ultimately inheres in organized physical matter—the physical world—or in logical and correct ideas. They ask whether reality is permanent and unchanging (absolute) or dynamic and evolving (relative). They ask whether reality exists apart from human experience, ***a priori,*** or prior to our ever encountering it, or ***a posteriori,*** only existing after and because we have experienced it. Do things have a distinct nature separate from human perception of them—are they objectively true—or do they exist only as we perceive and name them, subjectively?

We arrive at *a priori* conclusions through reason and analysis, while *a posteriori* conclusions come to us through direct sensory experience. We know, for example, that 2 + 2 = 4, an *a priori* truth that does not depend on having always to count a set of objects. But we don't know whether a particular method of teaching reading will work with a particular group of children until we try it and make our judgment *a posteriori.* For example, you may "know," that children need a good breakfast in order to focus on their morning lessons, but is this true because it is logical or because you have witnessed children who are hungry and are distracted from learning? Both *a priori* and *a posteriori* knowledge have value, but either may be incorrect. Sometimes our reasoning is faulty; sometimes our experience is narrow and incomplete. We may reason that children from single-parent households are more at risk for emotional and academic difficulties than children from two-parent homes, without including in our analysis the other variables—poverty, for example—that may be the actual cause of the difficulty, rather than the number of parents at home. We may also conclude that the earth is flat because it looks that way to us.

Some metaphysicians believe that the fundamental essence of reality is physical. To them, reality is fundamentally material, existing beyond or without the presence of human beings, and composed of matter. The material world—trees, wind, energy—exists independently, separate from our witnessing it, *a priori.* The existence of matter is permanent, originating before any particular individual or group who experience it, and lasting beyond the lives of individuals or groups. These philosophers believe that, if we are to understand reality, our task should be to come to know the physical world. The traditional philosophy called Realism is based on the conception of reality as physical; for centuries, this philosophy has grounded educators who would lead students to the truths within the natural and immediate world.

Others argue that physical reality can be illusory. Our ability to define or understand reality depends on the extent to which we perceive and think about it clearly. To these philosophers, trees are only defined as real because of how we conceive of them, as forms of life and as sources of shade and building materials. Matter appears and may disappear, as in the case of dinosaurs, who no longer roam the earth, or even trees, whose very definition changes depending on how human beings see, use, and speak about them. This second group of philosophers insists that a higher reality lies in coherent ideas. Fundamental reality is a reality of mind. To this group, mind or ideas or spirit are eternal, permanent, and orderly. If we are to understand reality, our task should be to apply our minds to uncover logical, generalized, universal truths. The traditional philosophy called Idealism espouses the conception of ultimate reality as a world of ideas. Idealism has produced educators who believe that the purpose of education is to help students see beyond the limits of their own experiences to arrive at general truths through critical thinking.

Metaphysical beliefs about the ultimate nature of reality influence decisions about the subject matter of education. They help address the question, What is worth knowing? Should the curriculum center on elements of the physical world—the sciences, historical events, the skills needed to understand and adapt to existing environments? Should it lead students to explore the world of "great ideas" in the arts, in literature, in philosophy? Should our goals for students be their mastery of facts and information, their ability to observe keenly life around them and act with decisiveness and effect? Should we expose them to the great ideas of great thinkers and teach them to use their own powers of critical thought and imagination?

Another metaphysical question addresses beliefs about basic human nature. Are people naturally good? Bad? Neutral? Do you think that children tend to be kind, or would you say that, "given an inch, they'll take a yard"? Or do you believe that their very character depends wholly on what they have been taught by their parents, their friends and neighbors, their religious institutions, and their teachers? Are children active decision makers in the development of their lives, or are they more or less passive receptacles to be filled up by experience? Do we have free will? Much has been written, by philosophers, psychologists, and educators, on the subject of children's natural proclivities, their moral development, and their orientation to learning. Some, like Jean Piaget, believe that children are born curious, driven by nature to explore and master their environment and to learn new things. Jean-Jacques Rousseau thought that "man is born free," but that society corrupts him so that . . ."everywhere he is in chains" (Rousseau, 1762, p. 1). John Locke (1692) was certain that only with positive environmental influences could children form positive social and academic habits and become kind, caring, and learned. A teacher's fundamental beliefs about human nature will influence the amount of freedom she allows students, the way she evaluates their learning, and her methods of classroom discipline. She may feel that too much freedom will lead to students taking over the classroom, competing with each other, treating each other poorly, and making bad decisions. A teacher with a different set of beliefs may assume that, given freedom to choose, children will make good choices for themselves and for each other—that they want to learn. A third teacher, adhering to the belief that how children develop depends completely on the environment they are raised and taught in, will assume that it is his responsibility to design a classroom and set tasks before students that invite and reward positive academic and social behavior.

Epistemology: How Do We Know What Is Real? What Is Learning? What Is Good Teaching?

The branch of philosophy known as **epistemology** asks, How do we know what is real? It is concerned with the processes of knowing and learning, processes central to the work of teaching. Epistemology helps answer the questions, What is learning? and What is good teaching? by guiding teachers in deciding the best approaches and methods to use to convey the truth to their students. To use the example from the opening of this chapter, many teachers who discussed the September 11 tragedy with their students first spent time researching what happened that day and possible reasons for it. In deciding what to present and how to present it, they needed to draw on some philosophical (epistemological) principles to assure themselves that they would be telling the truth. As a teacher I might have asked myself the following questions:

- Should I rely on accounts in the newspapers for the truth about what happened?
- On what basis do I think that CNN is a more valid source of information than Fox News?

- What else do I know about world politics that would help me understand why and how this disaster happened?
- To what extent can I rely on my own emotional reaction as a kind of truth?
- Is there some larger spiritual meaning in the events of 9/11?

Philosophers have many views (including authority, sensory experience, empiricism, logic, intuition, and revelation) on the most valid and reliable means of arriving at the truth of things, and these **ways of knowing** have led educators to use different instructional, or pedagogical, strategies in the effort to help students understand subject matter. Once the subject matter of the curriculum is determined, decisions about how to teach it are epistemological decisions.

Do we think that to know something is to have direct experience with it? Or are we more likely to want to expose students to a wealth of information that is wider than their own immediate experience? Some philosophers would opt for **knowledge by acquaintance,** believing that one can best understand a phenomenon through hands-on sensory experience. They would have students observe and record changes in a local plot of land to lead them to an understanding of seasonal changes in plant life, for example. Others who choose **knowledge by description** are concerned that if we limit students' learning to what they can see, hear, feel, taste, or touch, they will only come to "know" a small slice of reality rather than a general truth. To understand general principles of the effect of seasonal changes on plant life, students would need to have access to information from a wide variety of geographical areas through books, films, Internet sources, and the like. A knowledge-by-acquaintance orientation would have students learning about their own community, including its history, economy, and culture. A knowledge-by-description orientation would have them learn about life in China despite the fact that a field trip there is an unlikely possibility.

Kevin O'Reilly, an award-winning social studies teacher at Hamilton-Wenham Regional High School in Massachusetts, introduces his students to the difficulty of determining the truth about historical events, even when multiple sources are available and despite whether these sources "know" by description or acquaintance (cited in Swartz, 2000). O'Reilly presents the students with three accounts of "the shot heard 'round the world" on Lexington Common in 1775 and asks the age-old question, Who fired the first shot? The first account is an excerpt from an American textbook on U.S. history, which alleges that it was the British who fired first. In the second account, an excerpt from a British text, the blame is laid on the Americans: It was, says the British text, the rebels who fired the first shot. The third account is a memoir written by an elderly man who was on Lexington Green on April 19th. O'Reilly's students quickly agree that the old man's first-hand account should be believed, until he asks them to consider what they would need to know about this man before they accepted his version of the story. The students begin to list their concerns: How good is his memory? How far away from the battle was he? Was his father or brother or another male relative fighting on one side or the other? It becomes increasingly clear to them that a first-hand knowledge by acquaintance may be as limited as second- or third-hand knowledge by description. Both epistemological approaches have their place in education, though either or both may be flawed. A teacher concerned with presenting students with valid and reliable information would do well to use both direct and indirect sources of knowledge.

To better understand the epistemological method, let us take another look at how we discern what is real. Assume that you have been sitting indoors reading this chapter, in a classroom or library, in a dormitory or at home. How do you know that the ceiling overhead will not fall down in the next two minutes? On what basis do you continue to sit in this room believing that you are not in danger? Perhaps you say to yourself, a qualified architect designed this building and certified contractors built it; they knew how to construct a ceiling that would not fall down on my head. Or, you might look up at the ceiling to check for cracks or worrisome stains, or listen for sounds that would indicate trouble. Maybe the question disturbs you enough to find a ladder to climb up on so that you can push against the ceiling in several places to test for its solidness. Perhaps you reason that you have been in this room, and others like it, many times before and the ceiling has always stayed right where it should. Or, maybe you "just know" it will not fall down, or perhaps you just have faith. Whatever the method you used to confirm that the ceiling would stay up for the next two minutes is an epistemological method, a way of knowing that you feel comfortable with as a path to the truth. If you relied on the ideas, information, and experience of experts, you used **authority** as a way of knowing. Referring to authorities to determine the truth can involve asking people we think are more knowledgeable than we are, or reading books by authors whose credentials we find valid, even soliciting the advice of friends whose opinions we value. If you looked and listened for indications, you used **sensory experience.** You relied on your own immediate experience and your ability to perceive it clearly. If you actually tested the strength of the ceiling in one or more ways, you used empiricism. **Empiricism** as a way of knowing attempts to arrive at the truth through testing, often using a scientific method and standard guidelines for data gathering and analysis. If you thought through the question of whether the ceiling would fall down using reason, reflecting on and analyzing a number of facts and ideas, you used **logic.** You believed that clear, logical, coherent thought would lead you to the truth. If you "just knew" it would stay up, you were using **intuition,** what might be called self-evidence or subjective insight. And if you had faith (or perhaps even prayed), you were relying on **revelation** as an epistemological method, trusting that God or fate or a spiritual world beyond yourself plans and oversees our existence.

Most of us use all six of these ways of knowing at different times and in different contexts. For example, if my car fails to start some morning, my immediate response is to phone the local mechanic to come see what's wrong—an example of using authority as a way of knowing. (The mechanic would probably use a combination of sensory experience and empiricism to determine the problem.) On the other hand, my decision to write this book was made on the basis of logic (it covered the material in my Foundations of Education course, it offered the opportunity to put in writing some of my strong beliefs about education, I enjoyed past collaborations with my co-author) and intuition (I thought it might be fun to write). It is probably true, however, that we tend to rely more on some epistemological methods and tend to discount others. Some people hesitate to believe anything they have not directly experienced themselves. Others are skeptical of single experiences; they withhold judgment until they have fully studied all sides of an issue and thought through all possibilities. Still others trust their intuition to guide them toward what is true, and right, for them.

There is evidence that our ways of knowing may be influenced by our cultural backgrounds. For example, in communities where life is centered around the village square or the front porch, where doors are open to whoever comes by, close

Table 2.1 Some Ways of Knowing: What Is Learning? What Is Good Teaching?

Way of Knowing	Authority	Sensory Experience	Empiricism	Logic	Intuition	Revelation
Source of Knowledge	Knowledge can be had "at the feet of a master" or from a respected printed source.	Knowledge comes from direct observation. It depends on a report from the senses.	Knowledge is the product of testing. It is the outcome of "scientifically" guided study.	Knowledge comes from a systematic and orderly process of reasoning and analysis.	Knowledge comes through insight, personal judgment, and holistic impression.	Knowledge is revealed through faith in a supernatural higher reality beyond the rational or physical world.
Sample Classroom Application	Teachers' reading lists for children emphasize Newbury award-winners and "Junior Great Books" titles.	Students take observation notes to record seasonal changes in a plot of land near the school.	Students create and test hypotheses about factors affecting buoyancy by building toy boats of varying sizes, shapes, and materials.	Students defend a position on affirmative action after studying historical conditions, laws, statistics, and position papers.	Teacher refers a student to the school counselor to follow up on her feeling that "something may be going on at home."	Teachers mention that some believe in creationism (the idea that God created fully developed human beings) as an alternative to the concept of evolution.

social relationships may breed a keen ability to "read people" using a kind of intuition. Cultures where there are complicated encoded laws call for the exercise of logic. In cultures where people's livelihoods depend on the natural environment—the land, the sea, the weather—their sensory abilities may become highly developed. Many Native Hawaiian sailors are still able to guide their boats by the stars, using celestial navigation. One account of Aboriginal Australian ways of knowing, as the basis for their survival in "the bush" and their education, refers to both sensory and spiritual paths:

> God gave our Yulubirribi (salt and sand people) nation nutritious food supplies and miraculous medicines and the ability of our people to utilise these gifts by listening to his messages for managing weather, flora, fauna, environment, heavens, and each other. After creation, he then gave our ancestors knowledge to pass on through learned and natural expression the ways and means of existence without having to defeat his gifts. This expression is enjoyed by the Koenpil, Noonuccal and other nations' form of education for some hundreds of thousands of years (Ooodgeroo Noonuccal, in Martin & Birraboopa, 2001, p. 3).

The academic disciplines that constitute the subject matter of school curricula are characterized by modes of inquiry derived from epistemological beliefs.

Scientists, for example, usually follow strict guidelines in conducting empirical research, observing and testing before they report their conclusions. Poets and artists tend to rely on sensory images and intuition insight. Historians use primary and secondary authorities on past events, and mathematicians use logic. However, it would be a mistake to restrict our notions of the pursuit of truth in these various disciplines to one epistemological path. Great discoveries in mathematics have involved "sudden insights" and, at times, scientists use intuition to decide what among all possible factors they will test. Historians use scientific inquiry to help authenticate documents, date events, and locate historic sites. The success of poets and artists to make private "truths" available and meaningful to others is based on their ability to use language and media in authoritative and logical ways. As we make decisions about what modes of inquiry we ask our students to use, we need to remember that there are multiple ways to study and understand the same subject matter.

Axiology: What Is Right and Good in Society and Education?

Axiology is the branch of philosophy that asks the question, What is of value? It is divided into **ethics,** which is concerned with right conduct, and **aesthetics,** which addresses standards of beauty. Questions of value inform the expectations teachers hold for their students' behavior and the quality of their work. They inform the standards of behavior and expectations that teachers hold for themselves. And axiology helps educators define the purpose and value of schools in society: Toward what vision of the good society are we teaching? How can schools help new generations do their part to achieve that vision? Axiology, then, helps answer the question, What is the role of the school in society?

The authors of this book agree with many other thinkers and writers in the field of education who claim that education is never value free. Among the principles we listed in Chapter 1 that inform our point of view is the statement that "education is a moral enterprise." In the way we organize our classrooms and the codes of conduct we create for ourselves and our students, in the judgments we make about the form and presentation of artistic and academic work, we express our axiological assumptions about what is right, good, and beautiful.

A central axiological question is whether values are universal and unchanging (absolute) or appropriate to specific times and situations (relative). Is there an absolute standard of ethical behavior, which does not vary with an individual's particular culture, religion, historical setting, or economic or political situation? Is there a list of "commandments" all humans should follow? Those who say yes point to the universality of laws against murder and theft, for example, and find versions of the Golden Rule in the many religions of the globe. Others will argue that it may be right to kill another person under certain circumstances; for example, in self-defense or in "just wars." They may argue that, under certain circumstances, a student who asks a friend to help him with his homework is not cheating. Stealing might be justified if there is no other way to feed one's family or save a life. In mainstream American culture, spanking a recalcitrant child was an acceptable part of parenting (and even teaching) until recently. Now, in many parts of our country it is treated as a form of child abuse, and some immigrants whose culture allows spanking are surprised and confused to find themselves under attack for the practice.

The branch of axiology concerned with aesthetics, or the criteria for judging what is beautiful or pleasing, is illustrated by the following anecdote:

> In 1966 a high school English teacher asked her class, "What is the most beautiful building in our city?" Unaccustomed to being asked for their opinion, her students were reluctant to answer. Miss S_____ was always looking for "the right answer." One brave soul put up his hand: "City Hall?" "No," she replied with an amused look on her face. Another offered, "The new library?" "Hardly," she said with disdain, muttering to herself something that sounded like "modern monstrosity." After a few more stabs at trying to read their teacher's mind, the students went silent. They had exhausted the list of the city's major institutions: the art museum, the civic auditorium, the historical society, even the one established department store. What could the most beautiful building be? She shook her head, incredulous that they wouldn't know. "The Telephone and Telegraph Building," she announced, "is the most beautiful building in our city." None of her students had considered this possibility. In fact, very few had any impression of what the Tel and Tel building actually looked like. But whatever were the criteria Miss S_____ used to judge beauty in architecture, they were absolute, as absolute as the fact that the margins of her students' papers had to be one-half-inch wide and that the Easter bunnies their younger siblings crayoned in elementary school (whether or not they celebrated Easter) had to be white or pink. There could be no argument; standards were standards.

Education has come forward from the 1960s with a more flexible view of what is good, right, and beautiful. There are still, however, standards of conduct and beauty that we impose on students without room for negotiation. Schools have dress codes proscribing behavior that can lead to suspension or expulsion. Neatness still counts. In most classrooms, teachers ask students to raise their hands before speaking and use "inside voices." Many of these rules are imposed without much thought. Teachers tend to see them as practical adaptations to life in crowded classrooms and as opportunities to teach the conventions of behavior that students will need in adulthood. However, they are based on deep values that ought to be examined and articulated. When teachers insist on respect, they need to think about how they define the term. When teachers reward children for "good citizenship," they need to examine what values they are reinforcing: Helpfulness? Kindness? Participation? Initiative? Responsibility? Obedience? Compliance? Collaboration? Silence? As teachers consider whether they are teaching with integrity they must consider whether their practice is consistent with their own set of values. Given our belief that students are not passive recipients of information but active makers of their own meaning (see Principle 8 in Chapter 1), we would like to see teachers encourage students to examine values as well. Teachers who provide opportunities for discussions about values that lie within the curriculum and within the life of the school encourage students to think about and develop their own set of values. Chapter 10, on moral and social education, explores these issues in the world of the classroom.

Politics: What Is the Role of the School in Society?

Politics is the branch of philosophy that asks the question, What is just? Related to axiology, it assigns value to the allocation of power in society, the power relationships between individuals and groups, and the distribution of resources. Political philosophers debate definitions of concepts such as justice, fairness, equity, and authority and posit different ways of organizing society and rules and structures of governance that would ensure a just and reasonable distribution of power and resources. Applied to the arena of public education, our political beliefs help us answer the question, What is the role of the school in society? Later in this book (in Chapters 7 and 8 on school and society in American history, and in Chapter 9 on the problem of equity in education), we will discuss in detail how the various answers to this question and various political ideas have influenced the practice and outcomes of education in the United States.

As we indicated in the list of our guiding principles in Chapter 1, education is a political enterprise. Power relationships, or patterns of dominance and subservience, exist within classrooms, within schools and school systems, and within the societies that schools serve. Authority—who or what carries influence—may be vested in the person who occupies the position of teacher or may attach to whoever has the greater knowledge about a given subject. Resources in the form of funding, teaching personnel, and learning materials are distributed to students based on administrators' and teachers' decisions about what resources are available and who needs them.

In a nation built on the principles of equality and justice, life in schools for teachers and students is not always equitable or just. The questions are difficult: Does equality mean that everyone gets the same resources and the same power and has an equal voice? Should resources, too often scarce in public education, be distributed equally or based on who needs them most or who is likely to benefit most from them? Is it fair to spend more to educate students with special learning needs than to educate students without exceptionalities? Should students from groups who have been historically underserved and discriminated against receive extra consideration and funding to correct old injustices? Should classrooms be models of democracy where students are allowed full participation in decision making? What are the limits on students' constitutional rights?

Teachers occupy positions of power over their students, dispensing their attention, making decisions about what tasks will be required of individuals and groups, evaluating their work and grading it. Some teachers share power with their students; these teachers invite students to help devise the classroom rules, allow them to choose subjects of study or the forms their projects will take, and ask them to evaluate their own and each other's work. Among students there are also power relationships. Some students wield power over other students: they are more popular or perhaps more assertive; they are group leaders or class spokespeople; they may even bully other classmates. Their peers may look up to them, try to earn their friendship, or be afraid of them. There are also relationships of equal power among students: friends sit near each other and help each other with their schoolwork; in cooperative groups, students collaborate to study or complete projects.

Teachers themselves are subject to differential power distribution and relationships. In some schools, principals run tight ships, making most of the decisions and closely monitoring teachers' work to make sure they are carrying out those decisions. School system superintendents may mandate the materials that teachers must use to teach particular subjects. In other schools and school systems, teachers write the curriculum and choose the materials of instruction. They are the administrators' decision-making partners. In many schools, parents exert political pressure on principals and teachers or are important participants in school decisions. They may have formal roles on school councils, or they may lobby their school boards, or they may just make many telephone calls to the principal. In other communities, parents are not consulted, and they may not feel comfortable or knowledgeable enough to voice their ideas.

Political philosopher Michel Foucault (1979) says that power in schools operates through discourse (conversation), where the ideas and actions of some (teachers, administrators, politicians) influence the ideas and actions of others (children) who unconsciously develop a world view and an identity based on the information they receive. Foucault claims this kind of power is invisible. Because it is difficult for either the dominant or subordinate group to see the power dimensions of school discourse, it is difficult for those in power to understand that they have it, and difficult for those influenced by the power of dominant groups to resist. Ideas and actions—for example, a teacher's mandate that students "line up" to leave the classroom or his practice of grouping students for instruction by their presumed ability levels—seem normal, just the way things are. While it is not impossible for teachers or children to recognize that things could be different—that, for example, despite having been placed in "low-track" classes, a child might indeed be "college material"—for the most part, power relationships in school are accepted and greatly influence children's futures.

Conceptions of authority in education are related to power and politics. According to Kenneth Benne (1970), educational authority is either positional, rule-bound, or anthropological. In some teacher's minds, a person's authority lies in his or her official position. Just as in a family, where a parent may assume authority over a child based simply on the fact that she is the child's parent ("because I said so"), in a classroom, a teacher may insist that his position creates his right as an authority. To other teachers, authority rests with rules; for example, a policy that students should not take weapons to school has authority over student conduct. Teachers who believe that authority is anthropological assume that knowledge carries authority, and that knowledge is always developing through the human exchange of information and experiences. The person with authority is the person who knows most about a particular subject; therefore, authority is only temporary. A student who can teach his peers or his teacher something that they do not know (e.g., what life is like in the Dominican Republic, or how money is collected on a paper route, or another way to solve a math problem) is an authority for that period of time. As he contributes his information and experiences to the group, and members of the group respond by sharing their own information and experiences, the group refines and develops new knowledge. When a student asks, "Why are we doing this?" a teacher who conceives of authority as positional may use the phrase, "because I said so." A teacher who sees rules as the basis of authority will say, "because that's the policy." And the teacher who holds anthropological views of authority may discuss the reasons behind the decision, which may also have been discussed by the class: "What we've decided seems reasonable."

The distribution of educational resources is a political issue. A teacher may decide that one particular group of students should have more time in the library or greater access to the computer lab, while another group needs to work more closely with him. She may divide her students into groups based on their achievement or their assumed ability and assign different work, time, and materials to each group. In some secondary schools, students are organized into different "tracks," from "honors" to "general," where they receive instruction in different subject matter. Some schools hire poets or artists "in residence," while other schools struggle to make sure there are enough textbooks for everyone.

When a student is asked to conduct a class or make a presentation, that student, rather than the teacher, is in a temporary authority position.
Source: © Elizabeth Crews

Sadly, there are vast differences in the quantity and quality of instruction and resources offered to students in the thousands of schools in the United States. These differences can exist among schools in the same small community or among school systems within one state. They exist among the many states of our nation. Part of the problem is the way schools are funded. Most school budgets depend on the financial resources of local communities; that is, the money that is raised through property taxes. Wealthier communities, whose residents own valuable property and run successful businesses, are able to generate tax monies adequate to pay good salaries to teachers, buy good teaching materials, and fund interesting enrichment programs. Poorer communities typically find themselves with underfunded schools that struggle with outdated materials and, too often, unqualified teachers. The economic issues that lead to differences in the school experiences of children of different communities and social classes will be addressed at length in Chapter 9 (The Problem of Equity).

Table 2.2 shows the branches of philosophy discussed in this chapter and gives examples of how teachers make classroom decisions based on their metaphysical, epistemological, axiological, and political beliefs. In reviewing the chart, think about which of the teaching strategies you might use and what beliefs may lie behind your decision. As you determine your beliefs about the nature of reality, ways of knowing, aesthetic value and ethical behavior, and justice, you will be begin to develop an organized system of principles that is your philosophy. In the next section, we review traditional philosophies and describe their implications for the field of education and the work of principled teaching.

Table 2.2 Branches of Philosophy

Philosophy	The Major Question	The Educational Question	Applied to Schools	Classroom Examples
Metaphysics	What is real?	What is worth knowing?	The curriculum emphasizes either "great ideas"	Teacher guides students' critical understanding of classic literature in book study groups.
			or	
			the physical world.	Students study how form affects function by examining models of simple machines.
Epistemology	How do we know what is real?	What is learning? What is good teaching?	Teaching strategies emphasize particular "ways of knowing" (e.g., authority, sensory experience, empiricism, logic) as pathways to learning.	Students manipulate objects to learn the concept of fractions (sensory experience). Teacher conducts PowerPoint presentation on the causes of the Civil War, including original documents and quotations. (authority).
Axiology	What is of value?	What is the role of the school in society?	School and classroom climates and rules of behavior reflect standards of ethics	Teacher holds a classroom meeting where all contribute to the designing of classroom rules and consequences.
			and	
			aesthetics.	Teacher requires that student research papers be typed or word-processed with one-inch margins.
Politics	What is just?	What is the role of school in society?	Allocation of decision-making power and distribution of educational resources reflect beliefs about justice, fairness, and equity.	Principal arranges the schedule of a poet in residence to ensure that all classes, including special education classes, have equal time with her.

Traditional Philosophies and Education

Philosophy may be as old as humankind itself. To the degree that people have tried to interpret the nature of the world and the meaning of their existence within it, they have been "doing philosophy." Because we humans live in particular times and places, our worlds and our existence have been bound by physical realities and historical and social circumstances. Our philosophies define world views that help explain the things we encounter and justify our actions. Our philosophies, then, are closely related to our cultures—the patterns of belief and behaviors that we have devised to help us adapt to the conditions of our lives. Traditional Native Americans, for example, whose heritage is closely tied to adaptations to nature, believe that life follows a cycle of birth, death, and rebirth, and that all parts of nature, including the physical, human, and spiritual worlds, are interdependent.

As a means by which cultures transmit their world views, values, and norms of behavior to new generations, education, too, is as old as humankind. In some cultures, the education of the young takes place in formal institutions called schools or academies. In many other cultures, the vehicles for education are more informal; for example, storytelling or mentor relationships, or the "walkabout" of the Aboriginal Australians. Cultures that have used written means of education have been called *literate,* while cultures relying on tales and other nonprint materials of instruction have been called *oral.*

In ancient China, education was both literate and oral. Male children selected for their imperial connections and their intellectual promise attended formal schools where they read Confucian classics that stressed personal virtue and loyalty—values expected to result in a harmonious society. Other children learned informally, from the elders of their kinship groups. The "good society" was one that was orderly and highly structured, where everyone knew the sustaining traditions and contributed to its maintenance. In India, the path to truth was internal, through focused meditation. The children of Brahmins, the highest rank of a strict caste system, attended formal schools where they studied the Vedas (Hinduism's sacred books) and practiced disciplined meditation.

Historically, Islamic education in the Middle East and Central Asia was both religious and secular, formal and informal. The educated person in Islam was one who had knowledge of the Koran, the sacred book that reveals God's ultimate truth, plus the skills needed to thrive in the secular world. Educated people were God-fearing, learned, and brave (Shorish, 1988). Because of Mohammed's decree that education should be universal and democratic, many Muslim lands offered free elementary school for both boys and girls, either in mosques or in separate structures, and scholarships for secondary education were available (Council on Islamic Education). The wide accessibility of formal schooling helps account for the historically great scientific and literary accomplishments of the Muslim world. More recently, of course, education in some Muslim countries has emphasized religious dogma and been limited by geography and gender (Shorish, 1988).

Traditionally, Native Americans, and many other indigenous populations, have educated their children using oral and physical means. They teach a view of the world that emphasizes harmony among all life forms—natural, human, and spiritual—through myths, stories, and examples. In the past, "school" was time spent observing plants and animals, watching adults make and use tools, sitting at the feet of the elders, and testing themselves in important skills related to survival and healing. Today's Native American schools incorporate the skill of observation, the value of tribal traditions and the experience of elders, and respect for the natural world.

The philosophies of the East and of native peoples have contributed to the portrait of American education today. The newer philosophies of Pragmatism and Existentialism have also left important marks, which will be discussed in later chapters of this book. Among the oldest, most enduring, and most pervasive philosophies, however, are Idealism and Realism. These two philosophies, rooted in the ancient Greek culture, which inspired American political life, have influenced the history of our education most directly. In the remainder of this chapter, we will use classic Idealism and Realism to illustrate how ancient ideas about what constitutes truth—and how one arrives at an understanding of it—appear thousands of years later in our contemporary decisions about the subject matter of education and the best teaching methods. The next section of the chapter describes Idealism and Realism, contrasts their metaphysical and epistemological orientations, and considers their contributions to American education.

Idealism

One of the oldest philosophies, Idealism is evident in the ideas of the ancient Greek philosophers Socrates and Plato, the Jewish rabbi Moses Maimonides, and the more modern European philosophers René Descartes and Immanuel Kant. Its legacy to education appears in the writings of Robert Maynard Hutchins, Mortimer Adler, E. D. Hirsch, and Diane Ravitch; in the establishment of "academies" and liberal arts colleges; in the practice of tenure and the idea of academic freedom; and in the notion of a core curriculum. The school that functions as an "ivory tower," where students and faculty read, discuss, and devise great ideas, where they pursue learning for its own sake unencumbered by the cares and concerns of workaday tasks, is the ideal setting for an Idealist education.

To the Idealists, reality lies in the mind. There is absolute truth, which is universal, eternal, unchanging, and linked to absolute virtue. This truth can be pursued, but it must be pursued through logic, through our power to reason critically and coherently. We arrive at true understanding through **deductive reasoning**—coming to conclusions based on firm premises and clear logic. The syllogism, All apples are fruit. All fruits grow on trees. Therefore, all apples grow on trees, is an example of a true conclusion based on valid premises and logical reasoning. A young child, however, may reason incorrectly that, All apples are fruits. All apples are red. Therefore, all fruit is red, based on a false premise limited by the fact that all the apples in his immediate, sensory experience have been red.

The Idealists believe that we already know the truth of things; that it lies within us, waiting to be discovered and applied to the phenomena of our experience. The Idealist teacher helps students uncover their natural capacity for sound reasoning. In Plato's words, "All inquiry and all learning is but recollection" (Plato, 360 BCE). We are born with wisdom; what lies in the way of our being able to unearth that wisdom are false premises, false assumptions, limited experience, and our tendency to define things based on our sensory experience or on what others tell us, instead of our own reasoning. We should be skeptical about what we think we know, because what we have experienced is not the whole truth. The ancient Greek philosopher Socrates urged his pupil to "[k]now thyself" by realizing what he *didn't* know.

The business of living, according to Idealism, is the examination of one's ideas and assumptions for their truthfulness. "The life which is unexamined is not worth living," says Socrates in Plato's *Apology.* The business of education is to help students discover whether their own ideas are valid and accurate representations of the truth. To Rabbi Maimonides (1190), the highest purpose of human beings was to "know" God, because God was the source of truth. The way to know God was by perfecting the human capacity for reason and thus understanding divine revelation. For Idealists, then, the highest form of human perfection is intellectual; the perfect man is perfectly reasonable. The most learned man is intellectually perfect. Maimonides said the highest form of human perfection—the development of the mind—supercedes other forms of perfection, including the physical ability to take care of our bodily needs, the material ability to make and amass the things we need to help ourselves live our lives, and the social or moral ability to behave ethically toward others. In Maimonides' traditional Jewish culture, to study and think about the deep meaning of the Bible was the way to hone students' capacity to think and reason, which allowed them to distinguish what was true and ethical from what was not.

The Idealists' educated person has had an education that presented critical questions about all of life's important issues according to the highest standards of what is true and right and good. Idealist teachers are models of high intellect and virtue who have prepared their students to come to their own conclusions, rather than accede to the opinions of others. Truth does not come to us because the entire world tells us something is true, but because we have reasoned for ourselves. To René Descartes (1641), the question of reality, of existence, can be answered only with reference to our ability to think. Searching for an epistemological way to prove that anything existed, even himself, he reasoned that if the question existed, then someone was posing the question, and, therefore, there was in fact a someone. If he could think, then someone was thinking: *"Cogito ergo sum,"* he concluded, "I think, therefore I am."

To Idealist teachers such as Rabbi Maimonides, the highest purpose of human beings was to "know" God, which could be achieved by perfecting the human capacity for reason and thus understanding divine revelation.

Source: The Granger Collection, New York

Idealism is concerned with general truths, not specific examples. To Plato, "Men come and go, but mankind lasts forever." By this he meant that, through logic, we could come to understand that our own immediate world is but a narrow and warped view of reality. If we base our knowledge of the world on what it looks like from our own backyards, we are doomed to false notions. We who live in Salem, Massachusetts, would "know" that winter is five months long and brings snow; that trees are deciduous and change color in the autumn; that most people are Catholic or at least Christian; that people live in crowded cities; that most families consist of fathers and mothers who go off to work and a couple of children; that final *r*'s are not pronounced. On the other hand, if you live in rural Arizona, your assumptions about the seasons are very different, as is your knowledge of people's ethnicity, language, and way of life. In each case, our experience is only a small part of a larger, more general reality.

To the extent that our generalizations were based only on our everyday sensory experiences, we would be wrong. To the Idealists, our incomplete understanding of reality cannot be corrected by traveling to distant places or meeting many different kinds of people, for our understanding would still be confined to what we had experienced in specific times and places, rather than what we might conceive of as a truth that is timeless and universal. To the Idealist teacher, it is not necessary (nor is it usually feasible!) to take students on a field trip to China to teach them about that country; while the trip would be highly interesting and informative, it would not give students an accurate picture of the entire country, all its people, or its history. A discussion of good books, maps, and documentary films on China might do that better. The great Idealist philosopher Immanuel Kant never left his home town, the village of Konigsberg in Prussia. He never traveled and never married (Kuehn, 2001). From this rather remote spot, he read, reasoned, and wrote seminal treatises such as *The Critique of Pure Reason,* becoming one of the world's authorities on the philosophy of science and ethics.

Seeing Beyond the Shadows: Plato's Allegory The ancient Greek philosopher Plato described the difficulty of ridding ourselves of false generalizations in his famous "Allegory of the Cave" (see Directly from the Source). In this section of *The Republic* (360 BCE), his attempt to design a society based on Idealist philosophy, he describes the liberation of the student from taken-for-granted assumptions rooted in one particular cultural world. Plato uses his own teacher Socrates in this allegory as an example of good teaching. Socrates tells his student Glaucon a story about people whose entire lives are spent in a cave. They are chained in place and forced to look only at what is in front of them. Behind them are real people engaged in daily activities. A fire burning behind them illuminates the shadows of these people on the wall in front of the prisoners, so that all that they see are these shadows of things, rather than the things themselves. The picture that Plato paints is a picture of the limited and faulty way that people perceive reality when they assume that their particular assumptions represent general truths—when they do not learn to think critically. In the allegory, Plato further describes what happens when one person escapes from the cave into the real world. Confronted with information and experiences that are different from what he has always known, he does not at first believe what he now sees, but gradually comes to understand that he lived previously in the dark. Now "enlightened," he returns to the cave to tell the others what he has discovered—that everything they think they know is inaccurate and narrow. His words inspire fear and anger in his comrades. Because he has thought for himself and achieved greater knowledge than his friends, because he has discovered a reality larger and more truthful than the shadowy world peopled by those without critical thought, the educated person in the allegory is in danger of losing his place in society, being censored, or worse.

Plato wrote *The Republic* in part to design a system that would ensure the welfare of all within it, including the intellectuals—teachers and students engaged in critical thinking and even in criticizing society. As an Idealist, he believed the wisest members of society (those who understood the importance of pursuing the Absolute Truth that lies beyond the limits of physical experience) would become ruling "philosopher-kings." Because Plato believed that the greatest knowledge included understanding the greatest good, he assumed that the philosopher-kings would make decisions justly, with concern for what was good for the entire society. Because philosopher-kings were not allowed to own property and were relieved of the burdens of everyday life—there was a class of military to protect them, tradesmen to provide needed goods, and slaves to attend to basic tasks—they could be concerned for the society as a whole, rather than for their own needs.

Plato's fears for the safety of social critics who challenged established norms and values were not unfounded. They were based on the experience of his teacher Socrates, who was forced to kill himself by drinking poison by leaders who found his ideas dangerous to their authority and to the established ways of doing things. Socrates' ideas are represented in much of Plato's work; the student Plato wrote on

Directly from the Source

Plato's Allegory of the Cave, from *The Republic*
by Plato

Source: Plato, "The Allegory of the Cave," from Book VII of *The Republic* (360 BCE). Translated by B. Jowett. (New York: Dolphin Books, 1960), pp. 105–108.

Dialogue between Socrates, the teacher, and Glaucon, the student:

And now, I said, let me show in a figure how far our nature is enlightened or unenlightened—Behold! Human beings living in an underground den, which has a mouth open towards the light and reaching all along the den; here they have been from their childhood, and have their legs and necks chained so that they cannot move, and can only see before them, being prevented by the chains from turning round their heads. Above and behind them a fire is blazing at a distance, and between the fire and the prisoners there is a raised way; and you will see, if you look, a low wall built along the way, like the screen which marionette players have in front of them, over which they show the puppets.

I see.

And do you see, I said, men passing along the wall carrying all sorts of vessels, and statues and figures of animals made of wood and stone and various materials, which appear over the wall? Some of them are talking, others silent.

You have shown me a strange image, and they are strange prisoners.

Like ourselves, I replied; and they see only their own shadows, or the shadows of one another, which the figure throws on the opposite wall of the cave?

True, he said: how could they see anything but the shadows if they were never allowed to move their heads?

And of the objects which are being carried in like manner they would only see the shadows?

Yes, he said.

And if they were able to converse with one another, would they not suppose that they were naming what was actually before them?

Very true.

And suppose further that the prison had an echo which came from the other side, would they not be sure to fancy when one of the passers-by spoke that the voice which they heard came from the passing shadow?

No question, he replied.

To them, I said, the truth would be literally nothing but the shadows of the images.

That is certain.

And now look again, and see what will naturally follow if the prisoners are released and disabused of their error. At first, when any of them is liberated and compelled suddenly to stand up and turn his neck round and walk and look towards the light, he will suffer sharp pains; the glare will distress him, and he will be unable to see the realities of which in his former state he had seen the shadows; and then conceive someone saying to him, that what he saw before was an illusion, but that now, when he is approaching nearer to being and his eye is turned towards more real existence, he has a clearer vision,—what will be his reply? And you may further imagine that his instructor is pointing to the objects as they pass and requiring him to name them,—will he not be perplexed? Will he not fancy that the shadows which he formerly saw are truer than the objects which are now shown to him?

Far truer.

www.

behalf of his great teacher Socrates, who never wrote anything himself. The "Allegory of the Cave" may have in fact been Plato's recounting of the events of Socrates' work, and death.

Plato's allegory provides a description of how difficult it often is to rid ourselves of long-held false ideas and replace them in our minds with new and truer ones. Old beliefs are hard to shake. We tend to see only the things that fit into our already-established ideas about truth and reality, and ignore the things that challenge those ideas. Plato was correct in understanding that changing one's conception of

And if he is compelled to look straight at the light, will he not have a pain in his eyes which will make him turn away to take refuge in the objects of vision which he can see, and which he will conceive to be in reality clearer than the things which are now being shown to him?

True, he said.

And suppose once more, that he is reluctantly dragged up a steep and rugged ascent, and held fast until he is forced into the presence of the sun himself, is he not likely to be pained and irritated? When he approaches the light his eyes will be dazzled, and he will not be able to see anything at all of what are now called realities.

Not all in a moment, he said.

He will require to grow accustomed to the sight of the upper world. And first he will see the shadows best, next the reflections of men and other objects in the water, and then the objects themselves. . . . And when he remembered his old habitation, and the wisdom of the den and his fellow-prisoners, do you not suppose that he would felicitate himself on the change, and pity them?

Certainly, he would.

And if they were in the habit of conferring honors among themselves on those who were quickest to observe the passing shadows and to remark which of them went before, and which followed after, and which were together; and who were therefore best able to draw conclusions as to the future, do you think that he would care for such honors and glories, or envy the possessors of them? Would he not say with Homer, "Better to be the poor servant of a poor master," and to endure anything, rather than think as they do and live after their manner?

Yes, he said, I think that he would rather suffer anything than entertain these false notions and live in this miserable manner. . . .

And if there were a contest, and he had to compete in measuring the shadows with the prisoners who had never moved out of the den, while his sight was still weak, and before his eyes had become steady (and the time which would be needed to acquire this new habit of sight might be very considerable), would he not be ridiculous? Men would say of him that up he went and down he came without his eyes; and that it was better not even to think of ascending; and if anyone tried to loose another and lead him up to the light, let them only catch the offender, and they would put him to death. . . .

No question, he said. . . .

But then, if I am right, certain professors of education must be wrong when they say that they can put a knowledge into the soul which was not there before, like sight into blind eyes.

They undoubtedly say this, he replied.

Whereas, our argument shows that the power and capacity of learning exists in the soul already; and that just as the eye was unable to turn from darkness to light without the whole body, so too the instrument of knowledge can only by the movement of the whole soul be turned from the world of becoming into that of being, and learn by degrees to endure the sight of being, and of the brightest and best of being, or in other words, of the good.

A Closer Look at the Issues

1. What do you think Plato means at the end of this passage by "the movement of the whole soul . . . turned from the world of becoming into that of being"?
2. Give some examples from your own life of how people can be trapped in a "cave" of taken-for-granted assumptions.
3. Describe in your own words Plato's notion of the educated person.

reality takes time and can be a lonely process. Only with great effort, with the opportunity to engage in dialogue with a challenging teacher and challenging peers, and with courage, can we ever hope to arrive at the true knowledge that "exists in the soul already." Elsewhere in this book, in Chapters 1 and 6 and in our Message to Future Teachers at the end of the book, we discuss the work of Parker Palmer (1995), who sees good teaching as a matter of recapturing our "spirits." Palmer says that if we teach "who we are," if we listen to our "inner teachers" as we engage ourselves and our students in a dialogue about interesting subject matter, we will then teach with identity, integrity, and effectiveness.

Most educators in the Idealist tradition emphasize the power of deep and involving subject matter to unleash the power of the student's mind. For modern Idealists, choosing this subject matter is essential. While Chapter 3 explores this issue in more depth, we offer in the next section some examples of twentieth-century educators whose work has been heavily influenced by the tenets of Idealism. You should recognize in their ideas the metaphysics, epistemology, axiology, and politics of the ancient master, Plato.

Robert Maynard Hutchins: Education to Widen Horizons Robert Maynard Hutchins (1899–1977) worked his way through Oberlin College and Yale University in the early twentieth century, eventually becoming president of the University of Chicago. As president, he was controversial for reorganizing the curriculum around the classic texts of the liberal arts. His Chicago Plan called for a wide-ranging liberal arts education based on a study of the "great books." Students would learn to read, write, and speak carefully and critically, using masterpieces of literature and philosophy as subjects of study and critique. To Hutchins, the purpose of education was to "unsettle the minds of young men, to widen their horizons, to inflame their intellects" (Hutchins, 1936a, p. 48). Teachers educated in the liberal arts themselves should engage a "community of scholars" in reading and discussing big questions, such as the nature of freedom and the nature of the good life.

Believing that knowledge and truth were universal and permanent, Hutchins felt that a liberal arts curriculum should be available to all students, no matter what career they were intending or their background or station in life. He was, therefore, against specialized, vocational, technical, or any career-oriented education as not being education at all, but mere training.

> The great books are then a part, and a large part, of the permanent studies. They are so in the first place because they are the best books we know. How can we call a man educated who has never read any of the great books in the western world? (Hutchins, 1936a, p. 78).

> [I]f we want to educate our students for freedom, we must educate them in the liberal arts and in the great books (Hutchins, 1943, p. 14).

Given his emphasis on the importance of critical thinking, Hutchins was a strong defender of the kind of academic freedom and unfettered exercise of critical minds that Plato insisted was essential to the work of educators. In 1950s anti-Communist America, Hutchins opposed the faculty loyalty oaths that some politicians were calling for. Even earlier, he sensed the danger in allowing the reality of politics to influence the content of education: "I am now convinced that the greatest danger to education in America is the attempt, under the guise of patriotism, to suppress freedom of teaching, inquiry, and discussion," he said in 1936 (Hutchins, 1936b, p. 121).

After his university presidency, Hutchins chaired the board of editors of the *Encyclopedia Britannica* and served as editor in chief of the fifty-four-volume *Great Books of the Western World* (1952), fulfilling his commitment to education in the Western intellectual tradition to the end of his life. The words of the philosopher Alfred North Whitehead attest to Hutchins's debt to Plato: "I think the one place where I have been that is most like ancient Athens," said Whitehead, "is the University of Chicago" (Whitehead, 1954).

Mortimer Adler: A Substantive Education for Every Child Plato's ideas also foreshadowed the work of Mortimer Adler (1901–2001), a twentieth-century philosopher and educational thinker who wrote that it was through "Socratic dialogue" that students would come to higher understandings of abstract concepts. Building on the basic skills and information that children learn in elementary school, high school and college teachers could help older students understand abstract concepts through the critical exchange of abstract ideas. Adler was greatly concerned that too many American children were missing out on exposure to the great ideas of great thinkers; they were missing out on a stock of knowledge that would enable them to understand concepts central to the functioning of our society, and that would allow them to converse intelligently with those who had such knowledge. To Adler, practices such as "tracking" high school students into "college," "general," and "basic" classes, and vocational curricula and special education programs that pull children out of regular classes leaving gaps in the information they receive, are responsible for gross inequities among students in opportunities to develop their minds.

A democratic education, said Adler, was "encyclopaedic," meaning, literally, "circle of instruction." The root *paideia* referred to the Greek notion that the purpose of education was to help students understand the truest and highest form of human nature. Adler's *Paideia Proposal* (1982) called for a universal high-quality curriculum in the humanities: the study of language, literature, and the fine arts, along with mathematics, the natural sciences, history, geography, and social studies. The curriculum should represent the soundest and most creative products of human thinking and lead students to the development of their own powers of mind. Since Adler was a professor of philosophy at the University of Chicago during Robert Maynard Hutchins's tenure as president, it is not surprising that he worked closely with Hutchins to develop the "Great Books" curriculum. Adler thought these great works should be at the heart of the general curriculum for high school students. They should be taught through the Socratic method, which would engage students in critical-thinking discussions, rather than ask them to be passive listeners.

Adler's ideas greatly influenced the educational reformers of the late twentieth and early twenty-first centuries, those who worked to strengthen and standardize curricula so that every community would offer its children an education that was substantive and deep. His *Paideia Proposal* influenced the 1983 Carnegie Institute report, "A Nation at Risk," which gave rise to new mandatory state subject matter frameworks in the late 1990s.

Diane Ravitch: A Focus on Academic Content New York University professor of education and former assistant secretary of education under President George H. W. Bush, Diane Ravitch (born 1938) has criticized American educators for "dumbing down" the curriculum in the guise of providing an education that is relevant and appropriate. Arguing against "life-adjustment" reforms, vocational-technical studies, and specialized programs for particular populations of children, historian Ravitch (2000, 1987) says American schools have not provided an education that is truly academic. She claims that schools have been compromised by three misconceptions: that it is their responsibility to solve any social problem, that only some children can benefit from high-quality academic study, and that the imparting of knowledge is less important than engaging children in interesting activities and first-hand experiences. Teaching children how to learn and how to find information has taken priority over giving them information of value, teaching them how to discern what is true from what is not, and helping them organize that information. The result, she says, is that the education we provide is diluted, unequal, and anti-intellectual. It aims at utility, rather than knowledge. And our standards and expectations for all students are too low.

Diane Ravitch, New York University professor of education and former assistant secretary of education under President H. W. Bush, argues that American schools have not provided an education that is truly academic.
Source: © Time Life Pictures/Getty Images

Ravitch wants teachers prepared in subject matter knowledge, not pedagogy (the skill of teaching), so that they will have important information to impart to children. Like Hutchins and Adler, she calls for the systematic study of language and literature, science and mathematics, history, the arts, and foreign languages (the liberal arts) to "convey important knowledge and skills, cultivate aesthetic imagination, and teach students to think critically and reflectively about the world in which they live" (2000, p. 15). Students deserve to meet and understand the great writers of the world, the developments of science, and the significant events and issues of the past.

> Certainly the college bound need these studies. But so too do those who do not plan to go to college, for they may never have another chance to get instruction about the organizing principles of society and nature, about the varieties of human experience. Even if they choose not to enroll in a university, they too need the knowledge and skills that will enrich their lives as citizens, individuals and members of a community (Ravitch, 2000, pp. 15–16).

In the tradition of the Idealists, Ravitch urges schools to reclaim their place as centers of learning and return to their fundamental purpose: to develop young people's intelligence and character.

The Legacy of Idealism: Academic Freedom, Critical Content, and the Ivory Tower Idealism is alive and well in some aspects of U.S. schooling today. Plato's utopian scheme to educate and protect philosopher-kings foreshadowed the notions of tenure (protection against dismissal for arbitrary or political reasons) and academic freedom (permission to come to intellectual conclusions that are different from or unpopular with opposing groups). It also gave rise to the idea of the "ivory tower" academy, a place where scholars pursue truth in dialogue with each other, unfettered by the sights and sounds and concerns of "real" life. The notion of the academy underlies many of America's private preparatory schools, our liberal arts colleges, and even our habit of building high schools and colleges on land far outside the centers of our cities and towns. Its subject matter of study, the classic works of human intellectualism and creativity, lives on in the "Great Books" curriculum of Robert Maynard Hutchins (1963) and the Junior Great Books version that many high schools use today. Idealism prevails in Mortimer Adler's (1982) proposal for a paideia, or general knowledge; in E. D. Hirsch's attempt to define a common canon of knowledge that "every American needs to know" (1987); and in what we call the humanities—the disciplines of literature, the arts, and philosophy—that embody human creativity. In Chapter 4 we include a fuller description of these and other approaches to school curricula. One major result of all these efforts is the establishment of new state curriculum frameworks across America. Another is the federal No Child Left Behind Act, established in 2001 to hold schools accountable for the teaching of a deep and common stock of knowledge.

The fundamental message of Idealism is two-fold: that the path to Truth lies in clear and critical thinking, and that we are born with a deep capacity to know. Challenging conversations help to develop that capacity. Elements of Idealism appear in the work of Lev Vygotsky (1978), who believed that children's conceptual thinking grew with the exchange of ideas and information in social learning settings (see Chapter 5 for a fuller discussion of Vygotsky's ideas about learning); and Lawrence Kohlberg (1984), discussed in Chapter 10, who claimed that students learned to think more critically about moral questions when they were exposed to the higher-level reasoning of classmates participating in group discussions about ethical dilemmas.

However, to the Idealists it is ultimately by focusing inward, away from what we and others take for granted as real, that we can uncover Truth. The process is difficult. The idea is ancient, appearing not only in ancient Greece but also in other non-western cultures. In an old Chinese tale that reflects both the power of mind—what Buddhists call mindfulness—and the Eastern conception of destiny, Chuang Tzu tells the story of "The Wood Carver," who describes his genius as the result of a meeting of his mind and nature, resulting in the crafting of a beautiful object:

> Khing, the master carver, made a bell stand of precious wood. When it was finished, all who saw it were astounded. They said it must be the work of spirits. The Prince of Lu said to the master carver: "What is your secret?" Khing replied: "I am only a workman: have no secret. There is only this: When I began to think about the work you commanded I guarded my spirit, did not expend it on trifles, that were not to the point. I fasted in order to set my heart at rest. After three days fasting, I had forgotten gain and success. After five days I had forgotten praise or criticism. After seven days I had forgotten my body with all its limbs. By this time all thought of your Highness and of the court had faded away. All that might distract me from the work had vanished. I was collected in the single thought of the bell stand. Then I went to the forest to see the trees in their own natural state. When the right tree appeared before my eyes, the bell stand also appeared in it, clearly, beyond doubt. All I had to do was to put forth my hand and begin. If I had not met this particular tree there would have been no bell stand at all. What happened? My own collected thought encountered the hidden potential in the wood; from this live encounter came the work which you ascribe to the spirits" (in Thomas Merton, *The Way of Chuang Tzu,* New Directions Press, 1976).

In this story, the wood carver attains the highest level of aesthetic expression by removing from his attention all outside distractions. Focusing only on the concept of the beautiful bell stand, the potential of his mind—or inner spirit—meets the hidden potential of the tree that is perfect for the task. What results is a perfection possible because of the pure and open interchange of the wood carver's mind and the subject of the bell stand. The message Chuang Tzu gives teachers is that students can arrive at deep understanding and great accomplishments if they are freed from physical and social distractions. While no twenty-first-century teacher would advocate fasting, the philosophical point is that understanding happens as a result of the meeting of a student's clear and open mind and the unbiased presentation of an authentic subject. A teacher can expose a student to Van Gogh's painting, "Starry Night," for example, allowing her to come to her own understanding of its meaning and the beauty of its form. Because of this exposure to the brilliant painting, the student may even be inspired to create her own painting, or a poem or piece of music. Chuang Tzu reinforces the western Idealist tenet that tells us that the connection between student and subject is at the heart of learning. The subject matter of education, prized by Hutchins, Adler, and Ravitch, helps students not only to understand reality but also to understand themselves.

The medium, or the subject matter, for the wood carver's task is, of course, the tree. It is a thing of nature, rather than an idea. We turn now to the second of the two traditional philosophies considered in this chapter, one that elevates the tree to an important position in the quest to understand and teach toward reality. To the Idealist, both the tree and the bell stand the wood carver fashions from it are vehicles for thinking about the truth of "big ideas," for example, what is beautiful. To the Realist, the tree itself is more than a vehicle; in its very nature, it is truth itself.

Realism

While to Idealists, reality lies in a world of ideas—of what can be conceived by a keen human mind—the philosophy of Realism holds that reality can be found in the world available to the senses. If we examine closely the particular things in our physical worlds, we can extract from our observations by orderly analysis a set of common features, generalizations, and rules that constitute reality. To Realists, the world is made up of parts that contribute to its sensible, orderly functioning. Things have material matter, but they also have form, which defines their ultimate usefulness. Everything in the world has a positive aim, or purpose, or reason. Everything progresses toward its ultimate purpose in a perfect, orderly world. The philosopher's task is to provide a rationale and a method for uncovering the principles that order the world. The educator's task is to help the student understand the world by learning from its observable parts, and to guide the student to live out his own inherent destiny. The learner, to the Realist, is a curious, intelligent, productive, and socially appropriate being.

In Realism, then, there is a natural world composed of physical matter and scientific principles available to the human mind if it is disciplined and observant. Rather than imposing ideas *a priori* to experience, Realism's epistemology assumes that careful study of the physical world will inductively lead to valid and better ideas. The truth comes from an *a posteriori* careful study of the natural world and then a structured reflection on that study. The assumption that everything has a place and a purpose leads Realists to conclude that axiological issues of value—for example, moral and social behavior—follow nature, as well. The virtuous person contributes her efforts to the community, is a good and responsible citizen, and behaves in ways that benefit the needs of particular societies and settings. The Greek philosopher Aristotle departed from the Idealism of his teacher Plato by insisting that truth, reality, and virtue lay in understanding the complex physical and social world as it exists in the "here and now," rather than in some world of speculation and possibility.

The philosophy of Realism developed and expanded from the work of Plato's student Aristotle, who founded his own lyceum to engage teachers and students in a search for reality in the material world, rather than in a world of ideas. Realists from Aristotle onward look to the information available to us through the exercise of our senses to answer the questions of meaning and purpose. The tenets of Realism are exemplified in the writings of Aristotle and, later, in the work of St. Thomas Aquinas (1485), John Locke (1692), Jean-Jacques Rousseau (1762), and Johann

Pestalozzi (1780, 1871, 1801). Its legacy to education includes such practices as "nature study" and "developmentally appropriate practice," and the idea that children learn best from direct and hands-on experience. The school that offers students field trips, a project-based curriculum, and community service opportunities, where what they learn relates to real-life problems and issues and where they are assessed on the outcomes of their work more than the principles that underlie it, is a school influenced by the philosophy of Realism.

Seeing Within the Shadows: Aristotle's Natural Order Born in 384 BCE in Macedonia, Aristotle enrolled in Plato's academy in 368 BCE, when he was seventeen years old, and stayed until Plato died in 348 BCE. After his academy period he traveled, supporting himself by tutoring young men, including one who grew up to become Alexander the Great. Returning to Athens, he founded his own school, the lyceum.

Although he agreed with Plato that reality was absolute and unchanging, Aristotle departed from his teacher in believing that the path to understanding the universal properties—or forms—of things lay in studying the characteristics of particular examples. Reality was not some vague notion superseding the sensible world; it lay in the midst of it, in the very real existence of particular things. For instance, to find out what is "human," Aristotle thought one should study many individual human beings and draw conclusions inductively, based on these examples, rather than deduce what might be human through the process of reasoning alone. To learn how plants grow, children should first study the structure of many different plants and their development in different environments. Their observations must be controlled, systematic, and carefully recorded. They should then use their powers of reason to draw conclusions about the functions of various plant parts and the conditions necessary for them to thrive. To Aristotle, truth lay in reason based on systematic observation.

Our universal concepts are not real things in themselves; they are merely the result of our collective human perception. A wooden object with a flat top and four legs, for example, is a "table" because we have decided it is a "table" and have given that concept subjective meaning: something to serve food on, to write on, to sit and talk around. We distinguish a table from another flat-topped, four-legged object that is smaller and that appears in a classroom with many others like it; this second object we call a "desk," and define it as something used for writing and reading, rather than for serving and eating food. To use a classroom example, in a study of plant life, teachers might label some plants "flowers" and others "weeds," based on whether we typically include them in our gardens or dig them up and throw them away. Whatever their form—whether we consider them weeds or valuable ornamentals—the concept we have of these plants lies in our use of them, rather than in their natural characteristics, their *matter.*

While Plato believed that the study of particulars would limit our full understanding of reality, Aristotle argued that such a study, if undertaken in a systematic and thorough fashion, would lead to conclusions that were true, proven by the very existence of the particular examples. Our conclusions would be workable and applicable because they would have been "based in reality." But the process of arriving at the truth of things required the careful application of that function which makes humans human—our power of reason. Aristotle's epistemological approach combined sensory experience, empiricism, and logic in a reasoned, step-by-step approach to understanding. We must first examine the thing in front of us, then look at things that are similar and different, and draw conclusions based on our observations, using **inductive reasoning:** "the starting-point which knowledge even of the universal presupposes" (Aristotle, 350 BCE). Observing systematically, we must follow a line of thought until it is contradicted by experience and try to distinguish valid from invalid arguments to arrive at a universal truth.

To Aristotle, everything in nature has a positive purpose and proceeds to an end that is divinely ordered by God, whom he called the Unmoved Mover. In the opening book of his *Nichomachean Ethics,* he says, "Every art and every inquiry, and similarly every action and pursuit, is thought to aim at some good; and for this reason the good has rightly been declared to be that at which all things aim" (350 BCE). All things have innate and divine potential, purpose, and meaning within a grand design. A puppy becomes a dog and not a cat; a caterpillar becomes a butterfly and not a hyena; plants grow with sufficient light, water, and nutrients and do not become animals; the swallows fly to Capistrano and return. All things have potentiality and actuality; an object, or a person, has in it what it potentially needs to achieve its ultimate destiny, which, if the right conditions are provided, will be its actuality. The puppy, if well cared for, can become the healthy, affectionate dog we would like as a pet. The caterpillar, if it survives, emerges as a butterfly able to contribute to the ecological environment and add beauty to the world. The child, if it is nurtured and taught good habits of mind, body, and morality, will become a thinking, healthy, and ethical individual. The "ifs" are important, because achieving actuality is not inevitable; it depends on the conditions of existence, which can limit, misdirect, even kill, an object's fundamental destiny. To Aristotle, children have a natural curiosity and propensity to learn—a potentiality. To become knowledgeable and virtuous—to reach their actuality—requires good teachers, who will provide the right materials and the right guidance.

Aristotle included in the natural order of things the social order of human life. If all things have a natural purpose and destiny, he said, then so do men, women, and children. We are characterized not only by certain physical features, but by a set of drives, including the drive to feed and shelter ourselves, the drive to reproduce, and the drive to learn and adapt. Put positively, Aristotle saw humans as actively engaged in creating lives of safety, productivity, and meaning. Put more negatively—at least from a twenty-first-century perspective—he believed that men and women had predefined purposes that were different but complementary; men should go out and labor on behalf of themselves and their families, and women should stay home to live out their natural destinies as wives and mothers. The highest good was happiness, which he defined as achieving one's natural destiny. When we go against our natural purpose, or are kept from it, we suffer the consequences: we are wrong, we are uncomfortable, we are unhappy. Presumably, Aristotle would argue that women today who choose lives that do not include husbands and/or children will be unhappy, because their choice is against nature. In this regard, he departed from the avant-garde thinking of his teacher Plato, who believed that the intellectual capacities of women were equal to men and that children, at least of the higher classes, should be raised by the state rather than by their biological parents. Aristotle's stance on the differences between the destinies, and the education, of men and women was far more typical of his time.

Besides conformity with the natural order of things, Aristotle thought that happiness required balance. The happy person is rational, orderly, and avoids extremes. He is moderate in his behavior and in his thinking. He adheres to the "Golden Mean" by balancing the two parts of his human soul: the irrational part, which is both "vegetative" (seeking physical nourishment) and "animal" (emotional), and the rational part, which is the thinking, balanced, "reasonable" part. One task of the teacher is to guide the pupil toward developing the good habits necessary for living a balanced, virtuous, moderate life. Aristotle insisted that only if parents and teachers train children in the practice of good behavior will they actually develop what we call character:

> We learn an art or craft by doing the things that we shall have to do when we have learnt it: for instance, men become builders by building houses, harpers by playing on the harp. Similarly we become just by doing just acts, temperate by doing temperate acts, brave by doing brave acts. . . . Hence it is incumbent on us to control the character of our activities, since on the quality of these depends the quality of our dispositions. It is therefore not of small moment whether we are trained from childhood in one set of habits or another. . . . (350 BCE, Book II).

Aristotle's metaphysical belief in an orderly natural world made him a student of the sciences. His epistemology relied on the senses as the primary pathway to discovering how the universe was organized. To Aristotle, the business of education was to organize topics of study and material examples in ways that would depict their natural order and be accessible to students' inquiry through the exercise of their senses and by practice. Truth would be attained through direct experiences, recognition of the natural state of things, and a reasoned and structured understanding of those experiences. As filters of reality, the senses were the doorways to the mind's chronicling of it. While in Socrates' and Plato's opinion, the unexamined life was not worth living, Aristotle might have said the disorganized life is not worth living.

Aristotle believed that the path to understanding the universal properties—or forms—of things lay in studying the characteristics of particular examples.
Source: © The Granger Collection, New York

Aristotle's Realism informed the thinking of many philosophers and educators who followed him. In the following section, we review the thinking of a select few: John Locke, whose Realism not only addressed educational issues but also grounded political ideas that were later borrowed by the patriots of the American Revolution; Jean-Jacques Rousseau and Johann Pestalozzi, influenced by Realism to develop educational philosophies that used nature as a model for instruction and for moral character; and Thomas Aquinas, a thirteenth-century theologian who united Realism with religious belief. In chronological order, we begin with Aquinas.

Thomas Aquinas: Realism and Religion Thomas Aquinas (1225–1274), a Dominican friar and professor of theology, became a leading defender of Aristotle as a source of metaphysical support for the existence of God. His philosophy synthesized what had been assumed to be separate questions of reason and faith, and the physical and spiritual worlds. He thought that the natural world was living proof of the existence of God, who, as the Unmoved Mover had created a beautiful, orderly, and purposeful universe. Aquinas's epistemology was dualistic: the path to truth is first through divine revelation (the word of God), but God has given us the power to reason so that we can "rationalize" our faith in God and understand God's purpose (Aquinas, 1485). According to Aquinas, reality is both spiritual and physical, but spiritual reality is a higher reality. Faith is, by definition, above human understanding.

To Aquinas, the ultimate purpose of education is to guide human beings to perfect their souls and know God. The role of the teacher is to convey to students the majesty of God, to inspire in them the capacity for reason, which is God's gift to them, and to use that reason to know God by examining the physical evidence of his works on earth. Agreeing with Aristotle that we can derive universal truths from studying particular examples of the material world, Aquinas looked to the senses as ways to collect the evidence. The role of the teacher is to direct students' observation and reflection so that they might move from concrete observations to abstract conclusions. Aquinas's "Thomist" philosophy influenced a tradition of rigorous, formal education evident in Catholic schools and universities around the world.

Aquinas's ideas influenced the twentieth-century philosopher and political thinker, Jacques Maritain (1882–1973), a convert to Catholicism. Inspired by Aquinas, Maritain wrote that there is a natural law that derives from a divine or eternal law, and that the goal of human existence goes beyond life on earth. That natural law implies a set of God-given human rights. Societies ought to preserve and protect those rights, in order to allow human beings to achieve moral and spiritual perfection. This conclusion led him to a concern for issues of social justice, workers' rights, and advocacy of the right of a people to govern themselves (Maritain, 1951). He was a strong supporter of the 1948 United Nations Declaration of Human Rights, and his political thought has inspired many Catholic educators working to secure education and human rights for troubled populations around the world.

John Locke: Education for Right Habits and Self-Government

John Locke (1632–1704) wrote about the importance of inculcating good habits of mind and behavior in children. He believed that we are each born as a "**tabula rasa,**" or "blank slate," and that all we would become in life was determined by the experiences written on those slates. There are no innate ideas; we attain knowledge by reflecting on information derived from sensory experience and reflection. Therefore, parents and teachers should take care in the great influence they have over children's development, both in the models of behavior they present and in their direct teaching:

> The little, and almost insensible impressions on our tender infancies, have very important and lasting consequences; and there 'tis, as in the fountains of some rivers where a gentle application of the hand turns the flexible waters into channels, that make them take quite contrary courses, and by this little direction given them at first in the source they receive different tendencies and arrive at last at very remote and distant places (1692, p. 1).

Like Aristotle, Locke believed that both reason and good behavior developed from the daily practice of good habits, from learning to respond to everyday social situations in reasonable and socially appropriate ways:

> But pray remember, children are not to be taught by rules, which will be always slipping out of their memories. What you think necessary for them to do, settle in them by an indispensable practice, as often as the occasion returns; and, if it be possible, make occasions. This will beget habits in them, which, being once established, operate of themselves easily and naturally, without the assistance of the memory (1692, p. 66).

Locke was unusual for his time in understanding that children learned best from teachers who were gentle and positive. "[K]eep them to the practice of what you would have grow into a habit in them by kind words and gentle admonitions," he said, "rather as minding them of what they forget, than by harsh rebukes and chiding, as if they were wilfully guilty" (1692, p. 66).

Locke's student, like Aristotle's, was part of an orderly social world. In fact, Locke placed virtue, wisdom (which he saw as the ability to manage one's own affairs), and good breeding above learning in educational priority. An educated person was at home in the social world and functioned as a contributing member of his society. Unlike Aristotle, Locke's witnessing of the Glorious Revolution of 1688 in England influenced him to believe that the educated person was not wed to the idea of a "natural" social order. Locke's educated person was characterized by his ability to use sound reasoning, which he had learned from teacher and parent models. Locke advocated using reason with children, based on their growing capacity for thinking and their desire to be treated with respect, rather than simply dictating to them the rules that they must follow.

In seventeenth-century England, and at any time in history thereafter, Locke's educated person would rebel against any societal and governmental structures that he reasoned were unjust and ineffective at ensuring the rights and happiness of individuals. Education would equip men (in the sexist seventeenth-century world) with the right habits, social skills, and rational power to enable them to govern themselves. Locke's ideas would influence Thomas Jefferson to call for political independence from an unjust British crown in 1776 in the Declaration of Independence and to advocate public schooling to prepare thinking citizens of the new republic.

Johann Pestalozzi: Nature As the Best Teacher Johann Pestalozzi (1746–1820) was a Swiss educator who, though idealistic and utopian in his hopes for education's ability to improve society, was a Realist in his approach to instruction. He believed that children remembered what they saw much more than what they heard. He thought that their learning began with their responding to the concrete objects and experiences they encountered in their young lives. This led to a developing ability to make generalizations and understand abstract concepts, much in the same inductive fashion that Aristotle described. Pestalozzi was the originator of the **object lesson:** He began instruction by introducing his students to familiar objects, calling on them to use all their senses to examine those things, and then leading them to generalizations based on the objects' characteristics. The teacher might begin a discussion of seeds and propagation, for example, by presenting children with an apple and asking them to dissect it and examine its various parts. To introduce a lesson on the relationship between form and function in anatomy, she might have students observe and draw the bills and beaks of various birds. Nature, Pestalozzi thought, was the best teacher: "Lead your child out into Nature, teach him on the hilltops and in the valleys. . . . Let him fully realize that she is the real teacher and that you, with your art, do nothing more than walk quietly at her side" (Pestalozzi, 1780, quoted in Mayer, 1960, p. 268).

Pestalozzi echoed Aristotle in his assumption that the natural universe was a guide to the truth:

> The exercise of a man's faculties and talents, to be profitable, just follow the course laid down by Nature for the education of humanity. . . . [T]he man who, in simplicity and innocence, exercises his forces and faculties with order, calmness, and steady application, is naturally led to true human wisdom; whereas he who subverts the order of Nature, and thus the due connection between the different branches of his knowledge, destroys in himself not only the true basis of knowledge, but the very

> need of such a basis, and becomes incapable of appreciating the advantages of truth (Pestalozzi, 1780, quoted in Mayer, 1960, p. 269).

Pestalozzi was a social reformer. He was as concerned with teaching children to develop into moral adults as he was with academic learning. In his allegorical novel, *Leonard and Gertrude* (1781), he described the power of the mother-teacher Gertrude to reform the members of a family and, then, their whole village. In the book, the children in the family influence their parents to change their slothful ways, brighten up their home, and interest themselves in their own education and self-improvement. Pestalozzi was particularly interested in educating the children of the poor, which he did by establishing schools for them, designing classrooms as loving families, and teaching subjects that were practical and relevant to their experience. His model classroom took on the characteristics of a loving family.

Pestalozzi's pedagogy incorporated what later educators would call "the whole child," engaging her senses, her emotions, and her mind in activities such as drawing, writing, movement, and field trips. In this approach, he foreshadowed the twentieth-century work of William H. Kilpatrick, Maria Montessori, John Dewey, and Jean Piaget, and greatly influenced American education. Some "normal schools"—early institutions for the preparation of new teachers—such as the one established in 1861 at Oswego, New York (today the State University at Oswego), founded their teacher preparation programs on his ideas.

Jean-Jacques Rousseau: Education for Self-Reliance Pestalozzi's contemporary, the philosopher Jean-Jacques Rousseau (1712–1788), believed nature to be the best guide to the formation of reason, skill, and character. In his allegorical book *Emile* (1762), Rousseau argued that the ultimate lessons of truth are in the experience of confronting the reality of physical conditions. He taught his fictional student Emile to learn what is real and true by isolating him from the social influences that would corrupt his inherently good nature and positive instincts.

> Everything is good as it leaves the hands of the Author of things; everything degenerates in the hands of man. He forces one soil to nourish the products of another, one tree to bear the fruit of another. He mixes and confuses the climates, the elements, the seasons. He mutilates his dog, his horse, his slave. . . . He wants nothing as nature made it, not even man (Rousseau, 1762, p. 37).

www.

Building on what he thought was the child's natural capacity for learning, Rousseau would have Emile learn "the call of nature," because "[t]he first movements of nature are always right" (1762, p. 92). He should learn that he is his own master, limited only by the constraints of the physical world. When it rains, he will learn to cover himself. When he is hungry he will find ways to secure food. He will learn to depend solely on things, rather than on people, and will get what he needs not because he asked for it, but because he secured it himself. "[Y]our child ought to get a thing not because he asks for it, but because he needs it, and do a thing not out of obedience but only out of necessity" (1762, p. 89). Emile will earn the consequences of failure and success at his own hands. In learning how to take care of himself in the physical world, he will be self-confident and happy.

Rousseau disagreed vehemently with Locke's use of reasoning with children.

> [N]ature wants children to be children before they are men. If we want to pervert this order, we shall produce precocious fruits which will be immature and insipid and will not be long in rotting. We shall have

> young doctors and old children. Childhood has its ways of seeing, thinking, and feeling which are proper to it . . . and I would like as little to insist that a ten-year-old be five feet tall as to possess judgment (1762, p. 90).

Instead, Rousseau said, parents and teachers should be firm in their denials, letting children know that they are weak, and their guardians strong. "Grant with pleasure; refuse only with repugnance. But let all your refusals be irrevocable" (1762, p. 91). Rousseau wanted to banish from children's vocabularies the terms *obey, duty,* and *obligation,* and replace them with direct experiences of force, necessity, and constraint. He would keep children away from books, as they represent others' notions of reality, not reality itself. The exception was *Robinson Crusoe,* which offered children a model of human resourcefulness and self-sufficiency in the natural world.

In adolescence, Rousseau introduces Emile to society, where Emile tests himself against "flatterers" and "card sharpers," and learns from his failures. Rousseau has Emile help the poor and seek justice for the oppressed, for Emile is by nature kind and compassionate: "There is no original perversity in the human heart" (1762, p. 92). And Emile will fall in love, though in love he is still subject to the limitations imposed by the laws of nature. Like Aristotle, Rousseau believed that the laws of nature govern social, as well as physical, activity. To Rousseau, men and women were fundamentally different, fit by nature for different temperaments and roles. While he extolled the virtues of women, he saw their talents and their role in society confined by nature to raising and supporting men. His advice on the education of women is disturbing today:

> [T]he whole education of women ought to relate to men. To please men, to be useful to them, to make herself loved and honored by them, to raise them when young, to care for them when grown, to counsel them, to console them, to make their lives agreeable and sweet—these are the duties of women at all times and they ought to be taught from childhood (1762, p. 365).

Rousseau's Emile emerges from his education independent, level-headed, caring, and impatient with ideas that have no bearing on what is essential to human welfare. Confident, realistic, and trustworthy, this exemplary student enters adulthood ready to fulfill his own needs and to contribute to building a society that is just and egalitarian. In his portrait of Emile and his vision of the good society, Rousseau drew on some fundamental principles of Realism: the superiority of the natural world and its design and order over the world of ideas; the reliability of sensory experience as a pathway to the truth; and the idea that all things, including human beings, have potentiality and need time, experiences, and guidance to attain their ultimate actual form. For a comparison of Idealism and Realism, see Table 2.3.

The Legacy of Realism: Developmental Instruction, Social Learning, and Field Trips Realism has contributed much to modern-day educational thought. Among its legacies is the idea that children learn best by first experiencing what we want them to understand and then thinking about their experience. When we give them hands-on materials in mathematics—for example, Cuisenaire rods to visualize addition, or games to learn fractions, when we take them on a field trip to an arboretum or to a museum, we are operating on the premise that children need to see and hear first, and reason later. Pestalozzi's early "object lessons" found their way into the educational practice of twentieth-century teacher, principal, and professor William Heard Kilpatrick, who advocated

Table 2.3 A Comparison of Idealism and Realism

	Idealism	Realism
Metaphysics	The products of the mind (ideas) are more valid than the observations of the senses (physical reality)	The physical world (nature) is more valid than mental images (ideas)
Epistemology	The path to truth is by means of critical thinking	The path to truth begins with organizing sensory experience
Sample materials of instruction	Literature	Direct, sensory experience
Sample teaching strategies	Socratic dialogue, critical writing, discussion	Observation, field trips, research

a curriculum designed around group projects (1918). The projects engaged students in examining problems with real-world applications. They could be small construction projects such as building a kite, or larger problems, such as publishing a school newspaper. In either case, students were engaged in purposeful activity, in coming to know by working on real things, and in practicing for their adult roles as members of a cooperative society. Kilpatrick's project method contributed to the progressive educational movement that dominated much of the twentieth century and continues today in the form of constructivism and experiential education. The seminal work of progressive educator John Dewey, and the contemporary constructivist education, are described in detail in Chapters 3 and 5.

Realism also called on educators to pay attention to the natural unfolding of children's powers of observation and reason. It foreshadowed the work of psychologists such as Jean Piaget, who told us that children were not just small adults, but needed to be taught in ways that respected their developing stages of maturity. Children must be "ready" to understand the language we use with them, the concepts we want them to grasp, and the methods and materials of instruction we set before them. The Italian educator Maria Montessori, profiled in Chapter 6, constructed a method of instruction that paid heed to Realism's emphasis on children's natural curiosity, their developing physical and mental ability, and the importance of sensory exploration. In addition, Montessori education reflected Realism's assumption that reality is ordered and understood from the specific and concrete to the general and abstract. Today, Montessori classrooms have highly organized curricula and materials. Children learn the parts of a flower and the parts of speech. They classify birds and types of governments. They construct time lines as they study the history of the natural world. Five-year-olds practice the hand movements that they will use in handwriting by washing lunch tables. In the tradition of Aristotle, Locke, and Pestalozzi, they practice good habits of social behavior by working cooperatively and using quiet voices (Montessori, 1916; Soundy, 2003).

The classic philosophies of Idealism and Realism meet the essential questions about education that frame this book in the form of several philosophies of edu-

cation, which we discuss in the next chapter. We can thank Idealism for its focus on sound and coherent ideas as the basis for answering, What is worth knowing? and on critical thinking as a way to determine, What is learning? Idealism gave us the concept of the teacher as a model of intellectual and moral behavior. In answering the question, What is good teaching? Idealism told us that good teaching develops students' powers of mind and their ability to understand broad and deep ideas. And Idealism committed the school to the social role of educating all children toward higher-order thinking skills and cultural literacy. Realism added to the notion of, What is worth knowing? the importance of understanding the physical and social world. Realism told us that, What is learning? might include systematic scientific inquiry. Good teachers would pay attention to children's developmental ages and stages of understanding and carefully present the subject matter of study in ways appropriate to those stages. Realism also gave us the idea that the school could help create the good society by mirroring its values and social relations in the relationship of teacher to student and in the social organization of the classroom.

The philosophies of education presented in the next chapter do not follow Idealism and Realism in their "pure" forms but are variations and, at times, combinations of their elements and perspectives. However, it is remarkable how enduring the fundamental questions these two philosophical traditions raised are, and how relevant these questions are to modern times. In the field of education, we continue to question the nature of truth, the value of deductive versus inductive thinking, and the balance between emphasizing novel ideas or practiced habits of mind. Should we spend time teaching students to think logically and critically at the expense of the time needed to ensure that they master information? Should we nurture their powers of observation, using the real phenomena of the world around them, at the expense of wide reading and discussion? Is it our responsibility as teachers to be skeptics and social critics, or to inculcate in students the norms and conventions of contemporary society? We hope you understand from this chapter that the debate about these questions is centuries old.

SUMMARY

- The chapter opens with a discussion of the essential question, Who is the educated person? Answers to this question lie in the basic assumptions about what is real, true, right, and just, as contained in the branches of philosophy called metaphysics, epistemology, axiology, and politics.
- Metaphysical stances determine notions about children's basic nature and about the validity of the subject matter we ask them to master. They guide teachers and curriculum developers in deciding what is worth knowing.
- Epistemology distinguishes among different "ways of knowing" that some consider universally reliable and others would assign to different subject area disciplines or to different learners. Epistemology helps educators answer the essential questions, What is learning? and What is good teaching?
- Axiology includes aesthetics and ethics and defines standards of beauty and morality. Applied to education, axiological beliefs influence the criteria teachers use to evaluate students' work and the rules and norms of behavior they expect their students to follow.
- In asking the question, What is just? politics addresses the distribution of power and resources within classrooms and across schools and communities.
- The philosophical traditions of Idealism and Realism answer metaphysical, epistemological, axiological, and political questions differently.
- Idealism, exemplified in the writings of Plato, holds that truth lies in sound "big ideas," arrived at deductively through critical thought and dialogue. In the Idealist tradition, Robert Maynard Hutchins designed a well-rounded curriculum that emphasized

the Western traditions of literature and the other humanities; Mortimer Adler developed a *paideia* proposal to provide all children with a substantive education; and Diane Ravitch called on schools to refocus on academic learning. Idealism's legacies to education include a curriculum emphasizing the humanities and instruction based on discussion and reflection. The Idealist teacher is an intellectual and moral exemplar for her students.

- Realism, exemplified in the work of Aristotle, takes the physical world, nature, as the ultimate reality, available to human beings through sensory perception of ordered facts and direct experiences. Realists include Thomas Aquinas, whose philosophy made room for both the world of physical reality and the world of faith; and John Locke, who believed that the purpose of education was to prepare students with good habits of behavior and mind for an effective social life. Johann Pestalozzi and Jean-Jacques Rousseau believed that nature was the best teacher. The Realist teacher designs teaching–learning environments and materials that lead students inductively from concrete observations to abstract generalizations.

- The tenets of Idealism and Realism and the questions the ancient philosophers raised more than two thousand years ago, appear in the thought and practice of educators in the centuries since. Today's educators, engaged in an ongoing debate about standards, the subject matter of the curriculum, methods of instruction, and the fundamental purpose of education are participating in a conversation begun a long time ago.

QUESTIONS FOR REFLECTION

1. Are you more likely to depend on knowledge by description or knowledge by acquaintance to learn something? Are the two methods equally valid?
2. List some examples of Idealism in your school experience. Do the same for Realism.
3. What is meant by the idealist tenet, "the unexamined life is not worth living"? How might that apply to your own life?
4. John Locke believed that the end of education should be the development of a "citizen," while Jean-Jacques Rousseau eschewed the "citizen" for the "man." How did they differ in their views of the role that society played in the formation of the citizen and the man? What do you think are the limitations of each view?
5. Do you agree with Diane Ravitch that today's schools have strayed far from the fundamental purpose of education? Are today's schools producing the "educated person"?

APPLYING WHAT YOU'VE LEARNED

1. www. Consult the textbook website to view the diagrams of alternative classroom layouts, or draw a few of your own based on your observations of different classrooms and your memory of some of the ones you have experienced as a student. Hypothesize what might be the beliefs of a teacher who organizes the physical spaces in his or her classroom in different ways. You might refer to any of the following: metaphysical beliefs about what subject matter is "real" and "true," epistemological beliefs about effective "ways of knowing," axiological beliefs about ethics and aesthetics, and political beliefs about power and authority.
2. Using a Venn Diagram (overlapping circles), compare and contrast the views of John Locke and Jean-Jacques Rousseau on human nature, learning (epistemology), the use of reason, the educated person, and the social purpose of education.
3. How have the ideas in Plato's "Allegory of the Cave" been evident in your life? Try drawing a picture of your cave to illustrate your example.
4. Stage a mock meeting of a school board whose members are Plato, Aristotle, Robert Maynard Hutchins, John Locke, and Jean-Jacques Rousseau. Due to the need to reduce costs, the board must

vote on whether to cut the fine arts budget or the technology education budget. You will need to do further research to guess how they would each vote on this question.

5. Following the ideas of Pestalozzi, create and present an "object lesson" to teach a concept that is included in your local or state curriculum guidelines.

KEY TERMS

aesthetics, p. 40
***a posteriori* knowledge,** p. 34
***a priori* knowledge,** p. 34
authority, p. 38
axiology, p. 40
deductive reasoning, p. 47
empiricism, p. 38
epistemology, p. 36
ethics, p. 40
inductive reasoning, p. 58
intuition, p. 38
knowledge by acquaintance, p. 37
knowledge by description, p. 37
logic, p. 38
metaphysics, p. 34
object lesson, p. 61
politics, p. 41
revelation, p. 38
sensory experience, p. 38
tabula rasa, p. 60
ways of knowing, p. 37

WEBSITES TO EXPLORE

http://classics.mit.edu. Classic Greek, Roman, and Eastern texts on the Internet.

http://www.utm.edu/research/iep. Website of the *Internet Encyclopedia of Philosophy,* containing a comprehensive, alphabetized list of philosophers and terms with extensive description.

http://www.coreknowledge.org. Core Knowledge Foundation, founded by E. D. Hirsch to promote the dissemination of a standard stock of knowledge to educators and parents. Includes a "core knowledge sequence" and network of Core Knowledge Schools.

http://www.nctt.net. National Center for Teaching Thinking. Provides professional development to teachers in fostering higher-order thinking in students.

CRITICAL READINGS

Some Thoughts Concerning Education

BY JOHN LOCKE

I have said here, because the principal aim of my discourse is, how a young gentleman should be brought up from his infancy, which in all things will not so perfectly suit the education of daughters; though where the difference of sex requires different treatment, 'twill be no hard matter to distinguish. . . .

It seems plain to me, that the principle of all virtue and excellency lies in a power of denying ourselves the satisfaction of our own desires, where reason does not authorize them. This power is to be got and improv'd by custom, made easy and familiar by an early practice. If therefore I might be heard, I would advise, that, contrary to the ordinary way, children should be us'd to submit their desires, and go without their longings, even from their very cradles. The first thing they should learn to know, should be, that they were not to have anything because it pleas'd them, but because it was thought fit for them. If things suitable to their wants were supply'd to them, so that they were never suffer'd to have what they once cry'd for, they would learn to be content without it, would never, with bawling and peevishness, contend for mastery, nor be half so uneasy to themselves and others as they are, because from the first beginning they are not thus handled. . . .

Thus much for the settling your authority over your children in general. Fear and awe ought to give you the first power over their minds, and love and friendship in riper years to hold it: for the time must come, when they will be past the rod and correction; and then, if the love of you make them not obedient and dutiful, if the love of virtue and reputation keep them not in laudable courses. . . .

Esteem and disgrace are, of all others, the most powerful incentives to the mind, when once it is brought to relish them. If you can once get into children a love of credit, and an apprehension of shame and disgrace, you have put into 'em the true principle, which will constantly work and incline them to the right. . . .

I have seen parents so heap rules on their children, that it was impossible for the poor little ones to remember a tenth part of them, much less to observe them. . . . Let therefore your rules to your son be as few as possible, and rather fewer than more than seem absolutely necessary. For if you burden him with many rules, one of these two things must necessarily follow; that either he must be very often punish'd, which will be of ill consequence, by making punishment too frequent and familiar; or else you must let the transgressions of some of your rules go unpunish'd, whereby they will of course grow contemptible, and your authority become cheap to him. Make but few laws, but see they be well observ'd when once made. Few years require but few laws, and as his age increases, when one rule is by practice well establish'd, you may add another. . . .

www.

None of the things they are to learn, should ever be made a burthen to them, or impos'd on them as a task. Whatever is so propos'd, presently becomes irksome; the mind takes an aversion to it, though before it were a thing of delight or indifferency. Let a child but be order'd to whip his top at a certain time every day, whether he has or has not a mind to it; let this be but requir'd of him as a duty, wherein he must spend so many hours morning and afternoon, and see whether he will not soon be weary of any play at this rate. . . .

As a consequence of this, they should seldom be put about doing even those things you have got an inclination in them to, but when they have a mind and disposition to it. He that loves reading, writing, musick, &c. finds yet in himself certain seasons wherein those things have no relish to him; and if at that time he forces himself to it, he only pothers and wearies himself to no purpose. So it is with children. This change of temper should be carefully observ'd in them, and the favourable seasons of aptitude and inclination be heedfully laid hold of: and if they are not often enough forward of themselves, a good disposition should be talk'd into them, before they be set upon any thin. . . .

It will perhaps be wonder'd, that I mention reasoning with children; and yet I cannot but think that the true way of dealing with them. They understand it as early as they do language; and, if I misobserve not, they love to be treated as rational creatures, sooner than is imagin'd. 'Tis a pride should be cherish'd in them, and, as much as can be, made the greatest instrument to turn them by.

But when I talk of reasoning, I do not intend any other but such as is suited to the child's capacity and apprehension. No body can think a boy of three or seven years old should be argu'd with as a grown man. Long discourses, and philosophical reason-

ings, at best, amaze and confound, but do not instruct children. When I say, therefore, that they must be treated as rational creatures, I mean that you should make them sensible, by the mildness of your carriage, and the composure even in your correction of them, that what you do is reasonable in you, and useful and necessary for them; and that it is not out of caprichio, passion or fancy, that you command or forbid them any thing. This they are capable of understanding; and there is no virtue they should be excited to, nor fault they should be kept from, which I do not think they may be convinced of; but it must be by such reasons as their age and understandings are capable of, and those propos'd always in very few and plain words. The foundations on which several duties are built, and the fountains of right and wrong from which they spring, are not perhaps easily to be let into the minds of grown men, not us'd to abstract their thoughts from common receiv'd opinions. Much less are children capable of reasonings from remote principles. They cannot conceive the force of long deductions. The reasons that move them must be obvious, and level to their thoughts, and such as may (if I may so say) be felt and touch'd. . . .

But of all the ways whereby children are to be instructed, and their manners formed, the plainest, easiest, and most efficacious, is, to set before their eyes the examples of those things you would have them do, or avoid; which, when they are pointed out to them, in the practice of persons within their knowledge, with some reflections on their beauty and unbecomingness, are of more force to draw or deter their imitation, than any discourses which can be made to them. Virtues and vices can by no words be so plainly set before their understandings as the actions of other men will shew them, when you direct their observation, and bid them view this or that good or bad quality in their practice. . . .

Curiosity in children . . . is but an appetite after knowledge; and therefore ought to be encouraged in them, not only as a good sign, but as the great instrument nature has provided to remove that ignorance they were born with; and which, without this busy inquisitiveness, will make them dull and useless creatures. The ways to encourage it, and keep it active and busy, are, I suppose, these following: Not to check or discountenance any enquiries he shall make, nor suffer them to be laugh'd at; but to answer all his questions, and explain the matter he desires to know, so as to make them as much intelligible to him as suits the capacity of his age and knowledge. But confound not his understanding with explications or notions that are above it; or with the variety or number of things that are not to his present purpose. . . . As children's enquiries are not to be slighted; so also great care is to be taken, that they never receive deceitful and eluding answers. . . .

That which every gentleman (that takes any care of his education) desires for his son, besides the estate he leaves him, is contain'd (I suppose) in these four things, virtue, wisdom, breeding and learning. . . .

I place virtue as the first and most necessary of those endowments that belong to a man or a gentleman; as absolutely requisite to make him valued and beloved by others, acceptable or tolerable to himself. Without that, I think, he will be happy neither in this nor the other world. As the foundation of this, there ought very early to be imprinted on his mind a true notion of God, as of the independent Supreme Being, Author and Maker of all things, from Whom we receive all our good, Who loves us, and gives us all things. And consequent to this, instil into him a love and reverence of this Supreme Being.

Wisdom I take in the popular acceptation, for a man's managing his business ably and with foresight in this world. This is the product of a good natural temper, application of mind, and experience together, and so above the reach of children. The greatest thing that in them can be done towards it, is to hinder them, as much as may be, from being cunning; which, being the ape of wisdom, is the most distant from it that can be; . . . cunning is only the want of understanding, which because it cannot compass its ends by direct ways, would do it by a trick and circumvention.

The next good quality belonging to a gentleman is good breeding. There are two sorts of ill-breeding: the one a sheepish bashfulness, and the other a misbecoming negligence and disrespect in our carriage; both which are avoided by duly observing this one rule, not to think meanly of ourselves, and not to think meanly of others. . . . To avoid this these two things are requisite: first, a disposition of the mind not to offend others; and secondly, the most acceptable and agreeable way of expressing that disposition. . . . The latter of these is that decency and gracefulness of looks, voice, words, motions, gestures, and of all the whole outward demeanour, which takes in company, and makes those with whom we may converse, easy and well pleased. . . . The other part, which lies deeper than the outside, is that general good-will and regard for all people, which makes any one have a care not to shew in his carriage any contempt, disrespect, or neglect of

them; but to express, according to the fashion and way of that country, a respect and value for them according to their rank and condition. . . .

You will wonder, perhaps, that I put learning last, especially if I tell you I think it the least part. This may seem strange in the mouth of a bookish man; and this making usually the chief, if not only bustle and stir about children, this being almost that alone which is thought on, when people talk of education, makes it the greater paradox. When I consider, what ado is made about a little Latin and Greek, how many years are spent in it, and what a noise and business it makes to no purpose, I can hardly forbear thinking that the parents of children still live in fear of the school-master's rod, which they look on as the only instrument of education; as a language or two to be its whole business.

. . . Reading and writing and learning I allow to be necessary, but yet not the chief business. I imagine you would think him a very foolish fellow, that should not value a virtuous or a wise man infinitely before a great scholar. Not but that I think learning a great help to both in well-dispos'd minds; but yet it must be confess'd also, that in others not so dispos'd, it helps them only to be the more foolish, or worse men. . . . Learning must be had, but in the second place, as subservient only to greater qualities. Seek out somebody that may know how discreetly to frame his manners: place him in hands where you may, as much as possible, secure his innocence, cherish and nurse up the good, and gently correct and weed out any bad inclinations, and settle in him good habits. This is the main point, and this being provided for, learning may be had into the bargain, and that, as I think, at a very easy rate, by methods that may be thought on.

. . . [C]hildren may be cozen'd into a knowledge of the letters; be taught to read, without perceiving it to be any thing but a sport, and play themselves into that which others are whipp'd for. Children should not have any thing like work, or serious, laid on them; neither their minds, nor bodies will bear it. It injures their healths; and their being forced and tied down to their books in an age at enmity with all such restraint, has, I doubt not, been the reason, why a great many have hated books and learning all their lives after. . . .

The great skill of a teacher is to get and keep the attention of his scholar; whilst he has that, he is sure to advance as fast as the learner's abilities will carry him; and without that, all his bustle and pother will be to little or no purpose. To attain this, he should make the child comprehend (as much as may be) the usefulness of what he teaches him, and let him see, by what he has learnt, that he can do something which he could not do before; something, which gives him some power and real advantage above others who are ignorant of it. To this he should add sweetness in all his instructions, and by a certain tenderness in his whole carriage, make the child sensible that he loves him and designs nothing but his good, the only way to beget love in the child, which will make him hearken to his lessons, and relish what he teaches him.

. . . [H]aving had here only some general views in reference to the main end and aims in education, and those designed for a gentleman's son, whom, being then very little, I considered only as white paper, or wax, to be moulded and fashioned as one pleases; I have touched little more than those heads which I judged necessary for the breeding of a young gentleman of his condition in general. . . .

Source: from John Locke, *Some Thoughts Concerning Education* (1692) *English philosophers of the seventeenth and eighteenth centuries (Harvard Classics, no. XXXVII* (1910). New York: P. F. Collier & Son.

A Closer Look at the Issues

1. In the final paragraph of his treatise, Locke refers to the child as "white paper, or wax, to be moulded and fashioned as one pleases." What does this statement say about what he believes to be basic human nature? (Are humans born good, bad, or neutral?) Explain.
2. In several sections, Locke urges the tutor to observe what we would call today the child's "readiness" to learn. He says that children respond better to concrete examples rather than abstract principles. And he suggests that they be "cozen'd," rather than forced to learn. Reread those sections and consider some ways that teachers today demonstrate those precepts.
3. Locke's "educated person" is a person of virtue, wisdom, and good breeding, along with learning. Contrast his idea that a child should be raised to be a socially aware and appropriate being with Rousseau's contention that society tends to corrupt children. Whose ideas seem more valid to you?

Emile, or On Education

BY JEAN-JACQUES ROUSSEAU

Everything is good as it leaves the hands of the Author of things; everything degenerates in the hands of man. He forces one soil to nourish the products of another, one tree to bear the fruit of another. He mixes and confuses the climates, the elements, the seasons. He mutilates his dog, his horse, his slave. . . . He wants nothing as nature made it, not even man; for him, man must be trained like a school horse; man must be fashioned in keeping with his fancy like a tree in his garden. . . . In the present state of things a man abandoned to himself in the midst of other men from birth would be the most disfigured of all. Prejudices, authority, necessity, example, all the social institutions in which we find ourselves submerged would stifle nature in him and put nothing in its place (p. 37).

Observe nature and follow the path it maps out for you. It exercises children constantly; it hardens their temperament by tests of all sorts, it teaches them early what effort and pain are. Teething puts them in a fever; sharp colics give them convulsions; long coughs suffocate them; worms torment them. Almost all the first age is sickness and danger. Half the children born perish before the eighth year. The tests passed, the child has gained strength; and as soon as he can make use of life, its principle becomes sounder (p. 47).

The only habit that a child should be allowed is to contract none. Do not carry him on one arm more than the other; do not accustom him to give one hand rather than the other, to use one more than the other, to want to eat, sleep, or be active at the same hours, to be unable to remain alone night or day. Prepare from afar the reign of his freedom and the use of his forces by leaving natural habit to his body, by putting him in the condition always to be master of himself and in all things to do his will, as soon as he has one (p. 63).

To reason with children was Locke's great maxim. It is the one most in vogue today. Its success, however, does not appear to me such as to establish its reputation; and, as for me, I see nothing more stupid than these children who have been reasoned with so much. Of all the faculties of man, reason, which is, so to speak, only a composite of all the others, is the one that develops with the most difficulty and latest. . . . The masterpiece of a good education is to make a reasonable man, and they claim they raise a child by reason! This is to being with the end, to want to make the product the instrument. If children understood reason, they would not need to be raised. But by speaking to them from an early age a language which they do not understand, one accustoms them to show off with words, to control all that is said to them, to believe themselves as wise as their masters, to become disputatious and rebellious; and everything that is thought to be gotten from them out of reasonable motives is never obtained other than out of motives of covetousness or fear or vanity which are always perforce joined in the others (p. 89).

Do not give your pupil any kind of verbal lessons; he ought to receive them only from experience. Inflict no kind of punishment on him, for he does not know what it is to be at fault. Never make him beg pardon, for he could not know how to offend you. Devoid of all morality in his actions, he can do nothing which is morally bad and which merits either punishment or reprimand. (p. 92).

The first education ought to be purely negative. It consists not at all in teaching virtue or truth but in securing the heart from vice and the mind from error. If you could do nothing and let nothing be done, if you could bring your pupil healthy and robust to the age of twelve without his knowing how to distinguish his right hand from his left, at your first lessons the eyes of his understanding would open up to reason. Without prejudice, without habit he would have nothing in him which could hinder the effect of your care. Soon he would become in your hands the wisest of men, and in beginning by doing nothing, you would have worked an educational marvel. Take the opposite of the practiced path, and you will almost always do well. Since what is wanted is not to make a child out of a child but a doctor out of a child, fathers and masters can never soon enough scold, correct, reprimand, flatter, threaten, promise, instruct, talk reason. Do better: be reasonable, and do not reason with your pupil, especially to get his approbation for what displeases him. . . . Exercise his body, his organs, his senses, his strength, but keep his soul idle for as long as possible. . . . Let childhood ripen in children. And what if some lesson finally becomes necessary to them? Keep yourself from giving it today if you can without danger put it off until tomorrow (pp. 94–95).

I am, however, very far from thinking that children have no kind of reasoning. On the contrary, I see that they reason very well in everything they

know that relates to their immediate and palpable interest. But one is mistaken about their knowledge, ascribing to them knowledge they do not have and making them reason about what they could not understand (p. 108).

Let us see which of our two pupils resembles the slave and which resembles the peasant. Submitted in everything to an authority which is always teaching, yours does nothing unless given the word. He dares not eat when he is hungry, nor laugh when he is gay, nor cry when he is sad . . . nor move his foot except as has been prescribed to him. Soon he will dare to breathe only according to your rules. About what do you want him to think when you think about everything for him? Assured of your foresight, what need has he of any? . . . What need does he have to foresee rain? He knows that you look at the sky for him. . . . As for my pupil, or rather nature's, trained early to be as self-sufficient as possible, he is not accustomed to turning constantly to others; still less is he accustomed to displaying his great learning for them. On the other hand, he judges, he foresees, he reasons in everything immediately related to him. He does not chatter; he acts. He does not know a word of what is going on in society, but he knows very well how to do what suits him. Since he is constantly in motion, he is forced to observe many things, to know many effects. He acquires a large experience early. He gets his lessons from nature and not from men. He instructs himself so much the better because he sees nowhere the intention to instruct him. . . . This is the way one day to have what are believed incompatible and what are united in almost all great men: strength of body and strength of soul; a wise man's reason and an athlete's vigor. Young teacher, I am preaching a difficult art to you, that of governing without precepts and doing everything by doing nothing. . . . You will never get to the point of producing wise men if you do not in the first place produce rascals. This was the education of the Spartans: instead of being glued to books, they began by being taught how to steal their dinner. (pp. 118–119).

[Emile's] ideas are limited but distinct. If he knows nothing by heart, he knows much by experience. If he reads less well in our books than does another child, he reads better in the book of nature. His mind is not in his tongue but in his head. He has less memory than judgment. He knows how to speak only one language, but he understands what he says; and if what he says he does not say so well as others, to compensate for that, what he does, he does better than they do. He does not know what routine, custom, or habit is. What he did yesterday does not influence what he does today. He never follows a formula, does not give way before authority or example, and acts and speaks only as it suits him.

If he needs some assistance, he will ask for it from the first person he meets without distinction. He would ask for it from the king as from his lackey. All men are still equal in his eyes. . . . He will not stupidly question others about everything he sees, but he will examine it himself and will tire himself out to discover what he wants to learn before asking. If he gets in unforeseen difficulties, he will be less disturbed than another; if there is risk, he will also be less frightened. . . . Necessity weighs heavy on him too often for him still to baulk at it. He bears its yoke from his birth. Now he is well accustomed to it. He is always ready for anything. (pp. 159–161).

I hate books. They only teach one to talk about what one does not know. . . . Since we absolutely must have books, there exists one which, to my taste, provides the most felicitous treatise on natural education. This book will be the first that my Emile will read. . . . It is Robinson Crusoe. Robinson Crusoe on his island, alone, deprived of the assistance of his kind and the instruments of all the arts, providing nevertheless for his subsistence, for his preservation, and even procuring for himself a kind of well-being—this is an object interesting for every age and one which can be made agreeable to children in countless ways. . . . The truest means of raising oneself above prejudices and ordering one's judgments about the true relations of things is to put oneself in the place of an isolated man and to judge everything as this man himself ought to judge of it with respect to his own utility. (pp. 184–185).

Your greatest care ought to be to keep away from your pupil's mind all notions of social relations which are not within his reach. But when the chain of knowledge forces you to show him the mutual dependence of men, instead of showing it to him from the moral side, turn all his attention at first toward industry and mechanical arts which make men useful to one another. In taking him from workshop to workshop, never allow him to view any work without putting his hand to the job himself or to leave without knowing perfect the reason for all that is done there (pp. 185–186). I absolutely want Emile to learn a trade (p. 197).

Emile has little knowledge, but what he has is truly his own. He knows nothing halfway. . . . Emile has a mind that is universal not by its learning but by its faculty to acquire learning; a mind that is open,

intelligent, ready for everything. . . . It is enough for me that he knows how to find the "what's it good for?" in everything he does and the "why?" in everything he believes. . . . My object is not to give him science but to teach him to acquire science when needed to make him estimate it for exactly what it is worth, and to make him love the truth above all (p. 207).

Source: From Jean-Jacques Rousseau, *Emile, or On Education,* Trans. by Allan Bloom, New York: Basic Books, 1979.

A Closer Look at the Issues

1. Why does Rousseau consider books something to avoid in the education of children? Do you agree?
2. Do you agree with Rousseau that, in the education of children, habits should be avoided at all costs? Explain.
3. Rousseau vehemently disagrees with John Locke's emphasis on teaching children to reason by reasoning with them and modeling reason. How does this difference of opinion reflect their belief in how the mind develops?

REFERENCES

Adler, M. (1982). *The paideia proposal: An educational manifesto.* New York: Macmillan.

Aquinas, St. Thomas (1485). *Summa theologica.* Trans. by Fathers of the English Dominican Province. NY: Benziger Brothers, 1947.

Aristotle (350 BCE). *Nichomachean ethics.* Trans. by H. Rackham, Loeb Classical Library. Cambridge, MA: Harvard University Press, 1926.

Benne, K. (1970). Authority in education. *Harvard Educational Review,* 70 (3): 385–410.

Cahn, S. M., ed. *The philosophical foundations of education.* New York: Harper & Row.

Council on Islamic Education (n.d.). Education and the rise of universities in Muslim lands and Europe. http://www.cie.org/pdffiles/smplren2. Retrieved August 7, 2004.

Descartes, R. (1641). A discourse on method and meditations. In *The philosophical writings of Descartes,* ed. and trans. by J. Cottingham, R. Stoothoff, D. Murdoch, and A. Kenny. Cambridge: Cambridge University Press, 1991.

Foucault, M. (1979). *Discipline and punish: The birth of the prison.* Trans. by Alan Sheridan. New York: Vintage.

Hirsch, E. D. (1987). *Cultural literacy: Rediscovering knowledge in American education.* Boston: Houghton Mifflin.

Hutchins, R. M. (1936a). *The higher learning in America.* New Haven: Yale University Press.

Hutchins, R. M. (1936b). *No friendly voice.* Chicago: University of Chicago Press.

Hutchins, R. M. (1963). *A conversation on education.* Santa Barbara, CA: Fund for the Republic.

Kilpatrick, W. H. (1918). The project method. *Teachers College Record, 19,* pp. 319–334.

Kohlberg, L. (1984). *The psychology of moral development.* San Francisco: Harper & Row.

Kuehn, M. (2001). *Kant: A biography.* New York: Cambridge University Press.

Locke, J. (1692). Some thoughts concerning education. In *The educational writings of John Locke,* ed. by W. Adamson. Cambridge: Cambridge University Press, 1922.

Maimonides, Moses. (1190). *The guide of the perplexed.* Trans. by S. Pines. Chicago: University of Chicago Press, 1963.

Maritain, J. (1951). *Man and the state.* Chicago: University of Chicago Press.

Martin, K., and B. Mirraboopa (2001, September). Ways of knowing, ways of being and ways of doing: Developing a theoretical framework and methods for Indigenous research and Indigenist research. Paper presented at Australian Institute of Aboriginal and Torres Strait Islander Studies Annual Conference, Canberra, Australia. http://www.aiatsis.gov.au/rsrch/conf2001/PAPERS/MARTIN.pdf. Accessed March 13, 2004.

Merton, T., ed. and trans. (1976). *The way of Chuang Tzu.* New York: New Directions Publishing Corp.

Montessori, M. (1916). *The Montessori method.* New York: Schocken Books (1964 edition).

Palmer, P. (1995). *The courage to teach.* San Francisco: Jossey-Bass.

Pestalozzi, J. (1780). The evening hours of a hermit. In F. Mayer, (1960). *A history of educational thought.* Columbus, OH: C. E. Merrill Books, 1960.

Pestalozzi, J. (1801). *How Gertrude teaches her children.* Ed. and trans. by L. E. Holland and F. C. Turner. Syracuse, NY: George Allen & Unwin, 1894.

Pestalozzi, J. H. (1781). *Leonard and Gertrude.* Trans. by E. Channing. Cambridge, MA: Harvard University Press, 1885.

Plato (360a BCE). *Apology of Socrates.* Trans. by B. Jowett. http://classics.mit.edu/Plato/apology.html. Accessed July 29, 2002.

Plato (360b BCE) *The Republic.* Trans. by B. Jowett. New York: Dolphin Books, 1960, pp. 105–108.

Ravitch, D. (2000). *Left back: A century of battles over school reform.* New York: Simon & Schuster.

Ravitch, D. (1987). *The schools we deserve.* New York: Basic Books.

Rousseau, J.-J. (1762a). *Emile.* Trans. by A. Bloom. New York: Basic Books, 1979.

Rousseau, J.-J. (1762b). *The social contract.* Trans. by G. D. H. Cole. http://www.constitution.org/jjr/socon.htm. Accessed July 29, 2002.

Shorish, M. M. (1988, February). The Islamic revolution and education in Iran. *Comparative Education Review 32,* pp. 58–75.

Soundy, C. S. (2003). Portraits of exemplary Montessori practice for all literacy teachers. *Early Childhood Education Journal, 31* (2), pp. 127–131.

Swartz, R. J. (2000). Teaching thinking in the content areas. First Annual Thinking Qualities Initiative Conference, Hong Kong, June 23.

Vygotsky, L. S. (1978). *Mind in society.* Cambridge, MA: Harvard University Press.

Whitehead, A. N. (1954). *Dialogues of Alfred North Whitehead: As recorded by Lucien Price.* Boston: Little, Brown.

Philosophies of Education 3

ESSENTIAL QUESTION

What is worth knowing?

Talented teachers draw on many points of view to reach their students. Imagine a classroom with Mr. Thomson, who teaches ninth graders in a midwestern inner-city public school, where all of the kids love to go to his class. Mr. Thomson grew up in a public housing project that still exists in this city. As a humanist, Mr. Thomson believes all kids need to read the classics. He understands his students and appreciates what he needs to do to get them hooked on Shakespeare. He captures their attention by physically jumping on his desk, which he uses as a stage to present Shakespeare's plays to the class. This month, everyone is studying Romeo and Juliet. While only some of these students are gang members, all of them know about gangs, so he portrays the gangs in Romeo and Juliet to parallel his students' experiences of gang life. After several scenes, he stops and turns the production over to his students. The

classroom then becomes a theater in the round. Seats are in a circle; the stage moves from the teacher's desk to the center of the room. Mr. Thomson sets a scene with his readings, and then the students take on different roles. Students switch alternately from being the actors to being the audience. All are required to be engaged with the process of interpreting Shakespeare's work. The proper decorum for theater is set in guidelines previously drawn by Mr. Thomson and the students to provide a respectful tone in the classroom climate. Interpretations of the play emerge from personal experiences, particularly those related to the drama and tragedy of Romeo and Juliet. While the required readings of Shakespeare are also mandated in the school's standards-based curriculum, Mr. Thomson extends the scope of the standards when he ends the class by including other readings that reflect and emanate from the culture of his students. Today, he asks the class, "How might James Baldwin write this play?" ■

What Is Philosophy of Education?

The ideals of the humanist live in Mr. Thomson's classroom, in the insistence that all students read the classic works of literature. Yet, he values the personal experiences of his students, which is evident when he connects the body of literature to their lives. The students' active participation in the production of the play reflects a progressive's emphasis on student interpretation and hands-on learning. How would you describe Mr. Thomson's philosophy of education? Some have called him an elitist. Others have characterized him as a good, caring teacher not unlike Nel Noddings and other existentialists. What knowledge would Mr. Thomson define as worth knowing? As you read the philosophical approaches to education that are discussed in this chapter, you will have more ideas about Mr. Thomson's class. You might say that Mr. Thomson is a progressive who turns his classroom into a project-based curriculum; or that he is an essentialist who follows the standards-based education. Or, that he is a perennialist who wants to transmit a cultural heritage and values by reading the great books. Maybe Mr. Thomson's knowledge uses several philosophies of education that shape his approach to teaching.

How would you answer the question, What knowledge is worth knowing? Your response reflects your views on reality (your metaphysics), your notions of knowledge and the relationships between the knower and the subject to be known (epistemology), and finally, your values or beliefs (axiology and ethical system). (See Chapter 2.) Your philosophy of education defines what knowledge is important to you as well as how to impart that knowledge. If you are a traditionalist who believes that there is a common body of knowledge necessary for all people to learn, you might subscribe to theories that support classical studies. On the other hand, if you feel experiences are at the core of what one needs to know, your philosophy probably finds expression in social action, hands-on learning, or personal persuasions.

Defining Philosophy of Education and Its Purpose

Keep in mind the distinction between *philosophy* and *philosophy of education*. Philosophy is concerned with the theories, the ideas, and the notions of metaphysics, epistemology, and ethics. In philosophy, these theories and ideas are

challenge in labeling these isms, because similar elements are often ascribed to differing philosophies. Many philosophies intersect on common assumptions and beliefs, so you will find conflicting interpretations of the isms among authors of philosophy of education texts. The distinctions between schools of thought are not always clear-cut and are made with an individual's mindset and point of view. We offer our views with our own biases and dispositions and invite you to formulate and group yours.

Perennialism: A Curriculum for Cultural Literacy

Plants that bloom every year and express their beauty over time are known as perennials. Similarly, there are works, writings, findings, and truths that have stood the test of time and are considered the valuable body of knowledge that is worth knowing. The educated person possesses such knowledge. Educational philosophers who assume this position derive their name from nature, falling into the camp known as the perennialists. McNergney and Herbert (2001, p. 143) define a perennialist as one who holds that "there are principles of education so important, so central to the development of culture that they cannot be ignored, such as the universality of truth, the importance of rationality, and the power of aesthetics and religion to encourage ethical behavior," and "like realists, perennialists believe that such enduring principles exist in the physical world." Yet like idealists, perennialists begin with the ideas and principles of knowledge in their lifelong pursuit of education. Perennialists, then, can favor both realism and idealism. They revere the ideals of both Plato and Aristotle and their followers throughout the history of Western society. Perennialists prescribe the traditions of a classical education held in high esteem in western culture. This tradition reflects the cultural literacy of American society. American schools are responsible for preserving this cultural literacy as the heritage of western civilization and must transmit its values and knowledge base.

A Uniform Education Numbered among the perennialists are Robert Maynard Hutchins, E. D. Hirsch, Jr., and Mortimer Adler. For Hutchins, a liberal arts education includes the readings of the "great books," particularly those of western civilization. E. D. Hirsch identifies the readings he considers essential in his book, *Cultural Literacy* (1987). For Hirsch, in order for any learning to take place, there must be a shared body of knowledge that ensures meaning and communication. Adler presents his *Paideia Proposal* (1982) as a common curriculum for all students. All of these theorists argue that students share common needs and should receive a uniform education that can be passed on from one generation to another. Their curriculum favors the classic curriculum of literature, known as the western canon, which was passed down from the Western European legacy of study of the arts and sciences.

A core curriculum for all students is basic to this education, which places literature in a prominent position, along with the traditional subject areas of mathematics, science, languages, the social sciences, and the arts. Perennialists want the curriculum to include the body of knowledge that they feel sustains our world and reflects and transmits its culture. Since this knowledge has intrinsic value, it must be preserved in the curriculum, transmitted through the school, and studied for its own sake. This knowledge gives the learner a sense of identity, an enduring set of values, and insights into the workings of the universe.

While perennialists are in general agreement on the body of knowledge worth knowing, individual theorists express the philosophy in differing programs. We will discuss these in more detail in Chapter 4. It is sufficient to say here that they prescribe criteria for effective teaching but permit the delivery system to vary.

Paramount to the success of perennialist pedagogy is the informed and knowledgeable teacher who evidences a background of depth and breadth in the classics of western civilization, as well as in the subjects he teaches. Such a professional models in his scholarly pursuits an appreciation for learning for the sake of learning. In all professional endeavors he is expected to continue the traditions of an academic and to blend the best ideas of the past with those of the present.

Perennialists are often labeled as humanists. **Humanists** encourage their students to actualize their unique human potential to seek lofty goals for the betterment of all. These teachers are charged by society with the tasks to preserve and transmit the great ideas of our culture to each generation. Such teachers are considered the lights in a dark tunnel and the keepers of the keys to knowledge. These are the educators who understand that education means to lead. They are the leaders in Plato's cave who set the captives free to find truth. Fictional characters in literature and film like *Good-bye, Mr. Chips* and *The Dead Poets Society* portray the ideal perennialist practitioner.

What Might a Perennialist Classroom Look Like? The perennialist is more likely illustrated as a teacher of the humanities; but math teachers who pursue universal principles in their teaching and reflect the Platonic ideal of teaching math as part of the classical curriculum meet the definition of a perennialist as well. Throughout the centuries much emphasis has been on literacy as the sole definition of humanistic education to the determent and often the exclusion of numeracy. Therefore, we are offering a model mathematics class rather than the typical literature class as our perennialist model for the twenty-first century. So, welcome to Mr. Steves's sophomore math class. Poster-sized portraits of many of the great mathematicians in history are displayed around his room. Mr. Steves tells the stories of their lives to inspire his students to unlock the principles of life through their own study of mathematics. He uses biography as a storytelling technique to humanize his instruction by putting a face on key mathematical theories.

Mr. Steves wants all of his students to be highly skilled in mathematics and to appreciate the discipline for its own sake. For him, numeracy is as important as literacy for gaining knowledge about the world. He strives to pass on the legacy of the love for mathematics to his students. His high expectations for his students' achievements are fashioned by his own experiences as a student in an elite, private preparatory school. He has a strong belief that all students can attain the mathematical background accorded to him. To avoid defeatism and competition, he organizes his class into cooperative groups, in which students support each other in their quest. Each group member has an assigned role. Mr. Steves poses questions, provokes their dialogues, and assists in finding solutions. He demonstrates the value of their study when he challenges his students to use higher thinking skills in applying math to solving problems and making discoveries.

Today, the class is using algebra in statistical analysis. The group assignments are generated from happenings in the community and from news stories on the Internet or in daily newspapers. One group is comparing the Organization for Economic Cooperation and Development (OECD) tables that link levels of education with employment opportunities. Other groups are determining the statistical probability of the number of World Series championships the New York Yankees will ultimately win. Throughout the group work, the inherent value of mathematics is evident as the topics vary from group to group and change daily throughout the school year.

Essentialism: A Curriculum for Basic Skills

The philosophy of essentialism is often confused with perennialism. Essentialists also identify the knowledge worth knowing in a common core of knowledge with a heavy emphasis on western civilization. However, for the essentialists, this body of knowledge is not to be learned necessarily for its own sake, but for the skills derived by study and used in present-day living situations. For the essentialists there are essential skills necessary for the educated person to function successfully in society. These skills form the core of the curriculum and identify competencies that can be delivered in a standards-based education.

Realism and Standards-Based Education Essentialists are realists. In fact, they epitomize the realist's view of educational practice. The real world defines a basic core of knowledge necessary for successful living. Content areas address today's needs in society and the world of work. Teaching and learning can be measured objectively for success or failure. For the essentialist, accountability is critical to the teaching/learning process and is assessed in high-stakes testing schemes for recognition of levels of achievement. If a high school diploma is to have value, students must demonstrate a certain degree of knowledge and skills to warrant this award. Schools are judged as "good" or "underperforming" based on their students' performance on these tests. Administrators and teachers are responsible for meeting attainment targets, beginning in the elementary school years and continuing through high school. Teachers' and administrators' competencies also are measured by tests for certification.

Competent teachers transmit a **core curriculum** of basic skills, attitudes, and a body of knowledge through direct instruction and prescribed subject areas in defined programs of study. To do so, teachers must be thoroughly schooled in the core curriculum, well organized, and consistent in their presentation of material throughout the entire educational process. The rise of teacher testing for professional credentials is an international as well as national effort promoted by the essentialist movement worldwide.

The essentialist's rally call is "return to the basics." The school's mission is to transmit a critical mass of basic knowledge necessary for a moral and literate citizenry. Schools need to offer the skills and a knowledge base of the sciences and professional and vocation skills, along with communication, literacy, math, and civic understanding—all subjects that are necessary for participatory citizenship in a democracy and competent membership in the global work force.

Proponents of Essentialism At the end of World War II, there was a general concern about the disarray in American schools, which was blamed on progressive education. The works of William Bagley and Arthur Bestor, who demanded the restoration and promotion of an essential standard curriculum, fortified the essentialist movement. The *Sputnik* crisis of 1957 heightened the rhetoric of criticism of American education. The then–Soviet Union sent the first unmanned or artificial satellite—named *Sputnik*—into space, prompting Americans to pursue improvements in their science and technology programs to catch up with Russian achievements. The naysayers saw the U.S. educational system as falling behind in international circles. They clamored for American schools to focus more on mathematics and the sciences to assure equal footing in the "race in space."

Contemporary writers such as Alan Bloom, William Bennett, and Chester Finn continue the cause that sounds the alarm of failing schools in America and the need for a return to "basic essentials." The Council for Basic Education extends the movement of essentialism to a global audience. It disseminates programs that define and abide to world-class standards for curriculum and pedagogy among an alliance of educators. Themes that shape this philosophy and drive its curriculum are: multinational corporations' demands for a literate work force through programs that transfer skills from the classroom to the workplace, and governments' calls for fostering the skills, attitudes, and understanding necessary for educating an informed citizen.

What Might an Essentialist Classroom Look Like? Ms. Eliot is preparing her third graders for their first state standardized test in reading and literacy skills. She has revised the TV program *Jeopardy* to use in her class to practice word definitions for vocabulary development. In her rendition, the class is divided into teams. Each member of the team is to match the weekly learned vocabulary words to their proper definitions. Ms. Eliot holds up a flash card shaped like a TV screen to display a word definition. Then teams select a similar flashcard with the matching vocabulary word. The team with the most matches wins the game. The vocabulary comes from a required reading program designed to meet the state-mandated standards for reading in grade three. The children must also use the words in their daily writing assignments, which are generated through reading comprehension questions from the basal reading program assigned to each elementary school in the district.

Ms. Eliot wants her children not only to perform successfully on the test, but also to use the skills she teaches as a preparation for future study and work. She engages her children in many role-playing exercises that provide motivation for practice and drill in all of the basic areas of the curriculum. The results of her approach are evident in her class's increased word recognition and reading comprehension skills as well as improved performances in math and general science exams. Her peers have recognized her as a highly successful teacher by nominating her as the community's teacher of the year.

Behaviorism: Tabula Rasa and Mastery Learning

Behaviorism is more of a school of psychology than a philosophy. It shares a common ground with essentialism in its view of reality and its notion that we cannot ascertain the innate ideas of the idealists or the perennialists; nor need we be concerned with the notions of universal truths or principles. For the behaviorists, the *given* is human behavior, which they believe can be shaped and changed, conditioned and reconditioned, to reach carefully defined goals whose structured procedures lead to a mastery of learning. Behaviorists are realists who believe that knowledge is derived from the physical world and not from innate ideas or universal principles. Ideas and principles come from students' interactions with their world. The environment shapes the learner. By altering the environment, learning can be controlled or directed. In such an environment, behavior is manipulated by a series of reward/punishment experiences. Learning is the result of experimentation. Successful procedures or steps are identified to lead to a desired result. These steps require that the learner be conditioned to behave in a prescribed manner.

The foundation of this school was the work of Ivan Pavlov's experimentation in his study of the effect of "stimuli and responses" on dogs. Other theorists include John Watson, E. L. Thorndike, and B. F. Skinner (McNergney and Herbert, 2001, p. 140). All of these theorists predicated their work on a scientific basis. Stimulus/response, engineering the environment, operative behavior, behavioral objectives, and measured outcomes are some of the notions developed in behaviorism and are common practice in today's curricula. Tokens are given for good behavior in a preschool class. In many elementary classes you can find charts that list who has read the most books by displaying an array of stars next to the child's name. Prizes, trophies, honor rolls, and medals that cite desired achievement are ubiquitous in high schools throughout the country. While all of these rewards have motivational value for students to work for a goal, caution must be taken not to confuse the attainment of the reward with the acquisition of knowledge or skills.

Like their predecessor, the realist, John Locke, behaviorists view the learner as a blank slate, or "tabula rasa," which can be shaped and defined (see Chapter 2). While all behavior might be caused by the environment or experience, the cause is not important, only the resulting behavior. Usually, the cause of behavior cannot be determined, so causes are not the concern of the behaviorist. Behavior can always be changed through techniques and strategies that enforce and reinforce desired outcomes. Oftentimes, such strategies are individualized with an instructional plan that delineates a step-by-step process to structure appropriate behavior through intrinsic and extrinsic rewards systems.

The traditional practice of using grades to judge a student's work is another manifestation of the behaviorist rewards system. The practice is so entrenched in the schools that children soon learn what to do to get the good grade. In fact, the grade is the reward, rather than competency. Often, parents collude with the practice and encourage their children to elect easier courses for higher grades, instead of attempting a course that would be a challenge. We as professors have witnessed students devaluing assignments that are not graded as being unimportant. The conditioning factor has been in place throughout their entire careers as students. Knowledge for its own sake or pleasure has been jaded for them by the grading system. Even when education students study the irrelevance of the alphabet of grades—A, B, C, D, F—they look first for the grade on their own papers, rather than read the long, painstaking commentary from their professor. Likewise, when attempts are made to alter the system, to reverse direction by replacing grades with written evaluations or reports, students typically ask, But what did I get on this paper? Habits of the mind are difficult to change!

In the debate of nature vs. nurture, behaviorists favor nurture. All school problems, behavioral issues, and learning difficulties can be solved through programmed instruction and operant conditioning, teaching or conditioning with rewards for learning. In the educational field, these programs are represented by approaches such as formatted teaching, scripted learning, outcomes-based education, and the individual educational plan (IEP). This philosophy's impact on current instructional practices, counseling, and special education is evident; however, the behaviorist's influence is not limited to school. In counseling and psychology, the emergence of self-help literature and twelve-step programs find their genesis in the behaviorist school of thought.

Romantic Naturalism: The Child at the Center

Historically, romantic naturalism reflects the tone of the nineteenth century. In the world of music, literature, philosophy, and politics there was a growing optimism about the natural goodness of humankind. This optimism was interpreted with a romantic flair in the music of Beethoven, Schumann, and Chopin; in the art of the impressionists; in the books about the goodness of the "natural savage;" in the philosophies of the idealists and the transcendentalists; and in the changing political climate of the world. The movement was a natural reaction to the pessimism of earlier centuries when man was seen as depraved, in need of control, and saved only by God. As an outgrowth of the optimism of the Enlightenment Age—with its faith in science and the physical world, the discovery of its laws, and the exploration of the globe—romantic naturalism brought about an unbridled enthusiasm about humanity. New nations were emerging that replaced monarchy with democracy.

Educational reforms reflected this movement. Its spirit was captured in the works and writings of Jean-Jacques Rousseau, Frederick Froebel, Elizabeth Peabody, and Maria Montessori. All of these educators drew upon the works of earlier humanists, such as Erasmus and John Amos Comenius, with a belief in common sense, a benevolent treatment of the learner, and a confidence in students' good intentions and natural curiosity.

Romantic naturalists hold as a foundational tenet that the human condition is basically good. Any corruption of it is due to outside influences. For Rousseau, society was the corrupting factor. The child needed only to be freed from the bonds of society, allowed to be guided or tutored, and *he* would become enlightened and educated. His subject, *Emile,* the title name of his definitive book published in 1762, was to enjoy unlimited exposure and exploration of his world to develop and maximize his natural abilities. Unfortunately, "Emile's search for a proper life's companion in Book V" is the only mention of the education of a woman, whose goal is to enhance the life of Emile (Power, 1970, p. 486). Rousseau's writings were

Child-centered classrooms often involve students working at a variety of stations around the classroom, such as writing stations, art stations, science stations, etc. Although the teacher oversees the stations, he or she is not central to the activities taking place.
Source: © Elizabeth Crews

influential throughout the nineteenth century. Fortunately, his disciples did not emulate his gender bias.

Rousseau's views spearheaded a myriad of innovative educational approaches. These views focus on the child and the child's learning needs and styles. These alternative models are still prevalent in today's schools throughout the world.

Froebel Frederick Froebel was a Prussian philosopher, educator, and social activist. Framing his philosophy of education in *The Education of Man,* published in 1826, Froebel drew upon his philosophical beliefs in pantheism—the belief that God, the author of all being, exists in all of creation, including man. So, each one of us is divine as an extension of God's spirit. Awakening this intrinsic divinity was to begin when the child was young and unencumbered by outside influences. Froebel's defining achievement was the establishment of the *kindergarten:* a garden of children who will survive and strive for excellence if tended and nurtured as flowers in a garden. Froebel believed that within each child is a spirituality that unfolds and becomes evident, if the child is allowed to play in an environment that permits growth. Froebel's faith in play as the work of childhood and the medium through which children learn was a major breakthrough in early education pedagogy.

Prior to Froebel, theorists had speculated about the importance of play in childhood, but Froebel centered it in the educational process. The Greeks realized its importance, particularly at the secondary level, in which music, dance, and games defined the *gymnasium.* Other theorists valued play as an incentive or reward for learning. Froebel's unique treatment of play was his understanding of its value beyond an extrinsic mechanism. He defined play as being internally important to the development of the child. Through play, children learn about their world, themselves, and others. Play allows them to solve problems, explore ideas, socialize, and communicate. As a pantheist, Froebel identified God with nature or universal laws and was tolerant of others' beliefs and forms of worship. He added a spiritual dimension to play. His curriculum prescribes not only the kind of play that is important to the child but also the play materials that would best awaken and unfold the divine nature of the child.

While the spirit of the nineteenth century was ready for Froebel, the Prussian government was not, and it labeled his commune of educators as subversive. The disciples of Froebel who fled their repression in Prussia were welcomed in the educational circles of America and Europe. Also during this time, educators were beginning to accept childhood as separate from adulthood. Children were no longer seen as miniature adults. Childhood was beginning to be viewed as a special time of innocence, to be cherished and protected. The United States had opened its door to European immigrants who established Froebelian kindergartens in German-speaking enclaves. The first model German kindergarten in the United States was established by Margarethea Ronge Schurz, a disciple of Froebel who immigrated to Watertown, Wisconsin, during the 1850s. Elizabeth Peabody (and other educational reformers) was sympathetic to Froebelian writings and practices, which paralleled her own transcendental leanings. In Boston, she established the first English-speaking kindergarten, and with the backing of people such as Susan Blow and William T. Harris, she moved it from private supported philanthropy and its German ethnic endeavors to the sphere of public education open to all children (see Chapter 6 for further discussion).

Montessori Maria Montessori was also looking for a better method of education, in order to improve family living conditions and change social and political conditions in Italy. As a trained physician she designed a scientifically based educational system, with a curriculum and materials fostered by her understanding of the developing child. She differed from Froebel in his prominent use of play, as her didactic materials were intended for self-directed learning. *Play* is a term Montessori avoided, but as Froebel prescribed his play in what he called "gifts and occupations," Montessori designed sequential materials that matched stages of development in multiple domains, for example physical, social, and cognitive. These materials are the core of her method. The child is directed to be autonomous in implementing their use. The trained teacher in a Montessori school, known as a directress, demonstrates how the materials are to be used. While the child is free to choose materials to initiate instruction, he can use them only in the manner demonstrated by the teacher. Creative exploration is not an option. For example, the proper use of sound cylinders—a set of cylinders containing sand that are used to classify sounds from softest to loudest—is demonstrated by the directress. She models the prescribed steps for shaking each cylinder in the set to determine where to place it in the progression from the softest to the loudest. She repeats the activity by using a second paired set of cylinders, which is then matched with the first for self-correction. While the children have the freedom to choose these materials, they must follow the precise steps modeled by the directress for this classification activity. No optional exploration of the material by the children is permitted for creativity or problem solving.

Maria Montessori and her method moved geographically to all corners of the world. Her method continues to inspire child-centered programs. She began her work at the end of the nineteenth century, and promoted it through the middle of the twentieth century as a legacy for today's schools.

Child Study Pioneers Another child-centered approach, which was developed in the twentieth century and continues in today's schools, is the child study movement. Having less of a romantic notion of childhood, this movement bases its approach on the scientific study of children, the discipline of psychology, the use of psychometrics, and testing, observation, and prescriptive teaching. Benchmarks and milestones of development are identified to match the curriculum to the child's needs. Pioneers of this movement include G. Stanley Hall, Patty Smith Hill, and Lucy Sprague Mitchell, all of whom overlap with the progressive movement discussed in the next section.

Waldorf Schools Keeping the spirit of romantic naturalism alive was the visionary, Rudolf Steiner, an innovator of child-centered practices who designed a system of schooling built on the belief of the natural goodness of each child. Steiner was a social and political reformer who understood the relationship between school and society. He established the Waldorf School movement in Germany, which became a popular international model of child-centered teaching. The philosophy of learning is based on the **maturationist theory** that children's development is innate and grows naturally to its full potential in an environment with optimal conditions.

At the beginning of the twentieth century, Steiner designed his school for the children of employees of the Waldorf Astoria Cigarette Company to include a non-graded curriculum that centered on the child's "head, heart, and hand." Cognitive learning was linked with physical development and maturation. For example, in a Waldorf school, formal reading instruction does not begin until the age of seven, about the time a child has his second set of teeth appearing.

The same teacher remains with his class for the entire elementary years. The teacher knows his students well and implements the curriculum to reflect the needs and nature of each learner. Computer uses are deemed inappropriate for children's learning styles until the secondary school level, as the media is considered to be passive, unlike the active learning experiences so necessary for young children and middle school students.

Progressivism: Education for Democracy

A much maligned and misinterpreted school of educational thought, the progressives often have been wrongly considered a part of the romantic child-centered movement. The genesis of the progressives is rooted in the scientific and empirical school of philosophy known as pragmatism. John Dewey is credited with being the prophet of this movement in education. His philosophy is its foundation. Dewey's ideas framed the theory of pragmatism as an appropriate premise for education in a democracy. For Dewey, theory and practice were not separate but contingent upon each other. Likewise, educational practice was the living embodiment of educational theory. Education is not an end in itself, nor is it a lifelong goal or achievement. It is life itself. As Dewey states in *Democracy and Education* (1944, p. 9), "the very nature of life [is] to strive to continue in being. . . . Since this continuance can be secured only by constant renewal, life is a self-renewing process."

Education is central to that renewal process through experiences. Dewey's metaphysics disregards the *a priori* ideas of the idealist and the realist. Human experience defines reality. Knowledge is experiential. Knowledge is constructed through interaction. Education gives meaning to interactions that develop critical thinking skills and shape experiences. For Dewey and his followers, the learner has to be connected to what is to be learned. Discrete information in bits and pieces disconnects the subject from the object to be learned, while exposure to ever-broadening experiences creates opportunities to explore, discover, inquire, construct, and change.

Means and Ends Are Not Separate Dewey contended that means and ends are not separate: means *are* ends. Since education is life itself, education is not a preparation for the next stage, a job-training program, a course-load mastery of skills, a successful performance on high stakes tests, or the acquisition of knowledge for its own sake. Education is an active, rather than a passive, process that permits growth; the educational process needs to be relevant to engage the learner in solving problems, constructing meaning, and becoming involved. Dewey was seeking an education for democracy that used the sciences as well as the arts to produce an enlightened citizenry. Drawing upon the Aristotelian mandate that a citizen in a democracy had to be both a leader and a follower, Dewey wanted a school that permitted critical and creative thinkers to grow and effect change. His pedagogy had a healthy regard for curriculum content, but required the delivery of that content to be contextual with open-ended experiences.

Dewey's Predecessors and Disciples As Dewey had many followers who interpreted his work, he too was influenced by his predecessors. Charles Saunders

DIRECTLY FROM THE SOURCE

Waldorf Education . . . An Introduction

by Henry Barnes, former Chairman of the Board, Association of Waldorf Schools of North America

Source: Revised for this publication, this article by Henry Barnes, former Chairman of the Board, Association of Waldorf Schools of North America, originally appeared in the October, 1991, issue of *Educational Leadership Magazine.*

When children relate what they learn to their own experience, they are interested and alive, and what they learn becomes their own. Waldorf schools are designed to foster this kind of learning.

Waldorf Education has its roots in the spiritual-scientific research of the Austrian scientist and thinker Rudolf Steiner (1861–1925). According to Steiner's philosophy, man is a threefold being of spirit, soul, and body whose capacities unfold in three developmental stages on the path to adulthood: early childhood, middle childhood, and adolescence.

In April of 1919, Rudolf Steiner visited the Waldorf Astoria cigarette factory in Stuttgart, Germany. The German nation, defeated in war, was teetering on the brink of economic, social, and political chaos. Steiner spoke to the workers about the need for social renewal, for a new way of organizing society and its political and cultural life.

Emil Molt, the owner of the factory, asked Steiner if he would undertake to establish and lead a school for the children of the employees of the company. Steiner agreed but set four conditions, each of which

Pierce was one of Dewey's mentors for his doctoral study at Johns Hopkins. Pierce is credited with establishing pragmatism, and its premise on the value that experience gives meaning. Dewey predicated his work on Pierce's theories. Likewise, Francis Parker's experimental schools in Quincy, Massachusetts, and later in Chicago, paved the way for reforming education and promoting progressive practices as a foundation for Dewey's educational mandates.

We will discuss in more detail throughout the text many of Dewey's disciples who continue to implement progressive education. Here, we note several important contributions that have been made. John Kilpatrick in 1918 set forth his "project method," with its focus on the activity of the learner. His development of a project relevant to the learners and their environment as a viable strategy for teaching and learning has been replicated and renamed throughout the twentieth century and into the twenty-first. Today, this method falls under the rubric of thematic teaching or hands-on learning.

George S. Counts focused on the social message in Dewey's writings. He postulated that the problems of society need to be important components of the school's curriculum. Counts contended that in a democracy, education is the institution that transforms society. The informed citizen needs to deal with his world and improve it through change.

On the other hand, Lawrence A. Cremin credited progressivism for " the transformation of the school." In his book by that title, Cremin (1964, pp. viii–ix) defined progressive education's goals as:

1. "broadening the program and function of the school to include direct concern for health, vocation and the quality of family and community life"
2. "applying in the classroom the pedagogical principles derived from new scientific research in psychology and the social sciences"

went against common practice of the day: 1) that the school be open to all children; 2) that it be coeducational; 3) that it be a unified twelve-year school; 4) that the teachers, those individuals actually in contact with the children, have primary control of the school, with a minimum interference from the state or from economic sources. Steiner's conditions were radical for the day, but Molt gladly agreed to them. On September 7, 1919, the independent Waldorf School (Die Freie Waldorfschule) opened its doors.

Today there are more than 800 Waldorf schools in over 40 countries. In North America there are over 150 schools affiliated with the Association of Waldorf Schools of North America, and several public schools using Waldorf methods to enrich their teaching. There are also over 50 full-time Waldorf teacher-training institutes around the world; of these eight are in the United States and one in Canada. No two schools are identical; each is administratively independent. Nevertheless, a visitor would recognize many characteristics common to them all.

A Closer Look at the Issues

1. Why do you think Waldorf schools still have international appeal?
2. What math or science lesson might involve all three parts of a person: spirit, soul, and body?
3. What differences might you witness in a school where teachers have the primary control, not the government or administrators?

3. "tailoring instruction more . . . to the different kinds and classes of children . . . within the purview of the school"
4. "faith that culture could be democratized without being vulgarized, the faith that everyone could share not only in the benefits of the new sciences, but in the pursuit of the arts as well"

An Active Approach to Learning Like Dewey, progressives today regard content highly, but they seek active rather than passive approaches to the teaching/learning processes. Learning is not merely absorbing data; it requires constructing and using knowledge in life experiences. The educated person is a problem solver who can criticize, analyze, evaluate, synthesize, formulate, and create. The curriculum content is an integral part of the process. Knowing and doing go hand in hand. The challenge of the schools is to provide experiences that are relevant to the learner and promote both personal growth and intellectual understanding for the improvement of society. Schools need to offer that "renewal of life" cited by Dewey.

In a democracy, each citizen must be a critical thinker who has a voice in matters and the competencies to create change when necessary. Progressives include a diversity of teachers, educators, administrators, and theorists such as Jane Roland Martin, Ted Sizer, Cornel West, and Deborah Meier, to name a few. Each one of these theorists writes and practices the gospel of progressivism for their times and societal needs. Each does so with a personalized message.

What Might a Progressive Classroom Look Like? Mr. Richard uses an alternative approach to the typical wood shop class with his students, both male and female, in his town's high school. Most of these high school students have elected his course because the "regular" classroom holds little appeal to them. In the past, Mr. Richard selected as an annual project the restoration of historical community sites in need of repair. With that mission accomplished, his classes in recent years have been building wooden dories using the traditional practices of wooden boat builders in this seaside community. To keep this craft alive, the students not only have to develop hands-on carpentry skills, they also need to study boating traditions, acquire a background in maritime history, utilize math skills and computer technology to draw their plans, improve their oral and written communication skills in problem solving, create models that express their ideas, and develop a sense of teamwork. A tall and imposing figure to his students, Mr. Richard is a seasoned teacher. He fosters teamwork and models leadership skills. A man of many talents, he majored in languages in college, captained his college's basketball team, and played the sport at an international level of competition. After a period spent in the military and the business world, he decided to teach high schoolers the skills that as a youth he felt passionate about and learned from his own father. Instead of the routine assignments for shop class, he devised community-based projects that improve the community and enhance the lives of his students. His love of the craft is evident in the way he facilitates his students' approach to each project. Formerly, many of his students felt alienated in their public school, but in this situation they experience pride in their accomplishments. The course requirements are rigorous and demanding, but the students embrace the challenges.

Today, the students are resolving last-minute problems in the final stages of their work. As a class, they are preparing for the annual end-of-the-year exhibition in which the class showcases the dories. This acclaimed community celebration is for the entire town and open by invitation to all boating enthusiasts statewide. Some students are preparing those invitations. Others are helping with the publicity. With each student Mr. Richard is inspecting the boats for final approval to display. For Mr. Richard, the course is not a preparation for some vague future goal, but a life experience that opens doors for continuous growth in each of his students. His aim for the project is embedded in the means of the learning process that he directs and facilitates.

Existentialism: Learning for Personal Growth

Existentialism is an individualistic philosophy. For the existentialist, individual experiences, perceptions, and decisions structure the person. Reality grows out of existence and one's frame of reference. Existence defines the nature of being, the essence. As a school of philosophy, existentialists differ broadly from each other. For some, the frame of reference is embedded in religion. This is true for the founder of existentialism, Soren Kierkegaard, a Protestant theologian, and for Martin Buber, a Hasidic Jew, and Jacques Maritain, a Roman Catholic. Other existentialists, who have no religious affiliation or are agnostics or atheists, develop their ideas through literature. Most notable in this group are Jean-Paul Sartre and Albert Camus. For all existentialists, the educated person structures herself through her choices and the ranges of her experiences. Morality involves freedom of choice and responsibility for the consequences of one's behavior. In making decisions, each individual is structuring the nature of what it is to be human. In being one becomes. Each person is striving to be true to oneself and to others, which Sartre defined as being *authentic*. A lifelong process of introspection, which leads to self-knowledge, leads one to becoming authentic. This authenticity gives meaning to life. For Sartre, authenticity lends order to a world in which there is absurdity and chaos.

As a philosophy of education, existentialism strongly favors personalized instruction. Existentialists don't put much faith in particular methods, packaged programs, or the defined curriculum coursework found in many character education programs. **Character education** is a movement designed to counter the rising incidence of violence in the schools. The curriculum is designed around issues such as bullying, cheating, disrespect, and other self-destructive behaviors. The programs can be very prescriptive as to what and how to teach, with detailed teacher guides and lesson plans. In contrast, for the existentialist, such teaching cannot be packaged. Education requires a constant commitment to decision making, responsible choices, and risk taking. Literature, the arts and sciences, and especially the humanities, along with experiences that promote the affective domain, are the core of the existentialist's curriculum. Respectful interactions between teacher and students, cooperation among students, inquiry, and trust are critical components of this approach to education and permeate throughout the educational experience.

Martin Buber's "I-Thou" relationships are at the heart of this school of thought, which values affective development along with cognitive development. Cooperative experiences in which students and teachers recognize each other as another *thou or I* (a kindred spirit, another person) form a social consciousness for the individual and shape the individual's roles in society. A classroom is a learning environment in which people are not treated as *objects*—an *it* or the indefinite *they*—but always as persons, *subjects,* worthy of care and mutual respect.

The existentialist teacher supports individuals who take responsibility for themselves, for their commitments and contributions to the community. Dismayed by the violence and insensitivity of the world as well as the crass materialism of rampant consumerism, existential educators encourage students to love each other and to use things, not people, in relationships.

As a teacher, Nel Noddings seeks to create a caring community so that her students in turn become compassionate and competent individuals.
Source: Courtesy of Nel Noddings

The Teacher's Role The teacher's role in the educational process permits students to be honest and encourages caring for others. The teacher's primary concern is his students rather than completion of a prescribed curriculum by the end of the school year. The teacher's task is to know his students well enough to relate the curriculum to their lives. Nel Noddings's caring classroom and Maxine Greene's quest for freedom and authenticity through literature exemplify the best of existential educational practice. They both seek to connect the content areas to the human endeavor; content should not be learned in isolation or as subject areas to be mastered for their own sake. Noddings and Greene seek to shape the minds and souls of their students so they can become compassionate and competent individuals. Noddings strives for a caring community, while Maxine Greene includes the aesthetics taught through the fine arts. They would agree with Socrates that the unexamined life is not worth living. Like Socrates, they encourage their students to value being true to oneself. An existential education allows students to uphold beliefs, be steadfast in commitments, and dauntless in support of principles for social justice and personal freedom. "When we care, we accept the responsibility to work continuously on our competence so that the recipient of our care—person, animal, object, or idea—is enhanced. There is nothing mushy about caring. It is the strong, resilient backbone of human life" (Noddings, 1995, p. 369).

Summerhill School in Leiston, England was established on the existentialist notion of educating for personal freedom and choice.
Source: Courtesy of Summerhill School, www.summerhillschool.co.uk

The Student's Individual Responsibility A. S. Neill's experimental school, Summerhill, was established in 1921 as a private school in Great Britain and founded on the existentialist notion of educating for personal freedom and choice. His school permits students to decide and choose what is of interest and importance to learn. They are encouraged to follow their convictions, accept responsibility for their choices, and acknowledge the consequences of their behaviors. At Summerhill freedom implies responsibility. Students are not expected to submit to outside pressures, the influences of others, or to take the most expedient route, but to adhere to their personal principles in the face of adversity or rejection.

What Might an Existentialist Classroom Look Like? No two existentialist classrooms are the same. Finding one model classroom to represent such an individualistic philosophy presents many problems. A model could illustrate a classroom where the children decide the curriculum, set their own attainment targets, and work at their own pace. In light of recent school reforms, such a school is possible only in the private sector or in community-based alternative schools where the freedoms and choices accorded students at Summerhill have been interpreted to some extent. The model we have chosen focuses more on the existential messages of Noddings and Greene for building a caring climate in the classroom, making personal connections between the curriculum and the students, respecting students' values, and encouraging the students' voices in the implementation of the curriculum.

Ms. McGratton's sixth grade middle school classroom captures the spirit of existentialism in creating a caring community. Her children are currently studying migration and immigration as a unit in American history. Ms. McGratton wants her children to uncover the personal family stories and their particular contributions to American history. While she is a third generation American, her students' backgrounds vary. Many of her students are from families who have recently arrived from Mexico. Other families represent various places in the world including Asia,

South America, Europe, Canada, and Samoa. Two children are from families who migrated to the West Coast in covered wagons as pioneers of the western movement, while other children claim their families were Native Americans who were forced into migration. The students are to research their own heritage, interview family members for personal stories, and study the historical period in which their ancestors settled in their present community.

For today's class assignment the students are pretending to be one of their ancestors, in the appropriate period dress. They have used their family research to compose letters as if they were their ancestors writing to relatives they left in their homeland. The letters describe the students' perceptions of their ancestors' feelings and first impressions of their new home. Each student in turn shares a letter. In the letter-reading activity the children disclose sensitivity for their own heritage as well as empathy for their classmates'. They express delight in their ancestors' successes along with dismay for the hardships endured. It is evident from the children's involvement with the project that they now identify with their own cultural legacy when they describe with care and compassion their personal connections with past generations.

Reconstructionism: Global Education

Reconstructionism grew out of progressivism. George Counts, a disciple of Dewey, broadened Dewey's notions of education as a political endeavor necessary for a democracy. As reconstructionists, Counts and his followers, such as Theodore Brameld of Boston University, sought systemic changes of social conditions that would reconstruct society and fashion a new social order necessary for a democracy. Societal issues and concerns are the subject matter of their schools. The process of solving problems allows for growth in critical thinking and for affecting change. The educated person is a change agent for improving the human condition worldwide. The educated person seeks social justice that is inclusive of all peoples and nations. In Counts's scenario, schools transform society rather than simply transmit information reflective of the prevailing culture, values, and belief systems. He was optimistic that the sciences could provide tools and a methodology for solving worldwide problems, discovering equitable solutions, and enacting productive changes.

George Counts Counts was an internationalist who was sensitive to the impact of global issues. His concerns transcended national boundaries and challenged dominant cultures to be inclusive of multicultural voices. He was skeptical about the motivations of schools where values and information were imposed upon the learner by the prevailing culture. He questioned the educational process that was defined by some anonymous author, school board, or bureaucrat. He placed his faith in teachers to make appropriate choices. In fact, he challenged teachers to design schools that embrace and resolve the problems of society. Writing in the 1930s, when the American capitalist system was collapsing in an economic depression, Counts sought to build a "new social order" and to avoid the pitfall of an educational system that was one of indoctrination. His message has a contemporary ring. In his seminal work, *Dare the School Build a New Social Order?* (1932), he rallied teachers and educators to be advocates in difficult times to lead the transformation of society. His message was clear:

> As the possibilities in our society begin to dawn upon us, we are all, I think, growing increasingly weary of the brutalities, the stupidities, the hypocrisies, and the gross inanities of contemporary life. . . . The fact that other groups refuse to deal boldly and realistically with the present situation does not justify the teachers of the country in their customary policy of hesitation and equivocation. The times are literally calling for a new vision of American destiny. The teaching profession, or at least its progressive element, should eagerly grasp the opportunity which the fates have placed in their hands (in Reed and Johnson, 2000, p. 121).

Many Schools of Thought Later proponents of reconstructionism are more radical in their endeavors, less optimistic about the positive contributions of science and technology, and more politically focused on the struggle between the dominant culture of society and the subordinates. Reconstructionists come from many schools of thought. Some are labeled neo-Marxists, postmodernists, critical theorists, or liberationist educators. In the next section, we will explore the liberationist position.

Counts is surely one of the motivators for today's full-service schools which go beyond the purview of the cognitive side of schooling to embrace the community and families of their students. School leaders and teachers forge partnerships with other educational, social, and medical agencies to service all of the complexities of their children's lives and address societal issues prevalent in today's America. In such schools the spirit of social reconstructionism envisioned by Counts prevails.

Liberationism: Political Literacy

Influence from Counts, Brameld, Rugg, and other social reconstructionists is evident in the political and educational writings of the liberationists. Like social reconstructionism, liberationist education perceives the school as a social institution. The legacy of John Dewey is evident in this educational philosophy's pursuit to create democratic schools in the public sector with teachers who dare to challenge the status quo, expose the hidden curriculum, and balance the scales for equity and equality. The liberationist movement also reflects the political mantra of Karl Marx in the identification of the class struggle between the dominant culture and subordinate groups as it plays out in school and society. The movement focuses on the political issues of power and authority between various groups as determined by economic, national, ethnic, and gender factors. Critical theorists such as Henry Giroux, Lois Weis, and Peter McLaren can be considered liberationists. Their writings are fashioned after John Dewey's precepts on social reform. They, like Paulo Freire, champion the disenfranchised and the underclass in their call for student empowerment and political change through educational endeavors.

The Democratic School Liberationists are proponents of the democratic school—a place where teachers and learners have a voice and options. Michael Apple and James Beane (1995, p. 9) contend that a democratic school is a place where students "have a right to participate in the process of decision making;" a place where "[c]ommittees, councils, and other schoolwide decision-making groups include not only professional educators, but also young people, their parents, and other members of the school community. . . . [I]n classrooms, young people and teachers engage in the collaborative planning, reaching decisions that respond to the concerns, aspirations and interests of both." An external authority cannot mandate democratic schools; otherwise, propaganda and indoctrination ensue. Liberationists are concerned that in most educational systems, the prevailing culture controls minority voices through the dictum of the school, the hidden curriculum, and the imposition of contrary values that can prove destructive to subordinate peoples. These minority groups include people who share political, ethnic, linguistic, gender, social/economic, or sexual orientation differences from those of the dominant school climate. Activists from numerous persuasions empower such minority groups through their writings, including such social and political voices as Noam Chomsky and Jonathan Kozol, and educationalists such as Alfie Kohn.

Paulo Freire The champion of the liberation movement was Paulo Freire, whose defining work is *Pedagogy of the Oppressed* (1970). "One of the gravest obstacles to the achievement of liberation is that oppressive reality absorbs those within it and thereby acts to submerge men's consciousness" (Freire, 1970, p. 36). Having been poor and disenfranchised as a youth, Freire could identify with the plight of the underclass of his native Brazil. He recognized that the privileged class dominated the lives of the subculture. Through the educational process the dominant culture keeps "the masses 'submerged' and contained in a culture of silence" (in Reed and Johnson, 2000, p. 186). Freire sought to liberate the poor through a literacy curriculum that was socially and politically revolutionary. He used the language of his constituents to teach literacy, their culture and life experiences to break through the silence and give them a forum and a means of expression. He empowered his students to use their voice.

His approach to education was to counter what he called the "banking's model," in which students come to school with knowledge that they can deposit and bank to grow in value. The teacher possesses all the power to accept or disregard the student's knowledge. In most societies this model of teaching presupposes that the teacher possesses all the important knowledge and has earned the authority to teach the prevailing notions of the dominant society without any consideration of the contributions the students could make. The student relinquishes all power to the teacher. In these instances students are passive in the learning process. They receive information from the teacher, but do not internalize it or actively engage in acquiring knowledge that relates to their lives. Freire wanted to reverse that power structure by giving his students control of their own education, by having the teacher relinquish her authority to her students. Freire sought to free all students from domination and indoctrination. He wanted people of all socioeconomic classes to have an education that was relevant and guaranteed an active role in society. His notion replaced the traditionally held relationship between teacher and student. He wanted a reciprocal relationship in which there was a shift of authority, where power no longer belonged solely to the dominant culture. In Freire's scheme, teachers learn from students and students learn from teachers. He viewed the teacher as the teacher/student and the student as the student/teacher.

> [T]hinking correctly puts the responsibility on the teacher, or more correctly, on the school, not only to respect the kinds of knowledge that exist especially among the popular classes—knowledge socially constructed in communitarian praxis—but also to discuss with the students the logic of these kinds of knowledge in relation to their

> contents. . . . Why not, for example, take advantage of the students' experience of life (Freire, 2001, p. 36).

Freire taught adult literacy programs to the poor of his native country, Brazil, in the context of their own culture. He substituted the passive "banking's model" methodology with a problem solving approach for active learning. He focused on political awareness of legal rights for all citizens and advocated for social justice in a process he called conscientization (*conscientizacao*). His revolutionary approach encourages students to challenge the oppressors, question them, and oppose them by seeking fair and humane treatment of all. He brought his message to the world. His writings have been translated by one of his protégés, Donaldo Macedo, who continues Freire's mission in his own professional publications and teachings. However, Freire cautioned that his methods were not meant to be replicated elsewhere. Some were germane to their location. Their implications for others are to find the approach that liberates their subordinate group. His theories have inspired discussion, reflection, and application around the globe.

His methodology for teaching literacy is primarily a language experience approach. He encouraged his students to draw on their own words and their life experiences. "As we attempt to analyze dialogue as a human phenomenon, we discover something which is the essence of dialogue itself: *the word*" (Freire, 1970, p. 75). The word is a weapon against oppression when free expression is permitted. For example, the meaning of the word *plow* has a different connotation for the peasant than for the landowner. For the peasant it represents domination, while the landowner uses the term to describe a tool for working the land. The school must reflect and honor the students' culture. The classroom is a forum for the student to express his voice in his own words as well as that of the mainstream culture. Freire's sensitivity to words, the teaching of them and their usage, accounted for his success.

Teaching on Promise: Revisiting Your Pedagogic Creed

Your teaching practices will evolve from your value system, your beliefs, and your philosophy. To help you clarify your own philosophy of education, examine your basic assumptions and the principles that guide you through your life experiences. There are many schools of philosophy that shape the notions of education, define its mission, and prescribe its practices. Such schools of thought are the foundations of educational practices and the roots of the numerous philosophies of education—many of which were discussed in this chapter. Take some time to read the Voices of Principle and Promise and learn about two student teachers' pedagogic creeds. Then review your responses to the list of assumptions earlier in the chapter. Have your views changed after reading the chapter? Are you better able to describe and define your educational philosophy?

Because there are fine lines drawn between the different philosophies of education, there is not always agreement as to who belongs to which camp. Nevertheless, you might find yourself identifying more with one philosophical base than the others, or you might be eclectic in agreeing with many facets of different philosophies. Likewise, professionals change perspective depending upon their teaching experiences throughout their teaching careers. Dewey would consider such

Voices of Principle and Promise

Two Student Teachers' Pedagogic Creeds

My teaching philosophy stems from my belief that children learn best when they are actively involved in their own learning. Using the cooperative learning theory of Stuart Kagan, the multiple intelligences theory of Howard Gardner, and the guided release method in which the teacher models a specific action or task, I believe I can offer all children an equal chance to succeed. These models promote interdependence, individual accountability, equal participation, and guided practice defined by each child's learning style. I further believe that in conjunction with applying these theories, a teacher must be energetic, enthusiastic, and caring. A teacher must be able to listen to her students as much as she speaks to them. A teacher must also recognize that she still has to learn while she teaches *(Jaime Cronin, Student Teacher).*

It is my belief that beyond traditional curriculum, life lessons should be incorporated into the classroom. Unfortunately, there is still a great deal of intolerance in our communities and neighborhoods. I believe that respect and acceptance of other people's differences should be incorporated into classroom lessons. Teachers can use group work and partnership to help students value each other's attributes and accept shortcomings. Children in school today are undoubtedly our future tomorrow. I believe that every generation of children has the potential to strive harder and learn more than the generations before them. As a teacher it would be my job to teach all of my students learning strategies, self-esteem, and compassion for others. I truly believe in a better future, which starts in our schools today (Nicole Clayton, Student Teacher).

Questions to Consider

1. How do these pedagogic creeds reflect your thinking?
2. Do you agree that teachers must model active learning for their students? Would you agree with the statement "each generation can strive harder and learn more?"

change evidence of growth. It is imperative that educators reflect on their changing perceptions and analyze their own beliefs.

The following table reviews the key notions of the philosophies of education that we have examined. Use the table as a reference to help you formulate your pedagogic creed. Consider the promise that teaching holds out to you and the principles you might want to express in your pedagogic creed. Knowing what you believe gives substance to what you teach and helps you fulfill your promise as a teacher. Table 3.2 is a summary of the isms discussed in this chapter. Like all charts, it highlights only the key ideas of each ism and can be used as a guide to more in-depth reading.

We have presented a representative sample of leading philosophies of education. We invited you to consider different principles for teaching that define a choice of educational models and teaching practices. Our interpretations might differ from other writers. Thinkers might be identified with other labels or other schools of thought. The interpretations are open-ended. But we offer them to you for consideration in the building of your personal foundation to fulfill your promise for teaching.

Table 3.2 A Comparison of Educational Philosophies

Ism	Educated Person	Knowledge Worth Knowing	Role of School in Society	Good Teaching
Perennialism	Well read Pursuer of the arts and sciences	Liberal arts Knowledge for its own sake The "great books"	Schools transmit cultural heritage and values Aim: a just society	Humanist Teachers inspire discovery of knowledge through critical dialogue Subject matter centered
Essentialism	Competent master of basic skills and a core of knowledge for the better life	Preparation for life and national citizenship Vocational standards-based	Schools prepare for life, career options, and citizenship through transmitting cultural values Aim: the good life	Qualified professional Teachers demonstrate competencies and subject matter mastery Teacher directed
Behaviorism	Manager and controller of life situations	Skills and knowledge base that modify behaviors to control life situations	Schools prepare for living in society Aim: effective living and citizenship	Modifier Teachers define desired behavior and modify environments for learning Scripted and programmed teaching Teacher directed
Romantic Naturalism	Fulfilled person Maximized potentials gained through developmentally appropriate experiences	Experiences that unfold natural potential Knowledge that leads to discovery about life	Education improves society by removing barriers Aim: development of natural inclinations	Facilitator/director Teachers facilitate a student-centered curriculum that recognizes the *emergent* learner Student centered

Table 3.2 A Comparison of Educational Philosophies *(continued)*

Ism	Educated Person	Knowledge Worth Knowing	Role of School in Society	Good Teaching
Progressivism	Critical thinker Problem solver Meaning maker	Life Experiences that recognize change, permit inquiry, and lead to growth	Schools transform society Aim: a democratic society	Facilitator Teachers provide experiences and projects for students to engage in the scientific method to solve problems and process knowledge Interactive project method
Reconstructionism	Advocate Solves societal problems Uses knowledge to meet the changing challenges of life in the global village	Politics Social studies Environmental sciences	Schools reconstruct society Schools transform society by using real-life problems of the world as the curriculum Aim: world peace and betterment	Change agent Teachers advocate for improvement of society through active engagement Social action
Existentialism	Self-determined person The individual in pursuit of self-awareness and self-actualization	Process skills Elected study of subjects Uses knowledge and process skills to make informed decisions and responsible choices	De-schooling society Informal education that leads to building caring communities and improving society Aim: personal freedom	Facilitator Transfers authority to students to seek knowledge for personal learning and to make proactive decisions for oneself and society Personalized instruction
Liberationism	Change agent Seeks social justice for all segments of society	Political sciences Economics Cultural/global studies Class, race, and gender consciousness	Schools transform society by liberating and empowering minorities and the disenfranchised Aim: social justice	Liberator Teacher and student share authority that analyzes cultural reproductions and permits a multitude of voices in shaping a culturally personalized curriculum Empowerment of learners

SUMMARY

- Philosophy of education seeks to connect theory with practice, to develop philosophical theory as a foundation to educational pursuits. This lends purpose to teaching and provides goals for the learner. Both your philosophy of life and your philosophy of education structure what you value as the knowledge that is worth knowing. Your philosophy of education emerges from the assumptions you hold. Many of these assumptions reflect your personal experiences, and grow out of the culture of your society and its school climate.
- Perennialism pursues knowledge for its own sake through study of the traditional classical programs in the arts and sciences. Humanistic goals reflected in literature transmit to the learner a cultural heritage and reflect the aims of a just society.
- Essentialism prepares the student for life by teaching a core curriculum of basic skills, vocational education, and citizenship.
- Behaviorism is more a psychology than a philosophy, but has shaped educational practices based on a scientific view of human behavior.
- Romantic naturalism places the learner at the center of the education process and builds the curriculum based on theories of human development, with the goal that all students will actualize their innate potential.
- Progressivism promotes critical thinking through open-ended inquiries that use the scientific method for problem solving in a democratic society. Education is life, not a preparation; it is its own end, not a means.
- Existentialism is an individualistic philosophy in which self-actualization is central to the educational process in a school climate that is caring, personalized, and inclusive.
- Reconstructionism advocates for educating change agents who pursue social action for a democratic society. As in progressivism, problem solving is central to the educational process as schools transform society.
- Liberationism seeks social justice for all segments of society, particularly by protecting the rights of minorities or the disenfranchised with a curriculum that expresses class, race, and gender consciousness.
- Developing a pedagogic creed is based on understanding your assumptions and having knowledge about the range of educational philosophies. A pedagogic creed is essential to becoming a knowledgeable educator. Just as important is the ability for educators to reflect on their changing perceptions and analyze their own beliefs.

QUESTIONS FOR REFLECTION

1. What educational philosopher offers you the principles to guide your teaching and the promises you aspire to keep?
2. If you were to select books that best reflect the *cultural literacy* you wish to transmit to students, whose works and writings would you include?
3. Do you believe that there is a core curriculum necessary for all students to master? Discuss and defend your position. Describe what, if anything, you think should be included in your core curriculum.
4. Do you think schools change society or do they simply reflect society and its institutions?
5. What does "freedom" in an educational context mean to you? What authority do you think determines what is worth knowing?
6. What kind of educational experiences have been most meaningful to you? What kind of knowledge did these experiences provide? How have these experiences shaped your life?

APPLYING WHAT YOU'VE LEARNED

1. Think about a classroom where you have observed, taught, or perhaps even been a student. How is your classroom organized? Where are you in relation to your students? What kinds of resources do you and your students use? How do they access the resources?
2. Develop a checklist of important criteria for determining what knowledge you think is worth knowing. Evaluate your school against your criteria.
3. Visit a Montessori school or a Waldorf school. Compare its approaches to those of a school you have taught in or attended. Note the likenesses and differences. Consider combining the best of all practices.
4. Prepare a design for a website that illustrates your philosophy of education in practice.
5. www. Visit the companion website for this text. You'll find a link to *http://www.infed.org/archives/e-texts/dewey7.htm.* Read Chapter 7, "The Democratic Conception in Education," of John Dewey's seminal work, *Democracy in Education.* Discuss his famous quotation, "Society is one word, but many things." Then discuss its implications for teaching the children in today's schools. Consider how timely Dewey's chapter is to today's society. How relevant is it to your life?

KEY TERMS

character education, p. 91
core curriculum, p. 81
humanists, p. 80
maturationist theory, p. 86

WEBSITES TO EXPLORE

http://www.coreknowledge.org/Ckproto2/about/articles/breadthvsdepth.htm. An insight into E. D. Hirsch's *Cultural Literacy* through his article on what he considers important core knowledge.

http://www.theamericanenterprise.org/taema97e.htm. A defense of traditional educational approaches to schooling as proposed by E. D. Hirsch.

http://www.educationnext.org/2001sp/34.htm. An article against progressivism and why it is doomed to fail, written by E. D. Hirsch.

http://www.cortland.edu/c4n5rs/contents.asp? This website offers a definition of *character education.*

http://www.pragmatism.org/library/west/. This website provides a bibliographical sketch of Cornel West and reviews some of his works.

http://www.siu.edu/~deweyctr/. Southern Illinois University has a complete set of works about and by John Dewey. The Dewey Center holds his papers, publications, and awards. This is the center's website.

http://cuip.uchicago.edu/jds/. The John Dewey Society is found on this University of Chicago website. It offers up-to-date information on the society and its current officers.

http://www.montessori-ami.org. This website is developed by the Association for Montessori International. It offers background information about Maria Montessori as well as efforts to provide Montessori education worldwide.

http://www.greatbooks.org/. The Great Books Foundations presents this website to give an overview of programs, products, and services.

http://book.mirror.org/gb.titles.htm. This website provides a listing of the authors, and their works, recommended as part of the Great Books Series.

http://www.c-b-e.org/saw/overview.htm. A newsletter of the Council for Basic Education concerning their international program, Schools Around the World (SAW).

http://www.summerhillschool.co.uk/indexgo.htm. This website provides information about the current school that was based on A. S. Neill's book, *Summerhill.*

http://www.awsna.org/education-intro.hmtl. This website includes information about Waldorf education, addresses common questions asked about its philosophy and practices, and provides lists of schools in the United States and an outline of its K–12 curriculum.

http://www.capeannwaldorf.org. This website connects you to a model Waldorf School.

CRITICAL READINGS

Polishing the Progressive Approach: Why An "Endangered Educational Species" Should Be Protected

BY ELAINE WINTER

I've been thinking a lot lately about what brought me to the progressive independent school where I work. Why did I land here rather than somewhere else? I know the answer lies in the school's mission—not its mission statement, or its heritage, or image, though all these count, but in its defining purpose.

All the people at my school arrived here, I imagine, by different routes. Some always knew they'd be educators, some tried other fields. Some have taught around the globe, in other schools and with other approaches. Some are dyed-in-the-wool progressives. Whatever the path, we all now find ourselves the spokespeople for a tradition, a specific belief in children and philosophy. Today we are the protectors of an endangered educational species.

My own route began when I had children in 1972 and started to read educational writers of the 1960s like John Holt, Jonathan Kozol, Herbert Kohl, Robert Coles, George Dennison, and Ned O'Gorman. These writers made education, and teaching in particular, feel like a mission. In their own unorthodox ways, they were each helping children live more fully and work more resolutely to better their world. This soon felt like a meaningful career avenue for me—and so it has been. The progressive approach seemed to make sound child sense, though I didn't have a fully formed notion then of what progressive education actually meant.

In the early 1970s, as my sons started preschool, I got to know the Reggio Emilia pedagogy, and so gained another slant on empowering, bottom-up teaching. Among the many conceptually based underpinnings of this approach, three resonated for me at that time: respect for the learner's experience and current developmental perspective; a valuing of collaborative endeavor; and a use of the cultural surroundings as primary resource. I remember that teachers put children's quotes, verbatim, on the classroom walls for parents to read and that birthday books were made by the whole class for each child. These contained a drawing and a dictation; individual messages becoming a group gesture. And one of the richest activities I remember from that time was the class replicating the fall vendemmia, or winemaking process. Parents brought in plastic bags to cover children's feet, then the children stomped on a big bucket of grapes to make themselves grape juice. It was exciting because it was so relevant to the children's lives and culture. The approach valued children's voices and brought academic learning close to real-world experience. As parent and educator, I was won over.

This kind of thinking is summed up well in the following description of "the beliefs that underlie progressive methods" written by Carol Samuels Montag for the 1983 Miquon Conference on Progressive Education. They are:

- That intelligence is not fixed by genetic inheritance, but responds to experience.
- That to have the greatest beneficial effect, any experience the child gains must bear some relation to what he or she understands already, and be such that further new experience can be added to it. This means it may have to be individual. That children are geared towards growing up: They seek maturing experience.
- That education in situations based on experience and active individual participation may cut right across the barriers between "subjects." It all felt very different from the see-saw learning I'd had: learn/forget, learn/forget—all beneath an umbrella of angst. The learning of facts and putting them in correct form greatly outweighed decision making, problem solving, opinion forming and creative endeavor. There were good feelings, of course—satisfactions of being a good student, of doing well, of accomplishing—but the cost was high, and my dependence on teacher directive, nearly total. My education was about adult expectation.

When I began my first teaching experience in Rome, I wasn't sure about what role expectation should play in a progressive approach. I worried about drowning out children's voices, and so became guilty of slippery expectations, of leaving too much room for individual interpretation and having too much faith in the late-bloomer dynamic. I didn't realize that this approach only works if it works. In other words, if the education piece is of a very high caliber; stuff and substance that kids have to examine, understand, think over, and communicate are powerfully intelligent. Without high standards, progressivism loses its punch.

For most of its defenders, progressive education is a meaningful, even powerful approach to teaching. Yet I have referred to it as an "endangered species," a philosophy whose growth is currently threatened. By threats, I don't have in mind schools with different approaches. We all know there are many fine avenues. It's not my goal to promote a "one way only" kind of thinking. But there are fewer progressive schools than there were five years ago. While many schools have adopted progressive language, terms such as "child-centered" and "active," "integrated" learning, bits and pieces of progressive practice, they may not be committed to the philosophy itself. There are many parents who prefer more easily defined rungs for their children's educational progress—pages, scores and the basics. There's also an image problem that makes progressivism sound outdated and loose rather than challenging and current. There are many versions of misinterpretation: Last summer, Republican presidential candidate Bob Dole remarked that "while students in Japan are learning math, sciences and languages, our kids are getting in touch with their feelings. Let's get rid of all that PC stuff and move on." Progressive education is a hard read. Consequently, it is also easy to write off. It has been borrowed from, misread and maligned.

We now must ask what we can do to "polish the progressive approach" and make it shine so it can be appreciated for what it really is. I don't believe our mandate is to be more radical, but to be more consistent, united and clear; eloquent advocates of this philosophy. Through our work and our language, through children's work and the walls of our classrooms, we can make the statement that children are worth respecting; that meaningful teaching includes listening, questioning, responding and refocusing. By always clarifying what kind of learning is taking place and what kind of work is going on—because we all know that what is obvious to us is often unclear and unconnected for parents and other educators—by clarifying, we become leaders.

Certainly one cornerstone of progressive education is its respect for how children learn. We know that students want to learn to know and grow competent, to become their own brand of expert. Meaningful learning opportunities for them include problem- and conflict-solving, theorizing, defending a view and composing a poem; critical, analytical, reflective and creative thought. They also embrace organized work habits, neatness, clear communication and good form. And maybe even "getting in touch with feelings."

This foundation broadens to value social studies, as the hub of relevant learning—from the community of students to larger more diverse groups. So our philosophy embraces civic commitment and citizen-shaping activity. But does that stop at empathy and appreciation? I'm wondering if active response might be what we risk losing if progressive education falls by society's wayside.

Pat Carini, the former director of the Prospect Center, also spoke at the 1983 Miquon Conference on Progressive Education. She said: "Classrooms are bellwethers of society and anything in the atmosphere comes back to schools through children. Because of this, schools have an unusual opportunity to grapple, and I mean grapple, with the larger issues of society. Society's hopes, aspirations and values are right there before us—if we'll look. . . . Some of us may decide to go out and effect public policy, not all of us will, but in our classrooms we are shaping our common destiny and our individual perspectives right along and with the children."

At my school, we've been talking about the dynamic of educating activists, and I think that may be one corner of the educational platform still owned by progressive thought. It means being unafraid to take a community stand when it counts, no matter how uncomfortable or inconvenient that may be. It includes, but goes beyond community service. In her book, *Schoolhome,* Jane Roland Martin warns against what she calls, the "education of spectatorship" and talks about the difference between educating "consumers" and educating "voters."

She says, "Dewey wanted us to educate 'the whole child.' I have been talking about educating all our children in our whole heritage. That valuable capital includes ways of living as well as forms of knowing, societal activities and practices as well as literary and artistic achievements. It is all too easy, however, for school to instruct children about their heritage without ever teaching them to be active and constructive participants in the world—let alone how to make it a better place for themselves and their progeny. This is especially so in the United States, where school is thought of as an instrument for developing children's minds, not their bodies; their thinking and reasoning skills, not their emotional capacities or active propensities."

Ralph Nader said recently that "politics has been corrupted, not just by money but by being trivialized out of addressing the great, enduring issues of who controls, who decides, who owns, who pays, who has a voice and access." Maybe this is part of our mission.

Debbie Meier, a co-founder of the Central Park East Secondary School in New York City, describes schools that nurture citizens as those that promote skepticism, empathy (both an affective and cognitive quality), hope, and respect. She says what we know, that "it is doable to create schools that are respectful places." Which brings us to the stuff of a progressive community. Are we really a team that works together as we encourage our students to go; benefiting from the same dynamics of interdependence that color classroom life and curriculum design? In discussing this aspect of progressivism, the director of my school talks of "doing, dignity and diversity." Jane Roland-Martin speaks of "care, concern and connection." Both imply shared burden and shared gains, and are equally applicable to classroom and faculty communities.

One aspect of a progressive community is its group-decision making stance, which often requires a lot of effortful, time-consuming "process." But collaboration in a progressive community involves more than this. It calls for the kind of collegial support that enhances both our teaching and our school's leadership position. Really working together requires opening up and allowing oneself to share the rough edges with colleagues, not just the shiny gems of our programs. While that can be very hard to do, for a progressive school, interdependency is the starting point. For example, there are not desks in my lower school's classrooms—a statement about the value of collaborative endeavor. Though in true progressive fashion, we do also have an exception. We ask our students for collaborative effort across lines of race, class, gender and gender preference, age and family configuration. We also ask them for openness and flexible thinking—compromise and change, balanced by all-out stubbornness when it's called for; for respect for their own work and for others'—for accomplishments as well as good tries. We ask for willingness to take risks and explore what is new, for the ability to find pleasure in group work. And finally, we ask them to build an interdependent world and to start here.

Christopher Reeve, in a great moment from his speech to the Democratic National Convention last summer, remarked about how often in recent years he'd heard reference made to "family values." He'd been working to figure out what was meant by the phrase, he said, and he's come up with this answer: It means, Mr. Reeve said, that "we are all a family and we all have value."

In this "family" spirit, progressive educators need to think about ways we can let some barriers and defenses fall and help each other with our work. The answer lies not in a list of how-tos, but in the knowledge that progressive education can only survive within a truly progressive community. We can't fake it. By becoming a stronger community, we can make a stronger statement. That is a worthwhile goal to share.

Source: The Little Red Schoolhouse and Elisabeth Irwin High School. http://www.lrei.org/index.html. Accessed March 6, 2004.

A Closer Look at the Issues

1. Why does Elaine Winter think progressive education is "an endangered educational species"? Do you agree with her?
2. Why is group discussion important in a progressive curriculum?

The Idea of a University

BY JOHN HENRY NEWMAN

It is the education which gives a man a clear conscious view of his own opinions and judgments, a truth in developing them, an eloquence in expressing them, and a force in urging them. It teaches him to see things as they are, to go right to the point, to disentangle a skein of thought, to detect what is sophistical, and to discard what is irrelevant. It prepares him to fill any post with credit, and to master any subject with facility. It shows him how to accommodate himself to others, how to throw himself into their state of mind, how to bring before them his own, how to influence them, how to come to an understanding with them, how to bear with them. He is at home in any society, he has common ground with every class; he knows when to speak and when to be silent; he is able to converse, he is able to listen; he can ask a question pertinently, and gain a lesson seasonably, when he has nothing to impart himself; he is ever ready, yet never in the way; he is a pleasant companion, and a comrade you can depend upon; he knows when to be serious and when to trifle, and he has a sure tact which enables him to trifle with gracefulness and to be serious with effect. He has the repose of a mind which lives in itself, while it lives in the world, and which has resources for its happiness at home when it cannot go abroad. He has a gift which serves him in public, and supports him in retirement, without which good fortune is but vulgar, and with which failure and disappointment have a charm. The art which tends to make a man all this, is in the object which it pursues as useful as the art of wealth or the art of health, though it is less susceptible of method, and less tangible, less certain, less complete in its result.

Source: The Idea of a University, Discourse VII, New York: Doubleday, 1959, pp. 191–192.

A Closer Look at the Issues

1. What do you think Newman means when he says the educated person "has the repose of a mind which lives in itself, while it lives in the world, and which has resources for its happiness at home when it cannot go abroad"?
2. What knowledge do you think is worth knowing that would offer "the repose of a mind that lives in itself"?

REFERENCES

Adler, M. (ed). (1984). *The paideia program.* New York: Macmillan.

Apple, M., and J. Beane (1995). *Democratic schools.* Alexandria, VA: Association for Supervision and Curriculum Development.

Cremin, L. (1964). *The transformation of the school.* New York: Vintage Books.

Dewey, J. (1944). *Democracy and education.* New York: The Free Press.

Freire, P. (1970). *Pedagogy of the oppressed.* New York: The Seabury Press.

Freire, P. (2001). *Pedagogy of freedom, ethics, democracy, and civic courage.* Lanham, MD: Rowman & Littlefield.

Hirsch, E. D. (1987). *Cultural literacy.* Boston: Houghton Mifflin.

Kohn, A. (2002). The 500-pound gorilla. *Phi Delta Kappan,* October, pp. 113–199.

McNergney, R., and J. Herbert (2001). *Foundations of education: The challenge of professional practice,* 3rd ed. Boston: Allyn & Bacon.

Newman, J. (1959). *The idea of a university,* Discourse VII, New York: Doubleday.

Noddings, N. (1995). A morally defensible mission for schools in the 21st century. *Phi Delta Kappan,* January, pp. 365–369.

Power, E. (1970). *Main currents in the history of education.* 2nd ed. New York: McGraw-Hill.

Reed, R., and T. Johnson (2000). *Philosophical documents in education.* 2nd ed. New York: Longman.

Sadovnik, A., P. Cookson, and S. Semel (2001). *Exploring education: An introduction to the foundations of education.* Boston: Allyn & Bacon.

Webber, E. (1969). The kindergarten: Its encounter with educational thought in America. New York: Teachers College Press.

Winter, Diane. *Why an endangered educational species should be protected.* http://www.lrei.org/index.html Accessed March 6, 2004. http://www.awsna.org/education-intro.hmtl Accessed August 13, 2004.

Decisions About Curriculum

4

ESSENTIAL QUESTION

What is worth knowing?

Hillary is a first-year teacher in an inner-city school with a multicultural and ethnically diverse class of students, many of whom are English language learners. Yet, all of her fourth graders are held accountable for performing successfully on a state-mandated exam. As the year progresses, Hillary gets to know her students and realizes that before she can teach the content areas required for all fourth graders, she must gain their trust, understand their lifestyles, and teach them to care about each other. Likewise, she is constantly conflicted by the principles she acquired as a student teacher and the current demands placed upon her now that she is a practitioner. She feels she faces a dilemma of reconciling teaching for successful test performances with meeting the complex needs of her students. She is constantly grappling with the challenge of constructing a curriculum that addresses the achievement levels of the state testing program and is relevant to her students. ■

Constructing a Curriculum

Your philosophy of education offers a framework for constructing a curriculum. Your beliefs and assumptions shape what you value as suitable content or what you feel is worth knowing. Your philosophy of education also defines the method of delivery. The questions this chapter addresses are centered on the notion of authority in making these decisions about curriculum. We will explore six main questions:

1. Who makes decisions about curriculum design and construction?
2. What are some curriculum models?
3. What is the impact of standards-based education?
4. How do approaches such as developmental and community-based curriculum work?
5. How can curriculum address issues of language?
6. What are the advantages of a global curriculum?

How Is Curriculum Defined?

Expanding on the definition of curriculum in Chapter 1, here, we look deeper into the goals and aims of curriculum. Curriculum is the content, subject areas, topics, themes, or strands studied in a school or child-care center. The curriculum's goals and objectives are based on three domains of human development: the cognitive, the affective, and the psychomotor or physical/neurological. The aim of any curriculum is to have a purpose. This purpose determines the nature of the curriculum. In other words, Is the curriculum one that proposes self-actualization, good citizenship, vocational training, inquiry, or indoctrination? The scope of the curriculum gives an overview and reflects the aims of the curriculum, while the sequence outlines the steps to achieve the goals and objectives of those aims. The aims and the philosophy reflect the views of the authors who write the curriculum, structure its approach, and design its implementation.

Who Are the Players in Decisions About Curriculum?

There are several key players who decide curriculum (see Fig. 4.1). They include governmental agencies that determine laws and policies, professional organizations that can formulate curriculum and the constituencies of our schools, communities, and parents. Teachers also influence curriculum with their interpretation of mandates, their implementation of instruction, and their advocacy roles as professionals in the field.

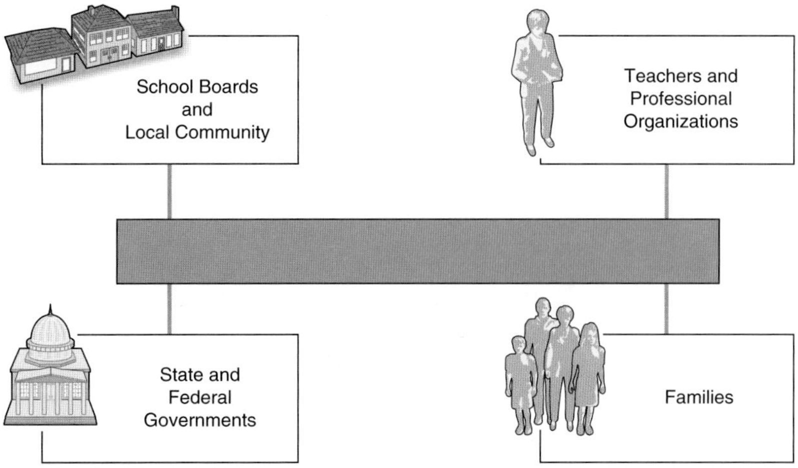

Figure 4.1

Who Are the Players in Decisions About Curriculum?

State and Federal Governments Following an international trend, the United States Department of Education is playing an ever increasing role in the decision making about curriculum. In this and subsequent chapters we will explore past and present federal legislation that has been promulgated to define national curriculum standards, to set minimum teacher qualifications, to determine accountability measures for schools to meet attainment targets for the curriculum, and to provide parental choice of schools for children. While the federal government's role in mandating curriculum is increasing, it is important to remember that federal curriculum standards are voluntary. State departments of education mandate compulsory curriculum standards. Only states that accept federal funding for education are required to meet the national government's guidelines. To date, all fifty states do have some form of curriculum standards for their public schools, but some states are challenging the current federal education act, No Child Left Behind, by noncompliance with certain measures.

Landmark Supreme Court decisions such as the 1954 *Brown v. Board of Education,* which desegregated schools; and legislative acts such as Title IX, which prohibits gender bias in schools, and the 1974 Bilingual Act, which allows parental input in developing programs for children with limited English language skills, have brought more diversity to the curriculum (see Chapters 7 and 9 for additional discussion of diversity). Likewise, the delivery of the curriculum now accommodates new populations of students with the passages of Public Law 94-142, the 1975 Education for All Handicapped Act, and the 1990 Individuals with Disabilities Education Act (IDEA). Both of these acts mandate equal educational opportunities for all students from age two to twenty-one to be available in the least restrictive environment. (see Chapter 9). Classrooms have become inclusive of students with learning differences and physical challenges. Individual Education Plans (IEPs) modify the curriculum to fit the special needs of these students. Classroom environments must be accommodated to provide conditions that support suitable instructional practices in a welcoming atmosphere conducive for all learners.

Professional Organizations Most of the states derive their curriculum standards from professional organizations and learned societies. For example, the National Council of the Teachers of Mathematics was the first of the learned societies to define national standards for teaching mathematics from kindergarten to grade twelve. Most states implemented their recommendations. In addition, textbook publishers followed the guidelines in their production of math series and programs. So, in essence, states and communities that adopt the textbook series are aligning their mandates with the recommendations of the professional organizations. Other learned societies that followed suit by creating standards in their disciplines include the National Council for Geographic Education, the National Council of the Social Studies, and the National Academy of Sciences. In specialty areas like early childhood education the National Association for the Education of Young Children authored standards for all of the fields, while the Council for Exceptional Children developed guidelines for adaptive instruction in inclusive classrooms.

Teachers and School Boards The local community's voice on curriculum resides in its elected school boards or committees. School boards represent the community in establishing local school policies and monitoring curriculum implementation. Often, local education boards modify statewide mandates to satisfy local cultural, political, and social stipulations. For example, local historical or community events can be highlighted over the national or state happenings in a social studies guide. Teachers also adapt state mandated curriculum when they design lessons to be relevant to their students. Most teachers address state standards in programs, activities, units, and special projects through studies of their community, field trips to local areas, and visits from local civic groups or guest speakers. Creative teachers weave their children's interests, current happenings near and far, and new ideas into their daily teaching of mandated curriculum.

Families and Community Families play a role in determining curriculum by their involvement in their children's schools. When there is a conflict between family values and school curriculum, complaints are registered at the school or through the school board, political officials, and the local media. Most controversial issues in mandated curriculum center around the teaching of character education, sex education, or world religions—subjects some families feel should be taught exclusively at home. On a positive note, families can influence curriculum through their presence as volunteers in the classrooms, visiting speakers, school councilors, and Parent/Teacher Organization (PTO) members. As informed constituents, they can affect changes, address concerns, and introduce new avenues of inquiry.

The sense of place is central to curriculum development. The tone of the community sets the school climate and determines its citizens' perceptions of education. Local environmental, economical, social, cultural, and geographical factors shape attitudes that can hinder curriculum growth or permit it to flourish. In a country as large as the United States, regional interests affect interpretations of curricula. For example, priorities at rural schools often differ from those of urban or suburban schools. Likewise, the various media outlets such as television, textbook publishers, news, the Internet, and the World Wide Web influence consumers and impact the schoolroom as well as the marketplace.

Paulo Freire called for community and family voices to be heard in constructing curriculum (see Chapter 3). In theory and practice, he stressed that the local people's language and personal community experiences should shape the curriculum. *Place education,* a curriculum model presented in this chapter, illustrates his teachings as an exemplar for developing curriculum around people, places, and happenings in a community.

Which Is More Important, Content or Process?

There is much controversy and debate in educational circles about curriculum in answer to the question, What is worth knowing? Many educators question what curriculum is most effective in meeting students' needs. Which approach is best? What teaching strategies work? How can success be assessed? Responses to these questions seem to fall into two major camps, those that favor direct teaching of content, and others that focus on the process of learning. Proponents from both sides debate the issue of what is more important: the content that you learn, or the process of learning how to learn. Those who favor content promote direct teaching approaches, while process orientation theorists seek open-ended-inquiry directions in which teaching is often indirect.

Direct instruction, scripted teaching, programmed learning, and standards-based education are built upon the content or the subjects to be learned. Some authority outside of the classroom—for example, governmental agencies, publishing houses, or, in private education, the school's mission and foundation—generally prescribes the content. Process driven strategies of cooperative learning, discussion groups, the project method, and experiential learning can address the same content or subject areas, but the approach is more open-ended. *How* is more important than *what*. The important lesson to be learned is based on process skills that can be acquired and applied. Such skills include observation, classification, prediction, inference, and communication. The content can be prescribed by an outside source or presented by the teacher, but more likely it is controlled by the learner. In both direct and indirect instruction, students, the teachers, and the subject areas all interact in different scenarios, with a varying emphasis on each.

Models of Curriculum

For both camps, the content approach and the process approach, there are three models as options for curriculum design and implementation. Each model involves the student, the teacher, and the subject matter, and how they interact. Each model addresses where the focus of authority resides, in other words, who or what determines the curriculum, what is the knowledge base for the curriculum, who imparts the knowledge, and what is the most feasible delivery system. The three models include the subject-centered model, the teacher-centered model, and the student-centered model (see Fig. 4.2).

The Subject-Centered Model

In this model, the subject matter is the heart of the curriculum. Interpretations of this model vary. For Parker Palmer, educational activist, teacher, and author, the subject matter brings the teacher and student together. For him, in "a subject-centered classroom, . . . teachers and students are more likely to come into a genuine learning community, a community that does not collapse into the egos of students or teacher but knows itself accountable to the subject as its core" (Palmer, 1998, p. 118). In Palmer's scheme, the subject matter is the meeting place for the learner and teacher to connect, explore, and discover together. But Palmer's notion of a subject-centered classroom differs from other subject-centered proponents. For the essentialist, basic skills or vocational training shape a core curriculum for

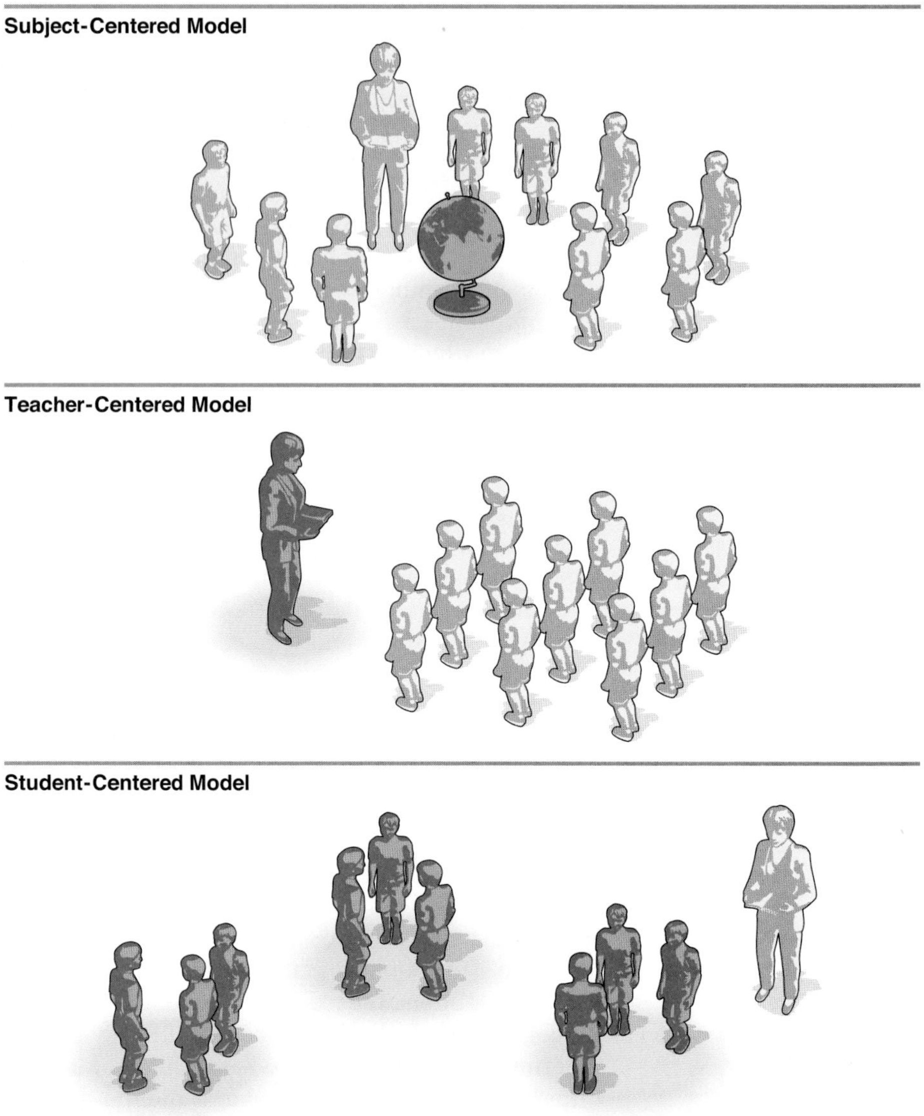

Figure 4.2
Three Teaching Models

charting the course of schooling. Behaviorists fashion their schooling around mastery of learning curricula through technology-enhanced educational designs, computer-assisted instruction, and/or programmed learning schemes. Proponents of standards-based programs, whether in the public or private sectors, identify strands of the subject areas that determine the curriculum, its goals, objectives, and assessments. In the subject-centered model schools can be seen as the agency for either transforming or reflecting society. Palmer might argue that subject-centered schools with teachers who have the courage to take on challenges and teach with conviction affect changes that transform society. Conversely, schools where teachers follow mandated protocols or a narrowly defined set of subject areas reflect the society they serve but with the aim of producing a literate, informed, employable, and competent citizenry.

grade twelve. Most states implemented their recommendations. In addition, textbook publishers followed the guidelines in their production of math series and programs. So, in essence, states and communities that adopt the textbook series are aligning their mandates with the recommendations of the professional organizations. Other learned societies that followed suit by creating standards in their disciplines include the National Council for Geographic Education, the National Council of the Social Studies, and the National Academy of Sciences. In specialty areas like early childhood education the National Association for the Education of Young Children authored standards for all of the fields, while the Council for Exceptional Children developed guidelines for adaptive instruction in inclusive classrooms.

Teachers and School Boards The local community's voice on curriculum resides in its elected school boards or committees. School boards represent the community in establishing local school policies and monitoring curriculum implementation. Often, local education boards modify statewide mandates to satisfy local cultural, political, and social stipulations. For example, local historical or community events can be highlighted over the national or state happenings in a social studies guide. Teachers also adapt state mandated curriculum when they design lessons to be relevant to their students. Most teachers address state standards in programs, activities, units, and special projects through studies of their community, field trips to local areas, and visits from local civic groups or guest speakers. Creative teachers weave their children's interests, current happenings near and far, and new ideas into their daily teaching of mandated curriculum.

Families and Community Families play a role in determining curriculum by their involvement in their children's schools. When there is a conflict between family values and school curriculum, complaints are registered at the school or through the school board, political officials, and the local media. Most controversial issues in mandated curriculum center around the teaching of character education, sex education, or world religions—subjects some families feel should be taught exclusively at home. On a positive note, families can influence curriculum through their presence as volunteers in the classrooms, visiting speakers, school councilors, and Parent/Teacher Organization (PTO) members. As informed constituents, they can affect changes, address concerns, and introduce new avenues of inquiry.

The sense of place is central to curriculum development. The tone of the community sets the school climate and determines its citizens' perceptions of education. Local environmental, economical, social, cultural, and geographical factors shape attitudes that can hinder curriculum growth or permit it to flourish. In a country as large as the United States, regional interests affect interpretations of curricula. For example, priorities at rural schools often differ from those of urban or suburban schools. Likewise, the various media outlets such as television, textbook publishers, news, the Internet, and the World Wide Web influence consumers and impact the schoolroom as well as the marketplace.

Paulo Freire called for community and family voices to be heard in constructing curriculum (see Chapter 3). In theory and practice, he stressed that the local people's language and personal community experiences should shape the curriculum. *Place education,* a curriculum model presented in this chapter, illustrates his teachings as an exemplar for developing curriculum around people, places, and happenings in a community.

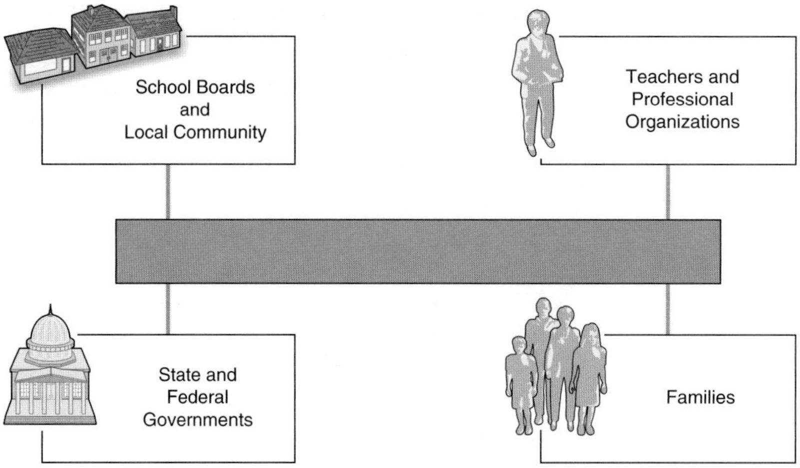

Figure 4.1

Who Are the Players in Decisions About Curriculum?

State and Federal Governments Following an international trend, the United States Department of Education is playing an ever increasing role in the decision making about curriculum. In this and subsequent chapters we will explore past and present federal legislation that has been promulgated to define national curriculum standards, to set minimum teacher qualifications, to determine accountability measures for schools to meet attainment targets for the curriculum, and to provide parental choice of schools for children. While the federal government's role in mandating curriculum is increasing, it is important to remember that federal curriculum standards are voluntary. State departments of education mandate compulsory curriculum standards. Only states that accept federal funding for education are required to meet the national government's guidelines. To date, all fifty states do have some form of curriculum standards for their public schools, but some states are challenging the current federal education act, No Child Left Behind, by noncompliance with certain measures.

Landmark Supreme Court decisions such as the 1954 *Brown v. Board of Education,* which desegregated schools; and legislative acts such as Title IX, which prohibits gender bias in schools, and the 1974 Bilingual Act, which allows parental input in developing programs for children with limited English language skills, have brought more diversity to the curriculum (see Chapters 7 and 9 for additional discussion of diversity). Likewise, the delivery of the curriculum now accommodates new populations of students with the passages of Public Law 94-142, the 1975 Education for All Handicapped Act, and the 1990 Individuals with Disabilities Education Act (IDEA). Both of these acts mandate equal educational opportunities for all students from age two to twenty-one to be available in the least restrictive environment. (see Chapter 9). Classrooms have become inclusive of students with learning differences and physical challenges. Individual Education Plans (IEPs) modify the curriculum to fit the special needs of these students. Classroom environments must be accommodated to provide conditions that support suitable instructional practices in a welcoming atmosphere conducive for all learners.

Professional Organizations Most of the states derive their curriculum standards from professional organizations and learned societies. For example, the National Council of the Teachers of Mathematics was the first of the learned societies to define national standards for teaching mathematics from kindergarten to

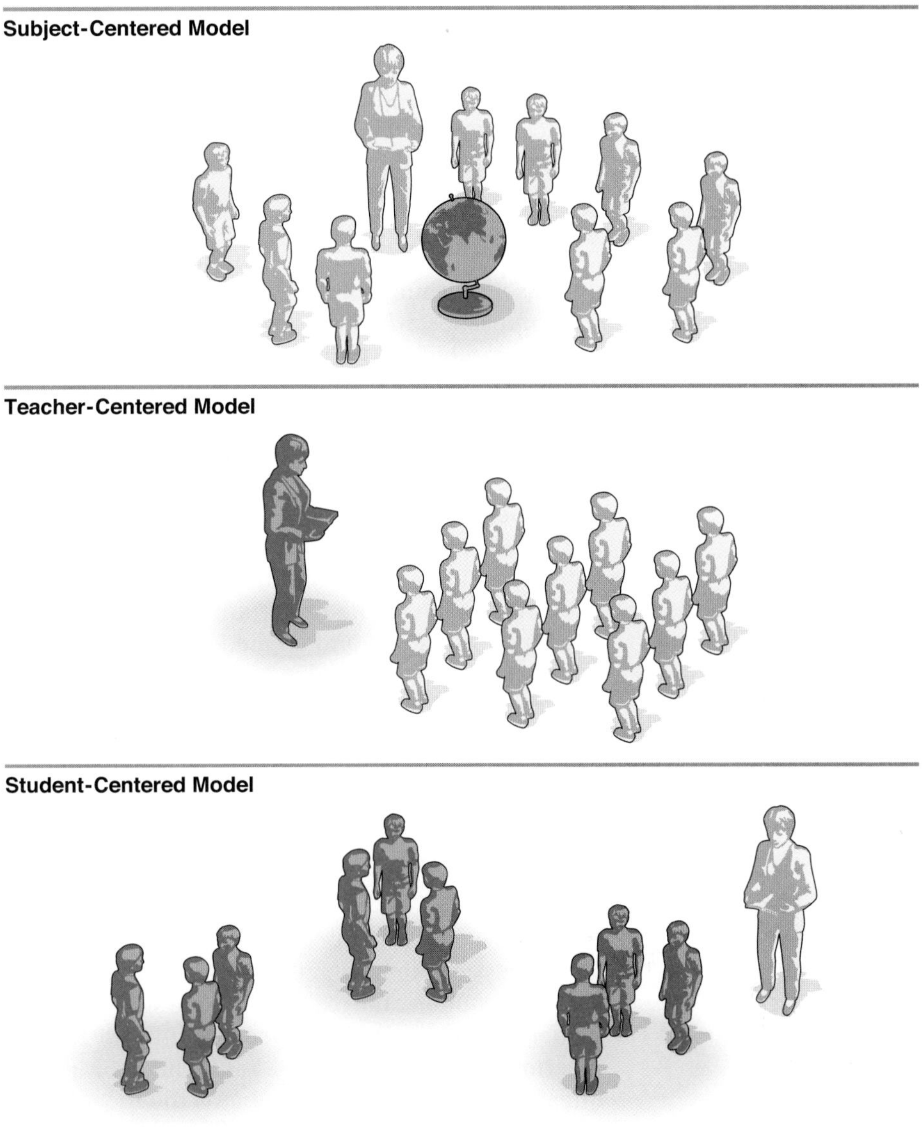

Figure 4.2

Three Teaching Models

charting the course of schooling. Behaviorists fashion their schooling around mastery of learning curricula through technology-enhanced educational designs, computer-assisted instruction, and/or programmed learning schemes. Proponents of standards-based programs, whether in the public or private sectors, identify strands of the subject areas that determine the curriculum, its goals, objectives, and assessments. In the subject-centered model schools can be seen as the agency for either transforming or reflecting society. Palmer might argue that subject-centered schools with teachers who have the courage to take on challenges and teach with conviction affect changes that transform society. Conversely, schools where teachers follow mandated protocols or a narrowly defined set of subject areas reflect the society they serve but with the aim of producing a literate, informed, employable, and competent citizenry.

Which Is More Important, Content or Process?

There is much controversy and debate in educational circles about curriculum in answer to the question, What is worth knowing? Many educators question what curriculum is most effective in meeting students' needs. Which approach is best? What teaching strategies work? How can success be assessed? Responses to these questions seem to fall into two major camps, those that favor direct teaching of content, and others that focus on the process of learning. Proponents from both sides debate the issue of what is more important: the content that you learn, or the process of learning how to learn. Those who favor content promote direct teaching approaches, while process orientation theorists seek open-ended-inquiry directions in which teaching is often indirect.

Direct instruction, scripted teaching, programmed learning, and standards-based education are built upon the content or the subjects to be learned. Some authority outside of the classroom—for example, governmental agencies, publishing houses, or, in private education, the school's mission and foundation—generally prescribes the content. Process driven strategies of cooperative learning, discussion groups, the project method, and experiential learning can address the same content or subject areas, but the approach is more open-ended. *How* is more important than *what.* The important lesson to be learned is based on process skills that can be acquired and applied. Such skills include observation, classification, prediction, inference, and communication. The content can be prescribed by an outside source or presented by the teacher, but more likely it is controlled by the learner. In both direct and indirect instruction, students, the teachers, and the subject areas all interact in different scenarios, with a varying emphasis on each.

Models of Curriculum

For both camps, the content approach and the process approach, there are three models as options for curriculum design and implementation. Each model involves the student, the teacher, and the subject matter, and how they interact. Each model addresses where the focus of authority resides, in other words, who or what determines the curriculum, what is the knowledge base for the curriculum, who imparts the knowledge, and what is the most feasible delivery system. The three models include the subject-centered model, the teacher-centered model, and the student-centered model (see Fig. 4.2).

The Subject-Centered Model

In this model, the subject matter is the heart of the curriculum. Interpretations of this model vary. For Parker Palmer, educational activist, teacher, and author, the subject matter brings the teacher and student together. For him, in "a subject-centered classroom, . . . teachers and students are more likely to come into a genuine learning community, a community that does not collapse into the egos of students or teacher but knows itself accountable to the subject as its core" (Palmer, 1998, p. 118). In Palmer's scheme, the subject matter is the meeting place for the learner and teacher to connect, explore, and discover together. But Palmer's notion of a subject-centered classroom differs from other subject-centered proponents. For the essentialist, basic skills or vocational training shape a core curriculum for

The Teacher-Centered Model

In this model, the teacher determines the curriculum. She is the warranted authority, who knows what needs to be taught, decides what approach is best for her students, and implements her strategies. The teacher selects the material to be taught, guides predetermined learning experiences with carefully constructed activities. Typically, the teacher models desired outcomes for class assignments and learning tasks. The teacher's expectations are clearly delineated for the students in rubrics or criteria outlines. Outside factors such as governmental requirements and regulations, educational publications, school traditions and mission, and the community's social, cultural, and economic climate contribute to her determinations. In a perennialist school, the dominant cultural heritage and its traditions influence the teacher, as it is incumbent upon her to transmit values as well as a common knowledge base. In this model, the school is a social institution that reflects society rather than one that attempts change or transformation. The curriculum's aim in this model is to impart wisdom through the study of the best ideas acknowledged over time for the education of an enlightened citizenry, scholars, and democratic leaders.

The Student-Centered Model

The student-centered model places the student at the center of the curriculum. The student's development, needs, interests, and/or cultural background are the critical factors for determining the curriculum and its implementation. Learning experiences need to be relevant to the lives of the learner for knowledge to be internalized. Typical theorists of this model include existentialists, liberationists, progressives, and child-centered romantics.

In Paulo Freire's proposal for "the education of the oppressed," the student has the authority to shape the curriculum; the student's culture needs to prevail over the dominant culture in reflecting the goals of the curriculum and the aspirations of the learner. For A. S. Neill at Summerhill, it is the student who decides about the options presented in the curriculum. The student is charged to take risks, to discover paths that reach goals, to not be swayed by prevailing opinion, and to accept responsibility for the outcomes of his choices and to learn from these outcomes. Maria Montessori 's method is predicated on the child's development. Her methods and materials were designed to match the developing rhythms of the child. The teacher is a *directress* who channels the learning experiences, while the child is autonomous in deciding what materials to select in the various learning activities. Progressives like John Dewey and the genetic epistemologist, Jean Piaget, recognize that the learner constructs knowledge and thus the curriculum content. For Dewey, learning results from experiences. The curriculum emanates from the student's experiences and must be relevant for the student in order to be productive. Students engage in projects that provide opportunities for growth, understanding, and appreciation. Students construct meaning of their world from these endeavors when they analyze, synthesize, criticize, explore, and create. Whether alone or in a group, the students direct the learning as the teacher facilitates. In this model, schools are often challenged to transform society and meet the challenges of constant change. The curriculum's aim is to educate self-actualized individuals who can participate and lead in a democratic society.

Table 4.1 Curriculum Models

Curriculum Model	Characteristics	Advantages	Cautions	Example
Student-centered	The curriculum matches the developmental needs and interests of the students. The students can design their own curriculum. Students are responsible for their learning. Students are active learners.	Engages students in their own learning experiences. Tailors instruction to make the curriculum relevant. Respects the voices of students.	Care needs to be given to ensure comprehensive and inclusive exposure to all areas of the curriculum by all of the children.	Kindergarten children in a two-way language class select experiences from a menu of choices written in English and Spanish for art projects placed at various learning stations. Each child reads the menu in the language she is learning and selects the project of her choice to work on at her own pace.
Teacher-centered	The teacher determines the curriculum and delivery of subject matter.	Teachers are accountable for their teaching and control the learning opportunities. Efficient approach for large groups and classes.	The teacher needs to engage students; otherwise the students are passive learners.	A seventh grade math teacher lectures to the whole class on how to balance a checkbook in a practical life application lesson.
Subject-centered	The curriculum can be derived from national or state standards or a program of study that defines the curriculum for each academic year. All students study the same subjects.	Continuity in the curriculum from grade level to grade level. Connects students and teachers to learning experiences. Spirals skills. Provides a uniform curriculum to all students.	Teachers need to plan lessons that accommodate their students' needs. Teachers need to make the subject relevant to their students. Students need to be engaged as active learners.	Students and teachers from an environmental studies high school class go on a field trip to collect and identify different kinds of rocks for a research unit prescribed in their standards-based science curriculum.

Technology's Role

Computers, the Internet, and the World Wide Web bring a world of resources to our fingertips. Along with the advent of changes in technology, schools experience the same political, social, economic, and cultural shifts present in all aspects of society. These new paradigms or patterns alter the school climate and change teaching practices and curriculum design.

Technology in education comes in many forms. School walls fall when replaced with distance learning through on-line instruction. Some classrooms use specific software programs to drill students on skills in grammar. With the advent of **assistive technology** students with learning differences and physical challenges are included in classroom populations from which they once were excluded.

Innovative and improved assistive technology devices include electronic communication aids, speech synthesizers, Braille writers, scanners, text readers, environmental controls, and touch windows, along with a myriad of computer software for all curriculum areas. These assistive technology devices enable teachers to adapt instruction to the needs of all learners as well as to encourage learners to be autonomous and active participants in class activities or individual projects.

Computer-based instruction in schools broadens horizons for both students and teachers. Now, resources that were once available only in libraries, museums, and other institutions can be accessed through the Internet. Computer-based instruction has altered approaches to curriculum implementation. Following is an illustration of the influence that technology is having on current teaching practices.

Teaching a Project-Based Unit with Technology

Charged by their state-mandated curriculum frameworks to teach the American Revolution, a team of teachers devised a project-based unit as a web quest for fifth graders. The web quest used computers and an array of software programs for classroom research, which provided student access to primary as well as secondary resources. Like most American Revolution units, this project-based unit began the study of the Revolution with a lesson on Henry Wadsworth Longfellow's legendary poem, "Paul Revere's Ride," but with a twist.

Most of us can recite the first line of this classic, "Listen my children, and you shall hear of the midnight ride of Paul Revere." It has been taught in American schools since Longfellow wrote it in the nineteenth century. Since the most commonly used technology of the past was "slate and chalk" and "paper and pen," teachers from previous centuries wrote Longfellow's renowned work on the chalkboard for the students to copy in notebooks and commit to memory. Now, technology has changed the paradigm.

Today, the fifth graders were presented the poem via the computer. Their task was to evaluate Longfellow's epic for its accurate portrayal of the ride, against an abundance of evidence provided in primary sources of the period such as personal letters, public documents, news reports, engravings, maps and even cartoons—all available on the Internet and easily accessed. The students took their charge seriously. Their computer searches for primary and secondary resources led them to the discovery that Longfellow took "poetic license" in his writing. They decided that the poem has perpetuated many myths about Paul Revere's ride. In their reports, they pointed out how and where the poem's account did not jibe with the evidence they uncovered. Yet this discovery did not dissuade the students from presenting an oral recitation of the poem. Many elected to memorize it for a school performance. Others took on the challenge to revise it for a more exacting rendition!

This computer-based instructional model illustrates that new technologies alter what we teach and how we teach. By using the computer as an instructional tool, this team of teachers enhanced their students' learning with opportunities that would not otherwise have been available. The web quest made history come alive and provided a hook that engaged the class to uncover and disclose truths about an important incident in the Revolution. For each assignment the students assumed the role of the historian as they sought to distinguish myth from reality. Their research abilities, decision making, readings, and investigative reports reflected high-level thinking skills. In their analysis of fictional portrayal and factual information, they compared and contrasted evidence gleaned through their computer searches for consistency and accuracy. Today's technology provided them with the same tools and experiences professionals employ to write and, when necessary, amend history.

Source: Based on *Massacres, Messengers and Misunderstandings,* by L. Patrie, F. Pomerantz, E. Prince, and E. Rittershaus, Project LEARN/21C, funded by the U.S. Department of Education's Preparing Tomorrow's Teachers to Use Technology PT3, 2004. www.pbubuilder.org.

Questions to Consider

1. How does this model make appropriate use of the computer?
2. How does this piece illustrate that technology can alter the curriculum and how teachers teach it?

Which Models Reflect Your Beliefs?

Throughout this chapter we invite you to consider which models reflect your personal beliefs, which models shaped your education, or which models are the educational milieu of your present teaching situation. You might also want to reconsider the assumptions you identified to define your philosophy of education as discussed in Chapter 3. The three models depicted in this chapter are based on philosophical perspectives of education and thus evoke debate about control of education (is the teacher in control, or the student?), question the standards or guidelines for an educational program, recommend divergent teaching strategies, and provide a variety of solutions to educational issues and concerns. In all of these models the learner is the constituent, but the purpose of the curriculum and the authors differ widely.

The Question of Standards in Education

Standards have many different meanings, yet by their nature they demand agreement among constituents. In this section, we will examine the definitions of standards, the models of education based on standards, and the ensuing debates about standards. Implications of international trends on standards will broaden the discussion of global studies and interpretations. Discussion of standards is also expanded upon in a later chapter when we consider changes happening in education due to school reforms (see Chapter 11).

What Is Meant by *Standards?*

Standards can be made complicated by the various meanings the term invokes. *Standard* is a term with many subtle meanings. When some educators refer to standards, they are setting high levels of achievement for students to attain, while other educators are setting a uniform or common curriculum for all learners. According to the *Merriam-Webster Collegiate Dictionary* (2003, p. 1216) a standard can be a "criterion, a gauge, a touchstone" or a milestone, all of which imply an attainment of quality or "a rule for excellence" measured by some authority. As an adjective, *standard* has a range of meanings from "sound and usable, but not top quality" to "having recognized and permanent value." When used in an educational context, the multiple meanings of standard spur debate. This chapter explores the arguments over whether educational standards promote high achievement or mere conformity and mediocrity. This debate has been prompted by the emergence of standards-based education.

What Is Standards-Based Education?

Standards-based education is an approach to identify the common body of knowledge and skills that need to be built into a uniform curriculum for kindergarten through grade 12 (see Chapter 11). The standards are attainment targets for achievement in defined subject matter areas. Each subject matter area can have several strands. For example, the social studies standards would include strands of history, geography, politics, and government. The standards for each subject area are defined in a framework or guide that serves as the foundation to support and structure the curriculum.

The educational process is driven by the framework to ensure conformity, continuity, and consistency in teacher expectations for student achievement. The anthem is: "All children can learn." Teachers are accountable for implementing the prescribed frameworks and are required to indicate the standards they are addressing in their written plans and programs of study. Attainment is measured through a battery of evaluations and assessments, including national exams, such as the National Assessment of Educational Progress (NEAP), and state-mandated tests, such as the New York Regents Exams. While standards-based education is predominant in the public schools throughout the United States, some private sector schools are equally prescriptive in defining and implementing their curriculum. Private schools are excluded from the mandates and therefore they have the choice whether or not to use standardized tests to measure student achievement or validate their curriculum.

Does Standards-Based Education Have International Implications?

Standards-based education is evident internationally in curriculum designs. School systems throughout Europe, and in countries like South Africa, South Korea, China, and Japan, adhere to a standards-based approach for their state schools. While there has been much rhetoric about *world-class standards,* attempts to define or formulate them as international guidelines for education have been difficult, due to differences in cultural values and national barriers. The World

Organization for Early Childhood Education (Organisation Mondiale pour L'Education Prescolaire, or OMEP) and the Association for Childhood Education International have been developing global guidelines for early education and child-care programs with limited success. Peter Moss, a professor of early childhood provision at the University of London, contends that international guidelines present many problems in "their denial of diversity and their potential for normalisation and control" (1999, p. 28). He is concerned that international guidelines "exclude alternative ways of understanding and interpreting the world [and] raise questions about power and power relations" (1999, p. 25). "I would argue that, within current power relations, attempts to produce international early childhood guidelines are likely to be governed by the dominant early childhood discourse, which is Anglo-American, and which is the product of the linguistic, cultural, economic, and technological structure of this one part of the world" (Peter Moss, p. 25).

Yet despite Moss's misgivings, many attempts to internationalize standards can be found in comparative testing programs such as the Trends in International Mathematics and Science Study (TIMSS). In 1995 and 1999, this study was conducted in thirty-eight nations at the fourth-, eighth-, and tenth-grade levels. As a major research project, it examined student testing performances in math and science, along with each country's curricula, instructional strategies, school policies, and teaching materials to formulate a league table that compared nations' overall achievements. A league is a comparative listing or ranking of schools based on some criteria such as test scores, achievement, etc. Findings showed that America's performances were less than stellar and our comparative standings in the rating scales indicated mediocre results. The perception of American students' abilities in mathematics has been unfairly skewed and maligned by the findings. For example, in many European systems, students leave secondary schools in the tenth grade, only selected students continue to the 12th grade. Thus comparisons for this level are skewed and not valid. Yet, the implications of the studies have spurred on the movement to restructure American schools with international benchmarks and to adapt some nations' educational practices. (see Chapter 11).

International standards are also found in the private sector of education, especially in schools that have spread worldwide, such as International Schools, Montessori schools, or Waldorf schools. To uphold their reputation internationally, these schools prescribe a common curriculum, methodology, and assessment means for quality assurance and commitment to their educational philosophy. Later in this chapter we will see how standards shape such schools to establish global recognition.

Is Standards-Based Education a New Initiative?

The notion of having standards for education is not new. Historically, educational movements have derived standards as the basis for curriculum. In 1586 the Society of Jesus drafted the *Ratio Studiorum,* which according to Edward Power is "the heart of Jesuit pedagogy . . . the instrument that guided Jesuit schools and Jesuit teaching and brought both to fame" (Power, 1970, p. 405). While the *Ratio* was adapted to place and changed over time, it served as the constant guide for the basic philosophy and practices of the religious order's schools and the standard-bearer of what constituted a Jesuit education. Jesuit schools, colleges, and universities identified themselves with the *Ratio* wherever in the world they were founded. Following the Jesuit tradition for a standard curriculum is the Montessori Method, which was developed at the end of the nineteenth century and is still a popular model in today's schools in both the private and public sectors.

Montessori schools today adhere to the method prescribed by Maria Montessori at the turn of the twentieth century. Deviation from her pedagogy or her delineated teaching strategies is a rare occurrence in today's Montessori schools. Likewise, Waldorf schools around the globe are aligned with the precepts of Rudolf Steiner, who early in the twentieth century designed a school and curriculum for the children of employees of the Waldorf Astoria cigarette factory in Germany. The more recent International Baccalaureate is a world class standard for an acceptable college and university preparation. Its rigorous course of study is detailed and devised to address the admission requirements of most of the elite universities and colleges worldwide.

As many governments became involved in the education of their young, centralized ministries of education evolved and standard curricula were established. Most notable of this group is France, but many countries have a ministry of education, which mandates guidelines for schooling. The United States has only lately joined the international community of public and private schools in defining national standards for achievement.

Setting the Policy for Educational Standards

The push for standards in education is a global movement. The international economic climate, the multi-national corporations, and the competitive edge of nations to perform successfully in the global work force have brought about a clarion call for world-class standards. In 1984, under a politically conservative push, the U.S. government produced a report entitled "A Nation at Risk," which highlighted the weaknesses in American public schools and the jeopardy of the United States falling behind its counterparts in the world (see Chapter 11). Other nations also felt challenged by societies whose schools performed better on international assessments; many of them began to create national standards where there had been none. Great Britain is a case in point. In 1988 the British Parliament passed a bill to establish a national curriculum to replace the 1944 proclamation that required only religious education in all local authority schools. Traditionally, head teachers and staff designed the curriculum and controlled the means of implementation. The British National Curriculum centralized education, setting up foundation courses in English, math, and science, along with history, geography, the arts, technology, and languages. These courses are basic for the education of all children from the school entry age of five to the school completion age of sixteen. Starting with a baseline assessment for school entry, each child's achievement is determined by a national assessment at "key stages." Schools are rated based on their students' performance and the ratings are charted in league tables for publication in the national and local press. Following a pattern similar to that of Great Britain, America 2000 was promulgated by President George H. W. Bush's administration and adapted by President William Clinton's administration as Goals 2000. Each mandate called for national standards in English, math, science, history, and geography, to be accompanied by rigorous testing that assured a high level of performance for all students in America by the year 2000. Statements that proclaimed American students would be first in the world in performance in subjects such as math and science were bandied about. Unfortunately, reality did not measure up to the rhetoric.

DIRECTLY FROM THE SOURCE

The No Child Left Behind Act of 2001

Source: U.S. Department of Education website: www.ed.gov/nclb/overview/intro.

The No Child Left Behind Act of 2001 (No Child Left Behind) is a landmark in education reform designed to improve student achievement and change the culture of America's schools. President George W. Bush describes this law as the "cornerstone of my administration." Clearly, our children are our future, and, as President Bush has expressed, "Too many of our neediest children are being left behind."

With passage of No Child Left Behind, Congress reauthorized the Elementary and Secondary Education Act (ESEA)—the principal federal law affecting education from kindergarten through high school. In amending ESEA, the new law represents a sweeping overhaul of federal efforts to support elementary and secondary education in the United States. It is built on four common-sense pillars: accountability for results; an emphasis on doing what works based on scientific research; expanded parental options; and expanded local control and flexibility.

What No Child Left Behind Does for Parents and Children

Supports Learning in the Early Years, Thereby Preventing Many Learning Difficulties That May Arise Later

Children who enter school with language skills and pre-reading skills (e.g., understanding that print reads from left to right and top to bottom) are more likely to learn to read well in the early grades and succeed in later years. In fact, research shows that most reading problems faced by adolescents and adults are the result of problems that could have been prevented through good instruction in their early childhood years (Snow, Burns and Griffin 1998). It is never too early to start building language skills by talking with and reading to children. No Child Left Behind targets resources for early childhood education so that all youngsters get the right start. Provides more information for parents about their child's progress.

Under No Child Left Behind, each state must measure every public school student's progress in reading and math in each of grades 3 through 8 and at least once during grades 10 through 12. By school year 2007–2008, assessments (or testing) in science will be underway. These assessments must be aligned with state academic content and achievement standards. They will provide parents with objective data on where their child stands academically.

www.

Alerts Parents to Important Information on the Performance of Their Child's School

No Child Left Behind requires states and school districts to give parents easy-to-read, detailed report cards on schools and districts, telling them which ones are succeeding and why. Included in the report cards are student achievement data broken out by race, ethnicity, gender, English language proficiency, migrant status, disability status and low-income status; as well as important information about the professional qualifications of teachers. With these provisions, No Child Left Behind ensures that parents have important, timely information about the schools their children attend—whether they are performing well or not for all children, regardless of their background.

Gives Children and Parents a Lifeline

In this new era of education, children will no longer be trapped in the dead end of low-performing schools. Under No Child Left Behind, such schools must use their federal funds to make needed improvements. In the event of a school's continued poor performance, parents have options to ensure that their children receive the high-quality education to which they are entitled. That might mean that children can transfer to higher-performing schools in the area or receive supplemental educational services in the community, such as tutoring, after-school programs or remedial classes.

Improves Teaching and Learning by Providing Better Information to Teachers and Principals

Annual tests to measure children's progress provide teachers with independent information about each child's strengths and weaknesses. With this knowledge, teachers can craft lessons to make sure each student meets or exceeds the standards. In addition, principals can use the data to assess exactly how much progress each teacher's students have made and to better inform decisions about how to run their schools.

Ensures That Teacher Quality Is a High Priority

No Child Left Behind defines the qualifications needed by teachers and paraprofessionals who work on any facet of classroom instruction. It requires that states develop plans to achieve the goal that all teachers of core academic subjects be highly qualified by the end of the 2005–06 school year. States must include in their plans annual, measurable objectives that each local school district* and school must meet in moving toward the goal; they must report on their progress in the annual report cards.

Gives More Resources to Schools

Today, more than $7,000 on average is spent per pupil by local, state and federal taxpayers. States and local school districts are now receiving more federal funding than ever before for all programs under No Child Left Behind: $23.7 billion, most of which will be used during the 2003–04 school year. This represents an increase of 59.8 percent from 2000 to 2003. A large portion of these funds is for grants under Title I of ESEA: Improving the Academic Achievement of the Disadvantaged. Title I grants are awarded to states and local education agencies to help states and school districts improve the education of disadvantaged students; turn around low-performing schools; improve teacher quality; and increase choices for parents. (For more about Title I, see the introductory paragraph to Q-and-As.) For fiscal year (FY) 2003, funding for Title I alone is $11.7 billion—an increase of 33 percent since the passage of No Child Left Behind. President Bush's FY 2004 budget request would increase spending on Title I by 48 percent since he took office.

Allows More Flexibility

In exchange for the strong accountability, No Child Left Behind gives states and local education agencies more flexibility in the use of their federal education funding. As a result, principals and administrators spend less time filling out forms and dealing with federal red tape. They have more time to devote to students' needs. They have more freedom to implement innovations and allocate resources as policymakers at the state and local levels see fit, thereby giving local people a greater opportunity to affect decisions regarding their schools' programs.

Focuses on What Works

No Child Left Behind puts a special emphasis on implementing educational programs and practices that have been clearly demonstrated to be effective through rigorous scientific research. Federal funding will be targeted to support such programs. For example, the Reading First program makes federal funds available to help reading teachers in the early grades strengthen old skills and gain new ones in instructional techniques that scientifically based research has shown to be effective.

Why No Child Left Behind Is Important to America

Federal Spending on K–12 Education under the Elementary and Secondary Education Act and NAEP Reading Scores (Age 9) Note: Appropriations for ESEA do not include funding for special education. Reading scores are the average scores for 9-year-olds, according to the National Assessment of Educational Progress (NAEP). A score of 200 implies an ability to understand, combine ideas and make inferences based on short, uncomplicated passages about specific or sequentially related information.*

Since the Elementary and Secondary Education Act first passed Congress in 1965, the federal government has spent more than $242 billion through 2003 to help educate disadvantaged children. Yet, the achievement gap in this country between rich and poor and white and minority students remains wide. According to the most recent National Assessment of Educational Progress (NAEP) on reading in 2000, only 32 percent of fourth-graders can read at a proficient level and thereby demonstrate solid academic achievement; and while scores for the highest-performing students have improved over time, those of America's lowest-performing students have declined (National Assessment of Educational Progress 2001).

The good news is that some schools in cities and towns across the nation are creating high achievement for children with a history of low performance. If some schools can do it, then all schools should be able to do it.

United for Results

Because of No Child Left Behind:

Parents will know their children's strengths and weaknesses and how well schools are performing; they will have other options and resources for helping their children if their schools are chronically in need of improvement.

Teachers will have the training and resources they need for teaching effectively, using curricula that are grounded in scientifically based research; annual testing lets them know areas in which students need extra attention.

Principals will have information they need to strengthen their schools' weaknesses and to put into practice methods and strategies backed by sound, scientific research.

Directly from the Source

The No Child Left Behind Act of 2001 *(Continued)*

Superintendents will be able to see which of their schools and principals are doing the best job and which need help to improve.

School boards will be able to measure how their districts are doing and to measure their districts in relation to others across the state; they will have more and better information on which to base decisions about priorities in their districts.

Chief state school officers will know how the schools in their states and in other states are doing; they will be better able to pinpoint where guidance and resources are needed.

Governors will have a yearly report card on how their states' schools are doing; they will be able to highlight accomplishments of the best schools and target help to those schools that are in need of improvement.

Community leaders and volunteer groups will have information they can use to rally their members in efforts to help children and schools that need the most help.

Note: For the purpose of discussion in this book, the terms "district" and "local education agency" are used interchangeably in discussing the agency at the local level that is responsible for maintaining administrative control of public elementary and secondary schools in a given area or political subdivision of the state.

*Reflects the President's budget request for 2004. (Source: U.S. Department of Education Budget Service and NAEP 1999 Trends in Academic Progress).

A Closer Look at the Issues

1. Do you think this overview offers realistic expectations to parents and communities for NCLB's impact on the education of today's students?
2. What might be some concerns about NCLB as it is implemented in the schools?

In January 2002, during the administration of President George W. Bush, new legislation was enacted called No Child Left Behind. This act's goals are to "improve overall student performance and close the achievement gap between rich and poor students" (Bainbridge, 2002). Schools are accountable for meeting the higher standards set for students. Provisions in the act use assessments as a tool for identifying underperforming schools and offer alignments for those schools to reach the bar set for achievement. This act engenders debate.

No one would argue with its intent: "In America, no child should be left behind. Every child should be educated to his or her full potential" (Bainbridge, 2002). In fact, the bill's passage in Congress was a bipartisan effort. Politicians crossed party lines and modified their diametrically opposed philosophical positions on conservative and liberal policies for a consensus on this legislation. Every citizen approves of the images drawn in this legislation for his or her future. Yet, educators question the soundness of the act and are concerned about provision of the necessary funding to support such an undertaking. Research points out that "all children can learn at some level." But the effects of poverty, the inequitable access to health care, and the lack of learning opportunities beyond the school for many children are realities that challenge "the belief that all children can learn the same curriculum, in the same amount of time, and at the same level" (Bainbridge, 2002). A summary of key components of the No Child Left Behind law (NCLB) is located in Directly from the Source; this overview from the U.S. Department of Education website informs parents of the benefits of the new law. (See Chapter 11 for more discussion on NCLB.)

Educational Standards for American Schools

Educational standards pose many questions for American schools, because the traditional seat of control of schools still lies mainly at the local, county, or state level. The federal government's U.S. Department of Education does not centralize education in the same fashion as its counterparts, the ministries of other nations. Education in the United States is like a pyramid, with the federal government's control on top, supported by the states, with the local authority of schools as the foundation. National standards in the United States are voluntary, but do have the sanction of funding attached. States that comply with the federal guidelines receive support, but not all states comply. Often, disputes arise over the content of the standards and the method of assessment of achievement. The voices of dissent come from various sources including educators, parents, students, and local and state politicians.

Voices of Dissent The cacophony of dissent arises from many voices in reaction to the "blame game" of educational politics. Everyone faults someone for underperforming schools. Teachers are the most obvious targets for criticism, while parents, administrators, the communities, societal values, and the students themselves are all singled out as a cause for the failure of American schools to educate its youth. The call for standards emerged as a way out of the quagmire to upgrade the educational process with set levels of high attainment, measures of common expectations, and means of assessment. The problem with the promulgation of standards is the lack of agreement among parties as to who will write the standards and how they will be implemented, assessed, and funded.

The most outspoken critics of the standards-based movement are "prominent leaders" such as Alfie Kohn, Susan Ohanian, Theodore Sizer, and Deborah Meier [who] "dispute the notion that all students, regardless of their backgrounds, interests, or location, should learn the same subject matter. They assert that part of being an educator is shaping school curricula according to the emerging conditions and local prerogatives" (Caron, 2002, p. 72).

Theodore Sizer, professor emeritus at Brown University, former dean of Harvard University's Graduate School of Education, former headmaster of Phillips Andover Academy, and Chair of the Coalition of Essential Schools, points to the uniqueness of each student. He feels strongly about the necessity for the teacher to know her students and address their needs with a curriculum that replaces rigidity with *personalized learning* (Sizer, 1999). Yet, he does adhere to an essential or core curriculum of skills and knowledge that all students should attain. He supports standards that are locally determined and personalized in teaching practices that are relevant to their students. (See Chapter 11 for a discussion of *The Essential School.*)

Alfie Kohn, teacher and author of many books on educational issues, attacks the standards movement on many fronts. He is most vociferous in his focus on the testing debates. He alludes to a conspiracy about corporate profits from the tests (Kohn, 2002). He agrees with Susan Ohanian (2000) and Deborah Meier (2000), both of whom question the relevance of mandatory subject matter, the abusive use of testing in the standards-driven schools, and the disregard for learning theory as it applies to practice. (See the Critical Reading in this chapter, where Deborah Meier argues against standardization.). They caution teachers to avoid teaching to the test, to keep the emergent learner as the focus of instruction, and to value themselves in the decision-making process regarding what and how to teach. Nel Noddings is concerned with the lack of moral education in the standards movement. She throws down her gauntlet when she declares,

> Our society does not need to make its children first in the world in mathematics and science. It needs to care for its children. . . . In direct opposition to the current emphasis on academic standards, a national curriculum and national assessment, I have argued that our main education aim should be to encourage the growth of competent, caring, loving and loveable people (Noddings, 1995, p. 366).

Noddings dismisses the value of the liberal education, which is narrow, controlling, exclusive, and undervaluing of women. She endorses an education "organized around themes of care rather than around the traditional disciplines," yet she does not jettison academics. For her the moral life is the aim of education. "Such an aim does not work against intellectual development or academic achievement . . . it supplies a firm foundation for both" (1995, p. 369).

Parents and students have opposed many of the standards-based initiatives, particularly the accountability issue of high-stakes testing. In Massachusetts, for example, lawsuits are under way regarding the legality and validity of the Massachusetts Comprehensive Assessment System (MCAS) as a requirement for a high school diploma. Protesting families and students are supported by teachers' unions and assessment consultants, like Walt Haney, "a professor of education at Boston College and a vigorous critic of test-based education" and Bob Schaeffer, "director of public education for FairTest, a Cambridge-based advocacy group opposed to high-stakes testing" (Pierce, 2003, p. 16). Taxpayers have joined the fray to decry the costs of testing and claim that money could be better spent on direct instruction, educational materials, and technology. They cite the 2001 study of the "Pew Center on the States that estimates the costs of testing to the states to be more than $422 million" (IBID). Newspapers like the *Boston Globe* have investigated "the school testing industry" and the profit motives for spawning high-stakes testing. The paper cited concerns in other states. In Arizona, Arizona State University conducted a study that showed successful results on standards-based tests from kindergarten through high school did not correlate with college entrance exam results. In Louisiana, the governor worries about funding the additional burden of mandated testing for No Child Left Behind (Pierce, 2003).

Voices in Support of Standards Contrary to the educational critics of the standards movement, many teachers favor the notion of standards as guides to their teaching. Teachers like to have a clear notion of what is to be taught, have defined goals and objectives for their instruction, and high expectations of their students. Yet, teachers' endorsements of standards are usually tempered by some concerns. Teachers question whether testing is the only measure of accomplishment and learning. They are particularly fretful of high-stakes testing in which one test determines the student's educational future. Surveys show that "teachers appear ambivalent about the totality of the [standards] movement . . . and report that at least partly as a result of the standards, their expectations are higher for students and students appear to be learning more. . . . [Yet] teachers also believe that concentrating exclusively on developing standards and testing policies in the core academic subjects disturbs the curricular viability of important nonacademic subjects" (Caron, 2002, p. 74).

Likewise, even Alfie Kohn, a former teacher, supports the kinds of standards that offer guidelines and "a change in the *nature* of instruction—a horizontal shift," like the national standards proposed by the National Council for the Teachers of Mathematics. But he is careful to contrast the *horizontal shift* with what he labels the *vertical shift*—those standards that are "proclamations . . . a claim that students ought to know more, do more, and perform better" (Kohn, 2000, p. 5).

The chorus of voices endorsing the standards-based education movement point to the need for a core curriculum for all students that ensures equity, that believes all children are capable of learning, and that motivates students to attain high benchmarks of achievement. The chorus of support is heard in the state departments of education across the nation. Forty-nine of the fifty states have put a standards curriculum in place, sanctioned by testing programs to determine the effectiveness of instruction and levels of achievement. Historically, New York is credited as the state that paved the way for the testing criteria route, with its famous Regents Exams.

A noteworthy proponent of uniformity in curriculum is E. D. Hirsch, in his promotion of a cultural literacy. Hirsch puts forth the argument that any society needs to have a base knowledge of prescribed literary examples, a core of curriculum areas, and a common background in order to be literate. Reading comprehension builds on this common background. To read an account in the newspaper, a novel, or a nonfiction book you must have common references to glean the meaning of the writing and the intentions of the author. For example, should a book refer to one's Achilles' heel, the reader must be familiar with the hero of Homer's *Iliad,* who epitomized the Greek ideal of strength but was fatally wounded in his heel, where he was vulnerable. Otherwise, the point of the reference is lost.

Hirsch (2001) borrows from James S. Coleman's report published in 1966 that concluded "schools could reduce the academic-achievement gap by becoming more 'intensive' by devising explicit academic standards for each grade, and making sure that every child meets those expectations." Based on Coleman's report, Hirsch's cultural literacy program prescribes a curriculum for each grade with literature, history, and science, and a systematic teaching of oral language and listening skills. For Hirsch, systematic direct teaching is the most efficient approach to reduce learning gaps among children and provide for equity in education. For children who have deficiencies, "explicit" teaching compensates for the gap. Teachers need "to break down each domain to be learned into manageable elements that can be mastered. Then systematically build on that knowledge with new knowledge." Knowledge becomes meaningful to children when it is taught in a "sustained and coherent way." Hirsch contends that direct teaching, formulated by explicit goals and sequenced objectives, results in effective learning. Such teaching is framed by the comprehensive scope of a defined curriculum that reflects and preserves the cultural foundations of a democratic society (Hirsch, 2001).

Supporters of cultural literacy and traditional time-tested approaches to standards-based education in curriculum back Hirsch. Educational leaders such as Diane Ravitch, Chester Finn, and William Bennett maintain that standards will equalize educational opportunity. (See the Critical Reading for Diane Ravitch's discussion of state-mandated testing.) They defend the accountability measures used in schools as the only route open for improvement of American schools. Each was a key player in the 1990s school reform movement that set the quest for standards and fashioned the means for accountability. In their recommended reforms, they called for the return to traditional measures of direct teaching, specifically defined strands of curriculum, core courses, and high-stakes testing.

The politics of education is evident in the standards debate. Traditionalists are typically conservative in their politics. Even reading instruction is politicized and polarized with pundits lining up on opposing sides. Conservatives favor phonics-only programs, while liberal groups look to multiple approaches that ensure comprehension. Conservatives endorse standards-based testing—beginning with four-year-olds in Head Start programs and continuing through high school—to measure benchmarks of achievement for the awarding of diplomas. They require teachers and administrators to be tested for certification or licensure. Liberals counter with research evidence that disputes the effectiveness of the "one test fits all" tactic of assessment. They also contend that since teaching is an art as well as a science, its effectiveness cannot adequately be measured by pencil and paper tests.

Many educators try to lend balance to the debate about standards. They predicate their support of standards on empirical evidence. They look to learning theory, research on intelligence, and ethnographic studies that identify effective teaching/learning practices as the foundation for developing efficacious standards, guidelines, and accountability for authentic educational experiences. They recommend many supplementary forms of assessment such as portfolios, performances, projects, and exhibitions.

Approaches to Curriculum

There are many curriculum models that are supported by standards. Some models use the standards to define expectations. Other models base their standards on developmental studies of children. Still others draw from the community to implement the standards. The following models are exemplars of such approaches.

The Efficacy Institute: Smart Is Something You Get If You Know How

Jeff Howard, founder of a national movement known as the Efficacy Institute, challenges the predominant belief that intelligence measures can define children's abilities. He opposes practices that "sort and select, in which children are consigned to places in a vertical continuum, of dullest to brightest, and lowest to highest achieving" (Blackman and Howard, 1999, p. 3). He calls for educators to abandon the bell curve, ability grouping, and the assumption that some kids just cannot perform in all areas. He asks educators to reconceptualize what he construes as "a system of miseducation" in which children are tracked into instructional levels. His efficacy model maintains that all children, regardless of background, have the innate abilities to succeed in school, rather than a fixed innate intelligence. According to Howard, if a child can learn language, which is a very complex cognitive task, he can handle the school's curriculum. Teachers must believe that children are not born smart, but can learn to be smart. The anthem of the Efficacy Institute is: "Smart is not something you are; it is something you can get" (1999, p. 4).

Teachers need to encourage children to believe in themselves and to work for results. High expectations are essential. Teachers need to hold all students to the same levels of expectation, in which proficiency is the goal. These proficiencies emanate from a common academic core curriculum and a persistent effort to develop work habits that result in successful outcomes. Teachers, students, families, and the community must "build consensus on the targeted outcomes that define success." For Howard, these outcomes are high achievement levels in which all students must perform, and include the ability to do calculus, write a research paper, read critically, and evidence insights into historical and present-day events in scholarly dialogue. Howard calls for the replacement of the "destructive . . . current American belief system about the distribution of learning capacity" with a "constructive belief system" that holds to high standards and accountability for all children (Blackman and Howard, 1999, p. 4).

Jeff Howard endorses school reforms that promote standards, demand high-level performance on achievement tests, and hold all students to the same expectations. These goals are expressed in the philosophy of his **efficacy model,** which contends that with effort all children can reach a high level of learning in any academic area. In dismissing the notion of the bell curve as myth for a measure for achievement, he challenges the deterministic nature of the achievement gap as being defined by class, race, and socioeconomic status. He replaces the notion that some students are smart and others are not with the goal for schools to hold all students to the same level of attainment. For Howard, all children can succeed in a core curriculum that demands high levels of achievement.

While the standards movement lends credibility to his model, the teacher is the key to success in Howard's model. He credits his own success in the world of academia to his fifth grade teacher, a caring and competent professional who valued the worth of each of her pupils and instilled in them not only the desire to learn but also the means. The teacher's encouragement and belief in her students are critical components of the model. Howard challenges teachers to relinquish long-held notions about teaching and learning. Teachers need to jettison biases and attitudes that stipulate that some children can't achieve in all areas of the curriculum. Howard contends that teachers should not group children according to ability or complain that some children just can't do math, write a coherent paper, or understand the complexities of an issue. He prompts teachers to acknowledge that with effort and coaching all children can realize a high level of scholarship across the curriculum. Teachers are to motivate all students to stay on task. The intent of the Efficacy Institute is to promote a resiliency in students to overcome barriers to learning through persistence and commitment to excellence.

Curriculum-Based Developmentally Appropriate Practices

The National Association for the Education of Young Children (NAEYC) has produced guidelines and standards for early childhood education identified as Developmentally Appropriate Practices (DAP). These standards are predicated on the research and writings of several theorists involved in cognitive development and the notion of intelligence. Jean Piaget, Lev Semenovich Vygotsky, and Jerome Bruner are three key figures in a curriculum approach to practices that attempt to match the standards of expectation and learning to the developmental stages of the learner. Piaget, a Swiss genetic epistemologist, formulated a theory of cognitive behavior that identifies four stages of development in people of any era and culture, namely:

1. The sensorimotor stage from birth to age two, in which sensory experiences and movement are key to the cognitive process.
2. The pre-operational stage from age two to seven, in which children are intuitive in their cognition and successfully recognize and use symbols in language and experiences.
3. The concrete operational stage from age eight to eleven, when children can begin to use logic to explain physical and concrete phenomena.
4. The formal operational stage from age twelve to adulthood, when abstract thought readily takes convergent and divergent directions.

Children move through these stages in an evolving process that requires interactive experiences—physical, intellectual, and social—that permit children to construct meaning and a knowledge base.

Consistent with Piaget, Vygotsky defined the zone of proximal development (ZPD), which is the point at which a child can act independently but needs assistance to move forward in areas where he cannot go independently. Teaching needs to address this transition to help the child move from dependence to independence. Teachers assess the child's emerging knowledge base and provide the critical experiences that fill in gaps and move the learner to the new level. Likewise, Jerome Bruner (1960, p. 33) explained that "[r]esearch on the intellectual development of the child highlights the fact that at each stage of development the child has a characteristic way of viewing the world and explaining it to himself."

Matching teaching with the child's developmental stage is critical in the design of a "developmentally appropriate curriculum," as put forth in the "Guidelines for Appropriate Curriculum Content and Assessment in Programs Serving Children Ages 3 Through 8," published by the National Association for the Education of Young Children in 1991 (Seefeldt, 2001). Play is the typical medium used for teaching the curriculum areas. Play provides opportunities for the teacher to observe the child, evaluate him, and model the kinds of play that enhance learning. Play engages children in activities that encourage active participation and it promotes intellectual processing skills of language development, problem solving, application, analysis, synthesis, and critical thinking. The model for selecting a suitable play-based curriculum that meets state and county standards was published by the Association for Childhood Education International. The practitioner and author of the model used "action research to document that [her] students could meet Virginia's tough new standards in a play based environment." In this constructionist view of learning, "play is the primary vehicle by which young children construct knowledge and understanding." In the author's K–1 classroom, intelligence is aligned with cognitive behavior and "interest centers reflect a multiple-intelligence framework" (Ritche, 2000, pp. 1, 6). Typical of early childhood educators, this author/practitioner implements curriculum mandates by integrating the subject areas to include all of the developmental domains of the child.

Many proponents of DAP oppose the 2003 initiative called Good Start Grow Smart, developed by the U.S. Department of Education and the U.S. Department of Health and Human Services for the federally funded Head Start program. The major contention lies with the testing of four-year-olds in Head Start to determine school readiness. Under this legislation, states are required to have "early learning guidelines" that are consistent with their state-mandated standards for kindergarten to grade 12. Some early childhood educators fear that these guidelines will push for a more academic approach in place of a play-based or child-centered curriculum for preschoolers. They note that standardized tests ignore the developmental needs of young children and are inappropriate measures of how young children learn and express themselves. On the other hand, optimists look to the federal government's initiative as a first step for improving articulation between preschool programs and kindergarten classes, which could assure smoother transitions. During the past decade studies indicated "a lack of articulation between what children and parents are accustomed to in prekindergarten programs and what they find once they enter formal schooling" (Lewis, 2003, p. 484). Community involvement, extension of health services, and social supports generally offered in Head Start are not guaranteed for the kindergartner (Lewis, 2003). Proponents of Good Start Grow Smart hope it will be a catalyst for more dialogue with the community and an extension of health care and social services to more families of early school-age youngsters.

Community-Oriented Curriculum Models

Most educators agree that the role of the community is central in decision making about curriculum. Resistance to changes in national curricula occurs when local voices are silenced or regional concerns are ignored. Jeff Howard maintains that community consensus is essential if all children are to achieve. Community consensus helps to avoid the gaps that divide children based on racial and socioeconomic backgrounds. Schools reflect their community, its goals, and aspirations for its children.

As a part of the community, parents play a vital role in curriculum decisions. When parents find their values honored and their expectations met, they embrace the school and its endeavors. A survey of parent and teacher expectations of children in their kindergarten (reception) year was made in the United States and the United Kingdom. In both countries, where there was agreement about expectations between the parents and teachers, satisfaction with the school and its curriculum was evident (Swiniarski, 1994). Schools that emphasize their connection to the community extend themselves to help parents, coordinate community services, and infuse the community into various curriculum areas. For example, the Full Service school reaches out to the community and "provides multiple avenues of support to the school's children, their families and community," which might include health care, social services, parent education, extended child care programs and family counseling (Breitborde and Swiniarski, 2002, p. 305). (See Chapter 11 for more discussion about Full Service schools.)

In the next section we take a close look at place-based curriculum. Place-based curriculum is built around the community to link the school with the daily lives of the students.

Place-Based Education

Does what you learn in school have any relationship to what you do at home and outside of school? Are you surprised to apply something you learned in school to your life? If your schooling has been disconnected, you have not experienced place-based education. If you have experienced place-based education, then you have personalized school experiences and internalized their lessons. **Place-based education** (also called pedagogy/curriculum of place) is simply the inclusion of the student's life, community, family, and culture into the curriculum.

Table 4.2 Characteristics of Place-Based Education

1. Teachers and parents use immediate and available phenomena as a foundation for curriculum and basis for comparison.
2. Students are creators rather than consumers of knowledge.
3. Students participate in defining their learning experiences.
4. Teachers guide and facilitate the learning process.
5. The community, its members, and the students interact, work together, and share expertise.
6. Students' work is valued and evaluated by its outcomes.

Source: G. Smith, Place-Based Education: Learning to Be Where We Are, *Phi Delta Kappan* 83(8) (April 2002), p. 593.

Curriculum of place has been explained as "an expression of the growing recognition of context and locale and their unique contributions to the educational project. . . . Using what is local and immediate as a source of curriculum tends to deepen knowledge . . . and gives a stronger impetus to apply problem-solving skills" (Annenberg Rural Challenge, 1999, p. 11). According to Gregory Smith, associate professor of education at Lewis and Clark College, place-based education can assume many formats, but it generally has six characteristics, which are listed in Table 4.2.

Place-based education is an old idea that is getting some new attention. John Dewey held a healthy regard for connecting the school to the community. He believed that education is not a preparation for life—it is life itself. Rather than study the river vicariously, Dewey would encourage the school to take the learner to the river. He was disconcerted by the "isolation of the school, its isolation from life" (Smith, 2002, p. 586). He realized that children conceptualize better with concrete experiences in a world that is familiar and relates to home, family, and neighborhood.

In the next sections, we discover several successful place-based curricula. They represent different regions of the United States. These featured models of place-based curriculum were developed around projects that reflect students' communities, lifestyles, and heritages.

The Foxfire Project Drawing on the lessons from Dewey, in the 1970s, the Foxfire Project of rural Georgia rekindled interest in using local folklore, customs, literature, personal stories, music, and community culture as a means of educating youth. The project began as an English topic that evolved into the publication of its own magazine and bestseller books. As a result, the Foxfire Project caught national attention. It was heralded as an innovative educational approach that taught literacy skills while it enhanced community life with the documentation of a rich regional heritage. Eventually the project reached New York City as a Broadway play production. The performance acclaim exceeded the expectations of Foxfire's original intent to teach writing skills and literature to rural high school adolescents in concert with their lives in Appalachia. The project has been adapted and replicated with success in other parts of the country. We recommend that you read *Foxfire* to determine the rich learning experiences the students captured in their writing and the skills they had to master to produce such a publication.

Aunt Arie Carpenter with Foxfire student Don MacNeil in the early 1970s.
Source: Reprinted with permission of Foxfire, Mountain City, GA 30562, www.foxfire.org.

The Annenberg Rural Challenge Building on the success of Foxfire, the Living and Learning in Rural Schools and Communities projects was funded by the Annenberg Rural Challenge under the direction of Vito Perrone at the Harvard University Graduate School of Education. This extensive project was set in several rural communities throughout the United States in an attempt to revitalize the communities by enriching the educational opportunities of their children. Each curriculum project was built upon the cultural heritage of the community, oral histories, environmental issues, social needs, languages, and art forms. Some projects involved the arts, while others centered on water and biodiversity, history, social action, technology, and integration. The students' work grew out of real issues, problems, and interests in the communities. The project's outcomes resulted in real-life resolutions, compilations of data for analysis and action, and community acceptance and appreciation. All subject areas were integrated and mastery was demonstrated in authentic life skills and applications. The teaching was personalized. Learning was internalized.

An exemplar of a local history project was The Tombstone Project of Frederick High School in Frederick, South Dakota. High school students documented 344 gravesites in their local cemetery to compile a database of information on the families that pioneered the region. Students were surprised to learn that the town's roots were Finnish rather than English. The early gravestones' inscriptions were in Finnish and needed the translation skills of older, native Finnish-speaking residents to decipher the information. The project soon became an intergenerational undertaking. Since it was such a successful community endeavor, plans were made for further work in other cemeteries in the Elm Valley District of South Dakota (Living and Learning in Rural Schools and Communities, February, 1999, pp. 67–68).

The Pack Your Bag Curriculum Any community can have a place curriculum, be it a rural, urban, or suburban setting. The fourth grade class of the Horace Mann Laboratory School in Salem, Massachusetts, has been working on place curriculum since the 1990s. The children, their teacher, and a college faculty member conceived of an exchange project that was centered on and set in their community. Activities took place in the community as well as the classroom and computer lab. They entitled it Pack Your Bag. The project got the children involved in using primary source documents, using the community as a resource, and interacting with family and community members. Students researched their family history with interviews and oral history. They examined community life with a focus on the geographical notions of location, place, movement, interaction, and region.

This project is now an exchange program in which a fourth grade is partnered with its counterparts in International Schools abroad. The results of the children's study are shared with their counterparts not only through a website, but also with samples and artifacts from their town that are packed in a bag and delivered abroad. Likewise, the partnered school reciprocates and repacks the bag with their findings about their community. The theme of the project might vary from year to year, but the cast of characters consistently involves family members, community leaders, businesses, museums, college faculty, artists, scientists, cartographers, and artisans. Visits throughout the community bolster the research and add to the resources available to the children. The project has received national attention at professional conferences and in publications as a modest attempt to keep alive the commitment of John Dewey—making the connections between the school and the life of the child.

The Phenomena of Language in Curriculum Design

Everyone agrees that the curriculum is communicated through language, yet controversy arises when people ask which language or how many languages, because language is closely tied to cultural identity. As one writer aptly stated: "We are our words" (Ackerman, 2004, p. 8). To sustain cultural identity, school systems around the world maintain minority languages along with the dominant language in their national curricula. For example, in Belgium there are two school systems, one uses French and another, Flemish. In Finland, the five percent of Finns for whom Swedish is their first language attend public Swedish-language schools. In the Canadian provinces of Quebec and New Brunswick, there are two dominant languages in schools, French and English. Many countries are preserving the languages of their indigenous peoples. Maori culture and language is taught throughout both islands of New Zealand. In Great Britain, the National Curriculum for Wales requires the teaching and speaking of Welsh in classrooms. In South Africa, children learn at least three languages, English, Afrikaans, and Swahili, along with their local dialect. Irish schools offer both Gaelic and English instruction. The children in all of these national schools are expected to be at least bilingual, if not multilingual. The motivation of these countries might well be political in nature, but their practices support the research findings that there are many cognitive as well as social and cultural benefits in being bilingual.

> Whatever language [children] hear becomes an indelible part of their lives, providing the words they'll use to know and be known. A bonus of bilingualism is that it forces a child to favor one set of rules while

> ignoring another, and that trains the brain early on to focus and discriminate, to ignore what's irrelevant and discover the arbitrariness of words (Ackerman, 2004, p. 8).

In the United States, studies show that immigrant children who continue to speak their native language at home and at school are more successful in learning English and less likely to drop out of school "than those who speak only English" (Miller and Endo, 2004, p. 786). Yet, there is much debate on whether immigrant or native peoples' children who are English language learners (ELL) should be allowed instruction in their first language. In fact across the country, the case for bilingual education has provoked debate and opposition.

The Debate over Bilingual Education

Ron Unz, a computer entrepreneur from California, mounted a national campaign known as the Unz Initiative. His goal was to replace **bilingual education**—instruction in two languages, including the student's native language and the dominant language—in American public schools with "English-only" immersion classes, where only English is permitted in all instruction and classroom communication. His campaign claims that the dismal results of American Latino students' achievement levels are due to the systemic failure of bilingual education. He further contends that these students linger in bilingual classes for up to seven years, only to consistently perform lower on standardized tests than many other subgroups. To date, he has persuaded such states as California, Massachusetts, and Arizona to pass legislation that prohibits bilingual programs in favor of English-only classes. In these states, children who are identified as limited in English proficiency (LEP) are given a year of immersion instruction in English with an English as a second language (ESL) teacher and then placed in a mainstream classroom. In these classrooms, English language learners (ELL) are faced with the daunting tasks of perfecting their newly acquired language while learning new subjects. Many of these children continue to fail state tests required by the rigorous goals of NCLB. Rebuttals and opposition to the Unz initiative can be heard nationally from professional educational organizations such as Teachers of English to Speakers of Other Languages (TESOL), as well as civic and ethnic communities such as the Colorado Parent Teacher Organization and the Navajo Nation Council in Arizona. These groups support other approaches for non-English-speaking students and endorse the following curriculum approaches to language instruction.

Curriculum Approaches to Language Instruction

There are many approaches to teaching English language learners. The following models represent the prevailing philosophies on how to acquire a second language. The models discussed are successful exemplars in many public schools throughout the country.

The Two-Way Program There are several curriculum approaches for teaching ELL students, be they newly arrived immigrants or indigenous peoples. One such program is a bilingual model that involves teaching ELL students and native English speakers together. Known as the Two-Way Program, this approach has experienced significant success in communities where there is a substantial number of non-English-speaking students. This program requires both English- and non-English-speaking children to acquire a second language in a team-taught approach to curriculum. Children are taught in their native language and a second language together. English-speaking children learn a second language alongside non-English-speaking children who are acquiring English language skills. In communities with a large Latino population it has affectionately been called the Amigos Program.

The Two-Way Program does not propose a quick fix or an easy answer to second language acquisition; rather it requires a lengthy time commitment on the part of the students and their families. Children begin the program in kindergarten and continue their study through grade eight or beyond. The program can be a school within a school, or a school of choice for families to select within a district. Teachers fluent in English team with teachers who are fluent speakers of the second language to present both populations of children all subjects in the two languages.

Sheltered Instruction A second option is Sheltered Instruction (SI), an "approach to teaching that extends the time students have for receiving English language support while they learn content subjects" (Echevarria, Vogt, and Short, 2004, p. 223). This approach is being introduced where ELL students are integrated with native English speakers in elementary, middle, and secondary school classrooms. Preparation and planning are key to the success of this program, as teachers need to differentiate their instruction in a three-part protocol entitled the Sheltered Instruction Observation Protocol (SIOP). The protocol is very detailed in outlining specific language objectives along with content goals for each lesson in all aspects of delivery and assessment. Teachers must consider the words they choose carefully, and use body language, gestures, and teaching aids to make the content comprehensible to all students (Echevarria, Vogt, and Short, 2004).

Immersion **Immersion** is often referred to as second-language immersion in that it presents the curriculum in two languages (Diaz-Rico, 2004). In Canada, where immersion is widely practiced in the provinces' public schools, French and English are spoken. English-speaking children are taught primarily in French as a second language along with English; French-speaking children are primarily instructed in English, with some French offered. The students are immersed in their second language so as to be sufficiently fluent for instruction in both languages. As in the Two-Way Program, the children begin the second language in kindergarten. Canadians base their success with this curriculum on the principle that knowledge of a second language enhances the analysis and learning of one's own native language (Swiniarski and Breitborde, 2003). This practice has been replicated as an alternative program in some American public schools and is a common approach in American private schools and the International Schools that focus on the teaching of world languages.

Native Languages and Oral Traditions Revisited Around the United States there is a movement to preserve and pass on the legacy of various subcultures by teaching through storytelling. Storytelling is an oral tradition that has been passed from generation to generation to teach, inspire, and entertain. Storytelling is an effective teaching method, as it helps the learner connect to a subject, organize content, and retain information (Raines and Isbell, 1999).

The growing interest in educating through storytelling has extended the definition of cultural literacy to include the legacies of many diverse populations in our country. A variety of artifacts are used as teaching tools to supplement storytelling. For example, the Pueblo stories from New Mexico were rekindled in 1963 by Helen

Educating through storytelling has extended the definition of cultural literacy to include the legacies of many diverse populations in our country.
Source: © AINACO/CORBIS

Cordeo when she crafted her storyteller dolls, which depicted the Hopi tradition of children clustered about their elders to hear folktales and legends of past ancestors. The dolls have since inspired the rewriting of many Hopi stories for literary anthologies and teaching programs prescribed in school curricula throughout the United States.

There has also been a revival in teaching languages of native and minority peoples. As a result of this renewed interest in local languages, many publications and multimedia materials have been produced for teaching topics across curriculum areas, including language arts, mathematics, social studies, and the arts. The Gullah language spoken by African Americans from the island of St. Helena, South Carolina, has been preserved through the efforts of the Sea Island Translation Team and Literacy Project of St. Helena, South Carolina. Hawaiian culture and language is integrated into the state school system's curriculum and is required in the privately endowed Kamehameha schools. Cajun storytellers continue to narrate tales and publish bilingual editions that retell classic favorites such as *The Three Pigs* and the lesser-known local tales from the bayous and plantations of the Creole world in Louisiana. Whether it be in the American Northeast or Southwest, Hispanic and Chicano literature written in Spanish and translated into English is listed as required reading in many state curricula. Often these selections reflect contemporary stories and personal histories of Latino students in today's schools.

Personal stories and native language instruction derived from a rich diversity of cultural heritages attempt to balance the Eurocentric slant of many state curriculum frameworks and enrich the learning experiences of all students. They promote empathy, appreciation, and understanding of oneself and others.

Multicultural and Global Education Curriculum

A primary component of any curriculum should be the culture of the students, the community, and the school. Culture determines the dimensions of the curriculum, the expectations of the community, the style of delivery, as well as the modes of assessment. Culture gives the curriculum identity. Culture has been defined as "the social backgrounds that imbue children with particular forms of knowledge, values, and expectations for behavior" (Swiniarski and Breitborde, 2003, p. 8). Through our culture we define "how the world works, what is normal, what is expected and what is the ideal way of living" (Swiniarski and Breitborde, 2003, p. 81). Factors that define our culture include our ethnic group, nationality, gender, age groups, lifestyle, geographic region, religion, and language. Based on this definition, it is safe to assume that most societies have a diverse population that is multicultural in some aspects. There are often prevailing or dominant cultures and subcultures within the society. To develop a curriculum connected to your constituents, their culture as well as the dominant culture must be integrated into the construction of the subjects, the instruction, and the assessments. To define multicultural education in this manner goes beyond the limitations of celebrating the holidays or foods of a particular cultural group.

Multicultural curricula begin at the local level and spiral outward to include a global perspective. Indeed, "global education and multicultural education are parts of a continuum: global education looks at the world as a community, while multicultural education sees the world in the local community" (Swiniarski and Breitborde, 2003, p. 10).

Guidelines for a Global Curriculum

Multicultural/global education brings consensus to the curriculum. Both multicultural education and global education teach perceptions of the world within a thematic view that sees unity within diversity. Global education is not a subject to be added to the curriculum, rather it is a perspective, a view of the world that can be infused in all subject areas beginning with the early childhood years through secondary education. The goal of global education is to move "students from a knowledge of the impact of social context of their own lives to an understanding of the impact of different cultures and contexts on others' lives, to a full understanding of human issues from a world perspective" (Breitborde and Swiniarski, 1999, p. 7).

We devised a framework to reach this goal that involves twelve principles of global education. These principles are multifaceted and embrace a broad scope to serve as a guide for curriculum development. These broadly stated principles "allow for alternative strategies for implementation and for discussion of the questions inherent in their articulation" (Breitborde and Swiniarski, 1999, p. 7). These principles are listed in Table 4.3.

Bringing the World Together

The world is becoming more homogenized, with McDonald's feeding a large part of the planet and The Gap's clothing marketed in shopping malls internationally; yet, ironically, neighborhoods are becoming more diversified. As more families are

Table 4.3 Twelve Principles of Global Education

1. *Global education is basic.* The messages of global education can be infused across the curriculum and in all academic areas.
2. *Global education is lifelong learning.* Like all learning, learning about yourself and others is a lifelong pursuit that begins with the early years and continues throughout adulthood.
3. *Global education is cooperative learning.* Living in a world with others requires cooperative learning to enhance the skills of collaboration and communication.
4. *Global education is inclusive of all.* Global education seeks to protect the rights of all of the world's citizens.
5. *Global education is education for social action.* Global education promotes knowing and doing in socially responsible endeavors.
6. *Global education is economic education.* World economics impacts lives in an interdependent and interconnected milieu.
7. *Global education involves technology.* Technology connects the world through communication in open-ended modalities such as computers, videos, films, etc.
8. *Global education requires critical and creative thinking.* Inquiry requires divergent and convergent thought to resolve world issues.
9. *Clobal education is multicultural education.* Cultural awareness at the local level is the foundation for learning about your world.
10. *Global education is moral education.* Global decisions require choices that reflect a moral code and ethical behavior.
11. *Global education supports a sustainable environment.* Caring for the environment, preserving natural resources, and protecting wildlife ensure a safe environment for the world's future.
12. *Global education enhances the spirit of teaching and learning.* Encouraging a sense of wonder promotes the emotional intelligence in learners of all ages.

Source: L. Swiniarski and M.-L. Breitborde, *Educating the Global Village,* 2nd ed. (Upper Saddle River, NJ: Merrill Prentice Hall, 2003).

pulling up stakes and moving from their homelands to other countries, all nations are becoming multicultural, while clamoring for some common ground.

Comparative studies of international models of curriculum spark debate and adaptation. For example, Italy's Reggio Emilia preschools have captured the imagination of early childhood educators in all corners of the globe. Their pedagogy has been translated into many languages for professional development, training in the field, and organized seminar groups. Periodic analysis of The International Mathematics and Science Study, which graphs the competitive results of high school achievements in math and science around the world, underscore the increasing international interest in how each country educates its population.

Collaboration among nations on international models of education that speak to the local needs within countries, as well as the global interests between nations, is evident in the common acceptance of the International Baccalaureate for university admissions worldwide. The economics of international education is studied by the Organization for Economic Co-operation and Development, headquartered in Paris. This organization collects data and publishes reports that change educational directives for curriculum development for the improvement of the economic well-being of its twenty-nine member nations, including the United States. The International Schools dotted about the globe prepare their students in multilingual tracks for reentry into their mother country, as well as for participation in world citizenship. Their curriculum ideas have been replicated in American public schools where the mission has been to globalize programs that prepare students for effective roles in the global work force. For example, the International Baccalaureate, developed through the International Schools' network, is a rigorous curriculum that has been incorporated into many public schools in the United States. It is a credential recognized for college and university admission worldwide for its high expectations for achievement in the study of the humanities, mathematics, sciences, and languages. The number of successful student exchanges and professional alliances highlights the need and interest in promoting daring global educational frameworks that reach out to all of the world's children.

SUMMARY

- There are multiple considerations to make in deciding about how the curriculum will be taught, what goals and objectives it will address, and how it is implemented.
- Many factors determine the curriculum: pedagogy, local and state standards, community input, and students having a voice in shaping the curriculum.
- There are many curriculum models. Three typical models are based on the central figure of the curriculum: the student-centered curriculum, the teacher-centered curriculum, and the subject-centered curriculum.
- The standards-based curriculum is a phenomenon of the worldwide school reform movement, which gained impetus during the 1990s in the United States and continues to dominate educational policymaking at the national, state, and local levels. There is a debate about the trends in standards-based education. There are opposing ideologies and philosophies and politics is also involved.
- The major controversy in the standards-based curriculum resides in the accountability measures of high-stakes testing. Conservatives align themselves with traditionally-minded educators in support of defined standards of high expectations for achievement benchmarks, validated by high-stakes testing. Proponents of the standards-based curriculum feel such standards will raise the level of expectations for all students. They feel that by having clearly defined curricula, teachers will be able to bridge the gaps that currently exist in communities where poverty prevails.
- Liberals decry the rhetoric of their opponents. As critics of the standards-based education they characterize the movement as a simplistic remedy for complex issues. While standards are designed to cover the gaps in achievement between children, based on race, class, and family lifestyle, critics depict the standards and their concomitant tests as punitive measures. While both sides agree that all children can learn, opponents to standards note that one size does not fit all. Personalized instruction, community culture, and the individuality of the learner should direct the curriculum's course. Both sides cite research and reports as support for their positions.
- There are many innovative curriculum models based on the culture of the community (place-based curriculum), learning theories, and internationally acclaimed practices.

- Technology has changed the mode of teaching for today's curriculum. New innovations help teachers and students access materials for research and in-depth study. Assistive technology promotes inclusion.

- Curriculum is communicated through language. Multilingual programs are common practice in other countries, but in the United States, debate over bilingual education prevails. Yet, there are many effective approaches being developed and revisited, such as Two-Way Programs, Sheltered Instruction, and oral traditions. It is important to balance the Eurocentric slant of offerings in mandated curriculum with a global perspective and sensitivity to the rich diversity of knowledge in America's multicultural heritage.

- *Multicultural curricula* means that students' culture as well as the dominant culture must be integrated into the construction of the subjects, the instruction, and the assessments. *Global education* stems naturally from multicultural education and teaches perceptions of the world within a thematic view that sees unity within diversity. Global education is not a subject to be added to the curriculum; rather, it is a perspective. The goal of global education is full understanding of human issues from a world perspective. To attain this goal, there are twelve principles of global education.

QUESTIONS FOR REFLECTION

1. What position do you take on the standards debate? Include in your discussion the reasons that support your position.
2. What type of curriculum model represents the experiences you had as a student? What model would best suit your teaching style?
3. How might you design a place-based curriculum for your community? Who would be contributors to the project?
4. Why is there a global effort to standardize educational practices in public education?
5. What is your position on high-stakes testing? Do you feel it helps teachers meet society's demands on today's schools?

APPLYING WHAT YOU'VE LEARNED

1. Research different state's standards for the grade level you teach or aspire to teach. Note similarities and differences in expectations, requirements, and recommendations.
2. Compare E. D. Hirsch's list of what every American needs to know to the list that you might make. Do you feel his "cultural literacy" reflects today's American society? What might you change?
3. Visit a school with a different standard base than one you have attended or have taught in. It could be a Montessori school, a religious school, a Waldorf school, or an International School. Observe the relationship between the teacher and students. Note the content of the curriculum. Describe the school climate. Compare the educational experience at this school with yours.
4. Design a curriculum that might work well for the children in your community. What core requirements do you prescribe? What pedagogical framework guides your choices and selections?
5. www What should be included in a multicultural/global curriculum? Is a good curriculum one that focuses on ethnic holidays and foods? What else should be included? Visit the book's website for articles and information, including pieces from the National Association for Multicultural Education (NAME) site. Read at least one of the articles about multicultural curriculum. Then make a list of criteria for a multicultural/global curriculum.

KEY TERMS

assistive technology, p. 115
bilingual education, p. 133
efficacy model, p. 127
immersion, p. 134
place-based education, p. 129
standards-based education, p. 117

WEBSITES TO EXPLORE

http://www.ed.gov/nclb/overview/intro/index.html. This site presents an overview of the text of No Child Left Behind.

http://www.fairtest.org/care/Standards_StandardsYes,_Standardization_No.html. This website covers much information on research and writings on standardized testing in particular Deborah Meier's essay reprinted from the *Rochester Democrat Chronicle.*

http://www.hooverdigest.org/022/ravitch.html. The Hoover Digest is an online publication of the Hoover Institute, which pioneered the standards-based reforms, in particular Diane Ravitch's defense of high-stakes testing in standards-based education.

http://www.nameorg.org/resources.html. National Association for Multicultural Education (NAME) is an organization for educators, business organizations, and community groups with an interest in multicultural education from all levels of education, different academic disciplines, and diverse educational institutions and occupations. NAME offers resource materials and educational strategies and establishes standards and policy statements for educational institutions, organizations, and policymakers.

http://www.pbubuilder.org. Website for computer-based units of Project Learn/21C, including Massacres, Messengers and Misunderstandings, by Petrie, Pomerantz, Prince, and Rittershaus. These projects can be replicated and were funded by the U.S. Department of Education.

http://www.gse.harvard.edu/principals. The Harvard University Graduate School of Education website for its Principals' Center, which offers numerous materials, professional development seminars, and conferences on curriculum issues, in particular the Efficacy Institute, English Language Learners Institutes, and conferences on standards-based education and mandated testing.

http://www.isb.be. The International School of Brussels website offers information about International School and the International Baccalaureate.

http://www.salemstate.edu/ngec. The Northeast Global Education Center at Salem State College offers professional development in globalization of curriculum frameworks and information on global education events, seminars, and workshops.

CRITICAL READINGS

Standards Yes, Standardization No

BY DEBORAH MEIER

After thirty years of work as a so-called school-reformer, I'm finding myself at odds with a lot what's now called reform. The inner-city schools I've led have been much touted for their extra-ordinary success with ordinary children. We learned some lessons from these schools. We learned, above all, that even "our way" wouldn't work if imposed unwillingly on others. If being well-educated means learning to exercise good judgment in a variety of disciplines and situations, then there's no short-cut around the need for young people to be in the company of grown-ups who are doing the same. We won't get high standards from kids if both parents and teachers are not trusted and respected to make important decisions. That's what we thought we had demonstrated loud and clear.

This is not a time to give up on the historic American idea that The People can be trusted—in the long run. Trust leads to trustworthiness and the reverse is equally true. Local control of schooling, and respect for practicing teachers are two ideas we should not abandon, and nothing suggests we need to. American schools are not a disaster when it comes to achievement. That's a myth, not substantiated by the data. Where we do look bad is the gap between our top and bottom students. But then we also look far worse than any other industrialized nation if we compare income, health care or money spent per child between the top and the bottom. These inequities are a national shame. So what do we need?

1. More contact between grown-ups and kids. Since education is a lot about the company we keep, we need to get more grown-ups into the act of keeping company with kids. That's the most efficient form of education. We need smaller schools—a lot smaller so folks know each other well. We need smaller classes. School-to-work and community-service programs are another way to broaden the contact between kids and grown-ups. In my lifetime we've gone from 200,000 local school boards—a million and a half citizens involved in running our schools—to less than 20,000. Meanwhile the population has more than doubled. Too many adults don't know our kids and their schools, and too many kids, especially adolescents, don't know many grown-ups or their worlds. We're living dangerously separate lives.
2. An end to the mandatory testing frenzy. Let's stop pretending we can make high stakes decisions (promotion, graduation, etc.) based on a single test designed by distant experts. Local communities should have the authority to give whatever tests they think will help them. When they want a second outside opinion they should be the choosers, and good state-sponsored school review options should be available. NAEP (National Assessment of Educational Progress) should continue to provide comparative data that local schools and the larger public might find useful on issues like equity, distribution of resources, long-range or state trends. Colleges and employers don't need public funds to test for their particular and different selection needs.
3. Choice within public education. We need sufficient public choices so that few parents will feel the need to opt out—except when they want things that our Constitution says they can't have at public expense (e.g. an all-white school). Standards yes. Standardization no. We should insist that schools exercise their right to define differently what they think it means to be well-educated and the best route for getting there. Plenty of public review, but far less public mandating.
4. Sufficient resources. We need sufficient resources so that poor kids and rich kids start on a more nearly level playing field—before, during and after schools hours. Do they go to school in buildings with similar facilities? Do they have teachers who are equally well-prepared and have the opportunity to continue to learn on the job? Good staff development is one place where international comparisons are embarrassing. Once again the gap between top and bottom is a national embarrassment.

I'm for raising the prestige of educational experts, but not by giving them the power to mandate what everyone must do. There will be fewer fads and more sustained reform once we invest more power in those whose first and foremost agenda is their collective children, not the many other agendas of corporations, politicians and academics worthy though they may be. There's sufficient well-financed pressure from colleges, employers and national media to insure that these powerful interests won't be forgotten. What's lacking is a counter balance to such impersonal, and often self-interested forces. If our definition of education includes teaching young people to exercise good judgment then they must be surrounded by grown-ups who are in the habit of exercising good judgment—who rarely have to say "Who me? I'm just doing what I've been told to do."

Deborah Meier is currently principal of The Mission Hill School, a new Boston public school. She was the founder and principal for twenty years of a network of kindergarten through twelfth grade public schools in East Harlem and author of *The Power of Their Ideas* (Beacon Press). She was awarded a MacArthur "genius award" in 1987 for her work in public education.

Source: Rochester Democrat Chronicle, Sunday, May 23, 1999.

A Closer Look at the Issues

1. How does Meier distinguish standards from standardization?
2. What is her position on the value of mandated testing programs?

On School Reform, Let's Stay the Course

BY DIANE RAVITCH

Recent reforms in Massachusetts show how we can improve our public schools by demanding excellence—from students and teachers alike.

Americans are famous for demanding instant results. Real school reform, however, takes time. Massachusetts embarked on a reform strategy in 1993, and only now is the state seeing results.

In 1993, the state legislature agreed to add $1 billion annually to education funding, with the expectation that students would thus be prepared to pass new state examinations 10 years later. After developing new standards and tests, the state began testing students on a trial basis in 1998.

Tenth-grade students were required to pass state tests (known as MCAS, for the Massachusetts Comprehensive Assessment System) in mathematics and English to qualify for a high school diploma. Those who failed had four chances to retake the tests.

The early returns of state testing were terrible. Half the 10th graders failed the math test, and a third failed the English test. The failure rates were even higher for minority students. Critics began attacking the reforms, charging that they stifled teachers' creativity and, worse, endangered minority youth, who might be denied a diploma. The Massachusetts Teachers Association launched a $600,000 advertising campaign against state testing, and the state's local school boards urged lawmakers to repeal the requirement that students pass the exams to graduate.

> Massachusetts has begun to reap the rewards of standards-based reform. The state bet that students could meet high expectations—and the most recent test results are beginning to prove the state right.

But state officials held firm. Their persistence was rewarded when the results of the 2001 tests were made public. Knowing that this was the first time that the tests counted for graduation, 10th graders took them seriously. Remarkably, the failure rate on the math test dropped from 45 percent in 2000 to 25 percent in 2001, and from 34 percent to 18 percent in English.

Minority students showed significant progress. The failure rate of African American 10th graders fell from 60 percent to 40 percent in English and from 77 percent to 52 percent in mathematics. Among Hispanic students, the failure rate dropped from 66 percent to 48 percent in English and from 79 percent to 58 percent in mathematics.

Many of those who failed received marks that were just below passing. With more effort and study, they will pass on their next try. The state has created remedial programs to help those who failed, and teachers know that they have a specific pool of youngsters who need extra help to master English and mathematics. With each retake of the tests, the number of students who fail will grow smaller.

The Massachusetts tests, it must be noted, are among the most challenging in the nation. The math tests are rigorous assessments of problem-solving skills, and the English tests have many essay questions based on excellent literature.

Massachusetts has begun to reap the rewards of standards-based reform. The state bet that students could meet high expectations, and it backed up its bet with serious new funding and excellent tests. State officials passed their own test, enduring a barrage of criticism and predictions of disaster.

The real winners in Massachusetts are the students. From now on, their diplomas will signify that they have mastered important knowledge and skills and that they are ready for college and the modern workplace.

Diane Ravitch is a research professor, New York University; distinguished visiting fellow, Hoover Institution; and member, Hoover's Koret Task Force on K–12 Education.

Source: Hoover Digest, 2002, No. 2, Spring Issue.

A Closer Look at the Issues

1. What evidence does Diane Ravitch use to support the practice of high-stakes testing?
2. Why does she think the students are "the real winners"? What do you think?

REFERENCES

Ackerman, D. (2004). We are our words. *Parade,* May 30, pp. 8–10.

Bainbridge, W. (2002). Commentary: Leaving children behind. *Technos Quarterly* 11(2), Summer.

Blackman, M., and J. Howard (2000). Proficiency for all: Can we ride the accountability wave to get there? *The Principal Advisor* 1(1), January, pp. 3–4.

Breitborde, M., and L. Swiniarski, (1999). Construction and reconstructionism: Educating teachers for world citizenship. *The Australian Journal of Teacher Education* 24(1), pp. 1–15.

Breitborde, M., and L. Swiniarski, (2002). Family education and community power: New structures for new visions in the educational village. *Educational Studies* 28(3), pp. 305–318.

Bruner, J. (1960). *The process of education.* Cambridge, MA: Harvard University Press.

Caron, E. (2002). Standards-in-practice: How understanding teachers should guide standards-based reform. *Educational Horizons,* 80(2), Winter, pp. 72–74.

Diaz-Rico, L. (2004). *Teaching English learners: Strategies and methods.* Boston: Pearson Allyn & Bacon.

Echevarria, J., M. Vogt, and D. Short (2004). *Making content comprehensible for English Learners.* 2nd ed. Boston: Pearson Allyn & Bacon.

Hirsch, E. D. (2001). Overcoming the language gap: Make better use of the literacy time block. *American Educator,* Summer.

Kohn, A. (2000). The case against standards. *The Principal Advisor* 1(1), January, pp. 5–6.

Kohn, A. (2002). The 500-pound gorilla. *Phi Delta Kappan* 84(2), October, pp. 112–119.

Lewis, A. (2003). Hi ho, hi ho, it's off to tests we go. *Phi Delta Kappan* 84(7), March, pp. 483–484.

Merriam-Webster Collegiate Dictionary (2003, p. 1216).

Meier, D. (1999). Standards yes, standardization no. Reprint in the *Rochester Democrat Chronicle* on May 23. http://www.fiartest.org/care/Standards_Yes, Standardization_No. html.

Meier, D. (2000). Educating a democracy: Standards and the future of public education. *Boston Review,* pp. 1–12.

Miller, P., and H. Endo (2004). Understanding and meeting the needs of ESL Students. *Phi Delta Kappan* 85(10), June, pp. 786–791.

Moats, L. (2001). Overcoming the language gap: Invest generously in teacher professional development. *American Educator,* Summer, np.

Moss, P. (1999). International standards or one of many possibilities. In World Organization for Early Childhood Education & the Association for Childhood Education International, *Early childhood and care in the 21st century: Global guidelines and papers from an international symposium* (pp. 19–29). Olney, MD: Association for Childhood Education International.

Noddings, N. (1995). A morally defensible mission for schools in the 21st century. *Phi Delta Kappan* 76(5), January, pp. 365–369.

Ohanian, S. (2000). Goals 2000: What's in a name. *Phi Delta Kappan* 81(5), January, pp. 344–355.

Palmer, P. (1998). *The courage to teach.* San Francisco: Jossey-Bass.

Patrie, L., F. Pomerantz, E. Prince, and E. Rittershaus (2004). *Massacres, messengers, and misunderstandings,* Project LEARN/21C. In http://www.pbubuilder.org.

Pierce, C. (2003). Who decides her future: (A) parents (B) teachers (C) the school testing industry. *The Boston Globe Magazine,* March 2, pp. 12–22.

Power, E. (1970). *Main currents in the history of education.* 2nd ed. New York: McGraw-Hill.

Raines, S., and R. Isbell (1999). *Tell it again.* Beltsville, MD: Gryphon House.

Ravitch, D. (2002). On school reform, let's stay the course, *Hoover Digest 2,* Spring, www.hooverdigest.org/022/ravitch.html.

Ritchie, G. (Spring, 2000). Meeting state and county standards and objectives within a play-based curriculum. *ACEI Focus on Pre-K & K 12(3),* pp. 1–3, 6–7.

Rural Challenge Research and Evaluation Program (1999). Living and learning in rural schools and communities: Lessons from the field: A report to the Annenberg rural challenge. Cambridge, MA: Harvard Graduate School of Education.

Seefeldt, C. (2001). *Social Studies for the Preschool/Primary Child,* 6th ed. Upper Saddle River, NJ: Merrill Prentice Hall.

Sizer, T. (1999). Personalized learning: No two are quite alike. *Coalition of essential schools* 57(1), September, np.

Smith, G. (2002). Place-based education: Learning to be where we are. *Phi Delta Kappan* 83(8), April, pp. 584–594.

Swiniarski, L. (1994). Parent and teacher expectations for the kindergarten; An international perspective. *Global Connection* 3(2), October, pp. 3–4.

Swiniarski, L., and M.-L. Breitborde (2003). *Educating the global village: Including the child in the world,* 2nd ed. Upper Saddle River, NJ: Merrill Prentice Hall.

U.S. Department of Education. Introduction: No child left behind. www.ed.gov/nclb/overview/intro/index.html.

Thinking About Learning

5

ESSENTIAL QUESTION

What is learning? What is good teaching?

Teaching is interaction, and it demands all the resources of my being. I have to decide whether to present information or stand back and let a student discover it. I have to know when and how to encourage, compel, accept, judge, nurture, admonish, humor, provoke, and inspire thirty individuals. . . . [I]f I really understand your kid, if I can see into his soul a bit, or if I can figure out how his mind works when he's wrestling with a particular concept or skill, or if I can find a way to make him passionately interested in what I teach, I just might be able to inspire him to real heights. But if I don't understand, I can damage your child. I can turn him off, or set him back, or crush his feelings, or stifle his opportunities (Ellwood, 1995, pp. 246–247). ■

WHAT IS LEARNING?

The title of this book, *Teaching on Principle and Promise,* reflects the authors' belief in the immense power of teaching to influence the lives of children and the future of the planet. Previous chapters addressed debates about what the goals of education should be and what should be taught in schools to support those goals. The curriculum, or the subject matter of schooling, is only one element in the business of educating children. We may offer students information that we think is important to know and introduce them to skills we think are important to have; however, the effect of the curriculum depends on the way we present it to the particular students in our classrooms, and how well they learn it. We join many who protest the idea that a carefully constructed standardized curriculum with prescribed materials and specific guidelines for teachers will make the curriculum almost "teacher-proof," enabling children to learn without the interference, or mistakes, of teachers (Sevener, 1997). We believe that the teacher is essential to the process of formal learning. Neither do we believe that learning happens without the active involvement of the learner. Teaching and learning are reciprocal and interdependent processes, as suggested in Chapter 1.

While the progressives and the existentialists believe that children are active makers of meaning and actors in their own experience, the behaviorists hold the view that teachers have considerable power over children's present and future educational lives. They can open doors of possibility to children, or close them. Teaching is by its nature an optimistic line of work; if we didn't think we could find ways for all children to learn, we would probably be doing something else. While teachers are well aware of the obstacles facing many children that compromise their ability and opportunity to learn, teachers go to school every day expecting to help them succeed.

However, good intentions are not enough. The ability to inspire interest, help children understand subject matter, and arm them with the academic skills they need to grow into capable adults rests on teachers' understanding of how children learn and on their mastery of a pedagogy that is responsive to differences in the way children learn. Teachers need to know how to engage children's attention; how to select, organize, and explain information; how to respond to children's learning needs with appropriate materials and strategies; and how to assess whether children have indeed understood. Fortunately, unlike teachers of old, we no longer have to rely on vague instincts or, worse, the birch rod, to guide us in our teaching. Today's teachers benefit from the growth of the field of education as a home for theory and research into the processes of teaching and learning. This chapter draws upon the growing body of knowledge about learning and teaching as we consider how children learn and how children's cultures, talents, and thinking styles affect the learning process. Within the framework of the discussion of children's learning, we include implications for how best to teach all children.

Learning as Shaped Behavior: Behaviorism

The classic "scientific" approach to the study of how children learn assumes that human beings are shaped by their experiences. What children learn, in school and out, depends on what lessons life teaches them, or, more specifically, what experiences parents and teachers arrange for them. To those who accept the approach to learning called **behaviorism,** what we learn and who we become depends on how we are nurtured. We take on, or learn, the knowledge and behaviors and values that we are exposed to and rewarded for displaying. Thus, one child is praised for being quiet in church, at the movie theater, or on the subway train and has little problem recognizing that the same quiet behavior is expected at school. If that behavior is consistently modeled by the adults and older siblings around him, the imitative child is rewarded, or reinforced indirectly, as well. If his older brother does homework faithfully and without complaint and is rewarded with good grades and praise, chances are he will, too. A four-year-old whose parents test her recognition of colors ("Do you know what color your shirt is? Purple, that's right!") learns to expect and respond to call-and-response questioning. In kindergarten, she will have no problem understanding why her teacher asks questions and what kind of answers the teacher expects. Another youngster whose home culture accustoms him to a different pattern of verbal interaction with his parents—perhaps giving and receiving information or directives—may wonder why his kindergarten teacher asks him questions she clearly knows the answer to, and he may not respond (Heath, 1983).

Classical and Operant Conditioning in Education Behaviorists see learning as a matter of classical conditioning or operant conditioning. In **classical conditioning,** an experience (conditioned stimulus) is paired with an emotional or physiological state (unconditioned stimulus). Over time, the individual responds to the conditioned stimulus with the same response he would have made to the unconditioned stimulus. Ivan Pavlov first described this phenomenon when he discovered that laboratory dogs accustomed to hearing a caretaker ring a bell to announce feeding time would salivate at the sound of the bell even if food were not provided. To use an all-too-frequent school example, if Janeen's first grade teacher berates her for her poor performance on an arithmetic test, Janeen may react with anxiety and fear. For years afterward the anticipation of a math test, or perhaps any request to solve a math problem, might engender in her the same anxiety that originated with the first unfortunate math test experience. Classical conditioning paradigms can be difficult to break, as they usually involve strong physical or emotional reactions that are often impossible to reason away.

Operant conditioning attempts to explain how individuals "voluntarily" respond to their environment with specific behaviors based on their having experienced the consequences of those behaviors; for example, rewards or punishments. B. F. Skinner was particularly interested in operating conditioning's application to education. He believed that children learn by being rewarded, or *positively reinforced,* for the behaviors adults want them to develop. If Janeen's teacher rewards her first graders for finishing their arithmetic work by praising them for their "good work habits," or giving them snacks or extra play time, presumably they will continue to work hard at math. Positive reinforcements can be physical (candy, money, grades) or social (praise, smiles, kind words). Behaviorists believe we are motivated to do things by these external outcomes, or **extrinsic rewards,** rather than because the action has some **intrinsic,** or internal, value by itself. To behaviorists, it is important that children experience success, rather than failure, for success provides a reinforcing sense of accomplishment and a set of effective skills. Skinner liked the idea of "teaching machines," or kits of sequenced tasks, that would allow children to practice correct behaviors (such as solving simple multiplication problems) and then, reinforced for their correct answers, move with confidence and skill to the next color-coded level (for example, division).

Operant conditioning also includes the possibility of negative reinforcement (the removal of something unpleasant), which behaviorists say will result in an increase in positive behaviors. For example, my teacher may offer a "homework pass," allowing students to skip homework if they have completed all their work during the day. *Extinction,* another operant conditioning paradigm, is defined as the removal of a positive reinforcer, resulting in an eventual decrease or disappearance of negative behaviors. If Jamal's teacher only responds to students who raise their hands and ignores students calling out for attention, Jamal will eventually stop calling out. Finally, *punishment* provides an undesirable consequence for a particular negative behavior, resulting in a decrease in that behavior. If I am grounded for tossing my clothes and toys around my bedroom, I will stop my messy clothes-tossing.

Other operant conditioning paradigms can pose problems. For example, punishment often results in the child's merely becoming angry with the punisher, rather than committed to improving his behavior. He may not be aware of the positive alternatives to the behavior that was punished. Furthermore, in the absence of the punisher, the negative behavior may well persist. Consider what happens when a punitive teacher is replaced one day by a hapless, unsuspecting substitute—certainly the negative behavior continues. Finally, extinction of the unwanted behavior can take a long time. Ignoring negative behaviors may for a while stimulate a child to escalate those negative behaviors, perhaps to gain the teacher's attention. The child who begins by calling out may, when ignored, turn to shouting, standing on her desk, or hitting other children.

Research shows that both positive and negative reinforcement can increase positive behaviors while extinction and punishment can decrease or eliminate negative behaviors. Many teachers use these contingencies to encourage children's academic and social learning, but with varying degrees of success. For one thing, rewards are only effective if children find them valuable. Not all children like pizza parties. For some, having pizza is hardly a special occasion. If a teacher is not well liked by her students, her praise may be worthless in their eyes. Candy and homework passes are also problematic; the first encourages poor nutrition, the second conveys the idea that homework is something to be avoided. More effective are social rewards such as the opportunity to spend private time with a well-liked teacher, or receiving the positive regard of one's peers, a smile, or a pat on the back.

The Role of Thinking in Behaviorism Behaviorist researchers after Skinner found that people do not need to experience the positive or negative consequences of behaviors directly. We can learn by watching what happens to other people and reasoning that the same consequences will befall us if we do what they do. Albert Bandura, who added the dimension of social learning to behaviorism, called this vicarious form of learning modeling (1977, p. 20). **Modeling,** or learning by witnessing other peoples' behavior and its consequences, is as effective as direct experience at changing behavior, and takes less time. The teacher who praises Jamal for raising his hand instead of calling out will not only increase Jamal's positive hand-raising behavior but also the hand-raising behavior of other students who have witnessed Jamal's positive reinforcement.

Robert Gagne, whose early works fall within the tradition of behaviorism, later included the place of thinking, or cognitive processing, in learning. He developed a theory and an approach to instruction that described several types of learning outcomes that teachers hope for in their students, including cognitive outcomes.

To promote thinking skills, Gagne suggested that teachers ask students to state facts, label or classify data, formulate rules and generalizations, or solve problems using higher-order concepts and skills. Teachers can set conditions that will enhance each of these cognitive learning outcomes; for example,

- stimulating student's attention and interest
- informing the student of the goals of the lesson
- drawing on students' recall of prior learning
- providing students with guidance as they think and learn
- giving students feedback and evaluating their performance (Gagne, 1985; Gagne, Briggs, and Wager, 1992).

The Behaviorist Teacher The teacher who subscribes to a behaviorist view of learning will probably use techniques that link specific materials and activities to specific learning objectives. He will arrange an orderly sequence of skills, concepts, and activities so that students will be successful, or reinforced, for learning in incremental steps. For example, students might need to complete a series of task cards or worksheets with a prescribed level of mastery before being allowed to continue on to more difficult tasks. The behaviorist teacher will be careful to provide a learning environment that reinforces the concepts, skills, and behaviors that he wants students to attain. He assumes that his students' learning depends largely on how he arranges that environment, what tasks he assigns, and whether he provides reward structures that encourage them to complete the assignments and move on. He will use physical rewards such as stars, grades, and "homework passes," and social rewards such as smiles, positive messages ("Good job!"), and invitations to sit at his desk or be "line leader."

The behaviorist teacher understands that his own behavior is an important source of learning for his students; he is an essential model. During "free reading" time, he will read. If he is concerned with modeling appropriate social behavior, he will be conscious of the way he interacts with other teachers, understanding that students will learn from what he does more than from what he says. He may use students as exemplars for their peers, complimenting them in public on their work and their behavior in the hope that others will follow the lead.

From a philosophical standpoint, behaviorist learning theory presumes that human nature is basically passive and that what and how children learn is entirely the result of external influences, or nurturing. While it is valuable to create an environment that stimulates and reinforces positive learning and behavior, our hope is that teachers will encourage children's intrinsic interest and motivation to learn. The following sections of this chapter describe the ideas of theorists and researchers who believe that learning is not a passive, reactive process, but is undertaken by a child who is, by nature, thinking and creative; and that learning depends in part on differences in children's interests, styles of thinking, and cultures.

Learning as Maturation: Child Development

Forward-thinking philosophers like Comenius, Rousseau, and Froebel (see Chapter 3) saw early on that children were not simply small adults who could be led to perceive and understand information using the same methods and materials that might be effective with adults. Instead, early proponents of what we now call **developmentalism** believed that children's powers of understanding and reason grew and changed with their growing and changing physical development. To developmentalists, children's physical, mental and social functioning is qualitatively different from adults' and develops in age-related stages, as part of the natural process of maturation.

In arguing with John Locke about children's capacity for reason, Rousseau wrote:

> Nature requires children to be children before they are men. By endeavoring to pervert this order, we produce forward fruits, that have neither maturity nor taste, and will not fail soon to wither or corrupt. . . . Childhood hath its manner of seeing, perceiving and thinking, peculiar to itself. . . . I would as soon require an infant to be five feet high, as a boy to have judgment at ten years of age (in Ulich, 1954, p. 397).

Cognitive Development and Piaget The idea that **cognitive development,** the increasing ability to think and solve problems, proceeds in predictable stages was fully expressed in the work of Jean Piaget (1952), probably the most significant figure in child development theory and research as they relate to the field of education. Drawing on his background in biology and on carefully documented observations of his own children, Piaget learned that children arrive in the world with an innate capability to learn. They are by nature curious and open to experience, driven by a need to discover and experiment. Left to their own devices and without any external stimulation, infants will spend time examining and experimenting with their own toes. Rather than tabula rasae (blank slates), as Locke would have us believe, children in fact influence the direction and content of their own learning. They do this by paying attention to selective aspects of new information presented to them, and by making sense of these new aspects by linking them to what they have experienced before. Because their physical capacities and their experiences are more limited than those of adults, what they "learn" may not be what we intend for them to learn. Nor are their conclusions necessarily accurate. To young children, all four-legged animals may be "dogs" and all round objects may be "balls," until more experiences (and the help of parents, siblings, and teachers) help them refine and distinguish concepts. By first experiencing directly the objects in their world and later by abstracting general principles from direct and indirect experiences, children learn about the world, draw conclusions, and refine and correct misinterpretations.

To Piaget and to many after him, therefore, learning was the result of the action of the individual child on the information or experiences presented by his or her environment. A child's active capabilities, however, depended on many factors; most important was the child's age. Piaget told us that how children learn and what they understand proceeds in orderly series of stages, which are described in Figure 5.1. Infants and young children learn through their bodies; thus, he called the period of birth through age two as the sensorimotor period of cognitive development. At this stage, children are motivated by basic biological needs. They pay attention only to the objects that they can touch, smell, hear, see and/or taste. They learn by sucking, grasping, banging, and shaking. Later, from age two through seven—the preoperational stage—Piaget said children demonstrate the ability to understand and manipulate symbols representing objects; for example, they play

Figure 5.1 Piaget's Stage Theory of Cognitive Development

Stage	Sensorimotor	Pre-Operational	Concrete Operational	Formal Operational
Age	Birth through age 2	2 to 7	7 to 11	11 to 15
Characteristics	Experimentation with objects, association of objects with characteristics. Schemata beginning to develop.	Understanding of symbols, including words. Forming of concepts (often partial and/or inaccurate). Egocentrism.	Organized thought, classification, problem-solving related to real events and materials.	Formal logic, abstract reasoning applied to ideas/information not part of immediate experience.
Learning Activities	Manipulating objects by sucking, grasping, banging, shaking. Recognizing recurring objects and people.	Building, pretending, identifying rules and patterns (often partial and/or inaccurate).	Role-playing, reading, simulating, experimenting, developing hypotheses.	Identifying themes, making generalizations, understanding underlying principles.

house, they build towers from wooden blocks, they use words to represent objects and ideas. Though they begin to form generalized concepts and hypotheses and can think about things that aren't actually in front of them, their focus is still on selected characteristics of objects and so their concepts and hypotheses are often half-formed or wrong.

> Any teacher of young children can tell a story about having carefully explained some phenomenon to a child, perhaps what caused the latest hurricane, and learning that what her listener heard was that the sign over the local bakery nearly fell down, leading him to conclude that hurricanes are dangerous for bakeries (Swiniarski and Breitborde, 2003, p. 135).

It is interesting for early childhood teachers to witness the processes by which children discover and apply rules and generalizations. As they begin to speak, and hear that past time is usually expressed by adding "-ed" to the ends of words, they will report to you that they "goed" to the store with their aunt and "buyed" a new Barbie. As kindergartners and first graders begin to write down their stories and observations, they apply the rules of phonics they have learned and try to spell all words phonetically. Parents and teachers present new information and model ways of behaving and then children modify their original generalizations; their speech and their spelling, for example, will come to follow adult-established rules.

Piaget called the period from age seven through eleven the concrete operational stage. Children in this stage of cognitive development show evidence of organized, logical thought. They are less egocentric, more open to possibilities beyond their immediate environment. They can sort and classify objects in many ways, and they can solve problems as long as these problems relate to concrete experiences. In mathematics, for example, they can understand the concepts of multiplication and division as long as they can physically group and regroup objects. They might understand aspects of life in ancient Greece, but only if the information were "made real" through, for example, role-playing, simulations, films, or a fictional account of a child living in that time.

It is not until age eleven (through fifteen) that a child is capable of abstract thought, according to Piaget. In this formal operational stage, children can use formal logic, abstracting principles from discrete examples or from a collection of ideas. This is the period of critical thinking, where children can detect general themes in literature, understand algebraic relationships, and draw conclusions about historical trends.

The Developmentalist Teacher Teachers who subscribe to developmentalist theories of children's learning believe that children come to teachers with already-constructed mental pathways (called *schemata*). These schemata are partially formed or misinformed at first, but proceed toward accuracy with more experience and under the careful guidance of parents and teachers. Teachers committed to developmentally appropriate practice will understand both the limits and possibilities of children's learning at different stages. Rather than expecting full and accurate "mastery" of concepts and skills, teachers will set lesson objectives that are aligned with the presumed stage of understanding that is characteristic of their students' age-mates.

Teachers of preschool and elementary-age children will provide concrete objects and direct hands-on experiences to help them begin to formulate generalizations. For example, a teacher might use math manipulatives—Cuisinaire rods, tangram shapes, and fraction pieces—to build children's understanding of abstract ratios. Or, a teacher might establish learning centers or stations in the classroom, where students can experiment and explore rocks and minerals or measuring tools, recording their observations, sorting and classifying, using the tools to measure dimensions in the classroom. A developmentalist teacher might begin a lesson with a discussion and examples drawn from children's own lives. For example, the class might begin a unit on insects by studying the caterpillar that a child has brought into school. Because Piaget and many of his followers believed that the age guidelines for concrete operational and formal operational learning were flexible, many middle and high school teachers will use these strategies with students who are "concrete learners" or still egocentric in their thinking.

Learning as Making Meaning: Constructivism

Many educators believe that Piaget underestimated the ability of young children to think abstractly. Building on Piaget's work, but influenced by the ideas of John Dewey (1938), Lev Vygotsky (1978), and Jerome Bruner (1990), many researchers and educators today—among them, Eleanor Duckworth (1987) and Catherine Fosnot (1996)—find that even preschoolers can make connections between facts and gain deep understanding of abstract concepts if they are led to reflect on what they are learning, ask questions, analyze, interpret, and predict. They espouse **constructivism,** an approach that considers learning as the active making, or constructing, of meaning from experiences and observations. Constructivists are interested in the process by which children pose questions, formulate hypotheses and make generalizations, and gather data to test their hypotheses. Teachers can best support children's learning by helping them ask clear questions using the techniques of investigation to discover answers. Constructivist beliefs are illustrated in the following classroom example.

> At the Salem State College Preschool, teachers tell the children that the college will soon have an important visitor: the world-renowned scientist and conservationist Jane Goodall will be giving a presentation on her life work studying chimpanzees. They describe Ms. Goodall's dedication to her work and her love for these animals, who exhibit human-like behavior and characteristics. Using principles from the Reggio Emilia approach to constructivist education, teachers lead the children in a month-long interdisciplinary investigation of chimpanzees in recognition of Earth Day, 2002.
>
> The project engages the children in exploring the following questions:
>
> - What is Earth Day and why is it important to celebrate this day?
> - Who is Jane Goodall and what did she learn about chimpanzees?
> - Where did she study chimpanzees for over 30 years?
> - Why are the chimps' habitats endangered?
> - What is a mammal?
> - What are some characteristics of chimps that are similar to humans?
>
> Books, posters, videos and a large new chimpanzee puppet greet the children on the first day of the project. Following the Reggio approach, teachers use various materials and modes to help children express ideas: clay, painting, drawing, sculpture, construction, music, movement, dance and shadow play. They use red balls to count the days until Earth Day, when they will display their project to the College community. On the globe, they locate the continent of Africa and find Tanzania and the Gombie National Park where Jane Goodall lives and studies chimpanzees. In the sand table, they create the savannah where tigers, zebras and elephants roam.
>
> They learn that chimpanzees are mammals and draw them, guided to observe carefully, beginning with a dot and a line and creating shapes. According to the Preschool teachers, children draw to learn, revisiting and revising their work to move to new levels of awareness. Using high-quality materials, they experiment with three-dimensional space. Helped with overhead projectors, they draw from life-like objects; paying close attention to detail, they discuss, as they draw, their ideas about the chimpanzees.
>
> Throughout the project, the Preschool teachers document the children's evolving understanding. Using tape recorders and taking notes and photographs, teachers collect the children's comments, questions and ideas. Using critical-thinking questions, they capture children's attention, provoke their creativity, watch and listen for unexpected responses. As the children work together to solve problems and make decisions, they learn to appreciate the thoughts, opinions and ideas of others and understand that their own ideas are valued.
>
> *Teacher:* What is the first thing you notice when you look at this chimpanzee?

Julia: He is eating and swinging.

Teacher: What else do you notice?

Julia: He is black and hairy. But not as hairy as my daddy. He has no hair on his hands. His hands look dry.

Teacher: What about his eyes?

Julia: His eyes are big and brown—just like mine. We have the same kind of eyes. His nose looks like ours but it has a dot at the end. The baby chimp's ears look like mine. The mommy has a weird ear. It looks like it was pinched.

Teacher: Tell me about their feet.

Julia: Their feet and hands look alike. Because they have to climb and swing.

Teacher: Do you know where chimps sleep at night?

Julia: In the trees on branches. And we sleep in beds with pillows and blankets.

Teacher: Talk to me about the chimp's habitat.

Abigail: They live in trees and build their big nests on the top. They use branches and leaves to make their nests.

Maija: They have night nests. They sleep up high in the trees so other animals won't see them. They use branches to get termites.

Teacher: Why don't the chimps want to be seen?

Abigail: So other animals won't eat them.

Teacher: Let's start the mural. What shape will you start with for the chimp's face?

Julia: A round or oval shape. I can't forget the heart shape. Now for his eyes and his pupils and 5 fingers and toes. I will draw hills for the termites. The termites are inside. Look, my chimpanzee is ready to eat them!

On Earth Day, the children showcase their work in the college library. There, they display the mural they have created together, their portraits of chimpanzees, and the conversations they have had with their teachers throughout the month-long project. The documented conversations show the college community the uniqueness of each child's construction of his or her experience, and the way that the group experience has contributed to their learning (contributed by Beverly Gerson, Director, Salem State Preschool).

This example illustrates several elements of constructivist belief about children's learning. Salem State College Preschool teachers assume that children as young as three years old can understand abstract concepts, such as the fact that all living things adapt to their environments and the nature of the work of biologists. They can observe and record, and compare and contrast the characteristics of gorillas and human beings. They can ask interesting questions and seek satisfying answers. They can demonstrate their learning by producing "reports" and detailed artwork. The conditions required for all this learning include an environment that invites children to question and explore, experiences and materials linked to real-world phenomena, the opportunity to hear other children's ideas, and teachers skilled in guiding individual curiosity and group investigation.

Constructivists believe that learning occurs when children pose their own questions, based on their natural curiosity, and when they are allowed to investigate to find answers without fear of making a mistake. Unlike the behaviorists, constructivists see errors as fodder for learning; mistakes are opportunities to seek more information, try a different strategy, or explore new ways of thinking. Learning is messy, say the constructivists, because real data are messy. Second grade students observing ladybugs and recording and graphing the number of wings on their specimens may report "two" or "four," until someone notices that a second pair is revealed when the ladybug spreads the first (Friedman et al., 1997). In the constructivist view of learning, it is essential that children discover this phenomenon themselves, but a discovery is more likely to happen if children are learning alongside their peers, observing and discussing their observations and questions in social groups.

The Value of Social Interaction in Education: Vygotsky The value of social interaction to children's construction of meaning stems from the work of Lev Vygotsky (1896–1934). Vygotsky (1978) theorized that children influence each other to pay attention to particular phenomena in their environment and to reason in particular ways about those phenomena. Later, the individual child reflects on that experience, makes his own internal sense or understanding of it, and acts upon that understanding. Learning, then, is both interpsychological and intrapsychological (1978). It is a process that involves all domains of functioning: affective (social and emotional), cognitive (mental) and behavioral (activity). A child's progress toward higher levels of understanding depends on social interaction during a stage that Vygotsky called the **zone of proximal development.** According to this concept, a child functioning at a cognitive level characteristic of his age can be induced to a higher level of cognitive functioning if he is exposed to reasoning that is at a higher level but still accessible to his powers of understanding.

Vygotsky's theory complements the research of the behaviorist Albert Bandura (1977), who stressed the importance of children's learning from observing others—modeling. It extends the work of Piaget on the role of ages and stages in cognitive development. In addressing the child as part of a social and physical world, Vygotsky reminds us of John Dewey, another theorist whose ideas have been built upon by constructivists. Dewey and Vygotsky agreed that what an individual knows and learns is *cultural,* in the sense that it is linked to what those before him knew and learned and to what others around him are discovering:

> [W]e live from birth to death in a world of persons and things which is in large measure what it is because of what has been done and transmitted from previous human activities. When this fact is ignored, experience is treated as if it were something which goes on exclusively inside an individual's body and mind. It ought not to be necessary to say that experience does not occur in a vacuum. There are sources outside an individual which give rise to experience (Dewey, 1938, p. 39).

One criticism leveled at constructivists is that they focus on the process of learning at the expense of content, or what should be learned (Cheney, 1997). Adherents of perennialist and essentialist education are concerned that constructivism's "patience" with children's incomplete reasoning and mistakes based on limited information allows children to come to wrong conclusions. Constructivists might respond by saying that learning based on natural curiosity and increasingly sophisticated thinking has more lasting value than memorization of information that children do not find meaningful or do not fully understand.

The Constructivist Teacher The constructivist teacher acts as a mediator between the learner and the learning experience. She respects and builds on children's natural curiosity and understands the importance of their questions. The constructivist teacher assumes that children:

- are capable of close observation and logical reasoning
- are capable of formulating hypotheses and testing them
- should be guided to reflect on their own process of discovery.

The constructivist teacher believes that her responsibility is to help children frame good questions and to pose open-ended questions of her own. She guides their attention and their discussion, and monitors closely the process by which they come to conclusions. She is not as concerned about the accuracy of their conclusions as she is about the breadth and depth of their thinking. Above all, she wants her students to be life-long learners, to retain their curiosity about the world and their resourcefulness in attempting to understand it.

What Are Some Differences in How Students Learn?

It can be argued that none of the above theories of how children learn pay enough attention to learner differences. Despite their attention to the processes by which individual children make sense of information, they may in fact assume that all children process information the same way. Classroom teachers know that children may need different information, different teaching strategies, or different materials to help them learn. These different needs may be due to individual differences in interest, talent, abilities, or styles of thinking. They may also result from social differences in values, traditions, and styles of behaving found in different cultures. The students who arrive in our classrooms are individuals, but also, as Vygotsky says, products of the social interaction that has characterized their families and communities. In this next section, we explore the ways that children's learning varies depending on their *learning styles, intelligences,* and *cultural backgrounds.*

Learning Styles

What is learning? The answer is not the same for everyone. As mentioned earlier in the chapter, learning happens in different ways for different people. It depends on learning style, culture, and who is guiding the learning. So what do we mean by learning styles? **Learning styles** are the ways we process information and the conditions we need to be able to pay attention. Some of us easily master information that is ordered and abstract. We had no trouble memorizing multiplication tables and understanding that they were a shorthand version of addition. Or maybe it was easy to read, understand, and remember the differences between the three branches of the federal government. For some, it's simple to apply the formula that provides the answer to where and when Dick and Ed would meet when traveling on the same highway from two different directions. Others of us needed to know where Dick and Ed were going and why they wanted to meet at all. To satisfy our curiosity about Australia, some of us would be content to read a good book about it; others would prefer attending a lecture by someone who had been to Australia; still others would want the direct experience of a visit. Some of our readers will study for an exam in this course by spending quiet time in the library reading through their notes and this text, perhaps writing out the answers to possible questions or making an outline of major points. Others will turn to study groups, needing the stimulation of discussion to motivate them to think about issues and concepts or to clarify their understanding.

Learning styles include the factors of physical environment, sociological setting, and modes of perception and mental organization. Many researchers and writers have proposed different schemes, or typologies, to define particular learning styles and talents. We will consider those typologies represented by the work of Herman Witkin, Anthony Gregorc, David Kolb, and Rita and Kenneth Dunn.

Witkin's Field-Dependence and Field-Independence Theory

Influenced by the classic work of psychiatrist Carl Jung on personality types (1921), Herman Witkin theorized that learners were of two types: field-independent or field-dependent. Using their Group Embedded Figures Test, Witkin and his associates (1977, 1981) asked subjects to trace simple geometric figures that were presented within complicated patterns. He found that subjects fell into two groups: those who could find the embedded figure quickly and those who had trouble discerning the figure from the pattern surrounding it. He called the first group, who could focus on a discrete phenomenon and not be distracted by its context, **field independent** perceivers; the second group, whose perception was strongly influenced by the field or conditions surrounding or linked to the phenomenon, were **field dependent.** Put briefly, his work suggests that some of us easily see the individual trees, while others first perceive the whole forest.

Applied to school learning, Witkin and later researchers determined that field-independent perceivers were more easily able to memorize and understand decontextualized, disconnected information than field-dependent learners, whose understanding required a view of how the information related to other information within a larger, connected picture. Field-independent learners might quickly memorize a page of multiplication "facts" and make sense of the algorithms governing them, while field-dependent learners might need objects to manipulate to understand the link between addition and multiplication and to embed the facts in their minds. Before deciding that field independence is always preferable to field dependence, consider that field-dependent people have perceptual strengths that field-independent people do not have. They can easily see the relationships between new information and old. They understand the impact of facts on associated situations. They would immediately consider, for example, how technological advances might impact human life. They tend to "read" the feelings of others more accurately than field-independent people, who might listen to a friend's words ("I feel fine") without noticing that her tone of voice and her expression would indicate that she does not feel fine at all.

Given traditional curricula and modes of instruction, where information is presented on paper in very organized and perhaps rote forms (for example, a list of the different responsibilities of the executive, legislative, and judicial branches of government), field-independent learners might have more academic success. On the other hand, curricula that present information in integrated formats and instruction that engages students in active discussions or applied tasks would help field-dependent learners achieve deep understanding. While it might seem that field-independent learners are oriented to mathematics and the sciences and field-dependent learners to the humanities and social sciences, it can be argued that any subject can be approached in abstract (field-independent) or connected (field-dependent) ways. Science, for example, can be taught as organized data and formal procedures, or it can be taught as an appreciation for nature and the way things work. Ideally, science teachers should design lessons and learning activities that reach both kinds of learners and enhance both kinds of perception.

Gregorc's MindStyles

Witkin's theory is only a portion of what we know about the differences in the way children learn. His theory was developed further by Anthony Gregorc (1985), who added new dimensions to Witkin's typology. Gregorc posited that differences in the way individuals perceive information address only part of cognitive functioning. Gregorc agreed that people perceive either the "trees" or the "forest," which he labeled concrete versus abstract perception, but he said we differ as well in the way we organize, or conceptualize, the information we perceive. Some of us organize information in linear, sequential, ways, while others organize information in more random patterns. Thus, rather than limiting our differences to two types, Gregorc posed four **MindStyles,** based on a combination of concrete or abstract perception, and sequential or random conception. One can be a "concrete sequential" information processor, or "abstract sequential" or "concrete random" or "abstract random," mindstyles that are described in Table 5.1.

Concrete sequential students are comfortable with tasks that call for learning and presenting discrete facts or physical objects. They tend to be neat and are good at sorting and classifying information. They have no trouble organizing their time and materials and prefer knowing what assignments are due at what time and in what form. They like expectations to be clear and precise and they like an orderly environment for learning. They might be the students who ask, "How many pages do you expect my story to be?" Our concrete sequential readers probably have neatly arranged notebooks; they rarely fall behind on their reading assignments or come to class late. They are lost without their weekly planners. In group work, they may function as the timekeeper or take the lead in delegating responsibilities and timelines for a group project. They are the conscientious performers among us.

Abstract sequential learners are organized, as well, but with respect to concepts and ideas, rather than materials. Their notebooks may not be as neat as their concrete sequential peers and they often forget to bring a pencil to class, but what's in their notebooks are comprehensive notes on theories and ideas. When they study, they tend to develop outlines of "big ideas." They are good at writing papers that ask for the application and interrelationship of course concepts. Abstract sequential learners are good at comparing, contrasting, analyzing, and evaluating. They are the critical thinkers among us.

Table 5.1 Gregorc's MindStyles

Perception +	Concrete +	Abstract +	Concrete +	Abstract +
Conception =	Sequential =	Sequential =	Random =	Random =
MindStyle	Concrete Sequential	Abstract Sequential	Concrete Random	Abstract Random
Teaching Ideas	Checklists, procedures, clear goals and deadlines, practical examples, concrete materials, and case studies.	Outlines, maps, flow charts, essay writing, reports, comparison charts and tables, analytical tasks.	Experiments, hands-on experiences, learning centers, field trips, art projects, simulations.	Choice of study topics, open-ended discussion, creative drama, and writing.

Concrete random learners like to experiment with objects and materials. They like learning activities that ask them to manipulate physical things. If they're interested in science, they prefer the laboratory work to the lecture and discussion. Some of them are artists, who like to "mess around" with different media. Others are more interested in mechanical things. These are the children who take apart radios and then try to put them back together, or wonder what's behind the panel covering the computer processing unit. They are creative risk-takers, happy with the process of discovery, less concerned about the outcome. They find planning difficult and can seem disorganized. They may need a lot of help with organizing time and tasks. They are the curious doers among us.

Like their concrete random peers, abstract random learners are spontaneous, but they operate in the realm of ideas. They surprise their teachers with thoughts that may seem to come from "left field." They make interesting new connections between concepts and are original thinkers. While abstract sequential learners easily order ideas in a logical fashion, it is sometimes difficult for others to follow the thought process of abstract random students. It may take abstract random learners a long time to figure out how to present information; they have little patience with traditional modes of organization. The abstract random students among us may take few class notes. While reading this book or listening to class discussions, their minds may wander off in new directions of their own devising. They are the creative dreamers in the class. Learners in each of Gregorc's four quadrants have strengths and weaknesses. Each has something to contribute to a group project or to the class as a whole. Without the concrete sequential learners, the project might never be finished on time. Without the abstract sequential learners, it might have little intellectual depth. Without the concrete random contributor, it might be presented in a format that was trite and boring. Without the abstract random learner, it might contain no new ideas. In traditional classrooms, where teachers present discrete information and expect to receive it back on traditional tests, sequential learners tend to be more successful than their more random classmates. For this reason, many teachers find concrete and abstract sequential learners easier to teach and to have in class. While the curiosity of the concrete random learner and the "dreaming" of the abstract random learner may be difficult for sequential teachers to work with, their talents should be recognized and encouraged. It can be argued that Albert Einstein, whose new ideas were responsible for revolutions in science and technology, was an abstract random thinker whose early

Table 5.2 Examples of MindStyle Learners

Concrete sequential learners work best when they

- have an orderly, quiet environment. *"My materials are organized. And I hate distractions when I study."*
- know the accepted way of doing things. *"If I know the procedure, I'm all set."*
- have exact directions and examples. *"I need to know what's expected of me and I need some examples to follow.*

Concrete random learners work best when they

- can try new approaches. *"I like to design my own experiments and figure out my own way to solve a problem."*
- are self-directed. *"I like to follow my own nose, work on the things I'm interested in."*
- can use trial and error. *"I'm happy when I can tinker and mess around until something works."*

Abstract random learners work best when they

- are free to develop their own ideas and share them with others. *"I have so many ideas—it helps to talk them out."*
- can create something original. *"I tend to think 'out of the box.'"*
- have a noncompetitive atmosphere. *"Why does everything have to be done for a grade?"*

Abstract sequential learners work best when they

- have reading references and expert sources. *"I like building on other people's ideas."*
- use traditional procedures and presentations: *"Just let me do a report."*
- discover broad themes and make connections: *"I'm good at putting ideas together in logical ways."*

school performance was disappointing to his teachers, who may have had a limited understanding of learning differences. Table 5.2 contrasts the learning orientations and preferences of Gregorc's types. In those descriptions you may recognize your friends, your family members, or yourself. You can anticipate that they will reappear in your future students.

Kolb's Experiential Learning Model

While Gregorc divided learners into four types based on the two processes of perception and conception, David Kolb's scheme (1975) divides learning into four related processes: concrete experiencing, observing and reflecting, forming of abstract concepts and generalizations, and experimenting with applying theories to practical action. Kolb believes that the learning process takes place in a four-stage cycle. First, the child actively participates in new activities (concrete experiencing), then considers those experiences from many perspectives (reflection). Third, he creates hypotheses, general principles, and tentative rules that integrate

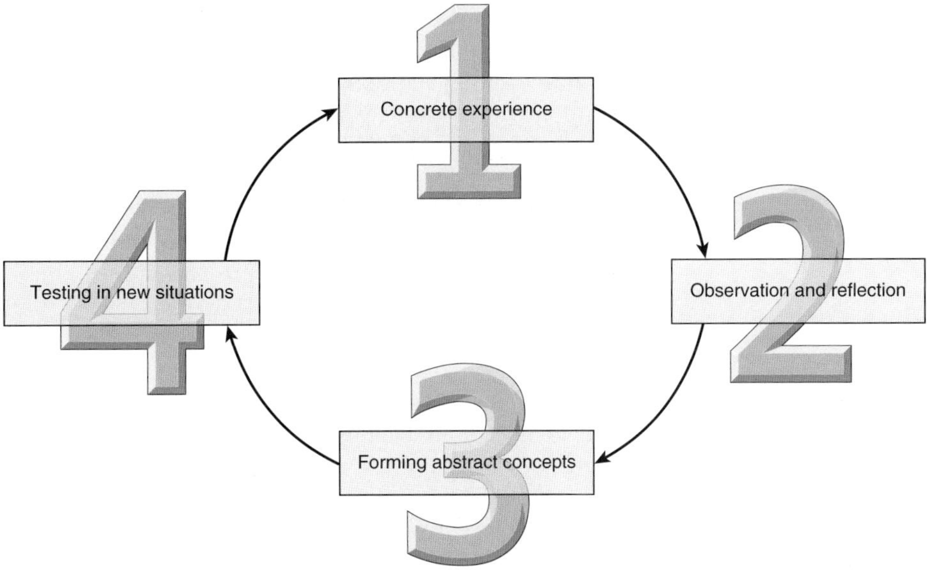

Figure 5.2

Kolb's Four-Stage Cycle of Learning

Source: Smith, M. K. (2001). David A. Kolb on experimental learning. *The Encyclopedia of Informal Education.* London: infed.org

his observations in some logical and meaningful way (abstract conceptualizing), and finally, he tests these theories in new situations to make decisions and solve problems (experimentation). Kolb's cycle is illustrated in Figure 5.2 (Smith, 2001).

According to Kolb, learners ideally need all four abilities, but they are not likely to have them in equal measure. Some people, he says, tend to be "convergers": they are more comfortable with abstract concepts than with concrete experiences and are better at applying concepts to specific situations than at generating broad principles. "Divergers" are good observers and reflectors; they are imaginative and creative and can see things from different perspectives. "Assimilators" have strong analytical abilities and are quick to develop theoretical models. "Accommodators" are risk-takers and experimenters, intuitive, and more comfortable with concrete tasks than theories and ideas.

While Kolb's model has been criticized as limited to the learning of certain kinds of information and for its assumption that learning always proceeds through a strict sequence of stages, the model's emphasis on the relationship between experience and reflection is an important message to teachers. Rather than categorizing learners as either concrete experiencing or abstract reflection, Kolb tells us that full understanding probably requires both processes. Children need an opportunity to engage in direct activity, and they also need to think about how that activity relates to broad and deeply understood concepts. For Kolb, good teachers provide the time, guidance, and encouragement necessary for children to engage in all aspects of the learning cycle.

Dunn and Dunn's Learning Style Preferences

Interested more in the modes and conditions that characterize individual learners than in the learning process itself, Rita and Kenneth Dunn and their associates have created a complex scheme of factors that constitute our learning styles. Based on observations and surveys of the ways people prefer to learn, they theorize that we vary in the conditions that we need in order to learn most easily. These conditions include our way of perceiving information, our physical environment, our emotional orientation, our sociological structure, and our biological needs.

Different Ways of Paying Attention Dunn and Dunn's research shows that individuals vary in the primary ways they pay attention to information. They believe that these preferred modes of perception, or ways of receiving information through the senses, are inborn. We may receive information more easily in visual formats, or auditorially (through hearing), or kinesthetically (using physical movement). Consider how you would prefer to find out how to drive to a place you've never been before: Do you ask for written directions or consult a map? If a friend simply tells you how to get there, will you remember? Do you have to write down what she tells you? Or will you master the route best if you follow someone else and "go through the motions" yourself? Think back to how you studied for your elementary school spelling tests. Did you try to conjure up a mental picture of the word? Did you write the word over and over? Did you learn it best by practicing spelling it aloud with a friend? Teachers who understand that students vary in perceptual learning styles might give their classes several different kinds of strategies for practicing their spelling words. For example, the teacher might ask them to turn the words into visual images, such as L ʘ ʘ K: or to practice spelling the word out loud with a partner, or even to use moving their bodies to create the letters of the word.

Physical, Emotional, Social, and Biological Factors It's important to adjust the physical environment to be optimal for learning. This includes varying the elements of sound, heat, light, and room design. For example, to help us concentrate on learning, some of us prefer to have music in the background, while others cannot focus unless it's perfectly quiet. Some of us concentrate better in cooler environments, others like to study where it's warm and toasty. Some like a dimly lit room, while others need bright light. And, of course, some of our readers are reading this book sitting upright at a well-organized desk, while others are sprawled out on a sofa or bed.

Emotional factors in learning style include motivation, responsibility, and persistence. Some of us need the external motivation of grades and awards, and are more comfortable fulfilling assignments that others have set out for us. Others learn

Children using kinesthetics as a way to enhance learning.
Source: © Ellen Senisi/The Image Works

better when they can choose their own topics of study and are intrinsically motivated by the work itself. Some of us prefer lots of responsibility; we readily volunteer to take on extra tasks and leadership roles and feel satisfied carrying them out. Others prefer to tackle one task at a time, perhaps at the behest of someone else.

Persistence refers to the way we carry out tasks to completion. Some children sit down to do their homework and don't get up until it's finished. Others aren't quite so single-minded. A young friend of one of the authors begins her math homework by doing a few problems, after which she might go to the kitchen for a snack. Rebecca will sit down to do a few more problems, then leave the table to practice her ballet steps at the barre in the hallway, return to her math, have a conversation with her sister, and finally finish the last few problems. The entire process might take two hours. For the author, whose style of persistence is to get the job done as quickly as possible and then move on to other things, it is painful to watch Rebecca do her homework. What is important to understand, though, is that she cannot do it any other way; she concentrates in short bursts on several different things. She may, in fact, accomplish as much as the author in that two-hour period, but in a different order. The importance of this is for the teacher to recognize, adjust to, and accommodate a variety of learning styles in the classroom. Sociologically, the Dunns say, some of us need the company of others to facilitate our learning, while others prefer to learn alone. According to Dunn, Dunn, and Perrin (1994) we are "self-oriented," "peer oriented," "adult oriented," or we combine all these sociological structures. We may like to work with others, enjoying the feeling of contributing to a group project, or we may like to get on with the task by ourselves. There are children who need to check in with their teacher from time to time. They ask, "Am I doing this right?" or "What do you think of what I've done so far?" The questions may come as much from a need for adult company and affirmation as from concerns about their performance. Without the social input, they may lose concentration. Conversely, the child who likes to work alone needs time and space to focus.

Finally, Dunn and Dunn note that we vary in the biological conditions that facilitate our learning. Some of our readers are more alert in the morning; others of you, late at night. The first group rises early and signs up for 8:00 a.m. classes. The second group hopes they never have a class before noon; but their friends can phone them at midnight, because then they are hard at work completing course assignments. Given our preferences, some of us do our reading and writing with a cup of tea or a bowl of popcorn at hand; food intake helps keep us on task. Some children can sit still for long periods of time at their desks, in an auditorium, or on the classroom rug. Others learn faster in a classroom that allows them to move around.

If you recognize and accept the differences in what Dunn and Dunn call "learning style" described above, it is logical to conclude that students in school classrooms have the same variations in the conditions they need and the modes in which they learn best. It is, of course, impossible for teachers to adapt classrooms and instruction to meet each pupil's particular set of preferences and needs; if a teacher decided to have music playing as students engaged in their schoolwork, she would be helping some students focus while distracting others. What good teachers do, however, is provide as much flexibility as possible in their modes of instruction and in classroom configurations. They can establish quiet "zones" and quiet times during the day; arrange seating to accommodate both small groups and individuals; allow for some freedom of movement and physical activity; present information in visual and auditory forms; and balance opportunities for student choice about what they will study, and when, with assigned topics and work periods, and change the schedule from time to time.

Howard Gardner's Multiple Intelligences Theory

Howard Gardner's groundbreaking work (1983) deepened learning style theory by exploring the meaning and nature of intelligence. Gardner dismissed the traditional notion that intelligence was a single trait that individuals possessed from birth to a greater or lesser degree than others. Intelligence was not a characteristic that could be measured on a single intelligence test, but there were, in fact, **multiple intelligences,** or many ways of being "smart." Researching the thinking processes of people talented in different ways, he concluded that some of us are highly intelligent quantitative thinkers, while others are highly intelligent at language or at art or at sport. Great athletes and dancers, he says, have a "bodily-kinesthetic" intelligence that allows them to "know" how to hold and move their bodies in purposeful and effective ways. One need only observe the ease with which some children who watch televised sports can immediately replicate a gymnast's movement or a pitching stance to see kinesthetic intelligence in action. Great therapists, says Gardner, have a high degree of social-emotional intelligence; great writers, linguistic intelligence; great sculptors, spatial intelligence. Having high intelligence in one area is no guarantee of having high intelligence in another. Einstein, an example of a logical-mathematically intelligent person, was famously inept at taking care of his person; kinesthetically "unintelligent," he dressed haphazardly and might forget to eat if someone wasn't around to prepare his meals. On the other hand, Gardner has found a connection between logical-mathematical and musical intelligence; the number of mathematicians who are also skilled musicians (Einstein was one) is, Gardner says, more than coincidental, perhaps because music involves mathematical relationships and patterns.

Gardner's original list of multiple intelligences included linguistic, logical-mathematical, musical, spatial, kinesthetic, and personal. Later, he divided personal intelligence into two categories: intrapersonal and interpersonal, based on his findings that some people were highly intelligent about others' feelings while fairly ignorant of their own, and vice versa. In the past few years, as he continues his research, Gardner (1999) has added an eighth intelligence to his list: naturalistic intelligence, describing the deep and ready understanding of the natural environment that farmers, gardeners, botanists, and geologists might possess. He is researching the possibility of a ninth "existential" intelligence, which would characterize people (philosophers, for example) who are oriented toward thinking about the big questions of life, many of which are explored in the first chapters of this book. To qualify as one of the intelligences, existential intelligence would have to meet Gardner's criteria. (See Table 5.3 for a list of the criteria.)

The multiple intelligences have a clear biological basis as well as very distinct manifestations in human behavior. Gardner believes, however, that each intelligence can be improved by practice. While he leaves decisions about curriculum to policymakers, he asserts that teachers can do much—in the way they present curricula and the learning activities they design for students—to address their students' several intelligences. At Harvard University's Graduate School of Education, Gardner and his colleagues are interested not only in how good teachers draw on students' strong intelligences to help them learn, but how, at the same time, they enhance students' ability to use the intelligences that are not so strong (Gardner,

Table 5.3 Gardner's Criteria for Intelligences

To qualify as an intelligence, a characteristic must:

- exist in living examples of savants, prodigies, and other exceptional individuals
- have an identifiable core set of information-processing operations
- have a distinctive developmental history, with definable "end-state" performances
- have a distinctive evolutionary history and plausibility
- be supported by experimental psychological research
- be supported by psychometric findings (psychological testing)
- be able to be encoded in a symbolic system; for example, mathematical equations, maps, and musical notation
- be able to be isolated in the brain; can be determined by the science of brain damage

Source: Howard Gardner, *Frames of Mind: The Theory of Multiple Intelligences* (New York: Harper-Collins, 1983) pp. 62–69.

1999). Harvard's Project SUMIT (Schools Using Multiple Intelligences Theory) collects information on lessons, units, and other teaching-learning activities that use the MI approach to help children understand curriculum content. A growing number of schools subscribe to the MI approach. At one particular school, for example, students learn about the South American rainforest by reading about it and writing essays and stories, listening to indigenous music and making up their own, tabulating the declining numbers of endangered animals, drawing murals depicting the biota, "climbing" through layers of the atmosphere, debating economic and ecological points of view, and creating fictional biographies of children living in the region. Classroom teachers work with art, music, and physical education teachers and with science specialists on the project. The children do independent research and writing, participate in group activities, and listen to whole-class presentations.

How Does Technology Influence Learning?

Children learn from a variety of media forms—interactive books, CDs, videos. All these media are used both in and out of school. The traditional children's books, with text and occasional illustrations, have been supplemented by newer versions whose pictures "pop up" or move or make sounds. Books are packaged with audiotapes and CDs. Many college textbooks, including this one, come with access to an accompanying website. Many early childhood educators wonder whether the virtual reality of computer activities diverts young children from exploring and enjoying the physical world or enhances their powers of imagination and logical thought. While the debate in early childhood classrooms goes on, however, in homes and libraries preschoolers sit down at computers to play games, hear stories, and even travel the world. And there is television, of course, to capture their time and attention, offering them more information and entertainment than generations before them ever had.

Many educators happily use audio, video, and computer resources to teach subject matter and skills in interesting and involving ways. They capitalize on what seems to be children's natural inclination to pay attention to sensory images and activity. The availability of these new media allows for a variety of intelligences other than the traditional linguistic and logical-mathematical to be used—for example, the spatial, musical, and kinesthetic. New media address the random and divergent cognitive styles that have been left out of the traditional classroom's sequential and assimilationist styles described by Gregorc and Kolb.

Technology and Learning: The Gender Gap

Despite the capability of these new technologies to respond to a range of learning styles and intelligences, there continues to be an interesting disparity between the enthusiasm that boys and girls hold for them. Girls are still underrepresented in high school and college technology courses and in technical and engineering occupations. The problem, says Sherry Turkle of the Massachusetts Institute of Technology, is the way that schools have considered and used technology:

> We believe that girls are not afraid but that they are uninspired and alienated by the way K–12 education presents computing to them. They see computing as an enterprise divorced from subject matter and from their interest in people. They see careers in computing as isolating (Turkle, quoted in Starr, 2000).

Ways of thinking about technology have reflected what Belenky and others (1997) have described as typically male ways of knowing. To Belenky, girls typically think in subjective terms, connecting what they know to their own lives and the lives of others, while boys are more typically oriented to objective analysis. Building on Belenky's work, Karen Zuga, an engineer, says that technology educators need to recognize girls' need to share their knowledge and experiences and apply technology to questions of value and action (Zuga, 1999).

Technology is hardly new to women, says Zuga. "Every woman has been a technological being, using and often inventing tools, materials, and processes in order to adapt and modify her world" (1999). In fact, say Turkle and her colleagues, in some ways girls are ahead of many educators in their concerns about the relevance of technology to education and society. Girls are "turned off" by video games, dull programming courses, and assumptions that technology careers are the province of "geeks" who work in drab and isolated cubicles on projects that have little to do with real people. Her report for the American Association of University Women, "Tech Savvy: Educating Girls in the New Computer Age" (Turkle, 2001) suggests that, while boys tend to be interested in how technology works, girls want to know how it can be used. Turkle says teachers can help reduce the technology gender gap by designing lessons and units that offer ways to use technology across all curriculum areas, including literature, the arts, and social sciences, as well as in mathematics and science. The general curriculum should use new technologies as proactive tools to find and interpret information that addresses interesting and important human questions.

Learning and Navigating in the Information Age

In the minds of some, children's exposure to media and technology is too long and too much. Newspapers are full of articles claiming that children watch too much television. Many teachers complain that students can no longer pay attention to anything longer than a fifteen-second "sound bite" or a thirty-minute situation comedy (interrupted by ten minutes of entertaining commercial advertisements). However, when new technologies such as computer-based simulations are used well, they encourage problem-solving, critical thinking, and experimentation (for example, Tom Snyder's "Decisions, Decisions" and "Diorama Designer" programs—see Websites to Explore at the end of this chapter). These are learning goals that Turkle, Zuga, and others would promote for both girls and boys. Internet-based research projects expose children to information not available to them via the traditional means of books and field trips. Teachers can create WebQuests or use existing ones (see Websites to Explore) to offer "safe" and prestructured Internet pathways to rich sources of information. In teacher-designed project-based units, students can find a whole series of lessons on a thematic topic, including background information, stories and music, video clips, art and data sets. Software such as Inspiration® helps students organize information by mapping concepts, using time lines, and graphing story elements.

If you believe that the ways in which children learn—their habits of mind—depend in part on what kinds of learning processes their environment provides, you might conclude that the plethora of multimedia images and "random" formats

Technology-based projects expose children to information not available to them through traditional means such as books and field trips.
Source: © Ellen Senisi/The Image Works

that characterize computer and video technologies have affected children's minds. Many believe that the age of linear ways of learning is coming to an end. They say that those whose minds are able to consider and store multiple sources of information will be more successful academically and that, in fact, they are the creative problem-solvers of the future. Seymour Papert, a pioneer in using technology to transform education, writes about the positive, and inevitable, ways that new technologies are impacting learning and teaching. He says that the technology-enhanced school is a place where students learn by engaging in projects that come from their own interests and their own questions. Such schools are places where students will want to be, where they can pursue subjects they want to explore and learn. He describes his vision of the school of the future in this way:

> The contribution of technology is that it makes possible projects that are both very difficult and very engaging. It is a place where teachers do not provide information. The teacher helps the student find information and learn skills—including some that neither knew before. They are always learning together. The teacher brings wisdom, perspective and maturity to the learning. The student brings freshness and enthusiasm. All the time they are all meeting new ideas and building new skills that they need for their projects. Some of what they learn belongs to the disciplines school has always recognized: reading, writing, mathematics, science and history. Some belongs to new disciplines or cut across disciplines. Most importantly, students and teachers are learning the art and skill and discipline of pursuing a vision through the frustrating and hard times of struggle and the rewarding times of getting closer to the goal (Papert & Caperton, 1999).

What Is the Impact of Culture on Learning?

What people know and how they come to know it depends on the information available in their environment and the tools available to access that information. At a more basic level, however, the history of the world's people is a history of adaptations to specific geographic contexts for satisfying biological needs. Surviving and thriving in the northern reaches of Quebec calls for a different set of skills than surviving and thriving in the heart of New York City. Based on ways of life in different parts of the globe, groups of people learned particular ways of perceiving, organizing, and responding to information in their environments. To the extent that one generation of members of a group shares common space, traditions, and a language, this common experience may have bred typical patterns of knowing and learning. In all cultures, elders take responsibility for teaching the young how to understand and survive in their particular time and place. In some cultures, education takes place in formal institutions—schools—through books and presentations. In others, children are educated at the feet of storytellers or in a series of physical tests. Everywhere, as you learned in Chapter 1, children also learn the knowledge, norms of behavior, and values of their cultures informally, from the precepts and cautions their parents share with them, from the actions adults model for them, and from the material that their environments present.

Schoolchildren in the United States bring with them into the classroom a wide diversity in patterns of knowing, learning, and communicating that are in part in-

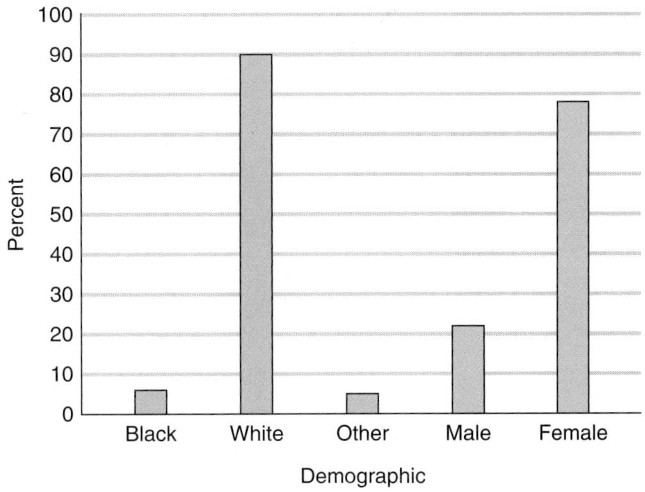

Figure 5.3

Cultural Backgrounds of Teachers in 2000

Source: National Education Association (2003). Status of the American School Teacher 2000–2001.

fluenced by the wide diversity of their cultural backgrounds. The fact that their teachers are overwhelmingly white, Anglo, and middle class means that there are bound to be cultural differences between what teachers and students know, the ways that they learn, and the languages they use to communicate. In Providence, Rhode Island, 95 percent of teachers in 2000 were Anglo, while almost half the students in their classrooms were Latino. Across the country in Los Angeles, with a school population that was 69 percent Latino, only 22 percent of the teachers shared this cultural background (Gordon, Della Piana, & Keleher, 2000). In general, the cultural and communication styles that characterize U.S. public school classrooms are typical of those found in white, middle-class homes. Children in the cities of Providence and Los Angeles who come from white, middle-class homes—where there is a "goodness of fit" between the cultures of home and school (Hale, 2001)—will find it easy to understand and learn in these classroom environments. Those whose home cultures are different from that of their white, Anglo, middle-class teachers may experience barriers to learning rooted in cultural incompatibility between teachers' and students' deep-seated habits of perceiving, behaving, and communicating. Chapter 9 will explore in depth the ways in which cultural differences affect the educational resources and opportunities that children are provided and the educational outcomes that result.

Culture and Learning Style

On the Navajo reservation in Arizona and in the Australian bush, far from the world of urban affairs, children are taught by tribal elders who weave stories and create objects in patterns that represent generations of spiritual traditions. Daily life involves making and growing things, repairing homes and vehicles, watching the weather, and keeping warm and dry. Children's knowledge of the physical world is acute and they understand that humans are small pieces of a much larger whole. Talk is limited to what is necessary; actions are more important. Children learn through observation of their elders and of nature, a process demanding patience and quietude. Long periods of study will optimize a child's success at attempting a new skill. First-time failure—for example, putting one's hand into a beehive or

Many teachers involve students in hands-on learning in order to optimize their understanding of different processes.
Source: © Bob Daemmrich

jumping into a lake without knowing whether the bottom is full of rocks—could have fatal consequences.

In many cultures, learning is defined as the ability to perform manual tasks and contribute to the physical welfare of one's family. Italian immigrants to America at the turn of the twentieth century valued hard and productive work, family loyalty, and religion over book learning or general knowledge—an attitude that characterizes many immigrant Caribbean Islanders today. Children of Dominican immigrants may take time away from school for three weeks to celebrate the Christmas season with their families back home on the island. Teenage sons commit to part-time jobs to help support their families, and middle-school girls may stay home to help out when their mothers are ill. Teaching approaches that seem to be effective for many of these Latino children draw on real-life experiences and make the pragmatic value of content learning clear. In one case, a teacher used the cultural concept of *familia* to create a personal, family-like environment in his classroom, where he assumed a father-like role (Abu-Nader, 1993).

Janice Hale (2001, 1986) proposes that many African Americans come from cultures that value spirituality, harmony with nature, expressive movement, creative thinking, interconnectedness, and person-to-person contact. Life in traditional African villages called for physical skill and the use of music, dance, and stories as modes of communication, for example. The "relational" learning style that Hale suggests characterizes many African American children, and provides them with a keen sensitivity to the emotions of others and a preference for kinesthetic learning, comes from their African roots. The more abstract learning style that characterizes most white Anglo-American suburban children, she says, fits better with the abstract teaching styles of most American classrooms, where students are expected to "do their own work" and focus on what Witkin called field independent tasks. Teachers who understand the roots of African American culture and its emphasis on creativity, physical stimulation, community, and oral expression will select materials and instructional strategies that respond to those cultural strengths. They will fit their teaching methods to the culture-based ways that many

African American children learn; for example, teaching mathematics using movement, hands-on materials, and real-world problem solving; teaching history through storytelling, group discussion and the arts; and encouraging children to work together and to help each other.

Culture and Language

Several researchers have examined the relationship between culture and language style, and discussed the implications of these differences for the school experiences of children in a variety of cultural groups. Susan Phillips (1983) found striking differences in the patterns of Native Americans and European Americans in the Pacific Northwest. Observing the language and nonverbal behavior of the two groups in separate community meetings, she noticed striking differences in the amount of speech each group used, as well as in the ways they interacted and came to decisions. European Americans varied in the amount and length of time each person spoke. They tried to relate their ideas to those of the person who had spoken just before them. They used all parts of their bodies—heads, faces, hands, and posture—to convey meaning, and continued the discussion until the whole group reached a resolution, either by vote or general consensus or an action plan. Among the Native Americans, on the other hand, the amount and time of members' speech was more evenly distributed. All members took a turn at expressing their ideas, unconcerned about whether what they had to say related to the previous speaker's point. They used few facial or body movements. When all who wanted to speak had had their say, the community members went home to reflect. Many weeks might elapse before the group reconvened to reach a conclusion. European American teachers of children from this reservation have mistakenly assumed that these children were resistant to learning, when in fact they were displaying the limited movement, the measured participation, and the extended time to process a response that is characteristic of their culture (Phillips, 1983).

In a study of both black and white Appalachian families, Shirley Brice Heath (1982) found differences in the way parents in the two groups asked questions and gave information to their children. While the white parents tended to ask rhetorical questions in a question-and-answer testing pattern ("What do I have in my hand? 'An apple!' Right!"), black parents told their children stories and gave them commands ("Share this apple with your sister"). According to Heath, these African American children were confused when they entered school and teachers asked them questions that seemed unnecessary. A black child might not respond to a teacher who asks, "What do I have in my hand?" because he believes that she must already know, and therefore, she could not really be asking for an answer. Heath believed that the question-and-response patterns of white families prepared their children for the language demands of public school.

The degree to which a culture is primarily **orally-based** or **literacy-based** (Ong, 1982) affects patterns and conceptions of learning. In some cultures, children are educated from generation to generation by elders who convey stories, chants, and myths representing great truths. Goss and Barnes (1989) refer to the call-and-response tradition of "testifying" in church, the brilliant rhetoric of Martin Luther King Jr. and Jesse Jackson, and the lyrical messages of blues and rap music as legacies of the African American tradition of teaching and learning through oral language. In contrast, Asian Buddhism, Judaism, Islam, and Christianity assume that truth is conveyed through "the word" of God as communicated in the

Voices of Principle and Promise

On Culture and Teaching
by Roda Amaria, Global Educator

Roda Amaria, originally from Bombay, India, completed postgraduate education (Master's and Ph.D. degrees) at the University of Birmingham in England. She taught high school in India, was a science resource teacher in England, and a professor of science education in Newfoundland, Canada, and the United States. As a Zoroastrian (Parsi), she was a religious minority in India. As someone who has traveled the world and taught on three continents, she considers herself a multicultural individual (Parsi, Indian, and English) living in America. In the following piece, she describes how her culture has influenced her as a person and an educator.

In my culture, you learn to listen to your elders, listen to what they have to say. You don't treat them as relics of the past. You can learn important lessons from the past, like how the Victorians treated the environment. Some of the things they did were incorrect; for example, they went on safari and killed all the animals in sight 'til the whole place was depleted. Some of us lived through that time. You don't just discard that information. This idea—that you integrate the past with the present and the future—is very important in developing countries.

Family relations are important. Not just your parents, but your aunts and uncles all have lessons to teach you. You listen with one ear, you make your own judgment and move ahead, trying not to make the same mistakes they did. In India, lessons are taught very subtly, through examples, through stories. My husband's father would tell him a story. That story had a lesson in it, but the reason he relishes the story is because it was told by his father.

In America we don't tell children how it was to live through the Depression. Instead we say, "Here's a toy. We never had it, but you can have as many as you want." It makes for a very wasteful society. In the Indian culture, every little article has value. When we're done using it, we pass it on to other members of our family or to the servants who need it. We mend the umbrella. Take a bicycle, for example—every member of the family learns to ride it. When they don't need it anymore, they fix the spokes and give it to the servant boy in the neighborhood, who maybe has to pedal it a little harder. When the time comes that it doesn't work anymore, it's dismantled and someone makes a new bicycle out of the parts of several old ones. In third world countries, paper is never wasted. Spokes are never wasted. There's a 1957

sutras, the Torah, the Koran, and the Bible, texts to be mastered only through careful and long study (Abramson, 2001). Children of literacy-based cultures may easily accommodate to abstract, book-centered teaching approaches and solitary study. Teachers of children from orally-based cultures can draw on this orientation by, for example, using children's own stories as reading material or teaching history through diaries and first-person accounts.

Language patterns in families often evince deep differences in cultural values and in expectations for behavior and orientations to authority. Black children accustomed to clear commands from their parents might not take seriously, or even understand, the kinds of commands that many white middle-class parents and teachers couch in rhetorical or interrogative forms. A teacher who asks, "Shall we get ready for art?" may assume that the children understand the question as a command to put away their things and line up at the door. While in some cultures all teachers have ultimate and absolute authority, in others a teacher's authority may depend on gender or tone of voice. In many Latino and Asian cultures, for example, teachers are treated with formal deference. Students will not use teachers' names, calling them "Teacher," or "Professor," and will not ask questions, fearing that questions might be taken as challenges to the teacher's authority. Children in

Fiat still in my family. My brother uses it. It's been redone, over and over. People get emotionally involved with things because they're precious and not readily available. We take pride in the fact that we're still using a refrigerator built in 1927. I've got a pair of scissors that my aunt gave me when I was in kindergarten.

My concern with not wasting the lessons or the things of the past has affected the way I teach. I would take children outside and ask them to think about how they could remove a bug without killing it. I would have them study the parts of a flower by picking up the ones that had fallen to the ground instead of breaking a new one. I would ask my teacher education students to think about the impact of technology on the environment; for example, all the pesticides that are sprayed on all the cornfields in this country.

You can't stop progress because people are curious. Humans are explorers. You cannot stop stem cell research or nuclear exploration. But the question of how that research is used is very important. You must consider the global view. I ask my students to go outside the school and look at a patch of ground, look at the biodiversity that's represented. What happens to the rainforest when people use up the trees to make elegant furniture? What happens around the transnational oil pipelines? Why do we need lawns that are "weed-free"? What's a weed to one person is really a wildflower.

A fact is a fact but the truth is interpreted by human beings as they conceptualize that fact. My truth is very different from your truth, so I have to be very true to myself and my beliefs. My culture has lots of rules. But my father was a strong individual and I chose a partner who treated me as an equal. Democracy means the same thing. You have to follow the rules, but you need to express your own viewpoint.

Source: Roda Amaria, retired secondary school science and math teacher and professor of education, North Port, Florida.

Questions to Consider

1. In what ways do you think Dr. Amaria's experience in her culture influenced her decision to become a teacher? How has it influenced her style of teaching?
2. How do you think she balances the respect for the past that characterizes her culture, and her idea that "you can't stop progress"?
3. Dr. Amaria says her culture has "lots of rules," yet she has lived in many places and done many things independently. Are you aware of other examples of people who honor their cultures but who have gone beyond their "boundaries"?

other cultures, where males are dominant, may perceive soft-voiced female teachers as more nurturing than authoritative. One of the authors recalls an incident in an elementary school where a young boy refused to mind his third-grade teacher. When the boy's parents were asked to discuss the problem, only the father came to school, bearing the request that his son be transferred to the class of a male third-grade teacher because, "In our culture, boys are not accustomed to obeying women."

The question of how to help the children of immigrants learn English and learn the subject matter of the curriculum has been a matter of significant debate for many years. In Chapters 7 and 8, we review the history of this debate and the changing attitudes toward bilingual education and teaching English language learners. At the present time, national and state policies oppose separate classes for beginning English speakers with content taught in native languages. English language learners are now to be included in regular classes. Teachers whose classes include limited English speakers must use special techniques to emphasize language learning and help the children try to understand the content at the same time. Whether this approach will help English language learners attain academic, linguistic, and social success remains to be seen.

The Culturally Responsive Teacher

Understanding the factors that affect learning and the processes by which individuals come to know things provides teachers with a foundation on which to design instruction. Once teachers determine what it is they want to teach, they must then find ways to bring the subject matter alive and make it meaningful to real students in real classrooms. Research into the processes by which children make sense of information and learn it, whether undertaken from the perspective of child development or behaviorist theories or constructivism, points to the importance of linking new concepts and skills to what children already know. This section of the chapter argues that what children already know depends at least in part on their cultural backgrounds.

To keep students "connected" to subject matter, **culturally responsive teachers** draw on their students' rich backgrounds and teach in ways that honor culture-based forms of expression and styles of learning. Lessons on geographical concepts and skills might engage students in mapping the routes their ancestors (or perhaps they themselves) took to reach America. Latino children's heritages are linked to early explorations of this country and the establishment of several territories and states. Our mathematical symbols, operations, and tools developed in Middle and Far Eastern lands. The English words we use every day and include in vocabulary lessons have origins in Arabic, Dutch, French, and many African languages. Certainly, there is a wealth of excellent multicultural children's literature whose themes and information express both the commonalities—unity—that characterize the human experience and the variations—the diversity—of expression that characterize different cultures. When teachers take the time to explore and share with their students the multicultural roots of the words, facts, and concepts they teach, they not only make them more meaningful to the children, but also nurture feelings of pride, self-esteem, and belonging that can make them care more about what they are learning.

Rather than adhering to one school of thought or approach to teaching, our experience with students of varying ages and stages, talents and interests, learning styles and cultural backgrounds, tells us that there is no one set of "best practices." Teachers should be familiar with a range of instructional strategies that they can tailor to students' learning styles. While it is essential to be aware of students' different styles, teachers must also have in mind the goal of strengthening the subject areas and "intelligences" that need improvement so that students will have the knowledge and skills that they need to thrive in society. Most important, culturally responsive teachers have high expectations for all learners. They communicate to all children their belief that, perhaps with varying strategies and tools and more or less help, they are all capable of learning and succeeding. Later chapters of this book will reveal more about how good teachers tailor curriculum and instruction to reach the particular students whose learning is their responsibility so that, in the introductory words of Cynthia Ellwood, they "inspire [them] to real heights."

SUMMARY

This chapter opens with the argument that "good intentions are not enough" in teaching effectively. To present subject matter in ways that are meaningful and important to children, teachers must understand how their students learn. In addressing the question, What is learning? we draw on philosophy, psychology, and anthropology to present theory and research on learning, and implications for classroom practice.

- Major learning approaches include behaviorism, child development theories, and constructivism. Each approach contributes to an understanding of the complexity of the learning process: Behaviorism offers insight into the importance of environmental conditions and paradigms. Developmentalism describes the impact of maturation on cognitive development. Constructivism deepens our understanding of how children interact with their environment and process experiences.
- Some learning style theories and models include Witkin's field-dependence and field-independence theory, Gregorc's MindStyles, Kolb's experiential learning model, Dunn and Dunn's learning style preferences, and Howard Gardner's multiple intelligences theory.
- New technologies have significantly changed the information available to students in classrooms, the ways in which they access that information, and, possibly, their habits of thinking. Many teachers use a variety of methods to present material—audio, video, and the Internet. This often addresses the range of learning styles in the classroom. There is a gender gap when it comes to technology. Girls tend to take fewer technology courses and are more interested in how technology is used than in how the technology works. Information and technology surround us, and those who can use multiple sources of information are likely to be more successful. Technology allows for more project-based learning and discovery, rather than the traditional approach of providing information to be memorized.
- A variety of factors influence the way individual children perceive, organize, and respond to the information presented to them in life and school, including their learning styles, intelligences, and culture. Teachers who understand the range of cultures represented by their students can select materials and instructional strategies that respond to those cultural strengths. Some cultures are primarily based in oral language, while others emphasize written language. Language patterns often reveal cultural values, such as deference for a teacher who may be perceived as having absolute authority. Teachers who have students with limited English proficiency in their classes can use techniques to emphasize language learning and help students understand content at the same time.

QUESTIONS FOR REFLECTION

1. Explain how children's learning can be influenced by their age, their individual learning styles and intelligences, or the social/environmental conditions of their lives.
2. What is your position on the existence of a "generalized intelligence" that operates across all contexts for learning?
3. Where do you stand on the nature versus nurture debate? Does one need to be born with the ability to become a fine pianist? Or, can anyone who puts their mind to it become a fine pianist? Can anyone become an excellent teacher, or are excellent teachers born with that ability?
4. How might your own ethnic background, including the traditional ways of life in your family's homeland or original culture, have influenced your beliefs about and orientations toward learning?
5. At this point in your reading and your classroom experience, how would you describe what it means to learn something? How would a teacher who shares your definition of learning design his classroom?

APPLYING WHAT YOU'VE LEARNED

1. Review the information presented in this chapter about classical and operant conditioning. Now, design a behavior modification program directed at some behavior you would like to change.
2. Spend some time in a preschool or day care center. Observe one child for half an hour. How does the child interact with other children? How does the child interact with materials? What evidence of the process of learning can you see? Now observe an older child in a school setting. Compare similarities and differences that might relate to their ages and stages of development.

3. Using the questionnaire on the learning style website below or another source, determine your own "learning style" or "intelligence."

4. Go to the Internet and research schools that are applying Gardner's Multiple Intelligences theory to classroom instruction. You might begin with the Project SUMIT website listed in Web Sites to Explore.

5. www. Explore one of the WebQuests contained in the textbook's companion website. What do you think of its value as a learning tool?

6. Observe an elementary classroom. How does the teacher accommodate instruction to students with a variety of academic needs and achievement levels?

KEY TERMS

behaviorism, p. 147
classical conditioning, p. 147
cognitive development, p. 150
constructivism, p. 152
culturally responsive teachers, p. 174
developmentalism, p. 150
extrinsic rewards versus intrinsic rewards, p. 147
field independent learner versus field dependent learners, p. 157
learning styles, p. 156
MindStyles, p. 158
modeling, p. 148
multiple intelligences, p. 164
operant conditioning, p. 147
orally-based culture versus literacy-based culture, p. 171
zone of proximal development, p. 155

WEBSITES TO EXPLORE

http://www.tolerance.org. The Teaching Tolerance project of the Southern Poverty Law Center maintains a site containing information and teaching activities to promote the teaching of tolerance and the prevention of hate crimes.

http://www.rethinkingschools.org. Rethinking Schools is an organization of educators whose goal is to provide curriculum and instructional strategies that promote equity and social justice. The site includes articles, position statements, resources, and teaching ideas.

http://www.cr.nps.gov/nr/twhp/. The United States National Park Service website. Teaching with Historic Places uses the National Register of Historic Places as a resource for linking curriculum to local communities. Teaching ideas are organized by national history standards and by location.

http://pzweb.harvard.edu/.

http://pzweb.harvard.edu/SUMIT/. The websites for Project Zero and Project SUMIT at Harvard University describe research projects on children's and adult learning using Howard Gardner's Theory of Multiple Intelligences and offer model schools and curricula.

http://pss.uvm.edu/pss162/learning_styles.html. Learning Styles website. A brief questionnaire allows viewers to assess their "intelligence" strengths and weaknesses.

http://www.tomsnyder.com/. Tom Snyder Productions's website reports on software and professional development for computer-enhanced, interactive instruction in a variety of curriculum areas. Snyder was an early advocate of the "one-computer" classroom.

http://www.inspiration.com. Inspiration Software, Inc., offers programs for all elementary and secondary students, using graphic organizers to enhance thinking skills and writing.

http://webquest.org/. Bernie Dodge at San Diego State University has developed a site to support teachers using WebQuests—self-contained pathways through the Internet that provide background information, lessons, and activities related to particular themes of study.

CRITICAL READINGS

Multimedia and Multiple Intelligences

BY SHIRLEY VEENEMA AND HOWARD GARDNER

Just 40 years ago, a new movement in science began to coalesce. Now termed cognitive science, this field seeks to integrate insights from several disciplines (including psychology, linguistics, artificial intelligence, and neuroscience) in order to put forth a more comprehensive understanding of the human mind. The approach fostered by the cognitive revolution has enormous, if not yet widely appreciated, implications for educational practice.

Even in science, one cannot have a revolution without an enemy. In the case of the cognitive revolution, there were two separate, though related, foes. The behaviorist perspective, as epitomized in the work of B. F. Skinner, disdained any concern with the mind and its contents: All that mattered, from the behaviorist perspective, was that an organism perceived a stimulus and responded to it or that the organism acted in some way and was positively or negatively rewarded for so acting. In education, the apotheosis of the behaviorist perspective was the teaching machine, which remains central in computer-assisted instruction today.

The second antagonist, from the perspective of cognitivists, was the view that what the mind contains is intelligence—more or less of it. Individuals, according to this perspective, are born with a certain amount of intelligence, which for better or worse is essentially fixed. Few asked just what intelligence was or how it could be improved, increased, or transformed—indeed, the not entirely whimsical definition put forth by psychologists was that "intelligence is what the tests test." The IQ test and its descendants, in such measures as the Scholastic Aptitude (now Assessment) Test, are the contemporary monument to this way of thinking. In direct response to these entrenched perspectives, cognitivists argue that individuals do not just react to or perform in the world; they possess minds, and these minds contain mental representations—images, schemes, pictures, frames, languages, ideas, and the like. Some of the mental representations that individuals are born with or form at an early age prove enduring, but many other representations are created, transformed, or dissolved over time as the result of experiences and reflections upon those experiences. The mind, like a computer, processes and transforms information, and it is vital to understand the nature of this computing machinery—or, perhaps more aptly, these types of computing machinery. . . . [T]wo central ideas in the cognitivist's arsenal do have important implications for education.

First of all, the mind is not comprised of a single representation or even a single language of representations. Rather, all individuals harbor numerous internal representations in their minds/brains. Some scholars speak of "modules of mind," some of a "society of mind." In our own work, we speak of the possession of multiple intelligences, which span the range from linguistic and logical intelligences (the usual foci of school work) to musical, naturalist, and personal intelligences. www.

According to multiple intelligences theory, not only do all individuals possess numerous mental representations and intellectual languages, but individuals also differ from one another in the forms of these representations, their relative strengths, and the ways in which (and ease with which) these representations can be changed. There are at least eight discrete intelligences, and these intelligences constitute the ways in which individuals take in information, retain and manipulate that information, and demonstrate their understandings (and misunderstandings) to themselves and others. For example, in their understanding of the American Civil War, some individuals would favor a linguistic or narrative approach; others can be most easily reached through an artistic depiction; and still others might resonate to the personal dimension—how an internecine struggle affects neighbors and relatives and even generates ambivalence within one's own self. While most individuals can use and appreciate these different perspectives and intelligences, over time each of us constructs our own amalgam of intelligences. Surprisingly (and counter to the claims of classical intelligence theory), strength or weakness in one area does not predict strength or weakness in other areas. And it is here that we encounter a seminal educational enigma.

Until now, most schools all over the world have been selection devices. These institutions have honored a certain kind of mind—ideally, one that combines language and logic—and tried to select individuals who excel in these forms. In most schools individuals who favor other mental representations have received little honor.

The cognitivist's acknowledgment of different kinds of minds opens up enormous educational opportunities. If individuals do differ from one another and if we want to reach as many of them as possible, it makes little sense to treat everyone in a one-size-fits-all manner. Rather, we need to understand the specific minds involved in an educational encounter; and insofar as possible, we should base our education, including choices of technology, on that knowledge. And so, whether the course be history or physics or dance, we should try to teach individuals in ways that are consonant with, or that stretch, their current mental representations. Equally, we should give individuals the opportunity to exhibit their understandings by means of media and representations that make sense to them.

A second, quite surprising finding from cognitive research is that many early representations are extremely powerful and prove very difficult to change. It is as if, in the first years of life, the mind/brain becomes engraved with a certain scheme or frame by which it apprehends parts of experience. Often this scheme is seen as inadequate, and so educators inside and outside of school seek to transform the initial engraving. They may well feel that they have been successful in bringing about this transformation because the student has acquired more information, especially more facts. Yet, in a majority of cases, even good students at good schools do not really alter their representations. Indeed, when students are examined outside the scholastic context, they often give the same answers as students who have not even studied the subject matter or discipline in question. It is as if school consists of layers of powder that obscure rather than alter the initial engraving; and once that powder has blown away, the original representations have changed very little. . . .

Traditionally, American history curricula include the battle fought at Sharpsburg, Maryland, on September 17, 1862, on account of its military and political significance. (Revealing the still charged nature of the encounter, even today northerners call this battle Antietam, while to southerners it remains the battle of Sharpsburg.) . . . Most textbooks present this material in such straightforward form. They may well provide an illustration or two. They generally convey the impression that there is a single, authoritative view of the battle, and, depending upon the background of the authors, often relate the battle from the perspective of either the North or the South. Assessments generally ask students to give back this information in factual form. Such a style of presentation and assessment is particularly appropriate for individuals who favor linguistic modes of learning. And such presentations rarely challenge the widespread assumption among students that there is a single objective account of a battle and that the Civil War featured a battle between Right and Wrong.

The CD-ROM *Antietam/Sharpsburg* uses accounts and representations from eyewitnesses to tell the story of the battle and offers a close-up view of the physical site and artifacts. Carefully selected primary source material in a variety of media highlights the idea that our knowledge of this battle comes from the representations left us by observers who encoded their impressions in specific symbolic forms, such as the written journalism of the time, photographs, drawings, and telegraph and signal reports.

Different observers saw particular aspects of the battle. George W. Smalley, correspondent for the *New York Tribune,* started the day near a cornfield where the fighting started and then moved on to several other sites, including General McClellan's headquarters. Felix Gregory de Fountaine, the correspondent for the *Charleston Courier,* identified his position as "upon the centre" where he could see little or nothing of the fight upon the left. . . . No single observer could see the whole battle and tell us the comprehensive story or give us one authoritative interpretation of what happened.

The idea that there exists a singular perspective is surprisingly hard to change. In fact, too often the seductive idea that there is a "right" view leads students to readily embrace the perspective of any perceived authority—teacher, textbook, or "expert"—instead of realizing that students themselves need to weigh the evidence, evaluate sources, and come up with interpretations and justifications. In [the CD] *Antietam/Sharpsburg,* an emphasis on multiple observers counters head-on the idea that there is a single interpretation and one "right" dramatic narrative.

Source: The American Prospect Online, 7 (29), November–December, 1996.

A Closer Look at the Issues

1. What does Gardner say are the advances that cognitive science has made in educators' and researchers' understanding of how children learn?
2. Gardner uses the example of a CD-ROM about a Civil War battle to describe the benefits of multimedia

learning. How might a multimedia CD-ROM help children who are stronger in non-linguistic and non-logical-mathematical intelligences understand subject matter?

3. How does this passage reinforce the idea expressed in this chapter that new technologies may be changing not only the way children learn but also the traditional roles of teacher and student?

Skills and Other Dilemmas of a Progressive Black Educator

BY LISA DELPIT

Why do the refrains of progressive educational movements seem lacking in the diverse harmonies, the variegated rhythms, and the shades of tone expected in a truly heterogeneous chorus? Why do we hear so little representation from the multicultural voices which comprise the present-day American educational scene? These questions have surfaced anew as I begin my third year of university "professoring" after having graduated from a prestigious university known for its progressive school of education. My family back in Louisiana is very proud about all of that, but still they find me rather tedious. They say things like, "She just got here so she's locked up in that room with a bunch of papers talking about she's gotta finish some article. I don't know why she bothers to come home." Or, "I didn't ask you about what any research said, what do you think?!"

I once shared my family's skepticism of academia. I remember asking myself in the first few months of my graduate school career, "Why is it these theories never seem to be talking about me?" But by graduation time many of my fellow minority students and I had become well trained: we had learned alternate ways of viewing the world, coaxed memories of life in our communities into forms which fit into the categories created by academic researchers and theoreticians, and internalized belief systems that often belied our own experiences.

I learned a lot in graduate school. For one thing I learned that people acquire a new dialect most effectively through interaction with speakers of that dialect, not through being constantly corrected. Of course, when I was growing up, my mother and my teachers in the pre-integration, poor black Catholic school that I attended corrected every other word I uttered in their effort to coerce my Black English into sometimes Hypercorrect Standard English forms acceptable to black nuns in Catholic schools. Yet, I learned to speak and write in Standard English.

I also learned in graduate school that people learn to write not by being taught "skills" and grammar, but by "writing in meaningful contexts." In elementary school I diagrammed thousands of sentences, filled in tens of thousands of blanks, and never wrote any text longer than two sentences until I was in the tenth grade of high school. I have been told by my professors that I am a good writer. (One, when told about my poor community and segregated, skill-based schooling, even went so far as to say, "How did you ever learn how to write?") By that time I had begun to wonder myself. Never mind that I had learned—and learned well—despite my professors' scathing retroactive assessment of my early education. . . .

Determined to use all that I had learned to benefit black children I abandoned the cornfields of Ohio, and relocated to an alternative inner-city school in Philadelphia to student-teach. Located on the border between two communities, our "open-classroom" school deliberately maintained a population of 60 percent poor black kids from "South Philly," and 40 percent well-to-do white kids from "Society Hill." The black kids went to school there because it was their only neighborhood school. The white kids went to school there because their parents had learned the same kinds of things I had learned about education. As a matter of fact, there was a waiting list of white children to get into the school. This was unique in Philadelphia—a predominantly black school with a waiting list of white children. There was no such waiting list of black children.

I apprenticed under a gifted young kindergarten teacher. She had learned the same things that I had learned, so our pairing was most opportune. When I finished my student teaching, the principal asked me to stay on in a full-time position.

The ethos of that school was fascinating. I was one of only a few black teachers, and the other black teachers were mostly older and mostly "traditional." They had not learned the kinds of things I had learned, and the young white teachers sometimes expressed in subtle ways that they thought these teachers were—how to say it—somewhat "repressive." At the very least they were "not structuring learning environments in ways that allowed the children's intellect to flourish": they focused on "skills," they made students sit down at desks, they made students practice handwriting, they corrected oral and written grammar. The subtle, unstated message was, "They just don't realize how smart these kids are."

I was an exception to the other black teachers. I socialized with the young white teachers and planned shared classroom experiences with them. I also taught as they did. Many people told me I was a good teacher: I had an open classroom; I had learning stations; I had children write books and stories to share; I provided games and used weaving to teach math and fine motor skills. I threw out all the desks and added carpeted open learning areas. I was doing what I had learned, and it worked. Well, at least it worked for some of the children.

My white students zoomed ahead. They worked hard at the learning stations. They did amazing things with books and writing. My black students played the games; they learned how to weave; and they threw the books around the learning stations. They practiced karate moves on the new carpets. Some of them even learned how to read, but none of them as quickly as my white students. I was doing the same thing for all my kids—what was the problem?

I taught in Philadelphia for six years. Each year my teaching became less like my young white friends' and more like the other black women's who taught at the school. My students practiced handwriting; I wrote on the board; I got some tables to replace some of the thrown-out desks. Each year my teaching moved farther away from what I had learned, even though in many ways I still identified as an open classroom teacher. As my classroom became more "traditional," however, it seemed that my black students steadily improved in their reading and writing. But they still lagged behind. It hurt that I was moving away from what I had learned. It hurt even more that although my colleagues called me a good teacher, I still felt that I had failed in the task that was most important to me—teaching black children and teaching them well. I could not talk about my failure then. It is difficult even now. At least I did not fall into the trap of talking about the parents' failures. I just did not talk about any of it.

In 1977 I left Philadelphia. . . . In graduate school I learned about many more elements of progressive education. It was great. I learned new "holistic" teaching techniques—integrating reading and writing, focusing on meaning rather than form. One of the most popular elements . . . was the writing process approach to literacy. I spent a lot of time with writing process people. I learned the lingo. I focused energy on "fluency" and not on "correctness." I learned that a focus on "kills" would stifle my students' writing. I learned about "fast-writes" and "golden lines" and group process. I went out into the world as a professor of literacy armed with the very latest, research-based and field-tested teaching methods. . . .

But then I returned to Philadelphia for a conference. I looked up one of my old friends, another black woman who was also a teacher. Cathy invited me to dinner. [She] began talking about the local writing project based, like those in many other areas, on the process approach to writing made popular by the Bay Area Writing Project. She adamantly insisted that it was doing a monumental disservice to black children. I was stunned. I started to defend the program, but then thought better of it, and asked her why she felt so negative about what she had seen.

She had a lot to say. She was particularly adamant about the notion that black children had to learn to be "fluent" in writing—had to feel comfortable about putting pen to paper—before they could be expected to conform to any conventional standards. "These people keep pushing this fluency thing," said Cathy. "What do they think? Our children have no fluency? If they think that, they ought to read some of the rap songs my students write all the time. They might not be writing their school assignments but they sure are writing. Our kids are fluent. What they need are the skills that will get them into college. I've got a kid right now—brilliant. But he can't get a score on the SAT that will even get him considered by any halfway decent college. He needs skills, not *fluency.* This is just another one of those racist ploys to keep our kids out. White kids learn how to write a decent sentence. Even if they don't teach them in school, their parents make sure they get what they need. But what about our kids? They don't get it at home and they spend all their time in school learning to be *fluent.* I'm sick of this liberal nonsense."

I returned to my temporary abode, but found that I had so much to think about that I could not sleep. . . . The next day at the conference I made it my business to talk to some of the people from around the country who were involved in writing process projects. I asked the awkward question about the extent of minority teacher involvement in these endeavors. The most positive answer I received was that writing process projects initially attracted a few black or minority teachers, but they soon dropped out of the program. None came back a second year. One thoughtful woman told me she had talked to some of the black teachers about their noninvolvement. She was pained about their response and still could not understand it. They said the whole thing was racist, that the meetings were racist, and that the method itself was racist. They were not able to be specific, she added, but just felt they, and their ideas, were excluded. . . .

In puzzling over these issues, it has begun to dawn on me that many of the teachers of black children have their roots in other communities and do not often have the opportunity to hear the full range of their students' voices. I wonder how many of Philadelphia's teachers know that their black students are prolific and "fluent" writers of rap songs. I wonder how many teachers realize the verbal creativity and fluency black kids express every day on the playgrounds of America as they devise new insults, new rope-jumping chants and new cheers. Even if they did hear them, would they relate them to language fluency? Maybe, just maybe, these writing process teachers are so adamant about developing fluency because they have not really had the opportunity to realize the fluency the kids already possess. They hear only silence, they see only immobile pencils. And maybe the black teachers are so adamant against what they understand to be the writing process approach because they hear their students' voices and see their fluency clearly. They are anxious to move to the next step, the step vital to success in America—the appropriation of the oral and written forms demanded by the mainstream. And they want it to happen quickly. They see no time to waste developing the "fluency" they believe their children already possess. Yes, they are eager to teach "skills." . . .

Progressive white teachers seem to say to their black students, "Let me help you find your voice. I promise not to criticize one note as you search for your own song." But the black teachers say, "I've heard your song loud and clear. Now, I want to teach you to harmonize with the rest of the world." Their insistence on skills is not a negation of their students' intellect, as is often suggested by progressive forces, but an acknowledgment of it: "You know a lot; you can learn more. Do It Now!"

I run a great risk in writing this—the risk that my purpose will be misunderstood; the risk that those who subject black and other minority children to day after day of isolated, meaningless, drilled "subskills" will think themselves vindicated. That is not the point. Were this another paper I would explain what I mean by "skills"—useful and usable knowledge which contributes to a student's ability to communicate effectively in standard, generally acceptable literary forms. And I would explain that I believe that skills are best taught through meaningful communication, best learned in meaningful contexts. I would further explain that skills are a necessary but insufficient aspect of black and minority students' education. Students need technical skills to open doors, but they need to be able to think critically and creatively to participate in meaningful and potentially liberating work inside those doors. Let there be no doubt: a "skilled" minority person who is not also capable of critical analysis becomes the trainable, low-level functionary of the dominant society, simply the grease that keeps the institutions which orchestrate his or her oppression running smoothly. On the other hand, a critical thinker who lacks the "skills" demanded by employers and institutions of higher learning can aspire to financial and social status only within the disenfranchised underworld. Yes, if minority people are to effect the change which will allow them to truly progress we must insist on "skills" *within the context* of critical and creative thinking. . . .

It is time to look closely at elements of our educational system, particularly those elements we consider progressive; time to see whether there is minority involvement and support, and if not, to ask why; time to reassess what we are doing in public schools and universities to include other voices, other experiences; time to seek the diversity in our educational movements that we talk about seeking in our classrooms. I would advocate that university researchers, school districts, and teachers try to understand the views of the minority colleagues and constituents. The key is to understand the variety of meanings available for any human interaction, and not to assume that the voices of the majority speak for all.

Source: Harvard Educational Review, 56(4), 1986, pp. 379–385.

A Closer Look at the Issues

1. Delpit's article seems to address the "fine line" teachers walk between sensitivity to cultural and linguistic differences and advocacy of uniform standards for all students. How does she resolve this apparent dilemma?
2. Teachers are often influenced by their own experience at home and at school. Describe how Lisa Delpit's "educational biography" influenced the development of her beliefs about teaching.

3. Teachers are influenced by their colleagues in the culture of the particular school they work in. Consider the ways in which Delpit's account of her own struggle with finding a way to teach her African American children effectively speaks of a certain kind of courage.

REFERENCES

Abramson, H. (2001). Studying the Talmud: 400 repetitions of the divine voice. *Thought & Action: The NEA Journal* XVII(1), Summer, pp. 9–18.

Abu-Nader, J. (1993). Meeting the needs of multicultural classrooms: Family values and the motivation of minority students. In M. J. O'Hair and S. J. Odell, (eds.) *Diversity and teaching: Teacher education yearbook I.* Orlando, FL: Harcourt Brace.

Bandura, A. (1977). *Social learning theory.* Englewood Cliffs, NJ: Prentice Hall.

Belenky, M. F., B. M. Clinchy, N. R. Goldberger, and J. M. Tarule, (1997). *Women's ways of knowing: The development of self, voice and mind,* 10th ed. New York: Basic Books.

Bruner, J. (1990). *Acts of meaning.* Cambridge, MA: Harvard University Press.

Cheney, L. (1997). Creative math, or just "fuzzy math"?: Once again, basic skills fall prey to a fad. *The New York Times,* August 11, p. A15.

Delpit, L. (1986). Skills and other dilemmas of a progressive black educator. *Harvard Educational Review,* 56 (4), pp. 379–385.

Dewey, J. (1938) *Experience and education.* New York: Macmillan.

Duckworth, E. (1987). *The having of wonderful ideas and other essays on teaching and learning.* New York: Teachers College Press.

Dunn, R., K. Dunn, and J. Perrin (1994). *Teaching young children through their individual learning styles.* Boston: Allyn & Bacon.

Ellwood, C. (1995). Preparing teachers for education in a diverse world. In Levine, D. ed. *Rethinking schools: An Agenda for change.* New York: New Press.

Fosnot, C. (1996). Constructivism: A psychological theory of learning. In Fosnot (ed.), *Constructivism: Theory, perspectives, and practice.* New York: Teachers College Press.

Friedman, L., F. Andrews, J. Stempel, A. Jehlen, C. Jackson, T. Erickson, V. Reilley, and M. Cheung (1997). Mathematics: What's the big idea? (videotape). South Burlington, VT: Annenberg/CPB Math & Science Collection.

Gagne, R. (1985). *The conditions of learning,* 4th ed. New York: Holt, Rinehart & Winston.

Gagne, R., L. Briggs, and W. Wager (1992). *Principles of instructional design,* 4th ed. Fort Worth, TX: HBJ College Publishers.

Gardner, H. (1983). *Frames of mind: The theory of multiple intelligences.* New York: HarperCollins.

Gardner, H. (1996). Multimedia and multiple intelligences. *The American Prospect Online,* 7 (29), November–December, http://www.prospect.org/print-friendlyprint/V7/29/veenema-s.html. Accessed May 3, 2004.

Gardner, H. (1999). *The disciplined mind: Beyond facts and standardized tests, the K–12 education that every child deserves.* New York: Simon & Schuster.

Gordon, R., L. Della, Piana, and T. Keleher (2000). *Facing the consequences: An examination of racial discrimination in U.S. public schools.* Berkeley, CA: Applied Research Center.

Goss, L., and M. E. Barnes (1989). *Talk that talk: An anthology of African-American storytelling.* New York: Simon & Schuster.

Gregorc, A. (1985). *Inside styles: Beyond the basics.* Columbia, CT: Gregorc Associates.

Hale, J. E. (1986). *Black children: Their roots, culture and learning styles.* Baltimore: John Hopkins University.

Hale, J. E. (2001). *Learning while black: Creating educational excellence for African American children.* Baltimore, MD: Johns Hopkins University Press.

Heath, S. B. (1982). Questioning at school and at home: A comparative study. In G. D. Spindler, ed. *Doing the ethnology of schooling: Educational anthropology in action.* New York: Holt, Rinehart & Winston.

Jung, C. G. (1921). *Psychological types.* Revision by Hull, R. F. C. (1976), Princeton, NJ: Princeton University Press.

Kolb, D. and R. Fry (1975). Towards an applied theory of experiential learning. In C. Cooper, *Theories of Group Processes.* London: John Wiley & Sons.

Ong, W. (1982). *Orality and literacy: The terminologizing* of the world. London: Methuen.

Papert, S., and G. Caperton (1999). Vision for education: The Caperton-Papert platform. Paper presented at the 91st annual National Governors' Association Meeting, August, St. Louis.

Phillips, S. U. (1983). *The invisible culture: Communication in classroom and community on the Warm Springs Indian Reservation.* New York: Longman.

Piaget, J. (1952). *The origins of intelligence in children.* (M. Cook, trans.) New York: W. W. Norton).

Sevener, D. (1997). How we've made our classrooms teacher proof. *Illinois Issues,* 23 (4), pp. 18–23.

Smith, M. K. (2001). David A. Kolb on experiential learning. *The encyclopedia of informal education,* http://www.infed.org/b-explrn.htm.

Starr, L. (2000). Is technology just for boys? *Education World.* http://www.educationworld.com/a_issues/chat/chat017/shtml. Retrieved August 20, 2004.

Turkle, S. (2001). *Tech savvy: Educating girls in the new computer age.* Washington, DC: American Association of University Women.

Ulich, R., ed. (1954). *Three thousand years of educational wisdom.* Cambridge, MA: Harvard University Press.

Vygotsky, L. S. (1978). *Mind in society: The development of higher psychological processes.* Cambridge, MA: Harvard University Press.

Witkin, H., C. Moore, D. Goodenough, and P. Cox (1977). Field-dependent and field-independent cognitive styles and their educational implications. *Review of Educational Research* 47(1), pp. 1–64. Witkin, H. A., and D. R. Goodenough, (1981). *Cognitive styles: Essence and origins.* New York: International University Press.

Zuga, K. F. (1999). Addressing women's ways of knowing to improve the technology education environment for all students. *Journal of Technology Education,* 10 (2), Spring. http://scholar.lib.vt.edu/ejournals/JTE/v10n2/zuga.html. Retrieved August 20, 2004.

6 The Nature of the Teaching Profession

ESSENTIAL QUESTION

What is good teaching?

I remember my favorite teacher quite clearly—Miss La Valley, my second grade teacher in a rural primary school in Vermont. I have such a vivid image of her. I can describe today what she looked like and what she always wore. She had a bubbling personality and was so enthusiastic about teaching that she made school fun. She managed to engage twenty-five lively children in hands-on projects for every subject she taught. A talented artist, she convinced me to believe I could be one as well. One art project I made in her class was a burlap wall hanging that I gave to my grandmother. Years later when my grandmother passed away, my mother found it saved among her cherished belongings. Now, it hangs as a family heirloom in my parents' home. While I am not a professional artist today, Miss La Valley gave me confidence in myself and encouraged me to share my accomplishments with others (Jay Eaton, Physical Educator and Trainer). ■

How Is Good Teaching Defined?

Why do you think Miss La Valley is remembered? What qualities of good teaching do you think this reminiscence portrays? To define good teaching, it is helpful to reflect on the teachers you have had. Think of those whose influence had a positive impact on your life. What difference did these professionals make in your life? What special qualities did these teachers have? David Shribman, a Pulitzer Prize winner, wrote a book about the memories of teachers who taught him to "think, to create, to dream" (2001). His book, *I Remember My Teacher,* is a compilation of 365 reminiscences of his own and those of people from all parts of the United States and Canada. Central to each person's story is a teacher or teachers who enriched their lives. Some of the memorable teachers were those at the beginning of the educational process in kindergarten, others in middle or high school, while some teachers were professors in undergraduate or graduate study. Such memories are a good place to start to answer the question, What is good teaching? Historical reflections of the ever-changing images of the teacher lend shape and substance to the definition of good teaching.

> I remember Mrs. Nowlin, my twelfth grade English teacher in San Antonio. She took me under her wing as a writer. She said one thing I always remember: Write what is in your heart. Lisa Cruz, publicist, San Marcos, Texas. (Shribman, 2001, p. 126).

Who Were the Good Teachers Throughout History?

Teaching as a profession has a long and impressive history. The images of the teacher change and differ according to time, place, and culture. In some ways, teaching is universal. However, the political, social, economic, and cultural factors provide variables in the role of the teacher in the educational process. A virtual trip back in time through a study of the images of teachers and the art, science, and craft of their profession lends an in-depth appreciation of the qualities required for good teaching, sheds light on the legacy of past practitioners, and identifies the challenges of today and tomorrow. In recent years, storytelling, memoirs, and personal narratives have been recognized as powerful resources for educational research. Mary Jalongo and Joan Isenberg (1995) have researched the value of using teachers' stories as an effective technique to structure theories of teaching. They found that teachers' stories provide opportunities for reflection on good practices, lend insights into the teaching/learning process, and document the development of the profession. As professionals and researchers, they examine individual teacher's stories to define and understand the dynamics of teaching. They contend that such narratives present multiple perspectives of teaching, shared values in the profession, and belief systems that serve as foundations to education. In light of their findings, we use teachers' stories to address the question, What is good teaching?

The following profiles of teachers include educators whose contributions to the profession had an impact on shaping the profession. While some are famous, others have not been given the customary recognition in traditional historical reviews of education. They are the educators that people have remembered for their dedication to the profession and their skillful teaching. The lesser-known educators' stories are told in this chapter to render a more personalized portrayal of the profession and to give tribute to the unsung heroes of teaching. For example, Louise Butterfield represents the spirit of teaching during the mid-twentieth century, while Donna Graham Harris models today's teacher who is creating a pathway by using technology in the twenty-first–century classroom.

You might add to our profiles the images of teachers that flash through your mind when you think of good teaching. You can add to our list candidates that you feel represent the good teachers in history. While reading the profiles consider the following questions:

- How do these teachers view teaching?
- How do they answer the call to teach?
- How did they change the profession?
- What qualities do they add to the definition of good teaching?

Greece

A kaleidoscope view of teaching over the centuries launches the journey that begins with Greek educators: namely, Socrates; his student, Plato; and Plato's student, Aristotle; all of Athenian fame. The Greeks reflected Middle Eastern, African, and Asian thought and preserved the combined heritage through the writings of their teachers. They borrowed from ancient Egypt its professional education of the military, engineering, medicine, the priesthood, and the scribe. Like Confucius, they held virtue and morality as aims of education. The Jews, whose laws grew out of their belief in monotheism as "the fundamental motivation for learning" (Power, 1970, p. 25) gave education a spiritual dimension; but the Greeks—particularly the Athenians—valued philosophy over religion and reason over mysticism (Power, 1970, p. 43). They pursued the study of the natural order with a "belief that one could reason one's way to the truth" (Reed and Johnson, 2000, p. 4).

Socrates Socrates (470–399 BCE), a teacher who gained fame through the writings of his students, notably Plato, is a role model not only for his "Socratic method," but for the notion of "academic freedom." Socrates used his method, a series of dialogues and probing questions, to find solutions to problems, inquire into the nature of things, and seek truths. He began his quest with a sense of his own limitations and liabilities. He is known for the proverb, "know thyself," which calls for a reflective life and an acknowledgement of what you know and do not know. Socrates is a model of good teaching in his pursuit of truth through inquiry, his engagement of students in the pursuit, and his personal courage to defend the freedoms to do so. When the Athenian city-state gave Socrates the option to retract his teaching or be executed, Socrates became a martyr for academic freedom, "not because of what he taught but because he refused to acknowledge the right of his accusers to dictate to him" (Power, 1970, p. 87).

Plato Plato (427–347 BCE), the student of Socrates, not only immortalized his teacher, but continued the tradition of the dialogue method and documented his teacher's and his own philosophy in his writings (see Idealism section in Chapter 2). Plato revered the world of ideas. He contended that education, rather than indoctrination, freed one to find the ideal virtues of temperance, courage, wisdom, and justice. Many of Plato's innovations have a contemporary ring. Contemporary character education programs still ask the questions Plato posed in his quest for the "just society." These programs attempt to replicate his teaching strategies for developing a moral dimension to the educational process. Plato wanted his students to use reason and knowledge for their pursuit of truth, not to be told what to believe. Plato's use of dialogue and questioning as techniques that provoke students to probe for answers rather than accept dictated solutions inspires today's teachers to avoid indoctrination, teaching with a prescribed point of view, as a substitution for learning.

Counter to Athenian tradition, Plato's Academy was open to women, emphasized the importance of mathematics and philosophy in the pursuit of knowledge with his "scientific humanism," and encouraged students to be responsible for their own learning (Power, 1969). In his work, *The Laws,* he raised early childhood education to prominence, with the prescription for each community to provide a sanctuary for children, beginning at age three. He has been credited with the maxim, "as the twig is bent so grows the tree" which is today's justification for early learning programs. But in Plato's early learning schemes no fantasy tales for young children were permitted, so as not to distort the pursuit of truth.

Aristotle Aristotle (384–322 BCE), Plato's student, expanded his teacher's theory of the idea as central to knowledge by noting that ideas originate in reality. For Aristotle, all knowledge comes first from the senses (see Realism section in Chapter 2). He, too, established a school, the Lyceum, where he developed a systematic study of logic through the use of the **syllogism,** a deductive form of argument based on logic. His major contribution is his "rational, systematic method for testing the logic of statements people make" through the use of a syllogism (Sadovnik, Cookson, and Semel, 2001, p. 185). The syllogism became the foundation in the Middle Ages for "scholastic philosophy"—also known as Thomism, due to St. Thomas Aquinas's adaptation of Aristotelian thought for the defense of Christian religious teaching.

The Sophists Not all of the Greek teachers pursued truth; some taught for money. Known as the Sophists, these teachers were looked upon with disdain by the likes of Socrates, Plato, and Aristotle, because they had little concern about the moral pursuit of their teaching. They taught what was practical or what people wanted to learn. They sold their knowledge and marketed themselves. In many ways, they were the precursors of today's capitalism.

Some historians feel that they have been unfairly judged, as many of the Sophists were sincere in their profession. Their legacy is evident in today's advertisements for schooling, tutoring services, and programs that promise guaranteed results for whatever the consumer demands.

Rome

Early Roman schooling was very practical, with its chief aim being the preparation for citizenship. As the Roman Empire grew, Greek influences in education became paramount, especially in teaching Greek language and literature as a foundation for Latin studies. But, citizenship remained a major theme in Roman education throughout its history. The **oratorical arts,** the ability to not only write well but to speak persuasively, were the mark of the educated person. Knowledge of Rome's famed writers—Virgil, Horace, and Cicero—was required in the education of the ruling class. Students preparing for positions of leadership in the Roman senate had to practice the art and craft of oratory. The Roman senator was required to deliver convincing speeches to his constituents, not unlike today's political leaders who try to convey their messages through the media as well as in political chambers. Only males were schooled to be such statesmen, with a curriculum that emphasized the importance of history along with the necessity of rhetoric—the art of persuasive public speaking. A definitive work for this curriculum, written by Marcus Fabius Quintilianus (known as Quintilian), was the twelve-volume *Institutio Oratoria (The Education of the Orator).*

Quintilian Quintilian (35–97 CE) was a Roman educator, whose twelve-volume work, *The Educator of the Orator,* sanctions the importance of early learning. For Quintilian, "relearning is more difficult than learning," so he endorsed the policy of beginning language instruction as soon as possible. In this policy he indirectly supported the education of women, who as nurses and mothers were the teachers of young children, by acknowledging the importance of their work. Yet he did not provide the necessary education for women in his scheme for early learning programs (Power, 1970, p. 183). Though Quintilian makes no mention of intentional education for women, he was quite progressive in his tenets for the education of males. Many of his recommendations have a contemporary tone, as he promoted humane approaches to discipline, a ban on corporal punishment, teaching practices framed by theory, support for literacy as the key component of a basic education, and the requirement that character education be modeled rather than preached by the teacher (Power, 1970).

Europe

As Europe and its nation-states emerged, much of the Greek and Roman legacy had been preserved in remote Christian monasteries or revived with the development of universities in such places as Paris, Bologna, and Montpellier. One early Christian educator of note is the Venerable Bede (673–735), who is credited as "the man who rekindled the flame of liberal learning on the Continent of Europe" (Power, 1970, p. 274). He is honored in his native Britain for translating Latin Biblical stories into English and devising an early precursor to the basal reader in his texts of reading selections with controlled vocabularies. The medieval university produced many fine scholars, such as Peter Abelard (1079–1142), who valued reason in the pursuit of truth, and Thomas Aquinas (1225–1274) who developed the philosophical system of scholasticism (see Chapter 2). The Renaissance brought classical humanism, through the efforts of Desiderius Erasmus (1466–1536) and Juan Luis Vives (1492–1540), who wrote on the value of education for women. The realism of modern education has many precedents in European educators such as Wolfgang Ratke (1571–1635), who attempted to structure a natural method for learning in his principles for teaching, and John Amos Comenius (1592–1670) who recognized the importance of visuals for teaching young children. Maria Montessori (1870–1952) introduced her scientific method for educating young children in Italy at the turn of the twentieth century. Her influence spread globally and her schools continue to flourish in the twenty-first century throughout the world.

The kindergartens of the nineteenth century were established for children from the ages of three to seven. The curriculum was play-based, with hands-on activities that were carefully delineated in Frederick Froebel's famous work, *The Education of Man,* and his lesser-known writing, *The Young Child.* Froebel devised a curriculum and a methodology that demanded an active role on the part of the teacher and the learner. Since the young child's self-activity is expressed in his play, play was the core of the child's development in the Froebelian design, and thus, the basis of his education (Swiniarski, 1976, p. 21).

"Play is the highest level of child development. It is the spontaneous expression of thought and feeling. An expression which his inner life requires. . . . It is the purest creation of the child's mind as it is also a pattern and copy of the natural life hidden in man and all things" (Froebel, 1967, p. 83).

Froebel's notion of play differs from previous uses of play as a motivational device for academic study, a reward for adequate completion of a task, or as an opportunity for physical exercise. For Froebel, play is the medium through which a child learns. (See Chapter 3.) During the early years of a child's life it is essential to learning. However, Froebel cautioned that play must be carefully prescribed in structured activities. Play is never left to the child's whim. Each play activity is to have a very specific objective that addresses varying levels of knowledge. He designed the materials and procedures for these activities, which he called *gifts and occupations.* The teacher's role is to select the appropriate activity by observing the child to determine his level of knowledge. Peabody fervently believed in Froebel's methodology**.** She replicated kindergartens throughout America to parallel the Froebelian model instituted in Prussia and implemented throughout Europe. She trained her teachers to be orthodox disciples of Froebel's teaching (Swiniarski, 1976).

Peabody's kindergartens were full-day options, with parenting programs that offered families a range of support and services. The role of the family was an important social doctrine in Froebelian kindergartens. Froebel did not wish to challenge the mother's role in the rearing of the young but to enhance it and strengthen the family base. Peabody took up his charge for parent education. She felt that "mothers had an instinct for educating the child, but that this instinct must be elevated into insight" (Peabody, 1894, p. 1). Parents needed a forum so Peabody sponsored Parents' Unions. *The Kindergarten Messenger,* a publication established by Peabody, was to be the voice of the Parents' Union with backing from the National Bureau of Education in Washington (Swiniarski, 1976).

> We have improvised this first number of our 'Kindergarten Messenger' with special reference to the Parents' Union that it has been proposed one should be formed in every neighborhood in the land, for the purpose of studying at their monthly meetings the Art and Science of Froebel's Nursery and Kindergarten (Peabody, 1873, p. 6).

Elizabeth Peabody's legacy lives on not only in early childhood education but also in the mission of today's full-service school. Her work on extending the walls of her kindergarten to include and involve families became common practice, particularly in neighborhoods with settlement houses—agencies for social and family services—throughout the country. She provided the foundation for today's **full-service schools,** which take responsibility for the total welfare of students, families, and community. She was a pioneer and role model for those who wish to further the cause of education of the young child.

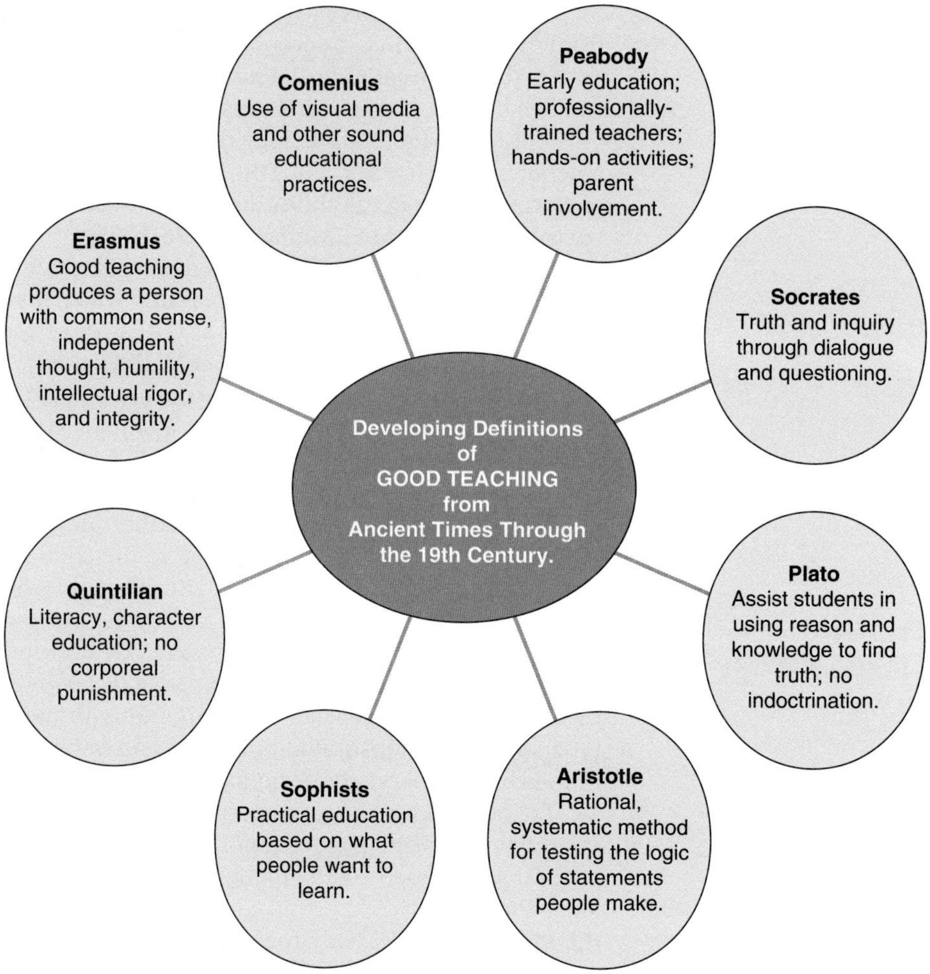

Figure 6.1

Developing Definitions of Good Teaching from Ancient Times Through the Nineteenth Century

Mary McLeod Bethune Born on a rice and cotton farm in Mayesville, South Carolina, Mary Jane McLeod (1875–1955) was the fifteenth of seventeen children, some of whom had been sold into slavery. Her parents, born slaves, had been able to buy their own land to farm and desperately wanted their children to be educated. When the Presbyterian Church opened a school for African American children, she walked the four miles back and forth to attend. An excellent student, she later attended Scotia Seminary in North Carolina and the Moody Bible Institute in Chicago on scholarship. When her original aim, to go to Africa as a missionary, was denied because of her race, she returned to the South to teach school and volunteer in the local prisons. Committed to educating African American girls, she opened the Daytona, Florida, Educational and Industrial Training School in 1904 with limited funds. Following the educational philosophy of the time, the curriculum was both academic and vocational: the girls learned the "home arts" of cooking and sewing, along with traditional subjects. The school grew to fourteen buildings and four hundred students and eventually included a working farm. In 1923 it merged with the male Cookman Institute in Jacksonville and became the coeducational Bethune-Cookman College. Mary McLeod Bethune's house still stands on the campus as a National Historic Landmark.

Bethune was an avid promoter of women's suffrage but she was frustrated by the domination of the movement by white women. Threatened by the local Ku Klux Klan, she nevertheless threw herself into the political cause, raising money to pay the poll tax and establishing evening classes to teach blacks to read well enough to pass the local literacy test, a voting requirement for blacks throughout the South. An excellent and vocal speaker, she was elected to the National Urban League's Executive Board and served as president of the National Association of Colored Women, the National Association of Teachers in Colored Schools, and the National Council of Negro Women. Presidents Coolidge and Hoover appointed her to their child welfare conferences. She was Franklin Roosevelt's Special Advisor on Minority Affairs from 1935 to 1944, a member of his "Black Cabinet," and a personal and professional friend of his wife Eleanor. Interested in the education and welfare of children all over the world, she helped design the charter for the United Nations. She received many honors for her contribution to African American education, women's welfare, and human rights, including honorary doctorates from both historically black and historically white colleges, and medals of honor from Haiti and Liberia. She is remembered also as a pioneer, a political activist, a consummate educator, and one of the outstanding women of her time.

Leonard Covello Leonard Covello (1887–1982) was a multicultural educator who was ahead of his time. Born in Avigliano, Italy, he emigrated with his family to New York City at the age of nine, where he attended schools designed to "Americanize" new immigrants. Covello dropped out of high school to help support his family, but later returned and graduated with honors. He attended Columbia University on full scholarship, and after graduating in 1911 he took a job as a French teacher at DeWitt Clinton High School. During World War I, he served as an interpreter in France, later returning to DeWitt Clinton, where he chaired the school's Italian department for several years.

Covello was a social activist as well as a teacher who was influenced by his own experience as an immigrant. He was sensitive to the conflict immigrant children faced trying to honor their family's heritage and, at the same time, separate themselves from their native culture and language in order to succeed in Anglo-dominated schools. To respond to that dilemma, Covello created Il Circolo Italiano at DeWitt Clinton, a club that promoted community service, recreational and cultural activities, and an Italian Parents Association, which extended a welcome to new families. He was appointed principal of the new Benjamin Franklin High School in East Harlem in 1934, and turned it into a community school, responding to the needs of the area's new Puerto Rican population. Franklin's Community Advisory Council, comprised of teachers, students, parents, and business and civic leaders, took on housing and sanitation issues, created social and educational centers, provided citizenship and adult education, and ran a summer school program. Its intercultural education program taught students to appreciate cultural diversity. In his retirement, Dr. Covello advised the Puerto Rican Department of Labor on literacy and citizenship education, community development, and cultural pride. His book, *The Heart Is the Teacher,* is still widely read. He is remembered for his commitment to cultural pluralism, his deep understanding of the importance of culture to learning, and his broad vision of the responsibility of schools to their larger communities.

Louise Hikel Butterfield Louise Hikel (1910–1988) was one of a family of nine children born to Syrian immigrant parents. The sons were given the opportunity to study at the University of Maine and the daughters could pursue professional training as a nurse or teacher. Louise became a teacher and a graduate of Gorham State Teachers College, a former normal school that is now the University of Southern Maine. She returned to her hometown as a credentialed junior high school teacher of language arts.

Although she is not as famous as the other educators profiled in this section, Louise Hikel Butterfield represents the spirit of the everyday teacher that Norman Rockwell portrayed in many of his depictions of American schools. In some ways, her story mirrors Dr. Covello's. As children of immigrant families, they both were educated in school systems that were not entirely welcoming of their cultural differences. Yet they each became teachers who created a climate in their classroom that embraced diversity and was inclusive of the wealth of heritage brought by all of their students.

Butterfield's rapport with her students could be compared to the teacher/student relationship captured by Norman Rockwell's illustration of "Miss Jones's Surprise Birthday"—a relationship of mutual trust and respect. Each day at the end of class, Louise would read favorite literary selections to her students to model her own love of reading. The readings bonded the class with their teacher and are fondly remembered by many of her students decades later.

Unlike Rockwell's Miss Jones, Butterfield eventually married, and because she had tenure and no children, she was allowed to continue teaching during America's Depression, World War II, and the postwar years. Most teachers of her era had to leave the profession, once married with children. For many teachers like Louise, her students were her children.

Butterfield spent her vacations in study to further her knowledge and improve her pedagogy. She modeled for her students and her community a professional demeanor, a moral code of behavior, and a commitment to academic scholarship. For her parents, Louise and her siblings epitomized the early-twentieth-century American immigrants' dream for their children to move into the professional class through education. She is remembered for her commitment to teaching and for being an exemplar of a true professional.

Jonathan Kozol, educator and author, continues to be a messenger of the problem of inequality in American schools.
Source: AP/Wide World Photos

Jonathan Kozol Jonathan Kozol (born 1936) is a teacher who left the profession to make his mark on education. As a young Harvard University graduate and recently returned Rhodes Scholar, Jonathan Kozol took a position as a substitute teacher in the Boston Public Schools during the early 1970s. Kozol was appalled by the conditions African American children faced in these de facto segregated schools. Despite the 1954 *Brown* vs. *the Board of Education* decision of the United States Supreme Court, school segregation—based on where the students lived—still existed decades later. In his first book, *Death at an Early Age* (1985), Kozol told the stories of racism in the public schools of the North. Now, as an acclaimed author of many books, he continues to be the messenger of inequality in American schools. While from time to time he has returned to the classroom to work with students at South Boston High School, he has continued to write prolifically about inequality in American schools. Kozol is a messenger with stories we might not want to hear, as one suburban high school English teacher wrote in her critique of *Amazing Grace.*

> Every once in a while, we hear about, watch, or read something, and we find it difficult to look at our world in the same way. Jonathan Kozol's book, *Amazing Grace,* is one of those books that forces its readers to face the realities of the world of the poor and underprivileged people and

> children of the South Bronx. It is a must read for all educators, Americans, and people of all ages and races (Kristina Shoulds).

Jonathan Kozol left the classroom to be an activist for just causes in education and a messenger whose stories might not be popular, but need to be told. He models for educators the critical role of the risk taker in advocating for equal education for all students. His major contribution to the image of teaching is that of the advocate. Many educational activists share similar concerns; they not only advocate for students whose voices are not heard, but put into practice the ideas Kozol endorses.

Pi 'ikea Miyamoto Another educational activist is Pi 'ikea Miyamoto, a native Japanese-Hawaiian special education science teacher at Castle High School, who developed an experiential environmental education program. The *Aloha 'Aina Program* connects her science curriculum to the restoration of the island, Kaho 'olawe, devastated by the bombing practices of the United States. She and her students formed work parties on the island to bring it back to life and in doing so the project brought pride and vision to her native students (de los Reyes and Gozemba, 2002, pp. 124–125).

Pi 'ikea Miyamoto exemplifies the tradition of Paulo Freire and other liberationists who base their teaching in the cultures of their students. She frees her students to use their own voice. She shares with them the authority for being responsible for their own learning experiences. Miyamoto's work with her special education classes on both the island and at her school has been cited as a "Pocket of Hope" in public education (de los Reyes and Gozemba, 2002). She models the ideals of the democratic school espoused by Michael Apple and James Beane (1995, p. 7) in her "concern for the dignity and rights of individuals and minorities." She instructs the students in native Hawaiian traditions to work with the land and preserve it for future generations. With her students she is reviving a native language and indigenous farming techniques out of respect for Hawaiian heritage.

> Miyamoto's students, who work their own farm at school as part of their Plants and Animals of Hawai'i special education science class, understand . . . the importance of taking care of the land so that it will take care of them. Their taro lo 'I (irrigated terraces) produce the staple crop of poi (pounded tar corns), marking both a political return to the culture's roots and healthy native diet. Their connection to nature is alive and ongoing: it is their love for the land—aloha 'aina.
>
> Her classroom and farm have become spaces where students participate with their teacher in shaping an ohana—an extended family that is there for them even when the school day ends . . . safe places they consider their own. A student carved a sign for the classroom that says simply "Our Place" (de los Reyes and Gozemba, 2002, pp. 122, 124).

Pi 'ikea Miyamoto honors her students' culture and dignifies their contribution to Hawai'i's past, present, and future.

Donna Graham Harris "Will the computer replace the teacher?" ask many educational critics. "NO!" replies Dr. Donna Graham Harris (born 1949), the 1995 Washington, D.C., Teacher of the Year Award recipient, (former) school administrator, and technology specialist in Washington's public schools. A graduate of the

University of Maryland, Howard University, and Catholic University, Donna Graham Harris furthers her education by keeping abreast of the constant changes in technology to advance her teaching and affect the maximum learning from her students. She would agree with Seymour Papert, of MIT, who developed the LOGO language, that a computer is a tool of instruction rather than a replacement for an instructor. She embraces Papert's goal of having a computer available for each child, much as pencils are supplied for every student (Papert, 1993). Dr. Harris used the platforms available to her during the award ceremony at the White House, as well as presentations, speaking engagements, and conference papers given across the United States, to promote equity access to technology for inner-city students (Swiniarski and Breitborde, 2003). She teaches and preaches the effective use of computers in the classroom and the need for educators to be computer literate and up-to-date with the recent technologies.

Through her teaching she models how technology can contribute to good teaching practices, while she shares her expertise in the field and her enthusiasm for the potential of technology. Since many students in her middle school do not have computers in their homes, she is an articulate advocate for computer competency and equal access for all children. Building on Seymour Papert's analogy of computers as modern-day pencils, she collects pencils—old and new and from near and far—as symbols of her cause that computers are tools to be used for teaching and learning in the twenty-first century. Dr. Harris believes that computers are changing—and will continue to change—the teaching process, but that they will not replace the professional whose skills and knowledge base determines their effective use.

Parker Palmer Parker Palmer, a contemporary teacher's teacher, gives permission to teachers to be themselves. As a senior advisor of the Fetzer Institute, he founded the Teacher Formation Program for K–12 teachers to assist them in personalizing their renewal as professionals. He is also a senior associate of the American Association for Higher Education. A prolific writer and speaker on the theme of teacher formation, Parker Palmer travels extensively from his Madison, Wisconsin, home giving workshops that encourage teachers to teach from their hearts, to teach what they believe, and to create a sense of community in their schools. His seminal work, *The Courage to Teach,* speaks to the spirit of teaching. Palmer revisits the notion of teaching as a vocation, a calling. For Palmer the calling comes from within, not "from a voice external to ourselves, a voice of moral demand that asks us to become someone we are not yet—someone different, someone better, someone just beyond our reach" (Palmer, 2001, p. 1). The teaching process involves the teacher, the student, and the subject matter. Through the subject matter, the teacher and student come together in the learning process . (1998, p. 102). The subject, that to be known, cannot be separated from the learner, the "knower"; otherwise, teaching falls victim to the "inert ideas" (1998, p. 52). Palmer admonished teachers not to succumb to the "culture of fear" (the anxieties, sense of failure, and rejection that riddle the classroom) and to avoid the "broken paradoxes" that separate "head from heart," "fact from feelings," "theory from practice," and "teaching from learning" (1998, p. 66). For him, good teaching requires a belief in oneself, reflection, and courage. Teaching is a spiritual endeavor. Teaching involves community building; "to teach is to create a space in which the community of truth is practiced" (1998, p. 90).

THE NATURE OF GOOD TEACHING

Each of the previous profiles illustrates the nature of good teaching but in doing so raises further questions. Are folks born to teach? Can anyone be taught to be a good teacher? You might say each educator depicted in the profiles was born to teach. But upon closer examination, it can be argued that they all learned how to teach from their predecessors. Plato used Socrates as the spokesperson in his dialogues to illustrate the Socratic method of teaching. While Aristotle took a different road in his systematic inquiry, he continued to seek moral solutions and principles for Plato's just society. The Roman curriculum is founded on Greek traditions, which Quintilian expanded upon to educate a literate society. The classical curriculum of Greece and Rome was the basis for European practices that have influenced the American school until today, when multicultural and globalization factors have grown in importance. Each generation of teachers has devised a **methodology,** a set of procedures, an analysis of principles, a body of rules or suggested approaches. This methodology borrows from the past and changes with each advance in technology and new perspective of school in society. Maria Montessori created a scientific educational methodology based on her background as a physician who worked with children.

Teaching Is Both an Art and a Science

There is no evidence that there is only one way to teach—the possibilities are limitless. For some educators, teaching is an art. The art of teaching is often described as having "insight." Teaching in this context is described as a creative endeavor like that of a painter, writer, musician, or actor. The art form of teaching emanates from what Palmer describes as "the spirit" of teaching: knowing how to connect students with the subject matter. Some educators describe it as a personal process in which insights are intuitive and emanate from the individual's own creativity.

Other educational theorists believe such insight comes from a wealth of experience in working with students, an enriched background in the content areas being taught, and a good grasp of teaching strategies. This scientific view of education asserts that good teaching begins with a respect for research in the field and a willingness to experiment with innovations. In this regard, education is considered a **discipline,** an academic area, with its own body of knowledge and set of principles called a **pedagogy.** Teachers like Elizabeth Peabody, Mary McLeod Bethune, Leonard Covello, and others pioneered the development of pedagogy. The process is ongoing. New frontiers in education are being explored by today's advocates: Jonathan Kozol, Donna Graham Harris, and Pi 'ikea Miyamoto. Their contributions expand the discipline of education to incorporate other areas of study, including sociology, technology, science, and literature.

While some people are intuitively good teachers, they usually need a relevant background to draw upon. Studies have indicated that teachers learn from formal study of educational theories and practice. For novice teachers, internships and practica shape their attitudes about teaching. Studies that analyzed attitudes of student teachers before and after their student teaching experiences document

Voices of Principle and Promise

Student Teacher
by Moira McNabb

As I look back on my practicum experience, I feel that I have grown tremendously from where I began my student teaching journey in my first placement at home in the United States to where I ended with my second placement in a reception class at the Sacred Heart Primary School in Ilkley, England. In my first student teaching experience, I realized that I was very distracted with other life commitments—running from one place to the other which left me with a lack of sleep, stamina, efficiency, planning and personal time. While I was in Ilkley, I made my own professional development my major obligation. I stayed focused on that task and devoted time to reflection and planning. Over time, I found myself growing confident in my skills and training while adjusting to cultural differences in the school and community. As the British accepted me and my ways, I embraced them and the opportunities they offered me. I executed successful lessons, worked closely with a small group of children lacking in phonemic awareness, and formed strong bonds with the behaviorally challenged students in the class.

At the end of the experience, my cooperating teachers were very impressed with my teaching techniques, but more importantly, so was I. You cannot be successful in any avenue of life unless you put your whole heart and soul into it. In Ilkley, I had that opportunity and took full advantage of it. My weaknesses became my strengths and my downfalls became my triumphs. I am truly a different person from when I began this journey. I have grown academically, spiritually and mentally. I now feel confident in my ability to become a future educator.

Moira McNabb, Student Teacher, Sacred Heart Primary School, Ilkley, West Yorkshire, England.

Questions to Consider

1. What growth as a teacher does this reflection illustrate?
2. What advantage did this student teacher have by teaching in two countries?

that novice teachers are positively influenced by practicum placements, particularly where they are allowed to test skills gained in coursework (Swiniarski and Breitborde 2001). Additionally, novice teachers gain self-confidence and positive self-esteem when they have welcoming opportunities to teach in another country or in a cultural setting different from their own (Swiniarski and Breitborde, 2001). No one teaches or learns in a vacuum.

Good teaching might be regarded as both an art and a science. Teaching is a multifaceted process. requiring the talents of the actor, the creativity of the painter, and the knowledge of the professional expert. Teachers need to master their disciplines in order to convey knowledge. They must keep abreast of new developments in their field and in the pedagogy of the profession. They must use creativity and compassion to get their students hooked on learning.

Is Teaching a Job, a Career, or a Profession?

> When I was an elementary school teacher and a principal, my colleagues and I experienced our work as a profession, even a calling. At the turn of the twenty-first century, I'm afraid that for all too many it has become a job. As a calling or profession, education offers much. As a job, it offers little (Barth, 2001a, p. 2).

Your reason for becoming a teacher is an indicator of what teaching means to you. For some, teaching is a good job with convenient hours for those with families. Others go into teaching to satisfy short-term goals, to experiment with a different occupation, or to try newly acquired skills. Many seek teaching as a career that offers distinct stages of development—a ladder of opportunities and advancement. Still others reflect Louise Butterfield's and Parker Palmer's ideals of commitment and a calling to a lifelong profession.

None of these notions of teaching is static. Research indicates that experiences in teaching alter one's concepts about career goals and personal expectations. Susan Moore Johnson and her Harvard University graduate students conducted a study of fifty first- and second-year teachers in Massachusetts. Their findings propose "a mixed model for the teaching career—one that would be responsive to the need of both teachers who envision long-term careers and those who envision short-term stays in teaching" (Peske, et al., 2001, p. 304). Their study indicated that today's teacher candidates are more flexible about career options than their predecessors. Expectations are that career changes are more the norm than lifelong commitments to a profession or organization, since teaching no longer provides the job security it once did. In fact, Johnson group's research findings suggest that, rather than regarding teaching as a calling to a lifelong commitment, many new teachers—both those who completed traditional teacher preparation programs and those who did not—approach teaching "tentatively or conditionally" (Paske, et al., 2001, p. 305).

The study calls for an extensive reevaluation of teacher recruitment and retention practices. Schools need to be restructured to provide incentives for short-term teachers in their initial years, along with compensation and differentiated career roles for those who stay the course. The job seekers and careerists tend to be influenced by contractual agreements set by teacher unions, the administration, and governing bodies. For them the classroom is the workplace, regulated by agreed upon conditions for employment. The school day begins and ends at designated times, with extra duties specifically defined. The job seeker and careerist typically view teaching as a livelihood protected by contracts that define rights and responsibilities. They are comfortable when the role of management and the duties of the teacher workforce are enforced. In contrast, the teacher-professionals decry their lost voice and are frustrated with constraints. Professionals want to cultivate a school climate that is conducive to reflective practices of teaching, encourages creative approaches to curriculum development, and permits the Socratic notion of academic freedom.

Teaching is a complex endeavor—an art form in its human relationships, a science in its use of research, and a craft in its skilled delivery. People enter the field of education with various strengths, some achieve success more readily than others, but everyone can grow and learn from one another through formal study. Novice teachers benefit from having a seasoned teacher as a **mentor**—a guide who counsels and advises them through the challenges and successes of the early years. If teaching is to be more than a job or career, but a way of life, it is important that teachers follow the lead of past models like Maria Montessori, by being change agents who chart a course for the profession.

What Are the Characteristics of a Profession? The notion of teaching as a profession depends upon how teachers regard themselves. Self-esteem and professionalism have been linked (Breitborde, 1981). Teachers who view themselves as professionals also consider their work to be as significant as the work done by those in the fields of law, medicine, journalism, and business. These teachers seek the same status as other professionals and expect similar recognition for their contribution to the community. Like any other profession, teaching requires many qualifications, including specialized degrees, licensure, accountability, and commitment. Unfortunately, the community often does not grant professional status to its teachers. Teachers are seen to have little authority in school management and no control over educational policy, and they receive comparatively low salaries. Historically, teaching has suffered a poor image from a long-held perception called the *Ichabod Crane syndrome* that taunts with the refrain: "Those who can't, teach." To refute these unwarranted criticisms, it can be argued that teaching possesses the major criteria that characterize a profession. A study that examined the criteria for defining professional work arrived at three conclusions, namely:

1. Professional work is based on knowledge derived from a body of coherent and scientific theory and requiring special and lengthy training and licensure.
2. Professional work is directed to the delivery of specific services to clients in need of them, and involves codes of practice that are stronger than any external or legal regulation.
3. Professional workers are autonomous decision makers, collectively determining occupational standards of performance, training and licensure, and work conditions, able to influence legislation pertaining to their field, and relatively free from lay control (Breitborde, 1981, p. 153).

In the next section we will examine teaching to determine if it meets these criteria and possesses the characteristics of a profession.

Does Teaching Possess the Characteristics of a Profession?

Teachers are learners who study both the subjects they teach and the discipline of education. It has been established that education is a discipline in its own right, supported by a theoretical framework with a set of principles. Its methodology is documented by research and practice and furthered through inquiry and investigation. In fact, education can boast of having many specialties within the discipline such as reading, special education, or school counseling. These specialties require a lengthy period of study at the undergraduate and graduate levels of university training. Teaching meets the criteria and possesses the characteristics of a profession.

Teachers need to be lifelong learners, continuing their formal studies in education and in their particular subject areas to obtain advanced degrees. They participate in professional development programs offered through their school systems or professional organizations. There are many opportunities for teachers to participate in continuing education in summer programs or in professional courses available during the school year. Governmental agencies such as the National Endowment for the Humanities and The Fulbright Program sponsor seminars, workshops, institutes, and travel programs to deepen teachers' scholarship and foster research in key areas.

Many programs throughout the country promote diversity in the teaching force. These projects provide both initial professional development and career ladder training. Grants from the U.S. Department of Education along with state monies and funds from private foundations support professional development programs that endorse the inclusion of various ethnic, linguistic, and racial populations in teacher training. Some programs focus exclusively on bilingual education, while others recruit for a broader multicultural scope. An innovative exemplar is the Big Horn Teacher Projects, offered through Montana State University in Billings to Native Americans interested in teaching. Through support from the U. S. Department of Education and the Office of Indian Education, the project has set out to increase the number of certified Native American teachers for the Native American schools in their area, to offer professional development on site in reservation schools, and to "integrate multicultural, bilingual and Crow language concepts . . . into the current curricula in Little Big Horn College's and Montana State University in Billings' teacher education program" (Big Horn Teacher Project, Indian Professional Development).

Teachers serve the community. Schools are a social institution through which teachers impart knowledge to the community. While teachers do not determine all school affairs, they are not powerless in school matters. To the contrary, teachers collectively influence schools through their learned societies, unions, and professional organizations when they set moral codes for the profession, lobby for educational legislation, develop standards, and determine curricula. Ironically, teacher unions and organizations are frequently criticized as being militant when they take a stance on educational issues.

In order to practice in the public schools, teachers, like other professionals, are licensed by the states. Under the new federal guidelines, all teachers in America must obtain certification as a qualified teacher (see Chapter 11). In most states, teacher certification or licensure requires that teachers hold at least a bachelor's degree from an **accredited institution**—a university or college that has been reviewed and approved by the state or professional agency. Additionally, teachers are tested for competency in their subject matter and pedagogy. This testing is administered not only at the entry level but also when teachers seek further credentials in specialty areas such as reading or additional fields of teaching. Some states prescribe their own tests for teacher competency, while others use a national

Table 6.1 Characteristics of the Teaching Profession

- Education is a discipline supported by a theoretical framework with a set of principles.
- Methodology is documented by research and practice, plus inquiry and investigation.
- Teachers are lifelong learners who continue their formal studies of education in their particular subject areas for additional degrees or in professional development programs.
- Schools are a social institution where teachers serve and impart knowledge to the community. While teachers do not determine all school affairs, they are not powerless in school matters.

  Teachers in the United States must have teacher certification. In most states, teacher certification or licensure requires that teachers hold at least a bachelor's degree from an accredited institution. Teachers are tested for competency in their subject matter and pedagogy.

DIRECTLY FROM THE SOURCE

What Teachers Should Know and Be Able To Do: The Five Core Propositions of the National Board of Professional Teachers Standards

National Board for Professional Teaching Standards (1989) *Policy Position* (Five Core Propositions) http://www.nbpts.org/about/coreprops.ctm (Retrieved March 22, 2005).

In this policy, the National Board presents its view of what teachers should know and be able to do—its convictions about what it values and believes should be honored in teaching. This expression of ideals guides all of the National Board's standards and assessment processes.

The National Board for Professional Teaching Standards seeks to identify and recognize teachers who effectively enhance student learning and demonstrate the high level of knowledge, skills, abilities, and commitments reflected in the following five core propositions.

- **Teachers are committed to students and their learning.**
  Accomplished teachers are dedicated to making knowledge accessible to all students.
- **Teachers know the subjects they teach and how to teach those subjects to students.**
  Accomplished teachers have a rich understanding of the subject(s) they teach and appreciate how knowledge in their subject is created, organized linked to other disciplines and applied to real-world settings.

model known as the **Praxis Series,** which is produced by the Educational Testing Service. Teaching certificates are no longer lifelong licenses to teach. In most instances they need to be renewed and validated. In order to renew a certificate, many states require that teachers submit documentation of continued study and scholarship. (See Chapter 11 for further discussion of teacher testing and certification requirements.)

The Professional Learned Societies

Throughout this text there are many references to educational organizations that endorse the professionalism of teaching. Two major players include the National Education Association (NEA) and the American Federation of Teachers (AFT). Both have state and local chapters and act as teacher unions. Their political arms lobby for educational affairs and teachers' rights at all levels of government. Their membership and leadership positions are made of teachers who are the voice and conscience of the profession. Each group has its code of ethics. See Directly from the Source for the code of ethics for the American Federation of Teachers.

Organizations that define teachers' professional competencies include the **National Council for Accreditation for Teacher Education (NCATE),** which determines competencies in the accreditation of professional education programs throughout the United States; and the **National Board for Professional Teaching Standards (NBPTS),** which provides a rigorous national certification process for experienced teachers. As with any profession, there are longstanding honor societies that recognize teacher excellence in scholarship and community service. Two noteworthy societies are Pi Lambda Theta and Phi Delta Kappa. Together they form an impressive alliance that testifies to the worthiness of teachers to join the ranks of other professionals.

- **Teachers are responsible for managing and monitoring student learning.**
  Accomplished teachers create, enrich, maintain, and alter instructional settings to capture and sustain the interest of their students and to make the most effective use of time.

- **Teachers think systematically about their practice and learn from experience.**
  Accomplished teachers are models of educated persons, exemplifying the virtues they seek to inspire in students—curiosity, tolerance, honesty, fairness, respect for diversity, and appreciation of cultural differences.
- **Teachers are members of learning communities.**
  Accomplished teachers contribute to the effectiveness of the school by working collaboratively with other professionals on instructional policy, curriculum development and staff development.

Accomplished teachers find ways to work collaboratively and creatively with parents, engaging them productively in the work of the school.

A Closer Look at the Issues

1. How can the Five Core Propositions serve as an effective guide in defining state requirements for professional licensure and in developing professional program in teacher education institutions?
2. How might you incorporate these propositions into your own teaching practices?

If teaching is more than a job, teachers need to define leadership roles for the profession. There are many routes to take to becoming a leader. You can be a visionary like Elizabeth Peabody, and pioneer new ways to teach, or an advocate like Kozol and Miyamoto, and disrupt the status quo. As change agents, teachers can remain within the profession or bring their professional training to other roles in society. In all instances, teachers need to join alliances and become involved in charting the course for the profession's future.

Teachers as Leaders

As in other professions, education has a variety of leadership roles that a teacher can assume. For educators, the typical leadership role is that of the school administrator or the college president. Other roles include agency administrators, center directors, policymakers, educational advocates, and legislative representatives.

What Does It Mean to Be a "Teacher-Leader"?

Leadership is not limited to management positions or designated positions within school systems. Leaders are people who assume responsibilities when others ask, What shall I do now? Leaders discover new avenues to explore, they create new ideas, and they take risks. They might be those educators who have no special title but who take on informal roles of leadership in the school. They might be the classroom teachers to whom other staff members look for mentoring, decision making, and problem solving. Teacher-leaders are the people who make a difference in the lives of their students and peers and in doing so leave their mark on the profession.

Sometimes they move to more formal roles of leadership, as principals, department heads, superintendents, or curriculum supervisors. They might even take their skills from the classroom to roles outside of the school that affect educational practice and policy.

Profiles of Teacher-Leaders

The following profiles of teachers, arranged alphabetically, reveal stories of some of the leaders who have shaped the world of schools, community and political organizations, and business with their visions for improving education. In most cases, they have credited their successes to their experiences as teachers. They have been selected here to represent the various roles that can evolve from teaching. In all instances they started their careers as teachers, but took paths that broaden the notion of the profession to include various possibilities they hadn't initially considered. Each profile illustrates the theme of public service, whether it be at the federal, state, or local level. The profiles testify to the fact that teaching—contrary to conventional wisdom—offers a career ladder and that being an educator is a multidimensional profession. These stories shed light into the prism of possibilities.

Cynthia J. Noon, Technical Assistant for the United States Department of Education Cynthia Noon has filled many roles in education since graduating with a degree in elementary education. She has been certified as a teacher for kindergarten through grade 8 on both sides of the country, in Massachusetts and California. She has taught in adult basic education programs as well as employment training courses. However, her current career in education took her out of the classroom to a federal governmental agency. She brought her teaching skills and commitment to the United States Department of Education as an Equal Opportunity Specialist. In this leadership capacity, she investigates complaints against U.S. Department of Education recipients, school systems, colleges, states, or local communities, performs compliance reviews of recipients, and provides technical assistance to recipients, communities, parents, students, and organizations.

Noon credits her teaching background and her educational training for the competencies and skills that enable her to assist her clients, to explain the complexities of the laws concerning disabilities, and to clarify policy information on racial and sexual harassment. As a referral agent who advises and counsels others on current informational programs, she continues her own professional development. For Cynthia Noon, being an educator is a lifelong pursuit. She believes that "teaching is a profession that can be carried out in many settings, not limited to the classroom; but the skills I learned in the classroom have served me well in my work for the federal government."

Milli Collins Pierce, Director of the Principals' Center at Harvard University Graduate School of Education Milli Collins Pierce personifies the evolving leader. She admits that initially she became a teacher to have more time with her sons. She went to college as a "returning adult" majoring in elementary education, only to find out "that good teaching takes a lot of your time." As a teacher in an inner-city classroom, her vision of teaching changed. She recognized that she wanted to make a difference for minority students. She began to realize that teaching is political, that leaders make change happen. She set sail to become a leader.

For her, the key position for making real changes in a school and the lives of the students is that of the principal. The principal sets the tone, is the instructional leader of the school, and is the catalyst to affect social and political policy. Pierce continued her formal study for this administrative role at Harvard University and became a school principal in Cambridge, Massachusetts. As a member of Harvard University's Graduate School of Education's Principals' Center, she was recruited by the board to be its director. For over a decade, Pierce has made her mission at the center coincide with her vision of equal opportunity for all students. She transformed the center from its regional origins to the international arena with a membership of principals from across the United States and has networked with school leaders around the globe. She shares with the membership her credo that "all children can learn to be smart in their world and I want principals to make schools a place where that can happen."

Pierce cultivates and brings together prominent members of the educational community for dialogue and discussion. At the Principals' Center, she has created a climate that is inviting, scholarly, supportive, and open.

John E. Mack, Professor of Management John Mack is a professor in a school of business administration. He has worn many hats: lieutenant colonel in the United States Army Reserves, owner of a teacher placement agency, and lecturer. He has worked in both the public and private sectors of education. He began his career as a junior high school social studies teacher in the 1960s. He became a "teaching-principal" of a rural elementary school and then a full-time principal in a parochial suburban school near St. Louis, Missouri, in 1969. After he completed his doctorate degree at St. Louis University, he assumed the responsibilities of a department chair of education in two different colleges. Eventually, he served as an acting dean of business administration, from 1991 to 1993 at Salem State College.

Now back in the classroom teaching, Mack brings to his business students the message of service. He advises his aspiring entrepreneurs and business managers that "it is what you do for people that is important, not making the dollar." He models a life of service. In addition to his military career, he spent time in Ethiopia as a member of the Peace Corps and worked as a community organizer in Putnam County, Florida, with the VISTA volunteer program. Professor Mack credits his success in these roles to the important lessons he gleaned from his teaching experiences: "It is important to be organized to make changes and to take action. To be successful working with people it is necessary to accept others at their face value and look for their strengths. Lastly, to make a difference in your endeavors, you need to be empathetic."

Judith R. Jacobi, Retired Teacher and Town Selectman Judy Jacobi was an elementary teacher for thirty-five years in urban and rural communities of New Jersey before she settled permanently in the New England enclave of Marblehead, Massachusetts, where she became a selectman. Jacobi loved teaching and enjoys politics. She maintains that "both situations continue to fulfill my life goals of being involved and making a difference in the lives of others."

For Selectman Jacobi, conducting town meetings at Abbott Hall is much like teaching in her classroom. She realized early in her career that education is political. She sees a clear connection between teaching and governmental service. Her teaching prepared her for the responsibilities she has assumed in town management and community outreach. Her roles as president of her teacher's union and its first female negotiator against unfair labor practices, as well as a stint as a state legislative aide, provided the apprenticeship necessary for her current position in local politics.

In both careers she had to build upon her organizational skills and her relationships with her constituencies. She is successful in her community work and has been reelected to her post annually since 2000. She credits her political accomplishments with the lessons she learned as a teacher. She contends that "a selectman, like a teacher, needs to be organized, do her homework, make decisions, get the job done, be thorough, listen to constituents, have a broad perspective of the community, be respectful of other voices, and see the commitment as a full-time endeavor."

Her leadership training began in her undergraduate education program at an all-women's college, Cedar Crest College in Allentown, Pennsylvania. In this supportive setting, she was encouraged to do her best, take chances, and try nontraditional roles. She continued her professional studies with graduate work at Rutgers University to enrich her scholarship and gain the confidence to implement her vision for making a difference in schools and society. She credits her leadership skills as outgrowths of understanding the political nature of teaching.

Shirley C. Raines, President of the University of Memphis The road to becoming a university president is a long one. For Shirley Raines the road took her around the United States in various academic roles and then back home to Tennessee. President Raines grew up on a farm in western Tennessee, where she decided on a career in teaching during high school.

Always a voracious reader, Shirley Raines taught reading as a second grade teacher in Louisville, Kentucky, and expanded her involvement with young children and their language development in a variety of administrative positions in early childhood education. Meanwhile, she continued her graduate study of the language arts to the doctorate level. Along the way, she became a professor and an author of numerous books and scholarly journal articles on the language arts, the teaching of reading, children's literature, and storytelling.

With each move within the United States, Dr. Raines assumed more responsibility. She has held administrative roles as program coordinator, chairperson, dean of the School of Education, and vice-chancellor at the University of Kentucky, before becoming the first female president of the University of Memphis. She was president of the Association for Childhood Education International, a professional organization whose mission is to improve the professional lives of teachers.

When asked what motivated her to pursue her goals, she readily credits the encouragement of colleagues, mentors, and friends. But she admits that she seemed to "grow into the possibilities—by observing the next step or office up close, I knew I could do the job." She has proven herself to be right. She meets each challenge with enthusiasm and determination. Currently, she is developing her presidency around three themes: "to invest in people through scholarship by giving faculty recognition and being inclusive of new people, to build concrete partnerships with the community, to promote interdisciplinary initiatives."

President Raines has the reputation of a caring leader who believes in people. She has reached out to all members of the Memphis community, welcomed new ideas for the university's goals, and held steadfast to her goals of fairness and equity in her administration.

Nancy D. Harrington, President of Salem State College Nancy Harrington began her route to the presidency of Salem State College as an elementary school teacher. She later became a college instructor, director of student teaching, laboratory school principal, dean of continuing education and the graduate school, acting vice-president of academic affairs, and finally, the first female president of Salem State College, in 1990.

President Harrington's administrative and higher education experiences were all at her alma mater, Salem State College. While this is quite unique, she feels it was a natural progression that grew out of her love of the college, rather than out of a lifelong goal. Her doctorate is in reading, rather than management and school administration. Her professional experiences provided her with on-the-job training. She feels she grew with each position she assumed; in each position, she realized she could meet the challenges of the next office. She had the self-confidence to risk leaving a comfortable job for a new opportunity. Encouragement came from family members, including her mother, who always promoted excellence in education, and her brother, who, as president of the Massachusetts Maritime Academy, was a role model.

Harrington wants to improve public higher education in the Commonwealth of Massachusetts by building Salem State College into an institution that offers opportunities to all who seek professional challenges and personal satisfaction. For those aspiring to be a college president her advice is "to get a broad education, be familiar with the academic side of the house, and realize that being a college president is plain hard work!"

Formal and Informal Leadership Roles for the Teacher-Leader

Each of the leaders sketched in these vignettes share many characteristics. All had a vision of education, a clear mission to accomplish, a sense of service to their constituency, and the self-confidence to take risks to accomplish their goals. Each story is one of a formal teacher-leader who left the classroom for a leadership role. Roland Barth, a teacher, principal, author, and the founder of Harvard's Principals' Center and the International Network of Principals' Centers, cites the many other ways educators can be leaders. He encourages teachers to be "informal leaders within the classroom" (Barth, 2001b, p. 444). He further maintains: "All teachers can lead. Indeed, if schools are going to become places in which all children are learning, all teachers *must* lead. . . . In order to create communities of learners teachers must model for students the most important enterprise of the schoolhouse—learning. A powerful relationship exists between learning and leading" (Barth, 2001b, pp. 444–445).

Informal leaders are those who influence others, make change happen, and dare to take on challenges. The informal leader is the "school-based reformer who works in the school and is seldom heard to say, 'They'll never let us' " (Barth, 2001b, 5).

Teacher leadership, both formal and informal, can take many forms. Teachers can join professional organizations to make a difference, to provide outreach, to improve curriculum instruction, and to network with colleagues. Numerous groups solicit teachers to become members, including the National Council of

Teachers of Mathematics, the National Council for the Social Studies, the International Reading Association, the National Council of Teachers of English, the National Association for the Education of Young Children, the Council of Exceptional Children, and the Association for Supervision and Curriculum Development, to name a few. There are learned societies like the Association for Childhood Education International and the Comparative and International Education Society that encourage educators to form international alliances. These groups publish an abundance of professional literature and invite teachers to contribute as authors and to sit on their editorial boards. All advocate for the improvement of the profession and the need for teacher-leaders to set policies, establish professional guidelines, and improve schools.

The Globally Literate Teacher

The world is becoming a smaller place. The theme of unity and diversity in global education "perceives the world as community while recognizing the world in the local community" (Swiniarski and Breitborde, 2003, p. vi) reconfigures the nature of good teaching. World events such as the immigration of vast populations of refugees seeking asylum, and the moral imperatives to protect and preserve human rights, are issues that call for professionals who are globally literate. Such a professional has knowledge about world conditions, sensitivity for the diversity of her constituency, and a willingness to advocate for just causes. The globally literate teacher is not only informed but is competent in communicating her message. Being computer literate and keeping abreast with technology's offerings and the use of multimedia approaches to teaching and learning are key components for the professional development of the globally literate teacher.

The globally literate teacher has many role models who experiment with new ideas and share their expertise with a worldwide audience. One role model to consider is Sylvia Ashton-Warner (1908–1984), who as a teacher and writer shared her innovative approaches for educating Maori children in New Zealand. Her method, which she called *organic teaching,* was embedded in the language, culture, and communal experiences of her students. She believed young children start to learn when they express personal experiences in their own cultural style and language. She also felt that the mainstreamed Anglican curriculum of New Zealand schools needed to incorporate not only the adult view of Maori culture but the experiences and vocabulary of her students. Her children began to read by writing their own books, which they published for each other to read and enjoy. Ashton-Warner's book, *Teacher* (1963), is a diary that describes in detail how her program has implications for teaching all children worldwide. Her ideas have had an impact on the teaching of minority children in the United States. Her strategies have been translated into effective practices that are still implemented in classrooms today.

Sylvia Ashton Warner on organic reading:

> Since I take original writing as a basis for reading, a strict watch is kept on grammar and punctuation [and] the handwriting has to be at least the best they can do, to save their own faces, when changing books.
>
> Organic reading is not meant to stand alone: it is essentially a lead up and out to all the other reading. As the child rises . . . further out to the inorganic and standard reading, there is a comfortable movement from the inner man outward, from the known to the unknown, the

A globally literate teacher, such as Donna Graham Harris, uses innovative technology as a way to engage teachers, researchers, and students from a variety of cultures.
Source: Courtesy of Louise Swiniarski

> organic to the inorganic. The thing is to keep it a gracious movement, for it is the extent that the activity is creative that the growth of mind is good (Ashton-Warner, 1963, p. 62).

The globally literate teacher demonstrates many competencies that define good teaching, including the following (Swiniarski and Breitborde, 2003, p. 17):

- ability to make connections and identify universal implications
- knowledge of world issues, affairs, and happenings
- sensitivity to the unity and diversity issues
- active attention to social issues
- involvement in local and international happenings
- openness to new ideas
- use of innovative technology
- willingness to share expertise with others
- employment of critical and creative approaches to problem solving
- adherence to a personal moral imperative
- positive spirit in teaching and learning
- reflective approach

Our Constituencies

First and foremost, our primary constituents are the students we teach. As teachers we are accountable to our students for their learning experiences at school. Various instructional models formulate the process. Some models place teachers at the center of the teaching/learning relationship, others put the students at the center, while still others center on the subject matter as the magnet that attracts to bring the student and teacher together. In each perspective, the teacher/student relation is key to the educational process.

In all teaching situations it is important to consider a broad band of constituents that includes your students, their families, and the communities you serve. Good teachers recognize education as a universal right for all children. To support their students' rights, teachers must know their students, respond to their needs, and respect the cultural heritages they bring to school. To do so, teachers need to educate themselves about the places and the people they teach—they ought to become globally literate teachers.

Teachers should reflect upon their teaching. In doing so, they assume responsibility for their students' progress while assessing the effectiveness of the teaching practices they use. They can improve their instruction methods by examining how well they meet their teaching objectives. As professionals, teachers need to cultivate a school climate that is conducive to reflective practices of teaching, encourages creative approaches to curriculum development, and permits the Socratic notion of academic freedom. Teachers are professionals who seek to make a difference in the lives of others.

As your teachers have touched your life, you can inspire your students. Good teaching from preschool to graduate school is an intellectual endeavor in which the teacher passes on from one generation to another the heritage of what it is to be a caring, competent, and knowledgeable person.

SUMMARY

- We agree with Roland Barth that teaching is about scholarship, modeling what you know and inspiring others to learn. Teachers who are leaders in their field need to be knowledgeable about what they teach; they must be sensitive to how students learn, and possess the skills to promote many "ways of knowing."
- Some of the prominent teachers in history include Socrates, Plato, and Aristotle from Greece. In Rome, Quintilian identified early learning as essential to education. European teachers included Erasmus, Comenius, and Maria Montessori. In the United States in the nineteenth and twentieth centuries, some of the prominent teachers were Peabody, Bethune, Covello, Butterfield, Kozol, Miyamoto, Harris, and Palmer.
- Good teaching is both an art and a science. Those who approach teaching as a profession want to cultivate a school climate that is conducive to reflective practices of teaching, encourages creative approaches to curriculum development, and permits the Socratic notion of academic freedom. A profession is an occupation that is based on scientific theory and licensure, in which services are delivered with a strong code of practice by practitioners who are autonomous decision makers. The professional societies in education include the National Education Association and the American Federation of Teachers.
- Teaching is risk taking. Teaching requires you to believe in yourself and teach to what Parker Palmer describes as your inner spirit.
- Teachers are formal and informal leaders who have a sense of mission and a vision. They respect their constituents. They reflect high standards of scholarship in their practice and expect the same of their students. As advocates of just causes they support the universal right of all children to have equal education.
- Teaching is a political and social experience with a global dimension. Teaching is a shared experience in which one can learn from the rich legacy of its past as well as from present-day leaders and current constituents.

QUESTIONS FOR REFLECTION

1. What is good teaching? What qualities would your role models possess that made them good teachers?
2. What do you think is required of a teacher to be a "teacher -leader"? How do you think such a teacher would reflect these criteria in the classroom?
3. What qualifications do you think are important to be recognized as a formal leader in education?
4. Which teachers whom you know would you add to the profiles offered in this chapter? What characteristics of good teaching do they exemplify?
5. What kind of teacher would you like to be? What qualities will you bring to the profession? What legacy would you like to leave?
6. For a second edition of his book, *I Remember My Teacher,* David Shribman (2001, p. 136) invites his readers to submit their stories about teachers "whose voices still speak to you, whose faces still smile (or scowl) upon you, whose lessons still breathe with you." What teacher story could you add for this second volume?

APPLYING WHAT YOU'VE LEARNED

1. www. Go to the textbook website and review the images of teaching through the ages. What universal qualities do you detect? How has teaching changed? What are your predictions for the future?
2. Interview someone who you feel is a "teacher-leader" or a "formal leader." The interview can be videotaped or audiotaped for viewing in class.
3. Find artwork that illustrates the legacy of teaching through the ages. Describe how it makes a social commentary on the manners and mores of the times.
4. Go to the websites listed below to find the codes of ethics for the professional associations. Draw up a composite code (based on three or four of the associations) that reflects the values you hold.

   Go to the website for the American Federation of Teachers http://www.aft.org or http://www.nea.org. Explore the offerings this union gives its membership and the causes it promotes for American education. What are the benefits of joining a teacher's union? What education concerns do teaching unions support?

KEY TERMS

WEBSITES TO EXPLORE

http://www.aft.org/history/histdocs/code.html. This website offers information about the American Federation of Teachers, AFL-CIO, as well as its code of ethics.

http://www.nea.org. The website for the National Education Association's code of ethics and information regarding membership and services.

http://www.acei.org. The website for the Association for Childhood Education International, its benefits, publications, conferences, and its journal, *Childhood Education.*

http://www.ciesoc.org. The website for the Comparative and International Education Society includes updates on conferences around the globe and the society's publications.

http://www.pilanbda.org. The website for the honor society, Phi Lambda Theta, and its publications, scholarships, and professional events.

http://www.pdkintl.org. The website for the Phi Delta Kappa honor society.

http://www.musbillings.edu/bighornteacherproj/abstract.htm. The Little Big Horn Project at Montana State University at Billings is described on the university's website, which provides information on the Native American education project and its mission, goals, and outreach.

http://www.quotegarden.com/teachers.html. A website for locating quotes about teachers and by teachers.

http://www.cies.org/about_fulb.htm. This website provides information about the Fulbright Scholar Program administered by the Council for International Exchange of Scholars and in particular the Fulbright Teacher Exchange Program.

http://www.neh.fed.us/projects/index.html. This website provides information about all of the National Endowment for the Humanities projects, including the Landmarks of American History Workshops for K–12 Teachers and the Summer Seminars and Institutes for School Teachers K–12.

http://www.normanrockwellmusem.org. The Norman Rockwell Museum's website gives information about the artist's work and special events for teachers and schoolchildren to learn about all forms of art.

http://www.socialstudies.org. The website for the National Council for the Social Studies, its publications, events, and updates on curriculum matters.

http://www.nctm.org. The website for the National Council of Teachers of Mathematics provides information on membership, conferences, publications, standards, and curriculum updates in mathematics.

CRITICAL READINGS

Preface to the American Edition of Maria Montessori's Il Metodo della Pedagogia Scientifica applicato all' educazione infantile nelle Case dei Bambini

BY MARIA MONTESSORI

In February, 1911, Professor Henry W. Holmes, of the Division of Education at Harvard University, did me the honour to suggest that an English translation be made of my Italian volume, *"Il Metodo della Pedagogia Scientifica applicato all' educazione infantile nelle Case dei Bambini."* This suggestion represented one of the greatest events in the history of my educational work. Today, that to which I then looked forward as an unusual privilege has become an accomplished fact.

The Italian edition of *"Il Metodo della Pedagogia Scientifica"* had no preface, because the book itself I consider nothing more than the preface to a more comprehensive work, the aim and extent of which it only indicates. For the educational method for children from three to six years set forth here is but the earnest of a work that, developing the same principle and method, shall cover in a like manner the successive stages of education. Moreover, the method which obtains in the *Casa dei Bambini* offers, it seems to me, an experimental field for the study of man, and promises, perhaps, the development of a science that shall disclose other secrets of nature.

In the period that has elapsed between the publication of the Italian and American editions, I have had, with my pupils, the opportunity to simplify and render more exact certain practical details of the method, and to gather additional observations concerning discipline. The results attest the vitality of the method, and the necessity for an *[Page viii]* extended scientific collaboration in the near future, and are embodied in two new chapters written for the American edition. I know that my method has been widely spoken of in America, thanks to Mr. S. S. McClure, who has presented it through the pages of his well-known magazine. Indeed, many Americans have already come to Rome for the purpose of observing personally the practical application of the method in my little schools. If, encouraged by this movement, I may express a hope for the future, it is that my work in Rome shall become the centre of an efficient and helpful collaboration.

To the Harvard professors who have made my work known in America and to *McClure's Magazine,* a mere acknowledgement of what I owe them is a barren response; but it is my hope that the method itself, in its effect upon the children of America, may prove an adequate expression of my gratitude.

Source: http://digital.library.upenn.edu/women/montessori/method.method.html

A Closer Look at the Issues

1. The preface by Maria Montessori was written for her seminal work, *The Montessori Method,* and translated from Italian into English by Anne E. George. What does this preface tell you about the historical significance of Maria Montessori's work?
2. Why might Montessori be considered a globally literate educator?

Educators As Learners: Creating a Professional Learning Community in Your School, Foreword

BY ROLAND BARTH

"Our school is a community of learners!" How many times do we see and hear this assertion, now so common in public schools? This is an ambitious promissory note, indeed.

The promise, is, first, that the school is a "community," a place full of adults and youngsters who care about, look after, and root for one another and who work together for the good of the whole—in times of need as well as times of celebration. I find that precious few schools live up to this mantle of "community." Many more are simply organizations or institutions.

As if "community" were not enough to promise, a "community of learners" is much more. Such a school is a community whose defining, underlying culture is one of learning. A community of learners is a community whose most important condition for membership is that one be a learner—whether one is called a student, teacher, principal, parent, support staff, or certified staff. Everyone. A tall order to fill. And one to which all too few schools aspire, and even fewer attain.

The big message of this little volume lies in its title: *Educators as Learners: Creating a Professional Learning Community in Your School.*

For when the adults within the schoolhouse commit to the heady and hearty goal of promoting their own learning and that of their colleagues, several things follow: They leave the ranks of the senior, wise priesthood, the learned, and become first-class members of that community of learners. And when the adults come to take their own learning seriously, value and promote it, students take note. And when students see some of the most important role models in their lives learning, they too will learn, even *achieve.* Hence, adults' learning in our schools is a basic, not a frill.

Schools exist to promote the learning of all of their inhabitants. Indeed, the central purpose of a school is to invent and then to provide the conditions under which profound levels of human learning can flourish. That's why we have them. To paraphrase the legendary coach Vince Lombardi: "In schools, learning isn't the most important thing; it's the ONLY thing." So just how do you transform a school into a community of learners?

Educators as Learners offers nothing less than a "lesson plan" for members of a school or school system to transform their institution or organization into a learning community. By offering abundant, explicit, useful examples and case studies; rich activities; imaginative processes; and thoughtful commentary, this book provides a coherent roadmap that will go a long way in helping a school make good on the promise, "Our school is a community of learners."

Source: Penelope J. Wald and Michael S. Castleberry, eds., Alexandria, VA. Association for Supervision and Curriculum Development. *Educators As Learners: Creating a Professional Learning Community in Your School,*

A Closer Look at the Issues

1. In this foreword Roland Barth speaks to another role of the teacher as that of the learner. What do you think Barth means by the *teacher-learner*?
2. Why do you think teachers are learners? How would you describe a *teacher-learner*?

REFERENCES

Apple, M., and J. Beane. (1995). *Democratic schools.* Alexandria, VA: Association for Supervision and Curriculum Development.

Ashton-Warner, S. (1963). *Teacher.* New York: Simon & Schuster.

Barth, R. (2001a). *Learning by heart.* San Francisco: Jossey-Bass.

Barth, R. (2001b). *Teacher leader. Phi Delta Kappan* 82 (6), February, pp. 443–449.

Breitborde (Sheer), M. (1981). *Teacher self-esteem and social vision: Conceptions of social role and responsibility.* Unpublished doctoral dissertation.

http://www.ascd.org/publications/books/2000waldbarth.html.

http://digital.library.upenn.edu/women/montessori/method.method.html.

de los Reyes, E., and P. Gozemba. (2002). *Pockets of hope.* Westport, CT: Bergin and Garvey.

Froebel, F. (1892). *The education of man.* Trans. by W. N. Hailman. New York: D. Appleton.

Froebel, F. (1967). The young child, in *Friedrich Froebel: Selections from his writings.* Ed. by I. M. Lilly. Cambridge, England: Cambridge University Press.

Jalongo, M., and J. Isenberg (1995). *Teachers' stories: From personal narrative to professional insight.* San Francisco: Jossey-Bass.

Kozol, J. (1985). *Death at an early age.* New York: Penguin.

McNabb, M. Reflections on student teaching in England. Unpublished document. Norman Rockwell Museum, (1999). *Resource packet for educators.* Stockbridge, MA: Norman Rockwell Museum.

National Board for Professional Teaching Standards (1989) *Policy Position* (Five Core Propositions) http://www.nbpts.org/about/coreprops.ctm (Retrieved March 22, 2005.)

Palmer, P. (1998). *The courage to teach.* San Francisco: Jossey-Bass.

Palmer, P. (2001). *Now I become myself.* http//:www.futurenet.org/17/work/palmer.htm.

Papert, S. (1993). *The children's machine: Rethinking school in the age of the computer.* New York: Basic Books.

Peabody, E. (ed.) (1894). *Mother play and nursery songs.* Trans. by F. Dwight and J. Jarvis. Boston: Lee and Shepard.

Peabody, E. (1873). Our hopes. *Kindergarten Messenger,* I, May, p. 6.

Peske, H., E. Liu, S. Moore, D. Kauffman, and S. Kardos (2001). The next generation of teachers: Changing conceptions of a career in teaching. *Phi Delta Kappan,* 83 (4), pp. 304–311.

Power, E. (1969). *Evolution of educational doctrine: Major educational theorist of the Western world.* New York: Appleton-Century-Crofts.

Power, E. (1970). *Main currents in the history of education,* 2nd ed. New York: McGraw-Hill.

Reed, R., and T. Johnson (2000). *Philosophical documents in education,* 2nd ed. New York: Longman.

Sadovnik, A., P. Cookson, and S. Semel. (2001). *Exploring education: An introduction to the foundations of education,* 2nd ed. Boston: Allyn & Bacon.

Shoulds, K. *Book summary and critique of Amazing Grace by Jonathan Kozol.* Unpublished document.

Shribman, D. (2001). *I remember my teacher: 365 reminiscences of the teachers who changed our lives.* Kansas City, MO: Andrews McMeel Publishing.

Swiniarski, L. (1976). *A comparative study of Elizabeth Palmer Peabody and Susan Elizabeth Blow by examination of their work and writings.* Unpublished Doctoral Dissertation.

Swiniarski, L. (1987). Elizabeth Peabody: A pioneer in the kindergarten movement in America. *Essex Institute Historical Collections,* 123 (2), April, 206–229.

Swiniarski, L., An unpublished series of interviews with Cynthia Noon, Shirley Raines, John E. Mack, Nancy D. Harrington, Milli Pierce, and Judith Jacobi, February–July, 2002. http://www.aft.org/history/histdocs/code.html. (Retrieved August 11, 2004.) http://www.musbillings.edu/bighornteacherproj/abstract.htm (Retrieved August 11, 2004.)

Swiniarski, L., and M. Breitborde, (2001. April). Teacher formation: Beginning with oneself, changing the world. A presentation for the 2001 Annual ACEI Conference on Education Odyssey: From Froebel to the Internet. Toronto, Canada (Case Studies by L. Swiniarski).

Swiniarski, L., and M. Breitborde (2001). Teaching formation: Beginning with oneself, changing the world. A presentation for the 2001 Annual ACEI Conference on Education Odyssey: From Froebel to the Internet, April, Toronto, Canada (Case studies by L. Swiniarski).

Swiniarski, L., and M. Breitborde. (2003). *Educating the global village: Including the child in the world,* 2nd ed. Upper Saddle River, NJ: Merrill Prentice-Hall.

7 School and Society in American History: The First Hundred Years

ESSENTIAL QUESTION

What is the role of school in society?

Just see wherever we peer into the first tiny springs of the national life, how this true panacea for all the ills of the body politic bubbles forth—education, education, education (Andrew Carnegie, quoted in Perkinson, 1991, frontispiece).

Despite frequent good intentions and abundant rhetoric about "equal educational opportunity," schools have rarely taught the children of the poor effectively. . . . [S]chools did not create the injustices of American urban life, although they had a systematic part in perpetuating them. It is an old and idle hope to believe that better education alone can remedy them. Yet, in the old goal of a common school . . . lies a legacy essential to a quest for social justice. (David Tyack, *The One Best System*, 1974, p. 12). ■

Education in the New Republic: The Ideal and the Pragmatic

In fashioning the United States as a democratic republic, the framers of the Constitution expressed lofty goals. We would have no king; we would have no entitled ruling class. We would insist on our "inalienable rights" as individual human beings. Rich or poor, we would be equal under the law and full participants in our own fate. The idea that common people could govern themselves was a radical experiment in the eighteenth century. Our founders had faith that the structures and laws embodied in a carefully written constitution would be enough to enable ordinary people to take on the extraordinary responsibility of self-government. Realizing that government by the people required an enlightened perspective, a fund of knowledge, and a sense of the common good, some of the founders thought public education would be essential to prepare Americans to govern themselves. Schools would provide citizens of the United States with the knowledge, skills, and values necessary to conduct the affairs of government, business, and society with wisdom and good judgment. Schools would respond to the "first tiny springs of the national life," to use Andrew Carnegie's phrase, by helping to create a uniquely new "American" culture and by fostering an ethical, just, and productive social order. Unfortunately, the lofty ideals of our forebears have been limited by the realities of life in American society. Their belief that the protection of individual rights would ensure social welfare was naïve and exclusive. Throughout our history, individual rights were unevenly applied. Under the guise of "protection," and for economic, social, and political reasons, many groups—among them, Mexican Americans, Chinese Americans, African Americans, disabled Americans, and women—were deprived of human rights and educational opportunities, or thought to be incapable of benefiting from them. While Jefferson and colleagues were penning a Constitution that ensured the rights of white males, settlers in this new land were focused more on the practical work of farming, learning a craft, building a business, and getting ahead than on finding ways to provide equal opportunities to everyone.

The individualism and pragmatism that characterize this nation have at times subverted its high ideals of equal opportunity and equal rights by—wittingly or unwittingly—supporting prevailing inequities in economic life, in social relations, and in political power. Though we agree with Andrew Carnegie that public education can lead the way to social change, educational historians like David Tyack, quoted above, show us that our public schools too often have colluded in maintaining these inequities, rather than acting as purveyors of opportunity and human rights. Subject to the influence of pragmatic politicians, businessmen, and taxpayers, the schools have often assumed a passive, transmissive, role with respect to society—transmitting whatever knowledge and skills the larger society thinks it should transmit to young people—rather than an active, or transformative, role as agents of social change.

The "panacea" that Carnegie hoped was American public schooling turned out to be imperfect (Perkinson, 1991). While we can be proud that our nation has led the world in providing access to schooling to all citizens, regardless of where they live or how much their families earn, the education provided by our schools has not been equitable. In a country touting the ideal that anyone can succeed, regardless of his or her background, research continues to reveal that the single most important factor determining the quality and outcome of children's educational experience is the socioeconomic status of their parents (Jencks, 1972; Berliner, 1995), with the level of income and education of their parents all too often associated with the color of their skin.

In other words, the sons and daughters of the wealthy have received a better education than the sons and daughters of the poor. The education of Native Americans was for a long time ignored. The schools that were eventually established for them robbed them of their cultural heritage; only in the past few years have Indians won the right to run their own schools. The abilities and aspirations of women were historically limited; their role was to support their husbands and children, not to educate themselves for their own benefit. Children of color, denied schooling outright in our early history, still too often receive an education that is inferior to that provided to children in middle-class, white communities. City schools and schools in impoverished rural areas have typically been more poorly equipped and staffed than schools in middle-class suburbs. There is evidence that the expectations that teachers and school administrators hold for poor and nonwhite children are significantly lower than those they hold for wealthier white children, resulting in different curricula, different modes of instruction, and different preparation for adult life and work (see Chapter 9 for a full discussion of this point).

In this chapter and in Chapter 8, we look through the lens of history to examine both the transmissive and transformative roles of schools in society and the social conditions that influenced those options. To illustrate the tension between the ideal and the reality of American public education, we describe particular events and the stories of particular people who are living examples of this tension. Always, the lens through which we look at the history of American education is colored by our conviction that schools and teachers are potentially agents of social improvement, and that the ultimate aim of public education is to improve life on earth for all people.

Education in Colonial and Early America: Religious and Social Order

From the beginning, America has been a nation of adventurers in a land whose vast natural resources offered opportunities for individual advancement. Even in colonial times, the geographical distance between Americans and their nominal European rulers made it relatively easy for them to govern themselves, or go their own way. Colonial leaders were concerned with the establishment of order and the imposition of standards of behavior on a population who had crossed the Atlantic seeking their independence and freedom. This was most important to the Puritan fathers who, after all, had not emigrated as individuals with a collection of many beliefs and lifestyles, but were bent on finding a place where they could practice their own version of moral, social, and religious order.

Life in the colonies was regionally diverse. There were great differences in the beliefs and characteristics of the groups who settled in New England, the Mid-Atlantic colonies, and the South, and there were great differences in their economies and social organization. These differences were reflected in the place and responsibility they assigned to education. Schools were governed quite directly by community people, whose decisions were made pragmatically and "instinctively," rather than through consciously constructed educational policy (Bailyn, 1960). Their structure and operation varied from region to region, governed by the prevailing cultures of the populations, their religious beliefs, and their socioeconomic organization. Nevertheless, common to all regions was the assumption that the social purpose of education was to strengthen morality, assist the growing economy, and preserve the social order—a rationale far more practical than intellectual. Despite changing and expanding notions of whose rights were "equal," this pragmatic sense of education's social purpose affected the character of American schools and the status and role of teachers.

The presumed purpose of schooling was modest. In an agrarian society, most people thought there was little need for "book learning." More important to those who argued for the establishment of public education were the twin goals of maintaining the order in the absence of executive authority and in the face of close communal relations, and teaching children to be God-fearing. Basic levels of reading and "ciphering" (arithmetic) were prerequisites for taking care of one's business affairs, succeeding at a trade, and understanding strict social and religious codes.

Schooling to Maintain Religious Order Believing that illiterate people were easy targets for Satan, the Puritans of the Massachusetts Bay Colony early on enacted laws holding families and communities responsible for educating their children. In 1642 the colony mandated that parents teach children the principles of religion and the capital laws of the commonwealth. Within five years, it had passed America's earliest law relating to schooling, the "Old Deluder Satan Act" of 1647, which required that every town of fifty or more families hire a primary school teacher for young children, and that towns of one hundred or more families appoint a Latin teacher to prepare promising young men for entrance into Harvard College, where they would be educated for the ministry. By 1683 anyone who had children under their guidance who had not learned to read and write by the age of twelve or learned a useful trade was charged a five-pound fine per child.

In many New England towns, primary education was accomplished in **dame schools.** Widows or women whose children had grown would take in a few local children and teach them basic lessons in reading, writing, and arithmetic. As the towns grew, they built schoolhouses staffed by one teacher for children aged six to thirteen or fourteen. Sitting on hard wooden benches, they read from their "hornbooks," which were horn-covered parchment paddles that contained the alphabet, phonetic spellings, and religious verses such as the Lord's Prayer. Once the children had mastered basic reading skills, they moved on to **primers,** reading books whose aim was to advance literacy in the context of moral and religious lessons. *The New England Primer* of 1777 included the following passages for reviewing the alphabet and gaining reading practice (reprinted in Johansen, undated):

A In Adam's fall,
We sinned all.

B Heaven to find;
The Bible Mind.

C Christ crucify'd
For sinners died.

D The Deluge drown'd
The Earth around.

A
In Adam's Fall
We Sinned all.
B
Thy Life to Mend
This Book Attend.
C
The Cat doth play
And after slay.
D
A Dog will bite
A Thief at night.
E
An Eagles flight
Is out of sight.
F
The Idle Fool
Is whipt at School.

Primers such as *The New England Primer* of 1777 were intended to advance literacy in the context of moral and religious lessons.
Source: The Granger Collection, New York

Interestingly, the overtly religious themes of such reading books persisted even after the framing of the U.S. Constitution, whose First Amendment in the Bill of Rights guarantees the separation of church and state. In the minds of political and educational leaders, economic and social stability were intimately linked to religion. The church was the source for the codes of moral behavior necessary for the basically sinful nature of human beings (Greene, 1965). The social historian Merle Curti (1959) quotes Dr. William Smith, "an earnest worker for education and the church," who, in his appeal for funds to educate the Germans of Pennsylvania, stated,

> Without education it is impossible to preserve the spirit of commerce. . . . Liberty is the most dangerous of all weapons, in the hands of those who know not the use and value of it. . . . In a word, commerce and riches are the offspring of industry and an unprecarious property; but these depend on virtue and liberty, which again depend on knowledge and religion (quoted in Curti, 1959, p. 6).

There was resistance, of course. The independent-minded "down-easters" in Maine, who before 1820 were part of the Massachusetts commonwealth, sent minister-teachers back to Boston in the name of "shak(ing) off all Yoake of Government, both sacred and civil" . . . One plainspoken fisherman informed a Massachusetts minister . . . "Sir, You Are mistaken, you think you are Preaching to the People at the Bay; our main End was to catch Fish" (Axtell, 1974, p. 271).

Not until the mid-twentieth century did educators take into consideration the provisions of the First Amendment ("Congress shall make no law respecting an establishment of religion or prohibiting the free exercise thereof . . . ") and the diversity of religious beliefs among Americans and, thereafter, prohibit the teaching of religion. While teachers may teach about religions and use religious materials to help students understand such subjects as literature, history, and the arts, they may not promote religious beliefs in schools. (See Chapter 10 for a full discussion of this issue.) Despite the Constitutional limits on teaching religion, many communities and school administrators in this country even today are loath to turn their backs on the idea that educated persons are good Christians.

Schooling in the Mid-Atlantic colonies of New York, New Jersey, Delaware, and Pennsylvania was the province of the several churches that predominated in each area. In New York (originally called "New Amsterdam"), the Dutch Reformed Church operated schools, and continued to do so even after the British won the colony. In Pennsylvania, the Quakers ran their own parochial schools, as did the Germans, whose schools were conducted in German. Therefore, middle colony schools were not only sectarian, but were also bilingual, reflecting the multiple ethnic cultures and languages of the population in general.

James Crawford (1999) argues that bilingualism is not a phenomenon new to American life or its schools. He points out that at the time the British took over New Amsterdam, at least eighteen tongues were spoken on Manhattan Island, not counting Native American languages, and that bilingualism was common among both the educated and uneducated classes of New York, Pennsylvania, New Jersey, and Delaware. When Pennsylvania General Assemblyman Benjamin Franklin, concerned about his inability to communicate with German-speaking voters, promoted the idea of free public schools in Pennsylvania under the auspices of the Society for the Propagation of Christian Knowledge, his German constituents refused to enroll their children when they learned that the common language would be English. Franklin warned that the assembly would soon need interpreters "to tell one half of our Legislators what the other half say; In short unless the stream of their importation could be turned from this to other Colonies . . . [Germans] will soon so out number us, that all the advantages we have will not in My Opinion be able to preserve our language, and even our Government will become precarious" (quoted in Crawford, 1999). Long after religious schools gave way to nonsectarian public schools, German remained the language of instruction in many of the schools in Pennsylvania and other states (for example, Ohio) well into the twentieth century. Given the controversy today about how best to educate new immigrants who do not yet speak English (now called "English language learners"), Franklin's words are eerily prophetic. Should English be the only language of instruction in public schools? Or should children with limited English be taught subject matter in their native languages?

Social Order for an American Identity For the first fifty years of the republic, access to schooling continued to depend upon where one lived and to what social class or ethnic group one belonged. The Northern states built primary schoolhouses in cities and towns, and academies for students whose gifts or social status allowed them to pursue secondary education. Local school boards oversaw the hiring of teachers and the distribution of funds. City schools were subject to the politics of ward bosses, who hired teachers as favors to constituents, secured funding for schools in politically important districts, and used their positions as steppingstones to higher office. As the nation grew, the Northwest Ordinance of 1785 required that the Midwestern territories set aside a section of land for educational purposes. As a result, each prairie township created one-room district schools and, later, the territories established colleges on large land grants to educate teachers and skilled professionals.

Education in the Southern colonies was limited to the privileged sons and daughters of plantation owners. In a region characterized by great physical distance between families, the children of small, backcountry farmers and tradesmen had little access to schooling. The children of slaves were prohibited from learning to read—a skill that slaveholders felt might endanger the status quo of the social and economic system. Plantation children received private tutoring in their homes or with other children on nearby plantations, or they were sent to boarding schools.

The purpose of education in the new nation was nominally to prepare all citizens for participation in the republic, to help develop the nation's resources and frontier land, and to help create an "American" culture (Ornstein and Levine, 2003, p. 166). The uneven but growing commitment in most parts of the country to providing the young nation's children with schooling was part of a conscious effort to create a culture that was distinct from our European roots. Noah Webster's contribution to creating a national language and form of instruction that was uniquely American was part of that effort. The "schoolmaster of America," who indeed began his career as a country teacher, published spelling books, grammars, and readers that replaced British spellings and pronunciations with new American ones, in lessons on morality and patriotism imbued with religious principles: "Begin with the infant in the cradle; let the first word he lisps be Washington" (Webster, 1783). A champion of the idea of publicly funded elementary schools (explored in the next section of this chapter), Webster saw schooling as an effective way to establish a strong national identity, an orderly society, and disciplined productivity.

> It is an object of vast magnitude that systems of education should be adopted and pursued which may not only diffuse a knowledge of the sciences but may implant in the minds of the American youth the principle of virtue and of liberty and inspire them . . . with an inviolable attachment to their country (Webster, 1790).

Webster was impatient with a classical education that would offer information of little use to a growing republic.

> When I speak of a diffusion of knowledge, I do not mean merely a knowledge of spelling books, and the New Testament. An acquaintance with ethics, and with the general principles of law, commerce, money and government, is necessary for the yeomanry of a republican state (Webster, 1788).

Like Webster, what most Americans had in mind for their children was to arm them with enough of the rudiments of reading, writing, and arithmetic to allow them to get ahead in the practical activities of life in a new nation. Richard Hofstadter, an eminent historian who believed that American society was fundamentally anti-intellectual, wrote:

> During the nineteenth century, when business criteria dominated American culture almost without challenge; and when most business and professional men attained eminence without much formal

> education, academic schooling was often said to be useless. . . . [A]n immediate engagement with the practical tasks of life was held to be more usefully educative whereas intellectual and cultural pursuits were called unworldly, unmasculine, and impractical (1962, pp. 33–34).

Textbooks emphasized the practical and the moral. They urged, "Little children, you must seek rather to be good than wise," and "We are all scholars of useful knowledge" (Hofstadter, 1962, pp. 306, 307). "Book learning" was limited, and only one small part of the total education offered by community institutions.

> Schooling—which farmers usually associated with book learning—was only a small, and to many, an incidental part of the total education the community provided. The child acquired his values and skills from his family and from his neighbors of all ages and conditions. The major, vocational curriculum was work on the farm or in the craftsman's shop or the corner store; civic and moral instruction came mostly in church or at home or around the village where people met to gossip or talk politics. A child growing up in such a community could see work-family-religion-recreation-school as an organically related system of human relationships (Tyack, 1974, pp. 14–15).

Teachers in Early America

With schooling relegated to a minor status among community institutions, the position of teacher did not carry much prestige. Teachers were paid little, worked for only a few months of the year, and had responsibilities that far exceeded the purely academic. The early New England schoolteacher was responsible not only for assigning and hearing "recitations," but also for keeping the schoolroom clean and tending the wood stove that provided the only heat. The teacher was charged with keeping order—no easy task in a classroom that included near-adult farm boys more interested in the crops than their lessons. The school term was short and attendance erratic, given the need for children to contribute to the family's economy. Discipline in those days was simple and physical; teachers controlled with the aid of a "switch," or a whip. Given the fact that teachers needed to be bigger and stronger than their students in order to carry out this form of discipline, most early schoolteachers were men. The short school term and low pay, however, meant that the men who became schoolteachers were either seeking temporary employment while they studied for the law or the ministry, or were incapable of plying a trade, managing a farm, or running a business.

> There was a train of stereotypes of this order: the one-eyed or one-legged teacher, the teacher who had been driven out of the ministry by his weakness for drink, the lame teacher, the misplaced fiddler, and the teacher who got drunk on Saturday and whipped the entire school on Monday (Hofstadter, 1964, p. 314).

Washington Irving described such a teacher in his fictional portrait of Ichabod Crane, in *The Legend of Sleepy Hollow:*

> The cognomen of Crane was not inapplicable to his person. He was tall, but exceedingly lank, with narrow shoulders, long arms and legs, hands that dangled a mile out of his sleeves, feet that might have served for

> shovels, and his whole frame most loosely hung together. His head was small, and flat at top, with huge ears, large green glassy eyes, and a long snipe nose, so that it looked like a weather-cock perched upon his spindle neck to tell which way the wind blew. To see him striding along the profile of a hill on a windy day, with his clothes bagging and fluttering about him, one might have mistaken him for the genius of famine descending upon the earth, or some scarecrow eloped from a cornfield (Irving, [1917], 2000).

Hofstadter argues that the sorry character of the early American male schoolteacher who was unfit for "real work" was evidence of both a lack of respect for the work of teaching and the nation's weak commitment to education. We urge our readers to remember the previous chapter of this text, where we have offered a fuller, more complex, and, we hope, more attractive, view of the vocation of teaching and the images of teachers in our history.

As the republic's first fifty years drew to a close with a heady expansion of its population and its territory, and with the growth of industrialization and a more specialized workforce, the need for an organized system of widely available schooling became more obvious. As we will discuss in the next section, those who succeeded in fashioning such a system used the same moral and economic arguments that characterized their forebears.

The Struggle for the Common School

The previous section describes the uneven picture of schooling in America during the eighteenth and early nineteenth centuries. The amount and type of education that children received—indeed, whether they received any at all—depended upon where in the nation they happened to live. With the exception of a few cities where elementary education was mandatory, white children who lived in cities and large towns went to school as long as they were not needed at home. Rural children might have access to schools, if there were sufficient numbers of parents who stopped working on the farm long enough to build a school and hire a teacher. Most black children had no schooling; in states where they were enslaved, any education they received was clandestine, and in most "free" states, they were largely discouraged from attending the local schools. Wealthy children might have tutors or be sent abroad for their education. Girls were not expected to seek an education beyond learning to read, write, and do simple arithmetic. Even in cities, district politics determined the quality and quantity of schooling a child would receive. In our new nation founded on the principles of democracy—"government by the people"—the people were not guaranteed access to the education they would need to participate in the experiment. It took the idealistic and dogged determination of a New England lawyer and legislator to convince the rest of the nation to create a system of **common schools**—available, equal, and with an "educational purpose truly common to all" (Cremin, 1957, p. 12).

Horace Mann, the "Great Equalizer"

By 1820 the Northeast, led by Massachusetts and Connecticut, was moving toward the establishment of organized school systems that were free and accessible to all children. In 1826 the Massachusetts Great and General Court (the state legislature)

Horace Mann was an active advocate of the common school and believed that the right kind of education would build individual character and thus eventually reform society.
Source: © CORBIS

enacted a law requiring that all cities and towns elect a school committee to oversee schools. The following year, the legislature expanded publicly funded education by requiring that communities provide a high school education for their children, and in 1836 it created the first state board of education, appointing one of its own members, Horace Mann, to the position of secretary to the board.

An advocate of temperance, women's rights, and the abolition of slavery, Mann believed that "the common school . . . may become the most effective and benignant of all the forces of civilization" because of its universality and because "the materials upon which it operates are so pliant and ductile as to be susceptible of assuming a greater variety of forms than any other earthly work of the Creator" (quoted in Mayer, 1965, p. 345). His early Calvinist upbringing (though supplanted later by the gentler Unitarianism); his experiencing of public insurgences, such as riots between Boston Catholics and Protestants; and the extension of the vote to white men of all social classes, regardless of whether they owned property (Spring, 1997) caused him to worry that "the unrestrained passions of men are not only homicidal, but suicidal; and a community without a conscience would soon extinguish itself" (quoted in Mayer, p. 346). But the right kind of education builds individual character ["Train up a child in the way he should go, and when he is old he will not depart from it" (Mann, 1848, p. 100)] and thus eventually reforms society. According to Mann:

> In teaching the blind and the deaf and dumb, in kindling the latent spark of intelligence that lurks in an idiot's mind, and in the more holy work of reforming abandoned and outcast children, education has proved what it can do by glorious experiments. These wonders it has done in its infancy, and with the lights of a limited experience; but when its faculties shall be fully developed, when it shall be trained to wield its mighty energies for the protection of society against the giant vices which now invade and torment it—against intemperance, avarice, war, slavery, bigotry, the woes of want, and the wickedness of waste,—then there will not be a height to which the enemies of the race can escape which it will not scale (quoted in Mayer, 1960, pp. 345–346).

As the first secretary to the Massachusetts Board of Education, and later as a U.S. congressman and then president of Antioch College, Mann committed himself to developing education's "faculties" and "mighty energies," working on everything from school curricula to the buildings themselves and to the education of the teachers who would staff them. He lived during a time of utopian thinking in America, associating with New England transcendentalists such as Emerson, Thoreau, and Bronson Alcott (who established his own experimental school), with the abolitionists who worked to eradicate slavery and fugitive slave laws, and with the early movement to equalize the rights and conditions of women. His marriage to Mary Peabody, sister of Elizabeth Peabody (see Chapter 6) and sister-in-law of Nathaniel Hawthorne, drew him into the circles of influential liberal thinkers and educators of the day.

Mann's sanguine belief in the promise of schooling as a means of enlightening and improving the life of ordinary (and poor) Americans marks him as an educational reconstructionist. The arguments he used to persuade taxpayers and the powerful business community to support expanded and systematized public schools were, however, politically circumspect. For one thing, the nation's ideology of individualism made many suspicious of any restraints on freedom and choice.

By 1820 the Northeast, led by Massachusetts and Connecticut, was moving toward the establishment of common schools, or organized school systems that were free and accessible to all children.
Source: The Granger Collection, New York

For another, the common school would require the financial commitment of individuals, communities, and states, in the form of significant new taxes. Realizing that he had to appeal to "pocketbooks," Mann used the traditional rationales of economic prosperity and societal preservation. He told businessmen that those who had attained economic success were the "stewards" of wealth. Their support for the education of the poorer classes was an investment; the common school would provide these children with the knowledge and skills that would make them productive and disciplined workers and ensure public safety and progress.

Mindful of the potential clash between social classes, Mann argued that, in educating the children of the wealthy and the poor side by side in the same classroom and teaching them a shared set of beliefs and values, the common school would "expand social feelings" and "disarm the poor of their hostility towards the rich" (1848, p. 87). It would also reduce the possibility of social divisiveness or revolution by increasing the general wealth of the population and reducing the gap between rich and poor. Education, "beyond all other devices of human origin is the great equalizer of the conditions of men, the balance-wheel of the social machinery," he wrote in his twelfth annual report to the Massachusetts State Board of Education (quoted in Cremin, 1957, p. 80).

Mann the Unitarian also hoped for a common moral education, but one that avoided the fierce denominational rivalries among the religious sects of the times. To escape being called antireligious, he accepted the contemporary association of morality with religion and argued for moral instruction in the tradition of a nonsectarian Christianity. There would be no references to the tenets of specific denominations, but all children would read the Christian Bible. "Common" in this instance meant the virtues shared by believing Christians. This is a stance that won him both support and criticism; the first, from those who appreciated the fact that he moved public education away from the various churches of specific regions; the

The advent of the graded school and the expansion of common schools across the country created a critical need for more teachers. The fact that it was acceptable at the time to pay women less than men for doing the same work attracted school system administrators to the idea that women teachers might be as good as, if not better than, men.
Source: The Granger Collection, New York

second, from those who deplored his insensitivity toward non-Christians and his refusal to separate religion from state.

Historian David Tyack's definitive book on the history of urban education, *The One Best System* (1974), describes the consolidation and systematizing of public schools in America. Though he portrays the road to the "one best system" as often rocky and not without its critics, he views the growth of the movement to replace politician-dominated ward schools, church-run town schools, tuition-funded academies, and nonexistent or inferior schools for children of color, as positive progress toward equal access and equal educational opportunity. While Horace Mann's legacy of common schooling is a clear advancement in American education, it did not fully accomplish its academic and social purpose: the creation of "one best system" that was right for everyone. The following sections of this chapter describe the continuing struggle for equality by and on behalf of women, African Americans, and Native Americans, and their teachers.

Women's "True" Profession

Among Horace Mann's contributions to American education was the upgrading of organizational structures to prepare teachers and to house the activities of education. He promoted the establishment of special state-funded post-secondary institutions called **normal schools,** named after the *Ecole Normale,* which was established in France in 1794 as a model for the training of elementary teachers. The first normal school was founded in Lexington, Massachusetts, in 1839. Mann helped build new and bigger schools that organized children into age-based grades. The new attention to education as a field of study included special preparation for school administrators (or "principal teachers").

With the goal of more efficient school administration, Mann promoted what has come to be called the egg-crate school, an architectural plan that persists today. Originating with the building of Boston's Quincy School in 1847, this plan replaced the multi-age one-room design with a more efficient assignment of students to separate rooms, based on the academic abilities that were presumably associated with their age. A separate office was established for the school principal. One benefit of this hierarchical structure was disciplinary: teachers could now more easily manage the behavior of children who were confined with others of similar developmental levels, and "unmanageable" children could be sent to the principal's office for correction. At the same time, the pedagogy available in the one- or two-year normal school programs prepared teachers to discipline with greater ease and confidence.

Paying Women Teachers Less The advent of the graded school and the expansion of common schools across the country created a critical need for more teachers. The fact that it was acceptable at the time to pay women less than men for doing the same work attracted school system administrators to the idea that women teachers might be as good as, if not better than, men. Though some communities balked at hiring women teachers, the Civil War, which took great numbers of men away to the battlefield, effectively ended the debate. Superintendents and school committees rushed to rationalize the hiring of women. The Boston School Committee praised its women teachers for their lack of ambition and their steadfast loyalty: "They are less intent on scheming for future honors or emoluments [than men]. As a class, they never look forward, as young men almost invariably do, to a period of legal emancipation from parental control" (quoted in Tyack, 1974, p. 60).

One Ohio superintendent wrote in the mid-1800s:

> Females do not expect to accumulate much property by this occupation; if it affords them a respectable support and a situation where they can be useful, it is as much as they demand. I, therefore, most earnestly commend this subject to the attention of those counties which are in the habit of paying men for instructing little children, when females would do it for one-half the sum and generally much better than men can (quoted in Rothman, 1978, p. 57).

The superintendent was correct in his mathematics. As late as 1905, according to a National Education Association survey of 467 school systems, salary differentials were startling. In the elementary schools, women teachers averaged $650 annually, as compared to $1,161 for men. In the high schools, women teachers earned $903, to men's $1,303. And the average salary for female principals of elementary schools was $970, while male elementary principals made $1,542 (Tyack, 1974, p. 62). Of note is the fact that salaries were differentiated not only by gender but by school level, a fact that compounded the problem for women, who were typically assigned to elementary schools. The assumption that women should earn less than men and be assigned positions lower in status and rank reflected their economic and social position in society as a whole. The hierarchical structure of schools and the paternalism of society "fit as hand to glove," says Tyack (1974, p. 60). When a teacher gave advice to a principal, coached a Denver superintendent, "it is to be [as] the good daughter talks with the father" (in Tyack, 1974, p. 60).

The emergence of teaching as a woman's job, however convenient, was not without controversy. The general relief at securing ladies of good character to teach children for modest salaries was balanced by a concern that feminizing the teaching force would adversely affect boys. The psychologist G. Stanley Hall believed women teachers would provide boys with a truncated view of the world, absent the realities of conflict and evil. According to Hall, the fear was that women teachers would instill in their male students the nurturing values associated with femininity instead of the aggressiveness that he felt was more appropriate, and more natural, in men (Hall, 1911, p. 540). The eminent educational historian Merle Curti described Hall's reservations about the influence of women teachers on adolescent boys:

> Women tended to inculcate certain qualities such as gentleness, and neglected to instill the virile traits so vital to the adolescent boy. The woman teacher refused to depict evil and its consequences. . . . No real boy, moreover, could safely be taught to love his enemies; the effects of such teaching were emasculating. He must fight, whip, and be whipped (Curti, 1959, p. 419).

The Feminization of Teaching Quite possibly the contemporaneous nineteenth-century movement for women's suffrage and the fear that great numbers of women teachers would soon be interested in professional advancement were additional factors compromising the complete acceptance of women as teachers. The city of Philadelphia created a "School of Pedagogy" for men only and established a policy that limited teaching positions in the top two grades of its elementary schools to men (Tyack, 1974, p. 64). While the academic requirement for elementary teaching was limited to graduation from grammar school and then completion of a one- or two-year normal school program, high school teachers had university degrees, a rationale used to justify pay differentials (Spring, 1997). The same National Education Association that conducted the salary survey reported previously, and which is the largest professional organization of teachers today, at first admitted only administrators as members. Teachers could attend meetings, but were confined to the gallery and could not speak. The NEA did not admit women until early in the twentieth century.

The rhetoric of female champions of women teachers is a curious blend of chauvinistic beliefs and advocacy for the education and employment of their gender. Catharine Beecher, founder of the Hartford Female Seminary in 1848, organized the American Women's Educational Association in 1851 to advance the role of women in the nation's development by arguing that women were especially fit to foster literacy and morality in the young. In teaching, Beecher said, women could express their "maternal capacity":

> Most happily, the education necessary to fit a woman to be a teacher is exactly the one that best fits her for that domestic relation she is primarily designed to fill (Beecher, 1835, p. 18).

Men, on the other hand, would be unhappy in the work:

> [W]hen we consider the aversion of most men to the sedentary, confining, and toilsome duties of teaching and governing young children; when we consider the scanty pittance that is allowed to the

> majority of teachers; and that few men will enter a business that will not support a family, when there are multitudes of other employments that will afford competence, and lead to wealth; it is chimerical to hope that the supply of such immense deficiencies in our national education is to come from that sex (Beecher, 1835, p. 18).

To Beecher, the preparation and hiring of women teachers met the dictates of both the different natures of the sexes and the natural order of society.

> [H]eaven has appointed to one sex the superior, and to the other the subordinate station . . . it is therefore as much for the dignity as it is for the interest of females, in all respects to conform to the duties of this relation (Beecher, 1851, p. 176).

It is not surprising that Beecher worried that giving women the right to vote and opening the doors to them into all the professions would threaten the social institutions of the nation. In the introduction to *Woman's Profession as Mother and Educator* (1872), she refers to "the false principles and false reasonings on the subject of 'women's rights' now working extensive evils that are little realized." Women's chief profession was mother and educator; but the suffrage movement was sending out women "of talents and benevolence" to lecture and "scatter tracts . . . advocating principles and measures destructive both to the purity and perpetuity of the family state." As nature ordained, women should be teachers, and should be educated to fit that role, but the political and legal power that might have prepared them for professional and policymaking leadership was left in the hands of men.

Table 7.1 shows that following the establishment of the common school, the majority of teachers were women, a percentage that increased over time so much that in the year 2000 women teachers comprised three-quarters of the teaching work force. The shift from male to female teachers in the mid-nineteenth century affected the nature of the work. Under the influence of women teachers, American schools' original emphasis on the mastery of information, the rote learning of rudimentary skills, and the practice of physical discipline grew to encompass a concern for the general nurturing of the young, including their social and emotional well-being. This shift contributed both positively and negatively to the status of

Table 7.1 Changes in the Teaching Work Force by Gender

Year	1870	1890	1910	1930	1950	1970	2000
Men Teachers (%)	39	35	21	16	21	32	25
Women Teachers (%)	61	65	79	84	79	68	75

Sources: U.S. Dept. of Education (1993), Office of Educational Research and Improvement (OERI); National Center for Educational Statistics (NCES), *120 Years of American Education: A Statistical Portrait;* and U.S. Dept. of Education (2002), OERI, NCES, *Digest of Educational Statistics,* Ch. 2 Elementary and Secondary Education.

women. On one hand, the subservience of most women teachers continued long into the twentieth century, helped by their own ambiguity about their chosen profession. In his classic work, *Schoolteacher* (1975), Dan Lortie documented women teachers' limited choices and limited ambitions. Many women reported to Lortie that their decision to teach had been determined by their parents, by the fact that they had been limited to local teachers' colleges for furthering their education, or by their own perception that teaching was work whose schedule was compatible with marriage and motherhood.

On the other hand, for a long time becoming a teacher was a great achievement and a step up the social ladder for the educated daughters of immigrant, poor, and working-class families (Rousmaniere, 1997). In addition, there are myriad examples of strong women in American history who chose teaching as a vocation and who, through their leadership, advanced the profession. Women led the fight for higher and equitable salaries and professional status for teachers (Tyack and Hansot, 1982), including:

- Margaret Haley, founder of the Chicago Teachers Federation
- Ella Flagg Young, appointed superintendent of the Chicago Public Schools in 1909, the first female superintendent of an American city school system
- Mary McLeod Bethune, organizer of the National Council of Negro Women, educational advisor to several presidents, and founder of the Daytona Normal and Industrial School for Negro Girls (now Bethune-Cookman College)

Elizabeth Peabody and other women created the first kindergartens in America (Swiniarski, 1987), established schools for freed slaves (Billington, 1981; Towne, 1901), brought education to the frontier (Hoffman, 1981), and led efforts to improve the education and social welfare of new immigrants (Antin, 1912; Elshstain, 2002). The portraits of teachers offered in the previous chapter provide examples of strong, committed women teachers who advanced the status and conditions of their work.

Female teachers collaborated with leaders of the women's movement, using its feminist rationales and political strategies to improve working conditions. Margaret Haley was an education reformer, labor activist, and feminist. She cofounded the Chicago Teachers' Federation with Catherine Goggin in 1897 as the first labor union for teachers, a feat that dramatically altered the future of teaching as a profession and teachers as a political force (Rousmaniere, 1999). In recalling a speech by her colleague, Haley described the strength of the suffrage message as a source of awakening women teachers to the conditions of their lives and work:

> [Goggin] brought home to the teachers in her unique, forceful way the revelation of their disadvantage as nonvoters. I remember the effect it had on the audience of teachers when she said, "Why shouldn't the City Council give our money to the firemen and policemen? Haven't they got votes?" There was no doubt but that this incident converted many a teacher to the cause of woman's suffrage (quoted in Spring, 1986, p. 263).

In the twentieth century this alliance saw important gains for women teachers. Today, women enjoy salary equity, increasing entrée into high-level school administrative positions, the right to participate in collective bargaining within the profession and to engage in political movements in the larger society, and, of course, the right to marry and keep one's job (Carter, 2002). However, the struggle for equal rights was long and hard, and complicated by a woman teacher's race, social class, and geographical location. In the story of one African American teacher of the mid-nineteenth century, we learn how gender, race, and social class, along with the events of history, influenced her determination to remove the barriers facing her people and her profession.

Charlotte Forten became the Salem Normal School's first African American graduate and subsequently devoted her life to improving the lives of her own oppressed people.
Source: Moorland-Spingarn Research Center, Howard University

The Story of Charlotte Forten: The Intersection of Gender, Race, and Class

One teacher who devoted her life to improving the lives of her own oppressed people was Charlotte Forten. She was a third-generation free African American. Her grandfather, James Forten, had learned sailmaking as an apprentice and had taken ownership of the shop in his thirties. As the inventor of a device to handle sails, he amassed a fortune, which allowed him to devote time and attention to the cause of abolition. As a child, Charlotte Forten was exposed to her grandfather's conviction that there was no biological difference between the races and that black slaves should be freed and educated to "take their place in American society" (Billington, 1981, p. 14). His well-appointed home on Lombard Street in Philadelphia became a gathering place for the great minds of the day; among them, the abolitionist William Lloyd Garrison and the poet John Greenleaf Whittier.

Forten was educated at home by tutors. The Quakers of Philadelphia offered education to blacks, but in separate schools. Seeking to provide her with higher education in an integrated setting, her family sent her to "grammar school" in Salem, Massachusetts, where she lived with an abolitionist family, once again in the company of prominent thinkers and political activists. Deciding to pursue a teaching career, she enrolled in the Salem Normal School, one of the earliest teacher-preparation institutions in the nation, and the present Salem State College. Forten became the normal school's first African American graduate.

Although she never enjoyed teaching, "Salem offered plentiful opportunity for her to pursue her real interests: abolitionism and learning" (Billington, 1981, p. 25). Regarding the latter goal, she became a student of several languages, a voracious reader ["sometimes as many as a hundred books a year" (Billington, 1981, p. 25)], and a writer of poetry and essays. In 1862 she embarked on arguably the most important experience of her life; leaving comfortable, cultured Salem, she made her way to the island of St. Helena off the coast of South Carolina, where she participated in a social experiment that would reveal the internal conflicts of her own life.

During the Civil War, the Union army's blockade of Charleston Harbor had resulted in the flight of wealthy white plantation owners from St. Helena, leaving valuable cotton crops in the hands of slaves who had been isolated from mainland, mainstream influences and were among the most oppressed of the Southern blacks. In 1862 Forten joined the ranks of a small group of volunteer teachers charged with bringing education and enlightenment to "her people." Excited by the prospect of "find[ing] my highest happiness in doing my duty" (quoted in Billington, 1981, p. 137), she soon learned that the conditions of her own life had left her in a position of social ambiguity and "homelessness." Her firsthand experience of the cruelty of prejudice and discrimination in Philadelphia, where she had been forced to sit in segregated sections of the city's streetcars and been denied access to restaurants, stores, and theaters, had reinforced her identity as an African American. Watching runaway slaves shackled by mobs, she developed a hatred of discrimination and a relentless racial consciousness:

> [H]er race was always uppermost in Charlotte Forten's thoughts. The color of her skin determined her attitude toward her fellow humans, toward her country, and toward her God. From the accident of pigmentation stemmed even her driving ambition. She must excel among the students of the . . . normal school. . . . She must read constantly. . . . She must master French, German, and Latin in addition to her regular school work. Every lesson learned well was a triumph not only for herself but for the oppressed Negro people of mid-century America (Billington, 1981, p. 8).

Forten herself wrote:

> I wonder that every colored person is not a misanthrope. Surely we have something to make us hate mankind. I have met girls in the schoolroom—they have been thoroughly kind and cordial to me,—perhaps the next day met them on the street—they feared to recognize me. . . . These are but trifles, certainly, to the great, public wrong which we as a people are obliged to endure. But to those who experience them, these apparent trifles are most wearing and discouraging; even to the child's mind they reveal volumes of deceit and heartlessness, and early teach a lesson of suspicion and distrust. Oh! It is hard to go through life meeting contempt with contempt, hatred with hatred, fearing, with too good reason to love and trust hardly anyone whose skin is white (quoted in Billington, 1981, p. 74).

Yet on arrival at Port Royal, the St. Helena island community where Laura Towne had started a school for newly freed children and adults, Forten was startled to find that the lives and backgrounds of "her people" were quite different from her own. Their language was unfamiliar; they spoke a dialect that combined the African languages of Mende, Kisi, Malinke, and Bantu tribes with the Southern English dialect of their slavemasters, a dialect that later came to be called "Gullah." Their African roots were still quite obvious in their clothing, their religious traditions, their food, and many of their cultural practices. At the outset of her experience on St. Helena, Forten refers to them in her journal as "these people," and remarks on their dark skin: "The mother is a good-looking woman, but quite black" (Billington, p. 150). All this was quite foreign to a wealthy, educated young woman whose lifestyle and values resembled those of upper-class white society far more than those of the Southern slaves of the sea islands. For example, in the attempt to bring the Northern, Christian, formally educated version of "civilization" to the freed slaves, Forten and her colleagues at Port Royal rushed to legalize island marriages in Protestant rites. Her description of the wedding of six couples on one day seems elitist and patronizing today:

> T'was amusing to see some of the headdresses. One, of tattered flowers and ribbons, was very ridiculous. But no matter for that. I am truly glad that the poor creatures are trying to live right and virtuous lives (Billington, p. 153).

Charlotte Forten went to St. Helena hoping to find a sense of belonging that had eluded her in the white-dominated world in which she lived in the North. Her initial startled reaction made her feel like an outsider once again, this time not because of her color but because of her social class. The journal she kept in her eighteen months there shows her growing connection to the people and appreciation for their way of life. From the first, she was sensitive to others' attitudes toward them:

> Some of the Superintendents seem to me strongly prejudiced against them, and they have a contemptuous way of speaking of them that I do not like. It shows a lack of sympathy with them. Such people sh'ld not come here (Billington, p. 165).

A musician herself, she was deeply affected by the singing at the "shouts," or prayer meetings: "'Look upon the Lord,' which they sang to-night, seems to me the most beautiful of all their shouting tunes. There is something in it that goes to the depths of one's soul" (Billington, p. 169). Meeting Harriet Tubman, a leader of Forten's own gender and race, was one of the highlights of her experience on the island: "She is a wonderful woman—a real heroine. My own eyes were full as I listened to her. . . . I am glad I saw her—*very* glad" (Billington, p. 180).

Her experience at Port Royal changed Forten's understanding of her own people—not only their problems, but also their strengths. She came to appreciate the music, the faith, the kindnesses, and the intelligence of the people who were originally strangers. Perhaps the experience ultimately gave her a wider sense of the African American community and a better sense of her own heritage. On St. Helena Island today, at the site of the original mission school, the Penn Center stands as a monument to preserving the culture of the black sea islanders. At this site is a plaque commemorating the contributions of Charlotte Forten to the liberation and education of her people.

Separate and Unequal: The Education of African Americans, Women, and Native Americans

Because of her wealth and the good fortune to have been born to educated free blacks in a Northern city, the quality of Charlotte Forten's education was unusual in the history of African American education. Most of that history is a sad example of two ideas proposed in Chapter 1: that education is always political, and that schools reflect the social, cultural, and economic conditions of the societies and communities in which they find themselves. Historian David Tyack (1974), social scientists Jeannie Oakes (1986) and Signithia Fordham (1995), and research statisticians David Berliner and Bruce Biddle (1995), among others, have convincingly documented our inability to live up to the promise of equal opportunity in the case of women, people of color, and the poor. Education for women in the United States has only recently received attention equal to that paid to the education of men. The shameful differences that persist today between the quality and outcomes of the education of children of the middle classes and the poor, and between white children and their black, Latino, and Native American counterparts, are rooted in the schism between the rhetoric of equality and the reality of social class and racism. We have held the door open to immigrants from around the world, but we have not taken good care of the poor and the people of color among us who may have lived in this country since its founding.

At times in the history of the United States, the public schools and their teachers have taken on transformative roles, revamping their policies and structures to be more accessible and inclusive and teaching in ways that promote social justice and social change. But too often, schools and teachers have served as transmitters of social inequality and institutionalized racism. The ideal of the common school offering equal educational opportunity to all children masked the reality of separate and under-resourced schools for black children in the South, Latino children in the Southwest, and Chinese children in California. It took lawsuits to force the public schools to open their doors wider to extend an equal welcome to all children. In the David Tyack quotation that opens this chapter, Tyack accepts that schools cannot alone correct the inequities and injustices of society, but he deplores their (mostly unwitting) role in perpetuating them. In the next section, we will explore the schooling experiences of three groups of American children who were left behind in a century characterized by the creation and expansion of free public schooling: African Americans, women, and Native Americans. In Chapter 8 we will address the schooling experiences of Latino Americans and immigrant minorities at a later point in the nation's history.

The Education of Black Americans

Before the end of the Civil War, most Southern states had laws prohibiting the teaching of reading to slaves. Therefore, black slaves seeking an education had to do so secretly or with the help of a few sympathetic whites. Black educational pioneer Booker T. Washington taught himself to read with the help of a Webster speller that his mother had managed to obtain (Washington, 1901). Some blacks ran their own illegal "schools" hidden in the fields or kept books hidden under their sewing. Even in the North, schooling for free blacks was hard to come by; poverty and distance and segregation kept many black children working at home.

Abraham Lincoln's emancipation of slaves in 1863 and the post–Civil War amendments to the U.S. Constitution—Amendment XIII, abolishing slavery, and Amendments XIV and XV, which granted African American males the rights and privileges of white males—did not ensure an adequate or equal education. Where schooling was available, it was most often segregated. In Boston, the hostility that faced black children in many integrated public schools led a group of black parents to request that the Boston School Committee set up a separate school for black children. Their request was eventually granted when private contributions from philanthropists such as wealthy white businessman Abiel Smith—who left his entire estate to advance the cause—could no longer be ignored. In time, parents of children in the new black school became disenchanted when it appeared that the quality of teachers, the instructional materials, and the physical condition of the school were inferior. Benjamin Roberts sued the city for barring his five-year-old daughter from attending any of the five white schools she passed on her way from her home to the black school she was assigned to. He lost the case in one of the first court rulings to state that separate schools were not inherently unequal. This line of reasoning culminated in the 1896 landmark U.S. Supreme Court case ***Plessy* v. *Ferguson,*** which affirmed the principle that political equality did not guarantee social equality—that separate facilities such as streetcars might well provide equal services. But the strong abolitionist movement in the Boston area worked to influence the Massachusetts state legislature to overturn the Roberts ruling in 1855, and to enact the first law prohibiting segregation and requiring that no child be denied admission to a public school on the basis of race. One year later, a law holding school committees liable for damages resulted in the integration of the Boston Public Schools by 1856.

Despite the emancipation of slaves in 1863 and subsequent amendments that were passed to ensure equal rights for African Americans, adequate education was not available to all black students. Where schooling was available, it was most often segregated, and the quality of education and physical conditions of the black schools tended to be inferior to those of the white schools.
Source: © CORBIS

Black parents, political leaders, and educators have argued about the relative merits of segregated versus integrated schools and the content of their curriculum since the end of the Civil War. A hallmark of Reconstruction was the establishment of the federal Freedmen's Bureau, which created thousands of schools across the South for the children of freed slaves, staffed mostly by Northern white teachers armed with Webster's spellers and McGuffey's readers. In the early 1870s, the percentage of black children enrolled in school exceeded the percentage of whites, a situation that reversed itself as Reconstruction failed at the hands of white Southerners who passed discriminatory laws, fearing the erosion of white supremacy (Spring, 1997).

The Debate over Separate Schools: Booker T. Washington and W. E. B. Du Bois Black leaders were divided over the issue of separate schools. Some, like Booker T. Washington, thought that the special circumstances of blacks called for a separate education that would prepare them for realistic employment so that they could establish themselves as contributing members of society and demonstrate their economic value. He argued against the traditional curriculum, which he thought was purely academic and of little use in the new industrial South, in favor of agricultural and industrial curricula, which would make blacks better farmers, tradesmen, and factory workers. Given the conditions of the times, Washington said, "the opportunity to earn a dollar in a factory just now is worth infinitely more than the opportunity to spend a dollar in an opera house" (Washington, 1901, p. 224). "Cast down your bucket where you are," he urged black and white audiences (Washington, 1901, p. 219). What was necessary for his people's ultimate advancement was a temporary compromising of their full integration and a yielding to the prevailing fears and prejudices of white Southerners: "In all things that are purely social we can be as separate as the fingers, yet one as the hand in all things essential to mutual progress" (Washington, 1901, p. 190). Black progress would be best accomplished through evolutionary, not revolutionary, means.

Washington had been born a slave in 1856. He spent most of his youth in Malden, West Virginia, working alongside other freed slaves in dirty and dangerous salt and coal mines, and teaching himself to read. In 1872 he was accepted into a new experimental school, the Hampton (Virginia) Normal and Agricultural Institute, whose founder, a white general named Samuel Armstrong, believed that an education in the trades was ideal for blacks. Washington became Armstrong's protégé, and carried his philosophy on to establish the Tuskegee (Alabama) Normal and Industrial Institute. Given minimal support from the community, Tuskegee would have to be self-reliant, as Washington hoped black people would be. Successful student-run agricultural, brick-making, carpentry, and printmaking businesses impressed white donors and politicians and made the school and its leader famous.

Washington the gradualist had his critics within his own community. The most famous and articulate was W. E. B. Du Bois. Born in 1868 in the North in Great Barrington, Massachusetts, Du Bois had never experienced the yoke of slavery and had no patience with compromise. To him, Booker T. Washington's industrial evolutionism would postpone perhaps forever blacks' civil liberties and their political, educational, and social equality, and would condemn them to lives of "permanent servility." In *The Souls of Black Folk,* published in 1903, Du Bois claims,

> Mr. Washington distinctly asks that black people give up, at least for the present, three things—First, political power. Second, insistence on civil rights. Third, higher education of Negro youth,—and concentrate all their energies on industrial education, the accumulation of wealth, and the conciliation of the South (1903, p. 16).

Instead, Du Bois argued that black liberation called for constant, conscious struggle for equal rights, political organization, and an education for potential leaders that was equal to what was available to white children of the highest social classes. He founded the Niagara Movement, precursor to the National Association for the Advancement of Colored People (NAACP), and refused to use streetcars or patronize services that were segregated (Du Bois, 1899). At first an advocate for the kind of integrated education he had experienced as a boy in Massachusetts, in his later life he became convinced that full equality would never be gained and he called for separate schools that would help develop an independent black culture:

> Education must not simply teach work—it must teach Life. The Talented Tenth of the Negro race must be made leaders of thought and missionaries of culture among their people. No others can do this work and Negro colleges must train men for it. The Negro race, like all other races, is going to be saved by its exceptional men (Du Bois, [1903] 1965, pp. 76–77).

Du Bois's philosophy was influenced by his racially and culturally mixed New England background and his own education. Valedictorian of his high school, he attended historically black Fisk University, where he met classmates who were the sons of slaves. He completed a Ph.D. in sociology at Harvard University, spending some years at the University of Berlin, where he marveled at the lack of color barriers in Europe. Committed to black liberation, he took a professorship at black Atlanta University (now Clark Atlanta University), where he wanted his students to become intellectuals—the 'talented tenth' who would lead others of their race (Du Bois, 1903, p. 25). The failure of Reconstruction and the gradual hardening of white control in the South radicalized him; the Southern states had enacted laws prohibiting intermarriage and mandating segregated schools, train stations, and public places (Lewis, 1994).

Du Bois wrote *The Souls of Black Folk* after his infant son died for lack of access to medical care. In it he says, "Well speed, my boy, before the world has dubbed your ambition insolence, has held your ideals unattainable, and taught you to cringe and bow" (Du Bois, 1903, p. 13).

Politics and Law: School Desegregation It took one hundred years before the Massachusetts law prohibiting school segregation on the basis of race established by the Roberts case became the law of the land in ***Brown v. Board of Education of Topeka, Kansas*** (1954). Represented by attorney Thurgood Marshall of the National Association for the Advancement of Colored People (NAACP), Oliver Brown argued that his daughter Linda ought to be able to go to the "white" elementary school four blocks from her Topeka home, rather than walk a mile through a railroad yard to the black children's school across town. Combining the Brown case with similar cases on its docket that challenged school segregation in five other states, and armed with facts detailing the vast differences in the quality of black and white schools, the U.S. Supreme Court threw out the "separate but equal" presumption contained in ***Plessy v. Ferguson.*** Chief Justice Earl Warren delivered the opinion, stating that "segregated schools are not equal and cannot be made equal, and hence they are deprived of the equal protection of the laws."

For Linda Brown's family, the original outcome was simple: "It only meant to me that my sister wouldn't have to walk so far to school the next fall," said her sister fifty years later (Stahl, 2004). The Supreme Court's ruling was one of the most significant events in America's progress toward equalizing education, and civil liberties in general. "I don't think any of us realized how far-reaching this would become. . . . It was not simply about a little girl wanting to go to school. It put race on the agenda" (Stahl, 2004, np). Nine Supreme Court justices could prohibit **de jure** (legal) **segregation;** they could not, however, ensure that black children would henceforth be guaranteed an equal and integrated education.

In the years following *Brown,* schools in the segregated South were forced to integrate, often with the intervention of federal troops. Martin Luther King, Jr., and other black leaders, using the tools of nonviolent protest and garnering the support of progressive whites, brought the constitutional guarantee of civil rights home to the South and its schools. By 1965, President Johnson had used the school integration issue to further the cause of equality and to work toward improving health care, job opportunities, and education for poor Americans. As part of his War on Poverty, he signed into law an Economic Opportunity Act to provide job training, a Voting Rights Act to eliminate discrimination at the polls, and the Elementary and Secondary Education Act of 1965, which created programs such as Head Start and Title I to compensate what the Act called the special educational needs of educationally deprived children" (in Spring, 1986, p. 307).

Combating De Facto Segregation: Busing in Boston The problem in the North took longer to address. Schools in many Northern cities were segregated **de facto** (in reality) by virtue of residential segregation. Blacks and whites lived in different neighborhoods, sometimes by choice, sometimes because blacks were kept from buying homes in certain areas—often because they could not afford to do so. In cities like Cleveland, Detroit, and Boston, the battle for integration

Linda Brown attending a segregated school in the early 1950s.
Source: © Time Life Pictures/Getty Images

resulted in an uneasy set of proposed remedies. These efforts to draw black and white students to the same schools included establishing "magnet schools" designed to attract students to schools based on their special focus or academic theme (e.g., the arts), expanding school districts to encompass white suburbs surrounding black cities, and busing students across town. The difficulties of using schooling to create social change came to a head in the capital city of the state that had launched the first public schools, educated Charlotte Forten and W. E. B. Du Bois, fueled abolitionism, and enacted the first integration law: Boston.

The city was notable for its collection of distinct neighborhoods that functioned as ethnic enclaves. In 1974, the Beacon Hill–Back Bay section of the city was home to "old-money" Yankee Brahmins; Allston-Brighton housed college students and young white singles; the North End claimed first- and second-generation Italians; South Boston, Charlestown, and Hyde Park were Irish; and Roxbury and parts of Mattapan and Dorchester were African American. Each neighborhood had its stores and businesses, and schools, and there was little commerce between them. People from Charlestown and South Boston did not venture into Roxbury, and Roxbury kids admitted to being afraid to do the reverse. School committee members and city councilors were elected at large and, given the relatively small size of the black community, they were white. Although poverty existed in both black and white neighborhoods, the schools in black neighborhoods were grossly inferior. Jonathan Kozol exposed the deplorable conditions in a book he titled *Death at an Early Age* (1967), and thereby launched his career as a chronicler of "savage inequalities" (Kozol, 1991).

In June of 1974, following a suit brought by black parents and supported by the NAACP, a federal district court judge ruled that Boston school committees had for years "knowingly carried out a systematic program of segregation affecting all of the city's students, teachers, and school facilities and [had] intentionally brought about and maintained a dual school system" (HGSE News, 2000, p. 3), thus violating black students' constitutional rights. In an unusual attempt to create the change he sought, Judge W. Arthur Garrity, Jr., placed the school system under his receivership and mandated a desegregation plan for the city's two hundred schools that would include forced busing. The effect was cataclysmic. The *Boston Globe* later put it this way:

> The ruling was the opening act in a long-running drama that would tear apart the ancient fabric of the Puritans' city on a hill. The city that had succored the abolitionists, that viewed itself as a seat of progressive values, was soon cast before the world as a city riven by class and racial strife, where black children on yellow buses could be held hostage by white people of all ages with snarling faces and rocks in their hands, a city where a black man could be assaulted at City Hall by a white man using a pole bearing the American flag as a weapon (Mulvoy, 1997, p. 1).

The school system was reorganized into eight districts, with a ninth comprised of new thematic "magnet" schools. Universities partnered with districts to offer help with program development and professional development for teachers. Good intentions and real offers of help were eclipsed, however, by the violence that accompanied the busing of Roxbury children to South Boston schools. Despite heavy police presence, white parents and others threw stones at the buses full of children as they drove up to South Boston High School. Fights broke out daily inside the school building, and politicians used the media to rail against Garrity's dismantling of "neighborhood schools" with an anger and hatred reminiscent of the bitter battle over school desegregation in Little Rock, Arkansas, twenty years earlier.

Eventually, the violence abated and the sight of school buses moving across the city became commonplace. The impact of the crisis was lasting, however; many white parents withdrew their children from the public schools, enrolling them in new private "academies" or parochial schools, or moving to the suburbs in search of a more peaceful education for their children, or a better one, or, in a few cases, a "whiter" one. In the decades since, the white population of Boston, along with Detroit, Chicago, and other cities, has declined precipitously and the public schools are overwhelmingly nonwhite.

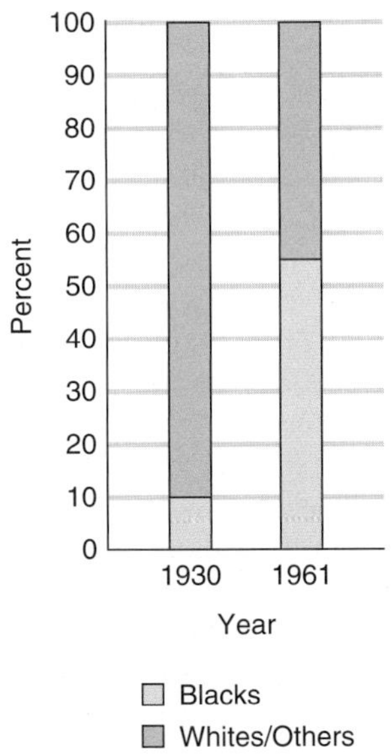

Figure 7.1

Exodus of White Families from Newark, New Jersey

Anyon, J. (1997). *Ghetto schooling: A political economy of urban educational reform.* New York: Teachers College Press.

Jean Anyon's book *Ghetto Schooling* examines the effects of this demographic change, using Newark, New Jersey, as an example. As early as 1918, Newarkers were concerned about an exodus of affluent families to the countryside, which was reducing the property tax base that funded the public schools. The exodus continued: while blacks comprised 10 percent of the city in the 1930s, the percentage grew to 55 percent in 1961 (Anyon, 1997). In 1996, only 3 of the 628 children enrolled in Newark's prekindergarten in the 1995–96 school year were white. New Jersey schools are now among the most segregated of the nation, with white children filling suburban seats in some of the country's best schools and nonwhites in underfunded inner-city classrooms (Orfield & Yun, 1999). The differences in student achievement as measured by state tests are disturbing. Jonathan Kozol has for some years chronicled the effect on black children of the exodus of the white middle class, which has concentrated poverty and racial isolation in the cities (Kozol, 2001, 1995, 1991). His work will be discussed further in Chapter 9.

African American professor Derrick Bell (2004) argues that in *Brown v. Board of Education* the Supreme Court was wrong in focusing on integration. Instead of mandating racial balance, the Court should have mandated that the education of black children be equal to that of whites, whether or not they were schooled separately. Forced integration, he says, has merely resulted in white flight from the cities and not in the educational equality the Court had hoped for. Lately, some black Americans are calling for separate schools that focus on African American culture in order to address better the particular issues facing black youth in a white-dominated society and their particular learning needs. They want a return to neighborhood schools with high-quality programs (Ginwright, 2004; Joondeph, 1998). Molefi Kete Asante (1998), who has developed a curriculum to strengthen black students' knowledge of their rich African heritage, has helped stimulate a network of Afrocentric schools in cities such as Baltimore, Maryland; Akron, Ohio; Milwaukee, Wisconsin; Cambridge, Massachusetts; and Seattle, Washington. While Afrocentric public schools cannot exclude white children, their curriculum appeals to black parents seeking a culture-based alternative for their children.

Under the leadership of strong African American leaders and white social reformers, aided by changing interpretations of law, de jure progress has been made in the education offered to black children. The problem of unequal education continues, however, and is the subject of Chapter 9.

The Education of Women in the New Republic

"Remember the ladies," Abigail Adams wrote to her husband John in 1776, as he was helping to create a free and independent new republic:

> If you complain of neglect of Education in sons, what shall I say with regard to daughters, who every day experience the want of it. . . . I most sincerely wish that some more liberal plan might be laid and executed for the Benefit of the rising Generation, and that our new constitution may be distinguished for Learning and Virtue. If we mean to have Heroes, Statesmen and Philosophers, we should have learned women (quoted in Butterfield, Friedlaender, and Ryerson, 1963, p. 94).

Mrs. Adams's appeal to her husband to provide federal support for the education of children went unanswered. As you learned in the beginning of this chapter, the new Constitution made no mention of schools, either for children in general, or for "the ladies."

What education there was in early America was reserved for boys. Women's lives were confined to the home. They were to be good daughters, good wives, good mothers. They were supposed to bear and raise children who could help in the labors of the family. If their fathers and husbands were farmers, they had no need for book learning at all. If the men had trades or ran businesses, wives and daughters might be taught to read, write, and do simple arithmetic to help out. The New England colonies required that boys be taught to read and write, and that girls be taught at least to read—as part of the training they would need for domestic and economic life. Even in New England, however, only half the women could sign their names (Solomon, 1986, p. 3). Women were assumed to have smaller brains than men, and were assumed to have natures that were inherently dependent and emotional, rather than intellectual. Men were presumed to be aggressive and active; women, submissive and passive (Welter, 1976). When Anne Hutchinson, an educated woman, held Bible study meetings in her home that questioned the prevailing interpretation of the Bible, she was excommunicated and forced out into the wilderness, an act that led her to establish the colony of Connecticut.

Even in such repressive times, some parents and guardians saw fit to educate young women. In colonial Massachusetts, one Boston family provided tutoring in English, Latin, and Greek to a slave girl by the name of Phyllis Wheatley, alongside their own children; she later became a published poet. Anne Dudley Bradstreet, a white poet, was taught by her father, and supported in her further education and her writing by her husband, the Massachusetts Bay Colony's Governor Simon Bradstreet. Mercy Otis Warren, sister of a Revolutionary patriot and wife of a politician, wrote a history of the American Revolution, published in 1805. Judith Sargent Murray, whose father was a Gloucester ship owner, married the Universalist minister John Murray and proceeded to publish numerous essays and plays, many of which asked women to seek independence and education (Smith, 1998). All of these women lived with wealthy families; most were born into them. Anne Bradstreet wrote while raising eight children, but she had the help of servants.

As American cultural and economic life grew, there was more opportunity, need, and time for education. The question of educating girls became less a question of whether to do so, and more a question of what kind of education to provide. The need for literate male voters benefited both sexes, but most people thought a proper education for women—beyond the rudimentary skills—was in the arts that would make them more attractive to suitors (music, dancing, and needlework) and in morality—the virtues of modesty, piety, and obedience. In Louisa May Alcott's *Little Women,* set in the mid-nineteenth century, Marmee tells her rebellious daughter Jo how she learned to control her own temper. Jo asks, "How did you learn to keep still?" Marmee says that Jo's father helped: "He helped and comforted me, and showed me that I must try to practice all the virtues I would have my little girls possess, for I was their example" (Alcott, [1969],1936, p. 65). Ironically, both Alcott and her alter ego Jo are examples of women ahead of their times, who achieved financial and social independence, in large part the result of their education.

Despite the societal suspicion that women who pursued academic learning were selfish and neglectful of their primary duties to their families, there were personal and social factors that led women to seek education. During the Revolution, women who were left on their own when their men went to war had to transact business and otherwise tend to family financial affairs (Wilson, 1976, pp. 386–387). Aware of that fact, Benjamin Rush of Pennsylvania, who was an advocate of free public schools for both sexes, thought that women should know how to read, write, and keep financial records so that they could take charge of their husbands' property if need be (Rush, 1787, pp. 6–9). Of course, girls would have to learn these skills in addition to others that prepared them for their more traditional responsibilities. Dancing, for example, "render[ed] the figure and motions of the body easy and agreeable." Singing strengthened the lungs, was useful in church, and "sooth[ed] the cares of domestic life. . . . [T]he distress and vexation of a husband—the noise of a nursery, and, even the sorrows that will sometime intrude in to her own bosom, may all be relieved by a song" (Rush, 1787, pp. 9–10).

Women who did not marry—a special problem in areas where many men went out to sea or west to the frontier territories—needed skills to support themselves. The new textile mills and manufacturing plants of the Northern cities were employing more women, who were financially independent for the first time and could pursue an education with the wages they were earning. Population growth, industrialization, immigration, and the white settlement of the West created a dire need for schoolteachers.

In response to these developments, a group of forward-thinking women opened new schools and academies for women. It can be argued that it was this group—among them, Emma Willard, Zilpah Grant, Catharine Beecher, and Mary Lyon—that "ensured the permanence of female institutions" and the education of American women (Solomon, 1986, p. 17). New opportunities for higher levels of schooling led women to value education as a way to improve their social stations and the quality of their lives. Those who had hoped that educating women would make them more useful to men did not anticipate that schooling might give women a sense that "they might shape [their] destiny with their own minds and hands" (Cott, 1997, p. 125). Furnished with the new ideas and new perspectives that their education had given them, women "put their minds to work at other purposes than refining their subordination to men" (Cott, 1997, p. 125). The result was the feminism of the mid-nineteenth century, which argued that women were naturally and intellectually equal to men. Educational opportunity had proved the point.

Academies for Women In the early nineteenth century, while standards and funding for schooling for boys was improving, girls' education was still relegated to private and inferior institutions whose subject matter was deficient and insubstantial. Emma Hart Willard, who was born in 1787 into a family of seventeen, received an education unusual for the time. Her father, "a bookish Yankee farmer" (Solomon, 1985, p. 18), encouraged her to enroll in the academy in Berlin, Connecticut. She supported herself as a teacher until she married. Reading through her nephew's medical school texts, she learned geometry and philosophy, subjects of study not offered to girls at the time. When her husband suffered financial problems, she opened a boarding school in her home in Middlebury, Vermont, where she was determined to offer girls a curriculum that included what men were studying, as well as women. When Troy, New York, offered her space to expand, she founded the Troy Academy, now called the Emma Willard School. The curriculum was controversial; many people of the day thought that reading classical literature would expose young women to the "squabbling of heathen gods and goddesses" and distract them from the attributes of the one true God (Solomon, 1986, p. 23). In addition, the Willard Plan included the study of rhetoric—the art of declamation—even before these young women were able to use it in public. (Southerners Sarah and Angelina Grimke's public lectures against slavery in the 1830s were considered revolutionary, and improper, activities for women.) Troy Academy's curriculum—including science, math, history, and philosophy—served as a model for the first public high schools for girls established in Boston and New York City in 1826. That the student population was wealthy was intentional: Willard felt that young advantaged women were typically pampered, averse to useful work, and concerned only with frivolities. Her rigorous education would turn their minds and talents to social responsibility and good works.

Zilpah Grant and Mary Lyon met at the Byfield Academy in Massachusetts in the 1820s, where both were teachers. Grant was self-taught, and had begun tutoring children at age fifteen. She founded the Ipswich Female Academy in 1839, which, along with Catharine Beecher's Hartford Female Seminary, prepared teachers for the fast-increasing number of common schools and sent many West to teach in the district schools of pioneer settlements. Mary Lyon went on to found Mount Holyoke College.

The movement to establish female academies was not limited to New England. In the South, Emma Hart Willard's sister, Almira Hart Phelps, began the Patapsco Institute in Maryland. Betsey Mix Cowles, raised on a Midwestern farm where the contributions of women as well as men were valued, began the Rockford Female Seminary in Illinois after graduating from Oberlin College. Oberlin was the first higher education institution open to both men and women, blacks and whites. Its Christian founders wanted to create a religious community that would carry out God's work on earth. Cowles became a common school teacher and eventually a district superintendent in Ohio, a highly unusual role for a woman at that time. In addition to her commitment to teaching and teacher education, she was a women's suffragist, an ardent abolitionist, and a conductor on Harriet Tubman's Underground Railroad (Ross, 2004).

All of these academies promoted the Christian idea of womanhood and its values of piety, obedience, and domestic skills. Barbara Solomon, author of *In the Company of Educated Women* (1985), concludes: "Knowing well that men feared that a woman of learning would get out of hand, they promised that students would not be spoiled for family duties" (p. 25). Yet Solomon also points out that the education that women received had the unintended consequence of opening their minds to new possibilities for themselves and alternatives to traditional women's roles. Mary Lyon's directive that her students should be "willing to do anything and go anywhere for the good of others" (quoted in Solomon, 1986, p. 25), challenged the idea that women should stay home.

The choice in those days, however, was marriage or career. A woman could not carry out the duties of wife, mother, and homemaker and also undertake the demands of a job outside the home or a public life that might eclipse her husband's. Marriage changed everything for an educated woman. Even Mary Lyon said that, once married, "males should go forward in all public duties, the female should go forward in private duties" (quoted in Solomon, 1986, p. 26). For many years, then, the education a woman might receive would not necessarily allow her to use it in ways other than to encourage her husband and children to use theirs.

Those women who chose to contribute to the larger society did so as independent, single women, as widows, or, in a few cases, with the support of progressive male partners. Catharine Beecher's reading of her fiancé's mathematical papers in part inspired her to reform the education of young women; after he died, she remained single for the rest of her life. Mary Lyon became independent at the age of thirteen, when her widowed mother remarried and moved away, leaving her to keep house for her brother, who paid her for the work. Mary McLeod Bethune, profiled in Chapter 6, had only been married six years when she left the marriage and founded the Daytona Normal and Industrial Institute (now Bethune-Cookman College) for black girls in Florida in 1904. Bethune later served in the cabinet of President Franklin D. Roosevelt. Margaret Haley, responsible for opening teachers' unions and the National Educational Association to the ranks of women teachers and elementary school teachers who were barred from active membership, never married. In fact, most school systems would not hire married teachers until well into the twentieth century. A former teacher who taught in a one-room schoolhouse in Illinois in the 1950s reported that, had she not hidden the fact that she got married in March of her last year of teaching, she would have been fired immediately (Breitborde, 2003).

Legalizing Gender Equity The nineteenth century was a time of growth and change in the new republic. As the country expanded and the economy grew, families worked together to farm the land, establish businesses, and build new settlements. New industries enrolled both men and women to produce new goods.

The contributions of women were as essential as the contributions of men to American economic life, and their relationships became more equal. Women's right to vote, not provided by the Constitution's revolutionary authors, would be just a matter of time. In 1844 female textile workers in Lowell, Massachusetts, organized the Lowell Female Labor Reform Association to demand a ten-hour workday. In 1848 the first women's rights convention met at Seneca Falls, New York, to design a "Declaration of Sentiments and Resolutions." In 1851, former slave Sojourner Truth asked, "Ain't I A Woman?" in a speech to women's rights advocates in Akron, Ohio. The invention of a reliable condom in 1859 enabled women to reduce the number of children they bore. The Civil War, from 1861 to 1865, enrolled women in jobs formerly reserved for men. In 1872, Susan B. Anthony was arrested for attempting to vote for Ulysses S. Grant in the presidential election, and in 1890 the National American Women's Suffrage Association began under the leadership of Elizabeth Cady Stanton. In response to the great wave of immigration in the 1890s, Jane Addams and many other women established a network of settlement houses that provided a way for educated women to do meaningful work. The National Council of Jewish Women was created in 1893, the National Association of Colored Women in 1896, and the Women's Trade Union League of New York in 1903. In 1917, the people of Montana elected Jeannette Rankin as the first woman to serve in the U.S. House of Representatives, and in 1920, the Nineteenth Amendment, giving women the right to vote, was finally ratified, and the Women's Suffrage Association became today's League of Women Voters.

The vote would change the lives and futures of American women. It helped to improve the pay and work conditions for women teachers as well as for other female workers. It propelled many Americans to work for equal rights for women, including equal access to education. Following in the footsteps of those fighting for equality and civil rights for African Americans in the 1960s, activists for women's rights influenced the U.S. Congress to pass Title IX of the Elementary and Secondary Education Act in 1972. Title IX ensured that

> No person in the United States shall, on the basis of sex, be excluded from participation in, be denied the benefits of, or be subject to discrimination under any educational programs or activity receiving federal financial assistance (U.S. Dept. of Education, 1972 preamble).

Title IX was supplemented by the Women's Educational Equity Act of 1974, which provided federal funding to schools for model programs, training, and research aimed at "leveling the playing field" for young women.

In 1966, President Lyndon Johnson's daughter Luci had taken time off from her nursing degree program at Georgetown University to get married. When she tried to return to school, she was denied readmission on the grounds that the school did not permit married women to be students. President Johnson was a strong supporter of Title IX, although it was not passed until after he left office.

According to former Secretary of Education Richard Riley, Title IX has helped young women by equalizing opportunities in academic and athletic education, reducing high school dropout rates, strengthening their preparation in math and science, and opening up the professions. Figures from Riley's report, *Title IX: 25 Years of Progress* (1997), and from more recent National Center for Educational Statistics data support those claims (see Figure 7.2).

Myra and David Sadker (1995) and the American Association of University Women (AAUW) (1991, 1994) tell us that the legal injunctions of Title IX did not

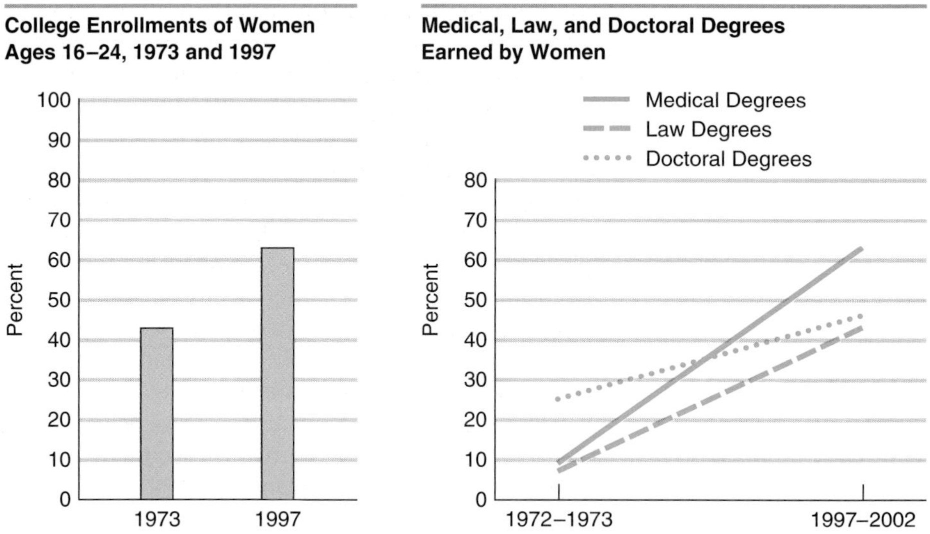

Figure 7.2

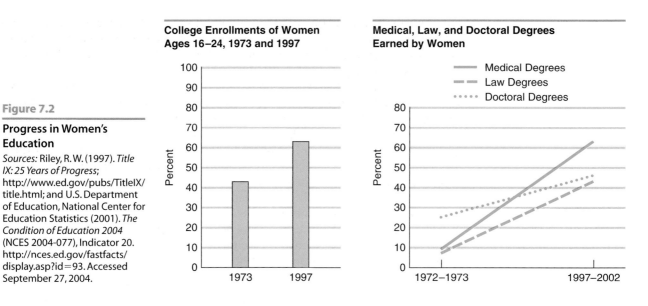

Progress in Women's Education

Sources: Riley, R. W. (1997). *Title IX: 25 Years of Progress;* http://www.ed.gov/pubs/TitleIX/title.html; and U.S. Department of Education, National Center for Education Statistics (2001). *The Condition of Education 2004* (NCES 2004-077), Indicator 20. http://nces.ed.gov/fastfacts/display.asp?id=93. Accessed September 27, 2004.

completely eliminate differences in the experiences of girls and boys in school. The Sadker husband-and-wife team's focus on gender equity began when they co-wrote articles in the late 1960s, only to have their professors and peers refer to them as "David's articles." David Sadker wrote about this experience:

> When Myra and I co-authored articles and proposals, faculty and students would refer to our co-authored work as "David's" article and "David's" proposals. When Myra said: "But I wrote it too!" a faculty member responded, "Of course, when we say 'David,' we mean 'Myra' too!" In class, a similar pattern developed as males dominated class discussion (me included). Female voices, if not silent, were quieter, less frequent, less influential. As Myra took her turn as editor of the school newspaper (another University of Massachusetts norm was rotating editorships), she wrote an editorial entitled "The Only Socially Acceptable Form of Discrimination." She discussed how it felt to be female, and invisible in a doctoral program. As chance (or was it fate?) would have it, that editorial was read by Lou Fischer, a professor who also edited a series of issues oriented books for Harper and Row. "Would you be interested in writing a book about what happens to girls in school?" he asked. And so it began (2000).

Research commissioned by the American Association of University Women (AAUW, 1991, 1994) shows that within the classroom, many teachers still give boys more attention and have higher expectations for them than for their female students. School boards spend more money on boys' athletic programs than on girls'. The curriculum refers far more often to male models and examples than to females. According to recent research commissioned by the AAUW, boys still outnumber girls in high school and college science and engineering classes and in the science and engineering work force (Ginorio and Huston, 2001). Those who attribute many of these differences to factors outside the school—for example, the emphasis in the media and in many communities on girls' social relations, physical attractiveness, and popularity over academic achievement—point to the benefits of single-sex schools, the same kind of education that Emma Willard and Mary Lyon promoted for girls.

There are dissenters: Christina Hoff Sommers (2000) argues that in today's schools, the balance has shifted in favor of girls. It is boys who are the "second sex," as evidenced by, for example, elementary school boys' reading test scores, which are well behind girls'. Likewise, women students now predominate on college campuses and high school girls outnumber boys in honor societies and in student government. More boys than girls are suspended, drop out of high school, and are diagnosed as having special needs. There is truth on both sides: The experiences of girls and boys in school mirror the differences and the issues that both groups face in society, issues that limit the expectations that others, and they themselves, have for their performance and, perhaps, for their future. But women face problems as adults that result from years of discrimination that were at least partly corrected by the federal education legislation of the 1970s. Secretary Riley summed up the impact of Title IX in this way:

> What strikes me the most about the progress that has been achieved since Title IX was passed in 1972 is that there has been a sea change in our expectations of what women can achieve. More important, women have shown skeptics again and again that females are fully capable of being involved as successful and active participants in every realm of American life. . . . The great untold story of success that resulted from the passage of Title IX is surely the progress that has been achieved in education. In 1971, only 18 percent of all women, compared to 26 percent of all men, had completed four or more years of college. This education gap no longer exists. Women now make up the majority of students in America's colleges and universities in addition to making up the majority of recipients of master's degrees. Indeed, the United States has become a world leader in giving women the opportunity to receive a higher education.
>
> Accompanying this untold story of success is the too frequently told story of the barriers that women continue to encounter—despite their history of accomplishments and despite the history of the legislation that protects them from such barriers. Too many women still confront the problem of sexual harassment, women still lag behind men in gaining a decent wage, and only one-third of all intercollegiate athletic scholarships are granted to women. Clearly, much more remains to be done to ensure that every American is given an equal opportunity to achieve success without encountering the obstacle of gender bias. But of this I am sure: somewhere in America today there are young women who are studying hard and achieving success on the athletic field who even now may be thinking hard about their careers as scientists, business owners, basketball players, or even the possibility of becoming president of the United States. They may not know of the existence of Title IX, but Title IX will be there for them should any of them encounter a skeptic who does not believe that they can succeed and be part of the American Dream (Riley, 1997, Introduction).

Cultural Replacement: The Education of Native Americans

In the first century after the founding of the republic, the federal government entered into several hundred treaties with the Native American nations. These treaties included provisions for federally funded schooling for the children of tribes that were "relocated." Schools were established on reservations in the middle of the nineteenth century, usually run by churches and missionary societies that were empowered by the government to Christianize the Indians. Attendance was mandatory and any language other than English was forbidden. Here are the words of E. A. Haytt, Commissioner of Indian Affairs, in 1869:

> Indians should be taught in the English language only. . . . There is not an Indian pupil whose tuition is paid by the United States Government who is permitted to study any other language than our own vernacular—the language of the greatest, most powerful, and enterprising nationalities under the sun (quoted in Jaimes, 1992, p. 380).

The government decided that the reservation schools were failing at teaching Indian children the language and culture of white Christian Americans; the influence of the tribal culture of the homes they returned to at the end of the school day was too strong. The children would have to be removed from that influence. Thereafter, in one of the most shameful periods in the history of Native American education, children were forcibly removed from their families to attend residential boarding schools hundreds and thousands of miles away.

In these off-reservation schools, Indian children received new "American-style" clothes—uniforms for the boys and Victorian dresses for the girls. Their long hair was cut off—a serious indignity. One Lakota girl wrote that she cried all night after her hair was cut, for "among our people, short hair was worn by mourners, and shingled hair by cowards!" (Zitkala-Sa, 1900). Speaking only English at school, and allowed visits home only during summers and at Christmas, boarding school children lost the ability to speak their native tongues. They lost the knowledge of native traditions and the values that characterized their native cultures. Many of them died in these schools, homesick, and after years away from home, victims of "white men's" diseases such as smallpox and tuberculosis. Many of those who survived and graduated had difficult lives, fully accepted by neither the white society nor the tribes whose languages and ways of life they had lost.

In some cases, tribal chiefs encouraged parents to send their children away, convinced by white educators that, if the children learned English and white American ways, they would better be able to advocate for the interests of their people. Among the recruiters were former abolitionists, Quakers, and other religious missionaries who believed that the only hope for Indian children was to remove them from the isolated poverty of reservation life, convert them to Christianity, and reeducate them in the ways of the dominant white culture. The story of the establishment of the first off-reservation boarding school illustrates the point that educational decisions that we consider today to be ill-founded and destructive were often made by well-meaning whites and tribal leaders who felt that they were acting in the best interests of Indian children.

The Carlisle Indian Industrial School After the Civil War, one retired Northern captain who had fought in the West, Richard Henry Pratt, took it upon himself to extend the principle of including African American freedmen in the mainstream of American society to the native peoples who were living in self-contained cultures on the reservations. Pratt thought that the Indians should be assimilated into mainstream society by being totally immersed in it. He did not ascribe to the prevailing belief that Native Americans and African Americans were genetically inferior to whites, but believed that the person one became was wholly a matter of environment—nurture, rather than nature.

> It is a great mistake to think that the Indian is born an inevitable savage. He is born a blank, like all the rest of us. Left in the surroundings of savagery, he grows to possess a savage language, superstition, and life. We, left in the surroundings of civilization, grow to possess a civilized language, life, and purpose. Transfer the infant white to the savage surroundings, he will grow to possess a savage language, superstition, and habit. Transfer the savage-born infant to the surroundings of civilization, and he will grow to possess a civilized language and habit (Pratt, [1892], 1973, p. 260).

If the Indians were to be integrated into the American society and become productive members of its economy, they would need to live within that new environment and be totally resocialized.

> The Indians under our care remained savage, because [they have been] forced back upon themselves and away from association with English-speaking and civilized people, and because of our savage example and treatment of them. . . . A great general has said that the only good Indian is a dead one, and that high sanction of his destruction has been an enormous factor in promoting Indian massacres. In a sense, I agree with the sentiment, but only in this: that all the Indian there is in the race should be dead. Kill the Indian in him, and save the man (Pratt, [1892], 1973, pp. 269–271).

To put his ideas into practice, Pratt convinced the federal Bureau of Indian Affairs in 1879 to allow him to convert an old army barracks in Carlisle, Pennsylvania, into the Carlisle Indian School. With funds provided by Quakers and former abolitionists, the school became the model for a system of federal nonreservation boarding schools that enrolled six thousand students by the beginning of the twentieth century.

Pratt visited reservations in the Dakota Territory to recruit children for his school. At the Rosebud Reservation, he met with tribal leaders Spotted Tail, Milk, Two Strike, and White Thunder.

> Spotted Tail was skeptical. He was reluctant to send his and others' children to be trained in the ways of the men who had violated their treaties and trespassed in their Black Hills. But Pratt was persistent and urged Spotted Tail to reconsider, using the argument that had his people been able to read the white man's words, the treaties would have been better understood and such violations might not have occurred. . . . Pratt also predicted that no matter what happened, the white man would keep coming and coming and that Spotted Tail's people must "be able to meet him face to face and take care of themselves and their property without the help of either an interpreter or an Indian agent." Spotted Tail consulted with his tribal headmen and after a long time, returned with

> his consent. "It is all right. We are going to give you all the children you want. I am going to send five, Milk will send his boy and girl, and the others are going to send the rest (Landis, 1996).

The curriculum of the Carlisle School was based on the philosophy of General Samuel Chapman's Hampton Institute, which Booker T. Washington had attended. The Carlisle School, like the Hampton Institute, taught vocational along with academic skills, in the hope of turning out graduates who had a useful trade with which they could earn a living and thus contribute to the American economy. Along with the basic skills of reading, writing, and arithmetic, Carlisle provided vocational training for boys and domestic science for girls. Boys as young as six years old learned to shoe horses, produce tin ware (for example, pots and pans), make harnesses and bridles, and build furniture and wooden, horse-drawn vehicles. Girls learned to sew, cook, and do laundry. Shoes were required; no moccasins allowed. Students marched in formation to and from classes and the dining hall. They were ranked in military style, with some serving as officers and some as representatives serving on a student-run court. Children's reactions to their time at Carlisle were mixed. They were not always aware of how long they would be away from home, or why Luther Standing Bear was Carlisle's first student and the first Indian to be offered United States citizenship. A Lakota Sioux, he recounts his time at Carlisle in his memoir, *My People, the Sioux:* "It did not occur to me [. . .] that I was going away to learn the ways of the white man. My idea was that I was leaving the reservation and going to stay away long enough to do some brave deed, and then come home again alive" (1928, p. 128).

It was difficult at first to adjust to their radically new lives. One small boy wrote a letter to his father a month after he came to Carlisle. His letter shows his confused feelings about being away:

> My Dear Father:—I thought I would write you a few lines and I like the place very much and there was one Negro boy got killed on the railroad and we have a very nice farm and cold water to drink and would send my Bow and arrows and how is my little pony getting along I would like to know how are you getting and would please send me some money and we have a great many boy and is great many girls. . . . And I am coming home in two years from now if Capt. Pratt will let me and how are you getting along . . . when we got here I did not like the place but since I have being here two or three days I have got used to the place and I like it very well but when we got I felt very home sick and be sure and send my bow and some spike arrows. And we go to church every Sunday. And I have a blue suit to where and there was one Shyenne boy shot himself with a pistol and how is Mrs. Cornet folks getting along Mr. and Mrs. Blankshiy folks getting and the boys have a nice green lawn in which play Kicking a football and how are you getting along with your stock (Landis, 1996).

Ote Ke, a Lakota Sioux member of the first group of Carlisle students, became Luther Standing Bear when his teacher wrote a list of Anglicized names on the blackboard and asked him to point to one of them. Standing Bear wrote in his memoir, *My People, the Sioux* (1928) that when the new students were first given paper and pencils, they pulled their blankets over their heads and began to draw pictures of life on the plains—tribal scenes, buffalo hunting, and special cere-

Female students at the Carlisle Indian School in Carlisle, PA. Founded in 1879, the Carlisle Indian School became the model for federal nonreservation Indian boarding school.
Source: © CORBIS

Native American students learn blacksmith trade at a training school in Forest Grove, Oregon.
Source: © Bettmann/CORBIS

monies. He wrote: "When my hair was cut short, it hurt my feelings to such an extent that tears came into my eyes." On the other hand, he admired his new clothes: "How proud we were with clothes that had pockets and boots that squeaked! We walked the floor nearly all that night."

A letter from Luther Standing Bear to his father in February, 1883, reveals that Captain Pratt's plan to turn young Native Americans toward white culture and away from their own was working, and was affecting the children's relationships with their families:

> My Dear Father,
>
> We had a funeral this evening one of the scholars died. The grandson of Standing Bear, Ponca Chief. What do you think of that? you think we felt

> sorry and cried walked around and killed horses and gave them away the things which we have? or cut ourselves and crying for him every day because we love him? Now this is what I want to say something about that. You know it is not right to do that way. If we are truly civilized. We know it is not that way what we want to learn the knowledge of civilization. I want you must give up the Indian ways, you must turn to the good way and try to walk in it, the way of which is God love. Try to be civilized while we try to get a good education. I hope you have determined to do this. Don't think just your children shall be civilized and you just keep on the Indian way, because you are too old now. But you must go with us in the whites' road. I feel glad and happier when I look toward the way of civilization and I feel so sorry when I look back to my own way in the Indians way. Dear father think of this. There only about 250,000 Indians in all. In just one state in New York there are 5,000,000 people. Now if they don't take care of the Indians how can we live if we are not civilized. Father think of this and try to follow the white men's way. Do what I have told you, don't just hear the words . . .
>
> From Your Son,
>
> Luther S. Bear (Landis, 1996)

Carlisle students appreciated the support of Captain Pratt, who encouraged them to call him their "school father." Under the school's Outing Program, children spent the summer working for wages with white families, to further the process of assimilating into white American cultures. One summer, Maggie Stands Looking wrote this letter to her benefactor: "Dear Captain Pratt: What shall I do? I have been here two weeks and I have not bathe. These folks have no bath place. Your school daughter, Maggie Stands Looking." Pratt wrote back, advising her to use a washbasin and rub herself well, signing his letter, "Your friend and school father" (Landis, 1996).

Carlisle teachers viewed Indian children with a mixture of paternalism and appreciation of their culture and character. In the February 1890 issue of the school paper, *The Red Man,* Pratt wrote:

> Miss S. commends the Indian's 'true eye', also regards them as 'more patient and painstaking than white children.' She was struck at first with the marked stillness, the 'reposeful feeling' in a room full of Indian pupils. In the natural sciences, and in civil government—a favorite study—they are more at home. Miss W., teacher of the Juniors, declares that her pupils show superior ability in solving for themselves problems in physics and physical geography. . . . Discipline is universally admitted to be easier than in white schools. This may be explained partially by the fact that here the children are under continuous discipline, from which there is no appeal (Landis, 1996).

Interestingly, Pratt, who had believed that the totalitarian environment of a white-run boarding school would erase Indian culture from children whose future lay in their being able to function in mainstream American society, seems to have realized that change came at a cost:

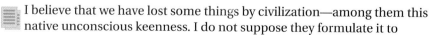

> I believe that we have lost some things by civilization—among them this native unconscious keenness. I do not suppose they formulate it to

> themselves at all, but instinctively, as it were, these children seem to size you up with wonderful quickness and accuracy. If they possess one quality, that is all but universal, among them and in which they are our superiors, it is that of personal dignity (Landis, 1996).

Although many students were won over, others found ways to resist the effort to rob them of their native cultures. David Adams's award-winning book, *Education for Extinction* (1995), recounts examples of the many ways that students at Carlisle and other boarding schools resisted the "replacement model of cultural change" by devising elaborate escape strategies, committing arson, or engaging in other active or passive ways to rebel. Perhaps these acts of rebellion, and the fact that graduates were not typically successful either in white society or back on the reservations, led to the changes in Indian education policies.

Self-Determination and Indian-Run Schools Some tribes undertook to educate their own children in their own way. The Choctaw and Cherokee Nations of Oklahoma created schools that taught the white man's language, but also skills that were useful on the reservations. The U.S. government supported and extended the initiative for an education that honored tribal cultures in the Snyder Act of 1921 and the Indian Reorganization Act of 1934, which mandated the teaching of Indian history and culture in schools. John Collier, commissioner of Indian Affairs, outlined a "new deal" for the Native American, part of President Franklin Roosevelt's New Deal program to combat the Great Depression. Collier thought that Indian education should stress native values and culture as well as skills that would allow Native Americans to adapt to the modern world and its available jobs. Indian schools in the 1930s were influenced by John Dewey's progressivism, which was popular in white schools. The curriculum was linked to the children's lives and culture. Academic skills were applied to real-world problems and tasks. Native arts and crafts became part of classroom life. Importantly, the Bureau of Indian Affairs directed schools not to interfere with native religious practices or ceremonies.

Unfortunately, progressivism disappeared from the curriculum of Indian schools during and after World War II in the same way that it disappeared from mainstream white schools. But the Civil Rights movement of the 1960s included recognition of the needs of Native American children and supported autonomy and cultural pride. In 1965, President Johnson's Elementary and Secondary Education Act included specially marked funding for Indian education, and the president also appointed the first American Indian Commissioner of Indian Affairs, Robert Lafollette Bennett. A 1969 Senate report admitted that the dominant policy of the federal government toward Native Americans had been forced assimilation, a policy that had had a devastating effect on the education of Indian children. Understanding that Native Americans had a right to run their own institutions and determine their own futures, Congress passed in 1975 the Indian Self-Determination and Education Act, which finally empowered the tribes to run their own schools. Today, Native Americans have autonomy over a system of reservation schools and tribal colleges that strengthen students' knowledge of their own history, language, and culture as they teach the standard skills and content common to all Americans.

Schooling and Social Change

The founders of our republic understood that the experiment in democracy would require an educated public. Their ideas about education were limited to teaching the basic skills of reading, writing, and arithmetic, along with the precepts of Protestantism, so that children would grow up God-fearing and able to manage their own affairs. Their ideas were also limited by their assumptions about the "natural" order of society that ranked only white Christian males and property owners as having the rights and responsibilities of full citizenship. Only this group of people was intelligent enough, moral enough, and responsible enough to govern themselves and, thus, benefit from an education to prepare them to do so. It was their duty to take care of the needs of the rest. Women were presumed to have a nature that fit them only for the work of the home; blacks were presumed to be property; Native Americans were deemed heathens. The first century of American education began with most of the country satisfied with educating the sons of gentlemen and tradesmen at home or at the hands of part-time schoolmasters. Massachusetts and the rest of New England led the new nation in raising local taxes to support public schools. It took the masterful efforts of Horace Mann to convince the rest of the country that good schools were good business; that the future of the economy and the democracy depended upon providing a "common" education to all children, no matter where they were born or to whom.

But the founders had set the stage for a society that would change and grow with the combined hard work of all its population—men and women, blacks and whites, natives and newcomers. They could not anticipate that the principles embodied in their Constitution would be reinterpreted as the nation grew to include in their embrace people who were originally excluded from the mainstream of society and from its schools. The twin principles of equality and individual rights would result in political and social movements that restructured social relationships and affected who was educated and how. In Chapter 8, we continue our account of the history of American schools and the path that led to today's emphasis on standardizing education so that "no child is left behind." We will begin with the test to American society and its schools presented by the great wave of immigration at the turn of the twentieth century. We will trace the impact of the great social and political movements of the 1930s and the 1960s on educational policy and curriculum changes. We will highlight the experiences of Latino and Asian American schoolchildren. Finally, we will describe the twentieth-century back-and-forth swings between progressive experimentation and essentialist "basics," culminating in the reform movements of today. Underlying Chapter 8 is the challenge that progressive educator George Counts posed to educators in 1932 during the Great Depression, a challenge that could have been posed in 1789 and should be posed today: "Dare the schools build a new social order?" As we stated at the opening of this book, we believe that American schools ought to lead the reconstruction of society in the direction of justice and equality, rather than merely responding to social problems as they arise. Given the complex events of our history, the changing faces of American schoolchildren, the growing knowledge of how children learn and how we might teach them, and the development of new technologies, the challenge to educators to be societal leaders has been difficult, but exciting.

SUMMARY

- The self-government propounded by the nation's founders required an educated public, while the ideologies of individualism and pragmatism limited the role of and access to public schools.
- Schooling in colonial America was spotty and varied across colonies and communities. Given that the twin purposes of early schooling were to preserve a moral and social order and to teach rudimentary skills required to advance the American economy, the established church in a particular region influenced school curricula and texts.
- Early schools operated only a few months of the year and were considered a small part of a child's total education, which included the family, the community, the church, and trade apprenticeships. This restricted place in society, and the prevalence of corporal punishment as the primary means of disciplining students, meant that most early teachers were men of limited promise.
- Horace Mann was successful in establishing "common schools" at public expense and at beginning to professionalize the preparation and work of teachers.
- With the advent of the "graded" school and the Civil War, teaching became "feminized," although dominated by male administrators. The suffrage movement and establishment of unions helped to correct male–female inequalities in the profession.
- The content and quality of schooling was unevenly distributed among children of different social groups.
- The legacy of slavery and racism limited black children's access to an education of high quality. Arguments arose both within and outside the black community as to the relative benefits of separate and integrated schools. Legal segregation, first banned in Massachusetts, persisted until a landmark 1954 Supreme Court case, with de facto segregation lasting much longer.
- Women's education was narrow and confined to instilling the skills necessary for their primary roles as wives and mothers and the values associated with "true womanhood"—piety, obedience, and domesticity.
- A group of forward-thinking women established academies to provide a more substantive and serious education for women and to prepare teachers for the growing number of common schools in the nation. Improvements in women's education came with advances in women's political rights.
- The education of Native American children was dominated by whites who promoted removing them to boarding schools where their tribal cultures would be replaced with white ways. Not until the late 1960s did the federal government empower Indians to run their own schools.

The chapter ends with the question of the social purpose of public schools and their potential to transform and improve society.

QUESTIONS FOR REFLECTION

1. Horace Mann sold the idea of the "common school" to taxpayers and businessmen as a benefit to the economy. Was he right in doing so? Do you think his arguments were correct?
2. In light of the history of the education of black children in the United States, do you agree with those who advocate special schools whose curriculum emphasizes African roots and African American heritage?
3. Do you believe female teachers are viewed differently from male teachers? Does the history of female teachers, or the history of how women have been viewed by society in general, have anything to do with assumptions people make about women teachers?
4. Schools for a long time discouraged Native American and immigrant children from speaking their own language. How might that policy have affected their families? What impact, if any, do you think it had on these children's sense of cultural identity?
5. Given what you have learned about the history of public education during the first century of this nation, do you think the social role of the public school was essentially transmissive or transformative?

APPLYING WHAT YOU'VE LEARNED

1. www The textbook website includes resources from the Library of Congress on Indian boarding schools. Read some of the memoirs and letters home written by boarding school children and record your thoughts in response to their experiences. Find information on an Indian-run reservation school of today to see how attitudes toward native culture and curriculum have changed.
2. Watch a video depicting the traumatic experience of school desegregation in the American South and, later, in the North. Suggestions are *Common Ground;* the PBS documentary, "Eyes on the Prize" or a segment of its video series on the history of education, *School* (see Websites to Explore). Record your impressions.
3. Find out what percentage of school principals, curriculum directors, and school superintendents in your area are women.
4. Assemblyman Benjamin Franklin argued for English as the language of instruction in the schools of colonial Pennsylvania. Two hundred and fifty years later, the question of "English-only" classrooms is still argued. Research current laws in your state regarding the education of English language learner (ELL) children. Do these children receive bilingual education, which provides first-language instruction in the content areas—math, science, social studies—while they learn English, so they do not fall behind their English-speaking age-mates? Or are they "immersed" in English-only classrooms? Search sources such as *Education Week* and newspaper articles to find arguments for both positions.

KEY TERMS

Brown v. Board of Education of Topeka, Kansas, p. 238
common schools, p. 224
dame schools, p. 219
de facto segregation, p. 238
de jure segregation, p. 238
normal schools, p. 227
Plessy v. Ferguson, p. 235
primer, p. 219

WEBSITES TO EXPLORE

http://www.cedu.niu.edu/blackwell/about.html. The Blackwell Museum of Educational History's site includes information on early teaching materials, one-room schoolhouses, and other artifacts.

http://my.voyager.net/~jayjo/primer.htm. Contains the entire text of *The New England Primer* of 1777.

http://www.hudsonvalley.org/education/Background/abt_irving/abt_irving.html. Historic Hudson Valley Educators' Sketchbook website contains the text of Washington Irving's *The Legend of Sleepy Hollow* and lesson plans.

http://www.pbs.org/onlyateacher/horace.html. Website of the public television series *Only a Teacher,* which includes information on historic American educators and video clips from the series.

http://www.pbs.org/kcet/publicschool/index.html. Website accompanying the Public Broadcasting Service's series *School,* containing a wealth of information about important figures in American educational history, curriculum, and classroom materials through the years, and the historical roots of contemporary issues such as school choice and bilingual education.

http://www.floridamemory.com/OnlineClassroom/MaryBethune/index.cfm. Information on Mary McLeod Bethune, who founded the Daytona Normal and Industrial School for Negro Girls, now Bethune-Cookman College. Includes transcripts of interviews, photographs, and lesson plans.

http://home.epix.net/~landis/index.html. Contains background information on the Carlisle Indian Industrial School, including history, primary documents such as letters from boarding school children to their parents, and information on alumni.

http://www.nativeculture.com/lisamitten/education.html. This website offers a list and links on Native American resources and organizations, including sites maintained by Indian-operated schools with Native American curricula.

CRITICAL READINGS

The Talented Tenth (1903)

BY W. E. B. DU BOIS

I am an earnest advocate of manual training and trade teaching for black boys, and for white boys, too. I believe that next to the founding of Negro colleges the most valuable addition to Negro education since the war, has been industrial training for black boys. Nevertheless, I insist that the object of all true education is not to make men carpenters, it is to make carpenters men; there are two means of making the carpenter a man, each equally important: the first is to give the group and community in which he works, liberally trained teachers and leaders to teach him and his family what life means; the second is to give him sufficient intelligence and technical skill to make him an efficient workman; the first object demands the Negro college and college-bred men—not a quantity of such colleges, but a few of excellent quality; not too many college-bred men, but enough to leaven the lump, to inspire the masses, to raise the Talented Tenth to leadership; the second object demands a good system of common schools, well-taught, conveniently located and properly equipped. . . .

Can the masses of the Negro people be in any possible way more quickly raised than by the effort and example of this aristocracy of talent and character? Was there ever a nation on God's fair earth civilized from the bottom upward? Never; it is, ever was and ever will be from the top downward that culture filters. The Talented Tenth rises and pulls all that are worth the saving up to their vantage ground. This is the history of human progress; and the two historic mistakes which have hindered that progress were the thinking first that no more could ever rise save the few already risen; or second, that it would better the uprisen to pull the risen down.

How then shall the leaders of a struggling people be trained and the hands of the risen few strengthened? There can be but one answer: The best and most capable of their youth must be schooled in the colleges and universities of the land. We will not quarrel as to just what the university of the Negro should teach or how it should teach it—I willingly admit that each soul and each race-soul needs its own peculiar curriculum. But this is true: A university is a human invention for the transmission of knowledge and culture from generation to generation, through the training of quick minds and pure hearts, and for this work no other human invention will suffice, not even trade and industrial schools.

All men cannot go to college but some men must; every isolated group or nation must have its yeast, must have for the talented few centers of training where men are not so mystified and befuddled by the hard and necessary toil of earning a living, as to have no aims higher than their bellies, and no God greater than Gold. This is true training. . . .

The Sixth Atlanta Conference truly said in 1901: "We call the attention of the Nation to the fact that less than one million of the three million Negro children of school age, are at present regularly attending school, and these attend a session which lasts only a few months. . . . Half the black youth of the land have no opportunities open to them for learning to read, write and cipher. In the discussion as to the proper training of Negro children after they leave the public schools, we have forgotten that they are not yet decently provided with public schools. This is not fair. Negro schools should be a public burden, since they are a public benefit. The Negro has a right to demand good common school training at the hands of the States and the Nation since by their fault he is not in position to pay for this himself." . . .

There was a time when any aged and worn-out carpenter could teach in a trade school. But not so to-day. Indeed the demand for college-bred men by a school like Tuskegee, ought to make Mr. Booker T. Washington the firmest friend of higher training. Here he has as helpers the son of a Negro senator, trained in Greek and the humanities, and graduated at Harvard; the son of a Negro congressman and lawyer, trained in Latin and mathematics, and graduated at Oberlin; he has as his wife, a woman who read Virgil and Homer in the same class room with me; he has as college chaplain, a classical graduate of Atlanta University; as teacher of science, a graduate of Fisk; as teacher of history, a graduate of Smith,—indeed some thirty of his chief teachers are college graduates, and instead of studying French grammars in the midst of weeds, or buying pianos for dirty cabins, they are at Mr. Washington's right hand helping him in a noble work. And yet one of the effects of Mr. Washington's propaganda has been to throw doubt upon the expediency of such training for Negroes, as these persons have had. . . .

Men of America, the problem is plain before you. Here is a race transplanted through the criminal foolishness of your fathers. Whether you like it or not the millions are here, and here they will remain. If you do not lift them up, they will pull you down. Education and work are the levers to uplift a people. Work alone will not do it unless inspired by the right ideals and guided by intelligence. Education must not simply teach work—it must teach Life. The Talented Tenth of the Negro race must be made leaders of thought and missionaries of culture among their people. No others can do this work and Negro colleges must train men for it. The Negro race, like all other races, is going to be saved by its exceptional men.

Source: Originally published in *The Negro Problem, a series of articles by representative American Negroes of today.* New York: J. Pott & Company, 1903, pp. 33–75. http://teaching americanhistory.org/library/index.asp?document print=174. Accessed May 23, 2004. Also, http://douglassarchives.org/dubo_b05.htm. Accessed May 23, 2004.

A Closer Look at the Issues

1. Explain what Du Bois meant by his contention, "the object of all true education is not to make men carpenters, it is to make carpenters men."
2. Do you agree with him that social change must proceed from the "top down"?
3. How does Du Bois's essay support the argument that his educational philosophy was rooted in Idealism?

Suggestions Respecting Improvements in Education

BY CATHARINE BEECHER

It is to mothers and to teachers that the world is to look for the character which is to be enstamped on each succeeding generation, for it is to them that the great business of education is almost exclusively committed. And will it not appear by examination that neither mothers nor teachers have ever been properly educated for their profession? What is the *profession of a woman?* Is it not to form immortal minds, and to watch, to nurse, and to rear the bodily system, so fearfully and wonderfully made, and upon the order and regulation of which the health and well-being of the mind so greatly depends?

But let most of our sex, upon whom these arduous duties devolve, be asked: Have you ever devoted any time and study, in the course of your education, to any preparation for these duties? Have you been taught anything of the structure, the nature, and the laws of the body which you inhabit? Were you ever taught to understand the operation of diet, air, exercise, and modes of dress upon the human frame? Have the causes which are continually operating to prevent good health and the modes by which it might be perfected and preserved ever been made the subject of any *instruction?* Perhaps almost every voice would respond, no. We have attended to almost everything more than to this; we have been taught more concerning the structure of the earth, the laws of the heavenly bodies, the habits and formation of plants, the philosophy of languages—more of *almost anything* than the structure of the human frame and the laws of health and reason.

But is it not the business, the *profession* of a woman to guard the health and form the physical habits of the young? And is not the cradle of infancy and the chamber of sickness sacred to woman alone? And ought she not to know at least some of the *general principles* of that perfect and wonderful piece of mechanism committed to her preservation and care?

Again let our sex be asked respecting the instruction they have received in the course of their education on that still more arduous and difficult department of their profession which relates to the *intellect* and the *moral susceptibilities.* Have you been taught the powers and faculties of the human mind, and the laws by which it is regulated? Have you studied how to direct its several faculties; how to restore those that are overgrown, and strengthen and mature those that are deficient? Have you been taught the best modes of *communicating* knowledge as well as of *acquiring* it? Have you learned the best mode of correcting bad *moral* habits and forming good ones? Have you made it an object to find how a selfish disposition may be made generous; how a reserved temper may be made open and frank; how pettishness and ill humor may be changed to cheerfulness and kindness? Has any woman studied her profession in this respect?

It is feared the same answer must be returned, if not from all, at least from most of our sex. No; we have acquired wisdom from the observation and experience of others on almost *all other* subjects, but the philosophy of the direction and control of the human mind has not been an object of thought or study. And thus it appears that, though it is woman's *express business* to rear the body and form the mind, there is scarcely anything to which her attention has been less directed. . . .

Another defect in education is that it has not been made a *definite object* with teachers *to prepare their pupils to instruct others.* For of how comparatively little value is knowledge laid up in the mind if it is never to be imparted to others, and yet how few have ever been taught to communicate their ideas with facility and propriety. That there is a best way of *teaching* as well as of doing everything else cannot be disputed, and this can no more be learned by *intuition* than can any of the mechanical arts. This can be made an object of instruction as much as any other art, and a woman, ordinarily, might be *taught* to converse with ease and fluency, and to communicate knowledge with accuracy and perspicuity, with far less time and effort than is now given to the acquisition of *music*. . . .

If all females were not only well educated themselves but were prepared to communicate in an easy manner their stores of knowledge to others; if they not only knew how to regulate their own minds, tempers, and habits but how to effect improvements in those around them, the face of society would speedily be changed. The time *may* come when the world will look back with wonder to behold how much time and effort have been given to the mere cultivation of the memory, and how little mankind have been aware of what every teacher, parent, and friend could accomplish in forming the social, intellectual, and moral character of those by whom they are surrounded.

Source: From *Suggestions Respecting Improvements in Education, Presented to the Trustees of the Hartford Female Seminary, and Published at Their Request.* Hartford, CT: Packard & Butler, 1829, pp. 7–16. http://www.britannica.com/women/pri/Q00177.html. Accessed December 14, 2004.

A Closer Look at the Issues

1. Catharine Beecher wanted to elevate the traditional role of women to the level of a "profession." What was her reason? To what extend do you agree or disagree with her?
2. Do you believe that a "selfish disposition" can be made "generous"? Can a "reserved temper" be made "open and frank"? "Pettishness and ill humor" be changed to "cheerfulness and kindness"?
3. How does Beecher's contention that good teachers do not teach by "intuition" support teacher education programs, and the science of "pedagogy"?

REFERENCES

Adams, D. W. (1995). *Education for extinction: American Indians and the boarding school experience, 1875–1928.* Lawrence: University Press of Kansas.

Addams, J. (1910, 1990). *Twenty years at Hull-House.* Reprint, with intro. and notes by James Hurt. Urbana: University of Illinois Press.

Alcott, L. M. (1936, 1969). *Little women.* Boston: Little, Brown.

American Association of University Women (1991, 1994). *Shortchanging girls, shortchanging America.* Washington, DC: Author.

Anyon, J. (1997). *Ghetto schooling: A political economy of urban educational reform.* New York: Teachers College Press.

Asante, M. K. (1998). *The Afrocentric idea.* Philadelphia: Temple University Press.

Axtell, J. (1974). *The school upon a hill: Education and society in colonial New England.* New Haven: Yale University Press.

Bailyn (1960). *Education in the forming of American society.* New York: Vintage-Random House.

Beecher, C. E. (1835). *An essay on the education of female teachers.* New York: Van Nostrand & Dwight.

Beecher, C. E. (1851). *The true remedy for the wrongs of woman; with a history of an enterprise having that for its object.* Boston: Phillips, Sampson. http://www.assumption.edu/wwhp/Beecher_True_Remedy.html. Accessed August 4, 2002.

Beecher, C. E. (1872). *Woman's profession as mother and educator, with views in opposition to women's suffrage.* New York: MacLean, Gibson. http://www.connhistory.org/beecher_readings.htm. Accessed May 18, 2004.

Berliner, D. C., and B. J. Biddle (1995). *The manufactured crisis: Myths, fraud, and the attack on America's public schools.* Reading, MA: Addison-Wesley.

Bell, D. (2004). *Silent covenants: Brown v. Board of Education and the unfulfilled hopes for racial reform.* New York: Oxford University Press.

Billington, R. A. (ed.) (1981). *The journal of Charlotte L. Forten: A free Negro in the Civil War era.* New York: W. W. Norton.

Breitborde, M. (2003). One-room schools of Illinois in the twentieth century: An oral history. Unpublished research. Available from author.

Butterfield, L. H., M. Friedlaender, and R. A. Ryerson (1963, 1993). *Adams family correspondence.* Cambridge: Harvard University Press.

Carter, P. (2002). *Everybody's paid but the teacher: The teaching profession and the women's movement.* New York: Teachers College Press.

Cott, N. F. (1997). *The bonds of womanhood: "Woman's sphere" in New England, 1780–1835,* 2nd ed. New Haven: Yale University Press.

Counts, G. S. (1932). *Dare the school build a new social order?* Illinois: Southern Illinois University Press.

Crawford, J. (1999). *Bilingual Education: History, politics, theory and practice.* Los Angeles, CA: Bilingual Education Services. http://ourworld.compuserve.com/homepages/JWCRAWFORD/BE.htm. Accessed July 31, 2002.

Cremin, L. A. (1957). *The republic and the school: Horace Mann on the education of free men.* New York: Teachers College Press.

Curti, M. (1959). *The social ideas of American educators.* Totowa, NJ: Littlefield, Adams.

Du Bois, W. E. B. (1899). *The Philadelphia Negro.* New York: Lippincott.

Du Bois, W. E. B. (1903). *The souls of black folk.* Chicago: A. C. McClurg. http://www.bartleby.com/114/3.html. Accessed August 6, 2002.

Du Bois, W. E. B. ([1903] 1965). The talented tenth. In Vassar, R. L. (ed.), *A social history of American education, Volume II: 1860 to the present* (pp. 68–77). Chicago: Rand McNally.

Elshstain, J. B. (2002). *Jane Addams and the dream of American democracy: A life.* New York: Basic Books.

Fordham, S. (1995). *Blacked out: Dilemmas of race, identity, and success at Capital High.* Chicago: University of Chicago Press.

Ginorio, A., and M. Huston (2001). *Si se puede (Yes, we can): Latinas in school.* Washington, DC: American Association of University Women.

Ginwright, S. (2004). *Black in school: Afrocentric reform, urban youth and the promise of hip-hop culture.* New York: Teachers College Press.

Greene, M. (1965). *The public school and the private vision.* New York: Random House.

Hall, G. S. (1911). *Educational problems.* New York: D. Appleton.

HGSE News (2000, September 1). Busing in Boston: Looking back at the history and legacy. Cambridge, MA: Harvard Graduate School of Education.

Hoffman, N. (1981). *Woman's "true" profession: Voices from the history of teaching.* New York: McGraw Hill.

Hofstadter, R. (1962). *Anti-intellectualism in American life.* New York: Random House.

Irving, W., 1917. *The Legend of Sleepy Hollow,* Vol. X, Part 2. New York: Collier; Bartleby.com, 2000. http://www.bartleby.com/310/2/.

Jaimes, M. A., ed. (1992). *The state of Native America: Genocide, colonization, and resistance.* Boston: South End Press.

Jencks, C. (1972). *Inequality: A reassessment of the effects of family and schooling in America.* New York: Basic Books.

Johansen, J. (undated). *The New England primer: Foreward and technical notes.* http://my.voyager.net/~jayjo/primer.htm. Accessed July 31, 2002.

Joondeph, B. W. (1998). Skepticism and school desegregation. *Washington University Law Quarterly 76* (1), p. 161.

Kozol, J. (1967). *Death at an early age: The destruction of the hearts and minds of Negro children in the Boston Public Schools.* Boston: Houghton Mifflin.

Kozol, J. (1991). *Savage inequalities: Children in America's schools.* New York: Crown.

Kozol, J. (1995). *Amazing grace: The lives of children and the conscience of a nation.* New York: HarperPerennial.

Kozol, (2001). *Ordinary resurrections: Children in the years of hope.* New York: HarperCollins.

Landis, B. (1996). Carlisle Indian Industrial School History. http://home.epix.net/~landis/histry. Accessed May 21, 2004.

Lewis, D. L. L. (1994). *W. E. B. Du Bois: Biography of a race, 1868–1919.* New York: Henry Holt.

Lortie, D. (1975). *Schoolteacher: A sociological study.* Chicago: University of Chicago Press.

Mann, H. (1848). Twelfth Annual Report to the Massachusetts State Board of Education. In Cremin, L., ed. (1957). *The republic and the school: Horace Mann on the education of free men.* New York: Teachers College Press.

Mayer, F. (1965). *The history of educational thought.* Columbus, OH: Merrill.

Mulvoy, T. J., Jr. (1997). Buses and bitterness. *The Boston Globe Online. http://www.boston.com/globe/specialreports/1997/mar/125/1974.htm. Accessed August 6, 2002.*

Oakes, J. (1986). Keeping track: How schools structure inequality. New Haven, CT: Yale University Press.

Orfield, G. & Yun, J. (1999). *Resegregation in American schools.* Cambridge, MA: Harvard University Civil Rights Project.

Ornstein, A. C., and D. U. Levine (2003). *Foundations of education,* 8th ed. Boston: Houghton Mifflin.

Perkinson, H. J. (1991). *The imperfect panacea: American faith in education 1865–1990,* 3rd ed. New York: McGraw-Hill.

Pratt, R. H. (1892). *Official report of the nineteenth annual conference of charities and correction.* Reprinted in R. H. Pratt, The advantages of mingling Indians with whites. In F. P. Prucha, ed., *Americanizing the American Indians: Writings by the "Friends of the Indian," 1880–1900.* Cambridge, MA: Harvard University Press, 1973.

Riley, R. W. (1997). *Title IX: 25 years of progress.* Washington, DC: U.S. Department of Education.

Ross, D. (2004). A message from the president. In *The freedom seekers: A publication of the Friends of Freedom Society.* Columbus, OH: Ohio Underground Railroad Association.

Rothman, S. (1978). *Woman's proper place: A history of changing ideals and practices, 1970 to the present.* New York: Basic Books.

Rousmaniere, K. (1997). *City teachers: Teaching and school reform in historical perspective.* New York: Teachers College Press.

Rousmaniere, K. (1999). Where Haley stood: Margaret Haley, teachers' work, and the problem of teacher identity. In K. Wieler and S. Middleton, eds., *Telling women's lives: Narrative inquiries in the history of women's education.* Philadelphia: Taylor & Francis.

Rush, B. (1787). *Thoughts upon female education (Address to the Young Ladies' Academy of Philadelphia).* Philadelphia, PA.

Sadker, D. (2000). Myra and me. *Excellent and Equity in Education,* 33(1). http://www.sadker.org/myraandme.htm. Accessed May 26, 2004.

Sadker, M., and D. Sadker, (1995). *Failing at fairness: How America's schools cheat girls.* New York: Scribner's.

Smith, B. H. (1998). *From Gloucester to Philadelphia in 1790: Observations, thoughts and anecdotes from the letters of Judith Sargent Murray.* Boston: Curious Traveller Press and Judith Sargent Murray Society.

Solomon, B. M. (1986). *In the company of educated women. The history of women and higher education in America.* New Haven: Yale University Press.

Sommers, C. H. (2000). The war against boys. *Atlantic Monthly,* 285 (5), pp. 59–74.

Spring, J. (1986). *The American school: 1642–1865.* White Plains, NY: Longman.

Spring, J. (1997). *The American school: 1642–1996,* 4th ed. New York: McGraw-Hill.

Stahl, J. (2004). Brown sisters recall landmark desegregation case. *The Princeton Packet.* http://www.zwire.com/site/news.cfm?newsid=11350323&BRD=1091&PAG=461&dept_id=425695&rfi=6. Accessed May 18, 2004.

Standing Bear, L. (1928). *My people, the Sioux.* Boston: Houghton Mifflin.

Swiniarski, L. (1987). Elizabeth Peabody: A pioneer in the kindergarten movement in America. *Essex Institute Historical Collections, 123* (2), April, pp. 206–229. Salem, MA: Peabody Essex Institute.

Towne, L. M. (1901). *Pioneer work on the Sea Islands.* Hampton, VA: Hampton Institute Press.

Tyack, D. B. (1974). *The one best system: A history of American urban education.* Cambridge, MA: Harvard University Press.

Tyack, D. B., and E. Hansot (1982). *Managers of virtue: public school leadership in America, 1820–1980.* New York: Basic Books.

U.S. Dept. of Education (1972). *Title IX Education Amendments of 1972.* Washington, DC: Author. http://www.dol.gov/oasam/regs/statutes/titleix.htm. Accessed December 14, 2004.

U.S. Dept. of Education (1993). *120 years of American education: A statistical portrait.* Washington, DC: Office of Educational Research and Improvement, National Center for Educational Statistics. http://nces.ed.gov/pubs93/93442.pdf. Accessed May 18, 2004.

U.S. Dept. of Education (2002). *Digest of Educational Statistics,* Ch. 2, Elementary and Secondary Education. Washington, DC: Office of Educational Research and Improvement, National Center for Educational Statistics. http://nces.ed.gov/programs/digest/d02/tables/dt068.asp. Accessed May 18, 2004.

Washington, B. T. (1901). *Up from slavery: An autobiography.* Garden City, NY: Doubleday. http://docsouth.unc.edu/washington/washing.html. Accessed August 6, 2002.

Webster, N. (1783). *A Grammatical institute of the English language: Part I.* Hartford: Hudson & Goodwin.

Webster, N. (1790). On the education of youth in America. ed., *A collection of essays and fugitive writings on moral, historical, political and literary subjects.* Boston. Reprint. Delmar, N.Y.: Scholars' Facsimiles & Reprints, 1977.

Welter, B. (1976). *Dimity convictions: The American woman in the nineteenth century.* Athens, OH: Ohio University Press.

Wilson, J. H. (1976). The illusion of change: Women and the American Revolution. In A. Young, ed., *Explorations in the history of American radicalism.* DeKalb, IL: University of Illinois.

Zitkala-Sa (1900). The school days of an Indian girl. *Atlantic Monthly, 85,* pp. 185–194.

Movement and Change in School and Society: The Second Hundred Years

8

ESSENTIAL QUESTION

What is the role of the school in society?

The Americans of all nations at any time upon the earth have probably the fullest poetical nature. The United States themselves are essentially the greatest poem. . . . Here is not merely a nation but a teeming nation of nations. Here is action untied from strings necessarily blind to particulars and details magnificently moving in vast masses. . . . Other states indicate themselves in their deputies . . . but the genius of the United States is not best or most in its executives or legislatures, nor in its ambassadors or authors or colleges or churches or parlors, nor even in its newspapers or inventors . . . but always most in the common people. Walt Whitman, preface to *Leaves of Grass* (1855) ■

The Beginning of the Second Hundred Years

The first century of the American republic was dominated by the interests and political power of those who were radical in their insistence on self-government and independence from England, but were wed all the same to their cultural roots in England and northern Europe. White, Anglo-Saxon Protestant males led a nation dedicated to the preservation of their individual rights, while women, Black Americans, Native Americans, Asians, religious minorities, and other groups were marginalized or ignored. The only route to economic and social success for these groups was **assimilation,** or absorption, into the dominant ways of life of the larger community—that is, if assimilation were even allowed them. The goal was that the language, culture, and behavior of immigrant and minority groups should become "similar to" those of the dominant groups of society.

The idea that the public should help educate their children—that all children should go to school at public expense, no matter their parentage or social class or color or gender—took leaders like Horace Mann many years to etch into public consciousness. His success was largely based on his argument that a national system of free, tax-supported common schools would be an efficient means of providing all children with an equal opportunity to learn the skills and values that were important to the development and preservation of the nation. His plan worked well for most white children in all parts of the land; the common school movement, which began in New England, grew to reach children in the South and in the new settlements of the West. As Chapter 7 described, it worked less well for children of color.

The last third of the nineteenth century saw the initiation of a period of tremendous demographic and territorial growth. Millions of newcomers came to America looking for work in new industries in the cities of the East and on the vast and fertile lands of the West. The promise that anyone could own his own labors and his own land drew people from countries where that was true only for a privileged few. The hope that one could advance one's own family simply by hard work and perseverance was enough to carry immigrants across the oceans, enduring all kinds of hardships for the sake of a positive future. Their arrival in the United States with new languages, religions, foods, trades, and traditions changed the face of the nation and the face of its schools. Within the country, supported by the 1862 Homestead Act, which gave citizens or would-be citizens 160 acres at low cost, tens of thousands migrated west across the prairies from the East Coast and the old South to create new lives and new settlements that changed the nation's very shape.

The wave of immigration and migration fueled by industrialization, western expansion, and the pioneer spirit that had characterized the United States since its inception created Walt Whitman's "teeming nation of nations." It also forced changes in the nation's schools. The new century would be a time of world-shaking historical events, revolutionary technological invention, and transforming social and political movements. American public schools would respond to these changes, at times adapting pragmatically to immediate crises, at other times acting as agents of social change. In this chapter we tell the story of changing and expanding schools in the context of a changing and expanding country. We begin with the settling of the American frontier.

School and Society on the Prairie

By the end of the nineteenth century, the American West was diverse; there were Native Americans indigenous to the area or removed from their Eastern tribal lands; Mexicans in all walks of life in the Southwest; African American, German, and Scandinavian farmers; Asians who had come to work on the transcontinental railroad and to establish businesses; and Mennonites, Mormons, and other religious minorities. There was room for all of these groups, and in many communities groups lived alongside each other harmoniously. But relationships among them were not always peaceful. There was conflict between whites and Native Americans. In Chapter 7 we described the negative impact white settlement had on the lives and education of the native people. The children of the Navajo and the Lakota attended privately funded reservation or boarding schools under contract with the federal government, whose mission was to strip away their language and their culture and replace it with something that looked more "American." There was discrimination against Asians. Not only were the living and working conditions of Chinese railroad and mine workers often deplorable and unsafe, but restrictive immigration policies left the men bereft of the families they were forced to leave behind in China.

African Americans came to the Midwest as freed men or as former slaves who had either bought their freedom or been emancipated during and after the Civil War. Some established communities that were separate and self-contained, such as Cheyenne Valley in Wisconsin (originally called Hopeful Valley). The area's rich soil and opportunities for fur trading, and the fact that Wisconsin openly defied the Fugitive Slave Act, attracted African Americans to the area in the 1850s (Cooper, 1977). Like their white counterparts in other communities, the black settlers' first order of business after staking out their farms was to build a church and a school, called Salem School, for their children. One farmer, who kept a picture of Booker T. Washington hanging in the hallway, became well known for his innovations, which included a tractor, an electric generator, and a round barn (Gould, 1997). In the late nineteenth century, Cheyenne Valley grew to include new white settlers from Ireland, Germany, and Norway, who lived, worked, and were schooled alongside the original black settlers without "even know[ing] we were integrated. We just didn't care about color. We would plant each others' crops, build their barns when they burned down. We'd share food if other families were starving. . . . Everyone was concerned about their neighbor" (Overview, 2001). The black and white families of Cheyenne Valley intermarried and shared churches and schools. However, in other communities in the Midwest, blacks were expected to be subservient to whites. Even in once-egalitarian communities, the invention of the automobile opened up these communities to the racism and prejudice at work in the larger society. The movement toward an industrial economy took many blacks away from their original communities to better-paying jobs and larger black communities in the cities. By the 1890s most African Americans had disappeared from rural farm communities in Wisconsin.

The District Schools

For the new settlers, work was a family affair, whether on the farm, in the house, or running the business. But parents, especially those who had migrated from East

Coast cities, understood the importance of providing their children with an education. In the early days of settlement, married women set up informal schools in their houses for their own and neighboring children. Some communities set up "dugout schools"—schools carved out of sod hillsides—and makeshift "lean-to" schools. Some churches established schools for the children of parishioners. As settlements grew, the idea that the community should support the schools also grew. In the Michigan Territory, which included the future states of Michigan and Wisconsin, an 1817 law mandated that the cost of building a school should come from district taxes on property, "but it could be paid in labor or materials instead of money" (Apps, 1996, p. 11).

The Northwest Ordinances of 1785 and 1787, which organized the territories that later became the states of Ohio, Illinois, Indiana, Wisconsin, and Michigan, established townships divided into thirty-six equal sections. Today, if you fly across the United States, you will see the evidence of the grids of those early Midwestern townships as you look down from the window of your airplane. As each new state was formed, its citizens had to set aside the revenues from the sale of the sixteenth section of each township for the support of public schools. Farming families in any part of a township could petition the county superintendent for permission to construct a **district school** (a small school serving their section of the township) and to hire a teacher. A school district could be as little as four miles square, with a school located in the middle. The idea that most children walked many miles to country schools is a myth; the goal was for children to walk no more than two miles to school (Apps, 1996; Fuller, 1994).

Since land was cheap, the revenues from the sixteenth section were generally not enough to support the school, so states enacted their own supplementary laws. Wisconsin's 1848 School Law (Apps, 1996, pp. 15–17) stipulated that elementary education should be free to everyone between the ages of four and twenty. Financing would come from the sale of the sixteenth section, from other federal sources, and from state, township, and district taxes. Township boards of supervisors could organize school districts within their townships, which had to be open for at least three months of the year in winter or summer, or both. The county superintendent would examine and certify teachers, who would offer a curriculum that included reading, writing, arithmetic, geography, English grammar, orthography (spelling), and whatever other subjects the board wanted to add. The superintendent would try to make textbooks uniform and "discourage sectarian teaching and the use of sectarian materials."

Local districts, then, had significant control over their own schools. While some public money was available, the people of the school district bore much of the cost and all of the labor. In Illinois, three members of the district were elected by their peers to serve as school directors, charged with hiring the teacher and providing necessary supplies: wood for the stove that heated the schoolroom, desks for teacher and students, slates, and chalk. Local control had both positive and negative results. The people of the district felt a strong sense of ownership and pride in their schools and, therefore, contributed much labor and attention to it. Many consider the establishment and control of schools on the prairie to be a prime example of American democracy (Fuller, 1994). But local control created disparities across communities. Some could not or did not want to tax themselves enough to furnish the school or pay the teacher adequately. The result was wide variation in the quality of the schools.

The district schools were typically one-room structures that housed students in the first through eighth grades. They were built by the farmers themselves ac-

A one-room schoolhouse in Minnesota, 1906.
Source: © Minnesota Historical Society/CORBIS

cording to a set of guidelines that specified the size of the building, the materials to be used, and the number of windows that would provide sufficient light for the "scholars" inside. For example, schoolrooms were to be twenty-three by thirty-one feet. Francis Blair, superintendent of instruction in Illinois, suggested that school directors should "jacket the stove" for more efficient heating and ventilation (Blair, 1910, p. 57). School architecture could affect academic learning and classroom order: "The only entrance to the coat rooms should be in view of the teacher" (p. 17). It could also influence morality. Blair was particularly concerned about the construction of outhouses. In his 1910 pamphlet for district school directors, he wrote that they should be screened by plantings of ivy, and that "the walls should be kept free from obscene language and pictures" (p. 74). He vehemently opposed "double outhouses," girls' and boy's outhouses contained in one building: "It is difficult to conceive of a worse architecture than these double-doored abominations. . . . Better expose the children to a deadly contagious disease than to subject them to the moral leprosy which lurks in these double outhouses" (p. 74). Some districts undertook regular improvements to the schoolhouse, adding bell towers to signal the beginning and end of the morning and afternoon sessions, enlarging the outhouses to separate the girls' from the boys' facilities, even adding basement kitchens with water pumped in from the well outside. Schools within growing towns divided into two and even three rooms, to attend to the different needs of primary, intermediate, and older students. The great majority of district schools, however, were in rural areas where, well into the 1950s , an outdoor pump provided the water for the common drinking bucket, teachers heated children's lunches on top of the wood- or coal-burning stove, and eighth graders studying algebra sat in the same room with first graders learning to read.

The School at the Heart of the Community

Along with the local church, the district school was the hub of community life and therefore a source of pride to everyone who lived there, whether or not they had children in the school. The whole community attended monthly potluck suppers and end-of-year programs, and the annual Christmas program was the highlight of the winter. Neighbors provided water and firewood, lent old textbooks to students who couldn't afford new ones, and raised money for instructional supplies. "Everyone who lived around the school came to the Christmas program, whether or not they were parents. Everyone went," said one alumna (Breitborde, 2003).

What went on in the school was the business of the community, and the business of the community affected what went on in the school. The yearly calendar revolved around the work of farming; school was in full force in the winter months, but rarely met during spring planting. If older children were needed at home to help with the plowing or harvesting, teachers understood they would need to miss school for a while and would send schoolwork home in the interim with neighbors or younger siblings (Breitborde, 2003). In some schools, students received special credits for chores done at home. In one Wisconsin school, among the tasks that would count for this special recognition were the following (Metcalf, Williams, and Pustina, 1976, p. 191):

- Building a fire in the morning — 1 credit
- Feeding the hogs — 2 credits
- Mixing and baking bread — 10 credits
- Bathing — 6 credits
- Carrying in wood for the day — 4 credits
- Cleaning a lamp — 1 credit

Teaching and Learning in the One-Room School

The district schoolteacher rang the opening bell at 9:00 A.M. For the rest of the day, until 4:00 P.M., she (most were women) managed to teach children as young as five and as old as fourteen in one room furnished with hard wooden benches or attached desks. She met with the children in each grade—sometimes there were one or two, sometimes none in a particular grade—for a fifteen-minute lesson. In the case of the little ones, she might spend the time reading to them and helping them make lists of words, which they would then go to their seats and try to copy and memorize. One alumna of a one-room school in the 1940s remembered that her teacher held her on her lap when it was her turn to read. She remarked, "What better way is there to learn to love reading?" (Breitborde, 2003).

Children learned by reading, writing, and copying. Older children demonstrated what they knew in "recitations," which meant that younger children were often exposed to the information and skills the older students were learning simply by overhearing their recitations. Many teachers took advantage of the multiage classrooms by engaging older students in helping the younger ones with their lessons. (These days, this technique would be called "peer tutoring.") As the Progressive Education Movement (described in a later section of this chapter) swept through the country, many teachers who had attended summer institutes or college programs that promoted progressivism added hands-on activities for their students: sand tables where children would experiment with measuring, "nature walks" to explore local flora and fauna, and group projects.

The curriculum included the fundamental subjects of reading, writing, spelling, grammar, arithmetic, and geography, and, for older students, algebra, geometry, physical science, and history. It was prescribed by the state and monitored by county superintendents. A look at a geography textbook from 1873 reveals how much the curriculum was affected by the biases and prejudices of the larger society, and how far we've come since then. Here is a passage from Monteith's *First Lessons in Geography* (1873), a popular textbook of the time:

> The first inhabitants of a place are called settlers, or colonists. . . . Many of the white settlers of this country suffered great cruelties from the Indians, who burned their houses and murdered men, women and children, as you see in the picture. At present there are no savages east of the Mississippi (p. 32).

Turn-of-the-century textbooks promoted the idea that the United States had the most intelligent, cultured, and moral people in the world and that the children were lucky to be living here:

> The people of the United States are famous for perseverance and inventive genius. A few years ago, people rode in stage-coaches over rough and hilly roads, but now they travel by steamboat and railroad (Monteith, 1873, p. 33).

Monteith made no effort at separating church and state, accepting the prevailing notion that the United States, and its schools, were Christian: "Where was our savior born? In the western part of Asia" (p. 60). Besides the fact that Jesus was born there, Monteith had little regard for the continent or its people. From Lesson LVIII on Asia:

> This is a picture of a heathen temple, or place of worship. It contains frightful looking objects, before which you see people falling on their knees and faces. They are idols, or false gods, which these people worship. . . . Such people are called idolaters, pagans or heathens. Missionaries have been sent from the United States and Europe to teach those ignorant people about the TRUE GOD" (p. 61).

Teachers worked hard. With the help of some older students, they carried wood or coal to the stove each morning and swept out the schoolroom and cleaned the blackboards in the evening. At lunchtime, they played outdoors with the children at games of Annie-Over, Red Rover, and Fox and Geese. Many schools had weekly baseball matches with other district schools on Friday afternoons and the teacher played, too. Teachers carefully documented all aspects of the curriculum, listing the subjects covered with allotted time, the books used, and the progress of individual students in annual comprehensive reports called "registers." They were evaluated informally by the local school directors, who received their information directly from the children. One woman who attended a one-room school in the 1930s recalls that, after she went home and told her parents that the teacher had struck her brother with a ruler, the teacher was fired the next day. It helped, of course, that her father was one of the school directors.

Illinois Superintendent of Instruction Blair gave his county superintendents and district directors some criteria on which to base their evaluation of teachers (1910, pp. 86–91). His list included teachers' own knowledge of subject matter, their interest in children, their ability to control children's behavior, and their skill at asking important questions during students' recitations. Personal qualities also counted: Teachers should be "natural" in the way they spoke to children, and they should have an "optimistic rather than a fault-finding" disposition. Finally, teachers should be concerned about what we today call professional development: "Is he progressive, trying to do better today than yesterday" (p. 91).

Preparing Teachers

Teachers for the district schools came at first from the East, then later from the prairie communities themselves. In the mid-1800s, female academies in New England and New York, such as Catharine Beecher's Hartford Seminary, sent hundreds of newly trained teachers out West. But by the end of the century, normal schools and public land-grant colleges sprang up and prepared young settlers to teach in their own communities. Many of those normal schools became "state teachers colleges" by the 1930s and are now comprehensive state colleges or state universities. Many of the land-grant colleges are now world-renowned research institutions.

Normal Schools State and county **normal schools,** or early teacher preparation institutions, offered one- or two-year programs of study for prospective teachers. Typically, those with high school diplomas completed a year of study and took a state or county test for licensure to teach in any common school. Those who had only an eighth-grade district school education would complete the two-year program and receive a license to teach, but only in the rural schools. What they studied in these programs were the subjects they would teach: composition, penmanship, arithmetic, geography, spelling, and American history. High school graduates, presumed to have already mastered most of those subjects, studied psychology, gymnastics, music, science, agriculture, civics, Latin, German, rhetoric, physiology, natural history, library methods, and "methods and observation." Greater emphasis was placed on knowing these subjects than on how to teach them. Some state normal schools had "demonstration rooms," which were replicas of one-room schools. Some arranged for excursions for their students, many of whom had never ventured beyond their own communities (Apps, 1996).

Between 1855 and 1875, the number of students in Indiana schools grew from 207,500 to over 500,000. State law increased the school year from 61 to 130 days. To prepare its own teachers, the state established a normal school. Indiana State Normal School (now Indiana State University) opened its Terre Haute doors to its first 21 students in 1870 (Lynch, 1946). By 1880, the study body numbered 330. Most were the children of farmers. Most had not completed high school. Students seeking admission to Indiana State Normal School in 1870 had to be at least sixteen years old and in good health. They had to have passed tests in reading, penmanship, spelling, grammar, geography, and arithmetic. They needed to provide evidence of "undoubted moral character." And, in return for their free tuition, they had to sign a pledge that, upon graduation, they would teach in the common schools of Indiana for a period equal to twice the time they attended the normal school. There were costs, however; students had to buy or rent textbooks and arrange for boarding with families in the community or in carefully monitored boarding houses.

Indiana Normal School provided different programs of study depending on a student's experience and intentions. Students who had already been teaching in country schools came for as little as one summer term of eight weeks to hone their skills. Those preparing to teach in the state's new high schools came for as long as four years. Many students never graduated, because they could no longer afford the tuition or because they were recruited for teaching positions in one-room country schools before they finished. The state's need of teachers was so great that a license was available to anyone who could pass the county superintendent's exams, whether or not they had a high school diploma, much less received formal training. The failure rate on these day-long exams was high; the tests took all day and covered many subjects (Fuller, 1994).

In the Midwest, as back East, most people believed that the education a schoolteacher needed was hardly more than the information a high school student would have, with a smattering of techniques to help young children learn to read and to keep order in a schoolroom where children of vastly different ages had to keep busy and study on their own for long periods of time. By the 1920s and 1930s, most states elevated the status of normal schools to college level and began granting bachelor's degrees. In addition to the growth and development of the state-funded normal schools, however, the federal government was aiding in the establishment of full-fledged colleges on grants of land. Though the focus of these first public colleges was on agricultural and technical training for future farmers and skilled industrial workers, many either provided a bachelor-level teacher preparation program or incorporated the local normal school under their mantles.

Land-Grant Colleges Because of the need to educate officers in the Civil War, President Lincoln signed the Morrill Act of 1862, "An ACT Donating Public Lands to the several States and Territories which may provide Colleges for the Benefit of Agriculture and Mechanic Arts" (Morrill Act). The Morrill Act granted thirty thousand acres of public land per Congressional representative to every state that had remained in the Union. With the proceeds of the sale of this land, the states built colleges on the remaining land to teach the "agricultural and mechanical arts," home economics, and military training (later ROTC). These colleges were known as **land-grant colleges.** Under the related 1887 Hatch Act, land-grant colleges were encouraged to set up experimental farms where faculty and students could conduct research into agricultural improvement. The original act excluded black Americans as well as the states of the former Confederacy, but both exclusions were eliminated by the second Morrill Act of 1890. Iowa State University's first African American student, in 1891, was George Washington Carver.

The Morrill Act extended higher education to the working people of the Midwest and the West, and provided for the first time direct public funding for college. It significantly changed higher education by emphasizing a practical education, rather than classic studies. At a time when half of the population of the United States lived on farms, it gave people a way to improve their own lives and, by extension, their communities. In fact, the land-grant colleges established "cooperative extension services" in every county which continue today to offer information and advice in areas such as plant development, biotechnology, natural resource management, and nutrition.

Many of the original land-grant colleges became large state universities, such as the University of Nebraska, Texas A&M, Purdue, the University of Illinois, and Louisiana State University. Many historically black colleges and universities such as Tuskegee Institute and Alabama State University began as land-grant colleges. In 1994, the federal government extended land-grant status to twenty-nine Native American tribal colleges and authorized endowments for them to provide long-term revenue. Today there is at least one land-grant institution in every state, the District of Columbia, and the territories of Guam, Puerto Rico, Samoa, and the U.S. Virgin Islands. Many of them have prestigious programs of world renown—for example, the engineering program at the University of Illinois and the veterinary school at Cornell University.

Social Change and School Consolidation

In land-grant colleges, and in factories, barns, and workshops, new technologies developed to make farming at once more efficient and more complex. The invention of the steam-driven reaper and the combine cut time and labor costs and allowed farmers to work larger acreages. Refrigeration, methods of insect control, better transportation systems, and new markets around the world meant that farmers needed more specialized knowledge. The changes in agriculture combined with the new opportunities for work in new industries drove many people away from the farms to the cities. District school enrollments decreased dramatically. Illinois Superintendent Blair bemoaned the fact that in country schools that once enrolled forty or fifty students, there were by 1910 often fewer than ten. The contrast between the wood stoves, water pumps, and outhouses of the district schools and the central heating, running water, and electricity available in the towns and villages was unacceptable to many people concerned that all children have the benefit of a modern educational facility with well-prepared teachers. The children who attended the rural schools were largely unaware of what they did not have. "We never thought about who had more or less—we did for ourselves, we made what we needed" remarked one alumnus (Breitborde, 2003). Another former country school student remembers the sudden stigma she felt when she moved to town and attended the bigger school:

> I didn't know how poor we were until I came to [the town school] in 6th grade. In Dr. Phil's words, it was a "tremendous life-changing experience" for me. For instance, my wardrobe—every year when school started I would get two flannel shirts, two pairs of jeans, and a new pair of shoes, whether I needed them or not. And that was it. . . . [The town] has always been class conscious. I didn't feel that way in the country. It wasn't 'til I came to town that I was embarrassed by my wardrobe. In the country, you knew the K_______ kids didn't have a father, but that didn't matter; it just explained why they had less than we did (Breitborde, 2003).

The influential historian Elwood Cubberley thought little of the country schools:

> The country school lacks interest and ideas; it suffers from isolation. . . . Its site is usually unattractive; its building is too often a miserable, unsanitary box; it too often lacks the necessary equipment for proper instruction; its instruction is usually limited to the barest elements of an

> education, and lacks vocational purpose; its teacher is often poorly trained or entirely untrained, and is poorly paid (1912, p. 13).

Cubberley was one force behind a push to consolidate the small districts. From the late 1940s onward, states began offering financial incentives to districts to combine and establish larger and more modern schools, and punishments—for example, loss of funding—to school districts with low enrollments. The result was a steep decline in the number of country schools. Table 8.1 shows the decline in the number of one-room schoolhouses in four Midwestern states, from 1931 to 1954.

In 1958, twenty-six states still had more than one hundred one-room schools; eleven of those states had more than one thousand. Today, one-room schools still exist in remote parts of several states, including Maine, Vermont, Wisconsin, Montana, and the Dakotas.

There have been efforts to record the memories of former country school students and teachers (Apps, 1996; Breitborde, 2003). These oral histories reveal a general feeling that, though the district schools were limited in their curricula and their materials, they offered a solid base of information and skills to children in rural communities. Many graduates report that one-room schools taught them habits of independent work and helping others along with a love of reading and an appreciation for lifelong learning (Breitborde, 2003). They seem to have been far more than Cubberley's "miserable, unsanitary boxes." In fact, many of the qualities that distinguished the district schools—accessibility, involvement of the local community, peer tutoring and cooperative learning, mixed grades, and the possibility of independent work—are qualities that are valued by movements in education today. Those who call for "small schools," cooperative learning, and full-service community schools might consider looking into the past for lessons that can be learned from the district schools.

Parallel to the nation-expanding migration of settlers to the farmland of the prairie and then to its cities was the turbulent wave of immigration of people from other nations to our coasts. The next section of this chapter describes the impact of that immigration on the urban schools of the Northeast, a phenomenon that changed the goals and character of American schools once again.

Table 8.1 Change in Number of One-Room Schoolhouses in Four Midwestern States, as a Result of Consolidation

	1931–32	1943–44	1949–50	1953–54
Wisconsin	6,600	5,055	3,956	3,699
Iowa	9,279	7,563	4,173	3,594
Illinois	10,041	8,361	2,370	722
Indiana	1,830	636	375	150

Source: Wayne E. Fuller, *One-Room Schools of the Middle West,* Lawrence, KS: University of Kansas Press, 1994.

Becoming Americans: The Immigrants at the Turn of the Twentieth Century

America has often been called a land of immigrants. Emma Lazarus's "huddled masses" have landed on our shores since the beginning, sometimes in a steady trickle, at other times in great waves. In 1855, when Walt Whitman described the United States in his preface to *Leaves of Grass* (1900) as "not merely a nation but a teeming nation of nations," Chinese men were fleeing the poverty and repression of their homeland to find jobs building the new transcontinental railroad. Irish tenant farmers devastated by the nightmare of the potato crop failure and unsupported by their English landlords were beginning new lives in U.S. cities, where their labor was used for construction projects and in domestic service. Fisherman from Italy, Portugal, and Maritime Canada were starting over in the waters of coastal New England. Swedish farmers facing years of crop failures were lured by President Lincoln's 1862 Homestead Act to start over on the western prairies. Until the last decades of the nineteenth century, most voluntary immigrants came from northern and western Europe, especially Great Britain and Germany. Millions of involuntary immigrants, of course, had come from Africa in chains. Congress banned the slave trade in 1808, stopping the legal traffic, but slaves from western Africa were brought to the country illegally well after that date. In the case of Mexicans and Native Americans, involuntary "immigrants" found themselves citizens of a new land as a result of redrawn borders and lost battles.

The Doors Open to New Americans

The Industrial Revolution and the advent of steamships brought millions of immigrants to the United States between 1880 and 1920 from Eastern Europe, Central Asia, and elsewhere. Among them were Armenians escaping the massacres by the Turks, Russians Jews escaping the anti-Semitic violence of the czars, Mexicans escaping the revolution in their country, and Japanese contract laborers working the sugar plantations of Hawaii and the sawmills and railroads of the Pacific Northwest. Fear that keeping the doors of the country open to millions more would allow immigrants to take away jobs and take over the economy and political institutions, Congress passed laws restricting immigration in the 1920s. These laws were responsible for turning away Jewish refugees from Nazi Germany in the 1930s and during World War II. After the war, the problem of nationless citizens led Congress to pass the Displaced Persons Act, offering refuge to some of them. In the 1950s, this act admitted thousands of Hungarians, victims of the failed revolt against the Soviets.

While many in the United States appreciated the contributions that immigrants were making to the American economy, the welcome extended to immigrants often depended on their national and cultural roots. Notions of who was acceptable and "civilized" changed over time. In the mid-1800s, America took in millions of immigrants fleeing the potato famine in Ireland. They endured not only conditions of abject poverty but also the xenophobia of those who saw the "invasion" as a threat to the "American" way of life and to its schools. Here are the reactions of the Boston School Committee of 1846:

> There are great masses coming in upon us who are not educated, except to vice and crime; the creatures or the victims of the oppression, or the overpopulation of the old world. . . . Immigration is constantly countervailing the Puritan leaven of our people, and reducing the scale of public morality and public intelligence. . . . It is almost too much for the children of Puritans to bear. Out from the heart of our beloved Commonwealth are now to be graduated Jesuit priests—the O'Briens, the O'Flahertys, and the McNamaras. Ireland and Rome together make a combination of a not very attractive character to the sons of New England sires (Gardner, 1857).

In general, Asians were not as accepted as Europeans. The Chinese Exclusion Act of 1882, for example, resulted in a "bachelor society" of Chinese male workers stranded in their new country without the company of their families. Chinese men had left wives and families behind, hoping to return home or send for them with their saved earnings. Immigration laws, however, limited their activities in this country to the specific jobs they had been recruited for and thereby prevented them from bringing their families with them. After 1882, it was very difficult for the wives and children to join their husbands and fathers.

President Lyndon Johnson signed the Immigration and Naturalization Act of 1965, which removed the biased quota system that favored immigrants from Europe. Since that time, most of the immigrants to this country have come from Mexico and other Latin American countries, and from Asia. However, federal policy today favors immigrants who have professional degrees and skills. The definition of a "refugee" appears to be linked to U.S. alliances in the world. For example, boatloads of Haitians seeking asylum are returned to their homeland by officials who claim that the Haitians are fleeing poverty, not political repression (Swarns, 2004). The U.S. Asylum and Refugee Policy (U.S. Department of Justice, 1998) contains quotas for the number of refugees allowed from different parts of the world, with 48,000 spaces reserved for European refugees and 3,000 reserved for refugees from the Caribbean Islands.

Patterns of immigration have affected the public schools. At times of great waves of immigration—for example, at the turn of the twentieth century and in the 1980s and 1990s—the numbers of new immigrant students have stressed the ability of schools to provide sufficient space, teachers, materials, and staff who can communicate with their non-English-speaking parents. Despite the stress, public schools rarely turn away any student who appears at their doors. Whether the education offered the student is appropriate and equitable is a matter of concern, to be addressed in Chapter 9. In the next section of this chapter, we highlight the experience of immigrant children who entered into and changed the face of American schools in the mid- to late-nineteenth century. Consider the following questions as you read the next section.

- Does the United States have a duty to keep its doors open to new immigrants?
- Do our schools have a duty to educate undocumented immigrants in addition to those who are here legally?
- Are our public schools obliged to acknowledge and support the native cultures and languages of immigrant children?

- Should the goal of schools be to help new immigrants assimilate into the mainstream culture or to promote the creation of a new culture that includes the cultures of newcomers?
- What are the implications of the history of immigration for the education of immigrant children in U.S. schools today?

Schooling for Immigrants

In response to conditions of poverty and political repression in Europe and to a growing industrialization in this country with its promise of employment, millions immigrated to America at the turn of the twentieth century. They disembarked at the great cities of New York, Philadelphia, New Orleans and, in the West, Los Angeles and San Francisco. Often uneducated and unprepared for urban life, speaking little or no English, they lived many families to one tenement apartment, sharing cold-water baths. Everyone in the family worked, in local businesses or factories, or at home.

Jacob Riis, a photojournalist, focused his camera on the terrible living conditions in New York. His first book, *How the Other Half Lives* (1890) documented the poverty, the sweatshops, crime, child labor, and gangs that afflicted the new immigrants. His major focus was the masses of children living in unsanitary and unsafe environments. Other journalists such as Joseph Mayer Rice and Alice Shaw wrote many articles based on their observations of immigrant children in city schools. Their stories showed that, while a few schools and teachers offered children a menu of involving activities, including art and nature study, and interesting integrated subject matter, in most cases school consisted of dull drills, and punishment. While the immigrant groups differed in the priority they put on schooling—Russian Jews, for example, had much higher rates of attendance and graduation than did Southern Italians (Tyack, 1974)—for the most part immigrant

A family works at making fabric bouquets in their tenement apartment, 1908.
Source: © CORBIS

families saw mandatory, free, accessible schooling as an amazing and wonderful phenomenon and understood that, regardless of whether the curriculum was relevant or interesting, education was the route to economic prosperity in America.

Assimilation and Acculturation The goal of public schools in the first years of the twentieth century was to help immigrant children assimilate into American society. The schools would take in children from many lands, from many religious and cultural backgrounds, speaking many languages, and teach them how to assimilate, or fit in with, or be similar to, those who were already here. Assimilation implies that the child's cultural background, language, religion, and so on will be replaced by their American equivalents.

In time, they would **acculturate**—they would learn the "American" (that is, the white Anglo-Saxon Protestant) way of life, which would take the place of their native culture, language, and perhaps even religion.

As neighborhood institutions, schools were logical places to carry out the work of assimilation and acculturation, not only for the children but for their parents. Furthermore, schools could house many of the social and health services that immigrant families needed. "The school building is the center of the neighborhood. What reaches every child . . . can reach every parent," maintained George Creel in "The Hopes of the Hyphenated" ([1916] 1965, p. 223).

Along with conveying basic skills and academic information, schools taught hygiene, nutrition, proper dress, and patriotism—all in English, the language of the land. Creel asked the schools to house representatives of the federal immigration offices, employment exchanges, visiting nurse associations, legal-aid agencies, "infant dispensaries," the "milk station," and the library. He suggested they add a model kitchen and an art gallery and be election polling-places. Some of his ideas took root: schools added health facilities, playgrounds, nurses, lunch programs, and adult evening citizenship and English classes, reaching beyond children to their families and communities.

Some saw the expanded services as necessary for the preservation of order in the face of an influx of people who were "largely illiterate, often lacking in initiative, and almost wholly without the Anglo-Saxon conceptions of righteousness, liberty, law, order, public decency, and government" (Cubberley, [1909] 1965, pp. 485–486). Boston's Unitarian newspaper was quite blunt in assigning responsibility for the work of acculturation:

> The dominant race must regularize the incoming class . . . to dispel from popular use every foreign language . . . to print all public documents in the English tongue alone . . . to ordain that all schools aided by the State shall use the same language . . . to develop a high and vivid patriotism . . . to return the Bible to our common schools . . . to nationalize before we naturalize, and to educate before either (Gardner, 1857).

Expanding the Social Role of Schools Moving beyond the ethnocentrism of assimilationist goals, others thought that, in the spirit of freedom, new Americans could learn to survive in the dominant society and also hold onto their cultural traditions, language, and religion. These social reformers saw an expanded social role for schools and links to other community agencies as not only necessary and humane, but key to improving society. In educating the immigrants, the schools had the chance to strengthen the democracy by welcoming a culturally diverse group of newcomers and by providing the services they needed to participate

Voices of Principle and Promise

Mary Antin, a Russian Immigrant in School

Mary Antin, a poet and novelist, was born in Polotsk, Russia, in 1881 to a Jewish family. Victims of several pogroms—violent attacks on Jewish communities—her family emigrated to America, settling in Boston in 1894. There, Mary attended Boston's Girls' Latin School and wrote poetry. The following piece describes the difficulties she faced in school.

It is not worth while to refer to voluminous school statistics to see just how many "green" pupils entered school last September, not knowing the days of the week in English, who next February will be declaiming patriotic verses in honor of George Washington and Abraham Lincoln, with a foreign accent, indeed, but with plenty of enthusiasm. It is enough to know that this hundred-fold miracle is common to the schools in every part of the United States where immigrants are received (Antin, 1912, p. 206).

Mary Antin had had some education in Russia and had a proud and supportive family to cheer her on. She also had caring teachers, who worked overtime to ease her way:

Whenever the teachers did anything special to help me over my private difficulties, my gratitude went out to them, silently. It meant so much to me that they halted the lesson to give me a lift, that I needs must love them for it. Dear Miss Carrol, of the second grade, would be amazed to hear what small things I remember, all because I was so impressed at the time with her readiness and sweetness in taking notice of my difficulties. Says Miss Carrol, looking straight at me: "If Johnnie has three marbles, and Charlie has twice as many, how many marbles has Charlie?" I raise my hand for permission to

fully and equally in U.S. social and economic life. Jane Addams, who established Hull House in Chicago as a combination school/residence/vocational training/social service center—a settlement house—wrote about the importance of education to the cause of social justice:

> [R]esidents of Hull-House feel increasingly that the educational efforts of a Settlement . . . should promote a culture which will not set its possessor aside in a class with others like himself, but which will, on the contrary, connect him with all sorts of people by his ability to understand them as well as by his power to supplement their present surroundings with the historic background. . . . The educational activities of a Settlement, as well its philanthropic, civic, and social undertakings, are but differing manifestations of the attempt to socialize democracy, as is the very existence of the Settlement itself (Addams, 1910, pp. 436, 453).

Teachers' work naturally increased with the expanded social role of the school and under the pressure of trying to instruct large numbers of children who spoke no English. In classes numbering sixty or one hundred students in some districts (Tyack, 1974), teachers struggled to attend to their needs and their stories. Faced with unduly large classes, educational policymakers and administrators developed tests to sort students "efficiently" into different programs of study. The schools became laboratories for the social visions of men like Edward L. Thorndike, "father" of educational psychology. Thorndike believed that intelligence was determined by nature. The ideal social organization would scientifically match individual intelligence, or talents, with societal needs, allowing for a more efficient distribution of educational resources (Spring, 2005). Providing all students with a standard curriculum of study was wasteful and unjust, if some of them had the inborn intelligence to enter college and the professions, and others were speak. "Teacher, I don't know vhat is tvice." Teacher beckons me to her, and whispers to me the meaning of the strange word, and I am able to write the sum correctly. It's all in the day's work with her; with me, it is a special act of kindness and efficiency (p. 206).

Her shame at "incurring discipline" at the hand of a favorite teacher depicts the conflict that often arose between the desire to adapt to a new world and the desire to hold onto her own culture:

Great was my grief . . . when, shortly after my admission to [Miss Dillingham's] class, I incurred discipline, the first, and next to the last, time in my school career. The class was repeating in chorus the Lord's Prayer, heads bowed on desks. I was doing my best to keep up by the sound; my mind could not go beyond the word "hallowed," for which I had not found the meaning. In the middle of the prayer a Jewish boy across the aisle trod on my foot to get my attention. "You must not say that," he admonished in a solemn whisper; "it's Christian." I whispered back that it wasn't, and went on to the "Amen." I did not know but what he was right, but the name of Christ was not in the prayer, and I was bound to do everything that the class did. If I had any Jewish scruples, they were lagging away behind my interest in school affairs (p. 206).

The whispering resulted in her being punished, for the teacher, though sensitive to the issue at hand, knew "there was a time and a place for religious arguments, and she meant to help us remember that point" (p. 206).

Questions to Consider

1. In what ways did Mary Antin feel different?
2. How did she cope with these differences?
3. What were some factors in her background, her family life, her new environment, and within herself that helped her succeed as a student and a future citizen?

bound for the trades. This political philosophy fit well with the industrial models taking over the country's economy and the pressures on school budgets resulting from immigration. Thorndike gave us "aptitude tests," and a rationale for the establishment of vocational schools as alternatives to the more traditionally academic high schools.

Some schools forbade immigrant children to use their native tongues and more than a few teachers changed children's names to their English equivalents or shortened surnames that were too difficult to spell. Many teachers worked heroically to balance an introduction to American ways of life with a respect for their students' original cultures. We turn to the story of a Polish immigrant girl for an example of one child's eagerness to "become American" and reluctance to give up her heritage.

Mary Antin, a poet and novelist, was born in Polotsk, Russia, in 1881 to a Jewish family. Victims of several pogroms—violent attacks on Jewish communities—her family emigrated to America, settling in Boston in 1894. There, Mary attended Boston's Girls' Latin School and wrote poetry. *The Boston Herald* published one of her poems when she was only fifteen years old. In her book, *The Promised Land* (1912), she wrote about her childhood experiences as a Jewish immigrant, including the difficulties and joys of mastering English and succeeding in school. As you read Mary Antin's reminiscences in Voices of Principle and Promise, think about the difficulties she faced in school.

After Mary Antin's marriage, she was able to go on to college, attending Barnard College and Columbia University in New York until the birth of her children. Her Jewish culture valued academic study, and her high school was one of the best in the city of Boston. And she had the company of thousands of other new students who were part of a great wave of immigration to this country. While some Americans resented the influx of new populations speaking new languages and bringing new cultures and religions to our shores, most Americans, and their

Immigrant children salute the flag at Mott Street Industrial School, c. 1890.
Source: © Bettmann/CORBIS

social institutions, met the challenge with creative new social and educational programs. Still, even with these positive influences, the struggle to learn a new language and make a new life in a strange new land was difficult. Those children whose families did not support formal schooling, or who could not afford to, who found learning more difficult, or whose teachers were impatient and unfeeling or overwhelmed by class sizes of fifty or sixty students, were not as successful. Many left school well before high school graduation.

The issues that Mary Antin faced as a child new to the culture, whose language and religion were different, and whose parents were struggling to make ends meet in their new land, are the issues that immigrant children from the Dominican Republic, Mexico, Laos, Guatemala, and Sudan face in our schools today. But at the turn of the twentieth century, those of Mary Antin's immigrant classmates who did not succeed in school had other options for gaining the skills and opportunities needed to make a living; for example, doing "piecework" at home or selling newspapers in the streets.

In the early 1900s only 16 percent of schoolchildren finished high school, largely because most jobs did not require a diploma (Tyack, 1974). The economy of the country and the technology that supported it grew increasingly more sophisticated, however, requiring that workers have more skills to prepare them for more complex production and distribution of goods. Industrialization meant a shift away from rural farms and small villages to cities and factories. The growing population required an expanded service sector. There was a need for more teachers, doctors and nurses, dentists and lawyers, managers and technicians. More specialized jobs meant that work was now the province of individuals trained for particular jobs in particular workplaces, and less a matter of whole families working together. Spurred by reformers like Jane Addams and by the new unions that were defining workers' rights, the government enacted child labor laws to protect children against the demands of adult workplaces. One result of industrialization, urbanization, professionalization, and labor organization, was that children were freer to go to school and encouraged to stay longer. This meant more crowding and more confusion in already overstressed schools.

The Testing and Efficiency Movement

In the face of overcrowding, educators looked to new developments in science and technology for help. Industrialization had created the "business model," which prized efficiency and organization. Perhaps the schools might find a way to sort through their myriad students and efficiently move them along different educational pathways to the jobs they would be fit to do in society. Underlying this thinking was often the assumption that social class differences were inevitable, the result of mostly inherited individual differences, and required educational differences. The superintendent of schools in Cleveland, Ohio, claimed that working-class children would not want to attend school past the eighth grade (Cohen and Lazerson, 1973). One Michigan educator explained in 1921 how well the schools could serve society if they would only recognize the link between social class and intelligence:

> We can picture the educational system as having a very important function as a selecting agency, a means of selecting the men of best intelligence from the deficient and mediocre. All are poured into the system at the bottom; the incapable are soon rejected or drop out after repeating various grades and pass into the ranks of unskilled labor. . . . The more intelligent who are to be clerical workers pass into the high school; the most intelligent enter the universities, whence they are selected for the professions (quoted in Cohen and Lazerson, 1973).

The Michigan educator assumed that schooling would differ in length or quantity. It occurred to others that it might differ in quality, as well. Rather than offer all students a uniform curriculum—of academic, rather than practical value—perhaps schools ought to match particular curriculum tracks to students' presumed abilities and likely futures. Such a sorting-and-selecting plan would be far more efficient and useful than one that "wasted" academic education on children whose futures lay in more technical, and non-academic, spheres of work.

Early Intelligence Tests If students were to be selected for an educational track best suited to their needs, the criteria for their selection would have to be objective. During World War I, the U.S. Army was interested in an efficient way to classify recruits. Previous studies had looked at the relationship between measured intelligence and occupation, concluding that people who had completed more schooling had higher I.Q. scores and, eventually, higher-ranking jobs. The Army commissioned Lewis Terman to develop intelligence tests to help match soldiers with specialized military jobs. After the war, Terman and other psychologists such as Edward L. Thorndike offered their expertise to the schools. Ignoring the possibility that I.Q. might not be innate—that socioeconomic background, including poverty, the educational background of one's parents, one's native language, or racism, might impact I.Q. scores—or that there might be more than one kind of intelligence (see the discussion of Howard Gardner's work in Chapter 5), or that the tests themselves might be biased, educators seized upon the intelligence tests as a means of making efficient educational decisions. They began to use the tests as rationales for reorganizing school systems, categorizing and labeling children, and placing them in particular programs or schools.

Terman thought that the "mental tests," which purported to measure a person's "general" intellectual ability, were the fairest, most objective, and most accurate means of determining not only appropriate educational programs, but also social futures. In one famous study, he followed the lives of 1500 children whose scores on his Stanford-Binet Individual Test of Intelligence indicated that they were "geniuses" to see if they achieved professional and personal success as adults (Leslie, 2000). The results were mixed; and, in fact, he had excluded the only two Nobel Prize winners in the original test group based on their undistinguished scores. Among Terman's optimistic predictions about the future usefulness of the tests were

> that educational and vocational guidance will be based chiefly on test ratings, and that Hull's proposal to measure every important ability and personality trait and to "grind out" a hundred or more occupational success predictions for every youth is practicable and will be realized; that it will some day be possible to identify, largely by means of tests, the pre-delinquent and the pre-psychotic, and that effective preventive measures will result from this advance; that matrimonial clinics will become common and that couples in large numbers will submit themselves to extensive batteries of ability, personality, interest, and compatibility tests before deciding to embark together; [and] that within a few score years school children from the kindergarten to the university will be subjected to several times as many hours of testing as would now be thought reasonable (Terman, 1930, p. 331).

Given the current mandates of the No Child Left Behind Act and state legislatures, his last prediction was indeed prophetic.

The Results of the Testing Movement The popularity of the new intelligence tests resulted in significant changes in U.S. schools. The test developers had convinced educators that intelligence was mostly hereditary and unchangeable; therefore, the schools should offer a variety of different programs, either "tracks" within one school or a system of differentiated schools, to prepare children for their different futures. In Boston, for example, the school committee established an elementary school that was "prevocational" for children expected to go to work in factories. The school followed a "factory model": the curriculum resembled industrial work and students produced practical materials (Cohen and Lazerson, 1973). High schools sprang up offering vocational training or a curriculum emphasizing "commerce" for those students bound for secretarial or accounting or small business careers. "Classical" high schools still prepared the academically gifted—those with high I.Q. scores—for college and the professions. Outside the cities, rural high schools established separate tracks labeled "college," "commerce," "general," and "vocational."

One result of the testing and efficiency movement was the segregation of children we would now consider as having special needs. Low I.Q. scores were categorized: "idiots" had a mental age of under two years, "imbeciles" between three and seven, "morons" between seven and twelve. "Backward students" had an I.Q. between 70 and 90, enough below the norm of 100 to require separate classes but still be considered educable (Winzer, 1993). Most urban school systems had been housing special needs students in separate schools or classes; however, before the advent of testing, placements had been based on subjective and arbitrary criteria. As a result, new immigrants who couldn't speak English, children with hearing and speech defects, over-age students, and rebellious students often found themselves in classes with children of low mental functioning. Whatever their reason for being there, children in the special schools and special classes tended to be poor or working class. They had few articulate advocates and, as a result, they ended up in school basements, closets, and former warehouses, out of sight and stigmatized. In rural areas, they might be integrated into the heterogeneous one-room school, perhaps helped by their peers (Breitborde, 2003), or they might not go to school at all.

Moving Beyond Efficiency and Testing To some extent, the testing and efficiency movement was an overzealous attempt to apply the philosophy of pragmatism and the new scientific thinking and technological developments to social and educational problems. Charles Darwin and William James had influenced a new generation of philosophers, psychologists, and educators to use the tools of logic and experimentation to try to make education more meaningful, relevant, and feasible in a time of overwhelming stress on schools. John Dewey, on the other hand, read James's pragmatism and Darwin's evolutionism to mean that the problems in schools could not be diagnosed with individual tests or solved with models of efficiency. The larger problems lay in the false notions educators had about how children learn and the nature of what they should be taught. They lay also in the very purpose of schools, which, said Dewey, was disconnected from the social reality of children's lives and from the progress of society itself. Rather than considering students as a faceless group needing to be efficiently and practicably schooled, Dewey homed in on students as whole individuals—thinking, feeling, and doing—in real social settings.

The immigrant wave of the early twentieth century, along with urbanization and industrialization, influenced educators' notions about the role of schools in society and what students should learn. While some worked on finding more efficient ways of educating immigrant students in overcrowded classes, others were addressing the social problems they brought with them to school. Some schools expanded their role with respect to families and the larger community. They established "night schools" for adults and used the school buildings to provide health and social services. Some included workplace-related skills in the subject matter of instruction.

The next section describes the growing recognition that the school curriculum had to catch up with the great social and economic changes of the times. Educational philosophers began experimenting with new ways of organizing subject matter and new ways of teaching to make it more meaningful, relevant, and useful to an increasingly diverse population of children in an increasingly changing society. We described in Chapter 3 the basic principles of Dewey's philosophy of education, called progressivism. In this next section we will discuss the appeal of progressivism to the United States of the early twentieth century.

The Era of Progressive Education

In 1930 John Dewey wrote a book entitled *Individualism Old and New,* in which he wrote about the fundamental changes to the family and the community wrought by the new industrialization. Dewey thought that the industrialization of the early 1900s was robbing people of both a sense of individual identity and a sense of connection. In itself, industrialization was a good thing; in the service of humanity, its innovations could make life easier for people. But without any curbs on the individual gain of the industrialists, and without any sense of social responsibility on their part—to some, the goal of industrialization was merely to make the best profits possible—industrialization was causing great disparities in private wealth, alienation of workers from their work, and a breakdown in social institutions. Dewey saw that happening in the first decades of the twentieth century, where native-born and immigrant workers slaved in factories under dangerous conditions for the sole benefit of the entrepreneurs and industrialists who employed them for as long as they were needed. Women and children did piecework at home or in illegal shops, ruining their eyes, their health, and their chance for an education. The precarious situation culminated in the Great Depression that began in 1929, leaving millions out of work and on their own, without the social securities and benefits we have today.

Work was no longer a family affair or even a community affair. It was no longer a matter of seeing a product through from its creation to its completion. Fewer people were now growing corn from seed, designing and making clothing, or crafting tools from beginning to end. Work was now about using specific skills for specific parts of a whole product. And it was carried out by individuals who came from many different neighborhoods to work alongside people they would not see after the whistle blew at the end of the workday. Furthermore, because of the changing nature of work and the distances adults traveled to get to work, children were no longer seeing adults at work, and were spending less time with their parents in general. Always looking for ways to bring together the positive aspects of seemingly opposing forces—in this case, the individual versus the society, and industrial-technological progress versus the welfare of ordinary people—and always with the goal of supporting the democracy in mind, Dewey proposed a revolutionary education method that captured the imagination of educators then and now. From the 1890s to the 1940s, the progressive education movement of John Dewey and his colleagues influenced many schools to focus more on the individuality of the child, the process of learning, and the aim of using schools to improve society. Child-centered education and social reconstructionism would move a society that reinforced greed, corruption, and inequality toward one based on responsibility, compassion, and equality.

The Dewey School

Dewey argued that the school should prepare children to join the ranks of creative entrepreneurs and problem solvers, but with a sense of social responsibility. The new progressive school would be a model of social community, where the curriculum related to life experiences, drew on children's talents and interests, and taught the values and skills of communication and cooperation necessary for full participation in democratic social life. The school would be a place where children would learn to be socially responsible people. "It is useless to bemoan the departure of the good old days of children's morality, reverence, and implicit obedience," he said in *The School and Society* (1899, p. 11), if the only thing we do is bemoan it. Instead, we can create in the school an "embryonic community life, active with the types of occupations that reflect the life in the larger society, and permeated throughout with the spirit of art, history and science" (pp. 43–44). When the school "saturates [the student] with the spirit of service and provides him with the instruments of effective self-direction, we shall have the deepest and best guaranty of a larger society which is worthy, lovely, and harmonious" (pp. 43–44).

While the progressive school would teach children to be sensitive to the needs of others and aware of the need for cooperation, it would produce leaders, not followers. "Mere inhibition is valueless," Dewey said in *Moral Principles in Education* (1909, p. 54). Its graduates would be critical and creative thinkers who would use formal methods of inquiry to analyze a problem, hear others' ideas, and test solutions.

Following his own precept that learning comes only from doing—from applying and testing ideas in real situations—Dewey established the Laboratory School at the University of Chicago in 1896 to test his own theories. Nicknamed The Dewey School, it allowed university faculty and students to study how children learn and to try out new methods of instruction. Impatient with the traditional organization of the curriculum into disciplines, and with traditional methods of teaching that used only books and lectures, Dewey united the "academic" and the "vocational." The new curriculum integrated the subject areas into projects that had real-world usefulness. The school introduced students to information important to the history and culture of the nation, the world, and their own particular people; but also led them to apply the information to tasks that made the information meaningful and useful. According to his daughters, Dewey realized that "the most important parts of his own education until he entered college were obtained outside the school-room" (Tanner, 1997, p. 13). In the Dewey School, children learned chemistry, geology, and mathematics by cooking, surveying, and building. Teachers had to report their reasons for assigning particular activities and how those activities were connected to other areas of the curriculum and to the world outside the school (p. 73).

The value Dewey placed on uniting academic and vocational learning influenced Booker T. Washington and founders of the land-grant colleges and technical schools. His emphasis on experiential learning and an interdisciplinary, community-linked curriculum inspired like-minded colleagues, who established experimental schools around the country. In 1919 the Progressive Education Association was founded with the goal of reforming all of the nation's school systems.

Dewey's ideas reinforced the work of Francis W. Parker and were echoed by Ella Flagg Young. As superintendent of the Quincy, Massachusetts, public schools in the mid-1800s, Parker experimented with a child-centered and integrated curriculum. Influenced by the Swiss educator Johann Pestalozzi (see Chapter 2), Parker imbued his Quincy Schools with the goal of developing children's minds and souls. He insisted that his much-copied strategies drew on psychologists' research on how the mind worked, principles that were being used everywhere except in the schools (Parker, 1894). Dewey considered Parker the actual "father" of progressive education. Ella Flagg Young was Dewey's graduate student at the University of Chicago. She had been a teacher and later became superintendent of the Chicago Public Schools, the first woman to head a large urban system, and president of the

National Education Association—again, the first woman to hold that office. Dewey claimed that her ideas about schools as democratic communities with participatory decision making greatly influenced his own (Smith, 1994).

As the philosopher and educator most associated with progressivism, Dewey left a strong legacy in the idea that the most effective learning is "hands-on" and connected to the experience of the child. Modern educational ideas such as multiage classrooms, reading and writing across the curriculum, community service, and cooperative learning have roots in progressivism. Theodore Sizer and Deborah Meier, two educators well known for their efforts to make schools more learner-centered, cite Dewey as an inspiration.

His ideas about the social purpose of education, however, were more radical and shorter-lived. They were most popular during times of great social and economic crisis. Jane Addams, founder of Hull House, a full-service settlement house for new immigrants to Chicago, established an adult education program there based on Dewey's ideas. During the Great Depression of the 1930s, Dewey and his colleagues had an easy time convincing many educators that schools were agents of social change. William H. Kilpatrick, who taught with Dewey at Columbia University's Teachers College at that time, wrote about what teacher educators needed to do to prepare teachers for the work:

> [C]onsidering the great significance of the present economic and social situation the profession will join forces with other agencies in the effort to bring about such study of this situation as will mean an increasingly intelligent planning of the social and economic processes to the end that life may be better for all. As a first step . . . the profession must remake its own outlook so as to acquire one and all a truly social point of view. . . . All must come to expect social changes and adjust their thinking accordingly. If we are to meet the confronting situation, all must wish the common good. All must learn to criticize intelligently both existing and proposed institutions. The profession will endeavor to use educative procedures to improve any . . . bad effects and to promote the better (1932, pp. 78–79).

Dare the School Build a New Social Order?

In 1932 George Counts wrote a pamphlet entitled "Dare the School Build a New Social Order?" (1932), in which he urged teachers to lead their students to "create a vision of a future America immeasurably more just and noble and beautiful than the America of today" (p. 288). He was equally upset by the traditionally narrow academic schooling espoused by conservatives and the purely "child-centered" view of some of the progressive educators. Counts asked the progressives, who had been successful in building a network of schools that were child-centered and project-based, to carry out the social promise of progressivism as a "movement which would seem to be completely devoted to the promotion of social welfare through education" (1932, p. 275).

> If Progressive Education is to be genuinely progressive, it must . . . face squarely and courageously every social issue, come to grips with life in all of its stark reality, establish an organic relation with the community, develop a realistic and comprehensive theory of welfare, [and] fashion a compelling and challenging vision of human destiny. . . . In a word

> Progressive Education cannot place its trust in a child-centered school (1932, p. 277).

Counts criticized progressive education for not having social goals, a fact that he suspected was acceptable to those who actually sent their children to progressive schools:

> [L]iberal-minded parents . . . who are full of good will and humane sentiment, who have vague aspirations for world peace and human brotherhood, who can be counted upon to respond moderately to any appeal made in the name of charity . . . but who . . . have no deep and abiding loyalties, possess no convictions for which they would sacrifice over-much, would find it hard to live without their customary material comforts, are rather insensitive to the accepted forms of social injustice, are content to play the role of interested spectator in the drama of human history, refuse to see reality in its harsher and more disagreeable forms, rarely move outside the pleasant circles of the class to which they belong. . . . At bottom they are romantic sentimentalists, but with a sharp eye on the main chance (1932, p. 13).

Education, to Counts, must work toward a clear social goal unafraid of potential charges of indoctrination, for "freedom without a secure economic foundation is only a word: in our society it may be freedom to beg, steal, or starve" (1932, p. 285).

This call to schools to take responsibility for transforming society rang out loudly in the crisis of the 1930s, when old economic social structures proved to be inadequate to ensure our social security. But the call was controversial; many people felt that Dewey, Fitzpatrick, and Counts were coming too close to the communism of the Great Experiment that was being mounted in the new Soviet Union. In the 1930s, nearly half the schools in America were using Harold Rugg's text, *Man and His Changing World.* Despite a title considered sexist today, it was a progressive series of books that advocated social justice, positive race relations, and national economic planning. Included in its pages were discussions of the problems of unemployment, inequities, and consumerism, and some accompanying critical questions. By the 1940s, the National Association of Manufacturers, the Advertising Federation of America, and the New York State Economic Council had condemned Rugg's books and others like them, accusing them of "creeping collectivism" and of being too critical of private enterprise. Many school boards banned the series, some conducting public burnings. The 300,000 copies of Rugg's books in American schools in 1938 had dropped to 21,000 by 1941 (Spring, 2005).

The call for schools to reform society disappeared almost completely, as did progressive schools, with the advent of World War II, as the nation focused all its attention on patriotism and the war effort. The post-war division of much of the world into nations allied with either the United States or the Soviet Union led to a Cold War of competition and suspicion. When the U.S.S.R. launched the first artificial satellite, Sputnik, in 1957, a barrage of criticism fell on American schools: How had we allowed the Soviets to surpass us in scientific knowledge? Surely, American schools had become too "soft," too "child-centered." Progressivism, said many critics, had resulted in a lack of discipline and an avoidance of substantive subject matter. Progressive schools were simply too easy. Returning to teaching "the basics," with a new emphasis on science, schools turned their backs on domestic social needs. It would take the civil rights movement and the "social revolution" of the 1960s to rekindle Counts's fiery ideas.

America First: Post-War Education

The 1950s in the United States was a time of domestic growth and deep anticommunist suspicion. Many were concerned that Karl Marx's prediction of world communism would come true under the growing influence of the Soviet Union. After all, Soviet Premier Nikita Krushchev had announced, "Whether you like it or not, history is on our side. We will bury you," in 1956. Senator Joseph McCarthy and others formed the House Committee on Un-American Activities (HUAC) to root out communists from the ranks of American writers, actors, lawyers, and teachers. Many state legislatures imposed loyalty oaths for teachers, and some school districts fired teachers suspected of communist leanings. Textbooks were examined for seditious content. Because the Soviet Union had the capability to launch a nuclear attack, schools constructed bomb shelters and conducted air raid drills, despite the fact that survival following such an attack was unlikely. New York City issued metal nametags to schoolchildren so that they might be identified after an attack. The federal Civil Defense Administration produced an animated movie called *Duck and Cover* to teach children how to duck under their desks and cover their heads. In some home economics classes, girls learned the fine points of decorating bomb shelters (Altenbaugh, 2003, p. 288).

At the same time, the returning soldiers were settling down in new suburbs with their new families. There was a boom in housing construction, and business and industry expanded to produce the goods that the young families needed. Women who had taken traditionally male jobs to help out during the war were told to return home to care for their families. The pages of *Redbook* and *Ladies' Home Journal* were filled with images of the perfect family—mom, dad, two kids (all white), and assorted pets—living happily together in a new, Cape Cod–style house behind a white picket fence. These images were repeated in the pages of the "Dick and Jane" readers that taught schoolchildren to read. The fact that the lives of millions of Americans looked very different—that many women worked to help support their families, that many Americans lived in city apartments, that black Americans had little access to the new jobs and new suburban neighborhoods and their children went to poorly-equipped racially segregated schools, that rural American was mostly poor—was ignored. The United States was savoring its triumph over Germany and Japan and bent on maintaining its status as a global superpower and its image as the nation with the most appealing quality of life. Look at the photograph representing a "typical" American family of the 1950s. How would you describe the image of the American family that this photograph creates? What stereotypes do you see? How does this image reflect assumptions about the post-war economy of the 1950s? You might want to look at a contemporary primary classroom reader to see how children and families are portrayed today.

In *Educational Wastelands* (1953), Arthur Bestor argued with Counts that the route to an improved society was through an education that improved intellectual reasoning and disciplined effort in its citizens. All children were capable of such reasoning, whatever their background. The school was responsible for transmitting a respect for knowledge and the achievements of the prevailing culture. Progressivism had served only to reinforce the country's tendency toward

In textbooks and other publications throughout the 1950s, the American family was depicted as a Caucasian household consisting of a mother, a father, two children, and assorted pets.
Source: H. Armstrong Roberts/ CORBIS

anti-intellectualism and its impatience with serious study. A strong curriculum that included literature, history, mathematics, and the sciences would train young minds to appreciate the traditions and ideals of American life and prepare them to face the social and scientific challenges of the post–World War II era:

> [B]uild a new social order [but] a social order in which intellectual training would be offered without discrimination to every citizen, in which respect for the highest cultural values would be universal, in which every man would be expected to bring trained intelligence to bear on personal and public problems, and in which scientific and scholarly effort would be . . . valued (pp. 26–30, 32–39).

Bestor rejected Dewey's interdisciplinary curriculum, claiming that it cost students the specialized knowledge offered by the subject matter disciplines. He claimed that over half of America's high schools offered no course in physics or chemistry; one-quarter offered no course in geometry. While in 1900, 84 percent of high school students took science courses, by 1958, only 54 percent were doing so. A similar decline had occurred in mathematics (Bestor, 1958). It was, then, no wonder that the Soviets, whose schools offered a superior education in mathematics and the sciences, had won the race to outer space.

While on the campaign trail in 1948, President Harry Truman told the crowd that "the best defense against the totalitarian system in our Government is education. No man who knows his ABC's and who has an honest heart can even consider being a Communist if he's educated. It's only suffering, misery, and ignorance that breeds communism" (Truman, 1948).

Voices of Principle and Promise

Schooling in the '50s: Dick and Jane Revisited
by Mary-Lou Breitborde

Granite Street Elementary School was a place of boundaries and rules. Even play had strict boundaries. The concrete playground out behind the school had a low wall around it to keep us from going out into the fields. And the playground itself was divided into two sections: one for the boys and the other for the girls. There was a boys' door and a girls' door on each side of the building, and a big front entrance that must have been used by important officials or our parents. Maybe the teachers—we never actually saw them come or go; they seemed to live in the building. Certainly, we children never used the front door.

The school was the typical "egg-crate" construction. Rooms for each grade lined the corridor, which ended in the principal's office. The "good kids" never saw the inside of Miss Johnson's office. You only went there to get rapped on the knuckles with her ruler if you'd been bad—talked in class, for example, or made a mess of your papers. Serious offenses might get you the mysterious "rat hand," or "rattan." (We never learned which, and I never knew anyone who had first-hand experience with it.)

The sex segregation was immutable. One day I was walking to school (everyone walked to school) with my little brother—a kindergartner—and my best friend. It was a lovely fall day and we were stopping now and then to gather up some of the beautifully-colored leaves that had fallen in our path. And so we were late to school. The bell had rung and everyone was inside. An otherwise obedient student, I was anxious to get inside as quickly as possible. The girls' door was nearest to us. I told my brother he'd have to come through it with us. He refused to go in the girls' door, but he was also too afraid to go around the other side to the boys' door by himself. Disgusted with him, I left him outside to make his choice. He chose to run back home. When I got home, my punishment was awaiting me. I don't remember what it was, but I do remember the trauma the incident caused my brother for years afterward.

We learned to read from the Dick and Jane series. Dick and Jane and their friends Sally and Tim didn't do much. They looked and saw. They came and went. They ran and helped and had fun with their dog Spot and their cat Fluff. Their mother was home all day, cleaning in her little black heels and bouffant dresses with their Peter Pan collars all buttoned up. Their dad worked, at something requiring a briefcase, and a suit and hat. There were stories entitled "Something Funny" about things that were not as hilarious as a child might hope. Maybe Spot got into the pail of water, or Sally hid the cat from Tim.

During reading time, our teachers would call a group of us up to the back of the room, where she had special posters and flash cards. We were supposed to memorize a list of "sight words" that we would then see in the next story. If our teachers had just done what the

Ten years later, under President Eisenhower, Congress passed the National Defense Education Act (NDEA) to strengthen American students' knowledge of mathematics and science in the face of the Soviet threat. NDEA began by finding that "an educational emergency exists and requires action by the federal government. Assistance will come from Washington to help develop as rapidly as possible those skills essential to the national defense" (Summary of Major Provisions of NDEA 1958, 2004). The act provided substantial funding for teaching mathematics, science, and modern foreign languages; for college loans; and for vocational programs "to meet the needs of national defense for technicians trained in science and technology" (Summary of Major Provisions of NDEA 1958, 2004). It required that funding recipients file an affidavit that he does not believe in, and is not a member of and does not support any organization that believes in or teaches, the overthrow of the United States Government by force or violence or by any illegal or unconstitutional methods Also, he must swear all oath of allegiance to the United States (Summary of Major Provisions of NDEA 1958, 2004).

publishers wanted, that would have been it—they'd have helped us practice the word cards and listened to us read. But they also taught us the sounds of the letters, prefixes and word endings, and other little tricks that would help us figure out how words were put together. I know now that they were breaking the rules. They were well-educated women themselves—graduates of Wellesley and Smith and Radcliffe—and they were using their own good common sense.

I tolerated Dick and Jane and their unfunny friends, but I thought the whole thing was boring. And too slow! In fact, my father and I got into big trouble one time over the speed at which we were progressing through the reader. I'd been sick for a couple of weeks (my mother had strict rules about not going back to school with a fever, though she'd probably kept my temperature up with all the tea she was pouring into me) and I had run out of books to read. Miracle of miracles, my father found *Our New Friends and Neighbors* in a downtown bookstore! I think he was concerned that I was missing so much school, but in the last few days of my convalescence I finished the book. When I returned to my second grade classroom and told my teacher, she was horrified! What would she do with me for the rest of the year? Somehow, I had done a very bad thing.

Despite these stories, I liked school. I liked the challenge of mastering multiplication tables and spelling rules and facts about China and the battles of the Revolutionary War. I knew the Presidents up through Lincoln and my penmanship was perfect, except for a period in fourth grade when I experimented with an early English script and earned a "B" for the term. I was aware that not everyone was happy. Those who couldn't carry a tune were labeled "hummers" and forced to the back of the class during music period. Those who couldn't make ruler-straight margins on their papers sometimes had those papers tossed into the wastebasket. Those who couldn't sit still or couldn't keep from rebelling found themselves carted off to someplace called "reform school." I have no idea what happened to children with special needs; we either didn't have them or they struggled without benefit of diagnosis. Schoolwork came easy to me, though. I was quiet by nature and so I fit in well. Years later, in high school and college, I had trouble volunteering my opinions in class and using the word "I" in my papers. But I knew when to use a semicolon and could rattle off the multiplication tables without a hitch.

Questions to Consider

1. Rudolph Flesch, Arthur Bestor, and others complained that schools were not rigorous enough and their curricula unclear and disorganized. Is that apparent in the reminiscence above? Explain.
2. How well does this passage conform to other accounts of schooling in the 1950s, perhaps by older folks in your family or community?
3. Evaluate this portrait of Granite Street School in light of the opinion of Will Rogers that "the schools ain't what they used to be and probably never were."

Back to Basics

The complaints about the laxness of U.S. schools extended to the very foundation of their curriculum: literacy. In 1955, Rudolf Flesch wrote a best-selling book exposing a shameful secret about U.S. schools: they were not teaching children to read. In *Why Johnny Can't Read: And What You Can Do About It,* Flesch decried the laissez-faire attitude of progressive educators, who were overly concerned with whether a child was "ready" to learn. Teachers were loath to impose learning on a child. Instead, they focused on waiting until a child was "ready" to learn to read:

> You take a 6-year-old child and start to teach him something. The child, as often happens, doesn't take to it at once. If you use a common-sense approach, you try again and again, exert a little patience, and after some time the child begins to learn. But if you are a 20th-century American educator, equipped with the theory of "readiness," you drop the whole matter instantly and wait until the child, on his own, asks to be taught.

> Let's wait until he's 7—until he's 8—until he's 9. We've all the time in the world; it would be a crime to teach a child who isn't "ready" (Flesch, 1955).

Parents who protested were themselves blamed, Flesch said. Colleges of education told prospective teachers of reading that if a mother "storms to the school . . . to protest . . . what she imagines is the failure to teach good old phonics" and the lack of her child's progress in reading, the teacher should understand that "it is likely that things have already happened in the home which are having a disadvantageous—indeed, sometimes a disastrous—influence on the pupil's efforts to learn (1955, pp. 14–15).

Flesch advocated teaching reading by teaching phonics—the sounds of letters that combine to form words. Reading instruction should be systematic, highly organized, and sequential, involving direct instruction and lots of practice. Progressives were afraid to provide direct instruction to children or make them practice and memorize information. Misreading Dewey, Flesch complained that progressives left learning to the children alone.

> Ever since 1500 B.C.—wherever an alphabetic system of writing was used—people have learned to read by simply memorizing the sound of each letter in their alphabet. Except 20th-century America. We have thrown 3500 years of civilization out the window (1955, p. ix).

Flesch's book was wildly popular and has never gone out of print. He published an updated version twenty-six years after the first, which, attesting to his continued frustration, bore the same title (Flesch, 1981).

In addition to the teaching of reading, the teaching of mathematics earned severe criticism. A 1957 *Saturday Evening Post* editorial castigated an elementary school for wasting time on an example of progressivism's learning-by-doing method. The school had established a school bank, with a bank president and cashiers taking turns behind cardboard counters. *Time* magazine reported that hundreds of Los Angeles high school students couldn't tell time and that more than half of eighth graders could not calculate the state sales tax on their purchases (Rothstein, 1998). *Life* magazine published a series of articles in 1958 entitled "Crisis in Education," which included a comparison between what a Russian high school student and his counterpart in the United States were studying. In light of the significantly higher expectations for Russian students, the magazine wondered how we could ever hope to win the Cold War (Rothstein, 1998).

Bestor and like-minded critics of the public schools founded the Council for Basic Education in 1956 to provide American schoolchildren with their "educational birthright"—public schools "devoted to mastery of the core disciplines of liberal learning: English, history, civics, geography, mathematics, the sciences, foreign languages, and the arts" (Council, 2004). The organization is now thirty-three years old. Its journal, *Basic Education,* publishes articles on topics such as the importance of grammar ("the profound connection between the nuts and bolts of knowledge and the brilliant scaffolding of intellectual and creative achievement" (Kalkavage, 1997). It sponsors many projects to strengthen liberal arts education in elementary and secondary schools. In the 1950s it was an early strong voice calling for higher standards and more content in public education.

Systematic Instruction

Reacting against what some felt was a lack of direction in the progressive curriculum and methods of instruction, educators in the 1950s sought to make instruction systematic, highly organized, even "programmable." In "The Science of Learning and the Art of Teaching" (1954), the behaviorist B. F. Skinner said that one teacher could not possibly provide the immediate feedback and reinforcement that her thirty students needed in order to learn—according to his theory of operant conditioning. (See Chapter 5 for a discussion of Skinner and the behaviorist approach to learning.) Therefore, Skinner designed a "teaching machine" that students could operate by themselves. Students pulled a lever on the machine and received a question to answer. If their answers were correct, they could proceed to the next higher level of questions. If their answers were incorrect, they would be directed back to lower levels or asked new questions. The idea was that individual students would be able to learn at their own pace and from an organized presentation of carefully sequenced concepts or skills.

Early Signs of Technology in Education The teaching machine never gained much popularity, perhaps because it required that teachers develop and load the questions, perhaps because it couldn't address more abstract concepts and discussions, or perhaps because it seemed to reduce teaching and learning to mechanical operations. The machine, though, was part of a larger effort called **programmed instruction.** Educational publishers produced kits to provide systematic, programmed learning activities with immediate feedback in all subject areas. Some of you might have used the SRA kits in elementary school that were typical of this instructional approach. Developed by Science Research Associates, the kits contained carefully sequenced, color-coded task cards, originally in reading but later in all subject areas. Students proceeded through the box, working on the cards and checking their progress. The cards provided information on a particular skill, with examples, and then required students to answer questions applying those skills. If students completed all the cards in one section with a prescribed level of success (usually 80 percent correct), they could proceed to the next section. The kits were designed to be almost "teacher-proof," allowing individual students to learn and practice on their own at a rate that was comfortable for them. Based on the behaviorist and mastery models of learning, the kits would not allow children to progress to learning new skills unless they had mastered the ones assumed to be prerequisite. Many children liked the challenge of seeing how fast they could move up through the skills cards; many others found the cards meaningless and boring. They were reflective of a significant move away from the applied, interdisciplinary approaches that the progressives had advanced.

Skinner's teaching machine also initiated an effort to turn teaching into "instructional design" based on research into learning and cognitive processing. It foreshadowed Robert Gagne's list of "conditions of learning," and Benjamin Bloom's "mastery learning." Bloom devised his Taxonomy of Educational Objectives in 1956 to organize and categorize curriculum goals along levels of thinking from concrete specific recall to abstract critical evaluation. The diagnostic-prescriptive teaching model that Madeline Hunter developed in the 1960s and 1970s, and today's standards-based instructional design, are also outcomes of the 1950s effort to systematize instructional design. (See Chapter 4 for a discussion of standards-based instruction and Chapter 5 for a general overview of models of teaching and learning.) Skinner's machine also foreshadowed the development of instructional technology, which applies engineering to curriculum design. In fact, the teaching machine is considered an early version of computer-assisted instruction.

By the end of the decade, domestic and world events were fomenting change in U.S. schools. There were still those who saw education as a tool for national defense against the specter of world communism. James B. Conant, a nuclear scientist and former president of Harvard University, blamed the United States' loss in the race to space on the small, underresourced American high school, where English teachers taught science in the absence of better-qualified colleagues. A consolidated larger school, with a variety of courses and up-to-date resources and a standardized curriculum, was the best way to regain footing in the world, he thought (1959). Conant's "bigger is better" opinion won over state legislatures and federal policymakers, who began supporting the construction of large, comprehensive high schools. But others were questioning the impersonal environments that schools were becoming and the lack of connection to the local or global community. By 1960, the nation was divided on many issues, including racial integration, human rights, and the Vietnam War. While Conant wanted the schools to help unify the nation and prepare for its defense in the world, others took the schools in the direction of facing and solving the social problems in the neighborhoods and the nation. The struggle for civil rights and the protests against a faraway war that marked the 1960s, entered the schools with full force.

The Pursuit of Equality and Justice

Preoccupation with the Cold War took a toll on American schools. Not only did the curriculum become narrower under right-wing political scrutiny, robbing teachers of their responsibility to educate children to think critically, but their budgets suffered as federal dollars went to military defense. In 1955, a year when America was not at war, the United States spent four times as much on defense as it did on assistance to public education (Tyack, 1974, p. 275). There was a great disparity in the resources available to schools in different areas of the country.

The G.I. Bill, which sent tens of thousands of World War II veterans to college, the availability of federal housing loans, and a new interstate highway system helped build suburbs on the outskirts of the old cities. These suburbs became increasingly popular places where rising white middle-class families with high expectations for schools wanted to raise their children. Left behind in the cities were new immigrants, ethnic minorities and people of color, the poor and the working-class, most without a higher education themselves and with limited power over their children's schools. Left behind in the rural areas were tenant farmers and miners who had neither the means nor the education necessary to migrate to new jobs in the cities or suburbs. Black, Latino, and Native children were largely underserved, many of them segregated either by law—de jure—as in the South, or in fact—de facto—because of patterns of residential segregation, as in the North. Children of the middle and upper classes went to well-equipped schools with up-to-date curricula and credentialed teachers. Poor children received a poor education.

In 1954 the landmark U.S. Supreme Court case, *Brown v. Board of Education of Topeka, Kansas,* brought an end to the legal segregation of black and white schoolchildren. In 1962 Michael Harrington published *The Other America,* which exposed the contrast between the affluence of the new suburban middle class in the United States and the one-quarter of its population that did not share in the economic boom. Harrington had "discovered poverty" (Isserman, 2001). The speeches and advertisements extolling the country's high standard of living ignored the fifty million who were living differently:

> The millions who are poor in the United States tend to become increasingly invisible. Here is a great mass of people, yet it takes an effort of the intellect and will even to see them. . . . Poverty is often off the beaten track. It always has been. The ordinary tourist never left the main highway, and today rides interstate turnpikes. He does not go into the valleys of Pennsylvania where the towns look like movie sets of Wales in the thirties. He does not see the company houses in rows, the rutted roads (the poor always have bad roads whether they live in the city, in towns, or on farms), and everything is black and dirty. And even if he were to pass through such place by accident, the tourist would not meet the unemployed men in the bar or the women coming home from a runaway sweatshop (Harrington, 1962, p. 191).

President John F. Kennedy read Harrington's book, and helped spur what became the War on Poverty begun by Kennedy and enacted by his successor, Lyndon Johnson. President Johnson's Economic Opportunity Act of 1964 and later legislation established Medicare, Medicaid, Legal Services, food stamps, the Job Corps, community action agencies, and VISTA (a domestic Peace Corps of volunteers) to help the "underprivileged," "because it is right, because it is wise, and because, for the first time in our history, it is possible to conquer poverty" (Johnson, 1964).

Compensatory Education

Legislators saw the school as a crucial weapon in the War on Poverty, both as a way to deliver new services to children and their families and as a route up and out of the ghetto, the ghost towns, and the backwoods. President Johnson formalized the role of the schools in combating poverty in the 1965 Elementary and Secondary Education Act (ESEA). For Johnson, the issue was also personal: he had been a teacher in Texas, and a child of rural poverty himself. With his own one-room country schoolteacher by his side, he proudly signed the landmark bill, which had passed both houses of Congress, with these words:

> As a son of a tenant farmer, I know that education is the only valid passport from poverty. As a former teacher—and, I hope, a future one—I have great expectations of what this law will mean for all of our young people. As President of the United States, I believe deeply no law I have signed or will ever sign means more to the future of America (Johnson, 1965).

The Elementary and Secondary Education Act (ESEA) The ESEA established a precedent that continues today to enlist the federal government's help in equalizing educational opportunity for all children. Over the years, ESEA has also provided federal funds for teacher preparation in math, science, and technology under the Eisenhower Professional Development program; bilingual education under Title VII; money for school libraries and textbooks; support for "safe and drug-free school" projects; special programs to aid Native American, migrant, and homeless children; and a federal office that conducts research and gathers data on school and student performance. The 2001 No Child Left Behind Act is the nickname for the reauthorization of this thirty-five-year-old program. Its 1965 introduction reads as follows:

> In recognition of the special educational needs of low-income families and the impact that concentrations of low-income families have on the ability of local educational agencies to support adequate educational programs, the Congress hereby declares it to be the policy of the United States to provide financial assistance . . . to local educational agencies serving areas with concentrations of children from low-income families to expand and improve their educational programs by various means (including preschool programs) which contribute to meeting the special educational needs of educationally deprived children (Elementary and Secondary Education Act, 1965, Section 201).

The 1965 ESEA and the 1964 Economic Opportunity Act would provide **compensatory education,** special programs that would compensate for the educational disadvantages of the home lives of poor children. These children were presumed to suffer from **cultural deprivation,** to lack the knowledge, habits of behavior, and values they would need to succeed in school. The Head Start preschool program would give them the developmental and social experiences their homes in the inner cities and isolated rural areas could not. As a result, they would be as ready for school as their wealthier peers because they would have more "culture." In Head Start classrooms, they would have books read to them; learn to count, recognize letters, and spell their names; visit the local fire station; and learn other things that suburban children were learning in their own homes and neighborhoods. The billion dollars allocated to schools in poor districts under Title I of ESEA would provide extra reading and mathematics teachers to help them catch up and keep up with their more advantaged classmates. But compensatory education was about more than providing remedial teachers; it was about filling the cultural void that supposedly characterized the home life of poor children.

The cultural deprivation theory eventually gave way to the idea that poor children came from families caught in a **culture of poverty,** which would keep them poor for generations to come, without a break in the cycle of low expectations, low education, and antisocial behavior. Anthropologist Oscar Lewis (1966) coined the term after studying poor Puerto Rican communities in New York and San Juan and, in Lewis's view, poor people created a culture that allowed them to adapt to their life conditions and survive. Their low occupational and educational expectations, for example, might be construed as realistic—a way to avoid the frustration of unfulfilled hopes.

Blaming the Victim Despite Lewis's intentions, many misread the culture of poverty as an indication that poor people were to blame, because of their own irresponsibility, misbehavior, and disorganization—behaviors typical of the culture of poverty. This point of view came to be called "blaming the victim." The culture of poverty was simply an inferior culture, nearly impossible to change. The social critic Christopher Lasch explained how this worked in some schools:

> When teachers in ghetto schools say that black children are "deprived," "disadvantaged," and "unteachable," they do show a "cultural smugness" —or better, a cultural aphasia—which makes them unable to talk to the children or to listen to what the children are saying. The schoolmarm's view of "culture" assumes that poems, for instance, should conform to certain rigid standards of grammar, meter, and sentiment. Thus a poem about "The Junkies," as Herbert Kohl notes, is dismissed as "the ramblings of a disturbed girl," whereas the same teacher praises "Shop with Mom" for its "pleasant and healthy thought." Similarly with music: some people can't hear jazz, blues, gospel, or "soul" because it doesn't live up to their arbitrary expectations of what "good music" should sound like (Lasch, 1968).

By **cultural aphasia,** Lasch meant that many teachers conveyed the idea that the then-dominant white Anglo-Saxon Protestant suburban culture was the ideal and the only culture worthy of attention. Remember that the teachers of the 1960s had come of age in the conservative 1950s. Perhaps the most famous example of what was actually a policy of deculturalization and institutionalized racism in many school systems in the early 1960s is Jonathan Kozol's description of the incident that caused his dismissal from the Boston Public Schools. As a fourth-grade teacher of black students in Boston's Roxbury in 1967, Kozol decided to add the poetry of Langston Hughes to the approved reading list. A white parent protested, and was supported by school officials, who told Kozol that "no poem by any Negro author could be considered permissible if it involved suffering." In any case, he had broken an important policy by including in his curriculum something that had not been approved by the administration. Instead, they said, he should have stayed within the prescribed list of materials, which included a geography book that described black Africans as "savage and uncivilized." An excerpt from Kozol's book *Death at an Early Age* (1968), including this incident, appears at the end of this chapter as a Critical Reading.

Civil Rights Come to School

Despite an expansion of public education in general, white children benefited far more than their black peers from the increased educational opportunities. The "black codes" legislated in the South following reconstruction in the late nineteenth century strictly segregated the schools. According to Henry Perkinson, Texas's public school funds were "exclusively for the education of white scholastics." Georgia educated "free white inhabitants" from age six to twenty-one. Arkansas free public education was "for whites only." Tennessee mandated separate schools for "colored children." In Florida, the state superintendent of schools claimed that whites "had a deadly hatred to the education . . . of the freedmen," but Florida offered a concession to Negroes: "If Negro males would pay a special tax of $1.25 per year, they could have their own public schools" (Perkinson, 1991, p. 21).

Meanwhile, the courts were affirming the right of states to segregate their schools (see Table 8.2). The "separate but equal" doctrine ruled the land until its repeal in the 1954 *Brown v. Board of Education of Topeka, Kansas,* when the Supreme Court recognized that separate schools for black Americans were ultimately not

Table 8.2 Timeline of Court Decisions on Desegregation

1877	1890	1896	1954
U.S. Supreme Court rules that states cannot prohibit segregated schools.	U.S. Supreme Court rules that states cannot require segregated schools.	*Plessy v. Ferguson* states "legislation is powerless to eradicate racial instincts" and schools could be "separate but equal."	*Brown v. Board of Education* repeals "separate but equal" doctrine.

equal. Presenting evidence that black schools were more poorly funded, staffed by less qualified teachers, and provided inadequate materials for instruction, the National Association for the Advancement of Colored People, led by the future Supreme Court Justice Thurgood Marshall, convinced the Court that segregated schools were inherently racist. Twelve years later, James Coleman would corroborate Marshall's point in a statistical report that attributed academic achievement to the socioeconomic background of both the child and the school he or she attended. Black students' performance improved if they went to school with white children. The Coleman Report (1966) supported racial integration and, later, the policy of affirmative action.

Brown v. Board of Education initiated a period of school desegregation in the South, a process that so reordered the entrenched ways of life that violence accompanied much of the process.

- In Little Rock, Arkansas, Governor Orval Faubus called out the state National Guard to try to prevent the integration of Central High School and President Johnson responded with federal troops.
- In Oxford, Mississippi, a white mob attacked the federal marshals sent to protect James Meredith, the first black student at the University of Mississippi.
- Governor George Wallace stood in the doorway of the University of Alabama on the day that two black students came to enroll, defying (unsuccessfully) federal intervention in state business.

In some communities, local police carried out the law despite the protests. Twelve black elementary students walked into six previously all-white schools in Nashville, Tennessee, on the morning of September 9, 1957, through a line of jeering white adults. One of the protestors—who, as it turned out, wasn't even from Nashville—threw a bomb that destroyed a wing of one school and was promptly jailed.

And in some communities, integration was accomplished without violence. In the North Carolina urban county of Charlotte and neighboring white suburban Mecklenburg County, residents voted two to one in favor of merging the two school systems. When a black parent sued the joint system for preventing his daughter from attending a nearby white school, the federal government stepped in and ordered that the schools devise a desegregation plan. *Swann v. Charlotte-Mecklenburg* established a precedent for federal oversight of desegregating school systems. Although the federal courts supervised the Charlotte-Mecklenburg school district for fifteen years, the system was remarkable for the relatively peaceful desegregation of its schools.

Brown v. Board of Education **initiated a period of school desegregation in the South, a process that so reordered the entrenched ways of life that violence accompanied much of the process.**
Source: © Bettmann/CORBIS

For a while, civil rights violations, including school segregation, were assumed to occur only in the South. Volunteers from the North went to Mississippi and Alabama and Georgia to join the ranks of the "freedom fighters," registering black voters and staging marches and sit-ins to protest Jim Crow laws and segregated schools. Once the de jure system of Southern school segregation was dismantled, however, the courts turned to the de facto segregation of the North. Federal courts began to rule that residentially segregated Northern school districts must achieve racial balance. They could use voluntary means, such as creating thematic "magnet" schools designed to attract children both white and black, or, involuntary methods, such as forced busing.

In Boston, white adults in South Boston and Charlestown pelted rocks at school buses carrying black children into their neighborhood schools for the first time, angry that their own children were no longer allowed to attend those same schools. Loath to put their children on buses bound for schools across the city in black Roxbury, many white parents pulled their children out of the public schools and enrolled them in parochial schools or new private "academies," or they moved to the suburbs. The outcomes of this crisis were significant: families torn apart by hatred, a white flight to the suburbs that left the city more impoverished and with a greater percentage of minorities, and feelings of bitterness and shame that continue today. Amidst the crisis, a few parents and students worked hard to reach across the racial divide to work together and form friendships. One community organizer now says it all could have been done differently, with more consideration and involvement of the people: "We need to act for what we feel is just, but try to understand where an opponent is coming from. We did not have the empathy and wisdom to . . . work it out in a better way (Finfer, 2004).

Mexican Americans and the Struggle for Educational Equity

While the primary target of the civil rights movement's attack on segregated schools was the de jure and de facto segregation of African American children, other children of color were attending separate and inferior schools in the nation as well. The 1848 Treaty of Guadalupe Hidalgo, which guaranteed the rights of Mexican Americans after Mexico was defeated in the Mexican–American War, included the right to an education. But the new states eventually created by the treaty (Arizona, New Mexico, Texas, and California) were slow to establish schools. When they did, the schools often did not respect the culture and language of the students. In many cases, communities established separate schools and separate "Mexican rooms" (Samora and Simon, 1995) for children on the assumption that their English was limited and required a special setting. The results were harmful. The children attended schools that were underequipped and ineffective, their teachers too often had low expectations for their academic success, and they were subject to prejudice and discrimination. Until the 1970s, many school districts prohibited Mexican American children from speaking Spanish in school and punished them for it.

Well before *Brown,* Mexican American parents in California had challenged segregated schools. In 1946, the state supreme court ruled in *Mendez v. Westminister School District* that separate schools for Mexican Americans and Anglos were illegal in California. In 1957 parents successfully sued one school district in rural Texas for class assignment practices that discriminated against Spanish-speaking children. The school system had been assigning them to separate Spanish-language classrooms for first and second grade, even if they were able to speak English. What was worse, these Mexican American children were retained in first grade for four years, followed by more years in second grade. Most students reached the third grade at the age they were expected to drop out of school to help their parents in the fields. The federal court ruled that the practice was "purposeful, intentional and unreasonably discriminatory" (Willoughby, 2004). Even in the 1960s, the U.S. Civil Rights Commission found that one-fourth of Mexican American children in California attended schools whose population was more than 50 percent Mexican American (Donato, 1997).

In California, Mexican Americans organized to advocate for more equitable schooling. Fueled by the Chicano movement of the 1960s, leaders such as George Sanchez and organizations such as the League of United Latin American Citizens (LULAC) worked to boost school attendance, provide scholarships, increase the number of Latino teachers and administrators, and establish Chicano studies programs. In Texas, Hector Garcia led the American G.I. Forum into court to battle discrimination against Mexican Americans in schools (Samora and Simon, 1995). Ruben Donato recounts in his book, *The Other Struggle for Equal Schools: Mexican Americans During the Civil Rights Era* (1997), the grassroots efforts of Mexican Americans in the town of Brownfield, California, to desegregate the schools and improve bilingual education. Mexican Americans fought a proposal to make school year-round, which would have been problematic for the migrant workers among them. Their efforts were largely unsuccessful, however, because they lacked political power. "They were marginalized from the political infrastructure of the community. . . . In most cases they were unable to influence educational policy decisions that were certain to have an effect on their children" (p. 152).

Legal help was imminent but proved to be imperfect. In 1968 Congress passed the Bilingual Education Act, which mandated that schools provide special assistance programs for language-minority students. Though the act required that these programs give students "full access to the learning environment, the curriculum, special services and assessment in a meaningful way," the structure and quality of programs varied widely from district to district. In too many schools, bilingual students were physically and educationally removed from the life of the school, sometimes confined to building annexes or basement classrooms.

In 1974 Chinese students sued the San Francisco Public Schools for not providing them with adequate help in learning English nor, in general, an education equal to that of the English-speaking children in the city's schools. The plaintiffs argued that the children were segregated in separate classes and schools and not allowed to participate fully in the district's educational program. In *Lau v. Nichols*, the U.S. Supreme Court found that the district was discriminating against language-minority students and held it responsible for remedying the situation.

But neither the Bilingual Education Act nor *Lau* specified how to accomplish the teaching of English to language-minority children while supporting their first language and culture and ensuring that they learn subject matter. There is no federal mandate for an education that is truly bilingual, though some states mandate such programs. Civil rights laws merely require that educational programs offer equal opportunities for language-minority children, based on sound educational research and providing adequate resources (History of Bilingual Education, 1998). Children whose first language is Spanish comprise the majority of language-minority children in today's schools, Mexican American children being the largest subgroup among them. The problem of the achievement gap between Mexican Americans and their Anglo peers, and the related issue of bilingual education, are discussed in depth in Chapter 9.

Radical Education for Social Justice

The combination of the War on Poverty, the civil rights movement, and the provisions of the ESEA in 1965 spurred discussion about what had been a traditional curriculum left over from the conservative 1950s. Once again the schools had vocal critics, but this time, the criticism was that they were irrelevant and disconnected from the real world of the students. In education circles, the ideas of relevance and community and personal growth brought back echoes of John Dewey. Writers such as Neil Postman and Charles Weingartner, authors of *Teaching as a Subversive Activity,* suggested that the curriculum be designed around students' questions because "the art and science of asking questions is the source of all knowledge" (1969, p. 172). Herbert Kohl refuted the idea that black children of the urban ghetto had cultural deficits when he recorded the extraordinary creative writing of his sixth-grade "unteachables" in *36 Children* (1967). Though others had told him that the children in his class had limited vocabularies, that they could not think abstractly, and that they were oriented to physical rather than mental activity, Kohl found that their writing about their own lives was powerful and insightful. He concluded that children will not write if they are afraid to talk, and they will not talk if they distrust their audience. In *36 Children* and the many books that followed, he asked teachers to use their influence to liberate and empower marginalized and underserved groups.

Radical educational reform in the 1960s called for a curriculum that addressed community issues and gave previously powerless groups the tools to advocate for themselves. Sometimes there were great political clashes between educators who felt they were working on behalf of children, and community activists who sought a stronger place in the schools. The Ocean Hill–Brownsville crisis of 1968 was an infamous and sad example. Ocean Hill–Brownsville was a mostly black neighborhood in Brooklyn, New York, that was experimenting with community control of its schools. When the black local school board tried to fire Fred Nauman, a white Jewish junior high school teacher and leader of the United Federation of Teachers, in defiance of both union and school administration protocol, the teachers struck. What followed were months of bitter battles in the schools, on the streets, and in the newspapers. Teachers were accused of racism, black community leaders of anti-Semitism and union busting. The battles pitted blacks against whites, blacks against Jews and Catholics, and the community against its teachers. When it was all over, the city would be divided by race, Jews who had fought alongside blacks in the civil rights movement would shift to the conservative right wing, and the experiments in community control would end (Podair, 2001). The biggest losers would be the schoolchildren.

Radical Education for Self-Actualization

By the end of the 1960s, many civil rights battles had been won. At the time of his death in 1968, Martin Luther King was addressing the issues of poverty and war—issues that affected both people of color and whites. The new decade began with the tragic deaths of student antiwar activists at Kent State University in 1970 at the hands of the Ohio National Guard, but within three years the United States had withdrawn from Vietnam. The assassinations of the two Kennedys and Martin Luther King, the Watergate scandal that resulted in the resignation of President Nixon, and an economic recession, among other events, led many young Americans to turn inward. They experimented with communal living, mind-altering drugs, and new forms of art and music. It was the "me generation," characterized by the new freedoms won during the revolutionary struggles of the 1960s—political, social, philosophical, sexual.

In the schools, teachers helped students "clarify their values" and become more "self-aware." High schools created elective courses in poetry, science fiction, sports literature, and "street law" to take the place of traditional survey courses such as "English I" and "Senior Civics." Teachers asked students to keep journals to record their impressions and feelings about the events in their lives. Educational researchers discovered that there were different styles of learning, and new materials and equipment appeared in classrooms to use visual, auditory, and kinesthetic modes of instruction. Congress enacted P.L. 94-142, the Education for All Handicapped Children Act, to ensure that special needs children would receive a free and appropriate public education. Teachers began thinking about their students' "individual needs."

Many educators who looked to the schools to foster independence of mind and individual freedom looked back to John Dewey's child-centeredness for inspiration. Unfortunately, some of them misread, or at least exaggerated, his ideas. Paul Goodman, author of *Compulsory Mis-Education* (1964) wanted no formal subjects of study until the age of twelve. Citing Dewey, Goodman wrote, "With guidance, whatever a child experiences is educational. . . . It makes no difference what is learned at this age, so long as the child goes on wanting to learn something further" (1969, p. 100). Dewey, of course, had imagined a much more active role for teachers and a curriculum that, while built on students' interests, moved beyond them and incorporated the teaching of information, skills, and methods of inquiry.

One Size Does Not Fit All John Holt's book, *How Children Fail,* sold widely throughout the 1970s and is still read today. Holt said that most children in school failed not only academically, but also "fail[ed] to develop more than a tiny part of the tremendous capacity for learning, understanding and creating with which they were born" (1964, p. 15). Children failed in school because they were bored and confused. The work didn't make sense to them and had no connection to their lives. Schools killed children's natural desire to learn; anyone who knew how quickly the excitement and curiosity of kindergartners became the "Do we have to?" of third graders would agree. Schools taught the same curriculum to everyone, regardless of their interests or their talents. Dewey, Piaget, and others had told us that children learn best when they are allowed to ask their own questions and find the answers. Instead of cultivating children's unique interests, schools were offering a "one size fits all" education that, Holt said, fit no one.

In his companion book, *How Children Learn* (1967), Holt described an alternative method of educating, which did not presume that there is one body of knowledge that all children should learn, but allowed children to explore the subjects that interest them. As natural learners and problem solvers, children could be trusted with their own education. Holt wrote in 1967 that teachers should only be passive facilitators. Later on, he concluded that schools would never allow children the freedom they needed to learn. School is bad for children, and so, it's best that they not even go.

> Almost every child on the first day he sets foot in a school building, is smarter, more curious, less afraid of what he doesn't know, better at finding and figuring things out, more confident, resourceful, persistent and independent than he will ever be again in his schooling. . . . In he comes, this curious, patient, determined, energetic, skillful learner. We sit him down at a desk, and what do we teach him? Many things. First, that learning is separate from living. "You come to school to learn," we tell him, as if the child hadn't been learning before, as if living were out there and learning were in here, and there were no connection between the two. Secondly, that he cannot be trusted to learn and is no good at it. . . . In short, he comes to feel that learning is a passive process, something that someone else does to you, instead of something you do for yourself (1969).

Holt was one of several educators in the 1970s to call for "home schooling." He established the *Growing Without Schooling* magazine in 1977 to support parents who wanted to educate their children away from the limiting influences of school. Although Holt died in 1985 and the magazine ceased publication in 2001, the movement continues to grow with the help of home schooling networks and Internet resources.

Humanistic Education: Free, Open, and Deschooled While they cited the philosophy of John Dewey for support, Goodman and Holt owed more to the existentialists, who believed that the only source of truth lies within the individual who was free to act and choose and create the conditions of his or her life. Existentialism gave birth to the "humanistic education" of the 1970s, a movement that saw the goal of education as fostering personal freedom and fulfillment. Abraham Maslow (1954, 1962) explained to teachers that human beings had a "hierarchy of needs," which progressed from physical safety to love and belonging, and culminated in "self-actualization." Teachers needed to nurture children's growth toward self-actualization by providing an atmosphere of safety and support, helping them understand themselves—their interests, their talents, and their values—and providing opportunities for them to experiment with how and what they learned and how they felt about it.

As Chapter 3 described, there was much in the philosophy of the existential-humanistic education that borrowed from the romantic naturalist Jean-Jacques Rousseau, the kindergarten pioneer Frederick Froebel, and the child-centered part of progressivism. The most radical of the existentialist-humanists promoted deschooling and free schools. Leading the deschoolers was Ivan Illich, who pioneered the **deschooling** movement with his 1970 book, *Deschooling Society.* It began with a chapter entitled, "Why We Must Disestablish School":

> Many students, especially those who are poor, intuitively know what the schools do for them. . . . The pupil is . . . "schooled" to confuse teaching with learning, grade advancement with education, a diploma with competence, and fluency with the ability to say something new. His imagination is "schooled" to accept service in place of value. Medical treatment is mistaken for health care, social work for the improvement of community life, police protection for safety, military poise for national security, the rat race for productive work. Health, learning, dignity, independence, and creative endeavor are defined as little more than the performance of the institutions which claim to serve these ends, and their improvement is made to depend on allocating more resources to the management of hospitals, schools, and other agencies in question. . . . [T]he institutionalization of values leads inevitably to physical pollution, social polarization, and psychological impotence: three dimensions in a process of global degradation and modernized misery (1970).

Illich's book described alternatives to school. Children could learn at home, in a series of apprenticeships, in museums and local libraries, and by exploring their cities, towns, and the countryside. They didn't need to be confined to a desk in a classroom for six hours a day, learning from paper representations of real things. Interestingly, Illich anticipated the development of new technologies and distance learning that now allow students, perhaps many of you, to learn away from traditional classrooms in independent ways. The deschooling movement never caught on as a serious educational alternative. **Free schools,** however, sprang up all over the world in the 1970s to give children complete charge of their own learning. The most famous of these schools was Summerhill. A. S. Neill founded the school in 1921, but it was in the late 1960s and 1970s that it became a model for many alternative schools established in the United States. Now eighty years old, Summerhill describes itself as "first and foremost a place where children can discover who they are." Teachers are available to help students learn, but students must first ask. In free schools, there are no requirements, no classes, no grades, because existentialist-humanistic educators believe that true learning is self-motivated. Summerhill and the American free schools that followed were self-governing, democratic communities, where everyone, including the youngest child and the oldest van driver, had a vote in determining school policies and rules. The primary goal of free schools is to create a climate that allows children the freedom and support to make choices and to learn from them (Summerhill School, 2004). Neill and his school inspired many educators to found similar schools in the United States. A few survive today, including the Sudbury Valley School in Framingham, Massachusetts, and the Albany Free School in Albany, New York. Free school ideas found their way into more traditional public school settings, as well. Many elementary schools built in the 1970s were constructed without interior walls. Students met in large and small groups, taught by one or two teachers, or by each other in cooperative teams. In these **open classrooms,** children chose the activities they wanted to do from among several learning centers. They had immediate access to materials, which included actual objects and books, rather than worksheets. Teachers paid more attention to children's feelings and were more willing to share their own experiences with their students. They began to hold classroom meetings to resolve conflicts and created opportunities for individual research projects. High schools added independent study options to their curricula and arranged for apprenticeships and internships. Some high schools had an "open campus," which meant that students could come and go from school during their free periods. Many of these existentialism-inspired initiatives disappeared from view in the 1980s, but you will recognize many others as existing today.

"A Nation at Risk"

As you might imagine, it was only a matter of time before politicians and policy makers hurled a barrage of criticism at the existential-humanistic education of the 1970s. The self-development approach to education was blamed for the poor performance of American children in international comparisons of subject matter tests, for declining SAT scores, for embarrassingly high levels of illiteracy among adults, and for the amount of money that businesses, industry, and the military had to spend on remedial education for workers. The prevailing educational philosophies of the 1970s had jeopardized national security: The Navy reported that one-quarter of its recruits could not read well enough to understand simple safety instructions and, without remedial education, could not hope to complete "the sophisticated training essential in much of the modern military" (National Commission on Excellence in Education, 1983, under "A Nation at Risk"). The dam of criticism broke with the 1983 publication of a report commissioned by the U.S. secretary of education to assess whether the "widespread public perception that something is seriously remiss in our educational system" (National Commission on Excellence in Education, 1983, under "Introduction') was accurate. In *A Nation at Risk,* the National Commission on Excellence in Education concluded that the United States' preeminence in industry and science was being overtaken by other nations who were offering their children an education far superior to our own. Our schools had lost sight of their basic academic purpose and of the disciplined effort needed to attain high expectations.

> If an unfriendly foreign power had attempted to impose on America the mediocre educational performance that exists today, we might well have viewed it as an act of war. As it stands, we have allowed this to happen to ourselves. We have even squandered the gains in student achievement made in the wake of the Sputnik challenge. Moreover, we have

> dismantled essential support systems which helped make those gains possible. We have, in effect, been committing an act of unthinking, unilateral educational disarmament (1983, under "A Nation at Risk").

"History is not kind to idlers," the commission said in its report. In allowing students to choose much of what they would learn and to evaluate their own success, the schools had been abdicating their responsibility and encouraging mediocrity. High school curricula had been "homogenized, diluted, and diffused to the point that they no longer have a central purpose." The "cafeteria style curriculum" offered "appetizers and desserts [that] can easily be mistaken for the main course." Students were reading science fiction and sports writing instead of the literary classics. They were opting out of challenging subject matter: only 31 percent of high school graduates in 1983 had taken algebra; only 6 percent, calculus. One-quarter of students' high school credits were earned in nonacademic areas such as health, physical education, cooking, drivers' education, work experience, and "personal service and development courses such as training for adulthood and marriage" (1983, under "Findings"). Teachers weren't assigning enough homework, and weren't well prepared themselves. The profession was not attracting the best and the brightest, and too many college teacher education programs were of poor quality.

Researchers like David Berliner and Bruce Biddle tried to refute what they considered to be the commission's "manufactured crisis," accusing the commission of using questionable statistical techniques, distorting findings, and suppressing contradictory evidence. Aware of the fact that the federal administration was Republican, and the educational establishment Democratic, they also charged the commission with political scapegoating: "The Manufactured Crisis was not an accidental event. Rather, it . . . was led by identifiable critics whose political goals could be furthered by scapegoating educators" (1995, p. 4).

Despite the protests, *A Nation at Risk* had a significant audience and has made a significant impact on public education since the mid-1980s. Chapter 11 describes its recommendations for changes to the curriculum of U.S. public schools. Along with other high-profile books and reports, such as Ernest Boyer's *High School: A Report on Secondary Education in America,* Mortimer Adler's *Paideia Proposal,* E. D. Hirsch's *Cultural Literacy,* and Allan Bloom's *The Closing of the American Mind,* and with the full support of President Reagan's Secretary of Education William Bennett, the report ushered in two decades of curriculum reform.

In the decades since the publication of *A Nation at Risk,* the initial emphasis on basic skills and deeper subject matter content expanded to include technological literacy. A growing and changing economy influenced by the rapid development of multimedia technologies required a new set of workforce skills. In the mid-1990s, these changes would lead President Bill Clinton to call on states to make technological literacy a standard for middle school graduation. To prepare a new generation to produce goods and services in new ways and to access the information available in cyberspace, Clinton added millions of dollars to the federal budget to help schools connect to the Internet, provide hardware and software for online learning, and train teachers in how to integrate technology into the curriculum (Johnston and West, 1996). The 2001 No Child Left Behind Act affirmed Clinton's goal by mandating that by 2006, every eighth-grade student be proficient in technology literacy skills. The federal initiative to use the public schools to prepare all children with twenty-first-century technology skills has been admirable, though it is incomplete. Funding cutbacks and the redistribution of funds under President George W. Bush have compromised the effort to close the "digital divide" between schools in poor and wealthy communities, described in Chapter 9 (Trotter, 2002).

Back to Basics, Part Two: The Standards Movement

ESEA committed the federal government to support the nation's public schools. At the turn of the twenty-first century, Congress had to vote to reauthorize the thirty-five-year-old act. While the ultimate goal of the act remains the same—federal support of the public schools and a concern for equality—the content of the Congressional debates about reauthorization was quite different. In 1965, the prevailing concern was about inequality. In 2001, the prevailing concern was about quality. The old question was how to meet the needs of underserved, undereducated populations—how to leave no group behind. The new question was how to raise standards for everyone—how to leave no child behind.

A Nation at Risk had recommended that schools offer more substantive academic subject matter, more requirements, higher standards, and tests to measure performance. They should administer standardized achievement tests at each major level of schooling and particularly at graduation from high school. The report also said that those who were preparing to teach should be required to meet high standards and be competent in an academic discipline. President George W. Bush's education secretary and sympathetic congressional leaders drew on the commission's recommendation to fashion a new version of ESEA, the No Child Left Behind Act, which incorporated their recommendations. The 2001 reauthorization requires annual statewide reading and mathematics assessments, public reporting of school performance, sanctions for a school's failing to make "adequate yearly progress," school choice for parents of children in failing schools, and the testing of prospective teachers.

In several chapters of this book we describe the current movement for standards and accountability in education and cite the concerns we and others have as a result. It seems, however, that, given the wide support both of Congress and of the public, the standards movement will be with us for quite a while. The question plaguing many teachers is how to balance the effort to provide a standard, high-quality education to all children with a respect for the cultural, social, and educational diversity that demands variety in school policy and practice. If learning is to be meaningful and effective, we must pay attention to the particular needs of individual children and the present and future conditions of their lives.

Purpose and Promise in American Education

The history of the role of the school in U.S. society has been cyclical. The old lofty ideal that public education would advance democracy and ensure an ethical and just social order too often has bent to accommodate the realities of politics, special interests, and hard times. Our faith in education is evident in the fact that we have built a system of public schools that is arguably the most accessible and comprehensive in the world. Having established that system, we look to education to solve whatever problems arise. "We are convinced that education is the one unfailing remedy for every ill to which man is subject, whether it be vice, crime, war, poverty, riches, injustice, racketeering, political corruption, race hatred, class conflict, or just plain original sin" (Counts, 1932, p. 274).

In Counts's words, we can see the social goals of educators in colonial times, in the common school era of Horace Mann, in the reform efforts of Charlotte Forten, Booker T. Washington, and W. E. B. Du Bois, in the advancing lives of immigrants like Mary Antin, in the words of the progressives and the sixties radicals, and even in the goals of No Child Left Behind. But the notions of education's social purpose that prevail today seem to focus on maintaining America's economic and political standing on the world stage, rather than on improving the world at home. To President Bush and many others, the public schools are neither realizing the promise of Horace Mann's common school nor ensuring our educational dominance in the world. To the extent that public schools are not independent of the structures and policies of other social institutions or the prevailing belief systems of the larger society, we believe it is naïve to assume they can correct social inequities and ills by themselves. But we will leave our readers to decide for themselves the extent to which public schools have succeeded or failed in their social role and purpose. Have we educated all our citizens well? Have we provided them with the information and skills necessary to survive and thrive in the times in which they lived, and to allow them to contribute to the survival and development of the nation? Have our schools responded adequately to social, economic, and political realities and needs? Have they helped lead the United States toward a society that is more just, more peaceful, more productive, and more supportive of its population? Can they?

SUMMARY

- The late nineteenth through early twentieth century was a time of expansion of America's population and territory. Western expansion, immigration, and industrialization called for a significant increase in the number of public schools and teachers.
- Prairie states established district schools for the elementary education of rural children that also served as social centers of the community. The quality of district schools varied depending on community resources and support for education.
- States established normal schools to prepare new teachers. The federal Morrill Act created land-grant colleges to educate an agricultural and technical work force.
- Local schools gave way to consolidated districts under the premise that "bigger is better," a premise that has been questioned by people who believe that small community schools better serve children and families.
- The wave of immigrants to the United States at the turn of the twentieth century severely taxed teachers and schools. Intelligence and aptitude testing became a way to sort and select students for various academic and vocational program tracks.
- Many people saw the role of the school as helping immigrant students assimilate into mainstream American society. Often students were barred from speaking their native language and given Anglicized names. Assimilation and acculturation sometimes resulted in conflict between immigrant schoolchildren and their parents.
- In many cities, reform-minded educators provided evening classes for immigrant parents and social and health services to families, along with a traditional academic curriculum for their children.
- Progressivism was a strong influence on schools in the first three decades of the twentieth century, giving rise to an emphasis on critical thinking about real-world problems, group projects, and interdisciplinary instruction. While some progressives were child-centered, supporting the education of the "whole child," others believed that the purpose of schools was to help create a new and more just social order. Progressivism fell out of favor with the

patriotism that attended World War II and the aftermath of the Cold War.

- The race to space won by the Soviets turned the schools' attention toward math and science. To strengthen basic skills, curriculum planners designed systematic and carefully sequenced programs of instruction.
- The civil rights movement of the 1950s and 1960s enlisted the federal government in the effort to equalize educational opportunities for children of color, including African Americans, Latinos, and Native Americans. The 1954 Supreme Court decision in *Brown v. Board of Education* dismantled de jure segregated schools in Southern states and, later, de facto segregation in the rest of the nation. In many cases, school integration was accompanied by violent protest.
- Congress passed landmark legislation in 1965 entitled the Elementary and Secondary Education Act, which provided compensatory education to children who had been previously underserved. In the 1960s, many children were labeled "culturally deprived," an ethnocentric label that dismissed their cultural and social class backgrounds.
- *Lau v. Nichols* in 1974 mandated that schools offer linguistic-minority children—among them, Chinese students in California and Mexican Americans in the Southwest—assistance in learning English and full participation in the life of their schools. The federal government did not specify the nature of that assistance and bilingual education continues to be controversial.
- Many educators in the 1960s and 1970s saw schools as vehicles for the radical reformation of society and for helping children achieve self-awareness and fulfillment. Some promoted "free schools" or education without institutionalized schooling (deschooling).
- The 1983 report *A Nation at Risk* introduced a return to academic content and basic skills. Nearly twenty years later, the back-to-basics movement culminated in the 2001 No Child Left Behind Act, which holds schools accountable for universal standards and testing.
- Conceptions of the purpose and place of the school in U.S. society have been cyclical, moving between the idea that schools should respond to the contemporary needs of the nation and the idea that they should be leading agents of societal reform. Public schools have been influenced by the structures and belief systems, and the inequities, of the larger society. To realize the promise of public schools, we need to address these influences as they affect school policies and practices and the lives of students.

QUESTIONS FOR REFLECTION

1. www How does Mary Antin's experience compare with what you know about the experiences of immigrant children in today's public schools? (You might consult the full text of Mary Antin's memoir, *The Promised Land,* available on this textbook's website.)
2. Rudolph Flesch and John Holt wrote books that were read not only by educators but by the general public interested in what was going on in the schools. Both books were critical, but written from quite different points of view about how children learn and about the responsibility of schools. Which point of view might you support at this point in your reading?
3. www Given what you know about John Dewey's philosophy, how accurate do you think the reformers of the 1960s and 1970s were in interpreting his ideas? You might read Dewey's *My Pedagogic Creed* (1897, available on this textbook's website and excerpted in Chapter 1) to help you answer the question.
4. The effort to break through the racial barriers of residential and school segregation was traumatic for many cities. One issue was the conflict between federal laws and states' rights. Another educational question was whether a child's right to attend a neighborhood school where he knew everyone was more or less important than his need to meet and learn about people different from himself. Given the historical context, what are your thoughts on these questions?

APPLYING WHAT YOU'VE LEARNED

1. Use the companion website to search the Blackwell Museum of Educational History and links to other sites describing one-room schoolhouses. Choose one of the schoolhouses to research. Find out about the history of the community, who went to the school and who taught there, and what subjects children learned using what materials.
2. Interview an elder in your family or community who experienced public schooling in one of the periods described in this chapter. Among the questions you might ask are: What do you remember about the school building? What do you remember learning? What were your teachers like? What kind of support did you get from home? Do you know what happened to any of your classmates? How did the events of the time affect what went on in school?
3. Compare the courses offered at a local high school in several different decades of the twentieth century. Check the school itself or the community library for help in locating the course lists.
4. Watch a video that depicts the struggles over the racial integration of public schools in the 1960s and early 1970s. (*Eyes on the Prize* is one choice.) Find out the extent to which the public schools are integrated today in one of the communities profiled.
5. How are Title I funds (part of the original Elementary and Secondary Act) used in the schools in your area?

KEY TERMS

WEBSITES TO EXPLORE

http://www.uft.org/?fid=65&tf=147. The United Federation of Teachers website chronicles the crisis at Ocean Hill–Brownsville in an article entitled, "Class Struggles: The UFT Story."

http://www.pbs.org/onlyateacher/timeline.html. The documentary series "Only a Teacher" explores the diverse faces and roles of the American teacher from the 1830s to the present. This site includes a timeline of major events in teaching.

http://wall.aa.uic.edu:62730/artifact/HullHouse.asp. The website for the Jane Addams Hull House museum.

http://www.cis.yale.edu/amstud/inforev/riistitle.html. *How the Other Half Lives: Studies Among the Tenements of New York (1890)* by Jacob Riis. This is a hypertext version of the book, with photographs by the author.

http://www.cedu.niu.edu/blackwell/. Northern Illinois University in DeKalb, Illinois, houses the Blackwell Museum of Educational History, which specializes in the history of one-room schoolhouses in the Midwest. The site offers information, historical photographs, schoolhouse artifacts, and links to other history of education and country schoolhouse sites.

http://www.cr.nps.gov/nr/twhp/wwwlps/lessons/58iron/58iron.htm. A site listed on the National Register of Historic Places, Iron Hill School was established in 1962 by the wealthy DuPont family of Delaware for rural African American children in the northern part of the state. This website offers readings, pictures, lesson plans, and an interesting collection of oral histories contributed by graduates of the school.

http://digital.library.upenn.edu/women/antin/land/land.html. The University of Pennsylvania's "Celebration of Women Writers" website, which contains the full text of Mary Antin's *The Promised Land,* recounting her childhood in Poland and her immigration to America, including her experiences in the Chelsea, Massachusetts, public schools.

http://www.uvm.edu/~dewey/. The John Dewey Project of the University of Vermont publishes articles and monographs on Dewey and progressive education, and materials for teachers who want to apply the principles of progressive education to their teaching practice.

CRITICAL READINGS

"The True Character of the New York Public Schools"

BY ADELE MARIE SHAW

Adele Marie Shaw, a high school English teacher turned journalist, wrote a series of articles based on her observations of New York City public schools during the height of the wave of immigration at the beginning of the twentieth century.

In a Brooklyn school not far from the Bridge I visited a room where sixty-five very small children were packed into a space properly intended for twenty. A bright-faced young woman was steadying a sleeping baby upon his third-of-a-seat while she heard the remaining sixty-four recite. By the end of the hour she had the sleepy one at the blackboard delightedly making a figure.

"He and his brother here are little Cubans," she explained. "They speak no English, but the brother can already imitate anything the rest can do."

I saw the same class a few days later and the two were already melted into the rank and file and were losing the distinctly foreign look. Soon they will begin to be ashamed of their beautiful Spanish names, and will revise its spelling in deference to their friends' linguistic limitations. Esther Oberrhein in the entering class changes to Esther O'Brien in the next grade. Down in Marion Street a dark-eyed son of Naples who came last spring as Giuseppi Vagnotti appeared in September as Mike Jones.

The adaptability of childhood modifies more than the names. Mr. Hewitt, in looking for "types" to photograph, remarked the extraordinary homogeneousness of uppergrade children, Swedish, Norwegian, Italian—all were *American.* With every "type" the primary teacher must deal. With the cruel-fingered boy who "fell from a window a year ago and isn't quite right," to the big girl just landed guiltless of any tongue save her native Yiddish, the same magic must be made to work; the fusing and amalgamating force of interest kept at white heat. It is exhausting labor. . . .

The good primary teacher has the power of making you forget your environment. It was in the cavernous dimness of a very dreary room that I became so absorbed I overstayed my hour. It was here that Garcia, Mendelssohn, and Joshua sat in the same row and made well-proportioned pictures with yellow crayons, and a nasturtium for model. . . . The teacher was a thin, delicate girl who gave her entire mind, and soul, and heart, and strength to her tasks. . . .

On the fifth floor of "No. 20" are the reading-room, library, sewing-room, cooking-room, girls' gymnasium, boys' gymnasium, modeling-room, draughting-room, and carpentry room. . . . If there is any place where a citizen may find hope for the solution of an apparently insoluble problem it is in the new schools of the lower East Side of Manhattan. Let him see the cheerful athletes on the roof playground of No. 1; let him watch the boys and girls fresh from the shower baths of 147; let him see the "little mothers" and the ambitious newsboys in the evening study rooms of the recreation centers; and let him visit that humane product of a real civilization, the ungraded class for the mentally handicapped at school No. 1. Such schools are making self-supporting men of probable paupers, good men and women of probable criminals, and good American citizens of thousands and thousands of children whose parents speak no English, and learn loyalty to government only by seeing what it does for their offspring. . . .

[But] New York children do not have equal chances, physically, in the New York schools. . . . [I]n nearly every classroom that I entered the atmosphere was foul. . . . A room in which forty-six little girls live and work five hours in the day contained only one outside window. The miserably flickering gas over their heads consumed the oxygen needed by starved lungs. . . . In one dim assembly hall I groped my way to a platform on either side of which was drawn a cloth curtain. Behind the curtains two classes went on in simultaneous confusion, and I talked with the principal in a kind of cloth-bound cave, with grammar on one side, arithmetic on the other, and a "bad boy" awaiting discipline down in front. . . .

Nor is there any greater equality in the conditions in which the New York public-school child develops mind and character. . . . In one class, the very way in which the teacher intoned "You—are—not—still" gave me a sensation of quick fright. . . . No child in this school ever "raises his hand" above the level of the shoulder excepting during the arithmetic recitation, when pencils that are not in actual use are held in the clenched fingers of the right hand, the right elbow resting on the desk, the left hand laid flat on the other side. . . . "You dirty little Russian Jew, what are you doing?" seems even more ruinous to a child's spirit and temper.

All servants of the Board are not like this, all buildings are not old, all teachers are not faulty. . . . In old buildings no less than in new are to be found a great corps of gently bred, enlightened teachers spending and being spent in the service of the city. . . .

There are certain injustices in the distribution of salaries. It is an injustice that a woman who is principal of a[n elementary] school of 2,500 children should receive $750 less a year than a man head of a high school department, and $150 less than a woman high school assistant. . . . Everywhere women teachers have to keep order for the men who are getting so many hundreds more for their virile authority!

Source: In *The World's Work, Vol. 7* (2), December, 1903, pp. 4204–4221. In N. Hoffman, *Women's True Profession* (1981). New York: The Feminist Press, pp. 217–232.

A Closer Look at the Issues

1. Shaw presents a complex picture of life in the New York City schools for immigrant children in 1903. How similar is that portrait to schools with great numbers of immigrant children today?
2. From her description, what would you surmise was the approach to teaching academic skills used by teachers in that time and place?
3. Shaw describes School No. 20 as including rooms for activities that offered more than traditional "basic skills." How did this school reflect the influence of the progressivist beliefs about education?
4. What factors and incidents in Shaw's account help explain why only 16 percent of all Americans finished high school in the early 1900s?

Where Ghetto Schools Fail

BY JONATHAN KOZOL

Jonathan Kozol, a prolific author of many books documenting inequities in education and society in the United States, describes in this passage the circumstances of his dismissal from his first teaching position in a Boston elementary school in the 1960s. The incident has become an often-cited example of a school system that shows more concern for rules and procedures than it does for its children or its teachers.

There has been so much recent talk of progress in the areas of curriculum innovation and textbook revision that few people outside the field of teaching understand how bad most of our elementary school materials still are. In isolated suburban school districts children play ingenious Monopoly games revised to impart an immediate and first-person understanding of economic problems in the colonial period. In private schools, kindergarten children begin to learn about numbers with brightly colored sticks known as cuisenaire rods, and second-grade children are introduced to mathematics through the ingenuity of a package of odd-shaped figures known as Attribute Games. But in the majority of schools in Roxbury and Harlem and dozens of other slum districts stretching west across the country, teaching techniques, textbooks, and other teaching aids are hopelessly antique, largely obsolete, and often insulting or psychologically oppressive for many thousands of Negro and other minority schoolchildren.

I once made a check of all books in my fourth-grade classroom. Of the slightly more than six hundred books, almost one quarter had been published prior to the bombing of Hiroshima; 60 percent were either ten years old or older. Of thirty-two different book series standing in rows within the cupboard, only six were published as recently as five years ago, and seven series were twenty to thirty-five years old. . . .

Obsolescence, however, was not the only problem in our textbooks. Direct and indirect forms of discrimination were another. The geography book given to my pupils, first published eighteen years ago and only modestly updated since, traced a cross-country journey in which there was not one mention, hint, or image of a dark-skinned face. The chapter on the South described an idyllic landscape in the heart of Dixie: pastoral home of hardworking white citizens, contented white children, and untroubled white adults. While the history book mentioned Negroes—in its discussion of slavery and the Civil War—the tone of these sections was ambiguous. "Men treasure freedom above all else," the narrative conceded at one point, but it also pointed out that slavery was not an altogether dreadful institution: "Most Southern people treated their slaves kindly," it related, and then quoted a stereotyped plantation owner as saying: "Our slaves have good homes and plenty to eat. When they are sick, we take care of them. . . . " While the author favored emancipation, he found it necessary to grant to arguments on the other side a patriotic legitimacy: "No one can truly say, 'The North was right' or 'The Southern cause was better.' Remember, each side fought for the ideals it believed in. For in Our America all of us have the right to our beliefs."

When my class had progressed to the cotton chapter in our geography book, I decided to alter the scheduled reading. Since I was required to make use of the textbook, and since its use, I believed, was certain to be damaging, I decided to supply the class with extra material in the form of a mimeographed sheet. I did not propose to tell the children any tales about lynchings, beatings, or the Ku Klux Klan. I merely wanted to add to the study of cotton-growing some information about the connection between the discovery of Eli Whitney's cotton gin and the greater growth of slavery.

I had to submit this material to my immediate superior in the school, a lady whom I will call the Reading Teacher. The Reading Teacher was a well-intentioned woman who had spent several years in ghetto classrooms, but who, like many other teachers, had some curiously ambivalent attitudes toward the children she was teaching. I recall the moment after I had handed her that sheet of paper. Looking over the page, she agreed with me immediately that it was accurate. Nobody, she said, was going to quibble with the idea that cotton, the cotton gin, and slavery were all intertwined. But it was the question of the "advisability of any mention of slavery to the children at this time," which, she said, she was presently turning over in her mind. "Would it," she asked me frankly, "truly serve the advantage of the children at this stage to confuse and complicate the study of simple geography with socioeconomic factors?" Why expose the children, she was asking essentially, to unpleasant facts about their heritage? Then, with an expression of the most honest and intense affection for the children in the class, she added: "I don't want these children to have to think back on this year later on and to remember that we were the ones who told them they were Negro." . . .

Not all books used in a school system, merely by the law of averages, are going to be consistently and blatantly poor. A large number of the books we had in Boston were only mildly distorted or else devastatingly bad only in one part. One such book, not used in my school but at the junior high level, was entitled *Our World Today.* Right and wrong, good and bad alternate in this book from sentence to sentence and from page to page:

"The people of the British Isles are, like our own, a mixed people. Their ancestors were the sturdy races of northern Europe, such as Celts, Anglos, Saxons, Danes and Normans, whose energy and abilities still appear in their descendants. With such a splendid inheritance what could be more natural than that the British should explore and settle many parts of the world and in time build up the world's greatest colonial empire?" . . .

Plenty of good books are available, of course, that give an honest picture of the lives of black Americans. The tutorial programs in Boston have been using them, and so have many of the more enlightened private schools. In the public schools of this city, however, it is difficult to make use of books that depart from the prescribed curriculum. When I made a tentative effort to introduce such materials into my classroom, I encountered firm resistance.

Earlier in the year I had brought to school a book of poetry by the Negro author Langston Hughes. I had not used it in the classroom, but it did at least make its way onto a display board in the auditorium as part of an exhibit on important American Negroes, set up to pay lip service to "Negro History Week."

To put a book by a Negro poet on display is one thing. To open the book and attempt to read something from it is quite another. In the last weeks of the spring I discovered the difference when I began to read a few of the poems to the children in my class. It was during a period in which I also was reading them some poems of John Crowe Ransom, Robert Frost, and W. B. Yeats. Hughes, I have come to learn, holds an extraordinary appeal for many children. I knew this from some earlier experiences in other classes, and I remembered, in particular, the reaction of a group of young teenagers in a junior high the first time I ever had brought his work into a public school. On the book's cover, the children could see the picture of the dark-skinned author, and they did not fail to comment. Their comments concentrated on that single, obvious, overriding facts; "Look—that man's colored." The same reaction was evident here, too, among my fourth-grade students: the same gratification and the same very vivid sense of recognition. It seemed a revelation to them that a man could have black skin and be a famous author.

Of all the poems of Langston Hughes that we read, the one the children liked the best was a poem entitled "Ballad of the Landlord." The reason, I think, that this piece of writing had so much meaning for them was not only that it seemed moving in an obvious and immediate human way, but also that it found its emotion in something ordinary. It is a poem which allows both heroism and pathos to poor people, sees strength in awkwardness, and attributes to a poor person standing on the stoop of his slum house every bit as much significance as William Wordsworth saw in daffodils, waterfalls, and clouds. At the request of the children, I mimeographed some copies of that poem, and although nobody in the classroom was asked to do this, several of the children took it home and memorized it on their own. I did not assign it for memory, because I do not think that memorizing a poem has any special value. Some of the children just came in and asked if they could recite it. Before long, almost every child in the room had asked to have a turn.

One day a week later, shortly before lunchtime, I was standing in front of my class playing a record of French children's songs I had brought in. A message-signal on the wall began to buzz. I left the room and hurried to the principal's office. A white man whom I had never seen before was sitting by her desk. This man, bristling and clearly hostile to me, as was the principal, instantly attacked me for having read to my class and distributed at their wish the poem entitled "Ballad of the Landlord." It turned out that he was the father of one of the few white boys in the class. He was also a police officer.

The mimeograph of the poem, in my handwriting, was waved before my eyes. The principal demanded to know what right I had to allow such a poem—not in the official course of study—to be read and memorized by children. I said I had not asked anyone to memorize it, but that I would defend the poem and its use on the basis that it was a good poem. The principal became incensed with my answer and blurted out that she did not consider it a work of art.

The parent was angry as well, it turned out, about a book having to do with the United Nations. I had brought a book to class, one of sixty or more volumes that told about the UN and its Human Rights Commission. The man, I believe, had mistaken "human rights" for "civil rights" and was consequently in a patriotic rage. The principal, in fairness, made the point that she did not think there was anything wrong with the United Nations, although in the report later filed on the matter, she denied this, and said, instead, "I then spoke and said that I felt there was no need for this material in the classroom." The principal's report went on to say that she assured the parent, after I had left the room, that "there was not another teacher in the district who would have used this poem or any material like it. I assured him that his children would be very safe from such incidents."

I returned to my class, as requested, and a little before two o'clock the principal called me back to tell me I was fired. She forbade me to say good-bye to the children in the class or to indicate in any way that I was leaving. She said that I was to close up my records, leave the school, and report to School Department headquarters the next morning.

The next day an official who had charge of my case at the School Department took a much harder line on curriculum innovation than I had ever heard before. No literature, she said, which is not in the course of study could ever be read by a Boston teacher without permission of someone higher up. She said further that no poem by any Negro author could be considered permissible if it involved suffering. I asked her whether there would be many good poems left to read by such a standard. Wouldn't it rule out almost all great Negro literature? Her answer evaded the issue. No poetry that described suffering was felt to be suitable. The only Negro poetry that could be read in the Boston schools, she indicated, must fit a certain kind of standard. The kind of poem she meant, she said by way of example might be a poem that accentuates the positive or "describes nature" or "tells of something hopeful." The same official went on a few minutes later to tell me that any complaint from a parent meant automatic dismissal. "You're out," she said. "You cannot teach in the Boston schools again. If you want to teach, why don't you try a private school someday?"

Other Boston officials backed up these assertions in statements released during the following hectic days. The deputy superintendent, who wielded considerable authority over these matters, pointed out that although Langston Hughes "has written much beautiful poetry, we cannot give directives to the teacher to use literature written in native dialects." She explained: "We are trying to break the speech patterns of these children, trying to get them to speak properly. This poem does not present correct grammatical expression and would just entrench the speech patterns we want to break."

A couple of weeks later, winding up an investigation into the matter, School Committee member Thomas Eisenstadt concluded that school officials had handled things correctly. Explaining in his statement that teachers are dismissed frequently when found lacking in either "training, personality or character," he went on to say that "Mr. Kozol, or anyone else who lacks the personal discipline to abide by rules and regulations, as we all must in our civilized society, is obviously unsuited for the highly responsible profession of teaching."

In thinking back upon my year within the Boston system, I am often reminded of a kind of sad-keyed epilogue that the Reading Teacher used to bring forward sometimes at the end of a discussion: "Things are changing," she used to say with feeling; "I am changing too—but everything cannot happen just like that." Perhaps by the time another generation comes around a certain modest number of these things will have begun to be corrected. But if I were the parent of a Negro child, I know that I would not willingly accept a calendar of improvements scaled so slowly. The anger of the mother whose child's years in elementary school have been squandered may seem inexplicable to a person like the Reading Teacher. To that mother, it is the complacency and hypocrisy of a society that could sustain and foster so many thousands of people like the Reading Teacher that seem extraordinary. The comfortable people who don't know and don't see the ghettos deliberate in their committee rooms. Meanwhile, the children whose lives their decisions are either going to save or ruin are expected to sit quietly, fold their hands patiently, recite their lessons, draw their margins, bite their tongues, swallow their dignities, and smile and wait.

"Where Ghetto Schools Fail," in *The Atlantic Monthly,* October, 1967, Volume 220, No. 4, pp. 107–110. Excerpt from Jonathan Kozol, *Death at an Early Age,* Boston: Houghton Mifflin, 1967.

A Closer Look at the Issues

1. School officials told Kozol that the literature that children should read should "tell of something hopeful" and model standard English. What is your response to these beliefs with regard to teaching fourth-grade children of color?
2. How do school committee member Thomas Eisenstadt's and Jonathan Kozol's conceptions of the social role and responsibility of a teacher differ?
3. Look up a description of the books that Jonathan Kozol has written since his first, *Death at an Early Age,* excerpted here. How might this first public school teaching experience have influenced the direction of his career?

REFERENCES

Altenbaugh, R. J. (2003). *The American people and their education: A social history.* Upper Saddle River, NJ: Merrill Prentice Hall.

Antin, M. (1912). *The promised land.* Boston: Houghton Mifflin. http://digital.library.upenn.edu/women/antin/land/land.html. Accessed August 4, 2002.

Apps, J. W. (1996). *One-room country schools: History and recollections.* Woodruff, WI: Guest Cottage, Inc.

Berliner, D. C., and B. J. Biddle, (1995). *The manufactured crisis: Myths, frauds, and the attack on America's public schools.* Reading, MA: Addison-Wesley.

Bestor, A. E. (1953). *Educational wastelands: The retreat from learning in our public schools.* Urbana, IL: University of Illinois Press.

Bestor, A. E. (1958). We are less educated than 50 years ago. *U.S. News World Report,* November 30.

Breitborde, M. (2003). One-room schools of Illinois in the twentieth century: An oral history. Unpublished research. Available from author.

Coleman, J. (1966). *Equality of educational opportunity.* Washington, DC: U.S. Government Printing Office.

Conant, J. (1959). The American high school. Cambridge, MA: Harvard University Press.

Cooper, Z. (1977). *Black settlers in rural Wisconsin.* Madison, WI: State Historical Society of Wisconsin.

Creel, G. ([1916] 1965). The hopes of the hyphenated. In R. L. Vassar, ed., *The social history of American education: Volume 2: 1860 to the present.* Chicago: Rand McNally, pp. 219–226.

Cubberley, E. P. ([1909] 1965). Changing conceptions of education. In R. L. Vassar, ed., *The social history of American education, Volume 2: 1860 to the present.* Chicago: Rand McNally, pp. 149–156.

Cubberley, E. P. (1912). *The improvement of rural schools.* Boston: Houghton Mifflin Co.

Dewey, J. (1897). My pedagogic creed. *School Journal, 54* (3), pp. 77–80.

Dewey, J. (1899). *The school and society.* Chicago: University of Chicago Press.

Dewey, J. (1909). *Moral principles in education.* Boston: Houghton Mifflin.

Dewey, J. (1916). *Democracy and education.* New York: Macmillan Company.

Dewey, J. (1930). *Individualism old and new.* New York: Minton, Balch & Company.

Donato, R. (1997). *The other struggle for equal schools: Mexican Americans during the civil rights era.* Albany, NY: SUNY Press.

Finfer, L. (2004). Boston and busing, 30 years later. *The Boston Globe,* 265 (175), June 23, p. A15.

Flesch, R. (1955). *Why Johnny can't read.* New York: HarperCollins. Updated, with a new foreword, New York: HarperCollins, 1981.

Fuller, W. E. (1994). *One-room schools of the Middle West.* Lawrence, KS: University Press of Kansas.

Gardner, H. J. (1857). Nativist address to the Massachusetts legislature. In C. L. Glenn, Jr. (1988). *The myth of the common school.* Amherst, MA: University of Massachusetts Press, pp. 65, 71, 72–73.

Gould, W. (1997). Black pioneers tamed rugged Wisconsin Territory, left legacy of achievement. *The Milwaukee Journal Sentinel,* January 13.

Harrington, M. (1962). *The other America: Poverty in the United States.* New York: Macmillan Co.

History of bilingual education (1998). *Rethinking Schools* 12 (3), Spring 1998.

Holt, J. (1964). *How children fail.* New York: Dell Publishing.

Holt, J. (1969). School is bad for children. *Saturday Evening Post,* February 8. http://www.pipeline.com/~rgibson/rouge_forum/newspaper/winter2003/HoltJohn1969.htm. Retrieved June 23, 2004.

Illich, I. (1970). *Deschooling society.* New York: Harper & Row.

Isserman, M. (2001). *The other American: The life of Michael Harrington.* New York: Public Affairs Press.

Johnson, L. B. (1964). Proposal for a nationwide war on the sources of poverty. Special message to Congress. *Public Papers of U.S. Presidents, Lyndon B. Johnson, 1963–1964.* Washington, DC: U.S. Government Printing Office, March 16, pp. 375–380.

Johnson, L. B. (1965). Remarks in Johnson City, Texas, upon signing the Elementary and Secondary Education Bill. *Public Papers of the Presidents of the United States: Lyndon B. Johnson, 1965.* Washington, DC: Government Printing Office, April 11, 1966, pp. 412–414.

Johnston, R. B., and P. West (1996). Clinton details school-technology initiative: Two reports. *Education Week,* February 21.

Kalkavage, P. (1997). The trouble with grammar. *Basic Education,* Vol. 42 (4), December.

Kirkpatrick, W. H. (1932). *Education and the social crisis: A proposed program.* New York: Liveright Publishing Corporation.

Kohl, H. (1967). *36 Children.* New York: New American Library.

Lasch, C. (1968). New York Review of Books, Vol. 10 (9), May 9. http://www.nybooks.com/articles/11702. Retrieved June 22, 2004.

Leslie, M. (2000). The vexing legacy of Lewis Terman. *Stanford Magazine,* July/August. Palo Alto, CA: Stanford Alumni Association.

Lewis, O. (1966). *La vida: A Puerto Rican family in the culture of poverty—San Juan and New York.* New York: Random House.

Lynch, W. O. (1946). A history of Indiana State Teachers College (Indiana State Normal School), 1870–1929. Indianapolis, IN: Bookwalter Co.

Maslow, A. (1954). Motivation and personality. New York: Harper.

Maslow, A. (1962). *Toward a psychology of being.* New York: Van Nostrand.

Metcalf, M., V. Williams, and M. Pustina (1976). *Schools of Iowa County.* Blanchardville, WI: Iowa County Bicentennial Education Committee.

Monteith, J. (1873). *Monteith's first lessons in geography.* New York: A. S. Barnes & Co.

Morrill Act (1862). *Basic readings in U.S. democracy.* http://usinfo.state.gov/usa/infousa/facts/democrac/demo.htm. Accessed June 4, 2004.

National Commission for Excellence in Education (1983). *A nation at risk: The imperative for educational reform.*

Overview of African American settlers (2001). http://www.hillsborowi.com/OVERVIEW.HTM. Accessed June 8, 2004.

Parker, F. W. (1894). *Talks on pedagogics: An outline of the theory of concentration.* New York: A. S. Barnes & Co.

Perkinson, H. (1991). *The imperfect panacea: American faith in education, 1865–1990.* New York: McGraw-Hill.

Podair, J. E. (2001). The Ocean Hill–Brownsville crisis: New York's Antigone. Paper presented at Gotham Center for New York City History, October 6, New York, NY.

Postman, N., and C. Weingartner (1969). What's worth knowing? In R. Gross and B. Gross, eds. (1969). *Radical school reform.* New York: Simon & Schuster.

Postman, N., and C. Weingartner (1969). *Teaching as a subversive activity.* New York: Dell.

Riis, J. (1890). *How the other half lives.* New York: Charles Scribner & Sons.

Rothstein, R. (1998). *The way we were: Myths and realities of America's student achievement.* New York: Century Foundation Press.

Samora, J., and P. V. Simon (1995). *A history of the Mexican-American people.* Notre Dame, IN: University of Notre Dame Press.

Skinner, B. F. (1954). The science of learning and the art of teaching. *Harvard Educational Review, 24* (2), pp. 86–97.

Smith, J. (1994). Ella Flagg Young. In M. S. Seller, ed. *Women educators in the United States 1820–1993: A bio-bibliographical sourcebook.* Westport, Connecticut: Greenwood Press, pp. 553–563.

Spring, J. (1986). *The American school: 1642–1865.* White Plains, NY: Longman.

Spring, J. (2005). *The American school: 1642–2004,* 6th ed. New York: McGraw-Hill.

Summary of major provisions of the National Defense Education Act of 1958 (2004). *Federal support for university research: 40 Years after the National Defense Education Act and the establishment of NASA.* Berkeley, CA: University of California. http://ishi.lib.berkeley.edu/cshe/ndea/ndea.html. Retrieved June 20, 2004.

Summerhill School. Introduction to Summerhill. http://www.summerhillschool.co.uk/pages/index.html. Retrieved June 23, 2004.

Swarns, R. L. (2004). Advocates for immigrants scorn Bush policy on Haitian refugees. *The New York Times,* February 27.

Tanner, L. N. (1997). *Dewey's Laboratory School: Lessons for today.* New York: Teachers College Press.

Terman, L. (1930). Autobiography of Lewis M. Terman. In C. Murchison, ed. *History of psychology in autobiography, Volume II.* Worcester, MA: Clark University Press.

Trotter, A. (2002). Technology programs in and out of Ed. Dept. take big hit in budget. *Education Week,* February 13.

Truman, H. S. (1948). Speech in Provo, Utah. Independence, MO: Truman Presidential Library, September 21. http://www.trumanlibrary.org/index.html. Retrieved June 20, 2004.

Tyack, D. B. (1974). *The one best system: A history of American urban education.* Cambridge, MA: Harvard University Press.

Whitman, W. (1900). *Leaves of grass.* Philadelphia: David McKay Co.

Willoughby, B. (2004). An American legacy. *Teaching Tolerance* 25, Spring, pp. 40–46.

9

The Problem of Equity: Culture, Class, and School

ESSENTIAL QUESTION

What is the role of school in society?

In a televised documentary created by graduates of New York City's public schools, a thirteen-year-old European American boy attending Intermediate School # ___ in the upper middle-class Riverside section of the Bronx tells the cameraman, "Anyone can make it in America, if they only try." His school has well-equipped science labs, a full band program, and an after-school center complete with a gymnasium, homework areas, and a game room. A mile away in the poorer Fordham section of the same city borough, an African-American seventh grader trudges out of the run-down building the last day of the school year, discouraged by the fact that his science teacher had neither the credentials nor the background, nor appropriate materials to teach science. His after-school recreation has been limited to playing video games in a local pizza parlor and pick-up basketball on the corner lot. "How am I supposed to do well in eighth grade science if I didn't learn anything this year?" he complains. His mother, who is with him, throws her hands up in the air. "If we can't move out of this neighborhood," she says, "he's not gonna make it. He's not gonna make it" (Moyers, 1994). ■

The Uneven Educational Playing Field

In their important book, *The Manufactured Crisis* (1995), David Berliner and Bruce J. Biddle launched a counterattack against those who say America's public schools are failing. Using statistical analysis, the authors cited evidence that, for example, the science and math performance of America's most talented students equals or surpasses the performance of similar students in other developed nations. While the average math and science scores of American high school students taking international tests is lower than the average scores of students in those other developed nations, Berliner and Biddle claim the comparison belies the great differences in the population attending school. America can be proud, they say, that since the era of Horace Mann's common schools, the nation has worked to include every child in public school classrooms. No matter where he lives or whatever her race, disability or income, an American child has access to free, convenient schooling. Of importance in international comparisons is the fact that America's school population is vastly diverse in income, culture, socioeconomic background, and way of life. Unlike high schoolers in other developed nations, American teenagers speak many languages, come from many places, present many talents and many learning handicaps, and have parents with widely disparate educations. Our shame, note the researchers, is that the quality of education offered to them is as diverse as their personal characteristics.

If American schools are ever to be places for equalizing opportunity by finding and educating talent wherever it resides, disparities in educational quality must be addressed. The "playing field" which grounds the educational experience of the two middle-school boys in the chapter's introductory anecdote is not level. In countless communities across the country, there are "good schools" at one end of town, and "bad schools" at the other, funded from the same central administrative budget, yet somehow unequal in what they offer children. Across many states, the quality of schools varies greatly from community to community, and across the country, similar differences exist between states. Largely because local communities fund their own schools from their tax bases, schools and school systems vary in the amount of money available for salaries and supplies, and state governments vary in their willingness to make up the difference. "Good schools" compete for well-qualified, credentialed teachers, while "bad schools" often must settle for teachers with little or no teaching experience or professional preparation. In the public schools of Chicago's South Side, many math, science, and special education teachers are "on waivers," meaning that they do not have the credentials or licensure required for their positions. Nearby, in suburban Winnetka, the school board can demand a master's degree of any new teacher.

In wealthy communities, parents are more available as classroom volunteers, political advocates, and fundraisers. Parents who are professionals and who are articulate consumers will work with educators to secure resources and keep the curriculum up to date. Well-educated themselves, they understand their children's homework and have the time to help them with it. In poorer communities, undereducated parents working several low-paying jobs may not have the time or the skills or even the knowledge of how to improve their local school. Their children come home after school to empty houses, perhaps responsible for taking care of younger siblings. They may work afternoons or evenings at part-time jobs to help with family finances. In America today, middle- and upper-class families are concentrated in affluent, largely white communities, leaving poor families—unemployed, perhaps immigrant, perhaps racially isolated—in inner cities. As a result, while suburban school districts are generally educationally and financially successful and wealthy urbanites send their children to expensive private schools, city public schools, and their students, are in trouble. This disparity is documented in a series of books by Jonathan Kozol, who portrays a poignant and disturbing picture of the lives of children in and out of school in New York and New Jersey (1991, 1995, 2001).

> The Number 6 train from Manhattan to the South Bronx makes nine stops in the 18-minute ride between East 59th Street and Brook Avenue. When you enter the train, you are in the seventh richest congressional district in the nation. When you leave, you are in the poorest (Kozol, 1995, p. 3).

At the elementary school that serves the Bronx's Mott Haven neighborhood and is the subject of a study by Kozol, seven of eight hundred children do not qualify for free school lunches, five of the seven obtaining "reduced-price" lunches that are designated not for the destitute, but for the merely "poor." This school ranked at the bottom of the city's elementary schools in reading scores (1995, p. 32). Children go to school next to dangerous hazardous waste dumping grounds and find limited resources inside. In one middle school, Kozol found girls using pieces of TV cable as their jump ropes and only fifteen licensed teachers in a staff of fifty-four. In some schools, classes were held in corridors and bathrooms and city officials acknowledge the presence of lead paint (1995, pp. 155–156). Mott Haven children understand the limitations of their neighborhood and know that there are luckier children elsewhere. " 'Life in Riverdale' " [a middle-class Bronx community] "is opened up," [Jeremiah] says. "Where we live, it's locked down" (1995, p. 32).

As Chapter 8 mentions, the reauthorized Elementary and Secondary Education Act of 2001 (No Child Left Behind) seeks to level the uneven playing field by holding all schools accountable for the education of the children in their care. "For too long, many of our schools did a good job at educating some of our children," admitted Rod Paige, the secretary of education when NCLB was passed (U.S. Department of Education, p. 9). The federal act mandates standardized testing at every grade level, and public reporting of school-level results. Parents of children in schools that do not make "adequate yearly progress" in improving average test scores may transfer their children to more successful schools at public expense. Using the "big stick" of high-stakes tests, the federal Department of Education expects to force poorly performing schools and school districts to improve, with the help of state boards of education and supplementary funding. NCLB assumes that mandatory standardized curricula and regular testing to determine whether schools have successfully taught that curricula to everyone will restore Horace Mann's goal of common schooling for all American children (see Chapter 7 for a full discussion).

However, there is evidence that holding schools accountable through high-stakes testing of students may be furthering the **achievement gap** between the educational success of children of different socioeconomic classes and races. Dan French, an architect of educational reform in Massachusetts, criticized the state tests that have been developed to hold schools accountable for students' academic performance without regard to the differences in the resources the schools have to teach them or the needs of their particular students. In a letter to the editor of *Education Week,* he wrote:

> The real story of the Massachusetts Comprehensive Assessment System—Massachusetts' high stakes test—lies in a deeper analysis by race and class. . . . Hispanic students are four times as likely, and black students are three times as likely, to fail the MCAS as are white students. Low-income students are three times as likely to fail the MCAS as are their more affluent peers. . . . MCAS has resulted in a decrease in the state's graduation rate [and] an increase of middle school and 9th grade dropouts. . . . In each case, the percentages of students are disproportionately black, Hispanic, and low-income. . . . These data demonstrate that the MCAS is widening the achievement gap by race and income. . . ." (2002, p. 39).

The current federal and state approach to leveling the playing field—to hold schools and communities accountable to present the same curriculum to all students and to hold them to the same high expectations for learning—may be simplistic and ultimately detrimental to the aim of equal education. It may not take into account important factors that compromise some children's ability to learn, factors that might lead educators to design policies and teaching strategies more likely to help all students succeed. In this chapter, we review the ways in which race, class, and culture have operated in schools and classrooms to limit children's education. Then we look at promising practices in using those very factors to provide an education that is more appropriate and effective.

Gender, Race, Class, and Education

The bumps in the uneven playing field of U.S. public schools have been encountered by the children of the poor and people of color. For many years, women, too, encountered the bumps, barred from enrolling in strong secondary schools and colleges, discouraged from studying higher mathematics and science, and often ignored in the classroom. There is evidence, however (NCES, 2003), that the climate for girls in schools has greatly improved since the publication of the AAUW Report, *How Schools Shortchange Girls,* (American Association of University Women, 1992 and the reports of researchers like Myra and David Sadker (1995). Gaps in the test scores of girls and boys have almost disappeared. Girls' reading scores are significantly higher than boys, and they outnumber boys in high school honor societies and in college enrollments. While differences in expectations and instruction still exist for girls in some schools, the significance of the problem has declined and may be as much attributable to expectations in the larger society as to what happens in school.

With regard to what schools offer to children and to their academic achievement, race and social class still seem to matter a great deal. There is a persistent gap, for example, in the test scores and in high school completion rates of white and black children, white and Latino children, and affluent and poor children.

Before we discuss this gap and the possible reasons for it, we will define our terms; that is, *race* and *social class.*

Race, Racism, and the Achievement Gap

Race is a term that is difficult to define. Historically, **race** has been used to describe physical differences among groups of people, mostly having to do with skin color or physical features. It has been used to describe social and cultural differences having to do with a group's traditions, foods, or language. It has been confused with religion and countries of origin. At one time, Irish people were described as being of a different race as were Jews, Portuguese, Native Americans, and others whose lives and ways were perceived by dominant social groups as different and, perhaps, "strange."

What Is Race? In the United States, *race* continues to be a problematic term—most often associated with groups that the U.S. Census Bureau describes as "white," "black," "Hispanic," "Asian," or "Native." But even the Census Bureau is refining its categories, recognizing that they are inexact. Does "black" include Haitian Americans? African immigrants? Dark-skinned immigrants from the Dominican Republic? Are light-skinned Dominicans "white"? Does "Hispanic" mean "Spanish-speaking" or "having Spanish ancestors"? If so, Portuguese-speaking Brazilians from South America are not "Hispanic." The general terms "Asian" and "Hispanic" blur important ethnic and cultural distinctions between, for example, Chinese-Americans and Cambodian Americans, or Puerto Ricans and Mexican Americans. Many people belong to more than one of the Census Bureau's groups or identify themselves as belonging to none of them, or "other." Many individuals are bicultural or multicultural. A glance at the beautiful faces of the children on the front cover of this book shows how difficult it is to identify racial background.

Racism While *race* is hard to define, *racism* is not. And it is unfortunately easy to recognize. **Racism** is an attitude that results in an action of actual discrimination against particular groups. The Office of the United Nations High Commissioner for Human Rights defines racism as follows:

> Any distinction, exclusion, restriction or preference based on race, colour, descent, or national or ethnic origin which has the purpose or effect of nullifying or impairing the recognition, enjoyment or exercise, on an equal footing, of human rights and fundamental freedoms; in the political, economic, social, cultural or any other field of public life (2000).

The commission includes in its anti-racism resolutions references to discrimination against blacks, Arabs, Muslims, and Jews. The World Conference on Racism in 2001 also recognized that,

> [r]acism, racial discrimination, xenophobia and related intolerance occur on the grounds of race, colour, descent or national or ethnic origin and victims can suffer multiple or aggravated forms of discrimination based on other related grounds such as sex, language, religion, political or other opinion, social origin, property, birth or other status (United Nations General Assembly, 2001, p. 96).

In North America, the Ojibway Nation incorporated the U.N. statements in its definition of racism as

> any communication, action or course of conduct, whether intentional or unintentional, which denies recognition, benefits, rights of access or otherwise abrogates or derogates from the constitutionally recognized rights and freedoms of any person or community on the basis of their membership or perceived membership in a racial, ethnic or cultural community. The fostering and promoting of uniform standards, common rules and same treatment of people who are not the same constitute racism where the specificity of the individual or community is not taken into consideration. The public dissemination of any communication or statement which insults a racial, ethnic or cultural community or which exposes them to hatred, contempt or ridicule also constitutes racism (Chiefs and Council, 1994).

Racism has affected the educational and civil rights of a succession of groups in the United States. In Chapters 7 and 8 we described the history of these restrictions as they affected the schooling of blacks, Asians, Latinos, Native Americans, and women. In the contemporary post-9/11 United States, Arab and Muslim children have been the victims of harassment, stereotyping, and ostracism in their public schools. In a report to the U.S. Commission on Civil Rights, the Illinois Advisory Committee conveyed testimony from educators and lawyers.

> We have issues of kids who had white friends for years, but they no longer want to be or play with our kids. We had kids in classrooms being invited to birthday parties except Arab or the Muslim children. . . . Girls are being picked on because they wear the *hijab.* Some students have been pulling them off their heads, and then teachers ignore it. There have been Muslim kids being picked on and hit after school, and no one saying anything about it (Illinois Advisory Committee, 2003).

Muslim students are faced with new levels of racism related to the U.S. war on terrorism. Teachers must be sensitized to the potential difficulties facing Muslim children.

Source: © Jeff Greenberg/The Image Works

The Achievement Gap Today, the academic achievement of U.S. schoolchildren is associated with their racial/cultural background, as well as their income level. Black, Latino, and Native American children as whole groups (not as individuals) significantly lag behind their white and Asian counterparts in academic success. The U.S. government's National Center for Education Statistics (NCES) reports that, although the gap between the academic performance of black and white children has narrowed since the 1970s, black children continue to score significantly lower on standardized tests of reading and mathematics achievement at every grade level. Furthermore, the gap between college completion rates of black and white students has increased. Based on their review of test scores, graduation rates, and college attendance in the past twenty years, NCES (2001) concludes the following:

- At every grade level, black children scored lower than white children on mathematics achievement tests. The gap widened as children proceeded through high school. Gaps were similar in size for boys and girls.
- At every grade level, black children scored lower than white children on reading achievement tests. The gap increased as children proceeded through high school, but at a rate lower than the mathematics gap.
- There is an eight-point gap between the percentage of white and black students who finish high school.
- The gap between blacks and whites in college attendance and completion has increased in the past twenty years.

Although there are important differences across individuals and subgroups of students labeled "Latino," the academic success of the group as a whole still lags behind that of Asian, white, and black students. Average test scores for Latinos are lower than for any other group. Fewer Latinos than whites, blacks, or Asians complete high school or attend college. Surveying the high school class of 2000, the Manhattan Institute for Policy Research found that the national graduation rate for Latino students who had begun high school four years earlier was 53 percent, compared to 55 percent for African Americans and 57 percent for Native Americans. Meanwhile, 79 percent of Asian students and 76 percent of white students graduated (Holland, 2003). Latina girls leave school at rates higher than any other group, often because of pregnancy, early marriages, family demands to help out at home, and gender role limitations that place a relatively low priority on education and a career for girls (Vives, 2001). Richard Valencia (1997) has outlined the problems that plague the education of Latino students. Along with relatively low academic achievement and high dropout rates, he includes school segregation, inequitable school funding, policies that exclude language and/or culture from the curriculum, a shortage of Latino teachers and placement in low-level courses, and vocational tracks that do not prepare them for college. In addition, Valencia says that Latino students who need special education may be unrecognized and underserved. High-stakes tests are based on Anglo concepts and experiences, and low scores result in grade retention, removal from sports and other activities, and denial of a high school diploma. Each year, NCES compiles the "Nation's Report Card," which reports to the public how American schoolchildren are progressing in reading and mathematics. Its 2003 report found that, while test scores are improving for all groups, black and Latino children continue to lag behind whites.

Table 9.1 The Mathematics and Reading Gap: White, Black, and Hispanic Students and Gender

Subject	White/Black Gap in Average Test Scores*	White/Hispanic Gap in Average Test Scores*	Gender Gap in Average Test Scores
Grade 4 Math	31%	26%	3% (M)**
Grade 8 Math	39%	32%	3% (M)**
Grade 4 Reading	34%	29%	10% (F)***
Grade 8 Reading	28%	26%	13% (F) ***

*White average score minus black or Hispanic average score.

**Boys outperformed girls, but the gap is not statistically significant.

***Girls outperformed boys.

Source: The Nation's Report Card: 2003 Mathematics and Reading Assessment Results. Washington, DC: U.S. Department of Education, National Center for Education Statistics, http://nces.ed.gov/nationsreportcard/.

Table 9.1 shows the gap between white and black students, white and Latino (Hispanic) students, and between males and females. Under the No Child Left Behind Act (NCLB), schools must report and publicize standardized test scores not only for their entire population but also for black and Latino subgroups. This mandate attests to the government's recognition of the problem of the "gap."

As much as race and culture are associated with academic achievement, there are important differences within racial/cultural groups. Achievement levels for immigrant students from Central and South America are higher than for Mexican Americans, Puerto Ricans, and Dominicans. While Asian students have been called the "model minority," the label is misleading and unfair. Students from China, Japan, and Vietnam on the average achieve a great deal of success in school. Hmong students and Cambodians have lower test scores and are more likely to drop out of school (Lee, 2001). There are factors that distinguish one subgroup from another; for example, the amount of schooling their parents had and the socioeconomic background of their families. Immigrants who arrived during and soon after the Vietnam War tended to be well-educated professionals escaping Communism who made education a priority and encouraged high academic achievement in their children. Cambodian immigrants, on the other hand, were escaping years of repression and rural isolation under the Pol Pot regime, which discouraged academic study and closed schools. The Cubans who emigrated to the United States were professionals who feared that their way of life would disappear under Castro. Even the subgroup of Mexican Americans is heterogeneous. Some Mexican American families are migrant agricultural workers whose children attend several schools in one year; others are university graduates whose children are following in their path. Though race and racism are statistically associated with academic achievement, other factors in children's backgrounds apply, including their families' educational level and whether their income supports their children's schooling or adds additional stress. We discuss these additional factors in the next sections.

Social Class and Achievement

In addition to reporting the test scores of black and Latino students, NCLB also requires that schools report the scores of children who come from low-income families. The federal government recognizes that, besides race or culture, socioeconomic factors affect the achievement of children. Educational sociologists use the term **social class** to distinguish groups of children whose families' social and economic characteristics affect their experiences in school. In *The Communist Manifesto,* written in 1848, Karl Marx and Frederick Engels used social class to describe the amount of power and control a social group had in society, especially the degree to which its members controlled the means of production of goods and services. The working class or "proletariat" were the producers of labor, and the "bourgeoisie" were the controllers (Marx & Engels, [1848] 1998). To the sociologist Max Weber (1958), social classes were part of the economic order of a society. A person's class depended on his or her relative wealth. But to Weber, social class also referred to how much prestige, or status, a group had, the lifestyles of the group, and its political power.

Generally speaking, social class, as used in the United States, refers to a group of people with a shared economic and social status; in the United States, where there is no royal or landed aristocracy, the two are linked. Many of our social and political leaders came from poor families. But in America, wealth and social position are also tied to education and lifestyle. Research indicates that social class is a primary factor in the quantity and quality of the education that a child receives. In an important book entitled *Inequality,* Christopher Jencks (1972) reviewed the factors that were statistically associated with a person's relative wealth and concluded that economic success depended more on family background than it did on educational opportunity. The sons and daughters of the rich became rich, and the sons and daughters of the poor stayed poor. Following a decade-long "War on Poverty" that saw education as the route to social and economic equality (see Chapter 8), Jencks's conclusions were disappointing; they seemed to say that making schools of equal quality would not equalize income. If we wanted economic equality, we should make policies that equalized income.

But others looked further into why schooling did not do more to equalize wealth and reduce the distinctions between social classes. They found that schools were not ignoring social class differences; they were responding to them in ways that simply maintained them. Samuel Bowles and Herbert Gintis (1976), Jean Anyon (1980), and Michael Apple (1995), for example, argue that schools offer selected types of curriculum knowledge to working-class, middle-class, and upper-class children, and that teachers use different instructional approaches. Anyon's work is discussed more fully later in this chapter.

Statistics bear out the importance of social class as a factor in unequal academic achievement. To track the achievement of children from various social classes, the National Center for Education Statistics compares the test scores of children who qualify for a free or reduced-price school lunch and those who do not. To qualify for a free lunch, a child must live in a family whose income is less than $24,000 (for a family of four); to qualify for a reduced-price lunch, the family's income must be below $34,000. This criterion is roughly comparable to the federal definition of "low income." Table 9.2 shows the NCES data on the income gap for mathematics and reading tests taken in 2003.

Table 9.2 The Mathematics and Reading Gap: Income

Subject	Income Gap*
Grade 4 Math	22%
Grade 8 Math	28%
Grade 4 Reading	28%
Grade 8 Reading	24%

*Average score of children not qualifying for free or reduced lunch minus the average score of children who qualified.

Source: The Nation's Report Card: 2003 Mathematics and Reading Assessment Results. Washington, DC: U.S. Department of Education, National Center for Education Statistics, http://nces.ed.gov/nationsreportcard/.

In addition to reading and mathematics gaps, there are gaps in other areas of the curriculum. Given the emphasis on increasing the subject matter knowledge of schoolchildren in the past several years, when the National Assessment of Educational Progress (NAEP) reviewed scores on standardized tests for eighth grade science in 2000, they expected to find signs of improvement. Instead, their comparison of 1996 and 2000 scores showed that, while the average scores for previously high-scoring schools had risen, the scores of previously low-scoring schools had declined. In other words, the gap in science knowledge had in fact increased. And it had increased for schools with significant minority and/or poor populations. NAEP found a significant and continuing gap between the science test scores of poor and nonpoor students (32 percent) and between white students and black and Latino students (37 percent) (Educational Policy Information Center, 2002).

The Interaction of Race, Class, and Achievement

Many factors operate separately and together in the myriad schools and communities in the United States. To understand the extent of the problem of the achievement gap and consider possible solutions to the problem, it is important to analyze and compare these factors. The information available to educators and to the public under No Child Left Behind and from the statisticians at NCES helps us do that. Let's look at two school districts in one state, the achievement of their children, and the characteristics of their communities.

Under the No Child Left Behind Act, all schools and school districts are issued report cards profiling the curriculum, staff, and facilities and the test scores of the children that go there. A look at the Illinois District Report Card for two school districts, available on the Internet, reveals striking differences across districts. In suburban Winnetka, referred to in the first section of this chapter, 98 percent of public schoolchildren are white. Black and Latino students account for less than 1 percent of the total population. One-tenth of one percent of students are low-income. One-third of one percent have limited English-speaking ability. Eighty-nine percent of Winnetka teachers have master's degrees or higher, and all are credentialed and qualified. The district spent $6300 per child in 2003. As measured by statewide achievement tests, 92 percent of Winnetka schoolchildren met or exceeded the

Illinois Learning Standards. In the nearby city of Chicago, 91 percent of the students are children of color. Fifteen percent have limited English. Eighty-five percent are low-income. Forty-one percent of teachers have master's degrees, and 15 percent have either emergency credentials or no qualifications at all. The Chicago Public Schools District spends $5200 per child. Only 38 percent of Chicago public schoolchildren met or exceeded the standards for tests.

Chicago and Winnetka are but two examples of how race and social class interact in particular locations. Fifty years after *Brown v. Board of Education* ruled that segregated schools were inherently unequal, Gary Orfield, director of the Harvard Civil Rights Project, reports that schools are "re-segregated," especially for black and Latino children and especially in our central cities and metropolitan suburbs. Moreover, he says,

> The vast majority of intensely segregated minority schools face conditions of concentrated poverty, which are powerfully related to unequal educational opportunity. Students in segregated minority schools face conditions that students in segregated white schools seldom experience (Orfield and Lee, 2004, p. 3).

As the data in this section show, race and social class are correlated with academic success. They appear both separately and together in statistical reports of reading, math, and science achievement test scores, high school completion rates, and college enrollment. Other factors may intervene; for example, whether a child lives in rural poverty, whether a child lives in a community or a state which provides sufficient funding for schools and education for teachers, whether a child speaks English or is given an adequate education until he or she does, whether a child has a diagnosed special need or is mislabeled as having one, and whether the education he or she receives as an exceptional student is substantive and equal to his or her peers. That race and social class correlate with academic achievement tells us only part of the story of why particular groups of children fare well or poorly in school. Furthermore, the correlation does not tell us how or why; it does not explain the cause of the problem, or what happens in the classroom. The next section describes theories that try to account for the differences in achievement of students of particular social or racial/cultural groups. We believe some of the theories are more helpful, and more valid, than others.

Theories Explaining the Achievement Gap

There are several theories that seek to explain the continuing disparity between the educational success of children of a variety of races, cultures, and social classes. Some claim the difference is rooted in biology. Other theorists believe the causes are cultural, or political. We explore each of these, but let's start with biology.

Biological Explanations

In the 1950s and 1960s, the educational psychologist Arthur Jensen (1969) tested black and Mexican American children on tests designed to measure conceptual intelligence and problem solving and determined that the trait occurred less frequently among blacks than whites, with the Mexican-American children falling somewhere in between. He concluded that 80 percent of intelligence was inborn and essentially unchangeable. He ascribed the differences between the measured intelligence of blacks and whites to differences in biology, rather than to the effects of poverty and discrimination. The 1969 publication of his genetic research results in the *Harvard Educational Review* touched off a controversy and a storm of protest that continues today. Jensen's argument reappeared in *The Bell Curve,* by Richard Herrnstein and Charles Murray (1994).

The Bell Curve In *The Bell Curve,* the authors conclude that there are substantial group differences in intelligence that are not easily remedied by education or experience. Herrnstein and Murray reviewed the research on tests of cognitive ability for people of a variety of cultural groups, including whites, blacks, and East Asians. They pointed out that the gap in measured IQ for whites and blacks of all socioeconomic levels has been a consistent fifteen points for decades—a gap that they, like Jensen, believe originates at least in part in genetic differences.

> In fact IQ is substantially heritable. . . . [T]he genetic component of IQ is unlikely to be smaller than 40 percent or higher than 80 percent. . . . [W]e will adopt a middling estimate of 60 percent heritability, which, by extension, means that IQ is about 40 percent a matter of environment. The balance of the evidence suggests that 60 percent may err on the low side (1994, p. 105).

The Bell Curve's stance is politically unpopular and has earned the authors epithets as racists and elitists. Some of their critics argue that the tests that have yielded consistent gaps are inherently biased. Others wonder whether the all-too-frequent low test scores are in fact the result of the low quality of schooling typically available to children living in poor communities. Many critics of Jensen, Herrnstein, and Murray question the very notion of intelligence that these theorists use to ground their arguments.

The Bell Curve defines "cognitive ability" as demonstrated by a score on an IQ test that measures "generalized" intelligence, or "g." Robert Sternberg (1988, 1997), on the other hand, has defined intelligence as "triarchic," including *analytical intelligence,* probably corresponding most closely to the abilities measured by traditional intelligence tests; *creative intelligence,* involving insight, synthesis, and the ability to react to novel situations in effective ways; and *practical intelligence,* which helps individuals understand and solve real-life problems in the context of everyday life via "street smarts." Sternberg thinks that intelligence is a process of thinking, rather than a static characteristic of individuals. Sternberg wants society to look at what people accomplish, not what they might or might not accomplish as predicted by intelligence tests.

> We have gotten into the somewhat ridiculous situation of even having constructs like "overachiever," which is talked about in education. Most societies wouldn't have that construct. What does it mean? An overachiever is somebody whose IQ is lower than their achievement scores. The idea is that they are achieving too much and that there is something wrong with them, and that they ought to be pushed back to their own size (Sternberg, quoted in Miele, 1995, p. 76).

Arguments Against *The Bell Curve* Contrary to *The Bell Curve*'s reliance on a single measure of a single generalized intelligence, Howard Gardner offers research to support the idea that there are "multiple intelligences." Gardner's analysis of people considered geniuses in several fields led him to the conclusion that there are many types of intelligence, most of which are unrelated to each other. (See Chapter 5 for a full discussion of Gardner's theory.) So far, he has found eight patterns of thinking that meet his criteria for intelligence, which includes evidence from experimental psychological tasks and tests and the ability to solve problems with ease (1983). For example, ace baseball pitchers whose bodies respond with lightning speed to complex conditions have "kinesthetic intelligence." Empathic psychotherapists who quickly grasp others' feelings from their fleeting facial expressions have "interpersonal intelligence." Interior designers who know how a room will look before they move a piece of furniture have "spatial intelligence." Poets who can convey strong images in a few well-chosen words have "linguistic intelligence." The fact is, says Gardner, people vary in their intelligences, which is a very good thing for a society. We need the writers, the musicians, the mathematicians, the artists, the athletes, and those with "people skills." Gardner and Sternberg refute the Jensen-Hernnstein-Murray notion that a single generalized intelligence describes people's talents or is even particularly useful to society.

The Bell Curve assumes that intelligence is inborn and largely unchangeable. In Chapter 5, we reviewed the work of Jean Piaget, Lev Vygotsky, and others who see intelligence, or cognitive ability, as developing over time. To Piaget, the ability of infants to think and understand things is different from that of older children and adults. Cognitive ability begins with a child's natural curiosity and develops with physical maturation. With increasing experiences, we refine our conceptions of the world. Vygotsky (1978) argued that having other people around to experience with us and share our ideas is necessary for the development of an accurate and sophisticated understanding of things.

To John Dewey, the pragmatist/progressive, experience was everything. To be intelligent, he said, means to be intelligent *about* something. There is no such thing as intelligence without an object; intelligence is not static, but applied to some problem or some activity. An intelligent reader understands what she is reading. An intelligent politician understands what people need and how to use power to get it. Human beings are actors; they think *about* things, they act *on* things, they solve the problems in their lives.

We agree with those who see intelligence as multiple, as developmental, and as applied. As educators, we believe that experiences affect the development of children's intelligences. Parents and teachers have important roles to play, in providing children with experiences that lead to greater understanding and encouraging them to exercise their talents and interests. We find the idea that the achievement gap is rooted in innate biological differences neither valid nor useful in helping to solve the problem. Other theories that look to social, cultural, and political factors offer deeper and more ethical explanations.

Cultural Explanations

Children living in poverty, of any race or cultural background, may not have the experiences that prepare them for traditional schoolwork. For example, they might lack experiences with books and museums and with travel to new places. This is especially true for those children whose parents or grandparents have had limited education. We know that broad experiences supported by print materials and verbal explanations expand children's conceptual knowledge. That conceptual knowledge helps children learn to read and to understand what they are reading (Neuman and Dickinson, 2003; Strickland and Shanahan, 2004).

Cultural Differences In the 1960s, the realization that some children came to school underprepared for the tasks they would find there led to the notion of **cultural deprivation** as the explanation for the achievement gap. Many believed that students of non-dominant cultures and children of poverty came to school without the knowledge, behavior, or values necessary to succeed in school. The federal government under President Johnson initiated programs such as Head Start and Title I supplementary instruction to provide compensatory education for children who, in its view, lacked the "cultural" ingredients necessary for academic achievement.

The 1980s and 1990s saw a celebration of individual differences and cultural diversity, with the result that the idea that some children were "culturally deprived" was discarded in favor of the idea that they all came to school with rich cultural backgrounds. Educators explained gaps in the educational achievement of children of various racial/ethnic groups as a matter of **cultural fit,** a match or mismatch between the cultural background of students—their knowledge, language patterns, culture-based learning styles, beliefs and values—and the culture of the school. Believing that schools must recognize and respect these differences and adapt the curriculum and instruction to make it more meaningful, educators tried to change curricula and methods of instruction to take into account the knowledge children already had, the language they spoke (Heath, 1982), and the way they learned (Hale-Benson, 1986). In this way, schools would respect cultural backgrounds and at the same time expose all children to new information. In Honolulu, for example, the Kamehameha Early Education Project (KEEP) used culturally compatible materials and methods of instruction to improve the reading skills of underachieving Native Hawaiian students. Teachers used the "talk story" format, in which listeners contribute to the development of a story in a collaborative way. Students learned in cooperative groups and used native designs to learn mathematical concepts such as symmetry and patterning (Au and Kawakami, 1985). James Banks (1993) advocated drawing on students' background cultures to find universal themes and relating those themes to information from cultures new to them. He urged teachers to address topics from the multiple perspectives of different cultures, using multiple resources to move beyond the Eurocentrism typical of traditional American schools and to include information and ideas from other peoples and other parts of the world.

Voluntary and Involuntary Immigrants The anthropologist John Ogbu (1991) offers an intriguing theory to explain why capable African American adolescent males seem to choose not to succeed in school. His research comparing African American adolescent boys' and African immigrant boys' attitudes toward school and their performance in school suggests to him that the difference lies in the varying expectations that the two groups have for the likelihood of success. He finds this difference rooted in the distinction between those people who have come to the United States, or become part of the United States, not by choice but through slavery, conquest or colonization, and those who have immigrated of their own free will. **Involuntary immigrants,** he says, have internalized the effects of historical discrimination and cultural denigration and do not expect to be accepted into the dominant white society, while **voluntary immigrants** perceive the conditions of their lives as not only far better than the poorer conditions of their homelands, but temporary and changeable.

Ogbu reports that many African American boys create an opposition culture to give them a sense of pride and belonging. Because of the long legacy of systematic racism and discrimination in the United States and their heritage as involuntary immigrants, African Americans, along with Mexican Americans and Native Americans, do not believe that they will be allowed entrance into the American mainstream. Their unwillingness to "act white" by engaging in academic activities, for example, is a kind of adaptive, cultural, response. If African Americans do not trust that they will be allowed to enter the dominant mainstream, they join groups whose behavior, language, and style of dress will define them as different; gangs are one result. In contrast, Ogbu says, voluntary immigrants from Africa and elsewhere—believe that, with hard work, they can learn "American ways" and succeed on those terms.

While Ogbu's theory has explanatory value and may apply to many students, he may have created his own stereotype of the adolescent black male. Pedro Noguera, a professor of education at New York University, a former teacher, and a Caribbean who considers himself a black Hispanic, challenges Ogbu's theory. Although he says that oppositional behavior and the fear of "acting white" is true for some high-achieving minority students, others are able to function in the two worlds of their school and their neighborhood, proud of their academic success and proud of their cultural backgrounds. He uses his son as an example. An excellent student, athlete, and musician throughout his childhood, Joaquin suddenly "took a nosedive" in tenth grade. He failed some courses, got into trouble at school and seemed constantly angry. His parents realized that most of Joaquin's friends, whose families were not as successful or supportive as Joaquin's, were dropping out of school. Moreover, the boy told his parents that on the streets of his city, he needed to appear tough in order to be respected and be safe from taunts and physical threats. He needed to be "cool" and "hang out with the right people."

Noguera realized that his son was constrained by the stereotypes of what young black males are like, and "they were pulling him down." Noguera was reminded of his own adolescence:

> As a high school student, I coped with the isolation that came from being one of the few students of color in my advanced classes by working extra hard to prove that I could do as well as or better than my White peers. However, outside of the classroom I also worked hard to prove to my less studious friends that I was cool, or "down" as we would say. For me this meant playing basketball, hanging out, fighting when necessary, and acting like "one of the guys." I felt forced to adopt a split personality: I behaved one way in class, another way with my friends, and yet another way at home (Noguera, 2003, p. 2).

Fortunately, this period in Joaquin's life passed and he finished school the same way he had begun, as an excellent and involved student with many interests and talents. Noguera's personal experience, however, and the research he has done with other adolescents lead him to question the stereotype of the anti-intellectual black student.

> [T]he vast majority of Black students I meet express a strong desire to do well in school. The younger students don't arrive at school with an anti-intellectual orientation. To the degree that such an orientation develops, it develops in school, and from their seeing these patterns and racial

> hierarchies as permanent. Because a great deal of this behavior plays out in schools, educators can do something about it (p. 3).

Noguera asks teachers to make sure that students of color are not segregating themselves in the classroom and that they are encouraged to enroll in advanced courses and activities that do not fit the stereotype of their group; for example, the debate team or the science club. In so doing, they will help to break down stereotypes and racial norms. He urges teachers to incorporate into their curricula material about the history and culture of their students, to help them develop an identity that includes cultural pride. Finally, he asks teachers to get to know students on a personal basis and urge them "to believe in themselves, to work hard and persist, and to dream, plan for the future, and set goals" (p. 3).

Political Explanations

Cultural explanations of the achievement gap focus on the academic behavior and expectations of students of various groups. Other explanations look at the institution of the American school itself as the source of inequities in achievement. Jean Anyon finds the explanation for persistent differences in achievement among children of varying social classes in the hidden curriculum of schools, which reproduces in new generations the dominance–submission relationships that exist in the American society and economy. In a classic research study (1980), she visited elementary schools in five communities with a range of socioeconomic levels, which she labeled working-class, middle-class, affluent professional, and executive elite. Observing the teaching–learning activities in each school as well as the nature of the verbal interaction between teachers and students, she found disturbing differences. Teachers in working-class schools emphasized rote learning and the importance of following rules and procedures. Children had little opportunity to make choices or participate in decision making, and were provided little in the way of explanation or rationale. Middle-class schools also stressed "finding the right answer," although children were sometimes asked to explain how they got it. In contrast, teachers in "affluent professional" and "executive elite" schools assigned creative and independent activities involving critical thinking, problem solving, and the application of concepts.

Anyon claims that these differences prepare children for their future "place" in society; working-class schools prepare children for blue-collar or subservient work, while higher-class schools prepare children to be economic, social, and political leaders. To the extent that the current demand for rigorous standards affects the curriculum in all schools, these differences may disappear. Anyon's observation, however, that many teachers come from social classes that match their students' may mean that some teachers need to overcome the assumptions about teaching and learning that they learned in their own schooling.

While Anyon believes that schools reproduce the culture which creates them, in the form of a curriculum which can't be seen, Michael Apple, who himself was one of the first to use the phrase "hidden curriculum," has lately refined his thinking. While he continues to believe that schools wittingly or unwittingly convey the unequal power relationships that exist in the larger society through unspoken norms and expectations, he wants us to understand that students don't accept this hidden agenda passively or automatically. Students are active agents of their own lives and futures, who accept school norms more or less or not at all.

> We need more interactive metaphors to talk about this. There is no real hidden curriculum that simply socializes students as if they were passive beings, puppets whose strings are being pulled by the major marionette. Institutions are arenas where there are various struggles, various conflicts, various cultural forums. . . . agreements and compromises, and students are pretty interactive players (Apple, 2000).

Anyon's and Apple's theories explain differences in academic achievement across social groups as issues of political power. How does political power operate in and around classrooms? We will describe three ways: in the resources that schools can provide their students, in the way students are grouped in classrooms and schools, and in the expectations teachers communicate to students about their academic abilities and their future prospects.

Unequal School Resources With respect to resource distribution among schools in a wide range of neighborhoods and communities, among program tracks, and among ability groups, separate is not equal. Students in low-level tracks and in schools in low-income districts with a preponderance of low-level courses tend to have teachers who are inexperienced and less credentialed than students in higher tracks and in more affluent schools with more high-level courses. This may be the result of school policies on assigning new teachers or seniority-based choices given to experienced teachers to request assignments. Adding statistical support to Jonathan Kozol's documentaries of life in New York's public schools reported earlier in this chapter, the federal government's General Accounting Office (GAO) has found that inner-city schools on the whole have higher percentages of first-year teachers, fewer library resources, poorer physical facilities, and larger enrollments than suburban schools (U.S. GAO, 2002).

Local taxes are the primary source of funding for school budgets. In communities with a limited tax base due to low property values or lack of business and industry, less money is available for schools, even though states will often supplement the budgets of low-income districts. While the per-pupil expenditures for city school systems is often higher than that of suburban communities, their financial needs are greater, because of the need for special services. Rural schools in communities with high levels of poverty are also in need of greater support but often pay teachers low salaries and provide limited resources. In more affluent districts, parents can raise money to provide materials and activities beyond the basic budget, such as field trips, artists-in-residence, technological equipment, and after-school programs. These parents are often strong advocates for the hiring of well-qualified teachers and a curriculum that includes an impressive array of courses and activities. In poorer communities, parents' support for their children's education is compromised not only by lack of funds, but also by their own lack of schooling (Howley, Strange, and Bickel, 2002).

The Digital Divide Today, new technologies not only make it easier and faster to send and receive information, but they also allow access to more information from more sources than ever before. We can get news from around the world, find out the best buys on the safest car, learn new skills, and write papers (and books) without moving from our computer. That is, if we have access to one. According to the U.S. Department of Commerce (McConnaughey et al., 1999), 40 percent of American households had a home computer in 1998 and one-fourth had access to the Internet. But families with incomes of less than $75,000 were nine times less likely to have a computer and twenty times less likely to have access to the Internet. Urban families were twice as likely to have access to the Internet as rural families, regardless of their income. Whites were twice as likely to have Internet access from home as African Americans or Latinos. By the year 2000, the majority of white households had a computer, but the number was significantly less for Latino and African American households (see Fig. 9.1) (U.S. Dept. of Commerce, 2000). Only 35 percent of African-American households and 50 percent of Hispanic households had access to the Internet from any location. Even in the very basic technology allowing access to the Internet—the telephone—there were stark differences, with Native Americans in rural areas having the fewest telephones, followed by rural Hispanics and rural blacks. Of the 103 million households in the United States, 6 million of them lacked basic telephone service.

Schools are beginning to make up for the difference in families' access to technology. According to the U.S. Department of Education (National Center for Education Statistics, 2003), by the fall of 2002, 99 percent of U.S. schools had access to the Internet. But there are still differences in the technological resources that schools can provide. The relative poverty of the community surrounding the school may account for the 8 percent without Internet access. While the 2003 federal Department of Education report includes no reference to differences in school characteristics, it reported three years earlier that 38 percent of classrooms in communities where there was a low incidence of poverty had no access to the Internet as opposed to 61 percent of non-poverty classrooms. (National Center for Education Statistics, 2000).

In 2004, at the Ford School in urban Lynn, Massachusetts—a school where 87 percent of the population are students of color and 90 percent qualify for a free or reduced-priced school lunch—middle-school students had no access to the Internet. Twenty miles away, in affluent white Westwood, every room in the high school is equipped with a digital white board and multimedia projector. Across the country, in a Latino neighborhood in Los Angeles, California, Ms. Miller's fifth grade students have no computer software; neither do they have "low-technology" crayons (Breitborde, personal correspondence).

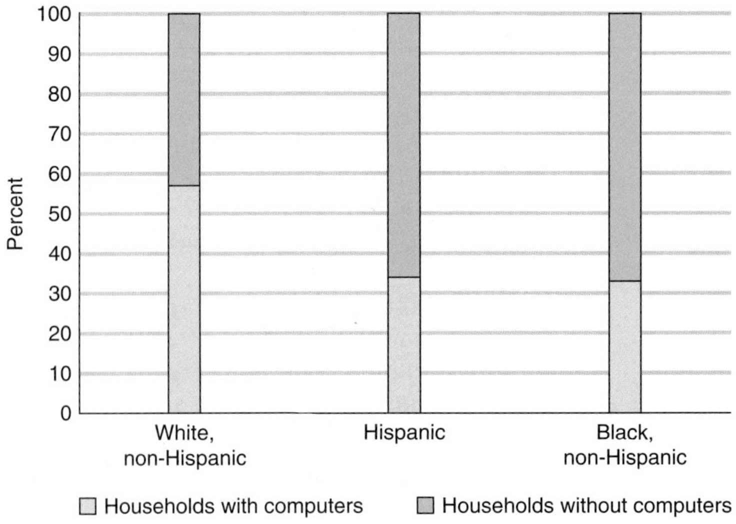

Figure 9.1

Percentage of Households with Computers by the Year 2000

Source: U.S. Department of Commerce, Falling through the net: Toward digital inclusion. October 2000.

The federal government has recently provided the means to wire schools and classrooms, but many schools in communities with limited tax bases or other resources still cannot afford to buy, install, or maintain the needed technology. If a school does have computers, it may not be able to afford to hire teachers and specialists who know how to use them in effective educational ways, or have the money to provide training to the existing staff. While the U.S. Department of Education report on technology in schools claimed that virtually all schools now had computers, Internet access, and professional development for teachers, they included at the end of their report the finding that only one-third of U.S. teachers felt prepared to incorporate use of the Internet in their classrooms. As Andy Carvin said in *Multimedia Schools* (2000), "the digital divide is about pedagogy. Internet access isn't worth a hill of beans if teachers aren't prepared to take full advantage of technology." Carvin notes that the continuing poverty that exists in the larger society is responsible for a continuing digital divide. The quantity and quality of technology available in the schools end up reflecting the differences in the larger society.

There are efforts to close the technological gap across school districts: local businesses, community agencies, and universities are partnering with under-resourced schools to provide equipment and training to teachers and children. Libraries allow free access to computers and organizations such as Boys and Girls Clubs provide after-school computer clubs. The federal government makes funding available to poor and rural school districts that want to wire classrooms. More needs to be done, however, to enable children without immediate home access to computers to use technology to support their present learning and their future careers.

Ability Grouping and Tracking Some researchers find the roots of persistent inequity between children of different races and social classes in the common practice of organizing students by so-called "ability" levels. Organizing elementary students for instruction into **ability groups,** based on their presumed ability to learn subject matter or skills, attaches labels to children that may haunt them for the rest of their lives. Children in the "low reading group" or "low math group" may assume that they will always be "poor readers" or "math phobic." **Tracking** students into groups such as "honors" or "college preparatory" or "vocational" results in patterns of "sorting" and "selecting" that can limit their futures. While teachers and school administrators may assume these placements will provide a curriculum suited to the needs of particular groups of students, the practice appears designed more for efficiency and ease of instruction than for the best interest of the students. Many teachers believe that it is easier to teach students of similar abilities because they can tailor the materials and pace of instruction to a level that is challenging but not overwhelming (Ballantine, 2001). But low-tracked students placed in general mathematics courses rather than algebra, for example, may find themselves locked out of certain science classes and the higher-level math courses required for college admission (Oakes, 1990). In elementary classrooms, children placed in low-level reading groups, with their slower instructional pace and more limited reading material, may never master the vocabulary or critical thinking skills necessary for higher-level academic work.

When viewed in light of race and class, tracking is not just a problem for individuals, but for social groups. Children from families of low socioeconomic class and children of color are more likely to be placed in low-ability groups (Colclough and Beck, 1986), based on the results of tests which may not accurately measure ability (Darling-Hammond, 1994). The number of nonwhite students in low-ability math and science classes is disproportionate to their numbers in the general school population (Ballantine, 2001, p. 81). The number of college preparatory classes available to students in particular schools seems to decline with the socioeconomic status of the school's neighborhood (Jones, Vanfossen, and Ensminger, 1995). The link between race/class and tracking is not new, but is newly troubling:

> Early on . . . low-level academics and vocational training were thought to be more appropriate for immigrant, low-income, and minority youth. . . . But things have changed considerably, and today most educators . . . are deeply troubled by the fact that sorting students into 'high' and 'low' tracks severely limits the educational and occupational futures of low-income, African-American, and Latino students and . . . perpetuates stereotypes of minority students as being less intelligent than white ones (Wheelock, 1992, pp. x–xi).

Children tracked into ability groups and school programs have different social experiences. Students in low- or average-ability groups have peers whose behavior is more disruptive and who are less likely to be interested in academic learning. Their teachers give them less praise than their higher-group counterparts, and fewer opportunities for creative work (Ballantine, 2001, p. 81). Evidence suggests that when students are placed in low-ability groups in early elementary school, they lose academic ground for years, perhaps for the remainder of their schooling (Hallinan, 1990).

The Teacher Expectation Effect Perhaps most importantly, tracking students carries with it differences in the expectations teachers have for students' intellectual understanding—expectations that students may internalize during their years in school. Ollie Taylor, an eleven-year-old African American boy eloquently expresses his feelings about being placed in a low-ability track in middle school:

> The only thing that matters in my life is school, and there they think I'm dumb and always will be. I'm starting to think they're right. . . . Even if I look around and know that I'm the smartest in my group, all that means is that I'm the smartest of the dumbest (quoted in Braddock et al., 1998, p. 127).

Even without formal tracking systems, children can come to believe their teachers' opinions about their academic promise, or lack thereof:

> Betsy hid her first-grade papers in her desk, wadded up and away from the eyes of her mom and her high-achieving older brother and sister. Full of black and red marks, they were clear evidence of her failure to learn. In school, she kept as quiet as she could, this child who at home created carnivals and made up stories and songs and was the social leader of her neighborhood. When her mother came in for a conference, her teacher discovered the hidden papers. She told Betsy's mom that her daughter would never learn to read and that she was a liar, to boot (Swiniarski and Breitborde, 2003, p. 124).

Ollie and Betsy are victims of what educational researchers have called the **teacher expectation effect.** The paradigm begins with the fact that teachers, as all human beings, have varying expectations for children, based sometimes on children's personal and social characteristics that have nothing to do with their actual academic work. A middle-school social studies teacher who has had four children from the same family in past years, all of whose classroom behavior was disruptive, will probably not look forward to the fifth sibling coming through her door come next September. A math teacher who had had positive experiences teaching Asian students may expect that a new student from China will do well in his Algebra I class. A fifth grade teacher who is being transferred from her long-time job in a school in a middle-class area to a downtown, inner-city school may assume that her new class will be much less motivated and much harder to handle. These three teachers might be wrong. The fifth sibling in the problematic family may turn out to be a "dream" student. The Chinese student may have trouble with math. The fifth grade teacher may fall in love with urban teaching. The force of their expectations, however, can significantly affect children's lives.

In the mid-1960s, Robert Rosenthal and Lenore Jacobson found that teacher expectations for differential achievement in students can result in differences in students' actual achievement. In a classic study reported in a book aptly entitled *Pygmalion in the Classroom* (1968), they gave intelligence tests to whole classrooms of elementary students. Without looking at the scores, they randomly selected a small group from each class and told the teacher that these children were her "late bloomers" whose high intelligence would be evident by the year's end. When the researchers returned at the end of the school year and retested the children, they discovered that the randomly-designated late bloomers did in fact score significantly better on the second round of intelligence tests. Rosenthal and Jacobson assumed that during the year, teachers had somehow caused the late bloomers to achieve more. Later researchers followed up on the Pygmalion study with classroom observations, recording vast differences in the expectations teachers had with varying groups of students, the quantity and quality of their interactions, and the impact these differences had on students' own expectations and performance (Brophy, 1983; Good, 1987, Obiakor, 1999).

In one early naturalistic study, Ray Rist (1970) spent time observing a group of children from the time they entered kindergarten through the middle of second grade. Rist found that the kindergarten teacher assigned students to high and low ability based on little more than her knowledge of family income levels, the quality of their speech, how well they were dressed, and, unfortunately, the shade of their skin. While all her students were African American, as was she, her "slow learners" came from poverty, spoke infrequently, and when they spoke it was in the vernacular dialect. They wore clothing inadequate for the weather, and had darker skin than those she considered her "bright" children. She drew these conclusions on the eighth day of their first year in school. Rist documented the ways in which the teacher interacted differently with the ability groups she had contrived; she gave those at the top more attention and privileges, more academic tasks, and more interesting academic tasks, and more support for their work. By the end of the kindergarten year, the higher-level children were beginning to read; the lower group had learned very little. Not surprisingly, they were passed on as slow learners to the first-grade teacher.

Expectations are natural and inevitable. When they remain in our minds, they are innocuous. When teachers act upon their expectations, however, they can seriously hurt children's progress and self-esteem:

Voices of Principle and Promise

Reflections of a Beginning Teacher, *by Nikki Miller, Los Angeles, California*

Last year was my first year of teaching. My school is in the Watts section of Los Angeles, California, a community mainly made up of Latino and African American families. Most are low-income, and parents work many jobs to survive. The school can't provide all the books and materials we need, so I bring in some extra things from home—art supplies and books and games. I struggled to answer my students when they asked me questions like, "Why is our community dirty?" "Why do other schools have better things than we do?" "Why did we run out of pencils?" How could I explain to them that their race and social class have something to do with it?

Despite these harsh realities, I saw our classroom as a community of young leaders who are going to change our society one day. My students' standardized test scores labeled them as below basic and not proficient, but I was blown away by the discussions that took place in our room about politics and literacy. I knew I had to try to bring up their test scores, but how could I also show the world how intelligent and thoughtful they were?

The first weeks of school were amazing. One of my students, who had a reputation as one of the most challenging in the school, came to school the first day excited and motivated. I had sent out cards welcoming my first class to our room and I think that won him over. We started off well. We had morning meetings every day where we focused on giving appreciations to one another and talked about social issues and feelings.

Unfortunately, the honeymoon period ended pretty quickly. Although I was determined to help the challenging student and not buy into the rumors about him, he was indeed hard to deal with. His test scores were low, though he could talk in depth about a story we'd read. His family was going through a lot and he was always getting in trouble in the schoolyard. I tried to get to know him and establish a relationship outside of school. I went to one of his baseball games, and I saw that he was brilliant in the ballpark, a real team player. I couldn't understand why he couldn't be that way in the classroom or out in the school yard. Maybe if the school-

> It seems that we teachers may form unfounded and unjust expectations of children depending on our surface impressions of them. We may use bright, quiet children as models for others, putting pressure on them to continue to be 'good' and perhaps alienating them from their peers. We may 'write off' others, assuming that 'they'll never get it.' We may show quick exasperation to some children, while working patiently with others to help them understand. We may look to one group of children to help us with putting up decorations or taking messages to the office and convey to another group that they have nothing to offer . . . or that they are not trusted (Swiniarski and Breitborde, 2003, p. 131).

When expectations evoke stereotypes and prejudices about children of particular social classes, races, or cultural groups, they contribute to pervasive patterns of discrimination that can affect generations. As America changes its demographic portrait, more and more children enter our schools from places unfamiliar to many teachers, speaking a language unfamiliar to them, and carrying experiences that are beyond their teachers' imagination. For this reason, we call upon you, as future teachers, to lay aside unexamined expectations and learn who your students are and where their talents lie. In the following sections we address the issue of this demographic shift and its implications for educational equity.

yard activities had been more structured, maybe if he had had an organized sport to play, he would have done better. He didn't do very well that year. Maybe the school didn't do its job. Maybe it's my fault for not being able to help him see what a strong leader he was. And our standardized testing just did not show his strengths.

There was also a young Latina student who came to school with a major chip on her shoulder. She had problems getting along with the other girls in the room and would yell at the boys. I just kept working with her on her attitude. I had many one-on-one conversations with her. Other students would help her by reminding her to say things nicely. She even would tell people she wanted to be more positive. By the end of the year, she was not so tough on her classmates. I felt like we all helped her, and she helped herself.

This is what I learned my first year: That you have to really prove you care about your students—prove it to the staff, to the parents and to the students themselves. It makes a difference when you do simple things like send home welcome cards or buy them school supplies. I think it made a huge difference to the children that my family came to visit the classroom a few times. That first year was tough and I sometimes felt burnt out. I woke up every morning at 5:30 a.m. to prepare my classroom for the day and I often went to school on weekends to catch up on my grading. Once, one of my students told me I was racist. That day I just came home and cried. But then there were the days when my students talked about our room being a family and I'd go home feeling great.

It's now a week into my second year of teaching in the school. Many of my old students have come in to visit me this week. I've seen at least 10 of them, some with their parents. Two of the girls even asked if they could volunteer in my room this year! How great is that?

Questions to Consider

1. Does Ms. Miller's experience reflect any of the theories that attempt to explain the achievement gap?
2. What evidence is there in this anecdote to support Ms. Miller's focus on the strengths in her students and their families?
3. After reading the rest of this chapter, consider some steps that this particular school could take to improve the school success of its students.

Immigrant Students in U.S. Schools

As described in Chapter 8, the end of the twentieth century saw a great wave of immigration to the United States. This new wave is part of a dramatic increase in migration worldwide. According to the United Nations High Commissioner on Refugees, more than twenty-two million people sought refuge in new countries in the 1990s (Yingling, 1999). World events have impelled the flight of whole families to asylum nations. From 1980 to 1990, for example, the United States admitted about one million refugees from the former Soviet Union, Iran, China, Central America, Haiti, Somalia, and other nations in political upheaval (Martorella, 1993). A continuing stream of refugees escaping war or political repression and immigrants escaping poor economies or in search of better educational opportunities for their families arrives daily from Mexico, the Caribbean, and tens of nations around the globe. The U.S. Census Bureau reports that seven million people entered the United States during the decade of the 1990s, many of them illegal, all of them seeking a better life in America.

A Changing National Portrait

The United States has always been a nation of complex and changing demographics. It is changing again. The fastest growing populations in this country are Asians and Latinos. The relative percentage of people who identify themselves to the U.S. Census Bureau as "white" is diminishing. Richard Rodriguez is a Mexican American with Spanish and Indian ancestry, who believes that this country has always been brown. A color made up of other colors, brown is the result of the mixing of European settlers, African slaves, Native Americans, and Latinos. In his book, *Brown: The Last Discovery of America* (2002), Rodriguez argues that while new immigrants become Americanized, at the same time they also change the face and culture of America.

> What interests me about the color brown is that it is a color produced by so many colors. It is a fine mess of a color. Initially, I had a sense that most Americans probably regard Hispanics as brown. But my interest was not in the Hispanic part of that observation but in the brown part of it—what is brown? And it seemed to me that the larger questions about America that the color raised is the fact that we are, all of us, in our various colors, our various hues, melting into each other and creating a brown nation (quoted in Hansen, 2002).

The idea that America is "browning" conjures up fears that immigrants drain economic and social resources. Some people believe that immigrants come to America only to take advantage of public welfare, public health, and other social services and, of course, free public education. Refuting the argument that immigrants sap American society, the *Boston Globe* reports that immigrants generally have a strong work ethic impelling them into the work force following a brief period of settlement (Blanton, 2002). Research studying the characteristics of Mexican American and Central American immigrant families shows that a strong work ethic is something that parents instill in their children, a value that can include the desire to work hard in school (Lopez, 2001; Orellana, 2001). Interesting data collected by the National Institutes of Health suggest that immigrants to the United States live longer, have healthier lifestyles, and use less medical care than people born here (Singh and Siahpush, 2001). In California, immigrants represent 31 percent of the labor force; in Massachusetts, they hold 40 to 50 percent of the manufacturing jobs, including high-tech industrial jobs. There is evidence that American business owners encourage immigration in order to fill a portion of skilled and unskilled jobs that would otherwise go unfilled (Blanton, 2002, pp. D1–D2).

A perhaps more troubling reaction to changing American demographics is the xenophobia that characterizes some who appear unprepared to deal with people of new and different backgrounds. In this land of perennial immigration, a negative opinion about newcomers is, unfortunately, not new. The educational historian Elwood Cubberley, writing at the turn of the twentieth century, complained that the new immigrants invading our shores from Ireland, Italy, Russia, and other European nations, were "almost wholly without the Anglo-Saxon conceptions of righteousness, liberty, law, order, public decency, and government" that characterized "true" Americans, and that "their coming has served to dilute tremendously our national stock" (1965, pp. 485–486).

Ironically, some of the children and grandchildren of these European immigrants are among those who bemoan the changing portrait of our people in the twenty-first century. Faced with recent statistics on the school achievement of immigrant children, Cubberley and others who make false assumptions about immigrants might change their minds. According to a study conducted by Stuart Anderson for the National Foundation for American Policy (Anderson, 2004), immigrant schoolchildren are among the highest achievers in math and science. In explaining why 65 percent of the country's top mathematics students and 60 percent of its highest-achieving science students are children of recent immigrants, Anderson cites their parents' emphasis on education as a way for the family to get ahead in their new life in the United States.

The Immigrant Child's Experience in School

Because immigrants and refugees tend to be relatively young, their children fill our schools.

- Twenty percent of the children in the United States are children of immigrants.
- Forty-eight percent of New York public school students live in households headed by immigrants. They speak one hundred languages.
- In California, 1.5 million children have limited English (Suárez-Orozco and Suárez-Orozco, 2001).
- The number of Latino schoolchildren grew 245 percent between 1968 and 1998 (Orfield & Lee, 2001).
- Language-minority students are expected to increase to 40 percent of school-age children by 2030. (Thomas and Collier, 2001)

The change is not limited to urban school systems; all over the United States, in rural and suburban school systems, the number of immigrant students is growing. In the Pacific and Rocky Mountain states and in the southern and southwestern areas of the country, 45 to 48 percent of school populations are children of color, many from immigrant families. Many veteran teachers have found it difficult to respond to the changes that new populations bring; it is essential that readers of this text who are preparing to teach in the next few years understand and welcome the diversity that awaits them in the classroom.

Immigration can be a lonely and confusing experience for children. The Harvard Immigration Project reports that almost half of all immigrant children were separated from parents during their move to America (Suárez-Orozco, Todorova, and Louie, 2001). Many grew up in detention camps in their own or foreign lands. Once here, the stress of finding a home and work and learning a new language affects all members of an immigrant family. The child with limited or no English can spend many months in his new school completely confused about what is going on in and out of the classroom and what is expected of him. A few years ago, one of the authors witnessed a young Cambodian first-grader gamely copying from the chalkboard week after week a list of spelling words whose alphabet, and meaning, were totally foreign. At the end of each week, he received grades of 0 or 10 percent. Every Monday, he would try again to do what was expected. Though sympathetic to his problem, his teacher unfortunately made no special provisions to help him.

Children learning English in school may have to serve as translators for their parents and grandparents, accompanying them to doctors' offices and job placement agencies, negotiating with landlords and bank personnel, and otherwise undertaking responsibilities far beyond their developmental capacities. They may miss school to help out at home. They may come home to empty houses in the afternoon or at night, where they watch younger siblings while their parents work at second or third jobs. Or they are put to work in family businesses, where their English skills and their extra set of hands are essential. Reporting the feelings of immigrant children with adult responsibilities, Alvarez (1995) writes about Seong Yang, who has memorized his family's new phone number and address, anxious that his family will get lost in their new home in New York City, and Elizabeth Tejada, who goes with her mother to factory after factory, embarrassed at having to ask for a job on her behalf. Schisms arise between immigrant children wanting to become American and their families hoping to hold on to at least some of their traditional ways. Sonia Nieto's book of case studies, *Affirming Diversity* (2000), is filled with examples of children whose loyalties are torn and for whom the parent–child relationship is turned on end.

In the lives of immigrant and refugee children, school is central. More than just a place to learn information and skills, school is also the place where they learn the language, the customs, the dress, and the values that will help them fit into their new land. And it is the place where they will learn whether their presence in this new land is welcome. In the case of Mary Antin, a young Russian Jewish immigrant in the early 1900s, whose memories are described in Chapter 8, supportive and sympathetic teachers made her feel optimistic about her future and proud to be a new American. While school is a positive experience for most immigrant children of today, there are some who must overcome the racism or ethnocentrism, or ignorance, of their teachers and classmates.

Too many teachers refuse to learn the correct pronunciation of their names, too many peers jeer at accents, "odd" behavior, or "funny" clothes. Too many administrators dismiss the values and beliefs of these students as annoying interferences with established policies and practices. Administrators may not understand the importance of family and religion in those cultures. Puerto Rican and Dominican children who travel with their families to the islands for a week-long Christmas holiday may be perceived as problematic. Principals who do not know that Hinduism prohibits the eating of beef or Islam the eating of pork may wonder why some children do not participate in the annual school barbecue. Teachers who complain that Cambodian parents do not come to the fall open house probably do not realize that many Asian parents believe that, out of respect, teachers should be left alone to do their work. Immigrant parents who do not attend parent–teacher conferences may be unable to leave their workplaces during the day. Parents who don't speak English are unlikely to carry out the home-reading programs that teachers assign to families.

Conditions of life in the country of origin may affect the educational achievement of immigrant children. Within the same national group, differences in socioeconomic and educational background, even in geography, make adjustment to American schools easier or more difficult. The first group of post-war Vietnamese immigrants, for example, were well-educated urban professional families whose children soared to the top of school honor rolls within a few years of their arrival, while the second wave of poor, unschooled villagers was far less successful academically. Cambodian immigrant children who grew up in Thai refugee camps typically missed years of schooling, which made the transition to American schools problematic. Among Dominican immigrants, children from the cities make faster progress learning English and academic material than do their agrarian counterparts, whose access to schooling on the island was limited.

In order to educate immigrant children effectively, it behooves teachers and school administrators to understand something about the backgrounds of the children in our ethnically diverse classrooms. The conditions under which they have immigrated to the United States will impact how well they fare in their new schools, how quickly they learn, how they feel about being there, and the amount of academic support their families can provide. We will present evidence in the next section of this chapter that educators also need to understand the differences that characterize their cultures in order to teach them effectively. The next section describes some of these cultural differences and how they influence academic learning.

CULTURE AND LEARNING

Arvizu, Snyder, and Espinosa (1980) provide a definition of culture that conveys the breadth and depth of its impact on everything we know, do, and believe. **Culture,** to these authors, is "a dynamic, creative, and continuous process including behaviors, values and substance learned and shared by people that guides them in their struggle for survival and gives meaning to their lives" (p. 5). Consisting of a set of norms of behavior, attitudes, values, and beliefs, culture gives a group of people a sense of identity and belonging, ways of communicating with each other, and clear guidelines for what is appropriate to do or say or think. Cultures arise in particular times and particular places, allowing people to adapt to those times and places in meaningful and effective ways. The ways we satisfy our need to survive, to get along and communicate with and learn from each other, may differ, depending on where we live and when. Even the words we use are tied to our cultures: commercial fishermen, for example, have many words that mean "boat." What looks like a rowboat to many of us may be a dory, a skiff, a punt, a pram, or a dinghy to a fisherman, with each type of boat having its own special function. The spirituals and songs of the Gullah people of the South Carolina sea islands incorporated the rhythms of African drumming that was forbidden by the slave masters. Their words were sometimes encoded messages of escape and freedom. Tropical villagers live much of their social life out of doors or in the nearby homes of extended families, while New Englanders nestle more privately in their insulated houses. Native American traditions convey the idea that human beings are but many small parts within a large physical world, which must be respected and sustained. European Americans often see nature as something to be subdued or used.

Culture guides parents in the raising of children, and children in learning how to behave toward adults. It prescribes standards of beauty and ways to decorate one's body. It defines for us how the world works, why the rain falls or doesn't, why people get sick, why some succeed and others fail, and what happens to us when we die. When we meet people from other cultures, we are often surprised and disconcerted at the difference between their assumptions and ours about what is normal.

The values and norms that characterize particular cultures affect children's experiences of school in many ways. In cultures that value "book learning," families may sacrifice to send children to the best schools. They will expect children to attend school every day, despite what may be happening at home or in the community; they will expect homework to be completed on time and that time be spent studying even when no homework is assigned. Cultures that place a high value on family may take children out of school to help out at home if someone is ill or otherwise in need of assistance. Some cultures traditionally assume that the responsibility for academic success or failure depends on the hard work of the individual. In other cultures, the "locus of control" is assumed to be external, attributable to whether the right services or conditions are provided; in the home or community environment; or in the mystery of fate.

Some researchers associate particular ways of thinking with specific cultures. For example, Janice Hale (1986, 1994) finds that the learning style typical of African American children is "relational." Hale believes that they tend as a group to want to make personal connections to subject matter, are highly sensitive to the nonverbal cues of teachers and other students, and are more intuitive than logical. Even patterns of social interaction embedded in particular cultures may affect learning. Researching the study and activity habits of a group of Asian American high school students, Asakawa and Csikszentmihalyi (2000) concluded that their high academic achievement might be enhanced by the values of their cultures, which included hard work, a focus on future goals, and membership in a community. The Asian students studied together and engaged in social activities that they perceived to be important to their future goals. These activities not only supported their academic achievement but also strengthened their self-esteem and sense of enjoyment.

Because most American schoolteachers continue to be white, Christian, and of European descent (AACTE, 1999), while fewer and fewer American schoolchildren meet that description, the cultural norms, values, and perceptions that teachers have may clash with those of their students. Serious miscommunication can result. Most teachers are unaware of cultural differences that may affect their children's learning and their own teaching. We believe that it is essential for teachers to look at how their own cultural backgrounds affect their assumptions about teaching and learning, and take the time to learn about the cultures of their students. There are many resources that help teachers do that, including books,

The cultural norms, values, and perceptions that teachers have may clash with or complement those of their students.
Source: © Elizabeth Crews

museums, electronic resources, community organizations, and the families of their students. In the next section we address some elements of culture that relate to education. Notions of family and authority and the use of language can directly impact teacher–student relations and children's success in school.

Culture and Family

Because teachers must interact with children's families and depend on them for academic support, they need to know how various cultures define family, and what is expected of their members. Conceptions of family differ significantly across cultures. White Anglo-Saxon Americans consider a family to consist of an intact nuclear group of parents and children, while Italians and Hawaiians would include extended relatives and even neighbors. African Americans include long-time friends, who can be closer than blood relations. The Chinese include past and future relatives—ancestors and descendants—in their list of family members, with husbands' family lines taking precedence over wives' (Hines et al., 1999, p. 70). Educators need to be aware of these differing notions of family as they plan and evaluate programs. In some African American families, for example, a child's grandmother is the primary caretaker and, thus, the parent with whom teachers should regularly confer. We will give you several other examples from our own experience.

Some years ago we visited a school readiness project based in the parks and playgrounds of Honolulu. When the project leaders asked for family members to participate with their preschoolers, they found that great numbers of cousins, uncles and aunts, neighbors, and local elders showed up at the park along with the children's parents and siblings. When one of us invited a group of teenage Colombian dancers to perform in an evening college class on multicultural education, they arrived not only with their traditional clothing and musical instruments, but also with several generations of supporters—grandparents to infant siblings. In the course of a research project that we conducted with a local elementary school, we found that two Cambodian first graders who lived together and called each other "brother" and "sister" had been recorded as siblings. It was later discovered that they had different mothers and fathers and were actually cousins whose families were sharing an apartment.

The strength and longevity of family bonds varies among cultural groups and can affect a child's schooling. In Latino families, loyalty and responsibility to the family is of paramount value, more important than schooling or personal achievement. Men assume financial responsibility not only for their wives and children, but also for elders, younger siblings, nephews and nieces. Adolescents are expected to contribute to the household; boys, by working at least part-time, and girls, by helping with the cooking, cleaning, and child care. Because they are considered adults at home and at their jobs, Latino high school students may chafe against teachers and administrators who, they feel, treat them like irresponsible children. The duration of family bonds also varies with culture. African American families, for example, value loyalty, but parents expect that their children will assert their independence in adolescence, experimenting and taking risks. And according to Hines and her colleagues, "[w]hile Italians and Greeks feel they have failed if their children move away, parents of British descent feel they have failed if their children don't (1999, p. 70). The latter group may encourage children to attend boarding schools, residential summer sessions, and study abroad programs;

Voices of Principle and Promise

Science Education on the Navajo Reservation: A Professor Confronts Culture

by Diana Beck, Science facilitator, Shiprock, New Mexico

For the past few summers, I have been teaching and learning at Atsa Biyaazh, a Bureau of Indian Affairs-funded elementary school on the Navajo Nation Reservation in Shiprock, New Mexico. The Navajo children are bright, curious and eager to learn, and have a great sense of humor. Working with them has been a delight. Knowledge is highly regarded in the Navajo tradition and teachers, as conveyers of that knowledge, are respected.

My colleagues and I hold summer school throughout most of June and July. In the mornings we work with the children in all sorts of science activities—mixing and experimenting with kitchen chemicals, constructing and swirling tornado tubes, studying living creatures in their natural environments, listening to stories, drawing maps of the school yard, and dying cotton t-shirts with native dyes. My goal is to bring culturally appropriate science into the classrooms, so I study Navajo traditions, culture, and taboos in order to help me meet that goal. At Atsa Biyaazh, as in almost all schools, students must be "tested" in order for the school to be accredited, and students are expected to meet state as well as federal "standards" (NCLB). I have those standards in mind as I plan lessons.

In the afternoons I work with the Navajo and Anglo teachers employed by the school. Since many elementary school teachers have a fear of science, I try to help these teachers shed their phobia by engaging them in the same activities that the students do. To insure that culturally appropriate science teaching and learning continue throughout the school year, the teachers design lessons and units that the group critiques.

While I look forward to my summers teaching the children and their teachers, I am also learning from them. I'm interested in investigating how children learn science and how they relate to scientific phenomena. Children make assumptions about scientific phenomena and about what they should do with it based on their own culture, experiences and traditions about what counts as knowledge. What children from one culture might do with any phenomenon will differ from what others might do, but this can happen in surprising ways. An intriguing example of this is the way the Navajo students "experimented" with tornado tubes.

in contrast, there are many examples of college students whose parents expect daily phone calls. The idea of a bright high school graduate's "going away" to college may be difficult for family members in some cultures to accept. Later in this chapter, you will read the account of a Mexican American man whose decision about which college to attend was based on how fast he could get home to his family if they needed him.

Culture and Authority

As discussed in Chapter 2, there are different conceptions of authority at work in social life and in schools. Kenneth Benne has described these as positional, rule-bound or anthropological. Cultures create patterns of authority within families, which are rooted in the political and religious structures of the homeland, in gender relationships, and in the relationship of young people to elders. Although cultures change, especially when their members migrate to a country with other cultures, the patterns of authority change with some difficulty and can cause conflict between generations. Children exposed to new conceptions of authority in school and in the larger American society may take on new ways of interacting with their elders that may cause conflict. It is useful for teachers to know what the tra-

Tornado tubes are 2 liter plastic bottles connected at their mouths with a short length of plastic tubing. The tubes are swirled so a vortex is formed as the water flows from one bottle to the other. Teachers use them in classrooms to demonstrate the altering of variables to achieve some desired end. Years spent in Anglo classrooms, where I had observed students modifying the tubes and racing to see whose tube emptied the fastest, had led me to expect that the Navajo children would also race their tubes. But that did not happen. As I watched the Navajo students spinning and flipping their tubes, I couldn't at first figure out what they were doing. As the children began crying out with delight as their tubes emptied, I realized that they were timing their "starts" so that all of the tubes emptied simultaneously. This meant that each person had to start spinning and flipping at a different time depending on whether s/he had a fast tube or a slow tube. Those with the fastest tubes had to start after the others. Coordinating this demanded that the children pay close attention to all the other members of the group as well as to the tube itself. This was, of course, the opposite of what I had seen in countless Anglo schools. It was not an individual competitive effort, but an organized cooperative way of "doing science."

In my time on the rez it has become clear to me that there is a conflict between much of Navajo culture and the values and practices of Anglo schools and science. As I watch these young Navajo students "doing science," I have to ask myself these questions: For a Navajo to succeed in the Anglo world of science, how much of his/her Navajo-ness needs to dissolve? The usual conceptual schemes of science fit the experiences and understanding of the Anglo world, not the Navajo's. Can we instill the values of Anglo science into Navajo children? Should we? What would be lost and what gained? Would this even be advantageous to them in the long run?

Questions to Consider

1. What do you think Diana Beck has learned from her time on the reservation?
2. What in the culture of Navajos might influence the children to use the tornado tubes in the way that they did? (You may have to do some research to answer this question.)
3. How would you answer Diana Beck's questions in the final paragraph?

ditional cultural patterns of authority are, either because many children may display them in school or because their parents and grandparents may expect them to.

In some cultures—for example, African American, Irish, and Greek—children do not argue with adults. Elders—women, in the case of African Americans; men, in the case of Koreans—are treated with respect for their wisdom and their ability to survive hardships. Caretaker roles are clearly defined, rules are consistent, and authority absolute. In return, children assume full responsibility for the care of aging parents. Adult authority may extend beyond the family to the "village," which might include adult members of the church and the neighborhood. In these cultures, adults do not feel bound to provide reasons for the orders and judgments they deliver to children. Their rationale is typically, "because I said so." On the other hand, in the Jewish culture, where family structures are relatively democratic and where positional authority gives way to the authority of the rules of logic, teachers may find children argumentative and challenging.

Notions of authority embedded within cultures impact life in classrooms. Children who grow up accustomed to clear, nonnegotiable directives and who are taught to respect and obey anyone in a formal position of authority will probably adhere to a teacher's demands more quickly than children who expect to be able to question these demands. While teachers may find the challenges of the second group frustrating, they may also find it difficult to elicit critical questions from the first group. To the extent that schools in low-income and working-class neighborhoods enroll large numbers of children from positional authority cultures, and to the extent that their teachers come from positional authority cultures as well, classroom activities and communication patterns may reinforce the kind of dominant–submissive relationships that Jean Anyon decries (1980, 1997).

Culture and Language

Language is the primary vehicle by which we convey cultural information. Language provides labels for identifying concepts and ideas and a framework for communicating with each other in mutually understandable ways. It identifies us as belonging to specific groups; at school or at work we may use a standard English dialect, while back home we fall comfortably into the language of the "hood." Students of nonwhite cultures who assimilate into mainstream white groups and give up, or never learned, the local dialect, are accused of snobbishness, or "acting white." In Hawaii, for example, the ability to speak pidgin English identifies one Nisei (second-generation Japanese-American) Hawaiian to another as a "local guy" (Kondo, 1996). A teacher need only listen to the special vocabulary and speech patterns of groups of middle- and high-school students to understand the importance of language in maintaining group membership. There are many examples of cultural groups who bemoan the loss of their native language as first-generation Americans work to assimilate into the English-speaking mainstream.

Language patterns in families often evince deep differences in cultural values, expectations for behavior and orientations to authority. As Shirley Brice Heath's research shows us, reported in Chapter 5, black children accustomed to clear commands from their parents might not take seriously the kinds of commands that many white middle-class teachers couch in rhetorical or interrogative forms. Asian immigrant children are accustomed to strict hierarchies of authority and a culture that discourages individual attention. Classrooms in their home countries regularly have forty or fifty students. They will often avoid asking questions of the teacher, fearing that questions might be taken as challenges to his or her authority. The verbal behavior of many Asian students in the classroom is limited and relatively formal. On the other hand, Latino students coming from cultures centered around *la familia* and village life may look for warm and personal interactions with their teachers and their classmates (Abi-Nader, 1993). Teachers of Latino students may be surprised at how much they like to talk with each other.

The language a child comes to school with has a great bearing on how quickly he will learn to read and write and on his academic success, in general. Since language provides labels for concepts, it is directly linked to thought. If we have a word for something, we can conceive of it; therefore, the more specific our language is, the more complex our cognition. The sociolinguist Basil Bernstein studied differences in the language use of working-class and middle-class English boys. When he presented the working-class boys with a series of pictures depicting a group who broke a neighbor's window playing ball, the boys described the pictures using short sentences with many pronouns without clear references: "They're playing football and he kicks it and it goes through there it breaks the window and they're looking at it and he comes out and shouts at them because they've broken it so they run away and then she looks out and she tells them off." The middle-class boys gave more elaborate explanations, using more precise nouns, adjectives, and adverbs, and qualifying clauses; "Three boys are playing football and one boy kicks the ball and it goes through the window. The ball breaks the window and the boys are looking at it and a man comes out and shouts at them because they've broken the window so they run away and then that lady looks out of her window and she tells the boys off" (Bernstein, 1971, p. 203).

Bernstein concluded that the "restricted speech codes" of the working-class boys resulted from life experiences that were largely limited to their immediate neighborhood, their friends and families, and the fact that, when disciplining them, their parents gave them little in the way of explanation. The middle-class boys had a wider variety of experiences with many more people in many more places. In the experiment, the working-class boys assumed that everyone would understand what they were talking about; the middle-class boys did not, leading them to more careful and more precise descriptions.

Bernstein surmised that the "elaborated speech codes" of the middle-class children would afford them an easier time recognizing the words presented in schoolbooks and reading lessons, and the concepts behind them. He urged his readers, however, not to assume that there were no benefits inhering in the restricted speech of the working-class children. Their assumption that everyone understood them implied a sense of security and feeling of belonging that Bernstein thought the middle-class children might well envy. Nor, said Bernstein, did restricted speech mean that working-class children did not have significant knowledge of the nuances of life in their families and neighborhoods. Both groups were knowledgeable; but only one had a knowledge base that would adapt easily to the traditional language patterns of school. Rather than treating working-class speech patterns as culturally deficient, we ought to appreciate a variety of speech patterns as functional in specific contexts.

Research and experience tells us that children are capable of speaking several languages; that is, they can learn the standard English that is used in school and in the wider society, while they preserve their own native tongue or dialect. Lisa Delpit (1995; Delpit and Dowdy, 2002) urges us to work toward this kind of bilingualism as an educational goal. From her premise that language is a medium for the exercise of power in society, she asks teachers to respect the dialect that children bring with them to school—and the culture that the dialect represents—and, at the same time, teach them the language conventions of the larger society that will allow them to succeed there. She wants teachers to assume that African American children, for example, are knowledgeable, competent, and worthy, and to build on their strengths and their experiences.

Delpit decries the well-intended but harmful effects of teaching approaches that ignore the "brilliance" as well as the needs of particular groups of children. Her audience consists mostly of white teachers who rely on research that white people have conducted to justify methods of teaching reading and writing that emphasize language fluency instead of the skills that African American children need. For example, the holistic "process" approach that has been emphasized in recent reading research may be inappropriate for black children. In her own teacher education programs, Delpit questioned the relevance of the research she was learning about. She asked, "Why is it these theories never seem to be talking about me?" (1995, p. 11).

One African American teacher that Delpit met voiced her frustration with white teachers who refused to teach black children the structures and conventions of reading and writing—phonics, grammar, and spelling—believing that direct

Directly from the Source

Silence
by Tu-Uyen Nguyen

Source: Teaching Tolerance, Spring, 2004, p. 34.

When I was a little girl,
I never said,
I want to grow up and be
Silent . . .
What?! Speak up!
I can't hear a word
Of what you're saying
Speak up!
For some,
Speaking comes so easily
Just open their mouths
And words come streaming out
For me,
Voice is like a lonely wanderer
Who rarely ever comes by
You see, to come, my wanderer
Must come through many miles
Miles of silent longing
Miles of silent struggling
Miles of silent tears
Miles of silent years . . .
So you tell me to speak up
Speak up! You say
You, not knowing the miles
I must trod everyday
How do I speak up?
When I don't even know how to speak down
Speak left or speak right
Speak even a sound
I've known only silent travels
All kinds of silent fears
I am so very tired
Of silence all these years
I don't mean the silence
Of dew drops, fragile
In the glistening dawn
Nor of a slowly falling leaf
Cradled as a boat
By gentle waves of wind
For these things speak of what they are
In their graceful natural beauty
No, I mean the silence
Of a child being told
Not to say how she feels
Why do you always talk so much?
Be quiet! Silence!
The silence of asking for a glass
And not getting one
Because the waitress didn't hear you
And telling yourself it's O.K.
Drinking your soda from the can
The silence of being invisible
In the eyes of those
Who only want to see
Their ready-made image of the Other
The silence of having others name you

instruction was limiting and "fascist": "So, I shut them out. I go back to my own little cubby, my classroom, and I try to teach the way I know will work, no matter what those folks say. And when I get black kids, I just try to undo the damage they did" (quoted in Delpit, 1995, p. 31). Delpit explains the teacher's rebellion:

> People of color are, in general, skeptical of research as a determiner of our fates. Academic research has, after all, found us genetically inferior, culturally deprived, and verbally deficient. But beyond that general caveat . . . there is little research data supporting the major tenets of process approaches over other forms of literacy instruction, and virtually

Internalizing the wrong pronunciation
Of what you want your name
To be.
Nujen? Ne gyen?
The silence of feeling trapped
In darkness
Between two worlds
Vietnamese hyphen American
American hyphen Vietnamese
Opposite ends of the alphabet
Outer edges of two cultures
The silence of emptiness
A hollow more vast than nothing
A void within history
Of the voices of women unheard
The silence of Lotus Blossoms
And Dragon Ladies
Of virgins and whores
Of battered women
I mean the silence
Of my own voice
Of the stories that are locked
In unspoken words
Of the pains and triumphs of women warriors
My mother, my grandmother, my great–
grandmother and her mothers
Yes, I mean the silence of
Not Existing
I've known only silent travels
All kinds of silent fears
My mind angry, disgusted
Of silence all these years
So you tell me to speak up
Speak up! You say
You think I haven't tried?
Day after aching day?
Breaking my silence,
Can't you see?
Not like you break an egg
It's not that easy
Takes more than dew drops
And falling leaves
Takes lots of heartache
With no reprieve
Takes many dreams
And remembering too
Takes my whole being
Takes also you
So open your ears
And listen, take heed
You can begin to hear my voices emerge
In chorus, with others no longer silent
Saying, we will be heard, we will be heard!

A Closer Look at the Issues

1. How is Tu-Uyen Nguyen defining *silence*?
2. To what extent was her silence influenced by cultural issues?
3. Ms. Nguyen is currently a doctoral student in community health at the University of California. How do you think her perception of herself changes by the end of the poem?

no evidence that such approaches are more efficacious for children of color. (1995, p. 31).

The problem, Delpit says, is that those who have power in society—white folks, including white teachers—are frequently the least aware of, or least willing to acknowledge, its existence. When white teachers ignore the power differences in society, they may ignore the strengths and the needs of the specific students in their classrooms. . . . Delpit's message—that teachers can prize the cultural backgrounds of all children while they provide them what they need to be powerful in the larger culture—speaks directly to the theme of this chapter: the role of the school in promoting equity and justice.

Latinos, Language, and Schooling

Culture and language are the central issues facing what is the largest subgroup of children in U.S. schools today. While Latinos include a number of groups—Mexican Americans, Caribbean islanders, Cubans, and immigrants from Central and South America—the issue of language has been of central importance to all of them and the subject of controversy in school policy. As Chapter 8 mentioned, the Bilingual Education Act of 1968 and the federal court decisions that followed never specified what kind of language assistance the schools should provide to language-minority students. All school districts implemented programs to teach English.

Language Programs Many states required **bilingual education,** a plan to provide instruction in the subject areas—math, science, and social studies, for example—in students' native language so that they would not fall behind their peers while they were learning English. Bilingual education has been the subject of strong debate. "Transitional" bilingual education programs aimed to support language minority students in both languages for three years, after which they would enter mainstream English classrooms. In a few cases, schools implemented "maintenance" bilingual education programs, which provided continuing instruction in both languages to support their long-term bilinguality and biculturality. Some school districts offer "two-way" Spanish bilingual schools where native English speakers learn Spanish, and native Spanish speakers learn English.

In 1998 Ron Unz, a millionaire software entrepreneur from California, upset by the number of Spanish-speaking immigrants in his own state and believing that the U.S. should officially be declared an English-speaking country, pronounced bilingual education a dismal failure. Too many Spanish-speaking children were never integrated into English-speaking classes and were learning insufficient subject matter. With the support of some Latinos who were upset with the poor quality of their children's bilingual education programs, Unz mounted a successful effort to pass referenda banning bilingual education in California and, later, in Massachusetts. The referenda replaced bilingual education with a one-year **sheltered immersion** program, which offers support to English language learners in regular classrooms. Many educators fear that sheltered immersion will not adequately address the needs of these children, who will simply be "submerged" in classes they can't understand.

Complicating the matter of English language learning is the fact that, in many regions of the country, Latino children are not attending school with native English speakers. While in rural areas and in the Northwest, Latinos are going to school with Anglo children, in the cities and in other areas of the United States, they go to school with children like themselves (Orfield, 2004). In his review of the status of school segregation in the fifty years since the *Brown* decision, Gary Orfield found that:

- In the Northeast, 45 percent of Latino students attend schools that are 90 percent or more minority; in the western states, 38 percent; and in the South, 40 percent.
- In the West, the term "minority" has become invalid: 51 percent of New Mexico schoolchildren are Latino, 45 percent of California children, and 42 percent of the children in Texas schools.

- Only one in four Latino children goes to a suburban school. In schools where 90 percent to 100 percent of the children are poor, 88 percent of the student population is black or Latino (2004).

Earlier in this chapter we discussed the interrelationship of race, class, and poverty in influencing educational achievement. Schools whose student body is almost universally poor are unlikely to offer a high-quality education. They are also less likely to provide children with qualified teachers. In Massachusetts, for example, a state where the great majority of teachers are highly qualified, the number of qualified teachers declines from 94 percent in white-majority schools to 78 percent in schools with large minority populations (Orfield, 2004).

Educational Opportunity for Latino Children To address the problem of disproportionately low academic achievement among Latino students, August and Hakuta (1997) studied schools that appear to serve Latino children well. The following common characteristics were identified in successful schools:

- a supportive climate
- the use of Spanish as well as English
- curricula that included both basic and higher-level concepts and skills
- systematic assessment of student learning
- the involvement of the family in the life of the school

Eugene Garcia (2001) adds that teachers of Latino children must support their ethnic identity and guard against any prejudicial attitudes they or other staff and students might have. Teachers should help students see the connection between academic achievement and future economic success. Garcia also asks schools to address Latino students' social, emotional, and health needs by establishing after-school programs and forging links with social service agencies.

Before the Spanish-American War, Mexicans living in what is now California, New Mexico, Arizona, and Texas were in fact living in a Spanish-speaking country. That arbitrary redrawing of boundaries and the sheer numbers of Mexican Americans who found themselves suddenly living in the United States created a strong and identifiable subculture whose language and traditions are sources of pride and identity. Some who have a sense of their own history even resent being called "immigrants." As more Spanish-speaking people enter the country from Central and South America and from the Caribbean, Spanish has become the second language of the nation's people. One indication is that throughout the nation's schools, Spanish is the first choice of English-speaking high school students who study a second language.

With increasing numbers has come an increase in political power. Latinos have become an influential group whose votes are solicited by presidential candidates. They are being elected and appointed to local, state, and national positions, including those associated with schools. There are more Latino teachers, principals, and superintendents, and Latinos serving on local and state school boards. Interest in the history and culture of Latino peoples is increasing and the arts are flourishing. Spanish-language television and radio, newspapers, magazines, films, and popular music are sources of pride as well as avenues of communication and

Voices of Principle and Promise

"Growing Up Mexican-American"
Xavier Romano, Vice President for Student Development and Dean of Students, Knox College, Galesburg, Illinois

There is no one Latino American experience. The Mexican-American experience is very different from the Puerto Rican or Cuban or Guatemalan experience. Your attitude toward education depends on your family experience, the role of education in the environment. And there are generational differences, which affect how acculturated you are. It also makes a difference whether you live in a Latino neighborhood or in a white-majority community. Mexican Americans no longer perceive themselves as politically or socially disempowered. There's been a demographic shift. Sales of salsa are ahead of ketchup. I once did a project with Carlos Fuentes—he described it this way: in the area from Monterrey, Mexico to San Francisco and then to the east and south to Arizona and New Mexico and parts of Texas, there's a "hyper-culture"—a synthesis of two cultures—American and Mexican. This is also true in Chicago, where there are 1.5 million Latinos from everywhere, from Mexico, Central America, Cuba, South America, Puerto Rico. Chicago is the Latino melting pot.

We now have political significance, economic significance. You can see it in the ads, in the fact that the Latino music awards are now carried on ABC. ABC isn't being nice. There's a market out there. But at the higher levels, our presence is small. In my field, higher education, among tenured faculty, deans, presidents, it's very small and not increasing.

Mexican Americans are always conscious of the fact that we lost a war—the Mexican-American War. After that war, these same individuals lived in the same place but under a new flag. So, tell me, Who's the immigrant?

We live in a global society, where monolingualism is death. To the English-only advocates I say, "Get over it." I have colleagues in Germany where kids graduate with three languages. Everyone learns English, either French or Russian—maybe both—, along with German. All citizens in this country should have a working command of English—it's the vernacular of society. But that's different from having an English-only policy. If kids also speak Mandarin or Khmer or Portuguese, I say, "Wow. More power to them." Kids should be allowed to learn in a language they understand and that is a part of their historic and cultural frame of reference. They should also learn to speak English. But we need to provide the resources.

My parents were from Mexico. Mom came from the city of Nuevo Laredo in the north. Her family name is Sanchez-Sandoval. They were Hispanic, among the first Spanish governors of what would become Taumalipas. Not surprisingly they were colonialists. My dad was born in San Antonio and educated in America, at St. Mary's University in Texas, and in Mexico City at the National University, during the radical 1950s. National University was the place of socialism, where the ideologies of Che Guevara and Fidel Castro were significant in the minds of the students. My father was a "radical artiste." My mother's family was not happy with him. I suppose that they didn't consider him fully Mexican. Also there were Sephardic Jews in his background, generations back in Spain.

They put down roots in San Diego in one of the beach communities where he found a good job as a window designer (he had a degree in interior architecture). There was a growing presence of Mexican-Americans there. But it was difficult for my mom. She just became a citizen two years ago. She was tired of her green card, felt like she'd invested and paid into this country and wanted the benefits. But she had to surrender her Mexican nationality, which was hard.

My family maintained ties to Mexico. We'd go back regularly. I had a bi-national upbringing. Evidently I had a heavy Mexican accent until my teens. In school, I recognized that I was a little different, but didn't know why. Other families came from Germany, England, mine was from Mexico. I went to public schools all the way, which were predominantly white at the time. I was a Mexican-American surf-rat. My hair bleached red from the sun. They called me "carrot-top."

My teachers were white. I found that weird. The curriculum made no mention of my heritage. My parents did a good job of making me aware of my family, our values. It was a shock coming back to my school from Mexico. For example, according to my school textbooks, the history of California started after the Mexican-American War. But I knew much more.

As an athlete, I was recruited by several universities all over the country. I thought it was strange that Boston University admitted me to the College of Basic Studies instead of directly to the College of Liberal Arts. You could transfer to CLA after two years if you did well. When I visited there as a prospective student, I noticed that all the students in the College of Basic Studies seemed to be students of color. I was a good student in high school, and I had strong ACT scores.

But the Latino thing kicked in—I couldn't go too far away. The question became, how fast could I get home if they needed me? My mom's English wasn't very strong and my dad's health wasn't all that good. I might be needed to translate at a time of a family emergency or simply be there for mom and dad. I had to be able to catch the train and get home quickly.

I went to the University of Oregon in Eugene. It was a time of great confusion. There were about 70 of us Latinos in a student body of 16,000, and very few African Americans. Most of us were athletes. I became particularly aware of my background as a Mexican-American. The Sephardic Jew part also surfaced—my father had told me all about that the summer after high school, before college. I got involved in Hillel. I wanted to learn as much about myself as I could. Who were these people I didn't know anything about? In Eugene I dated a Sephardic Jewish girl. But her parents told me that because my mother wasn't Jewish, the relationship wouldn't go anywhere.

I had a foot in multiple cultures, but a home in none. I was Mexican, sort of, but American. I was American, sort of, but Mexican. I was raised Catholic but I had Jews in my background. But because my mother wasn't Jewish, it didn't carry the appropriate weight. Once I came home and told my parents, "I'm Chicano." They were appalled. "You are not a "Chicano," they said. If you want to insult Mexicans, call them Chicanos. My parents saw themselves as Mexicans. They saw Chicanos as young people out of touch with their heritage, lost, looking for a new affinity.

I define myself as Latino, Mexican, but not Chicano. Chicanismo has its own literature, its own politics. It refers to a social and political movement. I've learned to value that movement, but it hasn't played a role in my frame of reference. My frame of reference is Latin America: its art and its history, including the Cuban revolution. My father ran in the same social circles as Diego Riviera and Frida Kahlo, the avant-garde Mexican university set of people who were, I understand, quite "electric" and engaged, socially and politically.

I understand why so many Latino students drop out of college here. They wonder, Where are the Latino faculty? Administrators? Where are the people who look and sound like me? It's lonely sometimes.

There are several reasons why Latino kids don't go to colleges like Knox. It's an enormous financial investment. They don't understand the value of the liberal arts, that it's about learning and thinking. Also, they won't go more than 50 miles from home, because of family ties. They assume a level of financial responsibility for themselves and their families, so they will start at a community college but then not finish, or not transfer to a four-year institution because they need to get out there and get a job. They're young and they marry young. They want to stay close by their girlfriends or boyfriends. Maybe somebody gets pregnant and so they need a job, an income.

A lot of Latino kids have a desire for the immediate reward—the clothes, the car—they want it now. But if you ask them about their futures, there's no dream. They don't understand where an education can lead them, who they are in the scheme of the world. They don't understand that knowledge is power—not a machete or a gun, but a different kind of power.

Once when I was working at Holy Names College in Oakland, California, I spent some time with some gang members down on 12th Street. They wanted to know why I had 'sold out.' Why I wore bow ties and oxford shirts, why I worked at the college up on the hill. They had no knowledge that the oldest university in the Western Hemisphere is National University in Mexico City. 'I'm actually being true to my history,' I told them. One of them, who had taught himself all about computers, ended up going to the community college in Oakland.

Recently, I went over to the junior high school in my community, which has a growing population of Mexicans. The kids didn't believe that I worked at Knox, never mind that I was a Vice President and Dean. We have to de-mystify what we do in the Academy. We have to be willing to mentor, role-model, leave our offices and hang in the community, so they can start to see themselves in us. We need to convince them that a bachelor's degree is a ticket that lets you get on board and find opportunities. But the messengers are critical—they have to be people who look and sound like they do. Whites can carry the message, but it will only be heard so far. At the end of the day, they will never believe that you know what it is like to walk in their shoes.

Questions to Consider

1. Why do you think Xavier Romano's family was so upset when he called himself "Chicano"?
2. What do you think of Dean Romano's reaction to the gang members accusing him of "selling out" in light of what you read about Pedro Noguera's account of his son's identity problems in adolescence (see the section Voluntary and Involuntary Immigrants)?
3. What do you think were the factors in Dean Romano's life that might have led to his academic and professional success?

expression. These not only serve the Latino population but also broadcast the culture to the rest of the public. All this can only help to make Latino children feel that they are important members of American society. Whether they will become equal members rests to a great extent on improving their education. You can witness the power of cultural pride and educational opportunity in shaping the success of a Latino child by reading Xavier Romano's account of growing up Mexican American.

Practical and Cultural Conditions for Family Involvement

Among contemporary educators it is a generally accepted belief that parental involvement is necessary for children's academic success. Many teachers complain about parents who don't show up for school open houses or conferences. Projects that children are supposed to complete at home do not get finished, notes don't come back signed, phone messages to parents go unreturned. These teachers notice that it is the parents of poor children and nonwhite children who don't volunteer in the classroom, who miss school events and rarely attend parent–teacher social functions. It's no wonder that these children aren't doing well, they say; their parents must not care.

In most cultures in the world, school is assumed to be the business of teachers, and so parents who contact the school are interfering with the teachers' work. The United States is in the minority in presuming that parents are and must be available at school. Yet there are also practical and cultural factors that discourage many families from active involvement in traditional ways. Many parents, for example, cannot secure time away from their two or three jobs to attend school conferences during the day. A third shift or lack of child care may bar some from attending evening programs, as well. Parents whose own schooling was minimal or unsuccessful or conflictual may feel intimidated at the prospect of being in a school and meeting with teachers. Many parents think that being asked to come to school is an indication that they or their children have done something wrong. If they have no idea that they might be asked to contribute to the solution of the problem, rather than be blamed for it, they may decide to stay away. Unfortunately, since teachers rarely ask families to come to talk about how well their children are doing, this last assumption is probably true.

In some cultures, women do not venture out in the evening without men. Parents whose English is limited may be uncomfortable talking with the teacher or principal. When they do attend conferences and meetings, they may not understand what the teacher is saying about their children, especially if that teacher is using education jargon. Language limitations and cultural beliefs may get in the way of parents' understanding or acceptance of special services that the school may want them to approve for their children. Some of the activities in the school may conflict with parents' traditional cultural norms and values, which may make them feel as though the school and family are rivals, rather than partners. Research into the effect of culture on special education services shows that cultural differences can impact whether parents will accept the existence of disability or understand it as something other than a failure on their part or as shameful "craziness" in their child (Lamorey, 2002).

Families who cannot or do not come to school for scheduled conferences, meetings, and social events, may well support their children's schooling in other ways. There is much evidence, for example, that parents in many cultures reinforce behavior and values associated with school success in the rules they establish at home and the expectations they convey (Lopez, 2001; Orellana, 2001). The assumption that parents demonstrate their involvement only by coming to school is false. Therefore, we believe that educators need to broaden the goal of parent involvement to include the involvement of families and communities, and reframe the definition of what constitutes family involvement. They should suspend the idea that a parent demonstrates caring only by showing up at school. In this regard, we agree with the editors of *Rethinking Schools,* who wrote:

> There is nothing inherently progressive about parental involvement. It was parents, for example, who threw stones at buses carrying African-American children in the mid-1970s in Boston as those children tried to exercise their right to attend integrated schools. It is parents who . . . shout the most un-Christian epithets as they try to prevent sex education, tolerance for gays and lesbians, and measures to counter the AIDS/HIV epidemic among adolescents in many urban areas. It is parents who . . . are quick to try to ban books such as *Catcher in the Rye, Of Mice and Men,* and *The Bridge to Terabithia* (1995, p. 236).

Eschewing traditional classroom volunteering and "pizza sales," the editors of *Rethinking Schools* want parent involvement to increase in the substantive areas of school governance and decision making, ensuring educational equity, improving the curriculum, and providing home educational support (p. 237). Joyce Epstein, a researcher in the area of family involvement, suggests that schools consider six ways in which they can engage families:

- as informed and supportive parents
- as sources of information and routes for communication
- as volunteers
- as supports for at-home learning
- as decision makers
- as partners in community collaboration (Epstein, 1995).

Schools should take all these roles seriously, working with parents to ensure that homework help, for example, means encouraging, listening, guiding, monitoring, and praising their children's schoolwork, not doing the work with or for them (cited in Allen, 2000, p. 8). Many efforts at whole-school educational reform enroll parents as members of school councils and educational teams (see, for example, Comer et al., 1996).

Schools need to consider the practical life conditions and cultural backgrounds of the families of the children enrolled and modify as necessary. They may well need to reach out and invite families in personal and direct ways to school for social celebrations and academic events. They might offer a more flexible schedule for conferences, and invite whoever in the family has an interest in or responsibility for the child. They might provide evening child care for families who cannot come to school during the day or leave young children at night. Translators should be readily available to facilitate communication with limited-English-speaking families. Newsletters and other school materials should go home in the language(s) dominant among the children's families, along with English. Teachers, special educators, and other staff should communicate to families that their culture is valued and respected and that the school can offer additional interpretations and resources for their children. Finally, using Epstein's model, family involvement should include those charged with responsibility for children's lives and should engage them in authentic, varied roles of support.

Achieving Equity

As part of the latest drive to reform education, policymakers are mounting efforts to close the gap between what is offered to and expected of children of a variety of races, cultures, and social classes. Unfortunately, the federal government's idea of solving the problem seems to be to hold schools accountable for closing the gap without providing the means for them to do it. Instead, the motivation is negative; schools that do not succeed in equalizing the education of the groups of children they are responsible for will simply be closed. As students move from a school that has failed to a new school across town, their success is not assured. Without the information and resources the new school needs to educate all students effectively, it may well be that that school, too, fails. In this chapter, we have attempted to describe many of the factors that put the bumps in the uneven playing field of American schools. Those bumps are being addressed by many schools across the nation where teachers and administrators have served black, Latino, Asian, and white children equally well. Educators like Deborah Meier, founding principal of Harlem's Central Park East Elementary and Secondary Schools and now principal of the Mission Hill School in Boston, Massachusetts, have worked with dedicated teachers to provide an equitable and exciting public education for students of color.

A Model of Equity: Mission Hill School

Mission Hill School is a public K–8 experimental pilot school that is part of the Boston Public School System and is committed to the principles of equitable education, democratic governance, small-school community, critical thinking, and authentic assessment. Of the 170 students, 58 percent are black, 22 percent white, 15 percent Latino, and 4 percent Asian. All decisions—from scheduling to the curriculum to school rules—are made by teachers and administrators together. The Parent Council, composed of "every parent, guardian and family member with a child in the school," meets monthly, with dinner and child care provided, to share information, coordinate volunteer opportunities and school events, and orient new parents.

The school's mission, which you can find on its website, included in "Websites to Explore" at the end of this chapter, is to "help parents raise youngsters who will maintain and nurture the best habits of a democratic society, be smart, caring, strong, resilient, imaginative and thoughtful." Mission Hill wants their students to be able to "defend intelligently that which we believe to be true and that which we believe best meets our individual needs and those of our family, community and the broader public" and to be well informed and "read well, write and speak effectively and persuasively, and handle numbers and calculations with competence and confidence." It wants children to be able to produce, perform, and invent their own art, because "without art we are all deprived." The school is committed to the principle of authentic assessment, which means that students must demonstrate what they know in real-world applications. To graduate from Mission Hill, students must show that they are ready for high school by preparing exhibits that showcase their knowledge through a portfolio of their experiences and a self-evaluation.

The size of the school is deliberately small, reflecting its membership in the Coalition of Essential Schools, part of the "small schools movement" that emphasizes personal relationships and a sense of community. Classrooms are wired to the Internet and have computers. The school uses outside resources to supplement its own offerings and to keep teachers and children connected to the community. For example, there are programs offered by the local branch of the Boston Public Library, and the Y.M.C.A. runs daily after-school programs, offers a full range of sports activities, and requires that students do community service. Middle-school students complete internships in the city.

The curriculum is structured around "essential questions" and organized into thematic topics that the whole school addresses in four-year cycles. The emphasis on critical thinking leads teachers to engage children in exploring primary documents and comparing and evaluating multiple resources for information, including local museums, libraries, and art galleries. Basic skills are incorporated into the curriculum themes. Mission Hill students are held accountable for the work habits that are part of what the school considers essential "habits of mind"; for example, they must meet deadlines, be on time, stay with a task until it's complete, and listen respectfully to the ideas of others. The curriculum reflects the respect that the school staff has for the community and cultures of the neighborhood. For example, in one schoolwide unit in American studies, students explored the struggles for freedom, economic justice, political justice, and equality from the point of view of African Americans and other people within the United States, from the perspectives of economics, government, art, literature, history, math, and science. Students studied particular topics that appealed to their interests and age levels. Mission Hill exemplifies an equitable school; it offers all students access to a curriculum that is multicultural and linked to issues in their own lives and in the world beyond, it holds high expectations for all students, and it involves all members of the school community in its governance.

What Does an Equitable School Look Like?

Drawing on the example of the Mission Hill School and other equitable schools, as well as from the research and theory that we presented in this chapter, we offer the following as a list of the characteristics of equitable schools. An equitable school:

- Addresses the racial/cultural/social-class achievement gap and the possible reasons for it in school policies, programs, curriculum, and instructional practice. Among these accommodations might be before- and after-school homework programs, supplementary skills instruction, a full menu of academic and extracurricular options for students, a number of teachers whose backgrounds are similar to the students', family outreach programs, school-linked social services, and small school and class size.

- Has a multicultural curriculum that includes information and perspectives from many cultures, including the ones represented within the school community. This curriculum emphasizes universal, global themes as well as cultural variations in the practice of those themes (Banks, 1993); for example, circumstances and celebrations of thanksgiving and independence, and standards of beauty. It employs a multicultural perspective, applied to all subject matter at all times, not just for special topics on special days.

- Makes sure that all students engage in content that is deep, substantive, meaningful, and connected to human experience.
- Respects the cultures represented in the local community—the history, traditions, and belief systems that have provided meaning to people's lives—and invites the community to share in and contribute to the activities of the school.
- Establishes policies and procedures that are sensitive to local cultures; for example, in developing the school calendar, in choosing the menu for meals and social events, and in scheduling conferences and meetings.
- Regularly celebrates the diversity of the school, the community, and the nation.
- Actively seeks out family participation in a variety of ways. Communicates with families orally and in writing in the language of the community, as well as in English.
- Makes sure that teachers and administrators convey high academic expectations to all students and helps them achieve those expectations.
- Uses culturally responsive pedagogy (instructional strategies), including teaching–learning practices rooted in the traditions of local cultures (Au and Kawakami, 1985), differentiated instruction, attention to multiple intelligences and learning styles, and a balance of cooperative learning, whole-class activities, and independent work.
- Showcases children's talents and strengths. Strengthens their areas of weakness without blame or shame.
- Provides many opportunities for informed student choice in academic study, social activities, and school procedures.
- Holds students responsible for their work and holds staff responsible for good teaching.
- Invites students to enroll in advanced classes and extracurricular activities, especially students who do not typically enroll in those classes, in order to equalize educational opportunities and break down racial/cultural norms and stereotypes.
- Ensures that students learn the skills needed to function and thrive in mainstream society, and teaches those conventions as useful means of expression equal in value to other forms and languages that may be used in their own communities.
- Functions as a participatory democracy by involving all parties (staff, students, and families) in governance and decision making.
- Establishes norms of community and practices them in all social interactions within the school. Builds into the curriculum community-building activities and skills that affect intercultural relations—for example, conflict resolution, tolerance of differences, and communication skills.

- Advocates for its student and community population, seeking out opportunities to secure additional funding and to broadcast stories of school successes.
- Employs teachers who are interested in learning about cultures other than their own, through study, travel, and from staff, students, and families.

We hope you have the opportunity to teach in such a school. We urge you to use your influence in the classroom and as a member of the school community to help your school be an equitable learning environment for all children.

The Social Role of the School and the Social Responsibility of Teachers

The No Child Left Behind Act of 2001 mandates standardized curricula and standardized testing across the country, which its authors hope will remove social class, race, and even geography as excuses for unequal schooling. Given the complex and changing demographic picture of schools and the external social and political factors that affect them, holding schools accountable through test results cannot alone improve the school experience of poor and ethnically diverse children. Educators must examine how race, social class, and culture affect the nature of children's experience in classrooms and provide the resources and strategies necessary to teach them well. We must lay aside the injustices inherent in tracking and other systems of conveying unequal expectations. We must eschew uniform notions of best practices that presumably apply to all children, regardless of what they know or what they need. Instead, we should look to the many programs and practices that have successfully closed the achievement gap for children of all social classes, races, cultures, and geographic areas.

In *Crossing the Tracks* (1992), Anne Wheelock provides a comprehensive description of successful "de-tracking" policies and practices. She offers myriad examples of teachers who set high expectations for all students. They teach heterogeneous groups of students of mixed interests, skills, and talents, sometimes in multi-age classes. They use challenging and varied materials and design creative, hands-on, multi-level lessons that are involving, meaningful, and accessible. Wheelock showcases Jim Reisinger, who teaches the same algebra course to his lowest-track math students that their upper-level peers get, using cross-age tutoring and student mentors for support. Steve Willette of Livermore Falls, Maine, teaches philosophy through stories posing ethical dilemmas to a heterogeneous class of middle schoolers. Sally Cotter emphasizes critical thinking skills such as predicting, problem solving, and decision making to Chapter I (remedial) fifth graders in Massachusetts. The teachers profiled in Wheelock's book demonstrate that all students are capable of high-level thought and sustained academic work.

Mike Rose traveled across the United States in search of excellent teachers. He found them in cities and suburbs and remote towns, in large high school complexes and one-room schoolhouses, in areas of wealth and poverty. They were white and black, old and young, and they used many kinds of teaching strategies. What they had in common was a faith in children's interest in and ability to learn, and a commitment to figuring out how to elicit that learning. They had a tendency to "push on the existing order of things" (1995, p. 429). They knew their students well as individuals and knew the social contexts of their lives—the history and economy of their communities, the cultural traditions and practices, the political relationships. These teachers' affirmation of the intellectual and civic potential of all children, including those from populations who have been historically devalued, gave to their work "a dimension of advocacy, a moral and political purpose." Rose says:

> We tend to forget what a radical idea this is in the history of Western political thought—this belief that all members of the state have an intellectual and civic contribution to make, have the potential for full participation in society. The shame of our schools is that, over time, we have denied such merit to so many. . . . Given the populations with whom many of our teachers choose to work, the enactment of egalitarian beliefs in their classrooms becomes a vehicle for social change, a realization of the democratic ideal in real time (p. 423).

Mike Rose believes that American public schools can lead society toward democracy and justice and that teachers are themselves agents of social change. We agree. More than institutions where children are socialized into existing societal norms, or where teachers transmit their knowledge to waiting students, schools are potentially places of personal liberation and social transformation. Until that potential is equitably realized, there is much work to be done.

SUMMARY

- This chapter addresses the gaps in the quality of schooling and the performance of children from a variety of social groups in this country, resulting from a "playing field" that is far from level.
- While the academic achievement of our most advantaged children in our best schools is second to none in the world, the inequities that persist in the education of certain social groups is perhaps the most serious problem facing American education.
- The education of children from lower social classes and minority cultures, children who are poor, and many who are immigrants is compromised by inadequate funding and resources, poor quality and limited teaching staffs, ineffective curricula and instructional practice, tracking, and low expectations.
- Theories explaining the achievement gap include biological explanations, explanations of cultural difference, and the conditions of immigration. In addition, there are political explanations—that schools have unequal resources and that students and schools have unequal access to computers and the Internet. Policies such as tracking and ability grouping can reinforce existing social inequities.
- Teachers' expectations impact the achievement of students.
- Schools should be more sensitive to the important and complex influence of culture and language on teaching and learning. White teachers need to be aware of their own cultural influences and their positions of power in order to understand and accept the strengths and needs of their students of color.
- Schools need to be aware of the cultural values and norms that each child brings with them or miscommunication can be the result. Notions of authority embedded within cultures impact life in classrooms—some children may be reluctant to challenge teachers or share private experiences, for example. Teachers must respect the language and the culture that the child comes to school with and build on these strengths.
- Immigrant students are becoming the majority and changing the portrait of the United States. The experience of immigrant students in the schools is an important consideration in achieving equity.
- The fastest growing populations in the United States are Latinos and Asians. The conditions under which they have immigrated to the United States will impact how well they fare in their new schools, how quickly they learn, how they feel about being

- there, and the amount of academic support their families can provide.
- Latino students' school success is affected by policies on second-language learning.
- Schools are responsible for implementing practices that allow families of all cultures and backgrounds to participate in the school and their child's education.
- Equitable schools share certain characteristics that include addressing the racial/cultural/social-class achievement gap, offering a multicultural curriculum, respecting cultures and diversity, providing opportunities for students, and advocating for them.
- The notion of "best practices" must be expanded to include a range of instructional approaches effective with students of various cultural and linguistic backgrounds.
- Families and communities must be integrally involved in schools in a variety of empowering ways.
- Closing the achievement gaps between children living in different communities and born into different social strata is the aim of the No Child Left Behind Act, which overemphasizes testing and accountability as vehicles for improvement.
- Schools can be places of personal liberation and social transformation if educators accept their potential roles as agents of social change.

QUESTIONS FOR REFLECTION

1. We often hear teachers say they are "color blind" and treat all students the same. Explain why not seeing a student's color or culture or social class may in fact not serve them well educationally.
2. How has your cultural background influenced your attitudes and orientations toward education? How might it affect your work as a teacher?
3. How does the digital divide contribute to the problem of the achievement gap? How might equalizing access to technology help reduce that gap?
4. In what ways have you or someone you know experienced the "teacher expectation effect."
5. What is your experience with tracking and ability grouping? How do you think this kind of grouping affects students?

APPLYING WHAT YOU'VE LEARNED

1. The companion website for this text contains the Harvard Civil Rights Project report on recent patterns of resegregation in U.S. schools. Consult the site to find the trends in your part of the country. What might this information tell you about equity in the schools in your part of the country?
2. Read Gerardo Lopez's article on parent involvement in Mexican immigrant families (see References). How does the article affirm the need to consider parent involvement in comprehensive or alternative ways?
3. Research the extent of recent immigration to your area and how it has affected your local schools.
4. You have read about the issues facing students whose native language or language patterns are different from those typically used in schools, and, in previous chapters, about how children learn. Explore several approaches to English-language learning (e.g., bilingual education, English as a Second Language, and immersion approaches), and take a position on their relative value.
5. Give some examples of how teachers might incorporate the cultural background of students or the culture of the community into curricula or learning activities. [You might use as a reference the Center for Multicultural Education's website listed below or James Banks's criteria (see References) for effective multicultural education].

KEY TERMS

ability groups, p. 337
achievement gap, p. 321
bilingual education, p. 354
cultural deprivation, p. 332
cultural fit, p. 332
culture, p. 345
involuntary immigrants vs. voluntary immigrants, p. 332
race, p. 323
racism, p. 323
sheltered immersion, p. 354
social class, p. 327
teacher expectation effect, p. 338
tracking, p. 337

WEBSITES TO EXPLORE

http://www.csos.jhu.edu/p2000/index.htm. Website of the Center on School, Family and Community Partnerships at Johns Hopkins University, where Joyce Epstein conducts research and development on six types of parent involvement. Includes guidance for schools and parents.

http://www.ed.gov/offices/OESE/reference.pdf. No Child Left Behind Act Desktop Reference.

http://www.gse.harvard.edu/~hip/. Website of the Harvard Immigration Project, including reports on the project's longitudinal study of the immigrant experience and resources on immigration and education.

http://www.civilrightsproject.harvard.edu/research/k12_ed.php. Website of the Harvard Civil Rights Project, including the full text of research reports on patterns of school segregation, integration and resegregation, and educational outcomes. Also includes studies of the effect of high-stakes testing and racial disparities in special education.

http://www.pbs.org/digitaldivide/. The Public Broadcasting System (PBS) website accompanies its series *The Digital Divide.* Site includes some research and statistics, multimedia resources, and information on initiatives to help close gaps in access to and education in technology.

http://depts.washington.edu/centerme/home.htm. Website of the Center for Multicultural Education housed at the University of Washington under the leadership of James Banks and Cherry McGee Banks. Includes samples of national programs and curricula.

http://www.missionhillschool.org/index.php. Website of the Mission Hill School in Boston, Massachusetts, a multicultural K–8 public "pilot school" led by Deborah Meier. The site offers information on the school's program, which emphasizes educating for democracy, participatory governance, and a curriculum organized around an "essential question" that engages learners in cross-disciplinary active learning.

CRITICAL READINGS

An Indian Father's Plea

BY ROBERT LAKE-THOM
(MEDICINE GRIZZLYBEAR)

Robert Lake-Thom (Medicine GrizzlyBear) is Karuk, Seneca, Cherokee, and Caucasian. He was a former professor at Humboldt State University in Arcata, California; an associate professor at Gonzaga University's School of Education in Spokane, Washington; and an associate professor at Eastern Montana University in Billings, Montana. (His ex-wife, Tela Starhawk Lakes, is an enrolled member of the Yurok Tribe of Northern California.)

Dear Teacher,

I would like to introduce you to my son, Wind-Wolf. He is probably what you would consider a typical Indian kid. He was born and raised on a reservation. He has black hair, dark brown eyes, olive complexion. And like so many Indian children his age, he is shy and quiet in the classroom. He is 5 years old, in kindergarten, and I can't understand why you have already labeled him a "slow learner."

At the age of 5, he has already been through quite an education compared with his peers in Western society. At his first introduction into this world, he was bonded to his mother and to the Mother Earth in a traditional native childbirth ceremony. And he has been continuously cared for by his mother, father, sisters, cousins, uncles, grandparents, and extended tribal family since this ceremony.

From his mother's warm and loving arms, Wind-Wolf was placed in a secure and specially designed Indian baby basket. His father and the medicine elders conducted another ceremony with him that served to bond him with the essence of his genetic father, the Great Spirit, the Grandfather Sun, and the Grandmother Moon. This was all done in order to introduce him properly into the new and natural world, not the world of artificiality, and to protect his sensitive and delicate soul. It is our people's way of showing the newborn respect, ensuring that he starts his life on the path of spirituality.

The traditional Indian baby basket became his "turtle's shell" and served as the first seat in his classroom. He was strapped in for safety, protected from injury by the willow roots and hazel wood construction. The basket was made by a tribal elder who had gathered her materials with prayer and in a ceremonial way. It is the same kind of basket that our people have used for thousands of years. It is specially designed to provide the child with the kind of knowledge and experience he will need in order to survive in his culture and environment.

Wind-Wolf was strapped in snuggly with a deliberate restriction upon his arms and legs. Although you in Western society may argue that such a method serves to hinder motor-skill development and abstract reasoning, we believe it forces the child to first develop his intuitive faculties, rational intellect, symbolic thinking, and five senses. Wind-Wolf was with his mother constantly, closely bonded physically, as she carried him on her back or held him in front while breast-feeding. She carried him everywhere she went, and every night he slept with both parents. Because of this, Wind-Wolf's educational setting was not only a "secure" environment, but it was also very colorful, complicated, sensitive, and diverse. He has been with his mother at the ocean at daybreak when she made her prayers and gathered fresh seaweed from the rocks, he has sat with his uncles in a rowboat on the river while they fished with gill nets, and he has watched and listened to elders as they told creation stories and animal legends and sang songs around the campfires.

He has attended the sacred and ancient White Deerskin Dance of his people and is well-acquainted with the cultures and languages of other tribes. He has been with his mother when she gathered herbs for healing and watched his tribal aunts and grandmothers gather and prepare traditional foods such as acorn, smoked salmon, eel, and deer meat. He has played with abalone shells, pine nuts, iris grass string, and leather while watching the women make beaded jewelry and traditional native regalia. He has had many opportunities to watch his father, uncles, and ceremonial leaders using different kinds of songs while preparing for the sacred dances and rituals.

As he grew older, Wind-Wolf began to crawl out of the baby basket, develop his motor skills, and explore the world around him. When frightened or sleepy, he could always return to the basket as a turtle withdraws into its shell. Such an inward journey allows one to reflect in privacy on what he has learned and to carry the new knowledge deeply into the unconscious and the soul. Shapes, sizes, colors, texture, sound, smell, feeling, taste, and the learning process are therefore functionally integrated—the physical and spiritual, matter and energy, conscious and unconscious, individual and social.

For example, Wind-Wolf was with his mother in South Dakota while she danced for four days straight in the hot sun, fasting, and piercing herself in the sacred Sun Dance Ceremony of a distant tribe. He has been doctored in a number of different healing ceremonies by medicine men and women from diverse places ranging from Alaska and Arizona to New York and California. He has been in more than 20 different sacred sweat-lodge rituals—used by native tribes to purify the mind, body, and soul—since he was 3 years old, and he has already been exposed to many different religions of his racial brothers: Protestant, Catholic, Asian Buddhist, and Tibetan Lamaist. . . .

It takes a long time to absorb and reflect on these kinds of experiences, so maybe that is why you think my Indian child is a slow learner. His aunts and grandmothers taught him to count and know his numbers while they sorted out the complex materials used to make the abstract designs in the native baskets. He listened to his mother count each and every bead and sort out numerically according to color while she painstakingly made complex beaded belts and necklaces. He learned his basic numbers by helping his father count and sort the rocks to be used in the sweat-lodge—seven rocks for a medicine sweat, say, or 13 for the summer solstice ceremony. (The rocks are later heated and doused with water to create purifying steam.) And he was taught to learn mathematics by counting the sticks we use in our traditional native hand game. So I realize he may be slow in grasping the methods and tools that you are now using in your classroom, ones quite familiar to his White peers, but I hope you will be patient with him. It takes time to adjust to a new cultural system and learn new things.

He is not culturally "disadvantaged," but he is culturally "different." If you ask him how many months there are in a year, he will probably tell you 13. He will respond this way not because he doesn't know how to count properly, but because he has been taught by our traditional people that there are 13 full moons in a year according to the Native tribal calendar and that there are really 13 planets in our solar system, and 13 tail feathers on a perfectly balanced Eagle, the most powerful kind of bird to use in ceremonial healing.

But he also knows that some Eagles may only have 12 tail feathers, or seven, that they do not all have the same number. He knows that the flicker has exactly 10 tail feathers; that they are red and black, representing the directions of east and west, life and death; and that this bird is considered a "fire" bird, a power used in Native doctoring and healing. He can probably count more than 40 different kinds of birds, tell you and his peers what kind of bird each is and where it lives, the seasons in which it appears, and how it is used in a sacred ceremony. He may also have trouble writing his name on a piece of paper, but he knows how to say it and many other things in several different Indian languages. He is not fluent yet because he is only 5 years old and required by law to attend your educational system, learn your language, your values, your ways of thinking, and your methods of teaching and learning.

So you see, all of these influences together make him somewhat shy and quiet—and perhaps "slow" according to your standards. But if Wind-Wolf was not prepared for his first tentative foray into your world, neither were you appreciative of his culture. On the first day of class, you had difficulty with his name. You wanted to call him Wind, insisting that Wolf must somehow be his middle name. The students in the class laughed at him, causing further embarrassment.

While you were trying to teach him your new methods, helping him learn new tools for self-discovery and adapt to his new learning environment, he may be looking out the window as if daydreaming. Why? Because he has been taught to watch and study the changes in nature. It is hard for him to make the appropriate psychic switch from the right to the left hemisphere of the brain when he sees the leaves turning bright colors, the geese heading south, and the squirrels scurrying around for nuts to get ready for a harsh winter. In his heart, in his young mind, and almost by instinct, he knows that this is the time of the year he is supposed to be with his people gathering and preparing fish, deer meat, and native plants and herbs, and learning his assigned tasks in this role. He is caught between two worlds, torn by two distinct cultural systems.

Yesterday, for the third time in two weeks, he came home crying and said he wanted to have his hair cut. He said he doesn't have any friends at school because they make fun of his long hair. I tried to explain to him that in our culture, long hair is a sign of masculinity and balance and is a source of power. But he remained adamant in his position.

To make matters worse, he recently encountered his first harsh case of racism. Wind-Wolf had managed to adopt at least one good school friend. On the way home from school one day, he asked his new pal if he wanted to come home to play with him until supper. That was OK with Wind-Wolf's mother, who was walking with them. When they all got to the little friend's house, the two boys ran inside to ask permission while Wind-Wolf's mother waited. But the other boy's mother lashed out: "It is OK if you have to play with him at school, but we don't allow those kind of people in our house!" When my wife asked why not, the other boy's mother answered, "Because you are Indians, and we are White, and I don't want my kids growing up with your kind of people."

So now my young Indian child does not want to go to school anymore (even though we cut his hair). He feels that he does not belong. He is the only Indian child in your class, and he is well-aware of this fact. Instead of being proud of his race, heritage, and culture, he feels ashamed. When he watches television, he asks why the White people hate us so much and always kill our people in the movies and why they take everything away from us. He asks why the other kids in school are not taught about the power, beauty, and essence of nature or provided with an opportunity to experience the world around them firsthand. He says he hates living in the city and that he misses his Indian cousins and friends. He asks why one young White girl at school who is his friend always tells him, "I like you, Wind-Wolf, because you are a good Indian."

Now he refuses to sing his native songs, play with his Indian artifacts, learn his language, or participate in his sacred ceremonies. When I ask him to go to an urban powwow or help me with a sacred sweat-lodge ritual, he says no because "that's weird" and he doesn't want his friends at school to think he doesn't believe in God.

So, dear teacher, I want to introduce you to my son, Wind-Wolf, who is not really a "typical" little Indian kid after all. He stems from a long line of hereditary chiefs, medicine men and women, and ceremonial leaders whose accomplishments and unique forms of knowledge are still being studied and recorded in contemporary books. He has seven different tribal systems flowing through his blood; he is even part White. I want my child to succeed in school and in life. I don't want him to be a dropout or juvenile delinquent or to end up on drugs and alcohol because he is made to feel inferior or because of discrimination. I want him to be proud of his rich heritage and culture, and I would like him to develop the necessary capabilities to adapt to, and succeed in, both cultures. But I need your help.

What you say and what you do in the classroom, what you teach and how you teach it, and what you don't say and don't teach will have a significant effect on the potential success or failure of my child. Please remember that these are the primary years of his education and development. All I ask is that you work with me, not against me, to help educate my child in the best way. If you don't have the knowledge, preparation, experience, or training to effectively deal with culturally different children, I am willing to help you with the few resources I have available or direct you to such resources.

Millions of dollars have been appropriated by Congress and are being spent each year for "Indian Education." All you have to do is take advantage of it and encourage your school to make an effort to use it in the name of "equal education." My Indian child has a constitutional right to learn, retain, and maintain his heritage and culture. By the same token, I strongly believe that non-Indian children also have a constitutional right to learn about our Native American heritage and culture, because Indians play a significant part in the history of Western society. Until this reality is equally understood and applied in education as a whole, there will be a lot more schoolchildren in grades K–12 identified as "slow learners."

My son, Wind-Wolf, is not an empty glass coming into your class to be filled. He is a full basket coming into a different environment and society with something special to share. Please let him share his knowledge, heritage, and culture with you and his peers.

Source: Teacher Magazine, Vol. 2(1), 1990.

A Closer Look at the Issues

1. What does Wind-Wolf's father think about the role of culture and language in education?
2. If someone had written to your teacher about the "full basket" that you brought with you into first grade, what would it have included?
3. Write back to Wind-Wolf's father to let him know how you will build on the "full basket" that Wind-Wolf brings to school with him in order to extend his knowledge and skills.

What Does It Take To Be a Successful Teacher in a Diverse Classroom?

BY GLORIA LADSON-BILLINGS, PROFESSOR, UNIVERSITY OF WISCONSIN–MADISON

I began teaching early adolescent students in a K–8 school in South Philadelphia in the late 1960s. Although I was a native Philadelphian, this part of the city was new to me. When I arrived about a month after the school year began, my classes were in chaos. The students were left to a series of substitute teachers and seemingly decided that school had not officially begun because their "real" teacher had not shown up. This disorganization was not surprising to me. I had no fond hopes that the students would be awaiting my arrival—attentive and prepared to move on in social studies and English. What was surprising was the "diversity" I experienced in South Philadelphia.

To the casual observer, I was teaching predominantly white, working-class students, along with a number of African-American students who were bused from West Philadelphia. I thought that myself. But as the year progressed, I learned that I was teaching white ethnic students—Italian Americans, Irish Americans, Jewish Americans, Polish Americans—of varied religious persuasions—as well as African-American students. I also learned that these differences mattered in specific ways, and any success I was to have in the school would be tied to my ability to develop a deeper understanding of the groups to which the children felt an affiliation. . . .

The diversity that today's new teachers face is qualitatively different from what I faced as a new teacher in the late 1960s. My students were clearly differentiated by their ethnic, cultural, religious, and racial differences during a time when such differences seemed more consequential; today, notions of diversity are broader and more complex. Not only are students likely to be multiracial or multiethnic, but they are also likely to be diverse along linguistic, religious, ability, and economic lines that matter in today's schools. . . .

In addition to the problems the students experience in their personal lives away from school, the schools create a whole new set of problems for children they deem different. As schools become more wedded to psychological models, students are recruited into new categories of pathology. Students who do not conform to particular behavioral expectations may be labeled "disabled" in some way, that is, suffering from attention deficit disorder, emotional disability, or cognitive disabilities. Students do in fact confront real mental and emotional problems, but we need to consider the way students' racial, ethnic, cultural, linguistic, and socioeconomic characteristics are deployed to make their assignments to these disability categories more likely.

Who are the teachers capable of transcending the labels and categories to support excellence among all students? Martin Haberman calls them star teachers; I call them dreamkeepers. But in both my work and that of Haberman, we have identified experienced teachers who knew how to teach well in challenging circumstances. Teaching well, in this instance, means making sure that students achieve, develop a positive sense of themselves, and develop a commitment to larger social and community concerns. Such teachers are inspiring and admirable, but their ranks are decreasing with each passing school year. The question facing most urban school districts is how to ensure a faculty of effective teachers when there is high teacher turnover and relative inexperience. . . .

The average white teacher has no idea what it feels like to be a numerical or political minority in the classroom. The persuasiveness of whiteness makes the experience of most teachers the accepted norm. White teachers don't understand what it is to "be ashy" or to be willing to fail a physical education class because of what swimming will do to your hair. Most white teachers have never heard of the "Black National Anthem," let alone know the words to the song. Most have never tasted sweet potato pie or watched the intricate process of hair braiding that many African-American girls (and increasingly boys) go through. And although African-American youth culture has become increasingly popular, and everyone can be heard saying, "You go, girl!" and believes she has the right to sing the blues, the amount of genuine contact these people have with African Americans and their culture is limited.

Similarly, the growing Latino population has forced a change in popular culture. Ricky Martin, Christina Aguilera, and Enrique Iglesias are enjoying huge popular success. But most white teachers cannot speak even rudimentary Spanish—enough even to signal an emergency or satisfy a basic need. More disturbing is the way Latinos are racialized into a unitary category. Few teachers (and prospective teachers) know the distinctive histories of Mexican Americans, Puerto Ricans, Cuban Americans, Salvadoreans, Guatemalans, Peruvians or the countless groups who originate in the Spanish-speaking Americas.

The indictment is not against the teachers. It is against the kind of education they receive. The prospective teachers with whom I have worked generally express a sincere desire to work with "all kinds of kids." They tell me that they want to make sure that the white children they teach learn to be fair and to get along with people different from themselves. But where is the evidence that the prospective teachers can get along with people different from themselves? When asked, most of my students admit that they have never gone to a movie or shared a meal or visited the home of a peer who is racially or culturally different. Some, because of program requirements or their own faith commitments, have worked in a soup kitchen or shelter or in other "helping" roles with people different from themselves.

But these brief forays into the lives of "others" often serve to cement the impression that others are always needy and disadvantaged. "Helping the less fortunate" can become a lens through which teachers see their role. Gone is the need to really help students become educated enough to develop intellectual, political, cultural, and economic independence. Such an approach to teaching diverse groups of students renders their culture irrelevant. There is nothing there to be learned, let alone built upon and developed. Certainly, every group has some "worthies" like Martin Luther King, Jr. or César Chávez, but even these cultural heroes have become sanitized to meet normative standards. Students are encouraged to be like (Martin Luther King, Jr., César Chávez, Sojourner Truth, Dolores Huerta, and so on) because they were "good Americans." Rarely are students invited to learn about the way such people stood up to America (not just to a "few bad people") and demanded that the country live up to its own democratic rhetoric. . . .

Helping students become culturally competent is not an easy task. First, it requires that teachers themselves be aware of their own culture and its role in their lives. Typically, white middle-class prospective teachers have little or no understanding of their own culture. Notions of whiteness are taken for granted. They rarely are interrogated. But being white is not merely about biology. It is about choosing a system of privilege and power. The white ethnic students in my first teaching job called themselves Italian or Irish or Polish. Their working-class backgrounds made it difficult, if not impossible, for them to identify with whiteness. In our current society, people with ethnic and cultural identities often find themselves *choosing* whiteness over those identities. Such a choice comes at a cost.

I gave a lecture at a local community college when a young man approached me at the end of the question-and-answer period and said, "You said a lot about Native American history and African-American history and Asian-American history, but what about white history—what about *my* history?" I followed up with a question that seemed to startle the young man "Are you white?" I asked. "Or do you have an ethnic or cultural heritage other than white?" He responded by saying, "I'm Irish." I then began to tell him about some of the aspects of Irish history—how the Irish were the first group the British exploited for slave labor in the Americas. I told him about the intricate clan structure the Irish had developed that allowed them to hold land in common and prevent exploitation. The young man knew nothing of this. I was not surprised. I suggested that he did not know his history because, somewhere along the line, his family may have chosen whiteness over all else. And when one chooses whiteness as a primary identity, one's ethnic and cultural history disappears. All he has left to signal his existence is something about a potato famine and St. Patrick's Day. . . .

Teachers who are prepared to help students become culturally competent are themselves culturally competent. They do not spend their time trying to be hip and cool and "down" with their students. They know enough about students' cultural and individual life circumstances to be able to communicate well with them. They understand the need to *study the students* because they believe there is something there worth learning. They know that students who have the academic and cultural wherewithal to succeed in school without losing their identities are better prepared to be of service to others; in a democracy, this commitment to the public good is paramount.

Source: Condensed from Gloria Ladson-Billings, *Crossing Over to Canaan* (San Francisco: Jossey-Bass, 2001). In Rethinking Schools Online. http://www.rethinkingschools.org/archive/15_04/Glb154.shtml

A Closer Look at the Issues

1. Why does Ladson-Billings think it's essential that teachers know their own cultures as well as that of their students? What do you think?
2. She says that teachers need to have "genuine contact" with the culture of the students in their classes in order to understand them. What do you think she means by "genuine contact"?
3. What is a "culturally competent teacher?"

REFERENCES

Abu-Nader, J. (1993). Meeting the needs of multicultural classrooms: Family values and the motivation of minority students. In O'Hair, M. J. & Odell, S. J. *Diversity and Teaching: Teacher Education Yearbook I.* Orlando, FL: Harcourt Brace.

Allen, R. (2000). Forging school-home links: A new paradigm for parental involvement. *Education Update, 42* (7). Washington, DC: ASCD, November, pp. 1–8.

Alvarez, L. (1995). Interpreting new worlds for parents. *New York Times,* October 1, pp. 29, 36.

AACTE (American Association of Colleges of Teacher Education) (1999). Teacher education pipeline IV: Schools, colleges, and departments of education. Washington, DC: AACTE.

American Association of University Women (1992). *The AAUW Report: How Schools Shortchange Girls.* Wellesley, MA: Wellesley College Center for Research on Women.

Anderson, S. (2004). *Children of immigrants: The multiplier effect.* Summer. Arlington, VA: National Foundation for American Policy.

Anyon, J. (1980). Social class and the hidden curriculum of work. *Journal of Education, 12,* pp. 67–92.

Anyon, J. (1997). *Ghetto schooling: A political economy of urban educational reform.* New York: Teachers College Press.

Apple, M. (1995). *Education and power.* New York: Routledge.

Apple, M. (2000). Coming to terms: Conversations on the hidden curriculum (video interview). In M. Gair, L. Montelongo, and G. Mullions (eds.). Conceptualizing the hidden curriculum in higher education: Theories of reproduction and resistance. Presentation at Sociology of Education Conference, Monterey, California, February 26. http://ether.asu.edu/peekaboo/presentation/slides/index.htm. Retrieved June 24, 2004.

Arvizu, S. F., W. A. Snyder, and P. T. Espinosa (1980). Demystifying the concept of culture: theoretical and conceptual tools (Vol. III, No. 11). Bilingual Education Paper Series. Los Angeles, CA: California State University, National Dissemination and Assessment Center.

Asakawa, K., and M. Csikszentmihalyi (2000). Feelings of connectedness and internalization of values in Asian American adolescents. *Journal of Youth and Adolescence, 29,* pp. 121–145.

Au, K. H., and A. J. Kawakami, (1985). Research currents: Talk story and learning to read. *Language Arts, 62,* pp. 406–411.

August, D., and K. Hakuta (1997). *Improving schooling for language-minority children: Research, policy, and practice.* Chicago: Charles C. Thomas.

Ballantine, J. (2001). *The sociology of education: A systematic analysis,* 5th ed. Upper Saddle River, NJ: Prentice Hall.

Banks, J. (1993). Approaches to multicultural curriculum reform. In J. Banks and C. Banks (eds.), *Multicultural education: Issues and perspectives.* Boston: Allyn & Bacon.

Berliner, D., and B. J. Biddle (1995). *The manufactured crisis: Myths, fraud, and the attack on America's public schools.* New York: Addison-Wesley.

Bernstein, B. (1971). *Class, codes and control, volume 1: Theoretical studies towards a sociology of language.* London: Routledge & Kegan Paul.

Blanton, K. (2002). A changing work force. *Boston Globe,* November 9, pp. D1–D2.

Bowles, S., and H. Gintis (1976). *Schooling in capitalist America: Educational reform and the contradictions of economic life.* New York: Basic Books.

Braddock, J., W. Hawley, T. Hunt, J. Oakes, R. Slavin, and A. Wheelock, (1998). Ollie Taylor's story: How tracking and ability grouping affects our children.

In H. S. Shapiro and S. B. Harden (eds.), *The institution of education.* Needham Heights, MA: Simon & Schuster.

Brophy, J. E. (1983). Research on the self-fulfilling prophecy and teacher expectations. *Journal of Educational Psychology, 75,* pp. 631–661.

Carvin, A. (2000). Mind the gap: The digital divide as the civil rights issue of the new millennium. *Multimedia Schools,* January/February. http://www.infotoday.com/MMSchools/Jan00/carvin.htm. Retrieved June 24, 2004.

Chiefs and Council, Saugeen Ojibway Nations Territories (1994). Racism defined, June 13. http://nativenet.uthscsa.edu/archive/nl/9406/0153.html. Accessed June 2, 2004.

Colclough, G., and E. M. Beck (1986). The American educational structure and the reproduction of social class. *Sociological Inquiry, 56* (4), Fall, pp. 456–73.

Comer, J. P., N. M. Haynes, E. T. Joyner, and M. Ben-Avie (eds.) (1996). *Rallying the whole village: The Comer process for reforming education.* New York: Teachers College Press.

Cubberley, E. P. ([1909] 1965). Changing conceptions of education. In R. L. Vassar, (ed.), *Social history of American education, Vol. 2: 1960 to the present,* pp. 149–156. Chicago: Rand McNally.

Darling-Hammond, L. (1994). Performance-based assessment and equation equity. *Harvard Educational Review, 64,* Spring, pp. 5–30.

Delpit, L. D. (1995). *Other people's children: Cultural conflict in the classroom.* New York: New Press.

Delpit, L. D. and J. K. Dowdy (2002). *The skin that we speak: Thoughts on language and culture in the classroom.* New York: New Press.

Educational Policy Information Center (2002). A deeper look at the NAEP science results. *ETS Policy Notes,* 11(1), Fall. Princeton, NJ: Educational Testing Service.

Epstein, J. L. (1995). School/family/community partnerships: Caring for the children we share. *Phi Delta Kappan 76* (9), May, pp. 701–712.

French, D. (2002). Letter to the editor. *Education Week* XXII (10), Nov. 6, p. 39.

Garcia, E. E. (2001). *Hispanic education in the United States: Raices y alas.* Lanham, MD: Rowman & Littlefield.

Gardner, H. (1983). *Frames of mind: The theory of multiple intelligences.* New York: HarperCollins.

Good, T. L. (1987). Two decades of research on teacher expectations: Findings and future directions. *Journal of Teacher Expectation, 38,* 32–44.

Hale, J. E. (1994). *Unbank the fire: Visions for the education of African-Americans.* Baltimore, MD: Johns Hopkins University Press.

Hale-Benson, J. E. (1986). *Black children: Their roots, culture and learning styles.* Baltimore: John Hopkins University Press.

Hallinan, M. T. (1990). The effects of ability grouping in secondary schools: A response to Slavin's best-evidence synthesis. *Review of educational research, 60* (3), Fall, pp. 501–504.

Hansen, S. (2002). The browning of America (interview with Richard Rodriguez). Salon.com, April 27. http://www.salon.com/books/int/2002/04/27/rodriguez/ Retrieved June 25, 2004.

Heath, S. B. (1982). Questioning at school and at home: A comparative study. In G. D. Spindler (ed.). *Doing the ethnology of schooling: Educational anthropology in action.* New York: Holt, Rinehart & Winston.

Herrnstein, R. J., and C. Murray (1994). *The bell curve: Intelligence and class structure in American life.* New York: Free Press.

Hines, P. M., N. G. Preto, M. McGoldrick, R. Almeida, and S. Weltman (1999). Culture and the family life cycle. In M. McGoldrick and B. Carter (eds.). *The Expanded family life cycle: Individual, family and social perspectives,* 3rd ed. Boston: Allyn & Bacon.

Holland, R. (2003). Study casts doubt on rosy reports of graduation rates. *School Reform News,* January 1. Chicago, IL: The Heartland Institute. http://www.heartland.org/Article.cfm?artId=11280. Retrieved August 30, 2004.

Howley, C., M. Strange, and R. Bickel (2000). Research about school size and school performance in impoverished communities, *ERIC Digest.* Charleston, WV: ERIC Clearinghouse on Rural Education and Small Schools (ERIC Document Reproduction Service No. ED488968).

Illinois Advisory Committee to the U.S. Commission on Civil Rights (2003). Arab and Muslim civil rights issues in the Chicago metropolitan area post-September 11. May. http://www.usccr.gov/. Retrieved August 30, 2004.

Jencks, C. (1972). *Inequality: A reassessment of the effect of family and schooling in America.* New York: Basic Books.

Jensen, A. R. (1969). How much can we boost IQ and scholastic achievement? *Harvard Educational Review, 39* (1), pp. 1–123.

Jones, J. D., B. D. Vanfossen, and M. E. Ensminger (1995). Individual and organizational predictors of high school track placement. *Sociology of Education, 68* (4), October, pp. 287–300.

Kondo, K. (1996). Language and needs for affiliation and achievement: A comparative study of English and Japanese bilingual and English monolingual Nisei students in today's Hawaii. Paper presented at the Western Conference of the Comparative and International Education Society, Honolulu.

Kozol, J. (1991). *Savage inequalities: Children in America's schools.* New York: Crown Publishers.

Kozol, J. (1995). *Amazing grace.* New York: Harper-Perennial.

Kozol, J. (2001). *Ordinary resurrections.* New York: HarperCollins.

Lamorey, S. (2002). The effects of culture on special education services: Evil eyes, prayer meetings, and IEPs. *Teaching Exceptional Children, 34* (5), pp. 67–71.

Lee, S. J. (2001). More than "model minorities" or "delinquents": A look at Hmong American high school students. *Harvard Educational Review, 71* (3), pp. 505–528.

Lopez, G. R. (2001). The value of hard work: Lessons on parent involvement from an immigrant household. *Harvard Educational Review,* Fall.

Martorella, P. (1993). Refugee issues in a globally interdependent world. *Educational Horizons, 71* (3), Spring, pp. 157–160.

Marx, K., and F. Engels ([1848] 1998). *The communist manifesto* (1848). New York: Oxford University Press.

McConnaughey, J., D. W. Everette, T. Reynolds, and W. Lader (1999). *Falling through the net: Defining the digital divide.* Washington, DC: National Telecommunications and Information Administration, U.S. Department of Commerce.

Miele, F. (1995). An interview with Robert Sternberg on *The Bell Curve. Skeptic Magazine, III* (3), pp. 72–80.

Moyers, B. (1994). *Listening to America: Unequal education* (video). Princeton, NJ: Films for the Humanities.

National Center for Education Statistics (2003). *Internet access in U.S. public schools and classrooms, 1994–2002.* Washington, DC: U.S. Department of Education Office of Educational Research and Improvement.

National Center for Education Statistics (2000). *Internet access in U.S. public schools and classrooms, 1994–1999.* Washington, DC: U.S. Dept. of Education Office of Educational Research and Improvement.

National Center for Education Statistics (2001). Educational achievement and black-white inequality. Washington, DC: U.S. Dept. of Education Office of Educational Research and Improvement. July. http://nces.ed.gov/pubs2001/2001061.PDF The nation's report card: 2003 mathematics and reading assessment results. Washington, DC: U. S. Department of Education. http://nces.ed.gov/nationsreportcard/ Retrieved June 24, 2004.

Neuman, S. B., and D. K. Dickinson (2003). *Handbook of early literacy research.* New York: Guilford Press.

Nieto, S. (2000). *Affirming diversity,* 3rd ed. New York: Longman.

Noguera, P. A. (2003). How racial identity affects school performance. *Harvard Education Letter, 19* (2), March/April, pp. 1–3.

Oakes, J. (1990). *Multiplying inequalities: The effects of race, social class, and tracking on opportunities to learn mathematics and science.* Santa Monica, CA: The Rand Corporation.

Obiakor, F. E. (1999). Teacher expectations of minority exceptional learners: Impact on "accuracy" of self-concepts. *Exceptional Children, 66,* pp. 39–54.

Office of the United Nations High Commissioner on Human Rights (2000). Racism, racial discrimination, xenophobia and related intolerance: Commission on human rights resolution. April 17. http://www.hri.ca/fortherecord2000/documentation/commission/2000-14.htm. Accessed June 2, 2004.

Ogbu, J. U. (1991). Immigrant and involuntary minorities in comparative perspective. In M. A. Gibson and J. U. Ogbu, *Minority status and schooling: A comparative study of immigrant and involuntary minorities.* New York: Garland Press, pp. 3–33.

Orellana, M. F. (2001). The work kids do: Mexican and Central American immigrant children's contributions to households and schools in California. *Harvard Educational Review, 71* (3), Fall.

Orfield, G., and C. Lee (2004). *Brown at 50: King's dream or Plessy's nightmare?* Cambridge, MA: Harvard Civil Rights Project.

Rethinking Schools, Editors. (1995). Beyond pizza sales: Parent involvement in the 1990s. *Rethinking Schools, VII* (3).

Rist, R. (1970). Student social class and teacher expectations: The Self-fulfilling prophecy in ghetto education. *Harvard Educational Review, 40* (3), pp. 411-451.

Rodriguez, R. (2002). *Brown: The Last discovery of America.* New York: Penguin.

Rose, Mike (1995). *Possible lives: The promise of public education in America.* New York: Houghton Mifflin, 1995.

Rosenthal, R., & Jacobson, L. (1968). *Pygmalion in the classroom.* New York: Holt, Rinehart & Winston.

Sadker, M., and D. Sadker (1995). *Failing at fairness: How our schools cheat girls.* New York: Touchstone Press.

Singh, G. K., and M. Siahpush, (2001). All-cause and cause-specific mortality of immigrants and native born in the United States. *American Journal of Public Health, 91* (3), pp. 392–399.

Sternberg, R. (1988). *The triarchic mind: A new theory of intelligence.* New York: Viking Press.

Sternberg, R. J. (1997). What does it mean to be smart? *Educational Leadership, 5,* pp. 20–24.

Strickland, D. S., and T. Shanahan (2004). Laying the groundwork for literacy. *Educational Leadership, 61* (60), pp. 74–81.

Suárez-Orozco, C., and M. M. Suárez-Orozco (2001). *Children of immigration.* Cambridge, MA: Harvard University Press.

Suárez-Orozco, C., I. Todorova, and J. Louie (2001). *The transnationalization of families: Immigrant separation and reunification.* Cambridge, MA: Harvard Graduate School of Education, Harvard Immigrant Project.

Swiniarski, L. B., and M. Breitborde (2003). *Educating the global village: Including the child in the world,* 2nd ed. Upper Saddle River, NJ: Merrill Prentice Hall.

Thomas, W. P., and V. P. Collier, (2001). *A national study of school effectiveness for language minority students' long-term academic achievement.* Santa Cruz, CA: Center for Research on Education, Diversity and Excellence.

United Nations General Assembly (2001). Report of the World Conference Against Racism, Racial Discrimination, Xenophobia, and Related Intolerance, Durban, South Africa, August-September. Geneva, Switzerland: Office of the United Nations High Commissioner for Human Rights.

U.S. Department of Commerce (2000). Falling through the net: Toward digital inclusion. October. Washington, DC: Author.

U.S. Dept. of Education (2001). No Child Left Behind Act. Washington, DC: Author.

United States General Accounting Office (2002). Perpupil spending differences between selected inner city and suburban schools varied by metropolitan area. December. Washington, DC: Author.

Valencia, R. (1997). Latino demographic and educational conditions. *ETS Policy Notes,* Winter. ETS Research Policy Information Center. http://www.ets.org/research/pic/v8n1a.html. Retrieved June 26, 2004.

Vives, O. (2001). Latina girls' high school drop-out rate highest in U.S. *National NOW Times,* Fall. http://www.now.org/nnt/fall-2001/latinas.html. Retrieved August 30, 2004.

Vygotsky, L. S. (1978). *Mind in society: The development of higher psychological processes.* Cambridge, Massachusetts: Harvard University Press.

Weber, M. (1958). Class, status and party. In H. Gerth and C. W. Mills, *Essays in sociology.* New York: Oxford University Press.

Wheelock, A. (1992). *Crossing the tracks: How untracking can save America's schools.* New York: New Press.

Yingling, P. (1999). Chair's report (introduction to special issue on refugees). *Peace and Freedom: Magazine of the Women's International League for Peace and Freedom, 48,*(4), p. 3.

10 Social and Moral Education: The Educated Person as a Member of Society

ESSENTIAL QUESTIONS

Who is the educated person? What is the role of the school in society?

To: Fifth-grade beginners
From: Melanie, fifth-grader

I know what your thinking your thinking that going to the fifth grade is going to be fun and not hard well I got something to tell you. You got to know every thing. You have to know your devition your time tables know how to do the dowy dowy decimal system. There are a lot of book she have read this year like The Hundred Dresses by Eleanor Estes, Greek Myths, Helen Keller, The Bat-Poet by Randall Jarrell and . . . and . . . you would find out the rest when you get here. You can not say shut up and you must follow the golden rule and you can not talk in the hall and you must not talk back at the teacher well I think that is anouf to let you know about the 5th grade life. Ta ta . . . (Codell, 2001, p. 1). ■

Melanie's message to the incoming fifth graders in her school is that there will be a lot to learn, both academic and non-academic. There will be multiplication tables to memorize and the Dewey decimal system to navigate. Along with the academic knowledge, though, she tells incoming fifth graders that they will have to master a set of rules of behavior in order to get along with the teacher and each other. Those rules are a kind of non-academic learning that underlies classroom life and includes values, expectations, and assumptions about what is proper and what is right. Along with new academic knowledge and new skills, schools teach children what is socially appropriate and what is morally correct or ethical.

Along with her "devition" and "time tables," Melanie had to learn not to say "shut up" and remember not to talk back to the teacher.

- What do you think Melanie's fifth-grade experience taught her about who has power in society and who does not?
- What did it teach her about what is important in the world?
- What did it teach her about what kind of behavior is right and honest?

Think back to your own days in fifth grade. What do you remember? What did you learn that year? Perhaps you remember that every day your teacher read to the class; you particularly liked C. S. Lewis's *The Lion, The Witch and the Wardrobe.* You had to be quiet while she was reading, but you could put your head down on your desk and close your eyes, if you wanted to. There was something about her voice reading that story that was comforting and personal, as though this wonderful story was a gift she was giving you. Maybe after the story, you remember that you had to show that you had memorized the capital cities of the fifty states. But the teacher made it into a game. The student who could rattle them off fastest got a prize, sometimes a free homework pass.

In fifth grade, if you didn't like to be called on in class, you might have learned that if you slunk down in your seat and stayed very quiet, the teacher would not call on you. Having your lunchbox and homework neatly arranged on your desk meant the teacher would think you "looked ready" and dismiss you to go home. Forgetting to do your homework might cost you recess the next day. Every morning, you tried to dress like Janelle, the most popular girl in the class, in the hope that you could be popular, too. And you had to avoid the boy with the short temper. Whenever he started to get angry, someone would say, "Look out! Here comes World War III!" But the teacher made an agreement with him that, if he made it through the day without an outburst, he could have extra time in the gym.

Schools do much more than simply transmit knowledge from generation to generation; they transmit deep messages about the way things work, or should work, in the larger society. Schools are socializing institutions, bridging the gap between the primary, personal world of the family and the secondary, adult world of work. They tell us how things should be in the world, where we fit in, and what we should do there. They present social messages about how people live in the world and how they might live and work alongside others. In many cases, these social messages carry moral meaning to children, lessons about the right way to live and the right way to behave.

In this chapter we will look beyond children's academic education to the social and moral education that schools attempt to provide, sometimes in ways that are clearly stated and even written down, but often in ways that are just part of life in classrooms. We will examine the characteristics, structures, and processes of classroom life that make classrooms places where social and moral lessons are taught. We will describe some debates about what those lessons should be and discuss the implications of those lessons for children's futures. As you recall your own fifth-grade experience, think about what it taught you about what kind of behavior is moral or proper. What did life in your fifth-grade classroom teach you and your classmates about how things work in society? About what is fair? About what is important? These messages are all part of what students learn in school, yet they are not included in the written curricula that guide teachers. They are part of what is called the hidden curriculum.

The Hidden Curriculum

What children learn in school can be divided into the overt curriculum and the hidden curriculum. The **overt curriculum** refers to the stated intentions of school administrators for what children will learn—the subject matter and the skills that are usually listed in a teacher's grade-level curriculum guide. Various notions of what the overt curriculum includes are described in Chapter 4. The **hidden curriculum,** on the other hand, is largely unstated. It includes the knowledge, values, attitudes, norms, and beliefs that children acquire in schools that are not stated in the formal, written curriculum objectives. It is what children learn in schools while they are supposed to be learning something else. What is learned may be about how society and human relations are organized.

For example, if the teacher always asks boys to fix the filmstrip projector, children may learn that part of an appropriate male role is being interested in and able to fix machinery; girls don't have to know how to fix it. Perhaps to be truly female, they shouldn't learn how. If a teacher asks for a simple recall of facts on exams, students may assume that their role as students is to memorize the ideas and interpretations of acknowledged and credentialed experts. On the other hand, if the teacher encourages critical questions and lively debate on controversial issues, students learn that their opinions are valued and expected. Teachers who engage students in formulating the "rules of the classroom" teach them that their ideas count.

The hidden curriculum carries with it messages of value. Students may learn that sharing with others is not only necessary in a classroom of twenty-five students, but the right thing to do. They may learn that people with disabilities should get special consideration. That it is wrong to question an authority figure, or, conversely, that it is right to do so. One teacher might assign many group projects and give group grades for the outcome, while another uses games in which students compete for first place. The first communicates to children that it is right and important to contribute your effort to help the whole group succeed; the other, that doing your best is paramount, and will be rewarded. In observing the way teachers interact with their students, their colleagues, custodians, and secretaries, students learn lessons about the right way to treat people.

David Hansen (1995) makes a convincing argument that seemingly simple things like the teacher's posture, whether she makes herself available to students who have questions or just want to say hello, and how quickly she gets down to the business of the class convey moral messages to students. In describing the first five minutes of a high school class, Hansen finds that in those five minutes a teacher can teach lessons about the importance of having a seriousness of purpose, respecting others' time and space, being responsible for one's work, and respecting the subject matter of the class.

In asking children to pay attention to particular people, ideas, and things, schools convey messages about what is valuable and important and what is not. Elliot Eisner thinks that what is excluded from the curriculum—the **null curriculum**—may be as influential on what children learn about subject matter, society, and themselves, as what is included. "[I]gnorance is not simply a neutral void; it has important effects on the kinds of options one is able to consider, the alternatives that one can examine, and the perspectives from which one can view a situation or problem" (Eisner, 1994, p. 97). In one example of the effect of the null curriculum, Samuel Totten (2001) argues that in teaching about the history of genocide and human rights, many teachers focus on the Nazi Holocaust of World War II, a significant and seminal event. But many of these same teachers ignore other genocides—those that targeted Armenians and Cambodians, and contemporary genocides against Bosnians and Rwandans. One result of this omission may be the idea that genocide was a one-time-only event perpetrated by an infamous madman (Adolf Hitler), rather than something that could recur today. Another potentially damaging message is that genocides affecting people of color or developing nations are not as important as those involving whites.

Teachers who ignore the racial and cultural background of their students—who claim to be "color-blind," for example—may convey the message that these differences are unimportant or embarrassing. Students who are homosexual have reported that a common reaction of teachers to incidents of harassment in the schools is to do "[n]othing. Nothing at all" (Bochenek and Brown, 2001), leaving gay and lesbian students to draw the conclusion that neither their sexuality nor their safety is important, and that prejudice and discrimination against gays is acceptable.

The hidden curriculum tells us that being educated is more than knowing the right things; being educated is also a matter of doing the right things and having the right character. In Chapter 1, we mentioned that the hidden curriculum is as important to children's futures as the stated curriculum (Principle 8), if not more so. The hidden curriculum can foster curiosity or apathy, participation or exclusion, equality or discrimination. It can teach students that education is fun, difficult, rewarding, or boring. It can teach them that learning is a matter of listening and understanding, or creating and shaping. It can teach them that life in general is predictable or chaotic, just or unjust, within one's control or not. It can teach conformity or creativity, assertiveness or passivity, competition or cooperation, the worth of the individual or the value of the group, and where to find the authoritative source for what is true and correct. In his classic description of the difference between the stated and the hidden curriculum, or between "the celebrated and the unnoticed," Philip Jackson wrote:

> School is a place where tests are failed and passed, where amusing things happen, where new insights are stumbled upon, and skills acquired. But it is also a place in which people sit, and listen, and wait, and raise their hands, and pass out paper, and stand in line, and sharpen pencils. School is where we encounter both friends and foes, where imagination is unleashed and misunderstanding brought to ground. But it is also a place in which yawns are stifled and initials scratched on desktops, where milk money is collected and recess lines are formed. . . . From the standpoint of understanding the impact of school life on the student, some features of the classroom that are not immediately visible are fully as important as those that are ([1968] 1990, pp. 4, 10).

The Social Characteristics of Classrooms

Jackson's book on the hidden curriculum of schools, called *Life in Classrooms* ([1968] 1990), argues that school prepares children for life beyond the family. It gives them practice in dealing with the less personal, more competitive world of work and society. It teaches them norms of behavior and values that are necessary to survive and thrive in the world. What distinguishes a child's school experience from her experience with family or friends is the fact that she must deny and interrupt her personal desires and wishes. No matter what the philosophy or organization of the school, Jackson says, classrooms share three characteristics that lead inevitably to that denial: *crowds, praise,* and *power.*

Crowds Classroom life is more crowded than even the largest of families. In any classroom, a child must vie with classmates for the attention of the teacher. In most cases, the student is one of twenty or twenty-five. But even in small classrooms—in a country school in Rio, Illinois, where there are ten students—each must wait a turn to ask a question, receive a book, look under the microscope, or use the restroom. This crowdedness means that schools have to establish rules, routines, and schedules—for example, lining up to enter and leave the classroom—that make classroom life as fair as possible for both teachers and students. Crowdedness also means that students must learn to be patient, take turns, and deny desire. They have to wait for the materials they need to complete their social studies projects. They may need to take turns using the paper cutter or the world atlas. Or, they might want to continue to work on a social studies project, but it's time to switch to mathematics. Students learn that "school is a place where things often happen not because students want them to, but because it is time for them to occur" (Jackson, [1968] 1990, p. 13).

In creating rules and routines to make the crowded situation manageable, a teacher not only teaches students the general norms and values of waiting patiently, respecting others' needs, and taking turns; he also conveys more specific social messages embodied in the rules. The teacher who prefers to dole out materials rather than allow students to get them on their own conveys a message about authority, responsibility, and trust. The teacher who regularly asks children to form two lines—a boys' line and a girls' line—to get her class outside for recess may be reinforcing a separateness or distinction between the genders. A high school that organizes its classes into six 45-minute periods, where one teacher meets with 150 students each day, limits the teacher–student relationship to one that is relatively impersonal. In the interest of efficient scheduling, high schools may end up organizing groups of students into programs that constitute career tracks; certain classes might be designated for students assumed to be headed for college and others for those assumed to be headed for business or manual trades.

Praise Even though children at home have chores and responsibilities for which parents and guardians praise or chastise them, most of the time they spend in their homes is judgment free. At home, children engage in activities of their own choosing. While behaviorists would say that all behavior is originally motivated by external results (for example, they would say that I love to play piano because my parents provided music lessons and praised me for practicing), most would agree that children at home are motivated more by an inner desire to do something than by external rewards or punishments. Within their families, children are generally accepted for who they are, not what they can do.

In school, however, acceptance is based on a child's performance of prescribed behaviors. Teachers give or withhold praise for how well a child reads, how polite he is, or how she demonstrates "good citizenship." The quality of a child's performance can lead to his being recommended for "the gifted program," or sent out of the classroom every day for "remedial reading." A child's very identity can be tied to being praised as "the brain" or chastised as "the class clown" or "the sped [special needs] kid." School praise—or the withholding of it—can affect a child's life at home. Many parents compound teachers' judgments by rewarding their children for their successes in school, or punishing them for their failures or transgressions. This was especially true in the past. Interviews conducted with graduates of Midwest country schools in the mid-twentieth century showed that "[i]f you were punished once in school, you got it twice at home" (Breitborde, 2003).

The centrality of praise in school, from a teacher's "good job!" to test grades, means that students are judged and motivated by something outside themselves. Many, including Jackson, say that this fact prepares children for the world of work, where good performances will earn them praise and financial reward. Others argue that external judgments undermine children's ability to motivate themselves. Alfie Kohn, whose ideas will be discussed later in this chapter, says that students have been "punished by rewards" (1999). Teachers who use a large amount of **extrinsic rewards**—external motivators, such as stars or stickers, used to reward learning or good behavior—convey to children the message that you learn something for what it gets you. On the other hand, **intrinsic rewards** convey the message that you learn something just because you want to learn it. External judgments also affect students' motivation to be creative; students who know how to earn the praise of their teachers will tailor their performance to "what she wants."

When children are asked which traits characterize a good teacher, they often cite fairness as a central quality. In other words, can they count on the teacher to respond to certain behaviors fairly and objectively? Or are some children praised more effusively or punished more severely than others? Unfortunately, as Chapter 9 discusses, evidence from research on teacher expectations and teacher–student interactions shows that, consciously or unconsciously, teachers distribute praise differentially. Recent attention to multiple forms of assessing children's learning, and the use of carefully designed rubrics that list the criteria for evaluation, are helping to clarify the bases for academic praise, and the distribution of it.

Power The primary dispensers of praise—the holders of power—in schools are, of course, teachers and principals. Even in the most democratic classrooms, where children participate in making class rules or choosing some activities, final power still rests in the hands of the teacher. The teacher issues end-of-term grades, decides whether to promote or retain a student, designs learning activities, assigns projects, can rob a child of recess if the child misbehaves, and might contact parents (those other holders of power over children). Teachers, administrators, and guidance counselors may determine whether a student can take algebra or play football—decisions that may affect his future. But students also exercise power over each other. The popular students, the bullies, the academic leaders, can make or break a peer's or a teacher's day.

"Education is a political enterprise," we said in Chapter 1. Politics involves the presence of power and the degree to which it is exercised justly. Following are some of the central questions about politics and power in education:

- How equitably is power exercised in schools?
- Who makes decisions about what children learn and about materials and school policies?
- Are materials, from books to computers, distributed equitably?

In schools and classrooms, the answers to these questions directly affect the degree of freedom, choice, and authority that children have. In your own school experience, for example, did all students get to use the computer lab? Did every class get equal time with the specialists or the poet- or artist-in-residence? In your observations in today's classrooms, do teachers help design the curriculum and set school policies? Do parents have a say about which classrooms their children are placed in from year to year? Do they sit on school councils? How much power do children, the primary stakeholders, have within their own schools? Is there a student government body with substantive responsibilities? How much choice do they have over their subjects of study, the topics for their research reports, the books they read? Many say that the power relationships in a school tell the children who go there how much power they will have as adults.

In some high schools, peer leaders help resolve conflicts among their classmates and act as advocates on student life issues. Many elementary teachers engage students in discussions about what behavior is appropriate for the classroom community and in solving problems that arise within it. In such classrooms, children may help devise the classroom rules and even the consequences for breaking them. These activities allow children to participate in creating their own social and moral communities, distribute power more equally among members of the community, and make the curriculum less "hidden."

Even the arrangement of classroom furniture carries messages to children about power and authority. In designing and outfitting his progressive Lab School at the University of Chicago, John Dewey recalled how difficult it was for him to obtain desks that invited learning, which he defined as active, social, and meaningful. At the time, there were no child-sized tables available that would allow a student to spread out multiple resources or art materials or that could be used for small-group discussions or project work. School furniture manufacturers only made desks for listening, he said:

> Some few years ago I was looking about the school supply stores in the city, trying to find desks and chairs which seemed thoroughly suitable from all points of view—artistic, hygienic, and educational—to the needs of the children. We had a good deal of difficulty in finding what we needed, and finally one dealer, more intelligent than the rest, made this remark: "I am afraid we have not what you want. You want something at which the children may work; these are all for listening" (1907, p. 50).

Classrooms where the teacher stands at the front of the room and lectures to students who passively receive directions teach children that teachers have power and authority over knowledge, and that the right way to learn is to listen, quietly. Such classrooms convey the message that society is organized hierarchically, with a few in charge of many followers.

While Philip Jackson claimed that all schools share the social characteristics of crowds, praise, and power, other researchers have explored the idea that these characteristics are present in particular forms in particular communities and are differentiated by social class and race or culture. In Chapter 1, we wrote that "public schools are linked to the social, cultural, and economic conditions of the societies and communities in which they find themselves." In poor and working-class communities, classrooms may be more crowded than classrooms in wealthier communities, for lack of funds to hire more teachers. In a school struggling with standardized tests, praise may be heaped on classes whose scores are good; in another community, where proficient test scores are taken for granted, praise may be heaped on students who ask critical questions or produce creative projects. Administrators in the first community may be so concerned about standardized test results that they may retain almost absolute power over the curriculum, limiting it to the basic information and skills that will be tested. Teachers there will have fewer choices about what they teach or how, and children will have fewer choices about what they learn and how.

The Social Educational Role of Schools in Society: Three Views

There are a number of theories about the social function of schools and the effect of the hidden curriculum on students' futures and the future of society. Each theory makes a judgment about the extent to which the information, values, attitudes, norms, and beliefs conveyed to students through the hidden curriculum influence the economic and social life they will have as adults. Are the schools simply doing their job in teaching children the social and academic skills they will need to be productive and responsible members of society? Or do they reproduce existing social, economic, and power inequities? Does the knowledge that students acquire in school fit them for a particular role or social status? Do children develop expectations for themselves based on what their schools expect of them? Or do schools liberate students to think for themselves, design their own futures, and reform society? In the following section, we take a look at three theories and their point of view on how the school functions to support or shape society: structural-functionalism, conflict theory, and resistance theory.

Structural-Functionalism Sociologist Robert Dreeben (1968) says that schools teach social norms that are important to a functional American society. Six structural aspects of schools help make them effective agents of social education through a process of "secondary socialization." These shared characteristics are:

1. non-kin adult–child relationships
2. time-limited school day
3. grade-leveling of students
4. transient teacher–student relationships
5. same-age peer interactions
6. high child-to-adult ratios

Dreeben says that these six characteristics allow schools to teach four norms that are distinctly "American": independence, achievement, universalism, and specificity.

Because their relationship to their teacher is impersonal and transient, because the high number of children in the room restricts attention to their needs, children in schools learn *independence*. They are expected to "do their own work," accept personal responsibility for their behavior, and act self-sufficiently, and they are tested on their individual performance. Second, they learn the norm of *achievement*. In the time limits set by the school day and the subject-matter period, they are expected to master content material and skills and compete against their age-mates according to some standard of excellence. Students learn the norm of *universalism,* meaning that they and their classmates are members of a group or category. They learn, for example, that all second graders are expected to sit still while the teacher talks, that all chorus members must practice their parts before rehearsals, that no matter who you are as an individual, you will lose your recess if you don't complete your homework. Universalism teaches the values of fairness and equality that Americans espouse. At the same time that students learn the norm of universalism, they learn *specificity,* which teaches them that different situations require different behaviors or knowledge. Students learn, for example, that the skills required to solve algebraic equations are not the skills needed to write good poetry, and that the math teacher may have rules for classroom behavior that are different from the poetry teacher's rules. Specificity means that while it may be fine to carry on a conversation about sports with your friends in the cafeteria over lunch, it is not fine to do the same thing in either your algebra or your poetry class.

Dreeben and other structural-functionalists look at the social, or hidden, curriculum of schools as a vehicle to teach the norms required for effective membership in American society. **Structural-functionalism** is the theory that a society that works (functions) needs to have a predictable and organized social order (structure) and a way of educating its members so that they have knowledge and skills that contribute to the preservation of that order.

Critics of the structural-functionalist approach say that it promotes the status quo of society without considering whether the status quo is good for all its members. They argue that some children will not learn the norms of independence and achievement if they need to feel personally connected to their teachers, classmates, and subject matter, and if they need more collaborative opportunities to understand subject matter and practice skills. They say that structural-functionalists don't pay enough attention to the content of the norms. The rule that children will lose their recess privileges for not completing their homework may ignore the fact that some of them don't speak English well enough to complete it. Differences in "universal norms" across schools matter: in one school without a cafeteria the norm may be that all students eat lunch at their desks and talking isn't allowed; across town, children can have a conversation with their friends at the cafeteria tables and then head outside to play when they're finished eating.

Critics of structural-functionalism claim that the social norms taught in schools are defined by dominant social groups with a vested interest in preserving the status quo. They say the theory does not account for who sets the norms and who preserves them by, among other things, teaching them in the public schools. While the structural-functionalists see the socializing role of schools as neutral or positive, necessary for the preservation of a functioning social order, conflict theorists look at the same process and judge it negatively.

Conflict Theory Some theorists regard the way that schools socialize through their hidden curricula as unfair and limiting. Samuel Bowles, Herbert Gintis, Jean

Anyon, and Joel Spring argue that the socializing, or acculturating, role of schools is not neutral, but is controlled by the dominant social class, who become elected school board members, policy formulators, and decision makers. They believe that the norms conveyed in schools vary across communities and, especially, with the social class of the students. Schools engage in **cultural reproduction,** mirroring in the relations between teacher and students the economic, social, and political relationships of the workplace, which are governed by the interests of the dominant group in society (Bowles and Gintis, 1976). A few highly privileged people (Marxists would call them the capital class) own and control most of the society's resources, leaving others to labor for them. This dominant group has a vested interested in preserving these unequal power relationships and looks to the schools to teach the skills necessary to continue the class-controlled production.

The idea that the process of school socialization becomes a way for the dominant group to maintain a status quo that reinforces social and political inequities is called **conflict theory.** Conflict theorists believe that there is a correspondence between the power relationships in schools and the power relations in the larger society. The relationship between school administrators and teachers, and between teachers and students, is much like the relationship between capitalists and laborers, or bosses and workers. Both settings, they say, are characterized by a hierarchy of authority and an unequal distribution of power and knowledge. Administrators dictate to teachers what they should be teaching and in what ways. Teachers have similar power over students: they determine what students will study, how they will be evaluated, and whether they will be rewarded. Someone decides what goes on in schools—what will be taught to whom, how students will be treated, how much freedom they will be allowed—and that someone is the dominant class. In contrast to the structural-functionalists, who assume that schools "work" for the good of the whole society, conflict theorists ask in whose interests the schools "work."

In the eyes of conflict theorists, teachers in many working-class schools consciously or unconsciously treat their students as subordinates, rewarding them for passive acceptance of rules and regulations, requiring that they adhere to schedules and routines, and restricting their decision-making opportunities. Students are "tracked" into programs that prepare them for subordinate jobs. Relationships with parents in these schools are "top-down," with school principals preferring to inform parents about school policies rather than ask for their input. Business leaders will influence school administrators to add computer literacy to the curriculum because they need workers who can use computers. According to the conflict theorists, schools promote the idea that things won't change, that "this is just the way things are." The best one can do is to learn the skills necessary to get a decent job.

Subordination and control were overt functions of schooling in the earlier years of this country (see Chapter 7). However, in modern times these goals are hidden behind an ideology of equal opportunity, despite the existence of persistent class conflict. Mostly unwittingly, the conflict theorists say, schools teach class-based values and norms. In subtle ways, through their hidden curricula, schools in working-class neighborhoods prepare children for a future of laboring for the upper class (Anyon, 1980). Practices that seem innocent or merely efficient, such as lining up to walk from class to class, or completing fill-in-the-blank worksheets instead of answering thought-provoking questions, or rewarding "good citizens" for their quiet attention in school assemblies, have a limiting and dampening effect on children's notions of what is possible or within their control.

Are these students being prepared for different futures?

Source: © Michael Newman/PhotoEdit (top); © Spencer Ainsley/The Image Works (bottom)

These practices, say the conflict theorists, keep children from asking too many questions, giving too many opinions, and considering too many possibilities for their future. On the other hand, schools that enroll the children of the dominant classes prepare them for the professional or leadership roles their parents expect in their futures. In these schools, children participate in deep debates, role-play legislative activities, and engage in detailed research projects, many of their own choosing (Anyon, 1980).

In many middle and high schools, various tracks, or levels—labeled, perhaps, as honors, college, general, basic, or vocational—serve to sort and select students for particular work futures by offering widely varying content and methods of instruction. Michael W. Apple (1995) argues that the knowledge and skills necessary for jobs that hold power and esteem in American society—for example, law, medicine, and management—are accessible only to advantaged social groups. This higher-level curriculum is withheld from others who are presumed to need more "practical" courses. Robert Moses, founder of the Algebra Project, is working to bring algebra to all students in the nation. At present many students, especially those of the underclass, are limited to "consumer math" classes and denied the chance to learn algebra and higher-level mathematics because they're in schools or tracks that don't offer those courses or because teachers assume they don't have the ability to do the work (Moses, 1994). Without algebra, students will be kept from taking higher-level math courses; without those courses, they may be counseled away from chemistry and physics. The end result may be that they don't have the courses required for college entrance and/or they are dissuaded from pursuing professional jobs that they might have enjoyed.

Conflict theorists see liberal reforms and compensatory programs like Head Start and Title I as ineffective long-term solutions to the problem of unequal educational opportunity. Compensatory programs will not succeed in correcting the problem because they do not address the socioeconomic class conflict that underlies our basically unequal society. Nor do they address the school's fundamental role in maintaining the inequities. Change is only possible, they say, with a redistribution of power and wealth in society. Only with significant controls on the amount of wealth one can amass and authority one can assume, only with a radically different organization of production and power, can we hope for a more equal society. If the producers of goods and services, and the students and teachers in schools, can participate in decision making and obtain their fair share of resources, then we will see changes in American society and its schools in the direction of equality.

Resistance Theory Those who adhere to **resistance theory** do not accept the assumption that what happens in schools perfectly corresponds with or reproduces the relationships in the larger society. They believe that individuals and minority groups can transcend the social messages that the majority or dominant groups in society attempt to convey through their institutions. To this group of theorists, individuals are not passive recipients of the social messages conveyed in schools and other social institutions. On the contrary, human beings are by nature active meaning makers and decision makers. Students can resist these messages and be agents of change in society and in their own lives, no matter what impediments school and society might present.

For example, if poor, working-class, or ethnic-minority students end up in schools with fewer resources and less qualified teachers than their white peers in wealthy suburbs, they may be fully aware that they are not getting the education they have a right to. If teachers impose rigid limitations on the kinds of questions students may ask, if they demand that students merely regurgitate lecture notes on tests instead of inviting their opinions and analysis, students may resist their teachers' views and understand that there are other viewpoints and more information to be had than what the teacher has provided. If no one in a child's family or neighborhood has ever gone to college or considered a professional career, that may not stop the child from having visions for herself that transcend the assumptions and expectations of the people around her.

To the resistance theorists, it is the teacher's responsibility to help students resist socializing norms and expectations that would limit their lives. Resistance theorists ask educators to use critical pedagogy to help their students understand their political and socioeconomic worlds and rise above potential socially limiting effects of overt and hidden curricula. Schools can be places that simply reinforce existing social, economic, and political inequities, or they can be places that promise new ways of life and new futures. The promise of schools to liberate students from old and hardened ways of thinking and doing lies in their intellectual premise—in the capacity for liberating minds. Schools can provide opportunities and models for critical thinking, intellectual courage, social imagination, and active citizenship. In other words, educators can "make hope practical and despair unconvincing," in the words of Henry Giroux.

> [T]eachers as public intellectuals can work to make the pedagogical more political by engaging in a permanent critique of their own scholasticism and promoting critical awareness to end oppression and forms of social life that disfigure contemporary life and pose a threat to any viable notion of democracy. Educators need to provide spaces of resistance within the public schools and the university that take seriously what it means to educate students to question and interrupt authority, recall what is forgotten or ignored, make connections that are otherwise hidden, while simultaneously providing the knowledge and skills that enlarge their sense of the social and their possibilities as viable political agents capable of expanding and deepening democratic public life . . . offering possibilities other than what we are told is possible (Giroux, 2002).

The first step is a **critical pedagogy** that engages students in examining the underlying social and political messages in textbooks, in the media, and in power relations in social institutions, such as school itself and the workplace, as a way of learning to use the important skills of reading, writing, and mathematics. The liberationist educator Paulo Freire, whose work was discussed in Chapter 3, devised a method of teaching reading that drew its vocabulary from the everyday lives of Brazilian peasants: words such as *tenant, plow,* and *labor.* His revolutionary method made the formerly illiterate peasants "critically literate" about their political and economic oppression and more effective and confident in expressing their unhappiness to landowners. When the political implications of his work drew the attention of government officials, Freire was banished from his native Brazil. You may recall that in Chapter 2 we discussed the position of Socrates and Plato that the educated person functions as the conscience and critic of society; what happened to Paulo Freire is an example of the age-old understanding of the risk that the critical educator takes when he challenges the status quo. Applied to today's classrooms, critical pedagogy is used to involve students in reading, writing, and research into the forces at work on environmental issues, racism, and the distribution of wealth in society.

Resistance theorists hold teachers accountable for recognizing their ability to influence political change and for liberating students from the taken-for-granted, and sometimes oppressive, conditions of their lives. As we stated in our guiding principles in Chapter 1, education is a political enterprise (Principle 2), and teachers are agents of personal and social change (Principle 11). We agree with Henry Giroux that effective change requires that educators work with parents, community leaders, and civil rights groups to "arouse public interest over pressing social problems, and use collective means to more fully democratize the commanding institutional economic, cultural, and social structures of the United States and the larger global order" (2002).

In the ancient tradition of Socrates, resistance theorists look to teachers as the conscience of their times. In that role, teachers cannot ignore the political conditions that affect their students' lives, as well as their own work. Sometimes, as Freire showed us, helping students to understand the power relationships at work in the larger society can make the curriculum more meaningful and important to them. At all times, political issues influence the curriculum, the quantity and quality of educational resources available to teachers and their students, and the values and judgments that are communicated inside classrooms.

Structural-functionalism, conflict theory, and resistance theory are united in linking the world of the school to the world of the society beyond it. They diverge in their analysis of society's interest in the schools and in their judgment of the outcomes. As you develop your beliefs about the purpose of education and the role of schools in society, and as you visit schools in various communities, consider whether schools limit students' futures in order to best serve social and economic needs, and whether they should. How can teachers prepare their students for a productive, responsible, adult working life and, at the same time, give them the knowledge and the tools to understand and correct society's faults? To begin to answer this question, teachers must understand the forces at work in society and the ways these forces affect the world of the school through its hidden curriculum. The following section addresses that part of the hidden curriculum that goes beyond the social messages conveyed to students as messages of value and judgment—the moral world of the classroom.

MORAL EDUCATION

> In a suburban middle school, an eighth-grade member of a student committee charged with recommending books for summer reading proposes that two critically acclaimed books be included on the list: Nancy Garden's *Annie on My Mind* and Marilyn Reynolds' *Love Rules.* Both books deal with the issues and problems facing homosexual teenagers. The school principal removes the books from the list, saying they are not appropriate. "We don't teach values," he explains. "When it comes to these kinds of value decisions, they are up to the individuals and their families" (Casselman, 2003, p. 1).

The principal portrayed in this anecdote believes that schools are value-free. Many educators would agree with him, arguing that schools should focus on the teaching of skills and information. But they ignore the fact that even in the subject matter they impose upon students, the materials they use to teach that subject matter, and the way they organize students to learn it, they are making moral judgments. Seemingly simple scheduling decisions such as allocating time for students proficient in reading to tutor classmates who are struggling conveys the message that helping others is important. When most of the students assigned to high school honors classes are white, while low-level classes are filled with students of color, educators might ask questions about what moral and social messages are being sent to students. In his action to ban two books, the school principal is demonstrating his belief that homosexuality is not a fit subject of study for eighth graders.

Schools are moral communities, in which particular values and attitudes are taught and rewarded, and others ignored or punished. In the preface to *The Moral Dimensions of Teaching* (1993), John Goodlad and his coeditors put it this way:

> Many educators and much of the community generally have come to eschew discussion of all matters moral and ethical concerning public schooling, preferring to focus instead on literacy and numeracy (as if such decisions did not rely on normative argument). Teaching the young has moral dimensions, however, simply because education—a deliberate effort to develop values and sensibilities as well as skills—is a moral endeavor (pp. xi–xii).

Addressing the moral questions that underlie school practices and policies is not easy in a pluralistic society that tries to ensure the rights and expression of beliefs of individuals and groups. "Schools and the people in them are caught up in a host of contradictions and the inevitable conflicts between individual and group interests and well-being" (Goodlad, Soder, and Sirotnik, 1993, p. xii). In this section, we will explore the many dimensions of the moral life of schools and classrooms and the debates about how schools can teach values that are consensual, yet respectful of differences.

The Moral Characteristics of Classrooms

"The domain of the moral begins where the domain of the social begins," said Emile Durkheim ([1925] 1961, p. xi). Many of our actions affect others; morality evaluates and regulates those that do. Durkheim thought that to act morally was to act unselfishly, with the interests of others in mind, or, as he said, on behalf of the "collective interest" (p. ix). When six-year-old Jaime pursues his own interests, building his castle and using all the blocks available, he is not acting immorally if he is by himself. As soon as Emma enters the scene, Jaime's interests may conflict with hers. Perhaps she wants to use some blocks to build a house. And there are not enough materials for both of them. Perhaps Emma wants Jaime's help or his company. Is it okay for Jaime to continue doing what he wants? Or should he stop and consider what Emma wants? As classrooms are social places, they are, therefore, places where moral decisions have to be made about what actions are ethical. Strictly speaking, decisions are moral, behaviors are ethical (or not). Social behavior is quite often **ethical behavior** based on moral judgments—behavior that we judge as right or wrong. Sometimes social behavior seems to be a simple matter of adhering to amenities and conventions. Raising your hand before you ask a question in class and keeping your desk neat are social conventions that are not right or wrong in themselves, but rather designed to make life in classrooms manageable. Sometimes the line between convention and morality is blurred, however. Even the hand-raising rule can embody moral messages: a teacher can impose the rule motivated by sheer control or as an occasion for education. Motivated by control, the teacher conveys the message that he is an authority figure who must be obeyed. Motivated by education, he can discuss with the class the reasons for a rule that enables maximum participation in a crowded classroom and asks everyone to listen to and respect each other. Lining up in the hallway can also have moral dimensions; if it is part of a general expectation that students are always regimented, always quiet, and always follow some leader, we would have to ask what they are being taught about their place in life and whether that lesson was moral. In schools, conventions that are incorporated into rules that govern children's conduct take on moral value. Durkheim thought that learning to abide by rules and conventions is a route to a moral character. Codes of conduct teach students discipline and a sense of duty:

> The child must learn respect for the rule; he must learn to do his duty because it is his duty, because he feels obliged to do so even though the task may not seem an easy one. . . . He must come to class regularly, he must arrive at a specified time and with an appropriate bearing and attitude. He must not disrupt things in class. He must have learned his lessons, done his homework, and have done so reasonably well, etc. There are, therefore, a host of obligations that the child is required to shoulder. Together they constitute the discipline of the school. . . . This then is the true function of discipline. . . . It is an instrument . . . of moral education ([1925] 1961, pp. 24, 149).

Whether or not you agree with Durkheim's conclusion that discipline and duty are important values, behind his conclusion was the understanding that classroom routines convey moral meanings. Everyday classroom routines indicate a teacher's style of working with students—her ways of responding to students,

Is this classroom one where raising hands is a rule imposed by the teacher to show her/his authority and control? Or is hand-raising a rule allowing maximum participation and respect for everyone?
Source: © Ellen Senisi/The Image Works

facial expressions, her gestures, and tones of voice—and the model of conduct she presents.

> Our daily actions emit moral messages. We often act unmindful of the fact that our actions presuppose a broader moral framework that says, in effect: this curriculum, this way of teaching, this way of conducting ourselves, and this way of treating human beings, is better than others (Hansen, 1996, p. 72).

While social behavior is often moral, morality is not always social. The decision to "do the right thing" may rest on a set of principles that are either religious or secular. Honesty, for example, may be valued as an abstract principle that includes being honest with yourself. A commitment to personal fitness does not necessarily affect others; nor does a commitment to prayer, or to emotional growth. In the classroom, however, the individual child is a member of an interactive community of youngsters learning how to interact in ways that will benefit them as they develop into happy, productive, and moral members of society. Teachers guide those moral decisions in the direct and indirect teaching of values and in the codes of conduct they institute in their classrooms.

Values **Values** are beliefs about what is important in life and how things should be. Values embody broad principles such as "the sanctity of the individual" or "private property" or "the common good," and include standards by which to judge whether something is right or good. Values vary across cultures and may also change over time. The philosopher Sissela Bok (1995), however, finds three categories of values that are universal: values that foster support and loyalty to their groups (families, communities, nations, and others), values that keep members of a group from doing actions that are harmful to themselves or others, and values that provide standards of justice and fairness. These universal categories apply to schools: Teachers teach students to help their peers and be proud of their class, their school, and their community. They teach students to be careful on the playground, stay away from drugs, and "keep their hands to themselves." And teachers try to demonstrate fairness in the way they interact with students and evaluate their work.

In multicultural, pluralistic American public schools, the question of which values or codes of conduct to teach is not simple. Goodman and Lesnick (2001) describe the moral environment of school as a "swarm of virtues," where values sometimes collide. As described in Chapter 9, some cultures may promote particular values that are opposed to the dominant values in public school classrooms. A student from Argentina, used to an environment where students must help each other to be respected and accepted, may have a difficult time understanding a teacher who stresses the value of "doing your own work." Students from families who are strongly religious may have a difficult time accepting scientific theories as explanations for the origin of life.

The "swarm of virtues" is not limited to culturally different sources. Sometimes a collision of values arises within the different interests of the people involved in the interaction.

> Raymond arrived at school looking tired and upset. He couldn't seem to pay attention to his work all morning, and, at recess, he kept to himself. In fact, he barely spoke to anyone, except to snarl at anyone who came close. Mr. Denis knew from the school records that there were problems

> at home; Raymond's father drank too much and sometimes stayed away from home for days at a time. Mr. Denis wanted to offer his help.
>
> "Is anything wrong at home?" he asked Raymond.
>
> No answer.
>
> "Is your father making things difficult?"
>
> "No," Raymond replied.

Mr. Denis stresses the value of honesty in his classroom. And Raymond has lied to him. But Raymond's mother has told him that family affairs are private, not to be discussed outside the home. To Raymond, the values of privacy and loyalty to family are more important than honesty. Was he wrong to lie to his teacher? Was his teacher wrong to ask him those questions? What if Raymond's friend Ana had overheard the questions and told Mr. Denis privately, later on, that Raymond's father had come home drunk two nights ago and then disappeared? Would her invasion of his privacy be right or wrong? Would she have been "tattling"?

Codes of Ethics Another dimension of the moral life of the classroom is its code of ethics. As Chapter 2 described, ethics refers to the standards that govern the conduct of the members of a group. They provide us with guides to judge whether an action is right or wrong, good or bad. Schools and classrooms have codes of conduct. Sometimes students have input into these codes, which define what behavior is acceptable and encouraged, and what behavior is unacceptable and punished. Teachers behave according to codes of conduct, as well.

A **code of ethics** is a collection of rules that are either presumed to be universal principles or judged to be good because they have positive outcomes. Teachers are themselves bound by professional codes of ethics that guide them in their work. The following Directly from the Source feature contains the code of ethics that the National Education Association (NEA) adopted in 1975 and stands by today. As you read through the NEA Code of Ethics, consider whether your own teachers or those you may be observing have lived up to these standards of conduct.

In the NEA Code of Ethics, the rule that a teacher "shall not misrepresent his/her professional qualifications" is probably based on the premise that honesty is a universal principle, good in its own right. Honesty would be an example of what the philosopher Immanuel Kant (1785) called a "categorical imperative," generally good and true (the example of Raymond, above, notwithstanding). The rule that a teacher "shall make reasonable effort to protect the student from conditions harmful to learning or to health and safety," is an example of a utilitarian, or pragmatic rule, whose value lies in its outcome: that students in schools will have conditions that allow them to learn and be healthy and safe.

The guidelines for what is ethical behavior in classrooms can be taught directly, through systematic instruction, or contained within the hidden curriculum as "taken-for-granted" rules. Many teachers post codes of conduct on their bulletin boards, reviewing their expectations with students at the beginning of the year and discussing with them the reasons behind the rules and the consequences for breaking them. To be based on *moral* principles, these codes of conduct must be more than mere conventions ("you must raise your hand to be recognized") but must embody principles of rightness and goodness—virtues—that the teacher has thought about and wants to instill in his students. Other teachers invite students into the process of creating the classroom rules, believing that codes of ethics are

DIRECTLY FROM THE SOURCE

Code of Ethics of the Education Profession, National Education Association

Source: Adopted by the NEA 1975 Representative Assembly (National Education Association (1975), Washington, DC).

Preamble

The educator, believing in the worth and dignity of each human being, recognizes the supreme importance of the pursuit of truth, devotion to excellence, and the nurture of the democratic principles. Essential to these goals is the protection of freedom to learn and to teach and the guarantee of equal educational opportunity for all. The educator accepts the responsibility to adhere to the highest ethical standards.

The educator recognizes the magnitude of the responsibility inherent in the teaching process. The desire for the respect and confidence of one's colleagues, of students, of parents, and of the members of the community provides the incentive to attain and maintain the highest possible degree of ethical conduct. The Code of Ethics of the Education Profession indicates the aspiration of all educators and provides standards by which to judge conduct.

The remedies specified by the NEA and/or its affiliates for the violation of any provision of this Code shall be exclusive and no such provision shall be enforceable in any form other than the one specifically designated by the NEA or its affiliates.

Principle I

Commitment to the Student

The educator strives to help each student realize his or her potential as a worthy and effective member of society. The educator therefore works to stimulate the spirit of inquiry, the acquisition of knowledge and understanding, and the thoughtful formulation of worthy goals. In fulfillment of the obligation to the student, the educator—

1. Shall not unreasonably restrain the student from independent action in the pursuit of learning.
2. Shall not unreasonably deny the student's access to varying points of view.
3. Shall not deliberately suppress or distort subject matter relevant to the student's progress.
4. Shall make reasonable effort to protect the student from conditions harmful to learning or to health and safety.
5. Shall not intentionally expose the student to embarrassment or disparagement.
6. Shall not on the basis of race, color, creed, sex, national origin, marital status, political or religious beliefs, family, social or cultural background, or sexual orientation, unfairly—
   a. Exclude any student from participation in any program
   b. Deny benefits to any student
   c. Grant any advantage to any student

not absolute and should not reflect the values of the teacher alone. In discussing the moral basis of rules and negotiating consequences, teacher and students are engaged in an approach to moral education based more on the power of reason than on a set of virtues.

While "moral education takes place, willed or not, planned or not," (Goodman and Lesick, 2001, p. 3), those schools and teachers who take seriously their role as moral educators have adopted several different approaches. These approaches reflect fundamental differences in beliefs about the nature of morality and about the school's responsibility to teach it.

7. Shall not use professional relationships with students for private advantage.
8. Shall not disclose information about students obtained in the course of professional service unless disclosure serves a compelling professional purpose or is required by law.

Principle II

Commitment to the Profession

The education profession is vested by the public with a trust and responsibility requiring the highest ideals of professional service. In the belief that the quality of the services of the education profession directly influences the nation and its citizens, the educator shall exert every effort to raise professional standards, to promote a climate that encourages the exercise of professional judgment, to achieve conditions that attract persons worthy of the trust to careers in education, and to assist in preventing the practice of the profession by unqualified persons.

In fulfillment of the obligation to the profession, the educator—

1. Shall not in an application for a professional position deliberately make a false statement or fail to disclose a material fact related to competency and qualifications.
2. Shall not misrepresent his/her professional qualifications.
3. Shall not assist any entry into the profession of a person known to be unqualified in respect to character, education, or other relevant attribute.
4. Shall not knowingly make a false statement concerning the qualifications of a candidate for a professional position.
5. Shall not assist a noneducator in the unauthorized practice of teaching.
6. Shall not disclose information about colleagues obtained in the course of professional service unless disclosure serves a compelling professional purpose or is required by law.
7. Shall not knowingly make false or malicious statements about a colleague.
8. Shall not accept any gratuity, gift, or favor that might impair or appear to influence professional decisions or action.

A Closer Look at the Issues

1. Have the teachers in your own school experience or teachers you may be observing now lived up to this code of ethics?
2. In which standards does the NEA code refer to subject matter? In your own words, what is the teacher's commitment to the content information that he or she is teaching?
3. Write your own standard to address an aspect of teaching that you think has been omitted from the code.

Approaches to Moral Education

Throughout the history of public schools in the United States, philosophers and moral educators have struggled with the question of whether there are broad universal values and ethical principles that teachers can refer to that are acceptable across cultures, times, and places; or whether what is right and good depends on the circumstances of culture, place, time, and particular situations. They differ also on the best way to teach children to think and act morally. Some see moral education as teaching children habits of thinking and acting in good and right ways. To them, moral education is about *doing* the right thing.

In 1924 William Hutchins (1924) devised "The Children's Morality Code," in which he told children how they could behave like "good Americans." Good Americans, Hutchins told children, control themselves. Therefore, children should pledge to "control my tongue and . . . not allow it to speak mean, vulgar, or profane words. I will think before I speak. I will tell the truth and nothing but the truth." Good Americans also try to gain and keep good health ("I will keep my clothes, my body, and my mind clean"). They are kind, they play fair ("I will not cheat. I will treat my opponents with courtesy. I will be a good loser or a generous winner"), are self-reliant, do their duty, are reliable ("I will be careful with money, I will do promptly what I have promised to do"), are true ("I will avoid hasty opinion"), are good workers ("I will not be satisfied to do slipshod, lazy, and merely passable work"), cooperate with others, and are loyal ("I will gladly obey my parents. I will do my best to help the friendly relations of our country with every other country").

More recently, Nel Noddings (1992, 1995) asks teachers to provide opportunities for children to demonstrate caring. She says that the curriculum should be organized around themes of care, rather than around the traditional academic disciplines, with academic content and skills taught in the context of caring relationships. Children should examine and practice caring for themselves, for each other, for their community, and for the earth. She argues that all children should be engaged in activities that reflect caring, and that moral education should be the main goal of education. Her work is excerpted at the end of this chapter as a Critical Reading.

While Hutchins, Noddings, and others view moral education as teaching children perspectives and habits of behavior, others see it as developing in them the capacity for moral *thinking*. In the view of cognitive-developmental moral theorists and promoters of the "values clarification" approach, the teacher's role in moral education is not to present particular values but to guide children to think about moral questions and come to conclusions based on higher-order reasoning. Psychologists Jean Piaget, Lawrence Kohlberg, and Carol Gilligan explored the ways that children make moral judgments at various ages and stages and experimented with ways that teachers might enhance the level of their thinking. Simon, Howe, and Kirschenbaum wanted teachers to help children think about what their values were, consider how their values affected their lives, and be willing to articulate and share them. The work of each of these developmentalists will be discussed in more detail later in this section.

A third group of moral educators focuses on the development of character in children, their very *being*. William Bennett and Thomas Lickona share the belief that schools should demonstrate, model, and directly teach a constellation of traits that presumably make up a person of "good character." These traits might include responsibility, fairness, integrity (both personal and intellectual), benevolence, bravery, tolerance, persistence, and altruism, among others. Some schools expose students to these traits by highlighting one trait at a time. A New Jersey school system celebrates a "trait of the month," with each school displaying banners advertising the trait and using the public address system to "broadcast" it. The schools also display literature and other materials related to the trait in the school library, provide whole-school speakers and dramatic presentations, and encourage classroom activities related to the trait, including researching famous people who display it. The idea is that students will be exposed to these traits several times throughout their experience in the school system.

There are many programs and products available to teachers who want to include character education in their curricula. Some use children's literature as models for teaching particular virtues. Others offer role-plays and simulations. Still others entail the direct teaching of principles. Websites to Explore at the end of this chapter lists the addresses for several character education programs.

The Virtues Approach Those who want teachers to help children "do" the right thing and "be" moral subscribe to a **virtues approach** to moral education. They find little difficulty in defining what it means to do or be good, differing only in the particular list of virtues that they would have children learn. William J. Bennett, secretary of education under President Ronald Reagan and later "drug czar" for President George H.W. Bush is convinced that the moral good is, for the most part, clear, absolute, and universal. He says, for example, that few people would argue about whether honesty is a part of good character, or whether courage is admirable (1993). A proponent of using the humanities to provide children with great models of truth and morality, Bennett collected classic stories to provide moral models for children. *The Book of Virtues* (1993) is a contemporary version of McGuffey's Reader, a collection of stories that Bennett feels present clear moral issues and instruct children in what are clear moral choices. "Children must have at their disposal a stock of examples illustrating what we see to be right and wrong, good and bad—examples illustrating that, in many instances, what is morally right and wrong can indeed be known and promoted." In his stories, good behavior is rewarded and bad deeds are punished.

The stories in Bennett's book are grouped into chapters whose titles are virtues: self-discipline, compassion, responsibility, friendship, work, courage, perseverance, honesty, loyalty, and faith. Each chapter has an introduction that describes the importance and universality of the virtue. The section on self-discipline begins: "There is much unhappiness in the world because of failures to control tempers, appetites, passions, and impulses. 'Oh, if only I had stopped myself,' is a familiar refrain" (1993, p. 22). Following Aristotle (see Chapter 2) and Durkheim, Bennett believes that we learn to discipline or "order our souls" through precept and practice. Teachers should provide both, furnishing students with principles and precepts in literature and history, and providing them with opportunities for practice by imposing clear and enforced rules of conduct. Critics have cited Bennett's emphasis on stories from the Western (European) literary tradition and the preponderance of male characters. They say he oversimplifies moral issues that can be far more complex than the stories portray. However, his book and its companion, *The Children's Book of Virtues* (1995), demonstrate how literature can be used to provoke discussions of moral issues and teach the consequences of one's actions.

Matthew Josephson's popular Character Counts program (see Websites to Explore) promotes "Six Pillars of Character": trustworthiness, respect, responsibility, fairness, caring, and citizenship. The pillars are presented as objective consensual values, enduring and universal, that distinguish right from wrong and define good character. The program "works to overcome the false but surprisingly powerful notion that no single value is intrinsically superior to another; that ethical values vary by race, class, gender and politics; that greed and fairness, cheating and honesty carry the same moral weight, simply depending on one's perspective and immediate needs." Josephson claims that his comprehensive program is helping to decrease the number of students who cheat, steal, and lie, and has also reduced drug use, detentions and suspensions, teasing, and the use of fake identification among students who attend Character Counts schools.

Like Bennett, Josephson believes that virtue is not inborn, but must be taught directly. We turn now to a different point of view—one that believes the business of schools is not to instill virtues, but to teach students to think about them.

Philosophy for Children The heated debates during the 1960s about whether the Vietnam War was moral convinced Matthew Lipman that many Americans could not think critically or formulate logical arguments. He thought that the discipline of philosophy had much to offer a democratic public where citizens were charged with making important decisions governing their own behavior and affecting the welfare of society. But it was too late to try to improve the thinking of adults; habits of clear thinking should be taught early. He thought the teaching of logic could begin as soon as children were capable of abstract thinking. Lipman developed an approach called **philosophy for children,** centered on a series of books for children ages eleven and older whose stories stimulated philosophical thinking. His first novel was *Harry Stottlemeier's Discovery* (1974), which taught the principles of logic in simple language describing everyday events in children's lives. His second novel, *Lisa* (1976), presented stories for older children that contained moral questions and ethical dilemmas. Lipman credits John Dewey and Lev Vygotsky as his sources of inspiration—specifically, their emphasis on teaching for thinking, rather than for memorizing.

Lipman's novels are at the heart of his philosophy for children movement, based at New Jersey's Montclair State University, where he is a professor. Philosophy for children engages philosophers in training teachers to use philosophical inquiry to lead their students to form concepts and ask and analyze questions. Lipman says children wonder about many of the same concepts that philosophers work at defining—truth, goodness, and justice. Using the novels, teachers and students create a community of inquiry where all members listen with respect and openness to each other's ideas and try to support their own with evidence and good reason. Children read *Lisa* aloud, raising their own questions and discovering general rules of morality using the principles of logic.

Rather than present lessons and moral precepts, Lipman wants to offer children guidelines and tools of inquiry so that they can come to their own reasonable conclusions about moral issues. Lipman does not advocate particular moral stances or virtues; he does, however, say there are right ways of thinking about moral issues, ways that philosophy can teach. The characters in *Lisa* debate questions such as: Can we love animals but eat them, too? Does giving someone something mean that they should give you something in return? This textbook's website includes an excerpt from Chapter 2 of *Lisa* in which Lisa, Harry, and their friends consider the second question. As you read the excerpt, consider what your contributions might be to the issues raised in the episode if you were one of Lisa's friends.

The Moral Development Approach Many would say that a basic aspect of moral behavior is the ability to think in morally sophisticated ways. Several psychologists concerned with the school's role in moral education believe that debates about which values schools should be promoting is neither appropriate nor central to the moral responsibility of educators. These psychologists look at students' willingness to act morally as the result of their understanding of moral questions, an understanding that develops over time with the help of adults. According to this **moral development approach,** teachers are important guides for children, whose moral thinking is expanding with their experience and their ability to comprehend abstract principles. Instead of directly teaching moral precepts ("be respectful," "don't lie"), the teacher's role as a moral educator is the same as it is for academic education: to create opportunities for children to enhance the level of their moral thinking.

Emile Durkheim ([1925] 1961), mentioned earlier in this chapter, said that because children were part of a social group, they learned the norms of the group as a preparation for membership in the larger society. But Jean Piaget (1965) rejected the idea that children simply internalized the norms and values that operated around them. He believed that children, and adults, arrived at their own values and moral decisions based on their struggle to solve problems and come to fair solutions. He extended his work on children's understanding of concepts to include their understanding of moral ideas. Based on his observations of children's application of rules when playing games, he decided that morality, too, is a developmental process. He concluded that children's thinking, including thinking about moral issues, proceeded through distinct stages, from concrete rules to abstract conceptions. Teachers, said Piaget, should provide students with opportunities to discover what is right and fair through problem solving, rather than indoctrination. In the 1970s, Lawrence Kohlberg and Carol Gilligan, developmental psychologists, expanded upon Piaget's conclusions and applied them to school settings.

Lawrence Kohlberg In the 1970s, Lawrence Kohlberg gained iconic status in the field of psychology for his groundbreaking theory of moral development. Kohlberg extended Piaget's theories to adult stages, researching how young people and adults answered questions about justice, human rights, and equality (Kohlberg and Turiel, 1971). Not content to limit his work to theory, Kohlberg wanted to use his research to help individuals make principled moral decisions and take principled moral action.

Kohlberg did not see morality as something adults impose on children, as in the view of psychoanalysts and sociologists like Durkheim, or as something learned through reinforcement or to avoid bad feelings, as the behaviorists believed. Instead, he thought that children made their own moral judgments. To Piaget and Kohlberg, cognitive development in general, and moral thinking in particular, entails reacting to experiences in our environment with organized thought limited by our particular developmental stage. Like Piaget, Kohlberg believed that when children are faced with new information that contradicts their previous world-view, they come to new conclusions based on a process called "equilibration." He used this phenomenon as the basis for his moral education strategy, presenting groups of students with moral dilemmas, and inviting them to debate solutions. Listening to the higher-order thinking of their peers—ideas that they would not have considered by themselves—enhanced the level of their original thinking. Kohlberg thought even young children were "moral philosophers," but that their reasoning depended on both their cognitive stage and the models of thinking present in their environment (Power, Higgins, and Kohlberg, 1989).

Kohlberg's initial research studied the responses of white boys to the dilemma of a fictitious Mr. Heinz, who steals a drug from a pharmacy to save his dying wife. Heinz cannot afford the exorbitant price that the pharmacist charges for the medicine that will save her. Refused legal remedies and unable to borrow the money, he

Table 10.1 Kohlberg's Hierarchy of Moral Reasoning

	Level	Stage	Social Orientation
Pre-Conventional	1	Obedience and Punishment	"I will be nice to my sister because my father said I should. If I'm not, I will have to go to my room."
	2	Instrumentalism and Exchange	"I am nice to my sister because she is nice to me," or, "I hit my sister because she hits me."
Conventional	3	Social Approval	"Being nice to my sister will get me my mother's approval," or "Being mean (or nice) to my sister will make me look good to my friends."
	4	Law and Order	"Helping my sister clean the table after dinner is right because that's the rule in my family."
Post-Conventional	5	Social Contract, Democracy	"Even though I don't want to help my sister with the dishes, I should, because everyone in my family needs to help keep the house clean."
	6	Universal Moral Principle	"It's important to be good to my sister because people should be kind."

From: *Moral Development and Behavior, Theory, Research, and Social Issues,* 1st edition by T. Lickona, copyright © 1976. Reprinted with permission of Wadsworth, a division of Thomson Learning: www.thomsonrights.com. Fax: 800-730-2215.

takes the law into his own hands and breaks into the pharmacy to steal the drug. Kohlberg asked the students whether Heinz had done right or wrong, but he was more interested in the reasons they gave than in their conclusion. Some said Heinz was wrong to steal the drug because he would end up in jail or because it was against the law or because personal property and privacy were individual rights. Others said Heinz was right because his wife would otherwise die, or because they loved each other, or because human life was more important than individual property. These answers reflected a three-level, six-stage hierarchy of moral reasoning, described in Table 10.1.

Table 10.1 shows examples of the types of reasoning made at each level of moral reasoning. Notice that a child who is able to conceive of general rules and the need for them (Stage 4, Law and Order) will conclude that "Helping my sister clean the table after dinner is right" because of the family rule. At the Post-Conventional Stage 5, the child understands the abstract idea that a society can function well only if everyone puts the welfare of the group ahead of their individual interests. Those individuals who attain the highest level of moral reasoning, according to Kohlberg, display a conscience and internalized ideals that transcend particular circumstances. The child will be kind to others because being kind is always the right thing to do; if she isn't kind, she will feel guilty. Applied to the Heinz dilemma, the argument that one can break the law when it will help one's beloved wife is a Stage 3 argument, while the argument that a human life takes priority over individual property places justice above unjust laws and, thus, is a Stage 6 argument.

Teachers who want to use Kohlberg's technique to raise the level of their students' moral reasoning can create their own dilemmas for discussion related to the students' lives in or out of the classroom. One example follows:

> Charlene gave her homework to her friend Emilio. Emilio was unable to do his own homework because he spent the night comforting his mother, who is severely depressed. Charlene knows that Emilio does not want to share his family problems with the teacher. Was she right to give Emilio his homework?

As you reflect on your own student experiences and observe children in today's classrooms, we encourage you to develop some scenarios that would engage students in meaningful moral discussions. You might try them out with your classmates and colleagues to reveal the questions, concerns, and thought processes that characterize moral decision-making. Listening to the discussion, try to find examples of various stages of moral thinking. Are your peers influenced by others' higher-order comments to move to a higher level of moral reasoning?

Carol Gilligan Kohlberg was less interested in his subjects' actual choices than in their moral reasoning, an indication that he opposed the kind of moral education that would have teachers teaching a set of "virtues" directly or through rewards. However, his highest stage tells us he believed in a set of "universal moral principles" transcending culture, gender, time, and place. He presumed that justice was more important, for example, than caring, and that higher-level thinking would lead anyone to that conclusion. His strongest critic was one of his former research assistants, later a professor of educational psychology, Carol Gilligan. In a now-classic book called *In a Different Voice* (1982), Gilligan challenged Kohlberg's research design, pointing out that all his subjects were male.

Gilligan's own research showed that female students' responses to moral dilemmas could not easily be categorized within the hierarchy of thinking that Kohlberg had designed. She concluded that males and females differed in their moral decision-making. When she presented young women with the Heinz dilemma, for example, many of them struggled to come to a firm conclusion about whether his theft was right or wrong. "It depends," they often said. Their concern was how Heinz felt about his wife, about the nature of their relationship, about the difficult conflict between doing for others and doing for themselves. Moral decisions were not black-and-white; there were shades of gray to consider.

To Gilligan's female subjects, an abstract concept like justice had no value in itself; what mattered were the real consequences for real human beings. Gilligan thinks that women appear hesitant and indecisive, even morally undeveloped, because they consider the complexities of relationships, the nature of people's feelings, and the social contexts of individual actions. In Kohlberg's terms, using his hierarchy, many women would be accused of being "stuck" at Stage 3, where reasoning addresses social relationships. While men may conceive of morality as fairness, rights, and rules, many women conceive of morality as compassion, care, and responsibility for others.

According to Gilligan, men's "justice orientation" has devalued women's "responsibility orientation," an orientation that has traditionally benefited the men (and others) in women's lives. Many men concerned with improving the quality of their own lives and of human welfare in general are now concluding that an ethic of care may lead to a healthier, happier, more peaceful human existence. When Daniel Goleman published *Emotional Intelligence* in 1995, the book was considered revolutionary. Howard Gardner (1993) gives "interpersonal intelligence" a status equal to "logical/mathematical intelligence." Ironically, says Gilligan, "[t]he discovery now being celebrated by men in mid-life of the importance of intimacy, relationships, and care is something that women have known from the beginning" (1982, p. 17).

Gilligan's concern is that girls' and women's "voices" have been lost in the moral development debate. She finds that, while young girls are confident about their abilities to stand up for themselves and others, adolescence for girls brings with it a period of self-doubt and denial of their own voice. Because women learn to nurture and put others before themselves, the outcome can be a desire to avoid conflict and refrain from causing pain, a suppression of their own needs, and silence. Schools, Gilligan says, have too often helped to silence girls, in insisting on "objectivity," dismissing personal feelings, and valuing autonomy over relationships. (In the authors' own high school educations, for example, we were told never to use the pronoun *I* in our essays.) Today's educators can help girls value their concern for others, retain a sense of self, and speak about what they think and feel. Gilligan asks teachers to listen to girls' (and boys') voices, to help them make personal connections with the subject matter of the curriculum, and to accept multiple points of view and shades of gray.

Critics of the Moral Development Approach Kohlberg's and Gilligan's developmental approach to moral education has its critics. Skeptical of the universality of the psychologists' described stages, some question the validity of the moral development research (Sommers, 2000). Others argue that moral development is not merely a cognitive process where thinking leads to moral actions, but is also emotional and social, depending on role models, direct teaching, and positive experiences (Ryan and Bohlin, 1999). In Kohlberg's "just democratic community," students participating as full decision makers may in fact need additional direct adult guidance: At the first meeting in one high school, students invited to choose a last-period elective from a given list decided that anyone who did not like any of the electives offered could leave school early (Power, Higgins, and Kohlberg, 1989). Finally, there is the argument that moral reasoning does not necessarily lead to moral behavior. If what we want is a nation of people who are willing to act on the courage of their convictions, teaching children to think morally is not enough. Values should be embodied in ethical conduct. Instructional strategies such as cooperative learning and schoolwide activities such as community service are ways to give students opportunities to practice moral behavior.

Urging educators and families to "overcome the culture of indulgence in America's homes and schools," William Damon (1995) asks us not to choose between teaching children to behave morally and teaching children to think about morality. He wants educators to resist polarizing children's capacity for careful reflection and their need for deeply embedded, continually practiced, good habits. As they mature into adulthood, they need to exercise both:

> In general, the vast majority of human social life is harmonious and well-regulated, beginning early in childhood. Children do not routinely rob, kill or lie. . . . They acquire, through nature and practice, habitual patterns of emotional and behavioral responding. For most children most of the time, such patterns trigger prosocial acts such as helping or sharing. . . . but [c]onditions change, and unexpected new circumstances suddenly appear. Strong new temptations may arise. Old habits become tested, or they no longer apply. At such junctures, children must turn to reflection in order to appraise their alternatives. These periods of reflective awareness can be crucial during key turning points in life. The deliberative choices that they engender can lead children to whole new levels of moral awareness and commitment (1995, p. 155).

The Debate About Character Education

President Bush's No Child Left Behind Act includes a "Partnerships in Character Education" provision (U.S. Dept. of Education, 2001, Sec. 5431) that awards grants to schools that will work with other community institutions to design and implement "character education" programs. The schools may choose to focus on select "elements of character" from the list of suggested elements that the federal law provides, as long as they "consider the views of the parents of the students to be taught under the program and the views of the students." The list of elements of character includes the following: caring, civic virtue and citizenship, justice and fairness, respect, responsibility, trustworthiness, giving, and "any other elements deemed appropriate by the eligible entity." Character education programs implemented under these grants must have clear, "scientifically based" (a NCLB phrase) objectives and will be evaluated according to whether they improve student discipline, academic achievement, and student and staff morale; increase participation in extracurricular activities; involve parents and the community; and result in a climate of inclusiveness and acceptance for all students.

In delineating so clearly the "elements of character" and the criteria for the evaluation of character education programs, the federal government presumes that character is something that can be objectively described in ways that most people would accept. It also assumes that extracurricular activity participation and academic achievement are potentially measures of improved character. This point of view holds that, while traditional American institutions such as the family and the church taught and reinforced these traits in the past, their lessons have been weakened by a combination of factors, including declining church attendance and a population increasingly diverse in both values and family structure. Children are faced with too many distractions, too many temptations, and too little guidance in navigating their way toward good decisions. The school captures their attention every day, and offers many opportunities for teaching positive social behavior and for learning about moral issues. Advocates of the direct teaching of character argue that the school is ideally positioned to fill in the gaps left by these other institutions.

The Direct Teaching of Character One advocate of the direct, systematic teaching of character is Thomas Lickona. He argues that children need specific instruction and constant practice in behaving ethically. Values such as honesty, fairness, tolerance, self-discipline, compassion, and cooperation—once taught without question in America's public schools—must again be carefully explained, modeled, and practiced in the classroom. Lickona blames the decline of the moral educational role of schools on several factors, including Darwinism, the philosophy of logical positivism, "personalism," and the increasing pluralism of the population.

> Darwinism introduced a new metaphor—evolution—that led people to see all things, including morality, as being in flux. The philosophy of logical positivism, arriving at American universities from Europe, asserted a radical distinction between *facts* (which could be scientifically proven) and *values* (which positivism held were mere expressions of feeling, not objective truth). As a result of positivism, morality was relativized and privatized—made to seem a matter of personal "value judgment," not a subject for public debate and transmission through the schools. In the 1960s, a worldwide rise in personalism celebrated the worth, autonomy, and subjectivity of the person, emphasizing individual rights and freedom over responsibility . . . delegitimiz[ing] moral authority, erod[ing] belief in objective moral norms, turn[ing] people inward toward self-fulfillment, weaken[ing] social commitments (for example, to marriage and parenting), and fuel[ing] the socially destabilizing sexual revolution. Finally, the rapidly intensifying pluralism of American society (Whose values should we teach?) and the increasing secularization of the public arena (Won't moral education violate the separation of church and state?), became two more barriers to achieving the moral consensus indispensable for character education in the public schools (1993, p. 6).

Lickona ascribes "the return of character education" to society's concern for "the decline of the family," "troubling trends in youth character," and "a recovery of shared, objectively important ethical values essential for our survival" (1993). To those who argue against a common set of values, he says that respect, responsibility, trustworthiness, fairness, caring, and civic virtue are perennial values that meet the test of reversibility, defined as the question, Would you want to be treated this way? and are universal, answering the question, Would you want all persons to act this way in similar situations? (1993, p. 8).

An effective character education program addresses the cognitive, affective, and behavioral domains of learning (See Chapter 5). Cognitively, children must be able to recognize moral dilemmas, see other points of view, and make thoughtful decisions. Affectively, children must be capable of empathy and humility, be able to control their emotions, and feel responsible for doing the right thing. Finally, knowing and feeling must lead to moral action. Children must be morally competent—for example, be able to listen and work with others—and have good moral habits. Lickona calls on schools to develop a systematic and comprehensive approach to character education, including adult modeling of moral behavior, the creation of a "moral community" where students respect and care about each other, rules that enforce the practice of moral discipline with children participating in decision making, the direct teaching of values through the curriculum—for example, through literature and history—the use of cooperative learning, and the teaching of conflict resolution (1993, p. 9).

There are many character education programs and curricula that propose to carry out Lickona's goals. Character Counts is a nonprofit coalition of schools and community agencies committed to teaching what they call the six pillars of character: trustworthiness, respect, responsibility, fairness, caring, and citizenship. Its Los Angeles office offers training seminars and materials, including books, videotapes, audiotapes, posters, play scripts, values kits, sheet music, and clothing. Willard Daggett's International Center for Leadership in Education in Rexford, New York, has a character education program built on the guiding principles of adaptability, compassion, contemplation, courage, honesty, initiative, loyalty, optimism, perseverance, respect, responsibility, and trustworthiness. The International Center's approach to character education relies on character-centered teaching that integrates these guiding principles into school curricula. Character-centered teaching asks that teachers recognize their influence as role models and character "coaches" and provides training in specific character education methods that the center claims will lead to academic success.

The National Center for Character Education offers teacher training programs and K–12 curriculum materials that address seven "core ethical values" (subdivided into "bedrock ethics" and "super values") linked to body parts: positive mental attitude (mind), respect (eyes and ears), integrity (mouth), compassion (heart), cooperation (hands), perseverance (stomach), initiative (feet). California's Jefferson Center for Character Education purports to teach children to accept the consequences of their actions using the "S.T.A.R." decision-making model: Stop, Think, Act, and Review. It assumes a universal set of eight common values: honesty, responsibility, courage, justice, respect, integrity, caring, and politeness. The Jefferson program teaches that attendance, punctuality, and reliability are aspects of personal responsibility. In its S.T.A.R. curriculum (Success Through Accepting Responsibility), teachers present themes such as, "Be On Time," "Be Prepared," "Be a Tough Worker," "Be a Goal Setter," and "Be Friendly." The Ethics Resource Center of Washington, D.C., offers Maximize the Moment, a curriculum for third grade through high school. This program offers schools weekly maxims with classroom discussion guides and links to related websites. Maxims may include, for example, "You never lose until you stop trying" (Chicago Bears coach Mike Ditka) or "The time is always right to do what is right" (Martin Luther King, Jr.).

The systematic approach to character education represented by the programs mentioned here is controversial. Many argue that the elements or principles or core values or maxims that make up "good character" are debatable and are the province of the home, rather than the school. Some claim that good character cannot be taught at all. Critics point to lists of values that govern programs such as the state of Georgia's. The state's 1997 list of forty-two officially adopted values included many traits that would be universally accepted, such as fairness, honesty, and kindness, and others that could be problematic or possibly even offensive, such as patriotism, cleanliness, and respect for the creator. In attempting to define "respect for the creator" in a way that would appeal to everyone, the state board said,

> [O]ur most basic freedoms and rights are not granted to us from the government but they are intrinsically ours. . . . This is to say that the founders of the republic recognized a higher authority, a power greater than themselves that endowed every human being with certain unalienable rights that no government or legal document could ever revoke or take away. In the Declaration of Independence Thomas Jefferson names this life form that permeates the universe and from which our unalienable rights stem the "creator," "nature's God," and the

> "supreme judge of the world." If we are to respect life, the natural rights of all people and the authority which the founders based their legal opinions on concerning our separation from Great Britain then there must be a respect for that creator from which all our rights flow. This cannot be interpreted as a promotion of religion or even as a promotion of the belief in a personal God, but only as an acknowledgment that the intrinsic worth of every individual derives from no government, person or group of persons, but is something that each of us is born with and which no thing and no one can ever deprive us of (Scerenko, 1997).

You will recall from Chapter 7 that the inclusion of religious references in character education programs is an old phenomenon in the history of public education in the United States. Many people find it difficult to consider character education devoid of religious roots, whether or not religion is actually mentioned in program materials and school policies. Others find the roots of character education in the inevitable moral life of a classroom community; we now turn to this more holistic perspective on character education.

Character Education as Democratic Community Alfie Kohn is a well-known critic of the direct teaching of character education. His concerns about teaching a set of "universal" or "natural" values are not appeased by statements such as those made by the state of Georgia, above. Kohn agrees that schools should, and do, in a broad sense, help children grow into good people. However, he is direct in his challenge to those who promote a narrower, more proscribed program of values instruction:

> What goes by the name of character education nowadays is, for the most part, a collection of exhortations and extrinsic inducements designed to make children work harder and do what they're told. Even when other values are also promoted—caring or fairness, say—the preferred method of instruction is tantamount to indoctrination. The point is to drill students in specific behaviors rather than to engage them in deep, critical reflection about certain ways of being (1997, p. 429).

Kohn cites examples of curricula that lead children to the conclusion that, "If it's Tuesday, it must be Honesty [Day]" (1997). He blames right-wing religious groups, "orthodox behaviorists," and curriculum publishers for promulgating the idea that children will not be good unless they are rewarded for being good; if they are rewarded for being good, they will become good people. Long a critic of teaching strategies that reward children for reading with pizza coupons, or acts of kindness with stars on a wall chart, Kohn says the kind of extrinsic reinforcement recommended by packaged character education programs "punish by rewards." Kohn supports his argument with reference to studies that show that people who have been rewarded for doing something good are not likely to think of themselves as caring or helpful people in general, and will more likely ascribe their behavior to the reward they received. Kindness cannot be bought, he says.

In addition to his criticism that most systematic character education programs rely on extrinsic rewards for practicing specific values-related behaviors, Kohn decries their social and political naiveté. The Character Counts program mentioned previously, for example, assumes that children can rise above negative social influences by the exercise of free will, an assumption that Kohn says represents a conservative political ideology. Moreover,

"That is the correct answer, Billy, but I'm afraid you don't win anything for it."

Source: © *The New Yorker* Collection 1986 Lee Lorenz from cartoonbank.com.

> If a program proceeds by trying to "fix the kids"—as do almost all brands of character education—it ignores the accumulated evidence from the field of social psychology demonstrating that much of how we act and who we are reflects the situations in which we find ourselves. . . . Set up children in an extended team competition at summer camp and you will elicit unprecedented levels of aggression. Assign adults to roles of prisoners or guards in a mock jail, and they will start to become their roles. Move people to a small town, and they will be more likely to rescue a stranger in need (1997, p. 430).

Kohn asks, "Whose values are being taught?" in systematic character education programs. He worries that the values promoted by most character education programs are really precepts supported by dominant business, industry, and religious leaders. "Good citizenship" can mean compliance. "Responsibility" can mean thoughtless conformity. While character education programs stress respect, responsibility, and citizenship, "these are slippery terms," he says, "frequently used as euphemisms for uncritical deference to authority. . . . I once taught at a high school where the principal frequently exhorted students to 'take responsibility.' By this he meant specifically that they should turn in their friends who used drugs" (1997, p. 432).

In contrast to programs such as Character Counts and the Jefferson Institute, Kohn supports a broader definition of character education, one that considers students to be full members of democratic school communities and gives them authority to participate in devising and evaluating the rules that govern their community. He is not against the idea of core values, but would limit them to skills that allow students to think critically and consider the welfare of others. He cites New York's Central Park East Secondary School, where Deborah Meier and Paul Schwarz offered two core values: empathy and skepticism. They wanted students to be able to see a situation from the eyes of another and to question the validity of what they encounter.

In Kohn's opinion, children learn right from wrong in natural environments. In fact, he thinks that children are basically good, and capable of high-level moral thinking. Promoting his alternative, holistic, vision of moral education, Kohn says educators must help students construct meaning about moral concepts that they share, plan, and reflect together. They need practice in "perspective-taking," listening, and participating in group discussions. Adults have crucial roles to play as role models, posers of challenging questions, and aids in helping children understand the effects of their behavior on others and the nature of experiences different from their own. He advocates regular class meetings, the use of literature to address moral themes, and a restructuring of classrooms to allow children more choice and more decision-making power. Agreeing with Kohn, Robert Nash wrote "There Is No One Best Way to Teach Moral Character" (2003), and he describes three paradoxes in character education that must be acknowledged and discussed. The first paradox, he says, is that we must teach virtues and ideals that we hold dear, knowing that it is possible that these virtues and ideals may be unteachable: "I know of no convincing empirical evidence that didactic teaching . . . has much effect on the actual formation of students' characters and subsequent moral behavior." The second paradox is that, "the less calculated character education is, the more effective it might actually be"; however, even in a "seamless, interconnecting moral web" of school, college, family, neighborhood, church, and peers, where virtues are "taught or caught," the formation of character is ultimately complex and unpredictable. Finally, Nash's third paradox is that "the character education most suitable for a reconstructed democracy might not be one that teaches a bag of predetermined dispositions, ideals, or practices, but rather one that grows out of a free-flowing, undominated, to-and-fro dialogue, necessitating continual compromise and consensus" (2003).

For Nash as well as Kohn, then, our democracy calls for virtues that prepare people to engage in active debate over issues such as the content of good character and the way to instill it. These virtues include courage, self-respect, hope, friendship, and trust.

Religion, the Schools, and the Law

In Chapters 7, 8, and 9, we explored the role and responsibility of the school in society and concluded that American public schools have always tried to influence the moral character of their students and, by extension, the nation. You may recall from reading those chapters that in early times, the schools unabashedly promoted a set of Judeo-Christian values that were assumed to underlie the "American" way of life. The idea that values could have nonreligious roots—in understandings about right and proper ethical behavior among individuals in a society, for example—was not part of the thinking of a population dominated by distinct church traditions. The "educated person" could not only read, write, and cipher, but was God-fearing, honest, persistent, ambitious, thrifty, and obedient to the rule of law. The stories and adages of the Christian Bible were used as primary reading texts. School began with prayer and many teachers' contracts included the expectation that they would attend church regularly. Wayne Fuller, who studied the history of country schools in the Midwest, says that the spirit that moved prairie pioneers to build little schools as soon as they had finished building houses and churches had religious roots.

> About moral values and their place in education there was no confusion in Midwestern one-room schools. They were largely Protestant-Puritan values, drawn from the Old and New Testaments, the Ten Commandments, and the Sermon on the Mount. These values were as readily accepted by most Midwesterners as democracy, with which they were closely allied (Fuller, 1994, p. 50).

The school day began with a prayer, a Bible reading, and the singing of a hymn. In 1899, when Daniel Freeman of Nebraska tried to forbid teachers from requiring children to engage in these religious exercises in the one-room school built on his land, he was forced to take his ideas to the state Supreme Court when the district court rejected them. Although the higher court's ruling in 1902 upheld the principle of separation of church and state, the local paper ran the headline, "Ignore the Court" (Fuller, 1994, pp. 50–51).

The 1960s ushered in an era of attention to differences among individuals and groups. In schools across the United States, values were no longer considered to be commonly accepted absolutes, but a product of group, and even individual, decisions. With the goal of fostering children's self-esteem and sense of uniqueness, programs such as the **values clarification approach** of Simon, Howe, and Kirschenbaum (1995) helped children identify and feel proud of their own particular sets of values. Critics argued that Simon and his colleagues were confusing deep values with shallow preferences in activities that, for example, asked children to list and share "the 20 activities you most like to do, with people or alone." Even stronger voices denounced the "values relativity" of an approach that seemed to accept whatever "values" or "preferences" children offered, no matter their social or legal consequences.

Despite the criticism, the effect of the movement to recognize and respect differences in religious, cultural, and personal backgrounds led the courts to enforce the principle of the separation of church and state embodied in the Bill of Rights of the Constitution. Supporting that principle, the U.S. Supreme Court banned official school prayer from public schools in 1962. In 1980 it rejected a Kentucky law requiring the posting of the Ten Commandments in classrooms. In 1992 it barred clergy from delivering prayers at public school graduation ceremonies, and in 1996 it included in that ban student-led prayers, arguing that, even if the majority of students voted to have a prayer at graduation, the rights of the minority needed protection. In 2000, the Supreme Court ruled that student-led prayers in public schools or at events sponsored by public schools, such as football games, were unconstitutional.

But the federal courts have distinguished between state endorsement of religion and the rights of individual students to express their religious beliefs. In 1996 the Supreme Court ruled against a Jackson, Mississippi, school principal who allowed students to pray using the school's intercom, saying that use of the intercom amounted to the message that the school promoted prayer; but two years later, in *Doe v. Madison,* a federal appeals court supported individual students who chose on their own to speak on the topics of religion and prayer at their high school graduation. The courts have supported state laws that provide opportunities for students to pray or meditate, as long as they don't require it; for example, in 2000, the U.S. District Court in Alexandria, Virginia, concluded that the state law that mandates a "minute of silence" was constitutional because it did not require that students use the minute of silence for prayer.

Under President George W. Bush, and under President Clinton before him, the U.S. secretary of education has been charged with providing guidelines to states and local districts on issues of religion and school prayer. President Clinton's education secretary, Richard W. Riley, issued guidelines entitled "Religious Expression in Public Schools" to all public school districts, in which he affirmed the "two basic and equally important obligations imposed on schools by the First Amendment": that schools may not forbid students from expressing their personal religious views, as long as they do not disrupt the instructional process or harass other students, and that schools may not endorse or coerce religious activity, through advising or coaching or compelling students to listen to religious speech. Schools may teach about religion, including comparative religion, the Bible (or other scripture) as literature, and the influence of religion in history and the arts. They may teach about religious holidays and celebrate their secular aspects, but they may not observe holidays as religious events (Riley, 1998).

Secretary Riley urged schools to invite parents, teachers, clergy, and the larger community to develop a systemwide policy on religious expression based on positive dialogue:

> Our history as a nation reflects the history of the Puritan, the Quaker, the Baptist, the Catholic, the Jew and many others fleeing persecution to find religious freedom in America. The United States remains the most successful experiment in religious freedom that the world has ever known because the First Amendment uniquely balances freedom of private religious belief and expression with freedom from state-imposed religious expression. . . . I encourage teachers and principals to see the First Amendment as something more than a piece of dry, old parchment locked away in the national attic gathering dust. It is a vital living principle, a call to action, and a demand that each generation reaffirm its connection to the basic idea that is America—that we are a free people who protect our freedoms by respecting the freedom of others who differ from us (Riley, 1998).

The No Child Left Behind Act of 2001 includes a special section on school prayer, which ties federal funding to the requirement that school districts allow for school prayer within the boundaries established by law. President Bush's law strengthens an individual's right to express religious beliefs or pray by mandating that school districts certify in writing that they have established no policy that prevents constitutionally protected prayer:

> As a condition of receiving funds under this Act, a local educational agency shall certify in writing to the State educational agency involved that no policy of the local educational agency prevents, or otherwise denies participation in, constitutionally protected prayer in public elementary schools and secondary schools. . . . The State educational agency shall report to the Secretary by November 1 of each year a list of those local educational agencies that have not filed the certification or against which complaints have been made to the State educational

agency that the local educational agencies are not in compliance with this section (U.S. Dept. of Education, 2001, Sec. 9524).

President Bush's first education secretary, Rod Paige, issued the "Guidance on Constitutionally Protected Prayer in Public Elementary and Secondary Schools" in February, 2003. Reminding local districts that voluntary prayer was constitutional, the secretary offered the following examples of legal policies on religious expression in school:

- Districts may not single out religious activities as more disruptive than other privately-initiated activities. Students may pray when not engaged in school activities or instruction, subject to the same rules that the district imposes to prevent disruption of the educational program by other activities. They may, for example, read their Bibles, say grace before meals, and pray with fellow students during recess, the lunch hour, or other noninstructional time to the same extent that they are permitted to engage in nonreligious activities.

- Students may organize prayer groups, religious clubs, and gatherings before or after school to the same extent that students are permitted to organize other non-curricular student activities groups. Such groups must be given the same access to school facilities for assembling as is given to other non-curricular groups, without discrimination because of the religious content of their expression.

- Districts that allow nonreligious student groups to advertise their meetings—for example, in a student newspaper, on a student activities bulletin board or public address system—must allow the same privileges to groups who meet to pray.

- Teachers may take part in religious activities where the overall context makes clear that they are not participating in their official capacities. Before school or during lunch, for example, teachers may meet with other teachers for prayer or Bible study to the same extent that they may engage in other conversation or nonreligious activities.

- Districts that excuse students from class on the basis of parents' requests for accommodation of nonreligious needs must not discriminate against religiously motivated requests for excusal. Schools may excuse students from class to remove a significant burden on their religious exercise, where doing so would not impose material burdens on other students. For example, schools may excuse Muslim students briefly from class to enable them to fulfill their religious obligations to pray during Ramadan.

- Students may express their beliefs about religion in homework, artwork, and other written and oral assignments free from discrimination based on the religious content of their submissions. A student who chooses to complete a poetry assignment by writing a poem expressing her religious beliefs, for example, should be judged on the basis of the poetic form, not the religious content.

Secretary Paige's guidelines tell school districts that the Supreme Court has interpreted the First Amendment as requiring that public school officials be neutral in their treatment of religion, showing neither favoritism toward nor hostility against religious expression. The No Child Left Behind Act (NCLB) reminds school districts that whatever policies they institute regarding disruptive activities or extra-curricular activities may not target religious activities for special prohibition.

The religion guidelines provided to districts by U.S. Education Secretary Richard Riley of the Clinton administration distinguished between the teaching of religion and the teaching of values. Schools should teach values, said the secretary, from a secular point of view, even though values can also be part of a set of religious principles. Teachers should understand the difference:

> Though schools must be neutral with respect to religion, they may play an active role with respect to teaching civic values and virtue, and the moral code that holds us together as a community. The fact that some of these values are held also by religions does not make it unlawful to teach them in school (Riley, 1998).

However, neither federal court rulings nor guidelines issued by the federal Department of Education have obliterated the belief that many Americans still hold, that morality must always come from religion. This assumption persists in many school districts today. Several states have recently challenged former Supreme Court rulings by passing laws mandating the display of the Ten Commandments in their schools. The United States House of Representatives, reacting to a spate of school shootings in the late 1990s, especially the tragic death of fifteen at Colorado's Columbine High School, voted (248–180) in 1999 along party lines (most Republicans voting yes and most Democrats, no) to promote the display of the Ten Commandments. A troubled Secretary Riley responded with the following statement:

> I am sure that this vote reflects the deep concerns of many members of Congress about the values of our nation's young people. However, the U.S. Supreme Court in 1980 ruled that it is unconstitutional for a state to require posting of the Ten Commandments in public schools. Addressing serious gun legislation must be a priority for Congress and this House action only serves as a diversion from keeping guns out of the hands of children (Riley, 1999).

The values curriculum of the first schools in America was quite obvious, or *overt,* and it was based on religion. Beginning in the latter half of the twentieth century, schools seemed to avoid any suggestion of imposing *any* values on individual children, religion-based or otherwise. Yet whether or not values are linked to religion or overt precepts, public schools cannot avoid the fact that they are institutions with moral messages. There is always a hidden curriculum, and that curriculum includes values, moral precepts, and norms of behavior that carry with them strong messages about what is right and proper. Despite the best attempts of the school principal mentioned in the anecdote that opened the moral education section of this chapter to claim that "we don't teach values," schools are, in fact, never value-free.

In the subject matter we choose to include and the subject matter we don't, the way we organize and teach students, the norms and rules of behavior we impose on them, the quality of our interactions with them and with our colleagues, the achievements we celebrate and the ones we do not, and in the celebrations we engage students in, we convey messages about what we think is important and right and good. These value messages are powerful, and influence not only the way children conduct themselves in school but also the goals and expectations they have for their futures. As John Dewey said, since we are "as a matter of fact" reinforcing one set of values or the other, we need to make sure we're doing it "intelligently, after a study of the situation and a conscious choice" (1935, p. 7).

Moral education has taken on more immediate and critical importance in today's schools in light of growing incidents of violence in society in general, and among youth in particular (Schwartz, 1996). Youngsters who once settled problems with fists now have easier access to guns. More youth are involved in gang activity; in the last thirty years of the twentieth century, the number of cities that reported gang activity grew tenfold and gang activity spread to include towns, villages, and counties in every state (Miller, 2001). Society has always looked to the schools not only to give children the academic skills they will need as adults but also to give them the social skills and moral orientations they will need to function as responsible citizens. In the past several years, the call to teach children how to get along with others and how to resolve conflicts peacefully is not merely idealistic. Violence has entered the American schoolhouse and resulted in physical injury and death. We end this chapter with a discussion of the problem of school violence and some efforts to make both schools and society safe.

Providing Safe Schools

Once thought to be islands of safety, off-limits to the problems outside their doors, schools in a variety of communities—urban, suburban, and rural, upper class and lower class, majority-white and majority-minority—are finding that the violence in neighborhoods is making incursions into schools. Tragic incidents in schools in Littleton, Colorado; Jonesboro, Arkansas; Paducah, Kentucky; and elsewhere have provoked concern at the highest governmental level. The federal government paired its Department of Education with the Secret Service under the Safe Schools Initiative in a combined effort to try to determine the indicators in individual students that might lead to school attacks (Vossekuil et al., 2002). Results are inconclusive; there seems to be no consistent list of characteristics, or behavioral warning signs, that show a particular student's potential for school violence (Lumsden, 2004).

On the other hand, there are initiatives that schools can take to prevent the possibility of violence, including teaching students and teachers to make thoughtful decisions, to recognize feelings, to respect differences, and to listen to each other. Schools should provide hallway monitoring during transition periods, behavior support plans for troubled students, and places where problems can be discussed in confidence. Caring and cooperative school environments not only support academic learning but also foster safety (Lumsden, 2004). We discuss in detail in the next section the extent of the problem of school violence and possible solutions.

School Violence and Student Fear

Too many students feel unsafe in school, afraid that their schools are becoming more violent, afraid of being hurt either inside the building or on the way to or from school. While some studies report that since 1995 there has been a decline in the number of students who say they are afraid they will be attacked in school, a significant number of children in both urban and suburban schools are still fearful.

Figure 10.1 shows data from the National Center for Educational Statistics on the percentage of students ages twelve through eighteen who reported they had been victims of crime in 1995 (the year of the Columbine tragedy) as compared with 1999. Figure 10.2 shows the percentage of students who said they feared being attacked at school.

According to public health researchers Tod Mijanovich and Beth Weitzman (2003), students' feelings of being unsafe in school constitute a serious and pervasive public health problem because they can lead to anxiety and depression, poor academic performance, and risky behavior. Surveying three thousand students, Mijanovich and Weitzman found that a substantial minority felt unsafe on any

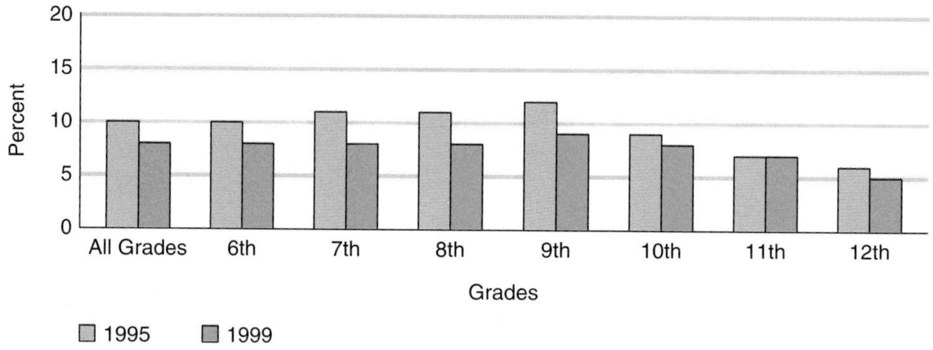

Figure 10.1

Percentage of Students Ages Twelve Through Eighteen Who Reported Criminal Victimization at School During the Previous Six Months, by Grade

Note: This figure presents the prevalence of total victimization, which is a combination of violent victimization and theft. "At school" means in the school building, on school property, or on the way to or from school.

Source: U.S. Department of Justice, Bureau of Justice Statistics; School Crime Supplements to the National Crime Victimization Survey, January–June, 1995 and 1999.

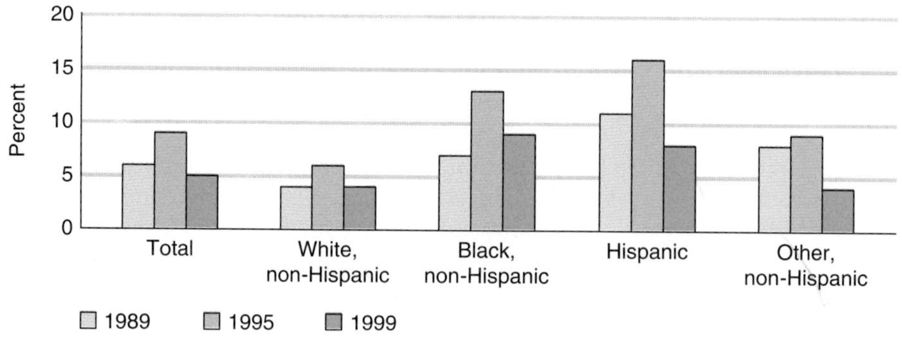

Figure 10.2

Percentage of Students Ages Twelve Through Eighteen Who Reported Fearing Being Attacked or Harmed at School During the Previous Six Months, by Race/Ethnicity, 1995 and 1999

Note: Includes students who reported that they sometimes or most of the time feared being victimized in this way. "At school" means in the school building, on the school grounds, or on a school bus.

Source: U.S. Department of Justice, Bureau of Justice Statistics; School Crime Supplements to the National Crime Victimization Survey, January–June, 1989, 1995 and 1999.

given school day. Students of low socioeconomic status and urban students (20%) were more fearful than students from wealthier families and suburban schools (10%).

The problem of school violence is both physical and psychological. Some fears are based on actual incidents of victimization or potential victimization. In the 1996–1997 school year, half of all middle and high schools in the country reported at least one incident of physical attacks, theft, larceny, or vandalism (Juvonen, 2001).

- In 1997, states reported to the federal government that 6100 students were expelled from the nation's schools for possessing firearms, only a fraction of the 370,000 high school students who reported that they had carried guns to school (Kingery and Coggeshall, 2001).
- In 1999, 7 to 8 percent of high school students reported that they were threatened or injured with a weapon in school (Juvonen, 2001).

But many students' concerns come less from actual incidents than from their sense that they are unprotected. Mijanovich and Weitzman (2003) found that the idea that their school was "disorderly" provoked fear and anxiety in many students. Physical conditions such as broken windows and organizational conditions such as inconsistent enforcement of school rules can make students feel unprotected by the adults who are supposed to be in charge. Large schools report more violence than small schools (Juvonen, 2001); detection of weapons and violent behavior is more difficult in large schools and students are less likely to have personal relationships with staff they feel they can confide in. Twenty to thirty percent of American schoolchildren report that they are either the targets or the perpetrators of bullying, which is a precursor of more violent crimes (Nansel et al., 2001). The problem is acute for sexual-preference-minority students, who are at even greater risk of being bullied than other high school students (Bochenek and Brown, 2001).

Though some administrators and local school boards would like to ignore the problem of violence, assuming that "it would never happen here," many are responding with a variety of policies and practices designed to keep children safe, prevent violence, and/or respond effectively when it occurs. The best of these responses involve families, community agencies, and the criminal justice system in the effort. In general, school efforts to prevent and respond to violence include the following initiatives:

- Physical surveillance, including weapons detection and security officers
- Punishment of students who perpetrate violence, including "zero tolerance" policies
- Programs designed to prevent violence, including bullying prevention
- Profiling of potentially violent individuals
- Counseling for students at risk of carrying out violent behavior
- Conflict resolution programs, including peer mediation

Zero Tolerance and Alternatives

In response to the spate of violent incidents in the 1990s, some schools added security staff and screening devices and many began requiring office check-in by visitors. To force schools to impose tough consequences for bringing guns to school, President Clinton signed the Gun-Free Schools Act in 1994, which mandated a one-year expulsion for students who carry weapons, as well as referral to the criminal or juvenile justice system. His action was an example of a **zero tolerance policy** which requires that schools strictly enforce rules against acts of violence and bringing weapons to school, without exception. The consequences for breaking this rule may include expulsion and referral to the criminal or juvenile justice system. Since the time of the original Gun-Free Schools Act, school districts have broadened the scope of the law to include a variety of objects defined as weapons, threats, and some types of fighting. Zero tolerance is a popular concept that is easy to understand and appears to offer a tough and immediate response to violence. But the policy has strong critics. In many instances, students have been suspended or expelled for bringing nail files, model rockets, toy cap guns, a plastic Halloween axe, and a kitchen knife carried in a lunchbox to cut chicken (Skiba and Peterson, 1999). Black students, Hispanic students, and low-income students, for years over-represented in school discipline cases in general, have been suspended or expelled in disproportionate numbers. Black students seem to receive more severe punishments for less severe behavior (McFadden et al., 1992; Shaw and Braden, 1990).

There is little evidence that zero tolerance policies have reduced student misbehavior or improved school safety. Between 30 and 40 percent of students who are suspended are repeat offenders; zero tolerance has not been a deterrent to their misbehavior (Costenbader and Markson, 1994). And students who are suspended drop out of school at greater rates than those who aren't (Ekstrom et al., 1987). There are calls for a more flexible response to students suspected of carrying weapons, tailored to the seriousness of the offense and the circumstances:

> We agree that zero tolerance sends a powerful message to the school community that violent, aggressive behavior will not be tolerated. We need strong, effective policies to protect our students and to help them feel safe. However, zero tolerance, despite its appearance of fairness, is inherently an unfair policy. A doctor is not fair if he prescribes chemotherapy for two patients with headache—one with a brain tumor and the other with a sinus condition—regardless of the similarity of symptoms. When two students in school throw a pencil—one because he has finished his assignment and is bored, the other because he cannot read the directions and thus hasn't even started the assignment—we do not treat them the same, regardless of the behavioral similarity. Any intervention that treats dissimilar problems with similar behavioral outcomes the same is not only unfair but destined to fail. . . . We see no strength in a system that uses the already frail, those least able to benefit, as sacrificial lambs (Curwin and Mendler, 1999).

Claiming that "one size does not fit all," Curwin and Mendler call for an alternative to zero tolerance; they recommend an "as tough as necessary" approach. In some cases, a school should respond to particular incidents with expulsion and the filing of criminal charges. In other cases, more appropriate responses might be counseling, parent involvement, restitution, behavioral training, conflict resolution, or suspension with training. They cite the example of a student who brought a gun to school after his drunken father had put a gun down his throat and threatened to kill both him and his younger brother. The student brought the gun to school to keep it away from his father. Without allowing him the opportunity to explain, the principal expelled him. Curwin and Mendler ask schools to develop a code of conduct that commits all members of the community to nonviolence, including the commitment that school will be safe, that differences will be resolved nonviolently, that everyone is responsible for preventing violent behavior, and that all persons, their property, and their feelings, will be respected. But, they say, to be humane and effective, schools should consider a range of circumstances before they impose a range of consequences.

Schools should do more to prevent violence before it arises by creating positive school climates. In such settings, students learn how to deal with their problems and conflicts in peaceful and socially appropriate ways modeled and counseled by the adults in the building, bullying is outlawed, and students who are potential perpetrators or victims of violence are identified early and receive counseling and behavior training (Dwyer, Osher, and Warger, 1998). The joint Department of Education–Secret Service study of school attacks concluded that schools should strictly enforce expulsion for weapons possession and have protocols for responses to threats and other suspicious behaviors that might lead to violence, but they should also foster climates where students are not afraid to communicate their concerns about violence-prone peers (Vossekuil et al., 2002).

Preventing Violence

There are many initiatives that schools can take within their academic programs to create a climate that discourages violence. There are curricula that teach students to manage their anger, resolve conflicts peacefully, and value the differences among them. One such program is Second Step, published by the Committee for Children in Seattle, Washington; it helps students recognize and understand their feelings, keep anger from escalating, and make positive choices using activity cards, simulations, and videos. Another is Resolving Conflicts Creatively, by Educators for Social Responsibility of Cambridge, Massachusetts; this program includes lessons, classroom management strategies, peer mediation training, and parent information. Professional development can help teachers respond to violence-prone children in ways that do not exacerbate the problem. Linda Albert's Cooperative Discipline approach (1996), for example, shows teachers how to identify the varying motives of individual students who misbehave—power, attention, revenge, or avoidance of failure—and how to use specific strategies that will help them get what they need in positive ways.

Teachers who understand that students experiencing constant failure in school may act out in frustration can work to make the classroom a more positive place for students with a variety of needs. They can provide materials and methods that reach students with a range of learning styles. They can implement tutorial arrangements and offer after-school, Saturday, and summer programs to those who need additional help. Opportunities for community-service learning and career exploration give students realistic reasons for paying attention to their assignments and staying in school. In one economically struggling rural district in Texas, administrators report that service-learning projects that engaged high school students in the community—including staffing a community health clinic and partnering with a company offering technology training—resulted in higher self-esteem and improved achievement scores (Pennington, 2001).

DIRECTLY FROM THE SOURCE

Musings in the Wake of Columbine: What Can Schools Do?

by Mary Anne Raywid and Libby Oshiyama

Source: Mary Anne Raywid and Libby Oshiyama, *Phi Delta Kappan,* February 2000, Vol. 81 (6), pp. 444–449.

There have been multiple attempts to figure out the reasons for the Columbine High School tragedy. The availability of guns has been widely blamed, as has the violence depicted in films and videos. Some analysts have turned their sights on parental failure. Others have looked to deep-seated personality problems within the young assassins, while still others have focused on the seductive power of hate groups. There is probably some truth in most of these explanations, plus others, with the choice among them being largely a matter of individual perspective. . . . Educators venture answers, too. . . . [T]here is a good bit of knowledge suggesting directions that schools can take in order to avoid more tragedies like Columbine. . . .

There is overwhelming evidence that violence is much less likely to occur in small schools than in large ones. In fact, not surprisingly, students behave better generally in schools where they are known. It is in large schools, where alienation often goes hand in hand with anonymity, that the danger comes. As James Garbarino of Cornell University, one of the nation's top scholars on juvenile delinquency, has put it, "If I could do one single thing [to stop the scourge of violence among juveniles], it would be to ensure that teenagers are not in high schools bigger than 400 to 500 students."[1] As suggested by all the standard indicators—truancy, dropout rates, involvement rates, graffiti, vandalism, violence—youngsters in small schools rarely display the anger at the institution and the people in it that was so blatant at Columbine and is evident in many high schools elsewhere as well. Larger school size is related to . . . higher levels of disorder and violence, student alienation, and teacher dissatisfaction.[2] Student social behavior—as measured by truancy, discipline problems, violence, theft, substance abuse, and gang participation—is more positive in small schools.[3] Research has consistently found that students at small schools are less alienated than students in large schools—and this positive effect is especially strong for students labeled "at risk."[4] Behavior problems are so much greater in larger schools . . . that any possible virtue of larger size is canceled out by the difficulties of maintaining an orderly learning environment.[5]

The reason why size is important is because the first lesson Columbine seems to urge for schools is the need to make them genuinely user-friendly places for all students—places where everyone is welcomed into a genuine community and each student is known well by at least one adult staff member who assumes responsibility for his or her positive growth and success. The student assassins of Columbine, by contrast, were outcasts who banded together after repeated acts of rejection and humiliation by two high-status campus groups, the "jocks" and the "preps."[6] And although they and others paraded around the campus in identifiable dress (black trench coats), gave one another Nazi salutes, and submitted assignments that should have spelled danger (videos on killing, poetry about death, violence-filled essays), no single faculty member was in a position to put the picture together, and evidently none felt a personal responsibility to address these particular aberrations. Indeed, with no one responsible for seeing and acting on the whole picture with regard to these boys, the multiple signs of trouble couldn't even be tallied. And the principal could report that he had actually never heard of the "trench coat mafia" in his school.[7]

This situation is not atypical of comprehensive high schools of nearly 2,000 youngsters. In such schools, many students remain virtually anonymous for their entire stay. Others are singled out by their peers for harassment and humiliation, which teachers typically find beyond their province—if they become aware of it at all. It is a mistake to assume that teachers in such schools don't care or that they are indifferent to students. We are reaping the results of the way we have organized schools and divided up staff responsibilities. We have apportioned things so that teachers' primary responsibility is not for youngsters but for content and grade levels. . . . No matter what we choose to focus on in articulating school organization—content or something else—it means that other things become less visible and may be obscured. Sometimes they are things that are centrally related to the kinds of human beings we are creating. . . .

What do high schools need to be . . . ? Small enough so that people can know one another. Small enough so that individuals are missed when they are absent. Small enough so that the participation of all students is needed. Small enough to permit considerable overlap in the rosters from one class to another. Small enough so that the full faculty can sit around a table together and discuss serious questions. Small enough to permit the flexibility essential to institutional responsiveness—to the special needs of individuals and to the diverse ways teachers want to teach. . . .

[I]t would help if schools modeled respect for individuals—that is, if all coming in contact with the school—students, parents, visitors—were consistently treated with courtesy and in such a fashion that their dignity remained intact. . . . It shows a lack of respect for schools to repeatedly assign youngsters to groups widely recognized to consist of "dummies" or "losers." It telegraphs another sort of lack of respect when lavatory doors can't be closed or locked—or when there is no toilet paper. Somewhat more directly, youngsters must be taught about and held responsible for respecting their classmates. This is a matter first just of physical respect. . . . It would be surprising if the ridiculing and the repeated rejections of the Columbine boys who became assassins were unrelated to their rage. . . .

We need to deliberately cultivate in schools the qualities associated with acceptance, such as empathy and compassion. . . . Again, these traits must be both modeled by staff members and deliberately cultivated among students. The major ways of cultivating them are, first, through the personal relationships that constitute school communities, but also through what is taught—certainly in the humanities. Literature can instruct eloquently in kinship, empathy, and compassion, as can people's history, to cite just two examples.

Over the years, schools have tended to focus on making youngsters more informed, more rigorously trained, more skilled. Perhaps we had better begin focusing on also making them more humane. The tragedy at Columbine would certainly recommend it. . . . Shifting to this perspective is not easy. But unless and until we do, we may well be headed for more tragedy and heartbreak. Until we make schools engaging learning communities whose members value those communities and feel welcome within them, we are right to think that the next Columbine could happen anywhere.

1. Quoted in Robert M. Gladden, "The Small School Movement: A Review of the Literature." In Michelle Fine and Janis I. Somerville, eds., *Small Schools, Big Imaginations* (Chicago: Cross City Campaign for Urban School Reform, May 1998), p. 116.
2. Ibid., p. 113.
3. Kathleen Cushman, "Why Small Schools Are Essential," *Horace,* January 1997, p. 3.
4. Gladden, p. 114.
5. Kathleen Cotton, "Affective and Social Benefits of Small-Scale Schooling," *ERIC Digest,* Clearinghouse on Rural Education and Small Schools, Charleston, WV, December 1996.
6. Bruce Shapiro, "The Guns of Littleton," *The Nation,* 17 May 1999, p. 4.
7. David Von Drehle, "A Model School for Some, Cliques and Taunts for Others," *Washington Post National Weekly Edition,* 3 May 1999, pp. 7–8.

A Closer Look at the Issues

1. Raywid and Oshiyama claim that in large schools, many students remain virtually anonymous. In your experience, or the experience of your friends who attended large schools, is that true? Is there anything that large schools can do to make school a more personal environment for students?
2. The authors want schools to be "small enough so that the participation of all students is needed." What do they mean by that? Why is it important?
3. Making schools smaller is a necessary but insufficient condition for preventing the kind of alienation and violence that Columbine High School experienced. Why is reducing the size of schools not enough?

Smaller schools, well-cared-for schools, and schools with up-to-date resources have fewer incidents of violence (Schwartz, 1996). Smaller schools and smaller class sizes foster more personal and more supportive relationships between students and adults in the building. Mary Ann Raywid and Libby Oshiyama (2000) agree that schools that want to reduce the possibility of violence in their midst can do something very simple but very powerful: reduce their size. Citing research that large schools have more disorder, student alienation, truancy, discipline problems, and gang participation, and feelings of dissatisfaction among both students and staff, they find that small schools have a much better chance to teach students the values of tolerance, empathy, and compassion that deter violent behavior. See Directly from the Source for an excerpt from their article, "Musings in the Wake of Columbine: What Can Schools Do?"

Bullying

The federal Safe School Initiative study (Vossekuil et al., 2002), found that most of the students who had attacked their schools had been the subjects or perpetrators of bullying. Linda Lumsden (2002) defines **bullying** as the willful and repeated exercise of power over another with hostile or malicious intent. Bullying can be physical or verbal, direct or indirect, the last category including behaviors such as ostracism or rumor-spreading.

Traditional views that bullying is an unavoidable and temporary part of childhood experience have been challenged by research that finds bullying to have serious and long-lasting psychological, academic, and physical effects (Ballard, Argus, and Remley, 1999). Frequent victims of bullying may become depressed, suicidal, or even homicidal. Bullying, as a form of violence, may spawn violent responses in both bullies and victims. Many school bullies become adult criminals (Olweus, 1995). Yet, despite the fact that a significant number of students report that they have been bullied, teachers and administrators underestimate the problem and too often ignore it (Barone, 1997).

School peers have the power to reinforce or reduce bullying in their schools; in other words, they can exacerbate or diminish the problem. Bullies need a reaction and an audience. If schools work to create environments that strengthen a sense of community, acceptance, and positive relations, bullying becomes aberrant, unwelcome, and "weird." They need to establish a cultural ethos that makes ridicule and hurting others unacceptable and enforce this ethos with rules and consequences. Since many bullies come from families who model aggressive behavior, schools need to take responsibility to teach alternative behaviors to those who have not learned them at home; skills such as conflict resolution, anger management, and language that conveys respect. See Table 10.2 for suggestions for schools that want to be part of the solution.

Responding to Crises

In the event of violent incidents, schools must be ready with a coordinated and effective response. In schools that are prepared for the threat of violence, counselors, administrators, even custodial staff, receive training in responding to situations that may erupt into violence. Peer leadership teams or school staff teams meet with students experiencing difficulty to defuse emotions, solve problems, and resolve crises in peaceable and acceptable ways. Parent representatives work in part-

Table 10.2 How Schools Can Be Part of the Solution to Bullying

Schools Can:

- Consider themselves moral communities, where students participate in decision making and problem solving, and learn to think critically about ethical and social issues.
- Accurately assess the existence of violence in the school and the surrounding community, including gang activity and bullying.
- Create and enforce "zero tolerance" for abusive behavior.
- Model respect and acceptance in all areas of school functioning.
- Create and communicate clearly defined behavior codes, and enforce them uniformly.
- Provide academic instruction and support that helps all students learn.
- Teach the requisite social skills that students may not have previously learned.
- Incorporate family education into school violence prevention programs.
- Call on all the resources in the community for help and counsel, including social service, mental health, and law enforcement agencies.
- Provide programs and opportunities for positive social interaction and constructive after-school activities.
- Establish protocols and crisis response teams for helping violence-prone students and responding to violent incidents.
- Prepare to engage in a long-term effort.

nership with school staff to discuss problems among students and in the community. Administrators establish **crisis response teams** composed of counselors, psychologists, nurses, administrators, and law enforcement officials to deal with potential or actual problems. All these efforts are designed to make sure that lines of communication among students, teachers, staff, and families are open and effective.

Under the aegis of the U.S. Department of Education, the Center for Effective Collaboration and Practice (2001) has issued guidelines to help schools respond to incidents of violence. These guidelines call on schools to establish a prevention and response team to prepare and implement a violence response plan, composed of the principal, teachers, school psychologist or counselor, parent representatives, the school nurse, support staff, and youth officer or community police officer. The plan should include:

- Evacuation procedures to protect students and staff from harm, and designated safe areas where students and staff should go in a crisis.
- An effective, foolproof communication system with designated roles and responsibilities for particular individuals to prevent confusion.

- A process for securing immediate external support from law enforcement officials and other relevant community agencies.
- Training for all faculty and staff that includes an explanation of the plan and exactly what to do in a crisis, as well as a written manual and opportunities for practice.
- Training for all adults in the school building on violence prevention (e.g., being observant, knowing when to get help, and modeling good problem solving, anger management, and/or conflict resolution skills).

The guidelines also offer advice for how to deal with children, parents, and staff in schools that have experienced violence. These guidelines are useful not only when crises happen in and around the school, but also when violence in the community or in the nation inspires fear in students and staff. Schools are asked to do the following:

- Help parents understand children's reactions to violence. In the aftermath of tragedy, children may experience unrealistic fears of the future, have difficulty sleeping, become physically ill, and be easily distracted—to name a few of the common symptoms.
- Help teachers and other staff deal with their reactions to the crisis. Debriefing and grief counseling is just as important for adults as it is for students.
- Help students and faculty adjust after the crisis, including providing both short-term and long-term mental health counseling.
- Help victims and family members of victims—and students returning to school who were removed—reenter the school environment. Often, school friends and parents need guidance in how to act.

Violence is not the school's problem alone. The Committee for Children, which offers exemplary programs to schools committed to violence prevention, explains what we learned from Columbine:

> [W]hat goes on outside school has a tremendous influence on what happens in school. We need to focus on families and communities, as well as children's behavior in school, if we want schools to be safe and respectful environments where children can truly learn. We cannot ignore the fact that in every single one of these school shooting incidents, the perpetrators had free and ready access to guns in their homes. We can give kids better social skills, but children, by nature, will make mistakes as they grow up. Guns make children's mistakes irrevocable (Crawford, 2004).

And schools cannot alone prevent violence. They need to look to other organizations for help. In many communities, public health and social service agencies collaborate with schools to offer families resources and support and teach parenting skills, behavior management, and job preparation skills. Girls' and Boys' Clubs and YMCAs offer after-school programs to engage children in constructive academic, social, and physical activities. Community mental health agencies can help identify and provide services to students who are depressed or suffering serious emotional distress. Area colleges and universities have faculty and students who will volunteer as professional development providers and tutors. And local police officers can work with schools to offer substance abuse prevention and gang deterrence programs.

The authors of this text are involved in one such community–school partnership in Lynn, Massachusetts. At the Robert L. Ford School, an elementary and middle school, principal Claire Crane learned from her parent advisory team that local gangs were stepping up their efforts to recruit members from the sixth-grade class. In response, she called in local community police officers, who met with the sixth graders and with their teachers to discuss the problem. The principal also met with the children and some of their parents to warn them. She brought in recent graduates of the school, who offered ideas about how to avoid the gangs and told them about the clubs and activities they could look forward to in high school. A local college offers them a campus-based after-school program of activities that include computer courses, arts and crafts classes, and physical education activities. The result of this comprehensive effort was that the gang recruitment effort was unsuccessful.

A Comprehensive Approach to Social and Moral Education

In this chapter, we make the case that educators need to take seriously their inescapable role as social and moral educators. All aspects of school and classroom life offer opportunities: the subject matter of the curriculum, the organizational structures, the everyday classroom routines, the ways teachers interact with and evaluate students, the models of conduct that teachers present, even the physical condition of schools and classrooms convey social and moral messages. Good teachers are aware of the connection between the academic and moral climate of their classrooms. In reviewing progress toward creating safer schools, The Committee for Children reviewed what works in schools committed to promoting peace:

> The lessons we have learned over the last five years [since the Columbine shooting] tell us that the seemingly small but significant ways in which children hurt or exclude others, and the ways in which children who don't have strong social skills respond to such hurts, can make for a dangerously volatile situation that can lead to big violence problems if they're left unchecked. We've learned that we can't leave children on their own to figure out how to be socially competent people. We have to teach them, support them, cue and coach them very intentionally if we want them to grow up healthy and whole. . . . Teaching children social and emotional skills, including empathy, impulse control, problem solving, and emotion management, means that they grow up more able to cope with problems and treat others with respect. Training teachers and parents to model and reinforce these skills ensures that learning goes beyond the school walls (Crawford, 2004).

Teachers concerned with promoting the development of good character in their students and providing an environment for them that is safe, just, and peaceful should take a comprehensive, holistic view of the means available to them. Social and moral education combine the reinforcement of good habits with critical thinking about social and moral issues in a comprehensive approach that treats the whole school as a morally educational environment. Teachers can turn children's attention to social and moral issues throughout the curriculum, inviting discussions about, for example, the moral decisions faced by fictitious characters in literature and real characters in history, the ethical issues underlying developments in science and technology, and the ways that basic skills such as reading and mathematics can be used to promote positive social goals. They can teach and reinforce behaviors that foster caring and responsible communities. Teachers whose classrooms contribute to children's social and moral development are fair and flexible in negotiating classroom community rules with students. They engage students in critical reflection on their own lives and the society they live in and on the moral decisions people make in everyday life. They help students develop their capacities to act as effective social and moral agents (Nucci, 1987, 2001).

Chapter 12 extends this discussion by describing classroom strategies and whole-school programs that serve to create communities of learning and being, where both the stated and the hidden curricula combine to offer students the conditions to develop holistically—as knowledgeable, capable, and moral members of society. We end this chapter by expanding on Kevin Ryan's (1996) and the Committee for Children's (Crawford, 2004) ideas to offer the following general efforts that teachers can make to educate their students socially and morally:

- Serve as a model for positive social and moral behavior.
- Insist on respectful behavior toward self and others.
- Teach children how to identify and manage their feelings, and provide them with strategies and outlets when they are angry or afraid.
- Teach communication and conflict resolution skills.
- Directly teach the meaning of values such as responsibility, altruism, kindness, trustworthiness, and honesty.
- Encourage students to reason about moral issues, evaluate evidence, and consider the social and moral consequences of actions.
- Provide ways for students to be of service to each other and to the community.
- Create and maintain a safe, democratic, and cooperative classroom climate based on clearly defined ethical principles.
- Get to know students' talents and aspirations. Make sure all students have access to challenging subject matter and interesting co-curricular activities.
- Draw examples from history, literature, and students' own lives of both famous and "everyday" heroes, social and political conflicts, and moral issues.
- Incorporate into the curriculum a study of the social, economic, and political conditions and issues relevant to the community and the larger world.
- Involve families and communities in violence prevention and peace-making programs, giving children and adults a language for recognizing and solving problems.

SUMMARY

- Life in schools includes not only the stated, or overt, curriculum—written frameworks of study for each grade level and subject area—but also a hidden curriculum that is social and moral in nature. Often more powerful and longer lasting than the formal, stated curriculum, the hidden curriculum transmits deep messages about the way things work, or should work, in society, where we fit in, and how we ought to behave.

- Theorists differ on the effects of this hidden curriculum. Some see it as helping to socialize students so that they can become functioning, responsible adults. Others look more negatively on the socializing effects of schools, regarding them as tools of the dominant and powerful, distributing those resources, information, and skills that will prepare children of particular social classes for economic and political lives that resemble their parents'. In other words, schools reproduce existing inequities. A third theory sees the possibility of resistance to cultural reproduction, both in the potential that teachers have to change the lives of their students, and in the potential students have to resist other people's ideas about their futures.
- Schools are never value free. Moral education in early America was linked to religion, a link that loosened with the recognition of the Constitutional principle separating church and state. Following a period in the 1970s and 1980s of "values relativity" and fear of indoctrination, educators have responded to an increasingly loud call that they return the education of "character" to the curriculum.
- The federal government and the federal courts have affirmed the principle of the separation of church and state contained in the U.S. Constitution. Teachers are encouraged to teach about world religions and honor the religious diversity of their students, but not to teach or celebrate any particular religion.
- Psychologists such as Lawrence Kohlberg and Carol Gilligan and the philosophers Matthew Lipman emphasize the quality of children's reasoning about moral issues, rather than moral principles, as the appropriate province of schools.
- While some argue for systematic programs that directly teach a set of universally accepted virtues, others claim that there is no such universality, and that character education cannot be taught in the same way that, for example, multiplication can.
- As part of creating a positive moral climate and encouraging students to behave ethically toward one another, teachers can structure classrooms as democratic communities where power is shared, differences are valued, and social issues are part of the curriculum.
- Along with the debate about what kind of character education is possible and appropriate there is the very real problem of increasing school violence. Educators are responding to violence and bullying with preventive, proactive, and responsive strategies.
- Teachers concerned with promoting the development of good character in their students and providing an environment for them that is safe, just, and peaceful should take a comprehensive, holistic view of the means available to them, including the subject matter and materials of the curriculum, the organization of the school and classroom, and the ways they model positive social and moral behavior with students and each other.

QUESTIONS FOR REFLECTION

1. What can you remember about the hidden curriculum of your own K–12 schooling? How did crowds, praise, and power elements of the hidden curriculum affect you?
2. Discuss with your classmates incidents of cultural reproduction in your schooling.
3. Reread the section on the legal constraints around religion and the public schools. Have the schools that you have attended or observed adhered to the laws separating church and state and the guidelines provided by the U.S. Department of Education?
4. Respond to the section of the chapter that describes the problem of bullying, its origins, effects, and interventions, drawing on your own school experience.
5. How can educators prepare responsibly for incidents of violence without producing anxiety in students and staff?

APPLYING WHAT YOU'VE LEARNED

1. Research security measures in a local school. Find out whether there is a protocol in place for responding to incidences of violence or potential violence.
2. Search the Web to find examples of character education programs. Try to find evidence of their relative effectiveness. You might begin with the websites listed here and those mentioned in the text of the chapter.
3. www Refer to the textbook's website to read more of Thomas Lickona's and Alfie Kohn's arguments about character education. Hold a character education debate in class, with one team supporting Thomas Lickona's view and another supporting Alfie Kohn's.
4. Zero tolerance policies have their critics, who claim that there are sometimes extenuating circumstances that make these policies harmful in particular instances. Research examples where these policies have been applied controversially.

KEY TERMS

bullying, p. 420
code of ethics, p. 393
conflict theory, p. 385
crisis response team, p. 421
critical pedagogy, p. 388
cultural reproduction, p. 385
ethical behavior, p. 390
extrinsic vs. intrinsic rewards, p. 381
hidden curriculum, p. 378
moral development approach, p. 399
null curriculum, p. 379
overt curriculum, p. 378
philosophy for children, p. 398
resistance theory, p. 387
structural-functionalism, p. 384
values, p. 392
values clarification approach, p. 409
virtues approach, p. 397
zero tolerance policy, p. 416

WEBSITES TO EXPLORE

http://www.safeschools.org/. National Alliance for Safe Schools, a nonprofit organization founded by school safety officers that offers safety assessments, training, and technical assistance to schools seeking to improve their security and response systems.

http://members.tripod.com/~twood/guide.html. Creating Safe Schools for Gay and Lesbian Students sensitizes educators to the need to provide emotionally and physically safe environments for homosexual youth. Includes suggestions for eliminating harassment and establishing supports.

http://www.cfchildren.org/. The Committee for Children is a Seattle-based nonprofit organization promoting children's health and academic and social welfare. Its website describes award-winning curricula for violence prevention and social and emotional learning and contains articles and related research.

http://modelprograms.samhsa.gov/pdfs/FactSheets/Olweus%20Bully.pdf. The Olweus Bullying Prevention Program offers training for schoolwide, classroom, and individual interventions based on the extensive experience of Dan Olweus, a Norwegian researcher on the conditions that promote, or eliminate, bullying.

http://www.character.org/. The Character Education Partnership, whose members include many national educational organizations, is a resource center promoting eleven principles of character education. It includes an awards program, newsletter, and journal.

http://www.jeffersoncenter.org/. California's Jefferson Center for Character Education promotes the S.T.A.R. program—Stop, Think, Act, and Review—with eight common values. The website has the program's philosophy, materials, and teaching ideas.

http://www.charactercounts.org/backgrnd.htm. Matthew Josephson's Character Counts program offers teacher training and character development seminars and other supports to schools who want to build a character education program around his Six Pillars of Character.

http://www.devstu.org/. The Developmental Studies Center in Oakland, California, sponsors the Child Development Project, a comprehensive school reform model that includes the creation of "caring communities." The website describes all aspects of the reform model, including activities and resources for community building.

CRITICAL READINGS

A Morally Defensible Mission for Schools in the 21st Century

BY NEL NODDINGS

What do we want for our children? Most of us hope that our children will find someone to love, find useful work they enjoy or at least do not hate, establish a family, and maintain bonds with friends and relatives. These hopes are part of our interest in shaping an acceptable child. What kind of mates, parents, friends, and neighbors will our children be? I would hope that all of our children—both girls and boys—would be prepared to do the work of attentive love. This work must be done in every family situation, whether the family is conventionally or unconventionally constituted. . . .

In education today, there is great concern about women's participation in mathematics and science. . . . Women's lack of success or participation in fields long dominated by men is seen as a problem to be treated by educational means. But researchers do not seem to see a problem in men's lack of participation in nursing, elementary school teaching, or full-time parenting. Our society values activities traditionally associated with men above those traditionally associated with women.

Relations with intimate others are the beginning and one of the significant ends of moral life. If we regard our relations with intimate others as central in moral life, we must provide all our children with practice in caring. Children can work together formally and informally on a host of school projects and, as they get older, they can help younger children, contribute to the care of building and grounds, and eventually do volunteer work—carefully supervised—in the community. Looking at Howard Gardner's multiple intelligences, we see that children can contribute useful service in a wide variety of ways; some have artistic talents, some interpersonal gifts, some athletic or kinesthetic abilities, some spiritual gifts. A moral policy, a defensible mission, for education recognizes a multiplicity of human capacities and interests. Instead of preparing everyone for college in the name of democracy and equality, schools should instill in students a respect for all forms of honest work done well. Preparation for the world of work, parenting, and civic responsibility is essential for all students. All of us must work, but few of us do the sort of work implied by preparation in algebra and geometry. Almost all of us enter into intimate relationships, but schools largely ignore the centrality of such interests in our lives.

When I suggest that a morally defensible mission for education necessarily focuses on matters of human caring, people sometimes agree but fear the loss of an intellectual mission for the schools. There are at least two powerful responses to this fear. First, anyone who supposes that the current drive for uniformity in standards, curriculum, and testing represents an intellectual agenda needs to reflect on the matter. Indeed, many thoughtful educators insist that such moves are truly anti-intellectual, discouraging critical thinking, creativity, and novelty. Further, in their emphasis on equality, they may lead to even grosser levels of mediocrity. Second, and more important from the perspective adopted here, a curriculum centered on themes of care can be as richly intellectual as we and our students want to make it. Those of us advocating genuine reform—better, transformation—will surely be accused of anti-intellectualism, just as John Dewey was in the middle of this century. But the accusation is false, and we should have the courage to face it down. . . .

I have argued that education should be organized around themes of care rather than the traditional disciplines. All students should be engaged in a general education that guides them in caring for self, intimate others, global others, plants, animals and the environment, objects and instruments, and ideas. Moral life so defined should be frankly embraced as the main goal of education. Such an aim does not work against intellectual development or academic achievement. On the contrary, it supplies a firm foundation for both. How can we begin? Here is what I think we must do:

First, be clear and unapologetic about our goal. The main aim of education should be to produce competent, caring, loving, and lovable people. Stating such an aim does not standardize either the curriculum or a mode of pedagogy. It opens the way to continuous dialogue and debate: What do we mean by competence? What does it mean to care? What can we (as parents and teachers) do to develop children who are loving and lovable?

Second, take care of affiliative needs. There are many things we can do with little cost to meet these needs. We can keep teachers and students together (by mutual consent) for several years instead of the traditional (and arbitrary) one year. We can keep students together and in one building for considerable periods of time—long enough for them to think of the physical place as their own. Administrators and policymakers can support teachers in their efforts to care and legitimize time spent on building relations of care and trust.

Third, relax the impulse to control. This is a hard recommendation to make and an even harder one to follow in an era reeking of distrust and filled with demands for accountability. But, surely, if we value a truly democratic way of life, we must give teachers, students, and parents greater opportunities to participate and exercise judgment. . . . We can learn from responsible experimentation.

Fourth, get rid of program hierarchies. This will take time, but we must begin now to provide excellent programs for all our children. Programs for the non-college-bound should be just as rich, desirable, and rigorous as those for the college-bound. What a student wants to do or to study should guide what is required by way of preparation. . . . In addition to preparation for work or future study, we must also give all students what all students need—genuine opportunities to explore the questions central to human life.

Fifth, give at least part of every day to themes of care. If we want to decrease violence and increase responsibility, we simply must spend time in dialogue with our children about the full range of existential questions, including both moral and spiritual matters. In all classes, opportunities can be found to discuss common human predicaments, outstanding acts of compassion, examples of towering genius, and the great joys potential in everyday life. We can give students practice in caring and time to reflect on and discuss their efforts. To nurture caring in our children, we have to show, first, that we care for them. This means listening as well as talking, following their legitimate interests as well as guiding them away from dangerous and undesirable interests.

Finally, we must teach them, and show by our example, that caring in every domain implies competence. When we care, we accept the responsibility to work continuously on our competence so that the recipient of our care—person, animal, object, or idea—is enhanced. There is nothing mushy about caring. It is the strong, resilient backbone of human life.

Source: Noddings, N. (1985). A Morally Defensible Mission for Schools in the 21st Century. *Phi Delta Kappan* (January) 76(5) p. 365–368.

A Closer Look at the Issues

1. In the tradition of John Dewey, Noddings tries to bring together ideas that are often seen as opposites. How, for example, does she tie together the goals of competence and caring in education?
2. Some of her critics think that putting caring at the center of the curriculum is anti-intellectual. Offer some examples of the academic learning that can accompany learning to care for oneself, others, the environment, objects, and ideas.
3. Do you agree with Noddings that moral life as she defines it should be "frankly embraced as the main goal of education"?

How Not to Teach Values: A Critical Look at Character Education

BY ALFIE KOHN

. . . The phrase character education . . . has two meanings. In the broad sense, it refers to almost anything that schools might try to provide outside of academics, especially when the purpose is to help children grow into good people. In the narrow sense, it denotes a particular style of moral training, one that reflects particular values as well as particular assumptions about the nature of children and how they learn. Unfortunately, the two meanings of the term have become blurred, with the narrow version of character education dominating the field to the point that it is frequently mistaken for the broader concept. . . .

Let me get straight to the point. What goes by the name of character education nowadays is, for the most part, a collection of exhortations and extrinsic inducements designed to make children work harder and do what they're told. Even when other values are also promoted—caring or fairness, say—the preferred method of instruction is tantamount to indoctrination. The point is to drill students in specific behaviors rather than to engage them in deep, critical reflection about certain ways of being. This is the impression one gets from reading articles and books by contemporary proponents of character education as well as the curriculum materials sold by the leading national programs. The impression is only strengthened by visiting schools that have been signaled out for their commitment to character education. To wit:

> A huge, multiethnic elementary school in Southern California uses a framework created by the Jefferson Center for Character Education. Classes that the principal declares "well behaved" are awarded Bonus Bucks, which can eventually be redeemed for an ice cream party. On an enormous wall near the cafeteria, professionally painted Peanuts characters instruct children: "Never talk in line." A visitor is led to a fifth-grade classroom to observe an exemplary lesson on the current character education topic. The teacher is telling students to write down the name of the person they regard as the "toughest worker" in school. The teacher then asks them, "How many of you are going to be tough workers?" (Hands go up.) "Can you be a tough worker at home, too?" (Yes.)

Some of the most popular schoolwide strategies for improving students' character seem dubious on their face. When President Clinton mentioned the importance of character education in his 1996 State of the Union address, the only specific practice he recommended was requiring students to wear uniforms. The premises here are first, that children's character can be improved by forcing them to dress alike, and second, that if adults object to students' clothing, the best solution is not to invite them to reflect together about how this problem might be solved, but instead to compel them all to wear the same thing.

A second strategy, also consistent with the dominant philosophy of character education, is an exercise that might be called "If It's Tuesday, This Must Be Honesty." Here, one value after another is targeted, with each assigned its own day, week, or month. This seriatim approach is unlikely to result in a lasting commitment to any of these values, much less a feeling for how they may be related. . . .

Then there is the strategy of offering students rewards when they are "caught" being good, an approach favored by rightwing religious groups and orthodox behaviorists but also by leaders of—and curriculum suppliers for—the character education movement. . . . In general terms, what the evidence suggests is this: the more we reward people for doing something, the more likely they are to lose interest in whatever they had to do to get the reward. Extrinsic motivation, in other words, is not only quite different from intrinsic motivation but actually tends to erode it. This effect has been demonstrated under many different circumstances and with respect to many different attitudes and behaviors. Most relevant to character education is a series of studies showing that individuals who have been rewarded for doing something nice become less likely to think of themselves as caring and helpful people and more likely to attribute their behavior to the reward.

"Extrinsic incentives can, by undermining self-perceived altruism, decrease intrinsic motivation to help others," one group of researchers concluded on the basis of several studies. "A person's kindness, it seems, cannot be bought." The same applies to a person's sense of responsibility, fairness, perseverance, and so on. The lesson a child learns from Skinnerian tactics is that the point of being good is to get rewards. . . .

In short, it makes no sense to dangle goodies in front of children for being virtuous. But even worse than rewards are awards—certificates, plaques, trophies, and other tokens of recognition whose numbers have been artificially limited so only a few can get them. When some children are singled out as "winners," the central message that every child learns is this: "Other people are potential obstacles to my success." Thus the likely result of making students beat out their peers for the distinction of being the most virtuous is not only less intrinsic commitment to virtue but also a disruption of relationships and, ironically, of the experience of community that is so vital to the development of children's character.

Unhappily, the problems with character education in the narrow sense . . . are not restricted to such strategies as enforcing sartorial uniformity, scheduling a value of the week, or offering students a "doggie biscuit" for being good. More deeply troubling are the fundamental assumptions, both explicit and implicit, that inform character education programs. Let us consider five basic questions that might be asked of any such program: At what level are problems addressed? What is the underlying theory of human nature? What is the ultimate goal? Which values are promoted? And finally, How is learning thought to take place?

1. **At what level are problems addressed?** One of the major purveyors of materials in this field ... has produced a video that begins with some arresting images—quite literally. Young people are shown being led away in handcuffs, the point being that crime can be explained on the basis of an "erosion of American core values," as the narrator intones ominously. The idea that social problems can be explained by the fact that traditional virtues are no longer taken seriously is offered by many proponents of character education as though it were just plain common sense. But if people steal or rape or kill solely because they possess bad values—that is, because of their personal characteristics—the implication is that political and economic realities are irrelevant and need to be addressed. Never mind staggering levels of unemployment in the inner cities or a system in which more and more of the nation's wealth is concentrated in fewer and fewer hands; just place the blame on individuals whose characters are deficient....
2. **What is the view of human nature?** Character education's "fix-the-kids" orientation follows logically from the belief that kids need fixing. Indeed, the movement seems to be driven by a stunningly dark view of children—and, for that matter, of people in general. In fact, at least three assumptions are seen to be at work when the need for self-control is stressed: first, that we are all at war not only with others but with ourselves, torn between our desires and our reason (or social norms); second, that these desires are fundamentally selfish, aggressive, or otherwise unpleasant; and third, that these desires are very strong, constantly threatening to overpower us if we don't rein them in. Collectively, these statements describe religious dogma, not scientific fact.
3. **What is the ultimate goal?** It may seem odd even to inquire about someone's reasons for trying to improve children's character. But it is worth mentioning that the whole enterprise—not merely the particular values that are favored—is often animated by a profoundly conservative, if not reactionary, agenda.... [C]haracter education is vital, according to one vocal proponent, because "the development of character is the backbone of the economic system" now in place. Character education, or any kind of education, would look very different if we began with other objectives—if, for example, we were principally concerned with helping children become active participants in a democratic society (or agents for transforming a society *into* one that is authentically democratic). It would look different if our top priority were to help students develop into principled and caring members of a community or advocates for social justice. To be sure, these objectives are not inconsistent with the desire to preserve certain traditions, but the point would then be to help children decide which traditions are worth preserving and why, based on these other considerations.
4. **Which values?** Should we allow values to be taught in school? ... Just as humans are teeming with microorganisms, so schools are teeming with values.... Whether or not we deliberately adopt a character or moral education program, we are always teaching values. Even people who insist that they are opposed to values in school usually mean that they are opposed to values other than their own. And that raises the inevitable question: Which values, or whose, should we teach? ...

   Look at the way character education programs have been designed and you will discover, alongside such unobjectionable items as "fairness" or "honesty," an emphasis on values that are distinctly conservative—and, to that extent, potentially controversial. Who benefits when people are trained not to question the value of what they have been told to do but simply to toil away at it—and to regard this as virtuous? ... Character education curricula ... stress the importance of things like "respect," "responsibility," and "citizenship." But these are slippery terms, frequently used as euphemisms for uncritical deference to authority.... I once taught at a high school where the principal frequently exhorted students to "take responsibility." By this he meant specifically that they should turn in their friends who used drugs.... Following a lengthy article about character education in the *New York Times Magazine,* a reader mused, "Do you suppose that if Germany had had character education at the time, it would have encouraged children to fight Nazism or to support it?"
5. **What is the theory of learning?** The schools with character education programs that I have visited are engaged largely in exhortation and directed recitation [and] ... seem to regard teaching as a matter of telling and compelling. Character Counts walks teachers through highly structured lessons in which character-related concepts are described and then students are drilled until they can produce the right answers. Teachers are encouraged to praise children who respond correctly, and use multiple-choice tests to ensure that students have learned their values. For example, here are two sample test questions prepared for teachers by the Character Education Institute.... "Having to obey rules and regulations (a) gives everyone the same right to be an individual, (b) forces everyone to do the same thing at all times, (c) prevents persons from expressing their individually [sic]"; and "One reason why parents might not allow their children freedom of choice is (a) children are always happier when they are told what to do and when to do it, (b) parents aren't given a freedom of choice; therefore, children should not be given a choice either, (c) children do not always demonstrate that they

are responsible enough to be given a choice." The correct answers, according to the answer key, are (a) and (c) respectively. . . .

Does all of this amount to indoctrination? Absolutely . . . good character and values are *instilled in* or *transmitted to* students. We are "planting the ideas of virtue, of good traits in the young," says William Bennett. The virtues or values in question are fully formed, and, in the minds of many character education proponents, divinely ordained. The children are—pick your favorite metaphor—so many passive receptacles to be filled, lumps of clay to be molded, pets to be trained, or computers to be programmed . . . objects to be manipulated—rather than learners to be engaged. The goal is not to support or facilitate children's social and moral growth. . . .

[T]he process of learning . . . requires that meaning, ethical or otherwise, be actively invented and reinvented, from the inside out. It requires that children be given the opportunity to make sense of such concepts as fairness or courage, regardless of how long the concepts themselves have been around. Children must be invited to reflect on complex issues, to recast them in light of their own experiences and questions, to figure out for themselves—and with one another—what kind of person they ought to be, which traditions are worth keeping, and how to proceed when two basic values seem to be in conflict. . . . [But] to say that students must construct meaning around moral concepts is not to deny that adults have a crucial role to play. . . . Let there be no question: educators, parents, and other adults are desperately needed to offer guidance, to act as models (we hope), to pose challenges that promote moral growth, and to help children understand the effects of their actions on other people. . . .

What does the alternative look like? [W]e might suggest holding regular class meetings in which students can share, plan, decide, and reflect together. We might also provide children with explicit opportunities to practice "perspective talking"—that is, imagining how the world looks from someone else's point of view. Activities that . . . support the impulse to imaginatively reach beyond the self . . . [help] students become more ethical and compassionate while simultaneously fostering intellectual growth. Rather than employ literature to indoctrinate or induce mere conformity, we can use it to spur reflection. . . . Instead of announcing, "This man is a hero; do what he did," such teachers may involve the students in *deciding* who (if anyone) is heroic in a given story—or in contemporary culture—and why. They may even invite students to reflect on the larger issue of whether it is desirable to have heroes. . . .

Source: Phi Delta Kappan, February 1997, pp. 429–439.

A Closer Look at the Issues

1. How would you describe Kohn's beliefs about the nature of learning? Look back at Chapter 5 for reference to some major approaches to the question.
2. Kohn says that most character education programs aim at indoctrination, not education. What is the difference? Do you agree with him?
3. How would Kohn define the "educated person"?

REFERENCES

Albert, L. (1996). *Cooperative discipline.* Circle Pines, MN: American Guidance Service, Inc.

Anyon, J. (1980). Social class and the hidden curriculum of work. *Journal of Education,* 162, 67–92.

Apple, M. W. (1995). *Education and power.* New York: Routledge.

Ballard, M., T. Argus, and T. P. Remley, Jr., (1999). Bullying and school violence: A proposed prevention program. *NASSP Bulletin,* May 1999, 39–47.

Barone, F. J. (1997). Bullying in school: It doesn't have to happen. *Phi Delta Kappan,* September, pp. 80–82.

Bennett, W. I. (1993). *The book of virtues.* New York: Simon & Schuster.

Bennett, W. I. (1995). *The children's book of virtues.* New York: Simon & Schuster.

Bochenek, M., and A. W. Brown (2001). *Hatred in the hallways: Violence and discrimination against lesbian, gay, bisexual, and transgender students in U.S. schools.* New York: Human Rights Watch. Available online at http://www.hrw.org/reports/2001/uslgbt/toc.htm. Retrieved September 1, 2004.

Bowles, S., and H. Gintis (1976). *Schooling in capitalist America: Educational reform and the contradictions of economic life.* New York: Basic Books.

Breitborde, M. (2003). One-room schools of Illinois in the twentieth century: An oral history. Presentation to the Rural Development Task Force, Galesburg, Il, October 30. Available from author.

Casselman, B. (2003). Masco administrators censor books with gay content. *Salem (MA) News,* June 11, p. 1.

Center for Effective Collaboration and Practice, *Early warning, timely response: A guide to safe schools.* Washington, DC: U.S. Department of Education, Office of Special Education and Rehabilitative Services, Office of Special Education Programs. http://cecp.air.org/guide/guidetext.htm. Retrieved July 10, 2004.

Codell, E. R. (2001). *Educating Esme: Diary of a teacher's first year.* Chapel Hill, NC: Algonquin Books.

Costenbader, V. K., and S. Markson (1994). School suspension: A survey of current policies and practices. *NASSP Bulletin,* 78, pp. 103–107.

Crawford, M. (2004). Columbine five years later: Have we made our children safer? (Press release, April 20.) Seattle, WA: Committee for Children. http://www.cfchildren.org/aboutf/mediaf/prf/colfive. Retrieved September 12, 2004.

Curwin, R. L., and A. N. Mendler (1999). Zero tolerance for zero tolerance. *Phi Delta Kappan,* 81 (2), pp. 119–120.

Damon, W. (1995). *Greater expectations: Overcoming the culture of indulgence in America's homes and schools.* New York: The Free Press.

Dewey, J. (1935). The teacher and his world. *The Social Frontier,* I, p. 7.

Dewey, J. (1907). *The school and society.* In M. S. Dworkin, *Dewey on Education.* New York: Teachers College Press, 1959.

Dreeben, R. (1968). *On what is learned in school.* Reading, MA: Addison-Wesley.

Durkheim, E. ([1925] 1961). *Moral education.* Glencoe, IL: Free Press.

Dwyer, K., D. Osher, and C. Warger (1998). *Early warning, timely response: A guide to safe schools.* Washington, DC: U.S. Department of Education.

Eisner, E. W. (1994) *The educational imagination: On design and evaluation of school programs,* 3rd. ed. New York: Macmillan.

Ekstrom, R. B., M. E. Goertz, J. M. Pollack, and D. A. Rock (1987). Who drops out of high school and why? Findings from a national study. In G. Natriello, ed., *School dropouts: Patterns and policies* (pp. 52–69). New York: Teachers College Press.

Fuller, W. E. (1994). *One-room schools of the Middle West.* Lawrence, KS: University Press of Kansas.

Gardner, H. (1993). *Multiple intelligences.* New York: Basic Books.

Gilligan, C. (1982). *In a different voice: Psychological theory and women's development.* Harvard University Press: Cambridge.

Giroux, H. A. (2002). Democracy, freedom, and justice after September 11th: Rethinking the role of educators and the politics of schooling. *Teachers College Record,* January 16(online). http://www.tcrecord.org/Content.asp?ContentID=10871. Accessed December 9, 2003.

Goleman, D. (1995). *Emotional intelligence.* New York: Bantam Books.

Goodlad, J. I., R. Soder, and K. A. Sirotnik, eds. (1993). *The moral dimensions of teaching.* San Francisco: Jossey Bass.

Goodman, J. F., and H. Lesnick (2001). *The moral stake in education: Contested premises and practices.* New York: Addison Wesley Longman.

Hansen, D. T. (1995). Teaching and the moral life of classrooms. *Journal for a Just and Caring Education,* 2 (1), pp. 59–74.

Hutchins, W. J. (1924). The Children's Morality Code. *Journal of the National Education Association, xiii,* p. 292.

Jackson, P. ([1968] 1990). *Life in classrooms.* New York: Teachers College Press.

Juvonen, J. (2001). School violence: Prevalence, fears, and prevention. Santa Monica, CA: Rand Corporation.

Kant, I. (1785). *Groundwork of the metaphysics of morals,* translated by H. J. Paton (1964). New York: Harper & Row.

Kingery, P. M., and M. B. Coggeshall (2001). School-based surveillance of violence, injury and disciplinary actions. Hamilton Fish Institute. http://www.hamfish.org/pub/incdrept1.pdf. Retrieved July 9, 2004.

Kohlberg, L., and E. Turiel (1971). Moral development and moral education. In G. Lesser, ed. *Psychology and educational practice.* Chicago: Scott Foresman.

Kohn, A. (1997). How not to teach values: A critical look at character education. *Phi Delta Kappan, 78* (6), 429–439.

Kohn, A. (1999). *Punished by rewards.* Boston: Houghton Mifflin.

Lickona, T. (1993). The return of character education. *Educational Leadership,* 51 (3), November, pp. 6–11.

Lipman, M. A. (1974). *Harry Stottlemeier's discovery.* Upper Montclair, NJ: Institute for the Advancement of Philosophy.

Lipman, M. A. (1976). *Lisa.* Upper Montclair, NJ: Institute for the Advancement of Philosophy.

Lumsden, L. (2002). Preventing bullying. ERIC Clearinghouse on Educational Management, *ERIC Digest* 155, March. http://ericcass.uncg.edu/virtuallib/bullying/1068.html. Retrieved December 16, 2003.

Lumsden, L. (2002). Profiling students for violence. ERIC Clearinghouse on Educational Policy and Management, *ERIC Digest,* 139, September. http://eric.uoregon.edu/publications/digests/digest139.html. Retrieved September 9, 2004.

McFadden, A. C., G. E. Marsh, B. J. Price, and Y. Hwang (1992). A study of race and gender bias in the punishment of handicapped school children. *Urban Review,* 24, pp. 239–251.

Mijanovich, T., and B. C. Weitzman (2003). Which "broken windows" matter? School, neighborhood, and family characteristics associated with youths' feelings of unsafety. *Journal of Urban Health, 80,* (3) pp. 400–415.

Miller, W. B. (2001). *The growth of youth gang problems in the United States.* Washington, DC: U.S. Department of Justice, Office of Juvenile Justice and Delinquency Prevention.

Moses, R. L. (1994). Remarks on the struggle for citizenship and math/sciences literacy. *Journal of Mathematical Behavior, 13* (1), pp. 107–111.

Nansel, T. R., M. Overpeck, R. S. Pilla, W. J. Ruan, B. Simons-Morton, and P. Scheidt. (2001). Bullying behaviors among U.S. youth. *Journal of the American Medical Association,* 285, pp. 2094–2100.

Nash, R. J. (2003). There is no one best way to teach moral character. *SER in Action,* Fall. Waterbury, CT: Society for Educational Reconstruction.

Noddings, N. (1992). *The challenge to care in schools.* New York: Teachers College Press.

Noddings, N. (1995). A morally defensible mission for schools in the 21st century. *Phi Delta Kappan,* 76 (5), pp. 366–368.

Nucci, L. P. (1987). Synthesis of research on moral development. *Educational Leadership* 44(5) February, pp. 86–92.

Nucci, L. P. (2001). *Education in the moral domain.* New York: Cambridge University Press.

Olweus, D. (1995). *Bullying at school: What we know and what we can do.* Williston, VT: Blackwell Publishers.

Pennington, J. V. (2001). Service learning sparks community and student achievement in Balmorhea. *SEDL Letter, XIII* (1). Austin, TX: Southwest Educational Development Laboratory.

Piaget, J. (1965). *The moral judgment of the child.* New York: Free Press.

Power, F. C., A. Higgins, and L. Kohlberg (1989). *Lawrence Kohlberg's approach to moral education.* New York: Columbia University Press.

Raywid, M. A., and L. Oshiyama (2001). Musings in the wake of Columbine: What can schools do? *Phi Delta Kappan, 81* (6), pp. 444–449.

Riley, R. W. (1998). Religious expression in public schools. Washington, DC: U.S. Department of Education.http://www.ed.gov/Speeches/08-1995/religion.html. Retrieved July 8, 2004.

Riley, R. W. (1999). Response to House vote on allowing states to publicly display the Ten Commandments. Statement by U.S. Secretary of Education Richard W. Riley, June 18. Available online: http://www.ed.gov/PressReleases/06-1999/housetc.html. Accessed September 14, 2003.

Ryan, K. (1996). Character education: A status report. *Journal for a Just and Caring Education, 2* (1), pp. 75–84.

Ryan, K., and K. Bohlin (1999). *Building character in schools.* San Francisco: Jossey Bass.

Scerenko, L. C. (1997). List of values and character education adopted by the State Board of Education. Atlanta, GA: Office of Policy and Communications, Georgia Department of Education, August. http://chiron.valdosta.edu/whuitt/col/affsys/valuesga.html. Retrieved December 31, 2003.

Schwartz, W. (1996). An overview of strategies to reduce school violence. ERIC Clearinghouse on Urban Education. http://eric-web.tc.columbia.edu/digest/dig115.asp. Accessed December 16, 2003.

Shaw, S., and J. P. Braden (1990). Race and gender bias in the administration of corporal punishment. *School Psychology Review,* 19, pp. 378–383.

Simon, S., L. Howe, and H. Kirschenbaum (1995). *Values clarification: Your action-directed workbook.* New York: Warner Books.

Skiba, R. J., and R. L. Peterson (1999). The dark side of zero tolerance: Can punishment lead to safe schools? *Phi Delta Kappan,* 80, pp. 372–376, 381–382.

Sommers, C. H. (2000). The war against boys. *Atlantic Monthly,* 195 (5), May, pp. 59–74.

Totten, S. (2001). Addressing the "null curriculum": Teaching about genocides other than the Holocaust. *Social Education,* 65.

U.S. Dept. of Education (2001). No Child Left Behind Act, P.L. 107-110. Washington, DC. http://www.ed.gov/policy/elsec/leg/esea02/. Accessed December 31, 2003.

Vossekuil, B., R. Fein, M. Reddy, R. Borum, and W. Modzeleski (2002). *Final report and findings of the Safe School Initiative: Implications for the prevention of school attacks in the United States.* Washington, DC: U.S. Dept. of Education, Office of Elementary and Secondary Education, Safe and Drug-Free Schools Program and U.S. Secret Service, National Threat Assessment Center.

11 Educational Reform

ESSENTIAL QUESTION

How do we determine what is worth learning?

My choice was to keep my son in a middle school with 160 other eighth graders or transfer him to a school with fewer students and more individual attention. Despite the possible trauma of changing schools for his last year in the middle school, my choice was right. I enrolled him in a charter school for his final year of middle school. This year, he has received more individual attention, feels more comfortable with his peers, and his grade in math has improved from D to B. (A parent's interview on reasons for moving her child from the local comprehensive middle school to a community charter school.) ■

What Are the Standards for a Good Education?

In this chapter we extend the discussion in Chapter 4 on standards to include the mandates that define the standards and their means of assessment in schools. Standards have been set to assure that all students are guaranteed access to good schooling. Accountability measures designed in rigorous testing programs are used to monitor schools and to identify those who do not meet expectations. In this chapter we address these questions:

- What are the mandates that define standards and assessment?
- What are the arguments for and against standards-based education?
- What is high-stakes testing and how does it work?
- How can schools be restructured to reflect standards?
- What are some models of change?
- What is the global age of school reform?

The debate on standards-based education discussed in Chapter 4 will be revisited along with the issues concerning testing and accountability. We will consider the notion of *choice* as it is interpreted in **voucher systems** and the charter school movement. To that end we will consider several educational models that have embraced change and are now in place throughout the nation. Throughout the chapter it is important to keep in mind that public education with all of its imperfections is still the foundation of American democracy as envisioned by our nation's founders and reformers. Alternatives can enhance it, but a commitment to support its mission of free education for all is imperative.

Change is inevitable, with each generation confident that its blueprint will improve the process of educating America's citizenry by determining what is worth learning. We can learn from the schemes of the past and the present to improve future schooling by examining each model, trend, or movement with an open mind, an appreciation of differing points of view, and optimism that public schools have the potential to prevail.

Standards-based education reforms are changes to the educational system that require schools to be accountable for the achievement of their students. This happens by creating a set of standards that each child must meet. The philosophy supporting standards-based education was articulated in the federal legislation entitled America 2000 and Goals 2000, which demanded that all children be held to high academic standards. These standards were designed to restructure schools, instruction, assessment, and accountability. The content of the curriculum must be aligned with the standards. States are accountable to the federal government to implement the guidelines to ensure funding for educational reforms. These mandates had their genesis in earlier reports and federal legislation, the most significant being the 1983 report, *A Nation at Risk.*

What Are the Mandates That Define Standards and Assessment?

During President Ronald Reagan's administration a national commission was appointed to evaluate the state of public education in the United States. The commission, known as the National Commission on Excellence in Education (NCEE), issued its report, *A Nation at Risk,* in 1983. Terrel Bell, secretary of education under President Ronald Reagan, named members to this commission. Diane Ravitch (2000, pp. 411–412) acknowledges the report as "a landmark of education reform literature" and "a call to action." In the next section, we examine the report.

A Nation at Risk

A Nation at Risk was a scathing censure of public education, as it focused on the pitfalls of American education, particularly student academic performances at the secondary level in comparison to counterparts in other nations. The report heralded the excellence movement, which sought to counter the erosion of standards in schools, replace a watered down curriculum with substance, raise levels of achievement as requirements for high school graduation, increase the hours of the school day, and improve teaching competencies. The legacy of the report is still evident in educational commissions and publications.

Fifteen years later, the 1998 report, *A Nation Still at Risk,* noted that the divide between socioeconomic classes was more evident in schools. Findings indicated that there remained an achievement gap. It appeared that schools in wealthier communities provided superior educational opportunities than those in deprived areas. To remedy the situation, the report recommended parental choice for schools and national assessment testing measures that would guarantee equality in schools (Watras, 2002, p. 373). Twenty years later, marking the anniversary of the publication of *A Nation at Risk,* an editorial entitled *Ever 'At Risk'?* published in *Phi Delta Kappan,* a professional journal in education, contended that the rhetoric of the report had outlived its intent (Smith, 2003). Yet, the impact of *A Nation at Risk* lives on in subsequent governmental reform measures, with its themes being reproduced and revised into the twenty-first century.

In *A Nation At Risk,* the commission made four major recommendations:

1. Graduation requirements need to establish a basic foundation in English, mathematics, science, social studies, and computer science.
2. Schools need to adopt higher standards of academic work that can be measured.
3. Students need to increase their time spent on learning.
4. Teaching as a profession needs higher standards for preparation and continued professional development (National Commission on Excellence in Education, 1983, under "A Nation at Risk").

America 2000 and Goals 2000: Educate America Act

During his administration, President George H. W. Bush launched an aggressive reform measure, America 2000, which defined national curriculum standards for math, science, English, history, and geography. This initiative was a joint effort of the Council of Governors, headed by the then governor William Jefferson Clinton of Arkansas. After his election to the presidency, Bill Clinton revised America 2000 in his Goals 2000: Educate America Act, which expanded the curriculum areas to include the arts, government, economics, physical education, and languages. Guidelines written by learned societies, such as the National Council for Teachers of Mathematics, served as voluntary federal standards. States could adapt their own standards into frameworks that comply with the federal mandates. To date, all fifty states have standards in place.

State and local implementation of Goals 2000 is focused on ensuring that all children meet high academic standards. This emphasis on result is embodied in changes in instructional and institutional systems—curriculum and instruction, professional development, assessment and accountability, school and leadership organization, and parental and community involvement—that are all aligned to content and performance standards. Because Goals 2000 represents the effective implementation of standards-based reform, the two are inextricably linked. Therefore, the success of Goals 2000 must be tied to state progress in implementing standards-based reform and its respective elements (U.S. Department of Education, http://www.ed.gov/pubs/G2KReforming/g2ch3.html).

Critics of both America 2000 and Goals 2000 cite the lofty rhetoric of the documents (see Table 11.1). Such declarations that by the year 2000 all preschoolers would be ready for school or that America would rank first in international comparative studies for math and science sound hollow. In reality, the rhetoric fell short of the targets.

Table 11.1 Summary of the Main Points in Goals 2000

By the year 2000 . . .

1. All children in America will start school ready to learn.
2. The high school graduation rate will increase to at least 90 percent.
3. All students will leave grades 4, 8, and 12 having demonstrated competency over challenging subject matter including English, mathematics, science, foreign languages, civics and government, economics, arts, history, and geography, and every school in America will ensure that all students learn to use their minds well, so they may be prepared for responsible citizenship, further learning, and productive employment in our Nation's modern economy.
4. The Nation's teaching force will have access to programs for the continued improvement of their professional skills and the opportunity to acquire the knowledge and skills needed to instruct and prepare all American students for the next century.
5. United States students will be first in the world in mathematics and science achievement.
6. Every adult American will be literate and will possess the knowledge and skills necessary to compete in a global economy and exercise the rights and responsibilities of citizenship.
7. Every school in the United States will be free of drugs, violence, and the unauthorized presence of firearms and alcohol and will offer a disciplined environment conducive to learning.
8. Every school will promote partnerships that will increase parental involvement and participation in promoting the social, emotional, and academic growth of children.

Source: U.S. Department of Education, http://www.ed.gov/pubs/goals/summary/goals.html.

DIRECTLY FROM THE SOURCE

U.S. Secretary of Education on the No Child Left Behind Act

Source: Rod Paige, Memo to Editorial Writers, Re: No Child Left Behind Implementation, Department of Education, March 11, 2004.

March 11, 2004
To: Editorial Writers
From: U.S. Secretary of Education Rod Paige
Re: No Child Left Behind Implementation

No Child Left Behind (NCLB) has been in the news a great deal in recent weeks. Our country has undertaken an important new course in terms of its commitment to educate every child, regardless of skin color, spoken accent or zip code. Educating close to 50 million children in a big, complex nation like the United States is bound to be a dynamic process. To help bring clarity to the process of the last two years and a sense of where we are presently in terms of implementing No Child Left Behind, I would like to offer the following specific information.

Although there is a great deal of hand-wringing in certain circles concerning the impact that the law is having, it is undeniable that in the two years since enactment, NCLB is having what I consider a transformative impact on our public education system. It is also undeniable that this transformation is taking place in large part due to the determined actions the Department and this administration have taken in implementing the law. For the first time in history, every state has an approved accountability plan to ensure academic proficiency for every child. Achievement gaps are being identified and addressed. The success of schools is now being measured on the academic achievement of all students so that children who need help aren't hidden in averages. Under-performing schools are getting the assistance needed to improve. In other words, in the two years since the bill was passed by Congress and signed by President Bush, we have begun to see critical movement in the public education system to address these important issues . . .

Through the debate on tax cuts, the change in leadership in the Senate, the terrorist attack on 9/11, and the closure of the congressional office buildings due to the anthrax "attacks," it was not until the end of 2001 that Congress moved to pass the bill. However, even after such a lengthy period, many of the intricacies of the law were intentionally left vague, with the expectation that the Department of Education, through the regulatory process, would smooth out the "rough edges."

. . . [U]nder my watch, the Department has undertaken aggressive efforts to provide comprehensive regulatory and technical guidance on many, if not most, of the complex issues in the law. Those endeavors take thoughtful deliberation, conversations with the people in the field, discussions with members of Congress and their staffs, and careful promulgation of regulations and guidance. The opposite tack—to promulgate rules and regulations, in a desire for speed, closeted in Washington without input from practitioners and key policymakers—was not an acceptable option to me. . . . To put our efforts in context, when this administration took office, only 11 states were in compliance with the 1994 ESEA. One of the first tasks we undertook was to address those states that were not in compliance with that law. In less than a year, we entered into compliance or timeline agreements with states to ensure that they would be in compliance with a law that had been in effect for seven years but really had never been enforced. This was critical, for, as you may know, many of the principles of NCLB (development of standards, assessing students, identifying schools for improvement, to name a few) have their roots in the 1994 ESEA reauthorization.

Upon issuing the new Title I NCLB regulations, it was our task to work with the states to institute accountability plans under No Child Left Behind in such a manner that balanced the interests of the states with the goals of the law. Considering that there are 50 different state educational standards and assessment systems in place and 50 different state governance systems overseeing more than 15,000 school districts, these negotiations were challenging, as I'm sure you can imagine. (You should also keep in mind that many of the state departments of education experienced changes in leadership during this time.) Yet we accomplished our goal, and on June 10, 2003—18 months after the law was enacted—all 50 states, plus the District of Columbia and Puerto Rico, had approved accountability plans in place. This was a historic day for our nation, our educational system and, of course, our children. It has been only eight months since those plans were approved, yet as of today we

www.

are seeing the impact of those state-driven accountability plans all across the nation.

Contrary to the perception in some corners, this historic achievement did not occur by happenstance but was due in large part to our extensive and unprecedented interactions with the states. We discussed with every state its unique education system and needs. At my invitation and at the expense of the Department, delegations from 47 states came to the nation's capital to meet individually with senior Department leadership. Then, an accountability peer review team composed of Department staff and experts in the fields of accountability, standards and assessments visited every state to review its accountability plan.

In the three years of this administration, the Department of Education has transformed its relationship with both the states and local school districts. The level of outreach and cooperation extended to the states on a range of issues has been unprecedented. And, unlike previous years, this administration is actively enforcing the laws that have been passed by Congress and signed by the President . . .

Since last summer, our technical assistance and outreach efforts on NCLB have expanded. At all levels—from senior leadership to staff-level experts—the Department is communicating on a daily basis with states, districts and schools. The following are just a few examples of this effort:

- The Department has issued guidance on numerous programs within NCLB. Since passage of the bill two years ago, 30 guidance documents on NCLB programs have been issued. In addition, we have sent almost 20 letters on NCLB implementation issues to chief state school officers, governors and other state officials.
- The Department recruited and trained 50 teachers, principals, district officials, representatives from higher education, and national policy experts to serve as members of the Teacher Assistance Corps (TAC). The TAC has rendered direct support and technical assistance to nearly every state in meeting the challenges of the highly qualified teacher provisions of the law and now has visited 49 states.
- In September 2003, President Bush and I announced the School Information Partnership, a unique public-private partnership designed to assist states in meeting the letter and the spirit of NCLB as it relates to educational data reporting. Through the financial support of the Broad Foundation and the Department, states have been given the opportunity, at no cost for the next two years, to report and analyze certain data through an easy-to-use Web-based service.
- The Department has provided technical assistance through conference calls, on-site visits, regional meetings, Listservs and the Comprehensive Regional Assistance Centers. In addition, the Office of Elementary and Secondary Education has held conference calls and meetings with state Title I directors, has for the first time initiated a program of national conference calls with local Title I directors, has held eight national conferences and has sent 500 different letters to various state and local offices on NCLB.
- Several organizations, such as the Council of Chief State School Officers and the Council of the Great City Schools, are working with the Department to provide assistance to states and districts.
- The Office of English Language Acquisition has conducted 52 video teleconferences and 35 on-site visits with the states to provide in-depth technical assistance. This effort facilitated the development and implementation of the integrated systems of standards and assessments, required by Title III of NCLB.

How states and districts use this wealth of information and technical assistance is a separate issue, as I am sure you recognize. States have tremendous flexibility in implementing this law, as outlined in a memo entitled "Charting the Course," which I encourage you to read at http://www.ed.gov/news/pressreleases/2004/01/01142004.html. This document outlines almost 40 elements of flexibility and decision-making that states have in implementing critical aspects of NCLB. . . .

The variety in state plans underscores the bipartisan intent of the law to build upon existing state accountability systems and reform efforts, not to dictate uniformity. As I think you will agree, this is a testament to the strength of the design of the law and to the methods that the administration pursued in implementing the law. Our overarching goal is to provide the maximum flexibility while remaining faithful to the spirit of the law. We continue to listen and examine issues being raised and will, if appropriate and consistent with the spirit of the law, address additional issues as soon as possible.

(continued)

DIRECTLY FROM THE SOURCE

U.S. Secretary of Education on the No Child Left Behind Act *(Continued)*

You should also know that more than any other time in its history, this Department is serious about enforcing the law. We have not issued waivers; we have withheld funds from states that have not complied with the law; and we have engaged in compliance agreements with those states that could not meet the law's timelines, including timelines that were instituted prior to NCLB. . . . Indeed, the chorus that there is inadequate funding under NCLB just doesn't wash. America's schools are experiencing record levels of federal funding. Under President Bush, funding for ESEA programs reauthorized by NCLB has climbed $7.4 billion, or 43 percent. What's more, with the flexibility added by NCLB, states, districts and schools can spend the money more freely than ever, as long as they do what works to improve student learning and achievement.

Bear in mind that these funds go into an environment where spending on K–12 education in general is already at unprecedented levels. In 1994, during the last reauthorization of ESEA, total K–12 spending in this nation was $286 billion. Now, we are investing more than $500 billion in K–12 education. Contrary to conventional wisdom, this is $125 billion more than our nation invests in defense. It averages about $100,000 for the life of a child in our K–12 system. We have spent $125 billion on Title I programs for disadvantaged students in the past 25 years, yet we have virtually nothing to show for it. The best way to win political support for more Title I funding is to demonstrate that it really works to raise student achievement.

Furthermore, three studies and the General Accounting office (GAO) all have found that NCLB is funded at a level to get the job done:

- A GAO study from May 2003 found that Congress is providing more than enough money for states to design and implement the statewide achievement tests required under No Child Left Behind. The report also shows education reform opponents are exaggerating estimates of NCLB's state testing costs by as much as $5.1 billion between fiscal years 2002 and 2008.

I do believe that investments in education are a priority for our nation if we are to maintain our economic security, not to mention our intellectual happiness as a people. The education of our children is one of the most important endeavors any nation can undertake. However, even after such increases over the last decade, we still hear the chorus of "more money" emanating from certain circles. That has always been and will likely always be the mantra of these organizations, for they chose to measure our commitment not by whether or not a third-grade girl can read on a third-grade level but by how much more money we are spending on the system. It reminds me of how Albert Einstein defined insanity: the belief that one can get different results by doing the same thing over and over again. It doesn't take an Einstein to see that all the money in the world won't fix our schools if the only plan is just to throw more money at them. To make a difference, you must first create a framework for change. That's what No Child Left Behind does—focuses our nation's attention on the appropriate bottom line—making sure our children are learning. Therefore, NCLB is absolutely leading us in the right direction.

Sincerely,
Rod Paige

A Closer Look at the Issues

1. Do you think that Secretary Paige's defense is a fair appraisal of NCLB?
2. How has the NCLB Act impacted your local school system?

No Child Left Behind

To counter the shortfall in closing the achievement gap, President George W. Bush extended the Elementary and Secondary Education Act to include his educational agenda, No Child Left Behind (NCLB). Republicans and Democrats, liberals and conservatives, embraced this bipartisan legislation when it passed through both houses of the U.S. Congress as law in January 2002. This initiative affects school policy, curriculum, and instruction in every American public school. Its intention is to close the continuously growing "achievement gap," which was first coined and defined in *A Nation at Risk*. The achievement gap refers to the difference in the continuous successful testing results of students from wealthy and middle class communities when compared with the levels of achievement in school populations from impoverished or minority households.

Accountability is a clause in the NCLB mandate that holds schools responsible for their students' achievement in literacy, mathematics, and science, as documented by unbiased assessments. Accountability is central to the mandate's requirement to test all students in public schools from the primary years through secondary school. While states can select the testing format, all schools are judged on their success in teaching reading and mathematics. Identification of underperforming schools is based on test results of all students in a school's Adequate Yearly Progress (AYP).

Exam results measure the achievement of the school's overall population as well as the performance of specific groups in the school population, such as special needs students and English language learners, to determine the ranking of the school. All segments of the school population must succeed. Parents can remove their children from schools designated as *underperforming*. Choice placements—options that parents have for their childrens' school assignments—are offered within the district in schools deemed successful, provided that they have openings available.

The NCLB Act identifies and expands its core academic subjects to include the following:

English

Reading/language arts

Mathematics

Science

Foreign languages

Civics and government

Economics

Arts

History

Geography

(U.S. Department of Education, http://www.ed.gov/admins/tchrqual/learn/hqt/ edlit-slide012 .html)

Because teachers are central to the success of any program, the legislation calls for "highly qualified teachers" in all classrooms from kindergarten through grade twelve. The law defines specific professional requirements for America's teaching force. To earn the status of being a highly qualified teacher, one must hold a minimum of a bachelor's degree, obtain full state certification or licensure, and demonstrate subject area competence in each of the academic subjects that one teaches (U.S. Department of Education, http://www.ed.gov/admins/tehrqual/learn/hgt/edlite-slice008.html). This information came from the U.S., Department of Education with no date given. Similarly, under the federal mandate, Good Start, Grow Smart, there is a move to require early childhood professionals to possess a bachelor's degree to strengthen Head Start programs, which provide child development services for low-income children, from birth to age five, and their families.

Along with the highly qualified teacher requirements the following four concepts summarize major components of NCLB:

Accountability: Testing and school status is determined for AYP (adequate yearly progress) reporting. By the year 2005–06 all children will be tested in math and reading beginning in third grade. In year 2007–08, science achievement will be tested.

Flexibility: The federal government will distribute funding. States and local authorities can determine how federal dollars are to be spent to improve their educational programs.

Proven Education Models: Federal funding will target "research-based programs" that have proven successful, particularly in the area of reading, notably the federally funded program called *Early Reading First.*

Parental Choices: Parents can transfer their children from schools identified as "in need of improvement" to a better performing public or charter school and use "supplemental education services" such as tutoring, after school and summer programs (U.S.Department of Education, http://www.nclb.gov).

The NCLB mandate is under constant scrutiny. While segments of American society hail the law as a milestone in the journey toward equal education for all students, others note the law's inherent flaws. Different factions clamor to change the law. The growing realization of the impact of NCLB on educational change has caused some states to reconsider adoption of the measures and suffer the consequence of losing federal funding. To address the critics, Secretary of Education Rod Paige offered a defense on page 442.

What Are the Arguments For and Against Standards-Based Education?

The success or failure of NCLB is still open to review. As noted in the previous section, response to this education act has its proponents and its critics. Proponents applaud the intent or spirit of the law in guaranteeing the right of all children in America to an equal and equitable education. Critics question the sufficiency of the funding, the assumptions about standards-based education, and the overemphasis on testing for accountability. All citizens have the responsibility to decide about the effectiveness of their schools. They must shift through the rhetoric of federal pronouncements by comparing evidence provided by test results against other measures of achievement. Community members need to make the government accountable for providing adequate funding to improve curriculum and restructure schools.

School and Community Response

Everyone has something to say about education—parents, families, business, governmental officials, boards of education, teachers, and students. Anyone who has attended school claims an expertise in defining what constitutes a good education and how to attain it. Parents want to be vested in their children's schools. Family members recall their own school experiences; some with fondness, others with discomfort. In either situation, parents are most comfortable with the familiar and uncertain about change. Often you hear families complain about new methods of teaching math or the lack of respect and tradition in schools.

Politically, governmental officials use education as a rallying call for support of their agenda. Politicians often promote innovations that they feel will resonate with their constituencies without regard for the merits of the change. People in general like to reminisce about past glories of public schooling and forget that each era has had challenges to meet. Yet many segments of society have recommendations on how to resolve the deficiencies in American education. The business community is vocal about their recommendations for improving schools. A recent article in *Business Week* illustrates this in its proposed "seven ideas" on how to "fix" schools:

- Pay teachers for performance
- Make schools smaller
- Hold educators accountable
- Offer variety
- Provide adequate funding
- Increase school time
- Use technology effectively (Symonds, 2001)

Few would argue with most of these sound recommendations, which reflect many of the goals of NCLB. There are various points of view on the recommendations about money issues. While some of the populace are willing to increase teacher salaries, they prefer to link students' performances to monetary rewards, such as bonuses or salary adjustments—a form of merit pay. However, merit pay is very controversial and not considered by teaching professional agencies as a fair way to acknowledge effective teaching. Teachers claim that student performance varies from year to year, dependent not only on teacher effectiveness but on factors such as the dynamics of the group. Indeed, students' achievement is affected by many variables, particularly socioeconomic conditions and linguistic or ethnic factors.

Likewise, there is no agreement as to what constitutes "adequate funding" for school reforms, particularly in an economic downtime. A disparity exists in funding educational endeavors. The cost of living differs in regions throughout the country. Adequate funding for Kansas or Florida might not be sufficient for California or New York. David Tyack of Stanford University contends that NCLB is a utopian vision: ". . . so long as school resources continue to reflect the gross inequalities of wealth and income in this country, major achievement gaps will persist between the prosperous and the poor, and too many students will continue to be, now as in the past, 'thoroughly trained in failure' " (Tyack, 2003, p. 126).

More Monies Needed

Much of school funding rests primarily with local and state resources. If tax revenues decline, educational innovations are often jettisoned. Lack of "adequate" reimbursement from the federal government jeopardizes the realization of the goals of NCLB, particularly in communities where it is most needed to fill the achievement gap.

Evidence shows that economics prevails when it comes to closing the gap. Children from wealthier communities consistently achieve higher test scores when compared with their counterparts from poorer urban and rural areas. Test scores are the basis for the rating of schools. So when federal subsidies fail to fill in the gaps with sufficient funds, reform becomes rhetorical. Yes, all children can achieve and learn, but only if the playing field is level and the opportunities are truly equal. While federal monies have been increased under NCLB, the prevailing sentiment in state governments is that more monies are needed to compensate for the discrepancies, in order to meet the varying needs in their communities.

Concerns About Standards-Based Education Reforms

As indicated in Chapter 4, there are many critics of the standards approach to school reform. Several prominent educators, such as Elliot Eisner, Deborah Meier, Alfie Kohn, and Susan Ohanian, criticize the standards movement as a "one size fits all" approach to teaching. They point to the need for more personalized schools with curricula that reflect key factors such as the culture of the community, parental input, students' needs, and autonomous teachers. They claim that the "sameness" of the standards-based approach is counterproductive in meeting the challenges of teaching a diverse population with a myriad of individual strengths and needs.

The dilemma of trying to ensure that all students receive the same education can lead to Paulo Freire's *banking approach* (where the teacher merely deposits information and the students are the depositories, patiently receiving and memorizing—as opposed to students who have a more active role in their education) for those students whose community and personal heritages differ from the mainstream (Lee, 2003). Somehow standards need to be personalized in reflecting the multicultural side of America. "The key is to link standards to the students' own ethnic, social and cultural lives" (Lee, 2003).

Many educators contend that the national and state mandates are simplistic remedies for complex problems, that they tinker with accidentals rather than grapple with substance, and that they produce misleading indicators as justification. John Goodlad cautions that "the most dismayingly scary characteristic of the current school reform era is the preoccupation with simplistic prescription devoid of diagnosis and purpose" (Goodlad, 2002, p. 23). Likewise, Elliot Eisner points out the pitfalls of school reform in which "superficial factors are addressed," resulting in short-lived reforms that "lead to no real reform at all" (Eisner, 2003, p. 657). The cycle will inevitably continue with yet another report and call for reform.

Educational policy and school reform needs to reflect the complex nature of American society and be grounded in research that is thorough, comprehensive, and reflective of the students' world. For example, reading specialists and educational psychologists question the promotion of Reading First as a standard approach to literacy instruction in the primary years, as mandated under NCLB. While teachers have found Reading First to be successful with some children, particularly those with learning differences, reading specialists do not give it a blanket endorsement for all children. Gerald Coles, an educational psychologist formerly at the Robert Wood Johnson Medical School of the University of Medicine and Dentistry of New Jersey, contends that the research supporting Reading First misrepresents the neurological research theories about the connection between functions of the brain and learning how to read. According to Coles:

> More than ever, claims about the research constitute an ideological barrier to a sounder understanding of the connections between brain activity and learning to read. More than ever, this work is a danger to the classroom both because it applies unproven labels to an ever-larger number of children and because it promotes a single kind of instruction that, based on the actual empirical evidence mustered for it, contains no promise for leaving no beginning reader behind. To all this, add the false and cruel expectations that these claims generate in parents (2004, p. 346).

Ron Brandt, former executive editor of *Educational Leadership,* wants to "separate standards from grade levels." He feels standards linked to grade levels are for the "convenience of teachers" and "partly for test makers, administrators and policymakers who want neat scorecards." He further concludes that such linkages mistake "common standards" for "high standards" (2003a, p. 20). Instead of excellence, he contends, common standards lead to mediocrity. Standards must reflect researched evidence that connects the standards to the academic needs of the students regardless of grade. Superficial learning of inconsequential facts can easily be mistaken for achievement.

To improve schools, teachers and principals and students need a voice in the reforms so as to build a school climate that suits the students and reflects the culture of the community and the heritages of its families. To replace the existing order with "break-the-mold" schools, communities, families, teachers, and principals need to shape goals that lead to scholarship, command high expectations, and encourage accomplishment. They must eschew top-down mandates that replace creativity with "kill and drill" methodology, creative teaching with scripted manuals, and substantive learning with piecemeal knowledge.

The Case for Standards-Based Education Reforms

Many educators put a positive spin on standards-based education. They recall with dismay the laissez faire days when teachers or communities decided what their students were to learn. Anecdotal references note the primary school in which the identical dinosaur unit was taught in kindergarten, grade one, and again in grade two; and the middle school that showcased the same unit on Japan for the past ten years as the school's annual global education project.

A more poignant anecdote is the case study of arbitrary grades. In a suburban district near Washington, D.C., the same annual end-of-course algebra test was administered in all secondary schools, but the results were treated very differently. A score of 66 would be worthy of an A in one school but would earn a B, C, or D in other schools. Teachers explained that circumstances (mainly socioeconomic) made the difference (Brandt, 2003a, p. 18).

Douglas Reeves (2003, p. 16) offers a cogent argument for standards that create a "level playing field in which expectations are consistent" and grades are determined objectively. He prefers matching students' achievement with a standard rather than using a **bell curve,** a statistical term for a normal distribution of any factor such as intelligence or achievement, used in comparing students to each other. To personalize the standards he encourages administrators, teachers, and communities to create "power standards," which are in effect "small subsets of state standards" (p. 20). He identifies the criteria of a power standard as (1) endurance—the standard provides knowledge of material that remains with the learner after the tests; (2) leverage—the standard presents ideas that cross many disciplines; and (3) leveling—the standard spirals knowledge and skills "required for the next level of learning" (p. 20).

Because teachers select the power standards, teachers are empowered to personalize instruction to the needs of their students while meeting the goals of the statewide mandates. Reeves insists that "the standards movement is a desire for fairness" and a remedy for the inconsistencies of the past, when teachers or schools did their own thing (p. 16).

What Does This Mean for Teachers and Students?

Teachers have a mixed reaction to standards-based education. Many appreciate the critics' positions, but realize that, at the end of the day, they are bound to implement the mandates. Support for standards has come from teachers who serve on their states' task force to write or review the standards. Some teachers maintain that standards help to set goals and clarify grading practices. They feel standards provide consistency because achievement is measured by clearly defined attainment targets. These teachers further note that although standards define uniform curriculum outcomes, they do not necessarily prescribe how the teacher must implement curriculum. While some teachers are inflexible and constrained to "teach to the test," others experiment with creative approaches that tailor the standards to their students needs. The following scenario illustrates a fourth-grade class in an urban school faced with an annual state-mandated test that measures the school's progress in attaining proficiency.

Scenario for State-Mandated Testing of Fourth Graders Mrs. Wadsworth's fourth-grade class has been working all year on project-based units designed to integrate the state's curriculum standards around themes and topics, along with direct teaching exercises for mastery of literacy and numeracy skills. Mrs. Wadsworth blended instructional strategies that allowed for practice and drill with creative expression and critical thinking through inquiry-based activities. Concept-building and test-taking skills have been fostered throughout the year in role-playing experiences. Family involvement has been encouraged as parents are expected to monitor homework assignments and are invited to school events, welcomed as volunteers, and provided with consultations.

The class is socially and economically diverse, with some English-language learners whose first languages include Spanish and Polish. Her community has school choice at the elementary level, so her parents have selected this setting for their children. The children live in neighborhoods throughout the city and come from homes of diverse incomes and social backgrounds. Families back the school and respect the teaching staff.

Like all fourth graders in their state, these children are required to take state examinations, as mandated by NCLB, to determine their achievement in reading and mathematics. The NCLB guidelines stipulate that all of the children are expected to pass the exam. Last year, the test performances were such that this school had been designated as an underperforming school. So now Mrs. Wadsworth and the children are under pressure to improve the class's test scores. A seasoned teacher, Mrs. Wadsworth has confidence in her approach and feels the children are prepared to meet the challenge. She tries to keep the tone of the class low key, to avoid any unnecessary anxiety among her children.

The tests were administered in May. While the results will not be reported until next fall, the students felt positive about their performance; as one youngster remarked, "There wasn't anything on the tests we didn't study. Mrs. Wadsworth taught us what we needed to know!" Let's wish them well.

What Is High-Stakes Testing and How Does It Work?

> Test scores need to take a back seat to more educationally significant outcomes. As long as schools treat test scores as the major proxies for student achievement and educational quality, we will have a hard time refocusing our attention on what really matters in education (Eisner, 2003/2004, p. 10.)

Among the reform mandates, testing requirements are very controversial. Many states are awarding high school diplomas only to students who achieve a passing grade on the state's designated standardized test—this is **high-stakes testing.** Such test scores are the sole criteria for accountability and measuring the school's, or

Many states use high-stakes testing as the sole means of measuring their success. Students are awarded high school diplomas only if they achieve a passing grade on the state's designated standardized test.
Source: © Michael Newman/PhotoEdit

school system's, success. Test results are calculated and published in local newspapers in league tables that rank community or individual school performance.

The Competitive Nature of Testing

Testing at all levels can be a contest. Children, regardless of age, are measured against one another. Comparisons are made. Judgments of the children are formed. When results are posted in newspapers and other media outlets, there are public postings of winners and losers, which can spark more rhetoric. The well-intended challenge made by a former governor of North Carolina for his state to be "First in America," echoes the reform rhetoric of the 1990s national mandates. "By the year 2010, North Carolina will build the best system of public schools of any state in America. By the end of the first decade of the 21st century, we will be first in education" (Hunt, 2002, p. 715).

The competitive nature of such pronouncements can diminish the goals of an education for democracy. The constant comparing, sorting, and labeling of school success based on test results can be more destructive than constructive in reaching the intended goals for America's schools. The tests, at best, are only one tool in the assessment process. They can diagnose and provide some measure of growth and learning. They can complement other forms of assessment such as a portfolio, performance, exhibition, production, or presentation. When test results are the only criteria determining the school's ranking, tests can become the sole determinant of the curriculum. No school or community wants to be the last on a public list. There is a strong inclination to teach to the test. A broader vision of education is warranted.

Alaska: A Case Study of High-Stakes Testing Alaska is one state committed to a high-stakes testing policy. The state's educational policy presents high-stakes testing as a means of bridging the achievement gap. "A high school exit exam is in place and has been given to 10th graders. . . . [T]he time line for using it as a graduation requirement [is] 2004. There are also tests given in grades 3, 6 and 8, called 'benchmark tests,' that are intended to gauge how students are progressing toward the exit exam." Scores of both the exit and benchmark exams are "the means of sorting and classifying schools into one of four categories: distinguished, proficient, deficient and 'in crisis' " (Jones and Ongtooguk, 2002, p. 499).

Supporters of such testing policy argue that a common test for all students raises the bar for all students' achievement levels, makes schools' accountability equitable, and avoids the inconsistencies of past practices. All students are held to the same expectations, with achievement demonstrated by their test results. The goal of the policy is to close the achievement gap, regardless of socioeconomic, racial, ethnic, linguistic, or class status.

Unfortunately, Alaska reflects the nation in that those gaps still exist. Rod Paige, the former U.S. Secretary of Education, noted these persistent gaps in his review of results of the National Assessment of Educational Progress (NAEP) annual national achievement tests. In a national comparative study of urban, suburban, and rural fourth graders' reading scores, findings showed that "only 32% of fourth graders can read proficiently and the proportion in urban areas is even lower" (Paige, 2002, p. 710). Ethnic differences were even greater. "While 40% of white fourth-graders read at or above the proficient level, only 12% of blacks and 16% of Hispanics perform as well" (p. 711). Proponents of high-stakes testing cite NCLB as

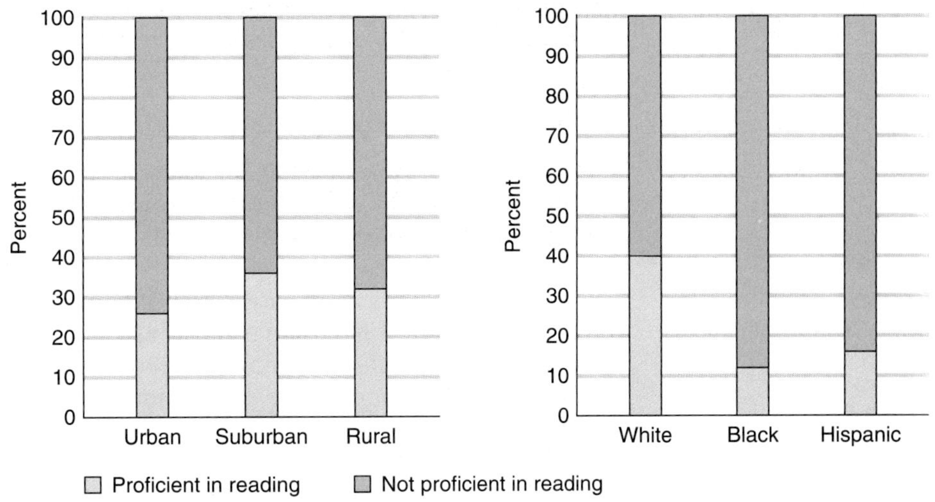

Figure 11.1

Percentage of Fourth-Grade Students Who Are Proficient in Reading

Source: R. Paige (May, 2002). An overview of America's education agenda. *Phi Delta Kappan* 83(9), p. 711.

a means to eradicate this difference by establishing a longitudinal record that tracks student progress in the reading and math tests from grades 3 to 8. Supporters contend this longitudinal record allows for "informed decisions" by administrators, teachers, and parents "to improve student performance" (p. 711) and prepare students for the exit exam in grade 10.

Critics label mandatory high-stakes testing policy as superficial and unfair. While they applaud the federal government's increased endorsement of equity, they voice many criticisms of a test-driven accountability process. Some question the validity and reliability of the standard tests used in many states. Teachers complain about the delayed reporting of results. In Alaska, studies show that cultural biases embedded in standardized tests put nonwhite students, particularly the native populations, at a disadvantage (Jones and Ongtooguk, 2002, p. 500). Alaskans are also concerned about their special needs students, who could be so disenfranchised by the process as to "leave school early, since there is no reward in sight for them if they stay" (McDermott and McDermott, 2002, p. 544).

Natural Skepticism Skeptics depict the "testing frenzy" as a conspiracy against public education. They also note that the inherent cultural biases of the tests deter success for nonwhite students, particularly those in poor urban and rural systems. They question the motives for the growing number of alternate choices such as charter schools, the demand for vouchers to support private schools, and the management of public schools by the "education-for-profit" industry as movements that undermine the mainstream public schools, yet draw from the public coffers for funding. These skeptics want the same testing requirements extended to the private sector, as is the typical practice in most states for charter schools.

Even though NCLB requires testing in elementary schools, there has been a move at the federal level to begin testing even earlier, at the age of four, with children in Head Start programs. The intent of the Head Start testing is to establish a baseline of skills development as a "school readiness assessment" to determine a smooth transition from preschool to kindergarten. Since private preschools do not include their population in the testing program for four-year-olds, early childhood educators raise some legitimate questions about the value of a testing program that is targeted for only one designated group.

Good Start, Grow Smart: When Should Testing Begin?

Debate mounts as to when to begin standard testing procedures for all children. What standards and assessments are appropriate for young children? Should testing begin before the child enters school?

The National Center for Education Statistics' (NCES) longitudinal study of young children indicates that the gap between low-, middle-, and high-income homes is evident with entrance into kindergarten (Lewis, 2003). As a result of that and other studies, the new federal initiative entitled Good Start, Grow Smart requires all states to produce "early learning guidelines" aligned to their K–12 standards (Lewis, 2003, p. 483). These early learning guidelines mirror the intent of Great Britain's Foundation Stages in regulating early childhood education at the preschool levels to provide for a smooth transition into kindergarten that bridges learning gaps apparent in young children.

Good Start, Grow Smart has three intentions:

1. Strengthen Head Start through an accountability process that assesses literacy, language, and numeracy skills.
2. Partner with states to improve Early Childhood Education by requiring state standards for alignment with K–12 curriculum.
3. Provide information to teacher, childcare providers and parent on current research and practices particularly in prereading and language curriculum development and teacher training. (National Child Care Information Center, 2002).

The British Foundation Stage replaced its preschool testing program with a longitudinal development profile that assesses the child from preschool through the reception class (kindergarten) year. The former entrance test into the reception class, known as Baseline Assessment, was a comprehensive evaluation of primarily literacy and numeracy skills. It was once required of all four- and five-year-olds upon entrance into the reception class. As of 2002, a developmental profile follows each child from age three in nursery school through age five in the reception class. The profile offers an overall developmental record of the child. It is designed to help children transition from a private or state nursery school program into the local authority schools. British early childhood educators saw no long-term instructional benefits of giving the "one-shot" screening assessment early in the reception class year (Swiniarski, 2003). America, however, has opted to test literacy and numeracy skills of all four-year-olds in Head Start as a predictor of academic readiness for kindergarten.

The overemphasis on academic readiness sounds alarms for early childhood educators and families. Educators concur with parents who worry about age requirements for school entrance. When preschoolers' birthdays fall near the cutoff dates, families fear that their children will not be ready age-wise to manage the academic demands of the kindergarten curriculum. To avoid early failure in school, some families decide to retain or "red shirt" their children for a year (Schulte, 2003). In response, early childhood specialists propose making schools ready for the "whole child" with appropriate standards that match the early stages

In England, a developmental profile follows each child from age three in nursery school through age five in the reception (kindergarten) class. The profile offers an overall developmental record of the child and is designed to help children transition from a private or state nursery school program into the local authority schools.
Source: © Elizabeth Crews

of all areas of development. They recommend multi-age classrooms or adaptation of the staggered admission policy of New Zealand, which allows each child to begin school in the term of his or her fifth birthday (Swiniarski and Brietborde, 2003, pp. 58–59).

In 1991 the late Ernest Boyer set forth a proposal in *Ready to Learn: A Mandate for the Nation.* Boyer was a spokesperson for values in higher education who headed the Carnegie Foundation for the Advancement of Teaching. He outlined a "seven-step strategy to ensure learning readiness for the entire nation's children" (Boyer, 1991, p. 135). The seven steps include:

1. a healthy start
2. empowered parents
3. quality preschool
4. a responsive workplace
5. television as teacher
6. neighborhoods for learning
7. connections across the generations

Boyer began his strategy with a national campaign for a healthy start to underscore the importance of wellness in the educational process. Like John Locke, Boyer believed education should begin early to build sound minds in sound bodies. To accomplish his goal he called for "good nutrition and access to basic health care for all mothers and babies" (1991, p. 31). Additionally, he recommended "family friendly work policies" that grant parent leaves, allow for flextime, and provide job-sharing and support for child care (p. 65). The workplace is a part of the larger community for families and children. Neighborhoods are learning environments, particularly those that offer well-supervised and creative playgrounds, children's museums with hands-on activities, libraries, zoos, or urban farms, resources that Boyer called "learning stations" (p. 99).

Likewise for Boyer, technology and the media play a role in the community's response to families' needs. "Next to parents, television is, perhaps, a child's most influential teacher" (p. 79). The community must regulate television programs, to enhance growth and spare children from "mindless mass communications" (p. 86). He commended the efforts of the 1990 Children's Television Act that mandated provision for children's programming with limited advertising time as a condition for a television station's license and renewal. He cautioned parents to be vigilant in monitoring their children's viewing. He applauded programs like "Reading Rainbow," of the Public Broadcasting System (PBS), as well as several Discovery Channel and Nickelodeon productions. Finally, he recommended that the education of youngsters connect with all members of a community, across generations.

> In the end, intergenerational connections may be the *real* key to quality in education. After all, a ready-to-learn campaign is not just about schools, or even about children. It's about building in this country a new network of support, creating a true community of caring for the coming generation. . . . [T]he steps—from a healthy start to connections across the generations—are bound together by the conviction that, if the future of the nation is be to secure, we must all come together on behalf of children (Boyer, 1991, p. 121).

Interestingly, Boyer offered no prescription for national or state testing schemes that measure intensive academic gains in literacy or numeracy skills. Educators concerned about the promotion of early testing and narrowly defined curricula have called for a renewal of Boyer's seven steps to ensure real reform in the beginning years of the educational process (Lewis, 2003, p. 484).

How Can Schools Be Restructured to Reflect Standards?

Many alternatives have been proposed to counter the eventuality that mandatory tests drive the curriculum . In this section, we consider several ongoing programs that personalize standards to meet individual student needs while raising the performance level of the entire student body. In all three of the following models, teachers are empowered to shape the standards through effective instructional practice with the conviction that all students can achieve.

The National Alliance on the American High School

The National Alliance on the American High School at Brown University in Providence, Rhode Island, has formulated instructional strategies for a standards-based curriculum that *personalizes learning* in America's high schools. The alliance has based its work on three recommendations of Theodore Sizer, one of which calls for a "demonstration of knowledge, not just testing" as a criteria for graduation and promotion (DiMartino, Clarke, and Wolk, 2003, p. vii). While the American Educational Research Association (AERA) has a position that there must be an "alignment between the test and the curriculum," the association "recommends using multiple test forms" to avoid "teaching to the test" and "a narrowing of the curriculum" (Sadowski, 2000).

A "Quiet Revolution"

In his bid for a "quiet revolution" Douglas Reeves challenges other states to follow the lead of Nebraska, which took advantage of the NCLB legislation's leeway of allowing each state to draw its own testing system. In Nebraska, district level assessments are written and scored by teachers to place the control and sanctions in the hands of the community and its educators. Reeves rallies other states to "create an assessment system that is flexible, teacher-created, teacher-scored and useful for immediate feedback in the classroom. Rather than rely on a single test, teachers would have multiple assessments on which to base the final judgment about the degree to which a student meets or fails to meet standards" (2003, p. 20).

Reeves's quiet revolution permits teachers to identify standards they feel have lasting value to their students, standards that can be taught across disciplines and that help to transition a knowledge base and skills from one grade level to the next. When teachers match students' achievement to a standard, rather than plot performance on the bell curve, all students are given the chance to succeed. Students are not then compared with each other but measured individually as they attain the targeted goals. Student performance need not be placed upon a distribution curve, the bell curve, in which some students are necessarily relegated as failures. Teachers do not have to adjust grades for performance along a distribution in which the majority of the class is rated average, the top range noted as superior and the bottom of the distribution a failure. Much like Jeff Howard's Efficacy Model discussed in Chapter 4, Reeves asks teachers to have the same expectation for all children to meet the established criteria.

A Credentialed Teaching Force

No Child Left Behind has defined its credentials for a highly qualified teacher, as discussed in Chapter 6, as someone who holds at minimum a bachelor's degree, state licensure, and a demonstration of knowledge of the subject matter to be taught. That demonstration is typically measured by tests designed for teachers from preschool to grade 12 in all academic areas and professional specialties, such as counseling, special education, administration, reading teacher, or teacher of English-language learners. Each state is given the flexibility to select or design its own tests for teacher competencies.

Teacher Testing: Credentials for Highly Qualified Teachers Not all standardized tests are intended for students. There are national and state tests for teachers. The nation is concerned about inadequately prepared teachers. The U.S. Department of Education claims only "forty-one percent of eighth grade math teachers majored in math," while one-fifth of "all public school students in grades seven through twelve were taught by teachers who did not have at least a minor in English literature, communications or journalism" (U S Department of Education) (http://www.ed.gov/admins/techrqual/learn/hqu/edlite-slides003 html) (004.html). Further, the U.S. Department of Education contends that "fewer than 36 percent of current teachers feel 'very well prepared' to implement curriculum" (U.S. Department of Education) (www.ed.gov/admins/tchrqual/learn/hqt/edlite-slide006.html).

To ensure professionalism in teaching and teacher competency states have required teacher testing as a sanction. Passing scores on such tests are required for the certification or licensure process administered by states across America. Each state chooses its own exam. As indicated in Chapter 6 some states use the National Teachers Exam or Praxis; others develop their own measures. The intent of all professional exams is to determine teacher candidates' levels of mastery in the subject areas to be taught; this, in turn, will help students perform because the teachers have been validated as being qualified.

What Does This Mean for Teachers and Students? Teachers for decades have taken the National Teachers Exam, but only when it was demanded by their schools of education as a degree requirement or by particular communities for hiring purposes. The difference now is that teacher testing is linked with licensure as a quality control criterion for being designated for the federal government's definition of a highly qualified teacher. Unfortunately, states do not readily grant reciprocity for licensure. The multiple number of tests teachers must take to satisfy each state's notions of adequate competencies can be daunting. Some common ground needs to be established among the states.

With each state using different exams, reciprocity among states for certification has diminished. There is uniformity only in the states that agree to accept the Praxis exam. For example, a passing score on the teacher's competency test in New York does not exempt a candidate from taking the test required in neighboring Pennsylvania. Experienced teachers as well as newly minted teachers are frustrated when they move from one state to another only to discover that their credentials are not valid. While there is a movement for national certification under the auspices of the National Board for Professional Teaching Standards, this is intended primarily for experienced teachers. To qualify for board certification, a teacher must be state licensed, possess a bachelor's degree from an accredited institution, and have at least three years of teaching experience. Other professional societies, organizations, and unions are investigating remedies for establishing reciprocal agreements among states. Meanwhile, teachers are faced with reexamination in any state that does not accept currently held credentials.

Hopefully, all of this assessment and credentialing means that schools are being restructured to serve their constituents. The winds of change continue to introduce new, promising models of education. Education now mirrors the commercial marketplace, with school choices for parents. Formerly only the family with means had options to educate their children in private or public schools, but now new directives are prevalent to place public schools in a competitive environment of choice for all parents. Now even families whose limited means once precluded options for private schooling can choose a school of preference. In the next section we examine some of the issues and the choices facing families.

What Are Some Models of Change?

In this section we examine model programs that were the result of school restructuring efforts in the past and those that continue to reach into the future. The models are representative of both private and public endeavors that present and debate a multitude of choices. The issue of school choice—offering parents an alternative to sending their children to the public school in their neighborhood—includes many options that we explore in the next sections. Parental choice of schooling in the public sector presents many basic changes to the system and the dynamics of how schools work. Among the choices are models of schooling that envision educational change for the future.

The Notion of Change

Central to reform is the notion of change. Dating back to the Greeks, philosophers have noted that change is as essential in social institutions as in nature. Heraclitus has been credited with the proverb, "You never step into the same stream, twice." Change is basic to John Dewey's concept of the aim of education for a democracy. For Dewey, change is a positive and progressive force leading to growth.

Robert Evans, a clinical and organizational psychologist, points out that change can be threatening. He tries to strike a balance between the positive gains from change and the optimism of reform with the sense of loss, confusion, challenge, and conflict change poses to people undergoing the process. He defines a *double duality* in change as "a public gap between what change means to its authors and what it means to its targets." He further contends that this double duality of change creates an ambivalence, which "needs to be seen as part of the solution [and] demands the attention and respect of all who seek innovation" (1996, p. 38).

Phillip Schlechty's work in defining five different roles people play in the process of educational change helps to reconcile Evans's duality. For Schlechty, these different roles in the change process are key at different stages of restructuring and require a different kind of training and support from educational leaders. The roles include those of the Trailblazers, who are the visionaries; the Pioneers, who take the risks; the Settlers, who follow though with encouragement and direction; the Stay-at-Homes, who resist change; and finally, the Sabateurs, who undermine efforts (Schlechty, 1993, pp. 47–50).

Recognizing all of these roles in most efforts for reform, Schlechty calls for a commitment on the part of school leaders to understand the motivation of each group. Evans would require a leadership that resolves to reconcile ambivalence to change. In this section we consider some models for change that have had an impact on school reform. We offer these models as choices teachers and parents have in improving learning opportunities for their children and in advocating for change in their community.

Having a Choice

The school reforms of the 1990s ushered in many changes. One offering was school choice. Despite the annual Gallup Polls, *Phi Delta Kappan* reports that while many Americans are satisfied with their local schools, evidence indicates that some families express dismay about conditions found in public education. Citing safety concerns, lackluster achievement results, declining test scores in literacy and numeracy skills, and conflict with family values, many parents demand alternative placements and choices.

Parents in urban settings are particularly frustrated by bureaucratic administrative decisions that affect the school placement of their children. They are given the opportunity to request particular placements, but "central office" policies rescind their choices with explanations that there is no room for their children in the chosen school. Also, school choice policies and procedures in large urban school systems are often so convoluted that families become frustrated while trying to navigate through the myriad levels of bureaucracy and end up accepting the status quo. Reports and studies suggest that more equitable options need to be available. Nationwide, several models for school choice have proven to be successful exemplars for future policy making as well as teaching practice.

Magnet Schools

Magnet schools are options that have been available for several decades. **Magnet schools** have distinguishing features and special approaches; they can specialize in a curriculum area such as the arts, offer an intensified math/science program, or expand their mission to include an international perspective to education. Some magnet schools offer a longer day and school year, including after-school programs on school premises, a technology base for curriculum instruction, or linkages to local colleges and universities.

Originally, magnet schools were designed to counter race-based school segregation. They were billed literally as *magnets* that attracted children from a broad spectrum of backgrounds, particularly in cities where there was de facto racial segregation based on neighborhoods. Their intent was to be an alternative to forced busing as a means for integrating schools.

One model in Connecticut is the Metropolitan Learning Center Magnet School for Global and International Studies, which draws from families in six communities of the Hartford area. Starting at grade 6, children are selected on a lottery basis to pursue their education through grade 12. According to a school brochure, the school was designed as a response to the *Sheff v. O'Neil* lawsuit to address "racial, ethnic and socio-economic isolation" through outreach to six urban, suburban, and rural communities. The mission statement reflects the purpose of the school "to provide a forum for global and international studies so that students experience the diverse cultural, linguistic, political and business perspectives of our world, while developing strong intrapersonal and interpersonal skills to be prepared citizens in the international workplace." The curriculum emphasizes the study of world languages along with its core subjects of English, math, social studies, science, the arts, physical education/health, and international/global studies.

The school holds membership in the Virtual High School Network; it requires **service learning** during the sophomore year, in which students work in the community as volunteers to improve living conditions and learn how governments and social agencies function; and it requires a senior project. High expectations of academic performance, an adherence to a dress code of appropriate business attire, team teaching, and a partnership with Yale University are featured elements of the school. The school's "graduation requirements are based on the New England Association of Schools and Colleges standards on teaching and learning, the pillars [in] *Breaking Ranks, Changing an American Institution,* . . . and the vision of the Connecticut State Department of Education's 21st Century work on Reconceptualizing Connecticut's High Schools" (Metropolitan Learning Center, nd).

Choice Communities

In addition to magnet schools, parents of children in public school are offered choices among school systems within a state. Communities can identify themselves as choice communities. Most of these choice communities are suburban schools that are presented as havens for students in disruptive urban school settings. Choice communities were established over a decade ago in the Commonwealth of Massachusetts. Parents decide on a school and request to send their children out of their district to a "choice" community. State payment of tuition to the choice community follows the child. Critics of this option warn of depletion of funds from needy school districts in favor of tuition payments to more privileged communities. Logistics such as transportation and school population shifts, and the fact that there are no guarantees of available slots, can put such a program in peril.

The Business Model and the Emergence of Vouchers

The business model for school choice views the parent as a consumer with schools as a commodity in a marketplace. This view is commonly extolled by conservative educational policymakers. John E. Chubb, currently of the Brookings Institution, the Hoover Institution, and executive vice president of Edison Schools is a proponent of this view of parents as consumers. Building on the premise that "the school allotment money follows the child," Chubb envisions a reorganization of public schools "according to the principles of competition and choice." His position is to place schools in the marketplace, where parents as consumers can choose which schools best suit their children. Just as the "principles of competition and choice" drive businesses, the fate of schools can thrive or die on the same principles. With choice, schools that meet the families' notions of academic achievement prevail, while schools that continue to fail to meet challenges close out of lack of demand. The choice can be within the public sphere or extend to private or religious schools in a community (Chubb, 2002).

Chubb's theory is predicated on his study with Terry M. Moe for the Hoover Institution and the Koret Task Force in 1990 of five hundred public and private schools. Their findings assert that free market principles would drive out poorly performing schools (Chubb and Moe, 1990). Their study noted that private education, with its autonomy, clearly focused goals, and tailored curriculum, prevailed over public schools, where centralized administration and bureaucratic regulations complicate the best intentions. Private schools get positive results by catering to the needs of their students and the demands set by their families.

To ensure equal education, all parents should have the opportunity to make choices and have a voice in the education of their children. Because of disparities in the financial means of families, Chubb eventually became a proponent of a voucher system for parents who cannot afford the choice of private education as an alternative. Generally, vouchers are based on per capita expenditure for each student in the public sector. Again, remember the principle of "the money follows the child." If a school system spends an average of $8600 per capita to educate each student in a public school district, the student can bring that $8600 in the form of a voucher to a private school of choice.

All is well if the allotment matches the private school's tuition, but more often there is a huge discrepancy between the public school per capita amount and the costs of private schooling. However, Roman Catholic parochial schools have lower rates than most private institutions. Since these religious school costs are more aligned with the voucher allotment, a U.S. Supreme Court ruling in June 2002 on a school voucher program in Cleveland, Ohio, allowed parents to send their children to Catholic schools rather than the "failing" Cleveland public schools. This Supreme Court decision has given a boost to the voucher movement. Chief Justice

William Rehnquist wrote in defense of the ruling, which he, Sandra Day O'Connor, Antonin Scalia, Anthony Kennedy, and Clarence Thomas approved:

> We believe the program challenged here is a program of true private choice. The Ohio program is neutral in all respects toward religion. It is part of a general and multifaceted undertaking by the State of Ohio to provide educational opportunities to the children of a failed school district (*Zelman v. Simmons-Harris,* 2002).

The ruling is controversial and has prompted arguments about the U.S. Constitution's separation of church and state. The decision also has implications for future attempts to support different religious schools, such as Christian, Jewish, or Muslim. Justice David Souter wrote the dissenting opinion for the minority vote against this decision in the U.S. Supreme Court. He maintained that the failure of Cleveland's public schools was not a sufficient reason to provide tax money for religious purposes (*Zelman v. Simmons-Harris,* 2002, www.cnn/LAW/06/27/scotus.schools.vouchers).

Critics of vouchers cite numerous concerns. The main fear is that vouchers might deplete funds for public schools that are already lacking adequate support. A second argument claims that vouchers cover only a fraction of the costs for most private schools. The support of religious schools with publicly funded vouchers has provoked legal battles in court over the separation of church and state and will continue to do so, as voucher supporters scramble to fashion their programs after the Cleveland model. Chubb's ideas continue to garner support among many Americans seeking alternative school placements for their children.

> Public opinion polls indicate that the concept of educational choice is supported by a majority of Americans, especially poor Americans and racial minorities who are often trapped—without choice—in collapsing urban systems. The business community is panicked about the quality of the work force and has grown impatient with traditional school reforms. As educators come to see that there is little hope for acquiring autonomy without also providing the accountability that choice allows, educators, too, may become supporters of the idea. In any event, choice will be the focus of educational debate over the next decade (Chubb, 2002).

Charter Schools

A charter school is a public school supported by public revenues that provides an independent option for parents. The school does not charge tuition. Its doors must be open to all who wish to attend regardless of race, religion, gender, learning differences, physical or emotional challenges, or language proficiency. When applications exceed the number of placements, an open lottery system governs admissions.

Charter schools have been described as grassroots initiatives that grow from a community's desire for a school with a particular kind of mission. Each charter school is to reflect a unique choice to the community. Individuals who want to establish a school with public support must write a proposal outlining the specific nature of their school and apply to their state for a charter; if approved by the state process, the school is funded. The school might be a former public school or it might be a new initiative. The charter school operates within the framework of its own charter through its own governing body. Charter schools can differ from state to state, as restrictions are shaped by the mandates of the individual state. Minnesota is credited with founding the first charter schools in the United States in 1991, spearheading the movement nationwide (Watras, 2002). However, the concept is not unique to America.

The school reform measure of the National Curriculum bill in Great Britain included a provision for the "establishment of grant-maintained schools." Such schools were once local primary schools; they required a school population of "more than 300 pupils" in order to opt out of the "local authority control." While there are some differences in the British provisions, the following justification for the measure has a familiar ring to those hearing messages in support of American charter schools.

> This [opting out] will widen choice for many parents in the State-maintained sector for whom all too often the only choice is take it or leave it. The wider choice will help improve standards in all schools as we introduce a competitive spirit into the provision of education (Haviland, 1988, p. 4).

As provisions in both America 2000 and Goals 2000, charter schools sprang up in all corners of the United States. In May 2000, President Bill Clinton established a National Charter Schools Week "to raise people's awareness of the contributions of charter schools" (Watras, 2002, p. 376). Some charter schools are conversion schools from the public sector, while others offer experimental approaches to education that can later be adapted to public schools. The verdict of their success is still open to review and interpretation. The National Teachers Association opposes the charter school movement, while the American Federation of Teachers pioneered advocacy of charter schools through the leadership of Albert Shanker. The National Education Association (NEA) has been reluctant to endorse the charter school movement. As publicly supported schools, charter schools dip into the same pool of taxpayer revenues as regular public schools; consequently, public school budgets become depleted as students brings their allotments to their charter school of choice. The NEA argues that current school funds are not sufficient to maintain both options.

Charter schools are at the center of controversy in many states. Though not all states subscribe to the charter school movement, some thirty-one states have opened charter schools with different state laws and varying degrees of success. Some studies point to the strength of the state laws as a predictor of a school's success (Center for Education Reform, 2004). Charter schools, like their counterparts in the public sector, are subject to ratings and scorecards for "success or failure." States have the option to close underperforming charter schools or to not renew the charter if a school does not fulfill its intended purpose.

The Essential School

An innovative model for middle and secondary schools is the essential school, founded by Ted Sizer in 1984 at Brown University through his initiative, the Coalition of Essential Schools. The **essential school** is based on ten "Common Principles" that guide personalized learning experiences and mastery of a few essential subjects and skills. A major feature of an essential school is its sense of community. Students are made to feel that they are accepted for their individual worth. Expectations for achievement are high. Sizer's primary goal for his model is "to create schools where students learn to use their minds well."

The movement is growing. In 1984, there were twelve schools in the coalition. Now there are approximately 250 full members, 275 schools in the planning stage, and as many as 500 schools exploring the possibility of joining the coalition. The success stories of schools that follow the model have aroused interest throughout the nation.

A Success Story: The Francis W. Parker Charter Essential School

A model charter school can be found in Devens, Massachusetts. Theodore Sizer and his wife, Nancy Faust Sizer, fashioned the school on the ten Common Principles of the Coalition of Essentials Schools, which Sizer pioneered at Brown University with a *personalized learning* approach to elementary and secondary school instruction.

> Personalization—meaning fundamental fairness arising from the differences among students—requires the expression of common, general "standards" in a variety of forms. Creating such standards is difficult work, far more difficult than saying that "high standards" are to be assessed by one "instrument" in one way and at one time. Time has to be made for it—the same sort of time that each of us prays happens among our physicians when they caucus to decide on a treatment for our disease. At its heart—"personalization" implies a profoundly different way of defining formal education. What is here is not the delivery of standard instructional services. Rather, it is the insistent coaxing out of each child on his or her best terms of profoundly important intellectual habits and tools for enriching a democratic society, habits and tools that provide each individual with the substance and skills to survive well in a rapidly changing culture and economy (Sizer, 1999).

In 1995, four parents from Devens, Massachusetts, lobbied for "a public high school of very high quality where kids enjoy school" (Jenkins and Keefe, 2002, p. 453). They secured the Sizers as co-principals of the school for the initial phases. The school reflects a progressive philosophy, as it was named the Francis Parker Essential School in honor of John Dewey's mentor. Like many public schools throughout the United States influenced by the work of Sizer and the Education Alliance of Brown University, this charter school follows the ten Common Principles of the Coalition of Essential Schools.

> The ten Common Principles guide the educational practices at the Parker School. Foremost among these are that teaching and learning should be personalized, that the governing metaphor should be the student-as-worker rather than the teacher-as-deliverer, and that credit is earned not for the time spent in class but only for the mastery of skills and knowledge (Jenkins and Keefe, 2002, p. 453).

Based on student performance on the Massachusetts Comprehensive Assessment System for grades 8 and 10, the Stanford Achievement Tests (SAT 9), and on the school's defined criteria for reaching the goals of its mission, the school has been recognized for its achievements and accomplishments (Jenkins and Keefe, 2002). This model is not unique to a charter school. As an essential school it has been replicated by many public schools throughout the country.

Table 11.2 The Ten Common Principles of the Coalition of Essential Schools

1. learning to use one's mind well
2. less is more, depth over coverage
3. goals apply to all students
4. personalization
5. student-as-worker, teacher-as-coach
6. demonstration of mastery
7. a tone of decency and trust
8. commitment to the entire school
9. resources dedicated to teaching and learning
10. democracy and equity

Source: Essential Schools, http://www.essentialschools.org.

Education-for-Profit Schools

> As technology continues to shrink our increasingly interdependent world, the future will belong to those who are to understand the languages, history, cultures, and dreams of people everywhere (International School of Minnesota).

The dilemma facing the Greek Sophists is alive and well in today's schools with the entrepreneurial movement known as education-for-profit schools. Can you or should you make money managing public education? "Yes," replies one entrepreneur, Chris Whittle, founder and chief executive officer of the Edison Schools, one of many companies established to run public schools, charter schools, summer and after-school programs, and to provide school management training—all for a profit. In fact, Edison Schools Inc. is currently the largest education-for-profit organization; it "serves more than 132,000 public schools in over 20 states" (Edison Schools, http://edisonschools.com/home/home.cfm). Like other education-for-profit companies such as the SABIS School Network, Edison Schools UK is extending its reach to a global constituency beyond the borders of the United States.

Edison Schools and other profit models—including Advantage Schools, Victory Schools, and Chancellor Beacon Academies—claim that they can run schools more effectively, efficiently, and economically while making a profit. The profit is based on the per pupil expenditure that is allotted by the school system—the money that goes with the child. These companies apply to school districts to manage individual schools or entire school systems, particularly in districts where schools are labeled as underachieving. The notion that a private management venture could turn around failing schools has challenged basic assumptions about the future of public education. The Edison project manages twenty of Philadelphia's public schools and is one of at least three companies hired by the district (*Time,* June 23, 2003). A growing number of charter schools use Edison's services to establish and administer their schools.

Table 11.3 Models of Change: School Alternatives

Type of School	Definition	Advantages	Cautions
Magnet schools	• Public schools that offer a specialty such as technology, the arts, math, or science to attract students with special interests or talents.	• A legacy of racially integrated urban schools that attract diversity in the student body. • Motivate students to follow their interests.	• Can be elitist, if admission requires testing or auditioning. • Enrollment is often limited.
Business model and vouchers	• The business model views families as consumers with options to choose schools as they would any commodity in the marketplace.	• Vouchers are awarded to families to select private sector schools when public schools fail.	• Vouchers do not cover the entire cost of tuition for private education. • Vouchers are controversial in regard to tax monies being used for religious schools.
Charter schools	• Charter schools are public schools with their own governing school boards and missions. • A charter school advisory board seeks a charter from the state to offer a unique approach to education.	• Charter schools grow out of community needs and interest. • Offer families an alternative approach to schools without tuition concerns. • Experiment with new school designs and initiatives. • Schools have more autonomy than other public schools.	• Limited spaces require a lottery system for admission. • Deplete funding for existing public schools. • Answerable to the state for high-stakes testing. • Teachers need not be certified.
Education-for-profit schools	• Designed educational programs for preschools to grade 12 and beyond to provide an array of services and school models to communities, but managed by a for-profit organization.	• Risk taking institutions that are willing to experiment with innovative designs and technology. • Promise state of the arts learning environments.	• Voices of concerns resonate when the bottom line is profit, rather than learning,
Full-service schools	• A full-service school expands the regular school beyond the school walls and into the community. • Its mission is to educate the whole child and outreach to serve families as well.	• Multi-service approach to education that includes many social agencies, educational institutions, and a myriad of services. • Educates the whole child and his family. • Empowers families and communities.	• Needs strong leadership from the principal to coordinate all the services and various professional liaisons. • Community cooperation is essential for funding and support. • Teachers must be committed to the mission.

While the companies boast on websites and in brochures about high success rates, there is no conclusive research to substantiate that they are more effective in raising achievement levels than public schools. Studies differ in their findings. While the companies detail their success stories, some school districts have cancelled contracts when delivery has not lived up to promises. The American Federation of Teachers questions the claims made by Edison Schools Inc. about their success rates in closing "achievement gaps" among nonwhite students and outdistancing their counterparts in achievement rankings on math and reading tests (AFT, 2003).

The notion of education-for-profit is not limited to school management companies. For-profit educational endeavors are evident everywhere. You need only look in your local paper, view television, or browse the Internet, to read advertisements for all kinds of schooling. Test preparation schools, tutoring services, language schools, trade schools, online courses, or "whatever you want to learn" schools are ubiquitous.

Reflecting the need to include more input from the community, there has been a global move to establish full-service schools. Known by many other titles, such as community schools, these schools are being established in rural areas of Tennessee and in urban cities across the Northeast, while some of their prototypes can be found internationally.

What Are Full-Service Schools? Historically, the kindergarten programs established in settlement houses and public schools during the nineteenth century were precursors of the full-service school. These early education efforts pioneered parental involvement, inclusion of social services in schools, and the notion of educating the whole child.

Internationally, the Nordic nations of Finland and Sweden were among the first nations to model full-service schools in community centers. Known as service centers, these facilities resemble shopping malls that were purposely designed and built to provide various services for all of their constituents in the neighboring community. In Helsinki, one center includes the neighborhood school, medical and dental offices, a library, the community auditorium, a café, a child-care center, as well as youth and senior citizens' drop-in programs (Swiniarski and Breitborde, 2003). Australia established full-service units in 1999 under its Department of Education, Youth and Family Services throughout the country and in Tasmania.

Public schools are the cornerstone of American democracy. Thomas Jefferson, Horace Mann, Charlotte Forten, Elizabeth Peabody, and John Dewey are but a few of the leading luminaries in American thought and education that gave credence to the value of public education. Public education deserves continued support and endorsement to carry out its mission of educating subsequent generations of Americans. Full-service schools have been replicated in private and religious schools; even in the for-profit sector, The Edison School offers it as an option. But primarily full-service schools have been nurtured under the auspices of public education and have served as exemplars for the others. They are one kind of public school that pioneers uncharted routes to learning and serves as a beacon for innovation.

Recognizing the widely held assumption in early childhood education that parents are the child's first teachers, full-service schools reach out to families in their mission to bridge the achievement gaps in America's schools. **Full-service schools** seek to improve education by empowering families. Typically, full-service schools provide after-school programs, medical services, social services, parenting courses, and counseling. Their mission is to involve the entire community and meet the needs of their constituents with an array of services that extend beyond the purview of the traditional school.

Full-service schools are a growing phenomenon. Throughout the United States, their message is resonating. Joy Dryfoos (1998) is a leading spokesperson who encourages schools to move beyond physical confines and into the community. She believes education does not happen in a vacuum. She recognizes that the education of at-risk students, in particular, involves a collaborative effort of many agencies that improve family life, provide health care, and offer social services. Tennessee, Florida, Illinois, and Massachusetts are some of the states fostering this movement for families that need support and for communities where unequal education exists.

Many full-service schools collaborate with local colleges and universities. One such model is the Partnership for the Educational Village Project, which links the pre-K to grade 8 Robert L. Ford Elementary School of Lynn, Massachusetts, with the departments of education, social work, and nursing at Salem State College. This model operates on the principle that achievement gaps narrow when schools and other agencies collaborate to improve the lives of their students and families by offering an array of services through the school to the community at large. The partnership's basic tenet is that schools can transform society when education is the social responsibility of the whole *village.*

The Comer Model James Comer, professor of child psychiatry at the Yale University School of Medicine's Child Study Center, has developed a model of community collaboration, known as the School Development Program, also called the Comer model. Comer directed his model at inner-city schools, which he sees as eroding due to breakdowns in and between schools and families. His goal is to bring a network of professionals, universities, colleges, schools, and families together to improve the total well being of children. Comer avoids the laying of blame for social and educational conditions on any one group (his no-fault principle for reform); rather he focuses on solving problems through team-building efforts, led by an enabling principal who permits shared decision making. Similar to Ernest Boyer's approach to educational change, Comer promotes both the physical and mental health of youngsters.

A basic tenet for Comer is that a nurturing environment and a caring community are vital to the good health of the child. All segments of society must collaborate in developing the whole child physically, psychologically, socially, ethically, and cognitively. Comer launched his program in 1968 and has persisted in grappling with the effects of abuse, poverty, and social alienation throughout the United States. In January of 2004 he was awarded the 7th Annual Smithsonian McGovern Award by Senator Hillary Rodham Clinton for his efforts.

Home Schooling: An Alternative Education

Home schooling, education that takes place in the home with family members and/or tutors, has received much publicity in the media. Although it is often depicted as a recent trend in the educational scene, home schooling is not new. In ancient Rome, Quintilian admonished families to avoid home schooling. He felt a child should be educated with others in a school. For him, the school is a social institution that brings students together to learn the roles of citizenship and to perfect socialization skills. He considered any form of education at home as too restrictive and lacking in socialization opportunities.

Yet, centuries later, many well-known people, such as Elizabeth Peabody and her siblings, were products of home schooling. The Peabody family's education was adequate for their sons' acceptances into Harvard University and laid the foundation for their daughters' work and advocacy of many social and political causes. Other home-schooled luminaries include Abigail Adams, wife of President John Adams; Agatha Christie, writer; and Jill Kerr Conway, former president of Smith College.

Home schooling is a universal phenomenon and generations of families continue to have children tutored at home. Sometimes it is a necessity. For families that live in remote places, it is often the only option for young children. In countries like Australia and New Zealand, **distance learning**—education via the computer, television, and radio—is a common practice on isolated sheep stations, where schools are inaccessible. Family members typically assume the role of teacher until their children are old enough to attend public or private boarding schools.

There are as many reasons for home schooling as there are families willing to take on the task (see Fig. 11.2). The reasons range from religious motives, parent conflicts with schools over family values, or concerns about safety and bullying issues. In many instances, parents express the confidence that they know their children and their children's needs better than an impersonal public school.

Families who are disenchanted with public schools and unable to afford private education for their children often elect home schooling. Some families employ tutors for specialized subject areas or form a consortium with neighboring parents for joint home teaching. Many families home school their children for short periods of time, while others educate their children from birth to adulthood. In all instances, home schooling is an enormous commitment on the part of parents. Usually, one parent must be at home full time to undertake the numerous tasks involved.

In addition to teaching, there are countless legal regulations families must address in providing home schooling, as education is mandatory for all children from

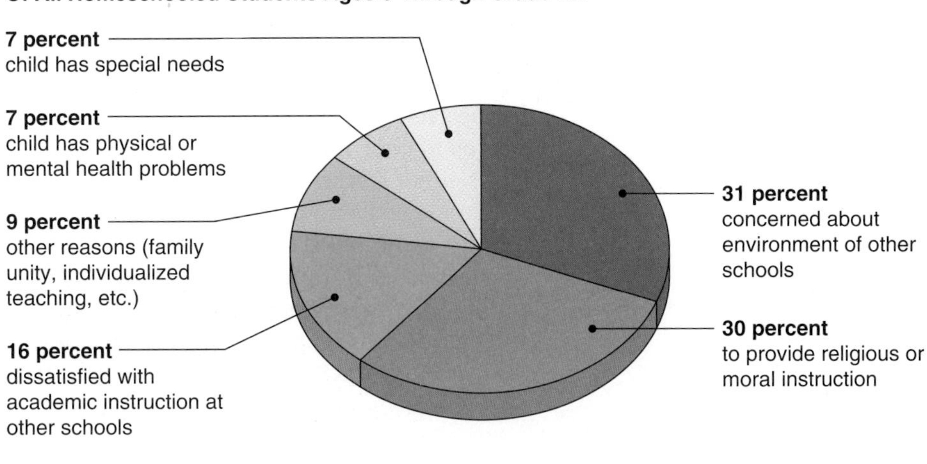

Figure 11.2

Reasons Parents Choose to Home School

Source: U.S. Department of Education, NCES. Parent and family involvement education survey of the 2003 national household education surveys program. http://nces.ed.gov/nhes/homeschool/#sec2.

age seven through age sixteen in the United States. Some states have no requirement that parents notify the state, while other states require parents to submit achievement test scores and have professional evaluations. Usually, parents submit a school plan to their local school district or superintendent for approval. To date, parents need not be certified as teachers or possess professional degrees.

To help parents, there is a multitude of home-schooling programs, teaching materials, and publications. The Internet and home-schooling newsletters provide references and resources. Home schoolers also frequent community "learning stations," as defined by Boyer, as well as community programs for sports, the arts, and public services. There are home-schooling options on the Internet that charge tuition fees and provide teaching texts and materials. Parents can also subscribe to home-schooling education services that provide programs, texts, materials, counseling, testing, and assessments. Membership in home-schooling organizations is available worldwide, including the National Homeschool Organization/USA, Cincinnati, Ohio; the Canadian Alliance of Homeschoolers, Toronto, Canada; The New Zealand Home Schooling Association, Auckland, NZ; and the Puerto Rico Homeschooling Association, Santurce, Puerto Rico.

At one time, home schooling was not considered a serious option for families and few engaged in the practice. Since the emergence of the Internet, however, and the support of theoretical frameworks that endorse the endeavor, the number of families that opt for home schooling has soared. According to the National Center for Education Statistics of the U.S. Department of Education, nearly 1.1 million students in the United States were reported to be home schooled in 2003, an increase of 29 percent over the number of home-schooled students in 1999 (*Boston Globe,* 2004). Theorists supporting home schooling include such well-known educators as Ivan Illich (1926–2002), a Roman Catholic priest and philosopher who disseminated his call for deschooling society through his Center for Intercultural Documentation (CIDOC) in Cuernavaca, Mexico, and John Holt (1923–1985), the former teacher who wrote extensively on alternative education and home schooling as an "underground railroad" escape from the banalities of formal schooling to freedom for learning.

Illich was a more radical reformer than Holt. His pronouncements rallied a global following whose contemporary voices are recorded in the writings of John Gatto, a former New York educator, and Matt Hern, editor, writer, and educator from British Columbia. The zeal and tone of Illich's mission is evident in the following excerpt from his work, *Deschooling Society.*

> Obligatory schooling inevitably polarizes a society; it also grades the nations of the world according to an international caste system. Countries are rated like castes whose educational dignity is determined by the average year of schooling of its citizens, a rating which is closely related to per capita gross national product, and much more painful.
>
> Neither learning nor justice is promoted by schooling because educators insist on packaging instruction with certification. Learning and the assignment of social roles are melted into schooling. Yet, to learn means to acquire a new skill or insight, while promotions depends on an opinion which others have formed. Learning is frequently the result of instruction, but selection for a role or category in the job market increasingly depends on the mere length of attendance (1971, pp. 8–9).

According to the National Center for Education Statistics of the U.S. Department of Education, nearly 1.1 million students in the United States were reported to be home schooled in 2003.
Source: © Ed Kashi/CORBIS

John Holt's promotion of home schooling evolved from his experiences as a teacher and a reformer of the educational system during the 1960s. He began to question teaching methods of both public and private sectors in his books, *How Children Fail, How Children Learn,* and *The Underachieving School.* By the early eighties, Holt endorsed home schooling in *Teach Your Own* and set the groundwork for the present burgeoning number of households living his legacy.

Andrew Goldberg's experience with home schooling (see Voices of Principle and Promise on page 470) defies many of the stereotypes about this option. And they are just that—stereotypes. Home schooling has been deemed by some to be isolating for children who won't be attending school with dozens or even hundreds of other students. Another stereotype is that religious families are the ones who most often choose to school their children at home. These stereotypes do not represent the reality of home schooling. There are many approaches to home schooling that include field trips, socializing opportunities, fulfillment of state regulations, and the provision of a great education for students.

What Is the Global Age of School Reform?

Educational reform is a global happening. Governments in many countries are changing policies to address new practices and requirements for their state educational systems. The economic globalization process has spearheaded a worldwide charge for educational reform. Each country is concerned about its future work force being competitive in the global marketplace and is forging ahead with a restructuring of its schools. Ironically, as Americans worry about how their schools measure up against those of other nations, change is evident in many parts of the world.

Voices of Principle and Promise

Reflections on Home Schooling, *by Andrew Goldberg, B.S., '04, Accountant*

My mother home schooled my brother and me from middle school through the high school years, when we moved from a suburban neighborhood to a nearby city. Because my mother was dismayed by the lack of academic challenges and the general demeanor of the students in our newly assigned urban school district, she explored the possibilities of home schooling us. As a single parent with limited financial resources, it was the only viable option she felt she had. Private schools were too expensive for our family budget even with support from possible scholarships. Additionally, my mother was concerned about the values expressed in many schools that were contrary to her own personal religious and moral convictions. As a graduate of a leading woman's college with a degree in biology and a former teacher at a prestigious private school, she had the confidence to undertake the responsibility of educating her sons, but realized she could not do justice to teaching the entire curriculum on her own. She joined a community support group of other families in our area who home schooled their children. Each parent taught the subjects in which they had some expertise.

At our home we often used the computer for self-directed instruction. My mother once said, "if you believe in your child's abilities, he will teach himself more than you can imagine." Well, my brother and I took her word for it, because we both spent a lot of time searching the internet and experimenting with ideas on the computer. My brother never wants to leave the computer for too long a time, so he is currently majoring in computer science at my university. Our home grown education was sufficient for both of us to gain admission and placements in a highly competitive university. I recently graduated with a major in business management and concentrations in accounting and finance. Now, I am employed as an accountant and looking forward to continuing my education at graduate school. My home schooling prepared me well for both my university studies and my career choice. It gave me the desire and skills to be a life long learner. My next challenge is to speak a foreign language.

Questions to Consider

1. Does Andrew's account of his home schooling change your opinion of this alternative approach to education? Explain.
2. Why do you think Andrew's experience as a home schooler prepared him for success in college?

Japan is adapting more creative approaches to their traditionally regulated schools. England has revamped the Foundation Stage of its National Curriculum to reflect a more developmental approach to the early years of schooling. South Africa, through its National Department of Education, is seeking to engage "stakeholders inside South Africa and world wide over a number of years" to develop a democratic approach to its national mandate, Curriculum 2005 (Tiley, 2000, p. 2). Nations with students terminating their formal education at age fifteen or sixteen are replicating practices of the American comprehensive high schools to retain students for extended schooling until age eighteen. Australia's Full Service Schools Units has designed projects for students aged fifteen through eighteen with links between schools, the communities, and the government, to increase the educational opportunities of its youth.

In any democratic society, equal opportunity and equity demand quality education for all of its citizens; failing schools deprive children of that opportunity. The goals to provide a competent global work force and offer equitable educational opportunities for all students motivate the school reform movement globally. In some cases the movement is a top-down mandate; other approaches are more inclusive of input from various segments of society. In all instances, citizens and educators everywhere must distinguish between the reality and rhetoric of the call for reform, particularly from the political arena.

The rhetoric of policymakers whose goal is to have their schools be named first in the nation or world in achievement does not reflect reality or produce results that improve instruction, meet the challenges of special needs children, support families, or close the achievement gap. These tasks are daunting. Simple lofty pronouncements do nothing to transform schools. Changes require the collaborative effort of all channels of society, as exemplified in full-service schools and recommended in the Comer model. A school's position in some arbitrary league table is a comparatively inconsequential assessment.

A British colleague recently commented that in his country, health care and education are key issues. If politicians want to grab attention, addressing these two topics is very likely to do the trick. Since costs and quality of care and education are concerns of constituencies throughout Great Britain, calls for reform dominate legislative agendas in Parliament. This scenario is not unique to Britain. The same can be said of the United States as well as other nations.

SUMMARY

- Throughout the final decades of the twentieth century, there was a plethora of reports and reforms to restructure the American public educational system, culminating in the 2002 No Child Left Behind Act. Standards-based education, high-stakes testing, school choice, vouchers, charter schools, and "highly qualified teacher" credentials are topics that continue to fuel debates for defining twenty-first-century schools among professionals, politicians, parents, and communities.
- Many issues are yet to be resolved. The achievement gap identified in the 1983 report, *A Nation at Risk,* is spiraling despite efforts to compensate for inequality and inequity in education. American students' academic performance is less than stellar when compared to their counterparts in international studies.
- Schools are perceived as unsafe with an escalation of violence and bullying. Public schools need more resources to fulfill their mission.
- Some critics cite inadequate funding as the primary cause of failing schools; others agree but differ on policy and philosophical issues.
- This chapter extends the debate on *How do we determine what is worth knowing?* in its analysis of current reforms and the recent restructuring of educational practices.
- Standards-based education is compared and contrasted with personalized learning in meeting the individual needs of students. Personalized instruction centers on the learning style of the student. It can have a core curriculum that is tailored for the student. Traditionally, standards-based education programs use the standards to drive the teaching/learning experiences.The positive and punitive natures of school accountability are considered in debates about high-stakes testing, the competitive nature of standardization, and the labeling tactics of schools-at-risk.
- Alignment in the standards debate depends on the philosophical dispositions of the participants. Conservatives support standards as a means to transmit a common cultural literary for a national identity, while progressives find standards to be counterproductive in transforming society for democracy. Moderates try to balance the goals of personal actualization with the teaching of a shared core of knowledge.
- Innovative models for American schools have resulted from debate and discourse. The spectrum of possibilities includes magnet schools, charter schools, for-profit ventures, and full-service schools. The home-schooling movement is gaining momentum in the United States and other nations among families seeking an alternative to mainstream

schooling practices. Families and educators must be vigilant in keeping choices viable and at the same time protecting the integrity of public education. To preserve our national heritage, our cultural "can do" attitude, and the goals of justice and equality, public schools must prevail. The public educational system is a cornerstone of American democracy. Although imperfect, such a system must be endorsed for the future well being of the entire nation.

- Educational reforms are being made in many countries throughout the world. Significant reforms can be seen in Australia, Britain, Finland, Sweden, Japan, and South Africa to eradicate illiteracy, educate a more effective work force, and provide equal opportunities for their youth. The global village can learn from each member nation, share successes, and grapple with common issues for feasible solutions.

QUESTIONS FOR REFLECTION

1. As a teacher, how might you personalize state-mandated standards for your school and its students? Find your state's mandates and choose three.
2. How might you define accountability? Do you support public publication of your community's average scores on state and national tests? Explain your response.
3. Do you believe that mandated testing measures are fair for all students?
4. Is the major responsibility of public schools to promote the self-actualization of each student, transmit a cultural literacy, or transform society? Explain.
5. At what age should children begin the testing process for literacy and numeracy gains? Support your answer.

APPLYING WHAT YOU'VE LEARNED

1. Conduct a survey to identify the number of charter schools in your school district. Find out what population these schools are serving, their mission, and their achievements. Decide how they provide an alternative to the public schools.
2. Brainstorm with fellow students or colleagues to define criteria you feel define a "highly qualified teacher."
3. Search the Internet for education-for-profit programs. How are they marketed? Visit a program in your community.
4. Consult the companion website for former U.S. Secretary of Education Rod Paige's memo to editorial writers on March 11, 2004, defending the No Child Left Behind Act. Has the former U.S. Secretary of Education provided a credible defense of the mandates in the No Child Left Behind Act? What issues might the current U.S. Secretary of Education address?

KEY TERMS

bell curve, p. 448
distance learning, p. 467
essential school, p. 461
full-service school, p. 465
high-stakes testing, p. 449
home schooling, p. 466
magnet schools, p. 458
service learning, p. 458
voucher system, p. 437

WEBSITES TO EXPLORE

http://www.nhen.org/. The National Home Education Network facilitates the grassroots work of state and local home-schooling organizations and individuals by providing information, fostering networking, and promoting public relations on a national level.

http://www.ascd.org. This site of the Association for Supervision and Curriculum Development provides many resources on issues relating to educational policy and leadership, including discussion of many parts of NCLB.

http://www.edweek.org/ew/ewstory.cfm?slug=01ayp.h23. This article in *Education Week,* "State Reports on Progress Vary Widely," discusses a provision in NCLB that requires schools to make "adequate yearly progress" on assessment tests.

http://www.washingtonpost.com/ac2/wp-dyn?pagename=article&node=&contentId=A15836-2003Sep15&notFound=true. An article in the *Washington Post* debating NCLB.

http://www.edletter.org/past/issues/2003-jf/nation.shtml. An article, "Teaching: From *A Nation at Risk* to a Profession at Risk?" from the *Harvard Education Letter.* This article takes a look at what it means to be a highly qualified teacher.

http://www.makingstandardswork.com. Website for the Center for Performance Assessment; updates research on holistic accountability and assessments. The center's aim is to work with governmental agencies to improve standards and accountability systems. Site includes an electronic newsletter.

http://www.aft.org. The American Federation of Teacher's website is a resource for publications and for updates on research in all areas of interest in education.

http://www.ed.gov/pubs/edpubs.html. This is the U.S. Department of Education website. Free publications on No Child Left Behind and other governmental mandates can be ordered online.

http://www.qca.org.uk/ca/foundation/?fp_clk. This website gives comprehensive information regarding the UK Foundation Stage and subsequent information of standards for early education in the UK.

http://www.edisonschools.com/home/home.cfm. This is the home page for Edison Schools Inc. It provides an overview and informational links.

http://www.marbleheadcharter.com/overview.hml. This home page for the Marblehead Community Charter Public School provides an overview and informational links.

http://www.Communityschools.org. For further information on full-service schools, the Coalition for Community Schools provides this website.

http://www.essentialschools.org. The national Coalition of Essential Schools is a network of schools committed to the principles of small school size, democratic decision making, personalized learning, and a curriculum structured around important, thematic "essential questions" that engage students in meaningful and active inquiry. The website offers descriptions of school sites and learning projects, along with information about its ten principles and its founding director, Theodore Sizer.

CRITICAL READINGS

Schoolhome: Rethinking Schools for Changing Families

BY JANE ROLAND MARTIN

Jane Roland Martin proposes a middle-of-the-road option between the traditional notion of school and home schooling as her reform proposal for meeting families' and children's needs.

It is time to leave our spectator's spot on the bridge and walk back into the world. Having seen with our own eyes the changed social realities, and having figured out what corresponding changes in American education will suffice, we need to ask ourselves what can be done here and now. *If* the world changes—*if* it is suddenly governed by domestic tranquillity—the Schoolhome will be the institution of choice. But I labor under no delusion that this nation will be transformed overnight. I know that we will not wake up tomorrow in a state of domestic tranquillity. The question is, Must we wait until the world is turned around for the Schoolhome on the promontory to become a reality, or can we begin the process of transforming American education right away?

We can begin now, provided we think of the transformation of the schoolhouse as a gradual process rather than an all-or-nothing affair and do not set our sights too high. Instead of trying to change the whole American school system in one fell swoop—or even the entire system of a city or township—we can concentrate on a single school. After all, Montessori built her Casa dei Bambini in the only too real world inhabited by Rome's poor. The Charles River Creative Arts Program that provided its participants with a moral equivalent of home exists in the United States we know. The Martin Luther King federally funded child care center was not a figment of Valerie Suransky's imagination. The Atrium School in Watertown, Massachusetts, which I recently visited, is not an invention of the alumna who wrote to her former teachers: "Every night I dream the same dream. It only lasts a second, but I always picture Atrium as one big hug. A huge crowd of people all hugging one another."

The first thing I noticed when I entered the third-grade classroom at the Atrium School was the silence: twenty-five girls and boys and not a single sound. Then I spied four small girls sitting in a row on a sofa, each reading her own book. Near them, two boys were curled up in an easy chair, one poring over Madeleine L'Engle's *A Wrinkle in Time* and the other engrossed in a thick paperback whose small print signaled its large vocabulary. The genre of the month was fantasy fiction, the school's founder informed me as she led me to a corner of the room where four more children, each one glued to a book, had stowed themselves away in the loft of a playhouse. "This is the time when the slow readers get private help from the teacher and the others read on their own," Virginia Kahn whispered. "Later today the children will discuss their books with one another." "Do they really want to talk about books?" I asked. "Oh yes," she said. "And they love to make recommendations to their friends." This is the woman who once told a group of parents, "Friendships are the other curriculum at school. Early friendships are like love relationships."

Last month's genre had been biography, I was told, with the high point of the unit a Biography Breakfast to which parents were invited. Each child came dressed as a character in one of the books he or she had read and prepared to answer questions about the book. By then, the children had already discussed different genres and story structures with their teacher. "Whose book has a good lead-in?" the teacher might ask. A volunteer would then read one aloud.

While one half of that third grade was reading fantasies, the other half was sitting at desks and tables writing in those black and white, hard-covered copy books that you and I also used when we were young. "Dear Mike," the teacher's entry in one bearing the boy's name began:

> Hi! Thanks for explaining what a rune is. Can the person using a rune make anything they want happen? Can they make good *and* bad things happen? Which of the three L'Engle books has been your favorite? Why? You are a *great* reader!
>
> What has been your favorite reading genre this year? Why? What has been your favorite book you have read this year? Why? I love hearing you talk about the books you have read because you can summarize and explain them so well. It has been great for

the other kids in our class to hear what you have to say about what you are reading and to get book recommendations from you. You are great!

Write soon and tell me about your book!

Love, Jessie

Before my eyes, twelve Mikes and Lucys were composing replies to their teacher about the plots of their fantasy books, the main characters, the genre they liked best.

On the bulletin board of the first-grade room I visited next there were photographs, including baby pictures, of one of the children. "Tania is the VIP of the Week," my guide told me. "She and her family brought in the snapshots and whatever information about her they wished—her favorite color, the sport she likes best, and so on." This much is done in many preschools, I was assured, but in the Atrium School's first grade every child is given a writing assignment—Tania and Her Pets, Tania and Her Friends, Tania's Summer Vacation. The teacher then interviews Tania and everyone has a chance to ask questions. By Friday, the children will have written their Tania stories, collected them in a looseleaf notebook, and presented their testimonial to the VIP herself. "You can't imagine what this means to the children. When they are eighteen they will be able to look at these books and remember their childhood. The parents are thrilled by the booklet too."

According to Descartes, the cause of anything must have at least as much reality as the effect. In education the smallest details—seemingly insignificant events—can have immense consequences. When I taught fifth and sixth graders the children in my class wanted to put on a play for the younger grades based on *Winnie the Pooh*. "Fine," I said. But when it came to casting, a girl who was far too shy, withdrawn, awkward, and inarticulate to play anybody asked if she could be Pooh. I was fully convinced that the play would be doomed if she were given the main role. Yet no one else volunteered and in good conscience I did not feel that I could deny her request. The scene the children decided to perform was the one in which Pooh eats too much honey and gets stuck in Rabbit's hole. Need I say that the child who would have been my last choice to play Pooh was a sensation? Everyone who saw the play laughed and cheered and wanted more. As an unknown actor on Broadway becomes a star overnight, my ten-year-old recluse, who before her debut had communicated her needs by grunting and had never looked me or her classmates in the eye, became a different person.

At the Atrium School a "grandmother" and a young boy are reading together. At the Chelsea, Massachusetts, Early Learning Center reported on by the *Washington Post* columnist Mary McGrory, white paper hearts on the wall record the children's acts of care, concern, and connection: "Josephine hugged Isaiah when he fell down." At the Czech school in England that Vera Gissing attended, group singing was a popular activity. At the Montlake Community Day School in Seattle where one of Ludtke's girls was a student, the third-grade teacher spoke to her class about an argument that had taken place during recess: "It might look macho. It might look chic, but we know better . . . You have choices to make. So grab for happiness. You're smart. Be wise. I love you and worry about you all the time. I want you to make good choices."

Small actions can have big effects. Inexpensive measures can have momentous results. But the process of transforming American education does not have to begin with a whole school. Individual classrooms can be moral equivalents of home even if the schools in which they are situated are not, for the American classroom is a relatively private place, its door closed to outsiders, its upkeep in the hands of its inhabitants, its ethos a function of the relationships and activities that constitute daily life within its walls. Acting on custom, a teacher in this "safe and sealed-off domain," as Tracy Kidder called it, can set about to tighten nuts and bolts and prepare the product under manufacture for the next station on the assembly line. Believing in the efficacy of the profit motive and in the values embodied in life on the other side of Woolf's bridge, he or she can instead create a micro-marketplace in which learning is a by-product of making money. Or, remembering the domestic vacuum in so many children's lives, she and he can create a small haven in a hostile world where education, affection, safety, and trust go hand in hand and the three Cs flourish. "These kids live in stark reality," that Seattle teacher said. "For most of them school is a sanctuary."

Who knows! If enough classrooms change, an entire school may be transformed. The idea of the Schoolhome includes major shifts in the way we think about—the way we define—teaching, learning, curriculum, and the aims of education, as well as about life in classrooms. Is it possible in that safe and sealed-off domain to bring new voices and perspectives into the course of study so that everyone will feel at home; to place at the center of the curriculum activities that integrate minds and bodies, heads and hearts, thought and action, reason and emotion; to make domesticity everyone's business?

With the cooperation of principals and supervisors and the support of parents, even such enormous changes as these can emerge from small beginnings. I am optimistic, in part because at Seward Park High School in Manhattan Jessica Siegel found the time for students in the required American literature course to listen to Martin Luther King's "I Have a Dream" speech. If she was able to do this, others may already have brought in *Betsey Brown* or *A Raisin in the Sun*. I am also optimistic because the Boston secondary school teacher I happened to sit beside at a play when I was writing this Epilogue explained at intermission that she was reading *A Raisin in the Sun* because it is now on her school syllabus. A week after this encounter I attended a conferences of the National S.E.E.D. Project on Inclusive Curriculum. The teachers there were not only bringing new voices into their classrooms, they were leading seminars on the subject in their schools. Examples like these make me think that our nation's inclusionary juices are starting to flow. That Siegel gave the members of her journalism class an experience something akin to the integrative one that stands at the center of the Schoolhome's curriculum, and that other journalism teachers—and drama teachers—have surely done this too, in turn gives me hope that coalitions dedicated to the integration of head, hand, and heart will soon begin to form.

What specific policy advice follows from the idea of school as a moral equivalent of home in which all children feel at home and learn to live in the world together? Perhaps just this: think small, think locally, think experimentally, and never forget the domestic vacuum in children's lives today. Keep in mind, too, the changed and changing composition of the population and the violence everywhere. And always remember that there is no single form that a Schoolhome must take, no foolproof recipe to be followed. The brief descriptions I have given of Montessori's schools in Italy, the Charles River Creative Arts Program, and the Atrium School show that what is needed in American education today is also possible. The scenes I have presented from that Schoolhome on the promontory are meant to suggest a new realm of possibilities.

By midmorning in that particular Schoolhome, domestic work and related study are in most cases replaced by the more central pursuits, each of which generates its own rhythms of work and play, living and learning. Lunch—a time for lively conversation about what the various groups have been doing—comes as a welcome break between the morning and afternoon segments of the curriculum. The free hour in which clubs meet and music and dance groups practice is also a period everyone loves, the major problem being how to schedule meetings so that the budding historians, debaters, auto mechanics, computer programmers can participate fully in the activities of the cultural clubs and in artistic endeavors too. Another especially happy time comes toward the end of the day when Huck, Betsey, Meg, Jo, Beth, Amy, and the others take the spotlight. Some of the most meaningful and profound conversations in the Schoolhome take place then. For some reason this is also the time when a music teacher is most likely to stroll by playing an accordion or guitar and students are apt to gather round for a "spontaneous" sing.

"We sang 'Zebra Dun,' " I told a classmate who had been unable to attend our elementary school reunion. "Do you remember 'Zebra Dun'?" his wife asked him. "Remember 'Zebra Dun.' Of course he does!" I exclaimed, and he nodded his agreement. Who is Zebra Dun? A horse, but that is not the point. As music has charms to soothe a savage breast, group singing can strengthen metaphorical bonds of kinship. When the songs are drawn from the many cultures whose people have come to the United States, as they were in my school, and celebrate a variety of ways of living on both sides of Woolf's bridge, music can make all our children feel that this land really is theirs.

I like to think that forty years hence the boys and girls from the Schoolhome on the promontory will return for a reunion feeling very much as my classmates and I did and as Gissing and her singing schoolmates also did. Gissing reported:

> The forty middle-aged passengers were talking away happily, without a trace of awkwardness, shyness or reserve. To any onlooker the scene would have appeared that of a large close-knit family, or of intimate friends. No one could have guessed that the last time we had all been together we had been no more than children, and that many had travelled great distances, some half-way across the globe, just to meet up again.

I like to think that in half this time, the small changes that are made right here and now will add up to the transformation of the American schoolhouse into the American Schoolhome.

Source: Jane Roland Martin, *Rethinking Schools for Changing Families,* "Epilogue: The Here and Now." Cambridge: Harvard University Press, 1992, pp. 205–211.

A Closer Look at the Issues

1. What power does language possess by simply changing the title for schools from *schoolhouse* to *schoolhome*? Explain.
2. Why does Martin's model evoke notions of home schooling?
3. How does the schoolhome proposal compare with Secretary Rod Paige's implementation proposal for No Child Left Behind? Are there any similar notions? How are the proposals different?

Seeking Common Ground Reflections

BY DAVID TYACK

Although Adlai Stevenson believed that public education was "the most American thing about America," many people do not share that view today. Some citizens speak of "government schools" as if they were alien invaders of their communities instead of longstanding neighborhood institutions. At the turn of the twenty-first century, people talk about the cash value of schooling or the latest innovation but rarely speak about the powerful ideas that link public schooling to our political past and future.

Daily, new get-smart-quick schemes to reform the schools pop up. Pupils should address teachers as "ma'am" and "sir." Schoolchildren should wear uniforms. School districts can raise money by giving Coca-Cola exclusive rights to tout and sell its sodas on campus. Students should fill in the proper bubbles on their standardized tests with no. 2 pencils, and if they don't, they should repeat the grade. Social promotion is out; nonsocial nonpromotion is in.

For more than a century public schools have been robust institutions, able to survive war, depressions, massive demographic changes, and even reformers. Amidst these trials, people retained a strong sense that education was part of the answer to problems, not the problem itself. But in recent decades, as schools have been drawn into the vortex of many social and political conflicts, and as an ideology of privatization has rapidly spread, doubts have arisen. Has public education failed the nation? Or, perhaps, has the nation failed education? The political and moral purposes that gave resonance to public education in earlier times have become muted, and constituencies that once supported common schools have become splintered and confused about where to invest their educational loyalties.

I am a partisan for the public schools—albeit a *critical* one, as this book indicates. I do not argue that public schools do a better—or worse—job than private schools in educating citizens (in any case we never have enough good schools, public or private, for the students who need them). But I believe that public schools represent a special kind of civic space that deserves to be supported by citizens whether they have children or not. The United States would be much impoverished if the public school system went to ruin. And one way to begin that impoverishment is to privatize the *purposes* of education.

The size and inclusiveness of public education is staggering. Almost anywhere a school-age child goes in the nation, she will find a public school she is entitled to attend. Almost one in four Americans work in schools either as students or staff. Schools are familiar to citizens as places to vote and to meet as well as places to educate children. Schools are more open to public participation in policymaking than are most other institutions, public or private. Once the most numerous public officials in the world—before consolidation of school districts—district trustees still represent the citizens who elected them to guide public education. When local citizens deliberate about the kind of education they want for their children, they are in effect debating the futures they want. Participation, representation, deliberation—these help to make schools places where adults can exercise their obligations as citizens.

In this book I have examined three issues in the creation of this civic space. The first is how leaders sought to educate republican citizens. The second is how they dealt with social diversity. And the third is ways of governing schools. A common theme runs through each of these topics: the search for common ground amid controversy and ethnoreligious diversity.

This history is in part a tale of persistent conflicts of values and policies. Whose values should be taught, whose history learned? Are pupils basically the same or different? To what degree should schooling be the same for all or differentiated? How should one diagnose and remedy academic failure? To what degree should school governance be centralized? Should experts or lay people govern the schools? Seen in the long view, such conflicts never seem truly settled, and for that reason I have called them unavoidable tensions. When you mix together common schools, a diverse society, and an open political system, you can expect disagreement and conflict. Occasionally, groups have engaged in winner-take-all policy combat, especially on heated issues such as Bible reading in the nineteenth century or racial desegregation in the 1960s.

But in the civic space occupied by public education, a political culture favoring accommodation and mediation has been common. For over a century, public schools have had a public mandate to teach children about civic and moral life. Horace Mann thought that school officials could avoid controversy in civic education by teaching only those civic and moral lessons on which everyone agreed—a common denominator. But often one person's unquestioned truth was another's sectarian myth or partisan story. Mann's solution of noncontroversial virtue worked best in socially homogeneous communities where citizens agreed on most moral and civic questions.

In socially diverse places the common ground in school policies was often procedural, a willingness to follow democratic rules in arriving at decisions. At its best, school governance was itself educational, as citizens debated with one another about how the community should educate the next generation.

Part of the deliberation, compromise, and reframing of issues needed in educational policy requires balancing the claims of innovation and conservation, looking both forward and backward. It is important to moderate the pendulum swings of fashion in policy that decree that schools should be larger (or smaller), that more (or fewer) courses should be elective, or that governance should be more (or less) centralized. Another important—and often neglected—job in educational politics and policy is to conserve what works in schools. There is no shortage of innovators with sure answers to educational problems. But when these reformers want to transform educational practices, few ask what might be lost in the process.

The word "conservationist" has an honorable ring when citizens struggle to preserve unspoiled habitats or fine old buildings. When real estate developers propose paving over wetlands, environmental activists are praised for stopping them. When people work to conserve what is good in education, however, they are often dismissed as mossbacks or stand-patters. Government requires environmental impact statements for construction projects—but not student and teacher impact reports for educational reforms. Who will defend endangered species of good schools, or good educational programs, from the relentless, if zig-zag, march of educational progress?

It is easy to become so preoccupied with what is not working—the cacophony of bad schools—that one forgets what makes many schools sing. Good schools are hard to create and nurture, for they require healthy relationships of trust, challenge, and respect, qualities that take time to develop. These values become embedded in institutions as part of the common ground that unites the members of the schools. When teachers, students, parents, and administrators create such schools, it's important to preserve what makes them work, to sabotage ignorant efforts to fix what ain't broke, and to share knowledge about how to create more good schools.

Decisions about schooling are made in many places—in the White House and the courthouse, the Congress and the state legislature, the blue-ribbon committee of business leaders and the teachers' lounge. Jefferson argued that there was no better school of citizenship for both adults and the young than deliberating about common needs and values in a face-to-face community. His model of educational governance was a town meeting; people could learn democracy by practicing it. I think there is still a good case for vesting decisions about education, as much as possible, with the people who have to live directly with the results of those decisions, in local districts and even in individual schools.

Democracy is about making wise collective choices. Democracy in education and education in democracy are not quaint legacies from a distant and happier time. They have never been more essential to wise self-rule than they are today.

A Closer Look at the Issues

1. What common ground does Tyack identify for America's public schools?
2. Who should make the key decisions for public schools in Tyack's plan?

REFERENCES

American Federation of Teachers (2003). Update on student achievement for Edison schools. February. http://www.aft.org.

Appalachia Educational Lab. http://www.ael.org/rel/csr/catalog/coalition.htm. Retrieved June 29, 2004.

Australian Government Department of Science and Training. http://www.dest.gov.au/schools/publications/2001/fss/index.htm. Retrieved July 10, 2004.

Boston Globe (2004). US reports increase in home schooling. August 4, p. A2.

Boyer, E. (1991). *Ready to learn: A mandate for the nation.* Princeton, NJ: The Carnegie Foundation for the Advancement of Teaching.

Brandt, R. (2003a). Don't blame the bell curve. *Leadership,* January/February, pp. 18, 20.

Brandt, R. (2003b). Will the real standards-based education please stand up? *Leadership,* January/February, pp. 17, 19, 21.

Center for Education Reform (2004). *Charter school laws across the states: Ranking and scorecard 8th edition.*

CES National Affiliate Schools. http://www.essentialschools.org/cs/schools/query/q/562?x-r=rennew. Retrieved June 29, 2004.

CES National Web Ten Common Principles. http://www.essentialschools.org/pub/ces-docs/about/phil/10cps/10cps.html. Retrieved June 29, 2004.

Chubb, J. (2002). Public schools. http://www.econlib.org.

CNN (2004). Supreme Court affirms school voucher program. http://www.cnn.com/202/LAW/06/27/scotus.schoo.vouchers/CNN.com./LAWCENTER. Retrieved June 29, 2004.

Coles, R. (2004). Danger in the classroom: 'Brain glitch' research and learning to read. *Phi Delta Kappan,* 85, 5, January, pp. 344–351.

Comer School Development Program. http://info.med.yale.edu/comer/. Retrieved July 3, 2004.

DiMartino, J., J. Clarke, and D. Wolk (2003). *Personalized learning: Preparing high school students to create their futures.* Lanham, MD: The Scarecrow Press.

Dryfoos, J. (1998). Full-service schools: A revolution in health and social services for children, youth and families. San Francisco: Jossey-Bass.

http://www.ed.gov/pubs/G2KReforming/gzch3.html.

Edison Schools. http://www.edisonschools.com/home/home.cfm.

Eisner, E. (2003). Questionable assumptions about schooling. *Phi Delta Kappan* 84 (9), May, pp. 648–657.

Eisner, E. (2003/2004). Preparing for today and tomorrow. *Educational Leadership* 61 (4), December/January, pp. 6–11.

Evans, R. (1996). *The human side of school change.* San Francisco: Jossey-Bass.

Goodlad, J. (2002). School reform. *Phi Delta Kappan* 84 (1), September, pp. 16–23.

Haviland, J. (1988). *Take care Mr. Baker.* London: Fourth Estate.

Hern, M. (ed.) (1996). *Deschooling our lives.* Gabriola, BC: New Society Publishers.

Holt. J. (1964). *How children fail.* New York: Pitman.

Holt, J. (1967). *How children learn.* New York: Delacorte.

Holt, J. (1970). *What do I do Monday?* New York: E. P. Dutton.

Holt, J. (1972). *Freedom and beyond.* New York: E. P. Dutton.

Holt, J. (1981). *Teach your own.* New York: Dell.

Holt, J. http://www.holtgws.com/johnholtpage.html. John Holt Page. Retrieved June 29, 2004.

Holt, J. http://www.mhla.org/HoltOrigins.htm. John Holt and the Origins of Contemporary Homeschooling. Retrieved June 29, 2004.

http://www.context.org/ICLIB/IC06/Holt.htm. *In Context: A Quarterly of Humane Sustainable Culture.* Retrieved June 29, 2004.

Hunt, J. (2002). Leadership in education: A view from the states. *Phi Delta Kappan* 83 (9), May, pp. 714–720.

Illich, I. (1971). *Deschooling society.* New York: Harper. http://homepage.mac.com/tinapple/illich/1970_deschooling.html. Deschooling Society. Retrieved July 5, 2004.

International School of Minnesota. http://www.sabis.com.

Jenkins, J., and J. Keefe (2002). Two schools: Two approaches to personalized learning. *Phi Delta Kappan* 83 (6), February, pp. 449–456.

Jones, K., and P. Ongtooguk (2002). *Phi Delta Kappan* 83 (7), March, pp. 499–503.

Lee, J. (2003). Implementing high standards in urban schools: Problems and solutions. *Phi Delta Kappan* 84 (6), February, pp. 449.

Lewis, A. (2003). Hi ho, hi ho, it's off to tests we go. *Phi Delta Kappan* 84 (7), March, 483–484.

Martin, J. (1992). *Schoolhome.* Cambridge, MA: Harvard University Press.

McDermott, T., and D. McDermott (2002). High-stakes testing for students with special needs. *Phi Delta Kappan,* 83 (7), March, pp. 504, 544.

Meier, Deborah. http://www.pbs.org/kcet/publi shool/innovators/meier.html.

Metropolitan Learning Center Magnet School (nd). Metropolitan center magnet school for global and international studies: A national magnet school of distinction. Bloomfield, CT: Capital Region Education Council.

National Center for Education Statistic, (2004). *1.1 Million homeschooled students in the United States in 2003,* U.S. Department of Education Institute of Education Sciences, NCES 2004-115, July. http://nces.ed.gov. Retrieved August 5, 2004.

National Child Care Information Center (2002). Good start, grow smart: The Bush administration's early childhood initiative. August 20. Washington, DC: U.S. Department of Health and Human Services.

North Central Regional Educational Laboratory. A Nation At Risk. http://www.ncrel.org/sdrs/areas/issues/cntareas/science/sc3risk.htm. Retrieved July 2, 2004.

North Central Regional Education Laboratory. New Leaders: James Comer's School Development Program. http://www.ncrel.org/cscd/pubs/lead12/1-2e.htm. Retrieved July 3, 2004.

Paige, R. (2002). An overview of America's education agenda. *Phi Delta Kappan,* 83(9), May, pp. 708–713.

Paige, R. (2004). Memo to editorial writers: Re: No Child Left Behind Implementation. U.S. Department of Education, March 11. http://www.reedmartin.com/usdoememonclbimplementation.htm. Retrieved July 10, 2004.

Ravitch, D. (2000). *Left back: A century of battles over school reform.* New York: Simon and Schuster.

Reeves, D. (2003). Take back the standards: A modest proposal for a quiet revolution. *Leadership,* January/February, pp. 16, 18, 20.

Sadowski, M. (2000). What the AERA says about high-stakes testing. *Harvard Education Letter,* 16 (5), September/October, p. 4.

Schlechty, P. (1993). On the frontier of school reform with trailblazers, pioneers and settlers. *Journal of Staff Development* 14 (4), Fall, pp. 46–51.

Schulte, B. (June 24, 2003). If a birthday's late, Should school be early? When to start Kindergarten prompts debate. *Washington Post.* p. AO6.

Sizer, T. (1999). Personalized learning: No two are quite alike. *Coalition of essential Schools,* 57 (1).

Smith, B. (2003). Ever "at risk"? *Phi Delta Kappan* 84 (8), April, p. 562.

Symonds, W. (2001). How to fix America's schools. *Business Week,* March 19, pp. 67–80.

Swiniarski, L. (2003). *A global perspective of school reform-USA/UK.* Unpublished presentation given in November at Bradford College, Bradford, UK.

Swiniarski, L., and M.-L. Breitborde (2003). *Educating the Global Village,* 2nd ed. Upper Saddle River, NJ: Merrill Prentice Hall.

Thirty Great Books on Education. The Schoolhome: Rethinking Schools for Changing Families. http://www.great-ideas.org/30-13.htm. Retrieved July 8, 2004.

Tiley, J., with C. Goldstein (2000). *Understanding curriculum 2005: An introduction to outcomes-based education for foundation phase teachers.* Sandton, South Africa: Heinemann Publishers.

Tyack, D. (2003). *Seeking common ground: Public school in a diverse society.* Cambridge, MA: Harvard University Press.

U.S.Department of Education. http://www.ed.gov/admin/tchrqual/learn/hqt/edlite.

U.S. Department of Education Goals 2000.http://www.ed.gov/pubs/oals/summary/goals.html.

Watras, J. (2002). *The foundations of educational curriculum and diversity: 1565 to the present.* Boston: Allyn and Bacon.

Zelman v. Simmons-Harris (2002). 536 U.S. 639. 6 U.S. 639.

12 Creating Educational Communities

My family farmed eighty acres for three generations. We still have the original deed. It was a Mennonite community. Both my sets of grandparents lived along the three-and-a-half-mile road to town. In the one-room country school I went to, most of us were related. When we had special programs—Christmas-time, for example—everyone who lived around the school came, whether or not they were parents. Everyone went. It's still the case: the whole town goes to Flanagan High baseball games. Harvest time was longer then—smaller machines, and family farms. My father considered himself lucky if he got the corn in by Thanksgiving. The older boys would miss school to help their parents. The teacher understood.

We all took our lunches, carried pails from home. The teacher would warm them up for us on the school stove. The older children helped the younger ones. In third grade I remember listening to a first grader read (there were only two first graders). And teaching one young man how to tie his shoes. My father met up with that man recently and he said he remembered that all through his adult life (Lee Farrar, age 62, in Breitborde, 2003). ■

Our Need for Community

Education is inextricably linked to the concept of community in two ways. First, schools are integral parts of the communities in which they find themselves, both limited by them and enriched by their cultural, economic, and political character. Despite state and national government assumptions that "no child will be left behind," if schools dictate the same standardized curriculum, strategies of instruction and paper-and-pencil tests for all children without attention to their cultural backgrounds and the characteristics of the communities they live in, these schools are doomed to fail. Research presented in Chapter 9 shows that academic achievement depends at least in part on the values, orientations to schooling, social and physical support, and even cultural styles of the families and communities who send their children to particular schools. Effective schools see themselves as collaborators with families and communities—partners in the education of children.

The second way we apply community to education is in promoting the idea that, to maximize children's learning, schools and classrooms themselves should function as communities. In Lee Farrar's reminiscence about the one-room country school of her childhood, she shares her strong memories of how the older children helped the younger ones not only learn to read, but to learn life skills such as tying their shoes. Students of all ages need a sense that they are supported and that they belong in the classrooms where they spend most of their days. This sense of security is fundamental to their feeling free to learn and confident about their success.

As you read this chapter, think about these two notions of community as they operate in the schools you observe now, and as they operated in your own education. To what extent have schools in your experience invited the local community to participate in education? Has the curriculum of the school included information and resources that pertain to local history or culture? Do teachers and administrators involve families in the educational life of the school? Do families and community representatives share in decisions made about school policies and programs? Is there a climate, or spirit, of community inside the building and its classrooms? Do the students feel it? Do staff members? What makes one school, or one classroom, seem to function more like a community than others? In this chapter, we examine how both notions of community affect academic learning and we describe ways that schools can reach out to the community beyond their walls and take care of the community within.

The Need to Invite the Community into the School

Successful schools take account of cultural, social, economic, and political factors, by inviting families to participate in school in ways that are feasible and meaningful to them and by providing the basic supports necessary for children to come to school regularly, pay attention, and learn. Rather than viewing families and local communities as antagonists, obstacles to the business of a separate, smooth-functioning "ivory tower," successful schools see families as partners and local communities as resources for meaningful learning. As evidenced by Lee Farrar's story, one-room schoolhouses in rural America understood their place as community institutions, and the value of involving the whole community in the school lives of the children. Adults provided the schoolteacher with whatever they could offer: firewood, help with repairs, a place to stay overnight during bad weather, a new furnace. The teacher kept the schoolhouse clean, taught the children games at recess, and heated up their lunches. Rural schools were sensitive to the prevailing economic needs of families—in Lee Farrar's prairie school, the teacher understood that the need for older boys to help on the farm, to ensure the family's basic survival, took priority over attending school during harvest time.

In contemporary times, the model of the rural community school reappears in some cities in the form of full-service schools, described in Chapter 11, where children and their families may find health services, counseling, English-language instruction, citizenship classes, and before- and after-school care under the roof of their local school. In some developing nations, the United Nations Education, Scientific and Cultural Organization (UNESCO) and its Children's Fund (UNICEF) support reciprocal partnerships between schools and their local communities, wherein the community provides funding, materials, and housing for the teacher and shares in making decisions for the school, while the school provides wellness programs, adult education, and space for the community (Shaeffer, 2000). In Chapter 9 we discussed the many ways that schools can involve families in the life of the school beyond the traditional "open houses" and in-school volunteering (see Epstein, 1995).

Bringing the community into the school means also including its knowledge, perspectives, and culture in the school curriculum. Schools committed to their local communities have rigorous academic standards that address both a common stock of knowledge and skills and information and resources that are specific to local community life. They teach reading, writing, and mathematics skills using culturally-relevant materials, they use local environmental issues to context the teaching of science constructs and research skills, they link broad concepts and patterns in the social sciences to local history and geography. Students in the seaside community of Gloucester, Massachusetts, have studied American economic and scientific development by researching the history, technology, and environmental impact of the fishing industry. Students in rural Nebraska can focus on the same broad issues by studying changes in the history and technology of farming, and the consequences for the social, economic, and physical health of the people of the region. In Waco, Texas, high school students work with Baylor University students and faculty to learn new technologies that might improve the water quality in Central Texas (Fogleman, 2003).

Abroad, UNESCO sponsors programs in several Asian countries, including Bangladesh, Cambodia, India, Thailand, and the Philippines, that teach ethnic minority students to read using their "mother tongues." Educators use instructional materials designed to help students improve their lives while they increase their literacy skills. Subjects of study pertain to health, nutrition, the environment, the preservation of local culture, and ways to increase income through the farming and marketing of goods and produce (UNESCO, 2003; de los Angeles-Bautista, 2000). In some parent-managed Zambian community schools, the curriculum includes life skills and HIV/AIDS information infused across curriculum areas (Zulu, 2000).

In an act that is progressive and responsive to the communities within the state, the Maine state legislature enacted a law in 2001 mandating that all Maine public schools teach children about the native peoples of the state as part of the required Maine Studies curriculum. Later in this chapter, we describe the standards used to teach contemporary and historic themes within "Wabanaki Studies" across the curriculum.

The Need to Create Community Within the School

The need to include community in education does not end at the schoolhouse door. Inside the building, teachers and principals can create a sense of community among students and staff so that those who spend their working and learning days there feel welcome, safe, encouraged, supported, and prized. The psychologist Abraham Maslow told us that we have a "hierarchy of needs," beginning with the physiological needs for food, water, shelter, and warmth; proceeding to the social-emotional needs for safety, love, esteem, and a sense of belonging; and ending with our highest need, the need for self-actualization (1970). (See Fig. 12.1.)

When our needs for safety, security, a sense of belonging, and esteem are satisfied, we are free to pursue our natural inclination toward growth and individual creativity. Deficiency needs dominate children who are hungry or cold, who are worried about their parents, who are afraid to ask questions or give a wrong answer, or who are ashamed or feel alienated from their classmates. Their brains are filled with anxious thoughts, reducing their capacity to process whatever academic information the teacher is presenting or to exercise their curiosity (Terry and Burns, 2001).

Thomas Sergiovanni, a former elementary school teacher who is now a distinguished professor of educational leadership, says that providing schoolchildren with a sense of security, belonging, and community is more than merely advisable. He echoes Maslow's love and belongingness stage in claiming that community is a fundamental and universal human need. Our need for community is so strong that, if we don't find it in our basic social institutions such as school, we will seek it elsewhere, in gangs or cults. Without community, we sink into loneliness and depression.

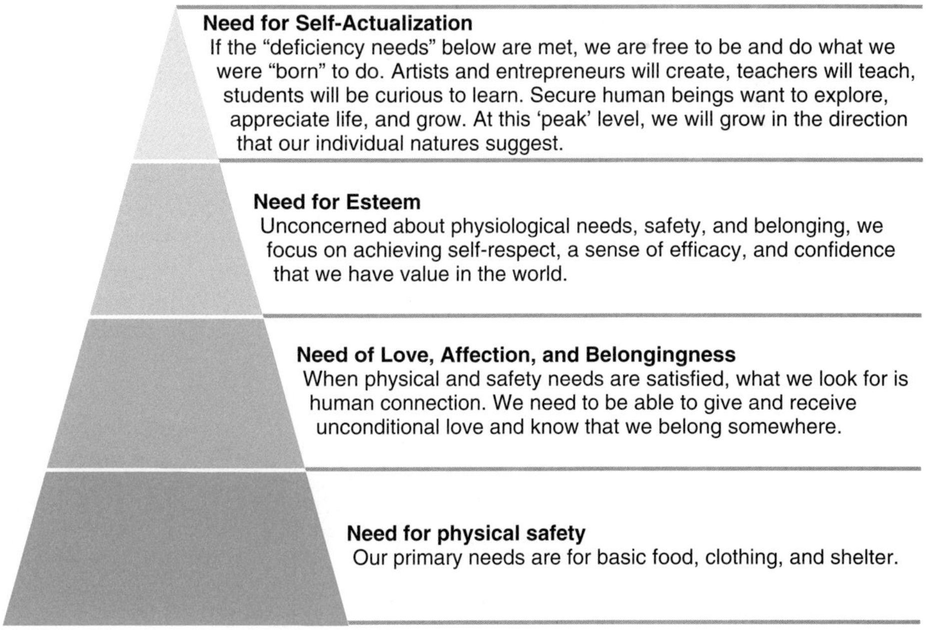
Need for Self-Actualization
If the "deficiency needs" below are met, we are free to be and do what we were "born" to do. Artists and entrepreneurs will create, teachers will teach, students will be curious to learn. Secure human beings want to explore, appreciate life, and grow. At this 'peak' level, we will grow in the direction that our individual natures suggest.
Need for Esteem
Unconcerned about physiological needs, safety, and belonging, we focus on achieving self-respect, a sense of efficacy, and confidence that we have value in the world.
Need of Love, Affection, and Belongingness
When physical and safety needs are satisfied, what we look for is human connection. We need to be able to give and receive unconditional love and know that we belong somewhere.
Need for physical safety
Our primary needs are for basic food, clothing, and shelter.

Figure 12.1

Maslow's Hierarchy of Needs

Source: Maslow-Frager, *Motivation and personality,* 3rd ed., © 1987. Adapted by permission of Pearson Education, Inc., Upper Saddle River, New Jersey.

> A sense of belonging, of continuity, of being connected to others and to ideas and values that make our lives meaningful and significant—these needs are shared by all of us. Their loss, for whatever reason, requires us to search for substitutes, which are not always functional (1999, pp. xiii–xiv).

Sergiovanni also says that creating community in classrooms and schools gives students and teachers a sense of purpose:

> Community is the tie that binds students and teachers together . . . to something more significant than themselves: shared values and ideals. It lifts both teachers and students to higher levels of self-understanding, commitment, and performance. . . . Community can help teachers and students be transformed from a collection of "I's" to a collective "we," thus providing them with a unique and enduring sense of identity, belonging, and place (1999, p. xiii).

Gemeinschaft and *Gesellschaft*

Sergiovanni uses Ferdinand Tonnies's classic sociological distinction between community and society to argue that schools have exhibited too little of the former and too much of the latter. Tonnies's ***gemeinschaft*** (community) is a world of face-to-face personal relationships offering a sense of kinship, shared place, and common mind. Its kinship aspect gives its members a feeling of being in a family—a sense of "we." The *gemeinshaft* of place is a shared habitat: this is "our" neighborhood, "our town," "our" school. *Gemeinshaft* of mind forges bonds by providing common goals, shared values, and shared conceptions of the way things are and ought to be (1887, cited in Sergiovanni, 1999, p. 6). Life in traditional societies can be characterized as *gemeinschaft.*

As the world advances, we drift further away from village and neighborhood life. Relationships become temporary and impersonal, institutions more complex. In the ***gesellschaft*** (complex society), contractual rules and relationships replace community values. People interact with each other for specific, instrumental purposes; we hardly know the person who checks our groceries or prepares our taxes or takes our movie ticket. Rather than being accepted for who we are as total beings, we are evaluated on what skills we have mastered and how we perform them for as long as they are needed. Some of you may know someone who was summarily laid off after working for a large corporation for many years. Except in times of great crises—hurricanes or national tragedies—we don't readily assume we will have help and support from the strangers who live nearby. In the *gesellschaft,* meaning is difficult to find. While we may live more efficiently and have more services, we run the risk in the *gesellschaft* of loneliness, isolation, and disconnection.

Schools where students are known only by their academic or athletic achievement or their alphabetical place on the class roster can be isolating, uncaring environments. In schools where teachers and other staff take the time to get to know all students and where there are organizational structures to engage students in a variety of activities and relationships, students are less likely to "fall between the cracks." The difference has important implications for everything from academic learning to the potential for conflict and violence.

Educational Community and Academic Learning

Sergiovanni is one among many educational thinkers who advocate the idea of schools and classrooms as communities. Some have suggested that a feeling of community is a protective factor that can foster resiliency in children at risk for academic failure. Bonnie Benard (1995) found that an atmosphere of caring, high expectations for all children, and meaningful opportunities for participation can help children to succeed academically despite social-emotional problems and other adversity in their lives. Other researchers have examined the impact that a spirit of community that engages families with schools can have on children's academic achievement. Susanne Carter (2002) reviewed studies over the past decade and found that family involvement and school-community collaboration significantly contributed to children's academic learning. Christenson and Sheridan (2001) discovered that schools that respected families as essential and interdependent partners in children's education maximized their academic success. The School Development Program reform model, which engages teams of parents and educators in school decision making using the principles of collaboration, consensus, and "no-fault" has produced academic gains for children (Haynes et al., 1996).

We described the position of well-known feminist educator Nel Noddings in Chapter 10, including her focus on creating an "ethic of care" in schools that function as communities. Noddings wants students to remain in one building for several years, in order to feel "ownership" and connection—what Tonnies would have called the *gemeinschaft* of place. Teachers should remain with a student group for three or more years, in order to come to know them well and to care deeply about them, and vice versa (Noddings, 1992). The important features of community, to Noddings, are a sense of belonging, a collective concern for everyone, individual responsibility for the common good, and an appreciation for the rituals and celebrations of the group (1996, p. 258). But not all communities will foster student learning. Claiming that there is a "dark side" to community, she warns against some communities' "tendencies towards parochialism, conformity, exclusion, assimilation, distrust . . . of outsiders, and coercion" (1996, p. 258). A learning community is a community that welcomes newcomers, respects differences, and is open to change and growth.

In Chapter 11 we described Theodore Sizer's essential schools movement, a critical component of which is personal relationships between students and staff. Sizer believes that, in order to learn happily and successfully, schools should be small enough so that every student feels there is at least one person in the school building who *knows* him. "I cannot teach students well if I do not know them well," Sizer says. Teachers, as members of the school community, must feel they are known as complete human beings as well. Sizer explains that teachers must have opportunities to express themselves beyond the boundaries of their specialties: "I am a teacher of mathematics. . . . I teach physical education. . . . I teach art. . . . I am a Dean of Students. No one of us . . . is to express and be held accountable for a general education—even as a "general education" is the ultimate goal for the students" (1999).

Deborah Meier, founding principal and spirit behind the noted Central Park East schools in Harlem, New York, now co-principal of the Mission Hill School in Roxbury, Massachusetts, complains that personalized education too often disappears after kindergarten:

> The kindergarten comes closest to encouraging openness and empathy, but each year thereafter schools strip away, one by one, all the kindergarten-like features that help sustain such qualities. Each year the classrooms look barer than the year before. They are less connected to the interests and passions of children, less social and collaborative in nature, and less kind to individual differences. The adults in charge are less and less likely to know each child and his or her family well, and the presentation of material is less and less likely to require the active use of children's imagination. As children move up through the grades, they are more and more judged in competition with one another, and displays of generosity and affection are increasingly seen as divisive and inappropriate. . . . We increasingly glorify "objectivity" over subjectivity, the impersonal over the personal, external standardization over the development of internal standards, certainties over ambiguities, and the one right answer over possible alternative paths (1996, p. 274).

In the schools that Meier has led, the idea of community became the reality of the way the schools were organized, the way decisions were made, and the nature of the relationship between the schools and the families and communities they served (1995). Teachers developed curriculum in collaborative teams and, in fact, ran the school. Families participated in making decisions about their children. Families and members of the community were invited to witness exhibitions of student work. Meier wants schools to recapture some of the personal, supportive relationships that existed in early schooling by creating communities where teachers, parents, students, and administrators talk to each other respectfully about things of importance to them (Meier, 2002a).

While Sergiovanni understands that schools must prepare children for the larger society beyond their doors, he sees them as needing to provide children with the sense of personal support they may have lost in the modern world. Schools cannot and should not substitute for strong, supportive families and neighborhoods, but "they can provide an important safety net" (1999, p. 13). Following his thinking, we ask these questions:

- How can school be more like a family? A neighborhood?
- What are our shared values and commitments?
- How will these values help us decide how to treat each other, what we should learn, what responsibilities we have to ourselves and each other?
- How can administrators foster community, collegiality, and caring among all school "stakeholders" (children, teachers, staff, families, and the larger community), so that they may serve as models for each other?

The answers to these questions may lead us to make changes in the way we organize schools, how we view the families and communities that send children to them, and the way we treat the students and staff inside.

The Elements of Educational Community

When a school capitalizes on its ability to create a community of learning and is connected to the larger community outside its doors, the result is a population of students and teachers and support staff who want to be there and want to participate in the activities of learning. But commitment to the idea of community in schools requires more than a phrase in a mission statement. In Sergiovanni's words,

> Authentic community requires us to think community, believe in community, and practice community—to change the basic metaphor for the school itself to community [so that] community becomes embodied in the school's policy structure itself, when community values are at the center of our thinking (1999, p. viii).

Schools can become caring and intellectually creative communities—communities of learning and mutual support for both students and teachers—only with focus and effort. The creation of an educational community requires that its leaders commit to:

- a shared mission
- an egalitarian distribution of power
- authentic and important dialogue among participants
- a teaching approach that is personal and centered on inquiry
- a respect for differences among its members and in the wider world
- a respect for the school's families and its local community

A Strong, Specific, and Articulated Mission

All members of a school community—students, families, teachers, administrators, teaching specialists, counselors, custodial staff, cafeteria workers—should be familiar with and understand the particular goals of that school and the programs and strategies designed to reach them. In a full-service school, for example (see Chapter 11 for a description of this and the following models), everyone should accept the premise that their school will provide children with the social and health services they need to be ready to learn. Everyone must understand that their school addresses the comprehensive needs of families, with the view that supported families will support their children's education.

In a school committed to the principles of the Coalition of Essential Schools (see Chapter 11), all members of the staff, as well as parents and the local community, should expect to participate in children's learning by, for example, attending exhibitions. Therefore, mission statements must be much more than material for hallway posters and brochures. Everyone in the building, including the students themselves, should know and be able to say what distinguishes their school's goals and programs from others', and understand how they can contribute to attaining those goals.

A shared mission gives a school community a reason to work together and a common vision of what success should look like. For example, the mission statement of Liberty Common School in Fort Collins, Colorado, reflects its membership in E. D. Hirsch's network of Core Knowledge Schools. The statement emphasizes the school's commitment to providing students with access to a common core of academic information and skills. All members of the school community understand and take pride in this commitment.

> The mission of Liberty is to provide excellence and fairness in education for school children through a common foundation by successfully teaching a contextual body of organized knowledge, the skills of learning including higher order thinking, and the values of a democratic society. Liberty recognizes the value of inclusiveness, or providing access to a broad cross-section of the community, so that students from all backgrounds can benefit from Liberty's educational offering. Liberty acknowledges the leadership of teachers in the classroom, and recognizes the responsibility of each student for his/her academic effort (Liberty Common School, http://www.libertycommon.org/about_us/mission/index.htm. Accessed December 21, 2004).

The mission statement of the Odyssey School in Denver looks very different. As an Expeditionary Learning School, Odyssey subscribes to the belief that learning means having direct experiences with real-world phenomena—for example, water resources—through interdisciplinary thematic investigations. Its mission statement refers to the school's emphasis on individual development within a community of "adventurers" in learning.

Fienberg Fisher Elementary School in Miami, Florida, is a full-service community school whose mission stems from the belief that a school should address the social, health, and educational needs of children's families in underserved communities to enable those families to support their children's academic learning. Its "controlling vision" reflects a commitment to working with the local community to provide comprehensive services to children and their families, many under the school's roof, with the ultimate aim of academic equity and excellence. In its mission statement, Fienberg Fisher declares its intention to develop independent, lifelong, academically successful, healthy learners by working in partnership with our families and community. (Fienberg Fisher, http://www.dade.k12.fl.us/fisher/community/community.html. Accessed December 21, 2004.)

Fienberg Fisher School's mission recalls the mission of the full-service settlement houses at the turn of the twentieth century (described in Chapter 8), which served as the "hub of multiple services" for the local community. The school sees itself as an integral part of, and resource for, the community, and makes little distinction between the community within and the one that surrounds the school.

Shared Power

Members of school communities are interdependent. They participate together in a variety of activities that account for their mutual needs and they make room for divergent and minority interests and points of view (Westheimer, 1998). Schoolwide policy decisions, focused on the school's mission, are collaborative efforts involving school staff, administrators, family representatives, and, when possible, students. Principals and curriculum directors must be willing to act as collaborators or facilitators as teachers take the lead in designing the curriculum they will be using in their own classrooms. Within the broad curriculum frameworks imposed by state boards of education and within the curriculum guidelines set by groups of teachers, students should be encouraged to make choices about what they want to learn, as well as how best they might present their learning. The social rules governing the classroom can be negotiated by its members—teacher and students. The sharing of power over curriculum, policy, and the rules and consequences of behavior gives students and their families a sense of their own effectiveness and empowers them for their roles as citizens of a democracy. Under Deborah Meier's leadership, in the Central Park East (New York) and Mission Hill (Boston) schools, teachers share responsibility for developing a curriculum that addresses broad questions, allowing students choice in specific topics of study and in the ways they will demonstrate their learning.

> The new schools that I've seen start and survive over time that have promised new approaches to teaching and learning . . . all have a strong sense of collegiality among the teachers rather than one strong leader. . . . Big decisions are made inside the school by the same people who have to implement them. Families have strong ties to the school and positive relationships with their children's teachers. For these reasons, parents generally do not become incensed if the school staff makes mistakes. . . . People feel appreciated for the work they do . . . [in] a more collegially governed school (Meier, 2002b).

Shared power requires a commitment from teachers and administrators to make the time to listen to the voices of all members of the school community. It requires a releasing of some of the control that they have assumed over decision making in schools (Merz and Furman, 1997). In meetings—whether staff meetings, parent-teacher meetings, or classroom meetings—everyone should be allowed to participate and to raise their own questions and concerns. Meetings should be small enough to enable all voices to be heard. Barb Aust recommends a "circle model," where a leader asks each participant to respond to the issue at hand until a consensus or an "agreement to disagree" is reached (Aust, 2003).

Students can share responsibility for each other's learning and welfare. Peer tutoring, peer leadership, and peer mediation programs structure student-to-student assistance in learning and solving problems. Peer helpers can assist teachers and administrators in running the school and communicating with students and families. In one school, students who were technology-savvy lent their expertise to administrators needing to learn more about how to design web pages, create databases, and use digital photography. Working with technology staff, they designed lessons linked to national technology standards and learned how to adapt instruction to the administrators' diverse knowledge and learning styles (Twomey and Schleicher, 2004). Students who are called upon to contribute meaningfully to decision making and operations within the school will increase their sense of efficacy and their commitment to their school, while practicing the skills of listening and understanding multiple perspectives and points of view.

Dialogue

Creating and maintaining a community require good communication. People must be as willing to listen as they are to voice their own thoughts and feelings. Discussions based on mutual respect and an interest in hearing others' points of view

Peer tutoring, peer leadership, and peer mediation programs structure student-to-student assistance in learning and solving problems.
Source: © Elizabeth Crews

will reflect a commitment to resolving differences constructively and peacefully. Children must be supported in expressing ideas without being ridiculed or dismissed. Teachers themselves must feel that their own opinions are welcome and solicited. Families must know what their children are supposed to be learning, and why, and how they might help. When the school is multilingual, all languages must be valued and interpreters should be made available to ensure school–home communication.

In classrooms characterized by shared dialogue, teachers invite children to ask their own questions, not just provide answers to the ones the teacher asks. These teachers know that the ability to ask questions is at the center of the ability to learn: "Once you have learned how to ask relevant and appropriate questions," Neil Postman and Charles Weingartner wrote in *Teaching as a Subversive Activity* (1969), "you have learned how to learn and no one can keep you from learning whatever you want or need to know." Questions are "powerful technology," says Jamie McKenzie (2000). They allow young people to make sense of their worlds, make decisions, solve problems, and invent and change things. In schools focused on teaching, students are like "passengers on someone else's tour bus. They may be on the highway, but someone else is doing the driving" (McKenzie, 2003). In schools focused on learning, where students exchange ideas in dialogue with their peers and their teachers, questions empower students to challenge traditional understandings of subject matter and act as creative citizens in a democratic learning community.

There are techniques that teachers and administrators can use to foster dialogue in schools. Two of these are active listening and dialogic listening. **Active listening** assumes that the listener is paying attention to what the speaker is saying, trying to make sense of the message, and responding to it respectfully and appropriately. When people talk to each other, they are often distracted because they are thinking about something else, because they are thinking about their own ideas on the subject, or because they assume that they know what the speaker wants to say before she says it. In active listening, the listener uses body language (for example, posture and eye contact) to show that he is listening, thinks about what the speaker is saying by relating it to previous information, repeats what the listener has said in his own words to confirm that he has understood, and then responds.

Dialogic listening focuses on the conversation as a shared activity. The participants in a true dialogue are joined in the process of co-creating meaning between them (Stewart and Thomas, 1995, p. 192), focusing on the present conversation, rather than on past events or future goals. Dialogic listening requires that students and teachers be "fully present" to their conversation partners and treat them as equals. Dialogue partners ask each other to "say more," to paraphrase, and to explore where each is coming from—in other words, to try to understand what in their past experiences, background cultures, and emotional lives has influenced their point of view. A listener might ask, "Why do you say that?" "What do you mean by that?" or comment, "In my experience, . . ."

Personalized Learning

In a community, people feel that they are known and understood. In a school that functions as a community, teachers and administrators know their students as individuals with their particular talents, interests, needs, and personalities. The curriculum makes room for the interests and talents of students, building on what they already know and can do and adding new knowledge and skills that are meaningful and important. It makes room for students' own questions and open-ended discussions. In other words, the learning is *personalized.* The student whose strength lies in the arts is invited to express himself artistically, as he learns and applies new material. The strong reader is introduced to new books, the athlete encouraged to learn in active, kinesthetic, ways. Teachers learn about their students' cultural backgrounds and use those cultures as important information about who they are as people and also as subjects of study. Students with learning exceptionalities are included in mainstream classrooms. Materials are adapted and modified to the way the teacher teaches to the specific learning needs. Teachers gauge learning success by using authentic assessment that allows students to demonstrate what they know in ways suited to their learning styles and talents—through exhibitions, artwork, oral presentations, and applied tasks. If learning is truly personal, students participate in assessing their own success by reflecting on what they learned and evaluating themselves.

One school that practices a personalized approach to instruction is the Thomas Haney School in Maple Ridge, British Columbia. In that grade 8 to 12 school, teachers have dual roles as coaches and advisors. Teachers work with small groups of advisees to help them set weekly goals, check their academic progress and discuss with them any personal information they want to share. As coaches, teachers work closely with students to help them master specific skills and content within the teachers' specialty areas. All students at Haney have personalized education plans based on their learning styles and achievement. Their weekly schedules can change as new needs arise. Teams of teachers have access to computerized databases of students' academic progress. Learning guides for all courses include varied activities geared to students' interests and skills needs, and students contract to do creative independent or group projects such as original poetry and news articles on subject matter topics. Students can redo unsatisfactory work; their learning is evaluated according to their own progress and assessed through exhibits and other demonstrations, in addition to traditional tests. The Haney School's commitment to **personalized learning**—including self-paced instruction, project learning, coaching and advisement, experiential learning, attention to individual learning styles, and authentic assessment—is evidence that the school "cares for students as individuals" (Jenkins and Keefe, 2002).

A Congruent Curriculum

By **congruent curriculum,**we mean a uniting of the cognitive, affective, and behavioral domains of learning: the head, the heart, and the hand. In teaching and learning, the medium is the message; the content and the process of education should work toward the same goals. Perhaps the most important rule for any teacher who wants the classroom to function as a community is to make sure the entire climate reflects the knowledge, behavior, and values she wants to teach. The stated and hidden curricula should be congruent and mutually reinforcing. Children must live things to learn them. For example, the teacher who gives lessons on pollution and world hunger and then uses Styrofoam plates for snacks and throws away usable food is undermining her own teaching. The message that "we should all respect each other" is undermined whenever a teacher ignores children's ethnic or homophobic jokes (or tells them himself!). Teachers need to consider all aspects of the learning environment—its physical contents and the organization of space, materials, and traffic patterns; the expectations teachers hold for students' behavior, the formal rules that guide that behavior, and the way these rules are implemented; the ways in which children are encouraged to work together or alone; the question of who "owns" the classroom materials, students' work, and the classroom in general; and the quality and quantity of teachers' interactions with students as individuals and in groups.

Teachers must also be willing to take the time to teach and help children practice the positive social behavior necessary to keep the community functioning. That means lessons in sharing, active listening, collaboration, problem solving, **conflict resolution,** and language that conveys respect and support. The time a teacher spends teaching the behavior requisite to community is well spent; in the long run, it will create an efficient, smooth-running classroom of independent, responsive, responsible learners, a classroom that "runs itself."

The overt curriculum is itself an opportunity to reinforce the idea of community. Subjects of study can include their impact on community life. Teachers can relate the conflicts facing characters in books and stories or lessons on scientific discoveries, for example, to real-world contemporary issues, perhaps in the children's own lives. Children might practice mathematical operations by solving problems in the classroom: How much paper might be saved by using the reverse sides? How many pizzas should the cafeteria staff order for next Friday's lunch? How should materials be divided among cooperative learning groups?

Collaborative Inquiry

A school community is a community of inquiry. To function as a learning community, schools must take the position that knowledge is created socially, by groups of people exploring questions together. While we believe that teachers using a variety of instructional approaches can create a sense of community in their classrooms, it is most easily fostered in a classroom characterized by a constructivist approach to teaching and learning. Constructivist teachers believe that there are many ways to interpret the world. In constructivist classrooms, learners generate their own questions and pursue the answers in active ways. The pursuit of knowledge is active, involving, and sometimes messy. The underlying assumption is that all members of the community have the power to contribute to the growth of knowledge. There are no "dumb questions," and neither is there one right way to arrive at the answers. Children can have questions that adults might not have thought of, and they may make discoveries that lead to new understanding for everyone. Constructivism is based on the idea that real learning is personal—that it comes from within us and changes our way of thinking. But constructivism also assumes that the exchange of questions and ideas in a learning community can lead each of us to higher levels of understanding than we can attain by ourselves.

Teachers who lead a community of inquiry use a hands-on, problem-centered approach to teaching and learning. They design lessons to engage students in inquiry and investigation, encouraging them to see themselves as "biologists" or "historians," rather than merely to memorize the information and ideas that other biologists and historians presented to them. Children learn the anatomical parts and functions of insects by examining insects, formulating hypotheses, recording their observations, and drawing conclusions from group discussions. They learn about the history of their community by posing questions and undertaking research about who came to live there and why, investigating the relationship between, for example, location and patterns of immigration and between scientific progress and economic development.

Inquiry classrooms are learning communities where everyone—students and teachers—are immersed in the pursuit of knowledge through the use of imagination and invention, interactive idea sharing and personal reflection. They are democratic environments that provide meaningful learning experiences for autonomous, equally respected, learners.

Respect for Diversity

In true communities, all members are valued. Despite a sense of "we," members also understand, and expect, that individuals will be different. They will have unique talents, skills, ways of thinking, cultural backgrounds, and personalities. Teachers who respect diversity provide opportunities for students to work cooperatively with peers who are different from them in many ways, by forming heterogeneous groups that collaborate on specific tasks. Following the tenets of constructivism, these teachers subscribe to the idea that a community is composed of a diverse group of individuals, and that understanding comes from a sharing of many different "heads," or multiple points of view. A group project, for example, draws on the variety of talents of the members of the group: the writers, the artists, the actors, the mathematicians. It might incorporate vocabulary from the native languages spoken by various members of the group.

Teachers who not only respect, but also use, the varying characteristics of their students teach with **multiple modalities.** Their teaching incorporates ways to reach students with a range of intelligences and learning styles. They use music, physical activities, field trips, dialogue and discussion, visual presentations, and a multimedia technology along with more traditional reading and writing materials. They use **differentiated instruction,** teaching the same content by adapting instruction and tailoring specific objectives to individuals and groups who have different

Voices of Principle and Promise

Welcoming All Families
by Melissa Correa-Connolly

Northeast Foundation for Children

Melissa Correa-Connolly presents the Responsive Classroom approach to schools. Before joining NEFC, she was an academic counselor at Academy Middle School in Fitchburg, Massachusetts, and taught bilingual and special education.

In the *Responsive Classroom* approach we believe that it's as important to know the families of the children we teach as it is to know the children. But in schools with a diverse population, there are special challenges in reaching out to parents. Many parents may work long or irregular hours; some may have limited English skills. Depending on their past experiences with education, school might seem like an intimidating place; teachers and administrators might be viewed as authority figures whose opinions and practices should not be challenged or questioned. All of this may prevent families from taking an active role. Here are some ideas for reaching out to parents:

- Make use of community resources such as cultural centers, multi-service centers, and libraries for learning about the cultural groups represented in your school community. Some useful things to learn about might be:
  - Cultural differences as they relate to learning style
  - Cultural views regarding education, family, and authority
  - Cultural values relating to time, respect, community, and male/female roles
- Meet parents as early in the school year as possible. Many schools begin the year with a barbecue, ice cream social, hike, or some other sort of gathering that parents and children attend together. This

achievement levels and specific learning needs. There are substantive, meaningful tasks for academically advanced learners as well as learners who need remedial help. Students with disabilities engage in meaningful activities with other students in the classroom.

Teachers who respect the diversity of the members of their classroom communities use teaching methods and materials that are culturally responsive. Geneva Gay (2000) defines culturally responsive teaching as using the cultural knowledge, prior experiences, and performance styles of diverse students in ways that build on students' strengths and make learning more effective and meaningful. In the classroom community, teachers treat the cultural heritage of ethnic groups as resources for interesting subjects of study and as positive influences on students' approaches to learning. They incorporate multicultural perspectives, information, and materials into the teaching of standard subject matter and skills. Students learn more about their own cultures and the cultures of their classmates. Textbooks and classroom literature reflect multicultural perspectives. Math exercises engage students in applying concepts and skills to the real-world conditions and experiences of populations of various cultures and social classes.

In classrooms that function as communities, students' native languages and rich and varied cultural backgrounds are valued and incorporated into lessons and units. In the Kamehameha Schools in Hawai'i, established for native Hawai'ian children by the legacy of the last descendent of King Kamehama, the curriculum includes Hawai'ian culture, language, history, and oral traditions. The program focuses on the student's physical, spiritual, artistic, and emotional growth along with academic progress. Its curriculum follows the Hawai'ian concept of *lokahi,* which allows families to meet school staff in an informal way.

- Think about how you'll communicate with families who might not be proficient in English. For example, whenever possible, translate written communication into the home language. If that's not possible, use graphics, clipart, or drawings to illustrate ideas. At conference time, encourage families to bring a friend or family member to act as interpreter.
- When talking with second language learners, use the following guidelines:
  - Speak slowly, enunciate clearly, and limit the use of complex words or slang
  - Offer clarification and ask for confirmation of understanding
  - Use contextual clues such as props, gestures, visuals, etc.
- Make sure that communication is ongoing and positive: classroom newsletters, "good news" telephone calls, etc.
- Invite parents to participate in a Morning Meeting. Encourage them to share something about their home culture or their family. Likewise, encourage children to share about their culture during "getting to know you" activities.

Source: Responsive Classroom, Spring 2003, 15 (2).

Questions to Consider

1. In what ways might Correa-Connolly's suggestions alleviate the fears of parents who find schools intimidating places?
2. How might you apply the principles of "active listening" described in this chapter to her ideas for communicating with students or parents whose English is limited?

speaks of balance, harmony, and unity for the self in relation to the body, mind, spirit, and the rest of the world. Kamehameha students, for example, study both Western and traditional Hawai'ian literature and learn to read using print materials but also the "talk stories" of their people. Students and teachers are treated as members of an *ohana,* or family.

Respect for Families and the Wider Community

A school that functions as a community does not ignore children's families or the larger community beyond its doors. Understanding that children's identities are bound up with their families and their neighborhoods, school administrators and teachers draw on the strengths and resources in family and community to honor children's whole lives, and to enlarge their learning and make it meaningful. These educators assume that all parents want their children to succeed in school. Conveying this positive attitude to parents is important to winning their trust. Schools with a community orientation find ways to involve parents who work long hours that prohibit them from attending traditional school programs such as afternoon parent–teacher conferences, or volunteering in their children's classrooms. These schools will provide child care during evening open houses. They will send weekly bulletins home to report on children's learning activities, in English but also in other native languages where they are spoken. If parents are not well educated or have limited English, teachers may host evening curriculum demonstrations, or ask children to read to their parents at night, rather than vice versa. Parents are encouraged to sit on school councils and advocate for school resources.

The Kamehameha Schools in Hawai'i focus on physical, spiritual, artistic and emotional growth along with academic progress. Its curriculum follows the Hawai'ian concept of 'lokahi,' which speaks of balance, harmony, and unity.
Source: © James L. Amos/CORBIS

Respecting the community culture means finding out about its cultural characteristics. In some cultures, "family" is not limited to the nuclear mother-father-children structure, but includes grandparents, aunts and uncles, and cousins. In many families, where parents work several jobs or where they are otherwise unavailable, the grandmother or the aunt or even an older sibling takes charge of the children; invitations to school conferences or presentations should be addressed generally enough to accommodate different family structures. In some immigrant communities, it is considered inappropriate or unsafe for women to venture out without men to accompany them, which may explain their absence from meetings or open houses. In most places in the world, parents are not expected to come to school; it may be considered rude or challenging to the teachers' authority to do so. These parents may consider "involvement" to mean making sure that children do their homework and get good grades. Schools should be sensitive to the many factors that might limit traditional parent involvement, and should value the many ways that families are involved in children's education in other ways.

All neighborhoods and communities have resources to offer schools. The means and materials for study can be found in both urban and rural neighborhoods, local markets, social agencies, fire and police stations, open land. Students can interview store owners and farmers, take architectural walks, explore cemeteries, study changes in plots of land, use town and city hall archives. Every town has a library whose staff is ready to help teachers and students find print and other media materials for research. Historical committees, environmental commissions, public works departments, and colleges and universities offer additional resources. Communities have unique and interesting economic, ethnic, and social histories that students should know and explore. A school that ignores all these resources for learning is missing important opportunities to make learning meaningful. In the next section we will describe specific ways to honor families and communities as educational partners in the learning community.

STRATEGIES FOR CREATING COMMUNITY

Teachers who understand the value of making their classrooms caring learning communities can accomplish this goal by looking hard at the way they organize students, choose topics for study and distribute the materials of instruction, and engage students in learning about the subject matter and about each other. Teachers who foster a sense of community establish a climate of care and inclusion in all aspects of classroom life—from the physical environment to the academic activities and the expectations for behavior. In the remainder of this chapter we offer some general guidelines and a sample of specific strategies that teachers can use to create and maintain educational communities.

Developing Groups

To perceive yourself as a member of a community, you must perceive yourself as belonging to a group. While children readily think of themselves as "second-graders" or "King School students," their ability to function as a positive, productive member of a group depends on a sense of belonging, but also on a set of skills they must be taught. If a child's previous experience was with teachers or parents who were authoritarian or individualistic, or if they come from a culture that does not promote shared decision making, they may not have learned how to collaborate with others, communicate openly and with respect, or value others' points of view. Teachers who stimulate open communication, shared decision making and problem solving, and cooperative work are more successful in creating functioning classroom groups.

The Johnson brothers (David, Frank, and Roger) have contributed research and many practical ideas related to the functioning of classroom groups. They found that classrooms can be characterized as having either cooperative, competitive, or individualistic goal structures. There are many instances where competition and individualism are appropriate and effective tools for learning. Classrooms that operate as communities, however, provide many opportunities for cooperative goal structures. Cooperation is created when teachers design activities that require children to work with and help each other in order to make sure that everyone achieves the learning objectives. Rather than simply asking students to work together, though, these teachers structure tasks that promote **positive interdependence** among members of a group. Positive interdependence can mean that individual students think that success means everyone has to attain the goals—the interactive effort of five basketball players comes to mind. It can also mean that resources are interdependent: each member of the group has one piece of information or set of materials which must be combined with what other members have in order for the group to complete its task. It can mean that members of the group function in different, complementary roles: note-taker or presenter, for example (Johnson and Johnson, 2000, p. 102).

In addition to positive interdependence, effective classroom groups require that their members feel individually accountable for their work. We have all had group experiences where one or two members do the bulk of the work, allowing others to "loaf." The result is both cognitive (not everyone learns the material) and affective (those who do more work feel resentful, and those who do little don't benefit from a sense of accomplishment). Each child should feel a sense of personal responsibility for contributing his or her efforts to the group goal. It should be clear where and how each member contributed. When individual responsibilities are clear, and children are held to, and rewarded for, their responsibilities, the social loafing effect (Johnson and Johnson, 2000, p. 117) disappears. One way to ensure both individual and group accountability and rewards is by evaluating, or grading, both the group product and the individual work that went into it.

Research in social psychology tells us that groups begin at different levels of functioning and develop through stages. "Development" implies an increasing capacity to do things. According to Richard and Patricia Schmuck, classroom groups develop four capacities (2001, p. 52):

- the capacity to welcome all participants into full membership and to afford everyone a secure and comfortable place in the group
- the capacity to share influence evenly in the group and to establish egalitarian relationships among all members
- the capacity to encourage and support one another in the pursuit of individual and group goals
- the capacity for "self-renewal"; that is, for all members to work together in changing the group's process when change means improvement

When students enter the classroom on the first day of school, they are concerned about questions such as: Who will I be with in this classroom? How will I fit in? Will I be accepted? What will I have to do to be accepted? Can I trust anyone in here? There are many exercises that engender the capacity for full membership and security. For example, students can learn about each other in an exercise that asks them to discover classmates who have particular attributes or experiences. A "make a new friend" worksheet, for example—with items such as, Find someone with red hair, Find someone who was born in another country, Find someone who has the same hobby as you, Find someone who has at least three siblings, and Find someone who speaks two languages—will encourage children to talk to each other and appreciate similarities and differences. The child who has a characteristic that makes her different from everyone else, such as red hair or immigrant status, becomes sought after, and this difference is suddenly a valuable asset.

Shared hobbies and interests might become the basis for a group research project or for forming literature groups. A small group "machine pantomime," where children imitate a common machine—a vacuum cleaner, for example—by representing its various parts, offers an opportunity for group problem solving and for otherwise hidden creative and dramatic talents to surface. In any group endeavor, teachers need to make sure that power is evenly divided and that relationships are egalitarian. Some teachers rotate group leaders to give everyone a chance at running things. Some use time tokens or wands to ensure equal time for comments, limiting "talk time" to the person who holds the wand. Round robins, where students give comments one by one around the group, ensure that everyone has the chance, and the responsibility, to participate. The "fishbowl" technique sets a small discussion group amid a larger circle of observers, who might join the smaller active group on a rotating basis. Teachers who make it their business to know the interests and talents of their students will structure cooperative work groups to include children with a variety of skills to contribute; a small group might include a good artist, a clear writer, a budding mathematician, and an interpersonally sensitive facilitator.

To promote student-to-student support, teachers use peer tutors, teach children how to phrase positive feedback and constructive suggestions, and encourage them to help each other when help is needed. Finally, "self-renewal" requires that teachers regularly convene class meetings to reflect on class rules, assess how group work is going and to brainstorm ways to solve problems that arise. Classrooms that function as community groups celebrate their successes, with exhibits, programs for the school and for families, and, of course, parties.

Designing Classroom Spaces

The physical environment of a classroom can encourage or discourage community. Teachers who decorate the classroom walls only with charts, posters, and pictures that they have chosen to display convey the message that the classroom belongs to the teacher, who alone decides what is important for students to look at during the school day. In classrooms where students are considered full members of a learning community, students' work is prominently displayed and they have a voice in deciding how to display it. While it is tempting for teachers to begin the school year with walls decorated with what they believe will be attractive to students, it is a far better idea to leave some blank spaces and invite students to contribute to the classroom décor as the year advances.

Furniture and seating arrangements can foster or discourage community. Classrooms that are arranged in *traditional* rows make helping, collaboration, and open communication difficult among students. They also convey the message that learning is an individual matter and that power and authority are in the hands of the teacher alone. While the "lecture-style" row arrangement is sometimes called for, other configurations offer more opportunity for creating community and should be used regularly. Figure 12.2 shows some other options including seminar style (or circle), clusters, and learning centers.

In a *seminar,* or *circle,* arrangement, students and teacher sit in a circle. There is no clear leader position; everyone's physical position is equal, and everyone can see everyone else. The circle invites open communication and full participation, though there may be some students who shrink from speaking to such a large group and time constraints may limit the number of participants. This arrangement lends itself to large-group discussions and classroom meetings. It conveys a clear sense of "we," and the idea that all members of the learning community have the right to contribute to the development of knowledge.

Similarly, the *U-shaped classroom* has students arranged along three sides of an imaginary square. The fourth side is left "open" to accommodate a presentation, perhaps by the teacher, or by other students. This arrangement has advantages similar to the seminar circle, in that it conveys the idea of equal status and participation and is oriented to whole-group learning. The U shape, however, adds the possibility that students may function as an audience for a whole-class presentation. While there is still a sense of "we," it is assumed that the community has a leader with greater knowledge and the responsibility to direct the group.

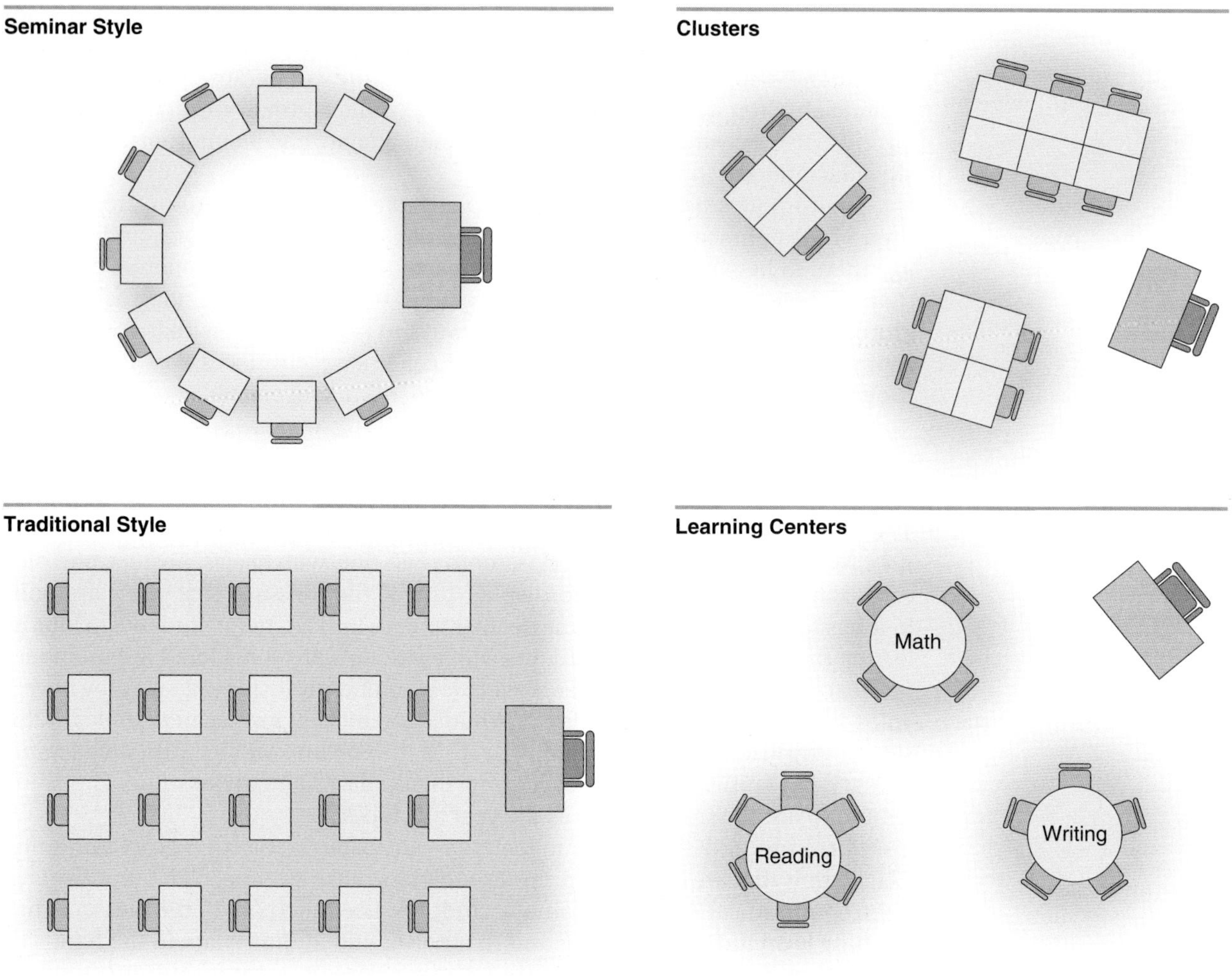

Figure 12.2

Seating Arrangements That Foster a Sense of Community

In a *cluster* arrangement, desks are arranged in small groups of four or six. It conveys the idea that learning is best done in groups. It invites small-group conversation and small-group cooperative work. The small group can function as a study group or do a project together. The teacher can also meet with a small group to help them work on a specific skill or coach them in their cooperative project. This arrangement may, of course, be problematic for students who need to limit distractions; it may be difficult for students to work independently and silently in such close proximity to their peers. Teachers using cluster arrangements need also to guard against the fragmenting of the classroom into groups, by making sure to create time for whole-class activities and discussions.

Learning centers divide the classroom into separate areas for subjects of study. They may be skills-based: designated as reading centers, writing centers, listening centers, or math centers, for example. Or they may be organized by content topics: a science center with a rotating display of seashore life or electricity; a literature center that displays poetry or biography; a social studies center focusing on African American history or the Bill of Rights. In all cases, learning centers house a collection of interesting visual materials and *realia* (real objects) as well as a set of tasks that children can complete using the materials; for example, a Venn diagram comparison chart to fill in, an experiment to complete, a note-taking or reflective writing activity, or a question sheet. A teacher who uses learning centers believes that learning is both personal and social, requiring "hands-on" materials. Teachers vary in the way they use learning centers, with some requiring all students to visit all centers and complete all activities, and others allowing for individual choice depending on student interest. Learning centers combine a sense of a community of inquiry while allowing for individual differences.

Teachers sensitive to the learning styles and needs among students will vary seating arrangements so that students have the experience of the independent choice offered by learning centers, the whole-class discussion advantage of circle and U-shaped arrangements, and the small group collaboration that clusters encourage. They will sometimes also use rows to present formal lectures and to accommodate students who need direct instruction and a quiet classroom. As Chapter 5 describes, a classroom of students presents a diversity of styles of learning; teachers should allow for these differences, while keeping in mind the effect of the physical environment on the creation of a sense of community.

Choosing a Multicultural and Meaningful Curriculum and Materials

Teachers interested in creating learning communities search the curriculum for opportunities for community-related themes. Even when school curricula must follow strict frameworks set by the state or the local district, teachers have some discretion about how to approach subjects of study. A community-strengthening curriculum includes subject matter that is deep and important and focuses on skills that empower students to learn from each other and work with each other, drawing on their separate and common experiences. The curriculum affirms, explains, and enhances the immediate worlds of students while it conveys to them the sense that they are part of the larger world community. Infused in the curriculum content are themes of human unity and cultural diversity, and the relationship of human beings to each other and to their environments. In the next section, we present a sample of curriculum themes and related activities and materials that teachers at all grade levels and in all subject areas can use to address the goal of community in their classrooms.

Exploring the Local and World Community Teachers in learning communities select materials that are rich in content, and use those materials in ways that involve students in shared exploration of their own experiences, their neighborhoods, and the world. *Sacred Places*, a beautiful book by Philemon Sturges and Giles Laroche (2000), is one example of a picture book that lends itself to this approach. A beautifully illustrated travelogue of "special places" where people of various cultures gather to worship and celebrate, the book encourages interdisciplinary learning, emphasizing world history, world religions, cultural practices, and the arts. In this book, children will find places and practices familiar to them and will be introduced to others that are new. They can consider how architecture, colors, and symbols express people's beliefs. Teachers can move from the book to a study of maps, of religions in history, of music, and of language and word origins.

Sacred Places has been used successfully in classrooms from elementary through secondary levels. While the illustrations beguile the younger students, the text and concepts hold interest for older students. The book is a valuable way to enhance the teaching of world religions and world history, topics included in many state curriculum frameworks. Secondary teachers can also use the book to introduce the study of materials science and engineering design. One high school geometry teacher turned the book, *Bridges Are to Cross,* into a geometry project. The students had to decipher the mathematical patterns used in the architectural principles to structure the bridges chosen to represent the diversity of designs used around the world.

Sharing with students some counting and alphabet books from different cultures provides opportunities to address numeracy and literacy as universal themes with specific variations in particular human communities that communicate using specific languages and dialects. Even when the same language is used in an alphabet book (English, for example), cultural differences are apparent in spellings, vocabulary, word usages, and dialectical syntax. We suggest that teachers and their students start a global collection of such books to expand their knowledge of how groups communicate and teach literacy and numeracy. In mathematics, students might consider how communities and cultures have used mathematical systems, procedures, and symbols. They might, for example, learn the origin of Chinese tangrams, depicted in Figure 12.3, using the wonderful picture book *Grandfather Tang's Story* (Tompert, 1990) or find out that the ancient abacus (counting frame) is still used in many countries.

When curriculum guidelines call for teaching geography and, specifically, the concept of cultural adaptation to physical environments, children might look at

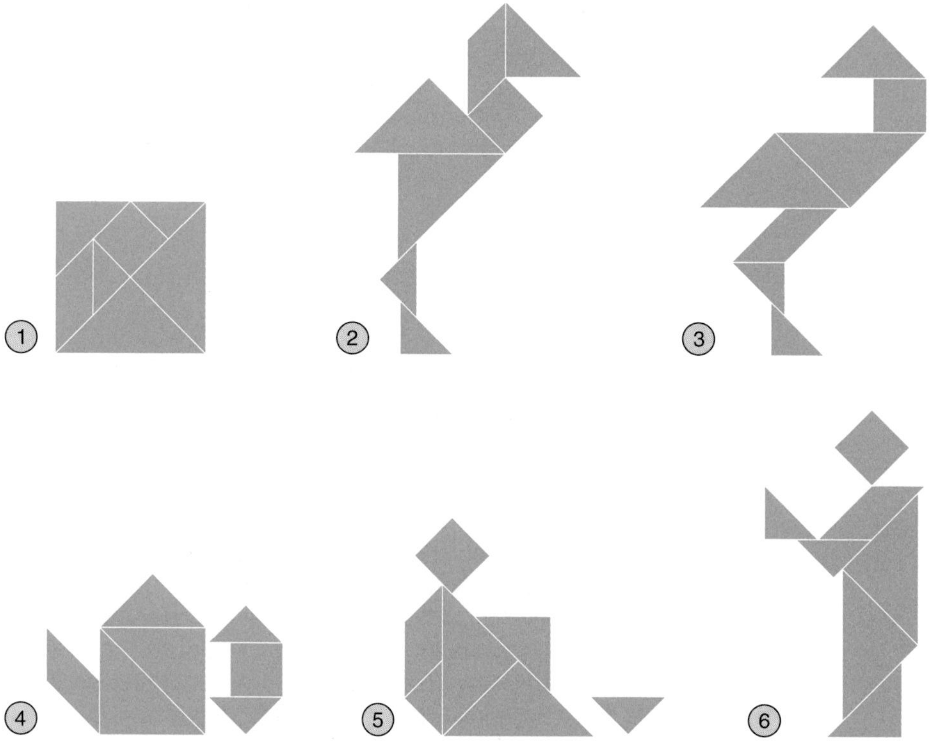

Figure 12.3

Traditional Chinese Tangram

how people from a variety of places, cultures, and times designed shelters for themselves and their communities—the materials used for housing and the ways in which housing design reflected functional adaptation to a physical environment and a way of life. They might learn that the word *bungalow* derives from the Hindu *bangla,* adapted by the British to mean a seasonal house suitable for warm climates; that the Georgian-style homes of the New England colonies were named for King George III; that later Greek revival architecture symbolized our new republic's admiration for the democracy of ancient Greece (Kassabaum, 1981); that the row houses in many communities were built to house immigrant boarders who were employed by the mills of the newly industrialized nation and shared rooms and meals with coworkers.

In the "Pack Your Bag" activity described in Chapter 4, (Swiniarski and Breitborde, 2003, p. 194) students learn about ways of life in faraway places by exchanging a package of artifacts and information about their local community with children in that other place. The activity engages them in researching the history, geography, demography, and economic characteristics of the city or town they live in, comparing their results with the reports of their faraway pen pals, and formulating hypotheses about the reasons for similarities and differences. Using communications technology, the "bag" might be enhanced or supplanted by multimedia presentations sent via the Internet. (We think, though, that there is no substitute for receiving real, "touchable," artifacts in the mail.)

Mapping activities help children to see their community from several perspectives. Teachers can display visual representations of the same location; for example, road atlases, topographical maps, aerial photographs, geo-information systems displays, and satellite images. Historic and contemporary maps and artifacts from different periods will show changes over time in their community. Another activity teaches the generalized concept of an "international address": Children divide a piece of paper into four sections; in the first box, they draw an outline map of their home on their street (street address), in the second, their street within their town or city; in the third, their city within their state; and in the fourth, their state within their country. This activity gives children a sense of their belonging to widening circles of community in the world. Figure 12.4 shows one child's depiction of his international address.

In one example of a large-scale initiative to integrate the study of the local community across the curriculum, representatives from the four federally recognized Native American tribes in the state of Maine convinced the state legislature in 2001 that the traditional Maine Studies curriculum left out the history, culture, contributions, and contemporary experience of the native communities of the region. Since that time, teachers from kindergarten to grade 12 have attended institutes each summer to learn about Wabanaki (Passamaquoddy, Penobscot, Maliseet, and Micmac) life from the natives themselves. Among their subjects of study are land use and current land issues; Wabanaki tribal governments; traditional and contemporary Wabanaki economic systems; and Wabanaki history, spirituality, languages, traditions, family structures, crafts, science and health knowledge, and oral and written literature.

Wabanaki Studies is linked to state curriculum frameworks and learning standards. The goal for educators is not only greater appreciation for the culture and contributions of the natives but also a greater understanding of native ways of thinking and learning, including their respect for honor and beauty. With help from Native American and white educators, teachers have developed lessons for

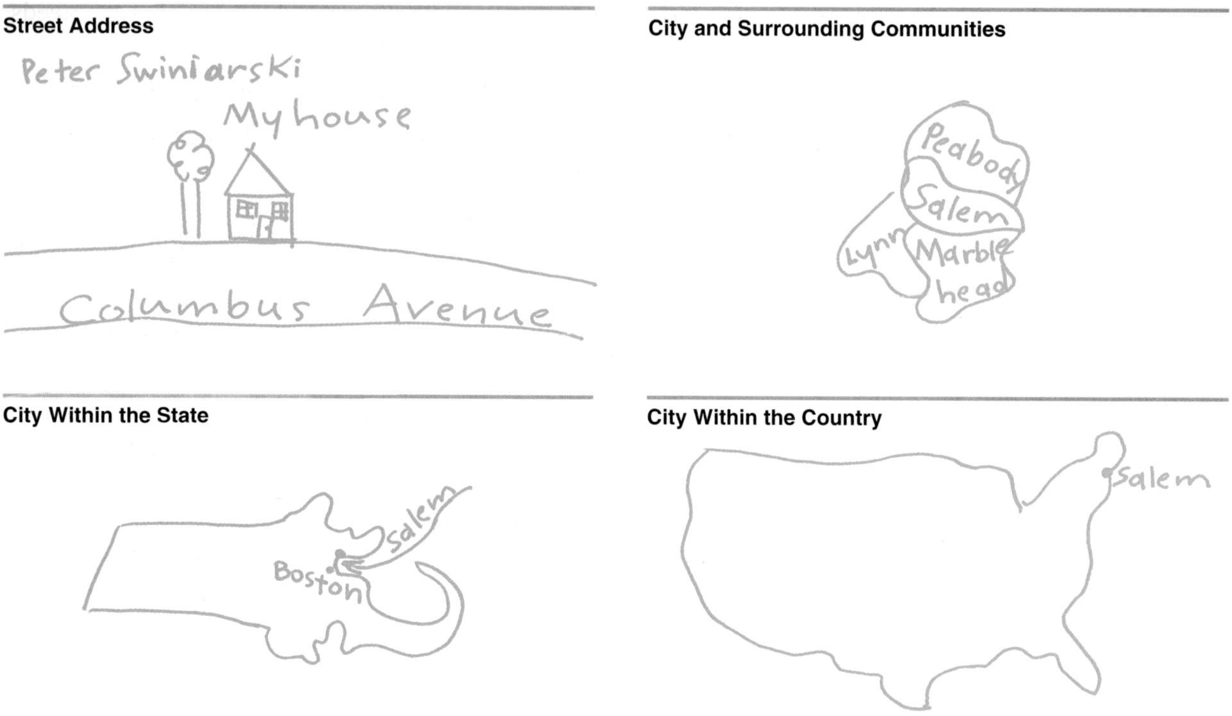

Figure 12.4

Mapping Your International Address

all levels and subject areas. For example, elementary students develop a historical timeline, middle school students examine native roles in the American Revolution, and high school students discuss the ethical issues involved in tourism and land use policy. The Wabanaki Studies Commission offers several principles and cautions in teaching Wabanaki Studies that serve as helpful guides for teaching about any culture, local or remote. As you read through the list, you may replace Wabanaki Studies with a reference to any local culture represented by a school's surrounding community.

Following are some principles and cautions in teaching about any culture:

- Everyone has a culture. Learning about another culture helps students understand their own culture. There tends to be an over-emphasis on artifacts in teaching about the Wabanaki people. The Wabanaki people and their culture are more than pretty, interesting objects.
- The issues of reality and authenticity are especially critical for culture.
- It is important to understand that there is diversity among the four Tribes in Maine.
- Thorough study about the Wabanaki people involves consideration of ethical issues. It is important to make it safe to discuss stereotypes, racism, genocide, and other things that make people feel uncomfortable.
- Wabanaki people must be involved centrally in designing curricula and in teaching about Wabanaki Studies.

- History sometimes tends to be a conglomeration of events and dates. It needs to come alive.
- Wabanaki Studies can challenge the notion that the victors write the history.
- It is important to incorporate oral histories and historical documents (such as treaties) into teaching.
- It is important for students to learn how to identify ethnic and cultural perspectives missing from historical accounts and to describe these points of view.
- It is safe to discuss some things about culture, but not others. Some parts of culture are private and spiritual.
- Teaching Wabanaki Studies should occur using a kaleidoscope of teaching approaches in a culturally competent manner both in and beyond the classroom.
- Training and support are essential to enable non-Native teachers to provide accurate, culturally competent information about the Wabanaki people.
- Simulations can be used to begin to understand complexities.
- Stories can be used to teach about the Wabanaki people (Wabanaki Studies Commission, 2003).

Sustaining the Environment and the Seas In a community-oriented classroom, teacher and students might consider the conditions for the sustainability of plant and animal life in their neighborhood and on the planet and the impact of science and technological change on people's lives. All state curriculum frameworks include the study of electricity, magnets, rocks and minerals, simple machines, plant and animal habits and adaptations, and the management of natural resources, among other topics. They refer to the teaching of scientific methods of inquiry, including careful observing, constructing hypotheses, testing, and measurement. Students can study these topics and skills in the context of their own classrooms and local communities. For example, they can explore, compare, tabulate, and evaluate what chemicals their families use in morning routines: in tooth-brushing, showering, washing the breakfast dishes, and doing laundry. The class might "adopt" a plot of land or a pond near the school, examine what grows and lives there and why, and observe and record seasonal changes. Tending to that plot of land will provide the class with an opportunity to work together and engage them in caring for the environment, a goal central to Nel Noddings's notion that care should be at the center of the curriculum.

The local community is a resource for the study of the influences of location, environment, and technology on the economic life of a community. In Seattle, Washington, students and parents at an alternative high school built a canoe with the help of members of the Haida tribe, using traditional methods. They hollowed out the canoe by hand, steamed the hull with volcanic rock, and painted totems on the bow and stern using native symbols. Along the way, they learned how human beings use the tools and technologies available to them, as well as math, reading, and the history of the region's native peoples. Students whose background includes Native American roots were able to learn more about their own culture. The school brought the boat to a Haida community in Alaska, who received it in an elaborate welcoming ceremony of singing, dancing, and the exchanging of gifts. The project began a relationship between Seattle and the Haida village, including plans for student exchanges (Toner, 2004).

On the opposite U.S. seaboard, Gloucester, Massachusetts, is a community historically dependent on the sea to sustain its families. The fishing industry, always important to Gloucester, has experienced major changes due to technological advances that have had both positive and negative effects on the fisheries and fishing techniques. Gloucester's location has influenced who immigrated there, how they supported their families, what community institutions grew, and how people adapted to change. Dr. Breitborde worked with Mary Kay Taylor to design a unit of study for local schoolchildren on ocean life and the changes in fishing techniques, inviting local fishermen to offer what they know and do. See the following description of a curriculum unit on the history of Gloucester fishing.

Children in farm communities might study the impact of science (chemistry, for example) and technology on agriculture and evaluate national policies such as farm supports and free trade agreements with neighboring nations. And children in city neighborhoods might study the physical conditions that contributed to the growth of their city and the ways in which science and technology help create and solve problems of community life such as health care, recreation, industrialization, resource distribution, and waste management. Even the practical problem of litter in the school neighborhood can be a subject of research and community action: Children can examine the problem, develop hypotheses about the causes, talk to local business owners and city officials, conduct observations and interviews, and formulate and test potential solutions.

Fishing Out of Gloucester: An Interdisciplinary Teaching Unit

"Fishing Out Of Gloucester" provides Gloucester, Massachusetts, fifth graders and their teachers with hands-on activities that illustrated the history and development of an industry that defined the culture of their city and a way of life on Boston's North Shore. The unit draws on the resources of local people and organizations, notably the National Historic Landmark schooner *Adventure*, the last of the great dory fishing "highliners," berthed in Gloucester. Unit objectives are linked to Massachusetts Curriculum Frameworks in science and technology, history, and mathematics. Some state curriculum strands addressed in the unit are:

History: patterns of emigration; use of primary and secondary sources

Geography: watersheds, ecological regions, and resources; effect of physical characteristics on industries and patterns of economic growth

Economics: stages of economic change in New England; international trade; local and international markets

Science: diversity and adaptation of organisms; impact of technology on the environment and society

English/Language Arts: identifying essential ideas; word choice and imagery

Mathematics: data analysis; proportional relationships and units of measure

The program consists of the following:

The Preliminary School Visit: a multi-media program on

- the geography of Gloucester Harbor and the Gulf of Maine fishing banks
- the nature and evolution of the fishing industry
- he lives of fishermen at sea
- the lives of fishing families

The school visit program introduces new vocabulary; provides reading material on the geography, history, economy, and technology of Gloucester fishing; and guides students to formulate questions and pose hypotheses about fishing and fish production in the past, present, and future. Teachers use materials for class discussions and activities following the visit.

Teacher Preparation Workshop: a two-hour workshop aboard the schooner *Adventure,* which presents teachers with

- a guided tour of the schooner and a fully equipped banks dory
- rotation through each of three learning stations (the place, the work, the life)
- a group discussion linking the stations to the state curriculum frameworks

Class Visits to the Schooner Adventure: a two-hour session where students are engaged in hands-on science, math, history, geography, economics, and language learning experiences. Students rotates through three learning stations.

Station One: The Place

Sample Activities:

"Where Are We?"

Locate your position using old and new technological tools (compass, global positioning system) and various types of maps.

"Buoyancy"

Experiment with flotation in salt and fresh water.

"Water Sampling"

Measure depth and salinity. Record marine organisms and the presence of pollutants.

"The Catch"

Compare tables of changes in fish stocks over time.

"The Debate"

Examine different points of view on fishing policies.

Figure 12.5

The Schooner *Adventure*

Station Two: The Work

Sample Activities:

"Simple Machines"

Experiment with six types of machines used on board.

"Knot Tying"

Examine the form and function of different knots.

"Be the Mast"

Simulate compression and tension.

"Net Design"

Identify and create nets to catch different species of fish.

"Chanteys and Work Songs"

Learn the function of the music by hoisting the sail to a work song.

Station Three: The Life

Sample Activities:

"They Came to Fish"

Map the routes the primary immigrant groups traveled.

"Life in the Foc's'le (Forecastle)"

Try on an oilskin. Experiment with water repellency. Pack a duffel bag for a fishing trip.

"Making a Living"

Calculate trip expenses and your pay share. Examine old catalogs to determine your buying power.

"Voices of the Community"

Listen to oral histories of Gloucester fishermen and family members; retell their story.

"Memoirs of a Fisherman"

Read excerpts from "A Childhood by the Sea." Compare with your own life.

Using World News to Explore Cultural Landscapes In high school English, geography, and government classes, newspapers from around the world provide students with an opportunity to explore diverse cultural landscapes. Teachers and students can collect newspapers from many nations and look at, for example, how the news is presented, who the noted celebrities are, what sports are highlighted, and which companies are advertising. By comparing the news from abroad to local editions, students can readily assess the impact of globalization on the cultural landscape as well as determine how nations are alike and different. While students can peruse the papers without knowledge of the various languages involved, the importance of being multilingual becomes apparent in this activity. In this activity, students who are bilingual usually are at an advantage. When this activity is a group assignment, bilingual students often gain recognition and appreciation from their peers for their linguistic skills.

Middle and high school teachers can adapt this activity to include the Internet for exploring other countries' coverage of world happenings. Web searches for primary sources reinforce practice in research skills. To enhance listening skills, teachers and students can turn, for example, to the radio news from the World Service of the British Broadcasting System (BBC). Students might compare its news coverage with that of an American broadcast to note the kinds of stories selected for reporting as well as the interpretation of events. Similarly, for an American studies class, students can investigate a collection of newspapers from various regions of our country to determine the extent to which American culture has become homogenized and what is still unique in American local and regional life. Old newspapers, magazines, and journals provide a wealth of resources for studying cultural issues in American history. For example, Norman Rockwell's numerous magazine illustrations chronicled social movements. The civil rights movement is poignantly captured in his works entitled "New Kids in the Neighborhood" and "The Problem We All Live With." Students might compare mass-market magazine coverage of national movements to local newspaper and other primary accounts to see the impact of these movements on the local community.

Using Toys, Games, and Folk Literature to Teach Global Themes

Toys delight everyone, young and old. They are a natural medium for teaching at all levels because they universally appear in the lives of children everywhere, in all cultures of the past and present. As artifacts of society, they reflect values, politics, lifestyle, and economies. Toys can be the centerpiece for a global education curriculum to teach concepts such as:

- global interdependence
- economics
- the sustainable environment
- peace education

Students can examine and create their own toys, research the toys' countries of origin, identify cultural traditions, or analyze the economics of the toy industry. Oregon teacher Bill Bigelow developed a high school social studies unit on global economics and the problem of child labor using a soccer ball (Bigelow, 1998). Students considered the concepts of transnational capital, environmental regulation, taxation, workplace conditions, profit, and social class, as they simulated corporate and social policy decision making. Toys can be organized into kits on various themes or concepts. A kit developed by Louise Swiniarski (1991) centers on the game of Monopoly, replicated in over thirty different national versions. The game promotes the curriculum areas of math, geography, economics, and social history, as it teaches about geographic and cultural differences. The Monopoly learning kit asks students to create new editions of the game using computer graphics.

Teachers can use folklore and folk literature to introduce the idea that human experience is both unified and diverse. Folktales and myths handed down through generations have provided people of various cultures with explanations of the physical world, moral lessons, and entertainment. A study of folk literature across cultures reveals universal themes such as good triumphing over evil, kindness and generosity prevailing over selfishness and jealousy, the value of hard work and persistence, and the importance of respecting the power of nature and one's elders. At the same time, stories from different times and cultures have characters and settings

Figure 12.6

Cendrillon and Ashpet

that take particular forms. Even high school students find it interesting to compare the many versions of the classic Cinderella tale that appear in various forms across cultures. There are many beautifully illustrated picture books that introduce students to Cinderella as a Caribbean washerwoman, a feisty independent Appalachian girl, even a young Irish boy beset by myriad problems. In reviewing Cinderella stories from Egypt, Vietnam, Germany, and elsewhere, teachers can guide students to examine the role of women, the balance of realism and fantasy, and multiple perspectives on what makes someone beautiful. In Fig. 12.6, a second-grade student compares the Caribbean Cendrillon with the Appalachian Ashpet, two Cinderellas:

Toys, games, folktales, and other local and global artifacts illustrate to students that the world is both a unified and diverse collection of communities. Activities such as those described here infuse the school curriculum with the idea that students are members of both.

Differentiating Instruction

Teachers whose classrooms function as communities understand that children have different learning needs and therefore need differentiated instruction. Carol Ann Tomlinson (1999) tells us that students of the same age can be at different levels of readiness, which affects how quickly they can learn specific material and how much teacher guidance they need. She advocates scaffolding or linking new material to the knowledge and skills students have already mastered, connecting subject matter contact to students' life experiences, and building a classroom climate that respects differences and promotes a sense of community (Tomlinson, 2003). Under these conditions, teachers can expose all students to important information by focusing on a common set of key concepts and skills, while they change the materials, methods of instruction, and assignments according to students' learning levels. The core of what students learn is shared; how they learn—to what degree of difficulty, in what working arrangements, with what help, and how they express learning—varies according to their readiness and needs.

Teachers begin differentiating instruction by assessing the learning levels and needs of their students. They then provide materials and activities that fit students' particular learning needs, such as books at a variety of reading levels, tasks that are organized either in small steps or as long-term projects, and support in the form of frequent teacher conferences or peer tutoring. They can differentiate instruction in three ways: by varying content, process, and/or product. Content differentiation means that students work on the same subject matter theme, but use different sources of information; for example, reading books written at different reading levels. Differentiation of process means varying the pace, amount, and style of instruction. Process differentiating teachers compact the curriculum for students who have already mastered a topic, so that they can move at a relatively quick pace through the topic, complete a test to determine mastery, and go on to more challenging materials and tasks. Students unfamiliar with the subject matter can learn at a more moderate pace, make discoveries as they learn, and benefit from teacher-directed instruction where appropriate. Differentiation by product means that the teacher provides different means of assessing student learning. While all students may be working on the same subject of study, they may choose from a variety of ways to demonstrate their understanding; for example, a poster presentation, a simulation game, or a written paper. Even in the case that all students are required to produce a written paper, they might be allowed to choose the format that would best allow them to express their understanding (e.g., personal reflection, expository essay, or a play).

As an example, a teacher undertaking a curriculum unit on life in colonial America might set the following key concepts as learning goals for all students: culture, historical change, and government. She might want them to arrive at the following generalizations: *Cultures are influenced by geography, political structures, beliefs, and resources. They in turn influence family roles, work habits, recreation, and ambitions. Cultures change over time. Government reflects a people's beliefs about power, authority, and the nature of a "good society."* The teacher may want to establish a set of vocabulary words for all students to understand—*colony, republic, social class, representative government, Puritan*—and important individuals to know—*Samuel Adams, John Adams, Crispus Attucks, John Hancock, Thomas Jefferson, Phyllis Wheatley, John Winthrop, King George III, George Washington.* Finally, a teacher may decide on a set of important skills for students to learn and practice:

using and interpreting primary sources, evaluating multiple sources of information, taking notes from written sources, writing persuasive essays, distinguishing between objective and subjective writing. Students may be required to produce a persuasive essay, but they might choose its form: a broadside, or a letter to the editor, or a letter to a friend back in "the old country." Or, they may be required to demonstrate what they have learned about colonial culture in a final project, but again, they may choose the form: a research paper, a poster talk, a set of journal entries. As an additional assessment of learning, the teacher will probably require a test.

A class session may begin with a broad question: How would your life be different if you lived in colonial times? Then, groups of children can each play a role in a fictitious family: "You are the oldest child of a small farmer in Pennsylvania." "You are the daughter of a seamstress living in Boston." "You are the son of a slave owned by George Washington." "You are a representative to the general assembly of the Commonwealth of Virginia." The scenarios may vary in complexity, based on the readiness level of the student. A teacher may provide specific questions and ask students to gather background information: What kind of education have you received? What are the economic concerns of your community? How do the patriot protest acts affect your life? How does what you eat reflect where and how you live? What is a typical day in your life? Each group may receive an additional general question with differentiated complexity. A relatively complex question would be, Why did colonial patriots believe they could experiment with self-government? Of medium complexity is, How did religion influence how colonial New Englanders lived? Less complex is, How is your life different today?

The teacher could provide for students' varying interests by allowing them to add questions of their own about children's games, tools and techniques in various trades, forms of art and music, country schools. She would differentiate the type and amount of resource materials available to each group: books with a range of reading levels, videotapes and audiotapes, copies of old letters and journals. She would provide varying degrees of help with organizing student research and writing: among these might be task cards, sentence starters, question sheets, study guides, graphic organizers such as Venn diagrams, note-taking outlines, and concept webs. She would provide coaching as needed through small group direct instruction, study groups, peer tutoring, and teacher–student conferences. While students will work independently and in small groups, the whole class participates in planning, discussing, debating, and reviewing concepts, vocabulary, and generalizations. Differentiation allows students to take different paths to the same learning destination. It reinforces the idea that they are part of a community of learners moving in the same academic direction, but that their own interests, talents, skills, and readiness levels count.

The Importance of Questions

In learning communities, students are full participants not only in gaining knowledge but also in developing it. Teachers are responsible for encouraging in students the habit of raising questions and seeking answers from a variety of resources, including each other's ideas and information. Teachers who create learning communities foster in students the habit of lifelong learning, strengthened by the ability to consider important questions.

Asking the right questions is a mark of the skillful teacher and an art form. Too frequently, teachers ask questions that students don't understand or teachers ask so many questions that students don't know how to respond. The kinds of questions teachers ask will not only assess what students learn, but also affect the way students think about information. If teachers always ask simple factual questions—for example, In what year was the Bill of Rights signed?—students may never develop the habit of critical thinking. A question such as, How does the First Amendment affect the rights of minority groups in the United States? asks students to analyze or evaluate information. Teachers should make time for students to ask their own questions and search for the answers to them. Questioning, therefore, is central to planning and assessing learning experiences, developing children's ability to think about their experiences, fostering their curiosity, and nurturing their positive feelings about learning.

Cruickshank, Bainer, and Metcalf define **effective questions** as those that "require students to actively process information and compose an answer." They contend that effective questions "increase students' engagement, raise the level of thought, help students organize their thoughts, guide students through tasks and allow teachers to monitor understanding and provide feedback" (1999, p. 338). Teachers who use effective questioning techniques first think about what their students already know and what level of difficulty is appropriate for them. Their questions are clear, concise, and thought provoking. Rather than demanding an immediate, perhaps unthinking, response, these teachers allow students a *wait time,* an opportunity to understand what is being asked and to reflect on possible responses. Effective questioners ask students how they arrived at their answers, in order to model a thinking process, analyze an incorrect answer, or limit "lucky guesses." For more complex questions, teachers might encourage students to develop their ideas in small groups before sharing them with the whole class. Effective questioners engage all students, drawing out the reticent participants, inviting all members of the classroom community to share their knowledge and their opinions. In this section we describe types of questions, questioning techniques, and ideas for how to formulate questions and use them effectively.

Bloom's Taxonomy of Objectives The kind of question you ask depends upon the kind of information you provide your students and your learning goals for them. For example, if you are teaching basic facts or want your students to identify, label, or recite what they heard or read, simple **recall questions** assess student's knowledge. Some examples of recall questions are: Can you name the colors of the rainbow? What is the product of 8 times 2? When was the Declaration of Independence signed? What are the directions I just gave you? Simple questions of this nature demand only a good memory. Recall questions might be important ways to assess basic knowledge and skills that children need to understand or work with new information; for example, remembering addition and subtraction facts quickly allows you to learn multiplication, make change, or compare historical time periods. But because recall is supposed to be fast and almost automatic, it involves a lower order of thinking skills or no thinking at all. In order to foster the habits of inquiry essential to a learning community, teachers must also ask **higher-order questions,** questions requiring students to think abstractly and make judgments; for example, to analyze, synthesize or evaluate information. Higher-order questions encourage more sophisticated thought and action.

Benjamin Bloom offered teachers a way to broaden the base of their questions by providing them with a taxonomy, or classification, of objectives that serve as building blocks for questions in all three of the domains of learning: the cognitive (intellectual), the affective (social/emotional), and the psychomotor or behavioral (physical) domains (Bloom, Englehart, Furst, Hill & Krathwohl, 1956). **Bloom's taxonomy** gradates cognitive, affective, and psychomotor/behavioral domains of development for planning curriculum goals, objectives, or outcomes. His six-level taxonomy of the cognitive domain is used most widely in schools to help children think about or act on information in increasingly sophisticated ways. The taxonomy, or list, of cognitive objectives entails the following levels:

Knowledge: Students know simple facts and recall information. In writing objectives and questions that measure success, teachers ask students to *define, describe, identify, label, list, match,* or *name* what they remember.

Comprehension: Students show insight and understanding of material. In writing objectives and questions that measure success, teachers ask students to *classify, convert, describe, discuss, estimate, explain, give examples, paraphrase, restate in their own words,* or *summarize.*

Application: Students apply and use knowledge or solve problems. In writing objectives and questions that measure success, teachers ask students to *collect, compute, construct, diagram, implement, graph, map, predict, prepare, produce, relate, report, show, solve,* or *use* what they have learned.

Analysis: Students examine the parts and components of the information, and identify patterns and relationships. In writing objectives and questions that measure success, teachers ask students to *compare, contrast, correlate, differentiate, distinguish between, infer, interpret,* or *summarize.*

Synthesis: Students use the information they have gained to generate new ideas and products. In writing objectives and questions that measure success, teachers ask students to *adapt, compose, create, design, devise, generate, initiate, integrate, invent, modify, plan, rearrange, reconstruct, reorganize, revise,* or *substitute.*

Evaluation: Students compare, discriminate, and make decisions, choices, and judgments. In writing objectives and questions that measure success, teachers ask students to *appraise, argue for or against, conclude, critique, decide, defend, judge, justify,* or *support* their judgments.

Table 12.1 provides examples of the kinds of questions a teacher might ask to generate various levels of thinking after his students have read E. B. White's classic book, *Charlotte's Web.*

Because questions should be linked to objectives or outcomes, Bloom's cognitive taxonomy provides a structure for formulating questions that engage students in using higher-order thinking skills in processing information. It asks teachers to consider thinking and learning as processes, rather than products. Using the model as a reference, teachers are encouraged to move from asking convergent questions such as, who? what? when? and where? to the why? and how? of analysis, discussion, and consideration of many possible answers. Higher-order questions tend to be more interesting to students, as they call on them to make connections to other experiences and subject matter and, perhaps, come to their own conclusions. They help teachers engage a community of learners in active inquiry into broad perspectives and deep understanding of subject matter.

Table 12.1 Bloom's Taxonomy of Cognitive Objectives

Level	Verbs	Sample Question to Students About the Book *Charlotte's Web*
Knowledge	*define, identify, label, list, match, name*	Who is the author of the book?
Comprehension	*classify, convert, describe, discuss, explain, give examples, paraphrase, summarize*	What did Charlotte mean when she spun the word "radiant" to describe Wilbur?
Application	*collect, compute, diagram, implement, graph, map, predict, prepare, produce, relate, show, solve, use*	Are you versatile? In what ways?
Analysis	*compare, contrast, correlate, differentiate, distinguish between, infer, interpret*	How are the personalities of Wilbur and Templeton the same? How are they different?
Synthesis	*adapt, compose, create, design, devise, integrate, invent, modify, rearrange, reconstruct, revise, substitute*	Pretend that you are Fern and you are helping Wilbur to write a poem in memory of Charlotte. Write the poem.
Evaluation	*appraise, argue for or against, conclude, critique, decide, defend, judge, justify, support*	In the last paragraph of the book, the author says "Wilbur never forgot Charlotte. . . . She was in a class by herself." What are some of the things in the story that show this is true about Charlotte?

Essential Questions Building on critical dialogue approaches and the notion that a learning community is the best context for developing knowledge, teachers use **essential questions** to define key concepts and outcomes and provide a focus for the learner. Essential questions are broad questions that develop deep understandings of the world we live in. They have no one right answer. They engage all students in thinking and learning, and make them investigators into provocative and meaningful issues. They connect information from several disciplines and connect what students are learning to their direct experiences and to larger world issues. Based on Theodore Sizer's idea that *less is better,* the essential question seeks to underscore the purpose of the curriculum project, unit, topic, or theme. For example, in teaching the principles and structures of U.S. government, teachers might begin with the general question, What influence does the U.S. Constitution have on people's lives? This essential question will serve as the focus of a unit of study and provide a base for subsequent questions raised by students, as well as the teacher. For example: How can an individual citizen influence government policies? What are the laws that ensure the right to practice one's religion? What are the rights of students in schools? How do we elect a new president?

For Heidi Jacobs, an "essential question is the heart of the curriculum . . . the essence of what you believe students should examine and know." She maintains that the essential question frames the whole curriculum and communicates

Table 12.2 Jacobs's Guidelines for Essential Questions

- The questions should be written in broad, organizational terms.
- The questions should reflect the teacher's conceptual priorities.
- Each question should be distinct and substantial.
- Questions should not be repetitive.
- The questions should be realistic, given the amount of time allocated for the unit or course.
- There should be a logical sequence to a set of essential questions.
- The questions should be posted in the classroom.
- All children should be able to understand the questions (Jacobs, 1997, pp. 30–32).

expectations to students (1997, pp. 26–28). In consultation with teachers across the United States, Jacobs proposed guidelines for composing essential questions in all subject areas at any age level (see Table 12.2).

Critically defined essential questions go beyond seeking answers. They stimulate problem solving, discovery of new ideas, and communal inquiry. The effective teacher uses such questions to gain insights into her students' perceptions. She links the abstract concept represented by the question to the concrete experiences of her students' immediate worlds. She is interested in the kinds of answers they offer. She encourages them to seek many approaches to find solutions, and to identify possibilities as well as to propose a response. Many teachers organize these tasks as project-based units of study, engaging students in investigations, searching multiple resources, and publicly sharing their results. For example, students might look into the problem of soil erosion in their community, tackle the issue of campaign financing, research the genius of Leonardo DaVinci, or answer the question, How old is the universe?

In some classrooms, students use WebQuests to search for answers to essential questions, drawing information from websites that are organized or developed by teachers. Developed by Bernie Dodge at San Diego State University, WebQuests are tools that are increasingly popular with teachers. Teachers use the Internet to empower cooperative teams of students to investigate topics of study by consulting with individual experts, searchable databases, and current reports in multimedia formats. Tom March, an associate of Bernie Dodge, says that WebQuests motivate and empower students to think for themselves and to use information, rather than look for it, using the higher-order thinking skills of comparing, analyzing, hypothesizing, synthesizing, and evaluating (1998).

Read "The Mitten Tale Retold" for an example of a teaching unit built around an essential question. Try writing some essential questions to guide topics of study for students in your future classrooms. You might want to follow Jacobs's guidelines or check with Bloom's taxonomy to see if your questions promote divergent thinking and a higher order of processing skills.

The Mitten Tale Retold: A Unit Model for Using the Essential Question

Drawing on the content of a state-mandated standards-based curriculum, I designed a unit on movement for a kindergarten class in which literature was to illustrate how ideas move from place to place. To help the concrete-thinking five-year-olds focus on the abstract concept that ideas move from one place to another through stories that are retold and rewritten, I formulated an essential question that asked, "How do stories move ideas from one place in the world to you?" Structured around this essential question, I developed activities drawn from numerous retellings of a popular Ukrainian tale, *The Mitten.* I read several versions of the tale to the class, including Jan Brett's (1989) and Alvin Tresselt's (1964) popular classic editions, as well as Yevonne Pollock's retold adaptation, *The Old Man's Mitten* (1994) and Steven Kellogg's *Missing Mitten Mystery* (2000). Children located Ukraine on a globe and traced a route the story could travel to reach their community. They noted the changes in the story as presented by different authors.

The essential question challenged the children to higher-order thinking tasks. They compared and contrasted the various treatments of the story's theme. They saw that a story can be alike and different when told in different places and at different times. In small group and class discussions, the children analyzed how the different authors and illustrators interpreted the story. They delighted in discovering many twists and turns to the tale. They synthesized their findings by acting out their own interpretation using a flannel board reproduction of the class's version of the tale. Throughout all of the experiences, the essential question was posed to the children as a focus for their learning. To culminate the unit, the children applied what they learned by writing and illustrating their own accounts of "what could happen to mittens you might lose." Then, in a shared reading and display of their work, they evaluated their own new adaptations of the tale.

Using the essential question provided coherence to the unit activities and avoided the common problem that a topical unit might merely be a collection of activities loosely tied together by a theme. The essential question's continuous focus structured the children's engagement in an in-depth study of the main concept.

—Louise Swiniarski

Promoting Positive Social Behavior

A classroom cannot function as a community if students lack the social skills that make for peaceful, respectful, and mutually helpful participation. Unfortunately, too many children arrive in classrooms without having learned how to get along with each other. Too many do not know how to get what they need without resorting to violent behavior and too many have not learned how to be patient, be polite, listen, or speak respectfully. Many children have poor social models, at home and in the media. Some are angry, and unable to control their anger or express it in ways that do not cause harm to others. We feel it falls to teachers to take the time to teach the social skills that promote supportive classroom communities for reasons both philosophical and pragmatic: because educators have a social, as well as an academic, responsibility to their students, and because it is time well spent. Teaching children what may be called the "new basic skills" of communication, cooperation, and conflict resolution (Breitborde, 1996) effectively results in a smoothly running and efficient classroom, where children can focus without fear and receive help and support from each other as well as from their teacher.

We caution teachers to identify language and behavior that are destructive to classroom communities as distinct from their own culture-based assumptions about what is polite and socially appropriate. Teachers may have notions of politeness and appropriateness that are different from their students', and therefore may mislabel students' language and behavior as disrespectful or rude. These differences may be due to cultural variations in language styles that are described in Chapter 9 or due to language styles that vary across families. Teachers raised in the South may expect to hear "sir" and "ma'am" from their students; if they teach in Northern schools where they don't hear those terms, they may think that their students are being rude. Teachers raised in homes where one did not argue with one's elders may find students who question and challenge them disrespectful, while those students may simply assume they are engaging in a reasonable exchange. As Chapter 9 describes, there are cultural differences in expectations and tolerance for the noise level of conversation. Many teachers avoid whole-class discussions or refuse to use cooperative learning, claiming "it doesn't work with these children." They blame poor parenting or the loss of religion or chaotic communities. Whether or not their accusations are correct, classrooms offer rich and constant opportunities to teach and reinforce the use of language and behavior that makes teachers and students feel valued and included.

Rather than relegate the teaching of social skills to special times—for example, as a separate social studies unit, or in a Friday afternoon class meeting—teachers should address these skills throughout the week, in all curriculum areas, with significant time devoted to them at the opening of the school year. Nel Noddings (1992) asks teachers to use every aspect of classroom life—from the curriculum to the playground used for recess—as an opportunity to teach children to care. In a new book, early childhood educator Marilu Hyson (2004) argues for a curriculum that unapologetically puts children's feelings at the center. In Hyson's "emotion-centered" classroom, there are warm relationships, feelings are expressed, and everyone demonstrates sensitivity and concern for others. The curriculum includes attention to individual and cultural styles of behaving and learning and emotionally relevant activities. Hyson wants teachers to model appropriate emotional responses and to help children understand their feelings and learn how to regulate them. Like Noddings, Hyson insists that a classroom that puts care at the center is a classroom that will promote learning.

One comprehensive approach to the teaching of social behavior that fosters community as well as responsibility is The Responsive Classroom, developed by the Northeast Foundation for Children (see Websites to Explore). The principles that guide the approach are included in Table 12.3.

The Responsive Classroom approach uses a set of structures and techniques to infuse the school day with the guiding principles. Teachers hold "morning meetings" with activities that build community and reinforce both academic and social skills. In morning meetings, students greet each other in fun and positive ways, share anecdotes about their lives, and play games that foster participation, communication, and an awareness of similarities and differences. Teachers and students together formulate a list of classroom "rules and logical consequences" that foster responsibility and self-control. A "guided discovery" to teaching and learning engages students in inquiry and teaches them to care about the school environment.

Table 12.3 The Responsive Classroom: Teaching Social Behaviors That Foster Community

- The social curriculum is as important as the academic curriculum.
- How children learn is as important as what they learn: process and content go hand in hand.
- The greatest cognitive growth occurs through social interaction.
- There is a set of social skills children need in order to be successful academically and socially: cooperation, assertion, responsibility, empathy, and self-control.
- Knowing the children we teach—individually, culturally, and developmentally—is as important as knowing the content we teach.
- Knowing the families of the children we teach and inviting their participation is essential to children's education.
- How the adults at school work together is as important as individual competence: Lasting change begins with the adult community.

Source: http://www.responsiveclassroom.org

Students have "academic choice" in topics of study to help them feel invested and self-motivated. Ideas for "classroom organization" include how to arrange rooms and materials to promote community and responsibility. "Family communication strategies" encourage teachers to involve families in many ways as partners in their children's education; for example, through classroom newsletters and the construction of family albums and projects such as collecting and displaying postcards from distant relatives. Teachers using the Responsive Classroom approach report that they not only feel more effective in maintaining a positive climate in their classrooms but also that they enjoy teaching more (Rimm-Kaufman and Sawyer, 2004).

Christine Mattise has developed a simple scheme to alert children to whether they are acting in ways that promote their own rights and the rights of others. She uses the symbolism of a rainbow of colors to promote a safe and inclusive classroom community. The children in her schools in the United States and in Kwa-Zulu Natal, South Africa, report that the "Rainbow of Safety" is "a rainbow that goes over the whole school. Everyone is under it; no one is left out" (2004, p. 20). The colors of the rainbow represent the decisions the students make about what they say or do. The children understand that "choices can be changed, turning mistakes and missed opportunities into better decisions in the future" (p. 21).

In Mattise's scheme, True Blue, the universal color of the sky, represents the best of humankind: equity, respect, acceptance, kindness, responsibility, and tolerance. She asks children to honor their bonds to each other by helping others when they are hurt, alone, or being teased. Growing Green, a "friendly color," encourages children to act humanely but understand they may fall short of this goal. Caution Yellow is a signal that children may have made thoughtless choices that have compromised someone else's rights or safety. Children should stop, think, and make different choices that will turn yellow behavior to green, by, for example, saying "I'm sorry. I'll try harder next time." Danger Red signifies a deliberate choice to hurt someone else and is never acceptable in the Rainbow of Safety. Mattise's classrooms have Rainbow of Safety traffic lights in hallways and classrooms, and on every student's desk. They are sometimes used to create behavior contracts for individual students. More than just reminding students how their behavior may affect others, the program asks them to be responsible peacemakers, intervening or getting adult help when the physical or emotional safety and rights of others are in jeopardy. Mattise is concerned that students learn not to be "spectators" in incidents of disrespect or bullying.

Many activities that educators can use to teach positive social behavior can at the same time address academic content and skills. To elaborate on ways to teach social skills directly, we will focus on what we think are four important abilities—effective communication, constructive anger management, and peaceful conflict resolution—and give examples of how these skills can be taught within the existing curriculum.

Effective Communication The words *communication* and *community* have the same root: the Latin word *communis,* meaning "shared by all or many." *Communication* means, literally, "to make common." Thus, communication is the basis for social interaction and for group functioning. Johnson and Johnson, champions of cooperative learning as a way to increase knowledge and skills as well as to build community, put it this way:

> The very existence of a group depends on communication, on exchanging information and transmitting meaning. . . . Through communication members of groups reach some understanding of one another, build trust, coordinate their actions, plan strategies for a goal accomplishment, agree upon a division of labor, conduct all group activity (2000, p. 142).

Good communication means that the message one person sends to another is interpreted by the receiver in the way that the sender intended. Poor communication happens when the sender's message is unclear or the receiver doesn't really listen. Sometimes this is the result of poor word choice, distractions that keep the parties from paying attention to what they are saying or hearing, or emotions that get in the way of clear speaking or objective interpretation. A speaker may be unwilling or unable to say exactly what he or she means; a listener may "hear" what he thinks the speaker "really" means or what he wants the speaker to say. Teachers can help students be more effective communicators by giving them practice with phrasing statements and requests in clear and polite ways. They can teach *active listening,* mentioned earlier in this chapter, which means the listener listens without interrupting, demonstrates that he is paying attention to the speaker by making eye contact with her and using appropriate body language, deepening his understanding of her message by linking it to his previous experiences or knowledge, reporting back to the listener what he heard her say, and giving her feedback. Teachers can also give students practice in speaking for different purposes; for example, to explain, to persuade, to debate. For many students, practice in pairs or small groups is preferable to the more threatening task of speaking before a large group. See Table 12.4 for guidelines for helping students communicate effectively.

Effective communicators know how to phrase and listen to requests, ideas, complaints, and responses in ways that do not demean another person. Effective communicators give speakers time to say what they need to say and listeners time

Table 12.4 Guidelines for Effective Speaking and Listening

Effective speakers:

- *Use first-person singular pronouns.* Using "I" statements, rather than referring to "most people," means taking responsibility for the ideas and feelings you express.
- *Describe their feelings.*
- *Make their messages complete and specific.* Good speakers give their listeners all the information they need.
- *Make their verbal and nonverbal messages congruent.*
- *Describe others' behavior without evaluating or interpreting.*

Effective Listeners:

- *Paraphrase accurately and non-evaluatively the content of the message.* "I heard you say . . ."
- *Describe their perceptions about the feelings of the sender.*
- *Negotiate with the speaker about the meaning of the message.*

Source: Johnson and Johnson, 2000, pp. 145–148.

to think about what they heard. In a classroom community, good communicators talk and listen to everyone with the same regard for their ideas and feelings. Finally, teachers are role models for effective communication, and, therefore, need to be careful to "do what they preach."

Constructive Anger Management In a peaceful community, members respond to their own and others' anger effectively. Anger is a natural and inevitable feeling that can be expressed in healthy or in unhealthy and destructive ways. Children vary in their tolerance to frustration, or their "boiling points," and in the ways they typically respond to frustrating circumstances. There is some evidence that emotional boiling points are physiological: some babies are born more irritable and sensitive than others. The differences may also be socially learned. Children who seem easily infuriated may live with adults who are "hot-tempered" and who are not skilled at emotional control. At home, these children may learn that the ordinary response to frustration is to yell or curse or attack. Other children may learn that it is not "nice" to express angry feelings and that it is better to keep frustrations inside, or to withdraw, or sulk. Children cannot always avoid situations that make them angry, but they can learn new ways to control their reactions. In the interest of maintaining a peaceful community, teachers can use strategies to teach **anger management,** the ability to express or control angry feelings in healthy, positive ways. Anger management strategies can include reporting feelings, cognitive restructuring (thinking differently), learning alternative responses, and relaxation techniques (see Table 12.5).

Peaceful Conflict Resolution In all communities, as in all human relationships, conflict is inevitable. Differences in interests, concerns, communication styles, talents, needs, and perspectives make us unique and able to complement each other. However, these differences will cause clashes from time to time. One

Table 12.5 Anger Management Strategies

- *Acknowledging and reporting feelings.* Children sometimes "act out" without knowing why. They may not understand that feelings are part of being human; they are neither good nor bad in themselves. Encouraging children to identify and express how they are feeling may be enough to help them relieve their frustrations. It can certainly open the door to a verbal resolution of the problem at hand.
- *Relaxation.* Deep breathing has the immediate physical effect of reducing emotional arousal. Teaching children to breathe deeply will help calm down their angry feelings and allow them to think through the problem situation.
- *Cognitive restructuring.* Angry children may not perceive the whole situation correctly and may need help with noticing details or considerations that will ease their frustrations. Telling them, for example, that "Remember that you had the recess ball yesterday," or "What Pablo actually said, was . . . ," or "Think about what will happen if you hit her" might help the angry child to feel differently and think more logically.
- *Time out.* Time away from classmates or in a different space need not always be a punishment. Teachers might provide a private area where children who are feeling angry can go and write, or walk around, or think for a specified amount of time—five minutes, for example. It is important that the child know that he or she can return to the teacher for help and to discuss the problem after the time-out period is over. This use of a time-out place respects the child's anger but provides a safe place to calm down.
- *Teaching alternative responses.* In one exercise called "anger brainstorm" (Kreidler, 1984), the teacher leads the class in listing, without prejudgment, all the things that people do to express anger. After the list is posted, children discuss which actions are never okay (e.g., hitting, cursing, name-calling) and why, which actions are sometimes okay ("venting" to a friend), and which actions are always good ideas (writing down your feelings, counting to ten). One benefit of this activity is that children will learn about behaviors they have never witnessed—for example, taking a walk, or writing in a journal. Another benefit is that they will consider the consequences of various behaviors, and the fact that some actions may be appropriate or inappropriate, damaging or not, depending on the circumstances. The activity offers new information to include in the behavioral repertoires children have available for reacting to different situations, while it reinforces the skill of critical thinking.

mark of a strong community is its ability to resolve those conflicts in positive ways. One mark of a good teacher is his ability to make peace.

William Kreidler has developed of programs for the national organization Educators for Social Responsibility to help teachers be peacemakers (see Websites to Explore). Kreidler, author of *Creative Conflict Resolution,* puts it this way:

> A teacher is a peacemaker. It's part of the job. Perhaps you and I never thought of ourselves as quite that; perhaps we're not even sure what peacemaking means. But conflicts occur in our classrooms, and we are expected to respond to them and restore peace, or at least order. That makes us peacemakers (1984, p. 1).

Kreidler promotes the teaching of strategies for conflict resolution to foster in students the ability to choose constructive, nonviolent responses to conflict based on the premise that conflicts are inevitable but solvable problems. He understands that "every classroom has conflict," but that "conflicts can be reduced through the establishment of a caring classroom community, and that the conflict remaining can be used for learning" (1984, preface).

Teachers who agree with John Dewey that education should be about life use classroom conflict as teachable moments. When conflicts arise, they offer opportunities for critical and creative thinking, and for social learning: Teacher and students can determine the root cause of the conflict (often not what it seems to be on the surface), think about it in light of the social contract and moral connection that the class has made to each other, and consider strategies to resolve it (Sergiovanni, 1999, p. 125).

To Kreidler, a peaceable classroom has five distinguishing characteristics: cooperation, communication, tolerance, positive emotional expression, and positive conflict resolution. Using this model, he finds the sources of classroom conflict as resulting from six types of problems:

- misuse of power by the teacher
- competition
- intolerance
- poor communication
- inappropriate expression of emotion
- lack of conflict resolution skills

In other words, what matters in creating classrooms where conflicts are resolved peacefully is an atmosphere where teachers' expectations are realistic, their rules flexible, and their attitudes positive. It's important to have a classroom where students learn to work with, rather than against, each other; where differences are expected and welcomed, rather than isolated and denigrated. A peaceable classroom is one where students know how to express their needs and listen to others', where feelings are expressed in effective, but nonaggressive, ways, and where students have a repertoire of strategies to handle conflict (1984, pp. 3–5).

People have different styles of responding to conflict. Some of us avoid it, others thrive on it. Some treat conflicts as objective problems to be solved, others tend to take conflicts very personally. Kreidler finds five approaches to conflict resolution (1984, pp. 9–11). These are described in Table 12.6. As you review these approaches to resolving conflicts, think about which approach you generally use when there is conflict in your life.

Clearly, all these approaches have their value in particular situations. Moreover, they all offer benefits, and they all have limitations. Children whose teacher takes authoritative responsibility for resolving their conflicts will feel well cared for. They will not, however, learn to resolve conflicts on their own. Smoothers may bring quick peace to a volatile situation; however, the conflict remains, and may reappear at a later time. A compromiser asks conflicting parties to bend in the name of preserving the peace, and the relationship; however, compromises can result in "lose–lose" situations where neither side is happy. The ignoring approach allows children to take responsibility for their own behavior and their own conflicts;

Table 12.6 Kreidler's Five Approaches to Resolving Conflicts

Which approach do you generally use when there is conflict in your life?

1. *The No-Nonsense Approach.* Teachers and others who use this approach would say they have the authority and the responsibility to decide what, and who, is right. They typically determine what the nature of the conflict is, and lay down the solution, trying to be as fair and as honest as possible. "Knock it off," is one no-nonsense response.
2. *The Ignoring Approach.* At the other end of the spectrum are those who see conflict as a part of human nature, and the ability to resolve conflicts as a developmental process. In response to an argument between children, for example, a teacher using this approach might say to himself, "Children need to learn how to work things out for themselves."
3. *The Smoothing Approach.* Many believe that conflict is bad for a community or a relationship, and, therefore, should be avoided at all costs. Before initial conflicts escalate, "smoothers" will try to distract the parties with humor or other diversions, and will try to keep them away from each other. "Soft words win hard hearts," say the smoothers (Johnson and Johnson, 2000, p. 382).
4. *The Compromising Approach.* Some people see conflict resolution as an either–or proposition, where the different sides can resolve the tension only by giving up some part of their position. "Better half a loaf than no loaf at all," say the compromisers.
5. *The Problem-Solving Approach.* Those who see conflicts as problems needing solutions treat conflict as an objective challenge. Teachers using this approach bring together the parties involved and encourage them to analyze the problem and come up with alternative ideas: "Come now and let us reason together," say the problem-solvers (Johnson and Johnson, 2000, p. 382).

however, where they lack skill in resolving conflicts peacefully and to mutual satisfaction, the results can be emotional, even physical, scars.

While these approaches have their uses, we believe that the problem-solving approach is best suited for classroom teachers concerned with children's learning and with maintaining a sense of community. To Johnson and Johnson, peaceful conflict resolution means two things: (1) the parties reach an agreement that satisfies both of them, and (2) they maintain their relationship (2000, p. 383). The following section offers a sample of four resolution strategies that meet these two requirements.

Classroom meetings are particularly useful for teacher–student conflicts; for example, when students are complaining about the curriculum or classroom procedures. Structure the discussion around one or two questions: Why is this happening? What can we do about this? Keep students focused on the conflict or problem, not on personalities. Remind them that a classroom discussion requires that they take turns speaking and listen respectfully to all points of view and all ideas. Try to end on a positive note, summing up the major points of the discussion and the helpful ideas, perhaps agreeing on a plan of action. Using the classroom meeting as a forum for resolving conflicts will only work if there is already an atmosphere of trust and mutual support in the class.

Negotiation is a conflict resolution strategy that teachers can teach children. A successful negotiation process involves several steps: First, each child needs to say what he or she thinks the problem is. (They may disagree.) Then each must say what it is he or she wants to see happen and what are his or her limits, if there were to be a compromise. The parties then try to work out an agreement that satisfies both of them.

Mediation is a process similar to negotiation, except that a third party intervenes to facilitate. That third party (a child, or the teacher) must stay neutral. As in negotiation, each child gets a chance to say what he or she thinks the problem is and what he or she wants to see happen. Then the mediator thinks of ways to solve the problem and discusses these ideas with the conflicting parties. Finally, the mediator chooses the solution everyone prefers.

Reverse role play is a technique in which the parties to the conflict first express their concerns and their needs to each other. Then they reverse their roles, and "speak" from these new positions. (Early childhood teachers might use actual footprints for the children to stand in while they consider how the other person might see things differently, how he or she might be feeling, and how he or she might express it.) Given the chance to see the "other side," the children might be better able to work together to find a mutually satisfactory solution.

Besides teaching children strategies for resolving conflicts peacefully, teachers must, of course, demonstrate peaceful conflict resolution in their own dealings with students, colleagues, administrators, and families. As discussed in Chapter 6, the most powerful teaching tool at a teacher's disposal is himself. We are crucial models of what is appropriate, effective, and right. Students watch teachers all day long. As you confront the conflicts and problems in your own teaching life in full view of a classroom of children, you offer them a chance to learn strategies for peaceful conflict resolution that they can carry with them into their futures.

Conflict resolution education offers students tools and models to address the inevitable problems that arise within communities and between them. In schools and classrooms that function as communities, it is important to recognize and help students with the diversity among them at the same time that they experience overarching principles of human unity. Educational communities are sensitive to the particular needs and conditions of their members—staff, students, and families—and consciously take on the task of responding to them.

Building a Peaceable Classroom Community

The human need for community is strong; the feeling that we belong, that we are connected, and that we share goals and values gives us a secure sense that there is something greater than ourselves providing meaning and order to our lives. We believe that, to learn and thrive, children need to be able to find that sense of community in their schools. We have described in this chapter the many ways that teachers and administrators can create school climates where everyone feels welcome, safe, and valued. We end the chapter with a list which offers some final suggestions for teachers who want to establish and maintain a classroom characterized by a spirit of community and peaceful relations.

1. Set clear standards for your classroom that promote dignity, respect, and equality. Be vocal about maintaining a physically, emotionally, and academically safe environment for everyone in the room. Maintain high expectations of behavior for yourself and your students.

2. Take action against prejudice and discrimination. Silence sends a message that racism, stereotyping, bullying, and discrimination are inevitable, tolerable, or correct. Intervene when you hear students making ethnic jokes or otherwise demeaning others. Sometimes, the best response is immediate; at other times, it is better to take students aside and hold a discussion in private, or use the incident to construct a learning activity, conduct a role play, or have a class meeting.

3. Do not avoid differences among your students or your colleagues. In ignoring the rich diversity of the American people, you will be ignoring their identities and their humanity. Convey the attitude that you welcome diversity by inviting students, their families, and school staff to share their traditions, their talents, and their interests.

4. Explore your own feelings and attitudes and the factors that helped construct them. Understand that prejudices develop from fear, from ignorance, and from accepting misconceptions without examining the facts. Be honest with yourself and get information or help when you feel uncomfortable handling particular situations. Educate yourself about people whose culture, sexual orientation, family structure, disability, or religion is unfamiliar to you.

5. Listen and respond to students' feelings, even those you find difficult to hear. But respect their privacy, as well.

6. Be a role model. Use language that is free of bias and treat people, including your students, with respect. Act in ways that demonstrate interest, compassion, and support.

7. Teach students the behaviors that foster a spirit of community and peaceful relations. Give them practice in alternative ways to communicate their needs, express their feelings, help others, and handle conflict. Structure opportunities for them to contribute to the welfare of the classroom and serve the community outside the school.

8. Talk to students about war and peace. Do not ignore difficult issues that arise within the classroom or those present in the wider society that affect students. When discussing conflicts in the world or the nation, ask students what they know and what questions they have. Help them gather accurate information. Use essential questions and moral principles such as those embodied in the United Nations Declaration of Human Rights to help them think about the issues and understand different points of view. Be sensitive to students whose family members might be involved in those conflicts, as military personnel or political figures or as immigrants or refugees. Let students know about organizations that are working to resolve important conflicts.

9. Practice democracy in your teaching. Share decision making with your students and treat their families as respected partners in education.

10. Advocate within your school, your school system, and your community for policies and programs that support justice, equality, and compassion. Use your potential as an educator to promote positive social change.

Within this list of strategies for creating a spirit of community in and around the classroom lie many of the principles that we have presented to you in the preceding chapters of this book: the ideal of teaching democratically, the need to respond to and celebrate cultural diversity, the goal of equitable and substantive education for all students, and the importance of the political and moral aspects of life in schools. The last item suggests that, as you begin to take on your professional role as an educator of future generations, you think of yourself not only as being responsible for the students in your classroom but also as a spokesperson for the welfare of children in the wider world community. Your knowledge of what it means to be an educated person and what education can truly contribute to the world if it is well done and well supported, is special and invaluable. We hope that the information and ideas we have presented in this book will help you undertake that responsibility with commitment and confidence.

SUMMARY

- Schools that take seriously their place in the larger community beyond their walls and their ability to create community within them set optimal conditions for children's learning. External communities—families, neighborhoods, local organizations, and landmarks—are necessary supports and rich resources for learning. Schools need to explore the many ways that families can participate as partners in their children's learning in both traditional and nontraditional ways that take account of their circumstances and lifestyles.
- Within the classroom, children need a sense of security and belonging in order to be able to focus on their schoolwork. Teachers who turn their classrooms into learning communities provide the important emotional and intellectual grounding for academic learning. The work of psychologists, sociologists, and educators such as Abraham Maslow, Ferdinand Tonnies, Thomas Sergiovanni, Theodore Sizer, Deborah Meier, and Nel Noddings, supports the idea that personal, supportive classroom relationships allow children to express their natural confidence and curiosity in learning.
- The factors that foster a sense of community in schools and classrooms include a shared sense of purpose or mission, shared power and decision making, participatory dialogue, learning that is personally meaningful and appropriate, overt and hidden curricula that are congruent and reinforce each other, respect for differences among people, and respect for the community that surrounds the school.
- Teachers can use a variety of strategies to build and maintain a sense of community in their classrooms: developing effective groups, space arrangements that foster community, the incorporation of multicultural materials and perspectives into the curriculum, differentiation of instruction that engages all students, the use of questions to stimulate learning and interaction, and the direct teaching of the social behaviors prerequisite to peaceful and productive community life.

QUESTIONS FOR REFLECTION

1. Consider your experience as a participant in group learning or group projects. What worked? What didn't? How might you improve the experience if you were the teacher organizing the groups?
2. Recall the physical arrangement and design of classrooms in which you have been a student. Did the setting affect your relationship with the teacher or with your peers? Which one(s) made you most comfortable? Why?
3. Some would argue that social skills, group development, and a sense of community are not the responsibility of schools, and that schools should focus on making sure that children understand substantive information and learn important academic skills. The theorists and educators mentioned in this chapter would clearly disagree. Which side are you on? Why?
4. How can the kinds of questions that teachers ask and the ones they invite from students foster a sense of community in the classroom?

APPLYING WHAT YOU'VE LEARNED

1. Make an annotated list of resources in the local community—for example, geographic landmarks, museums, organizations, historic places—that teachers might use to enhance specific areas of the curriculum.
2. Find the mission statement of a local school. Interview the principal to get a sense of how the mission is put into practice, and what "stakeholders" are involved.
3. Consult the print and electronic references for Bloom's taxonomy of educational objectives: the cognitive domain. Apply the taxonomy to a children's book or story and design questions based on each of the six levels.
4. Observe a classroom and talk to the teacher to determine who developed the classroom rules. Do the rules, and the process by which they were developed, reinforce a sense of community in the classroom?
5. www. Go to this book's website and review the free lesson plans offered by Educators for Social Responsibility to help students deal with prejudice and stereotyping. Select one lesson plan to try out with your classmates or in a classroom that you are observing.

KEY TERMS

active listening, p. 492
anger management, p. 523
Bloom's taxonomy, p. 516
conflict resolution, p. 494
congruent curriculum, p. 494
dialogic listening, p. 493
differentiated instruction, p. 495
effective questions, p. 515
essential questions, p. 517
gemeinschaft, p. 486
gesellschaft, p. 486
higher-order questions, p. 515
multiple modalities, p. 495
personalized learning, p. 494
positive interdependence, p. 499
recall questions, p. 515

WEBSITES TO EXPLORE

http://www.alaskanative.net/. The Alaska Native Heritage Center offers a wealth of information about Alaska native cultures, resources, and teaching–learning ideas.

http://www.stedwards.edu/cte/resources/blooms.htm. St. Edward's University (Austin, Texas) offers a multipage website with ideas for using effective questions, especially for enhancing higher-order thinking. Includes samples of questions based on Bloom's taxonomy.

http://www.tolerance.org. Teaching Tolerance, the educational arm of the Southern Poverty Law Center in Montgomery, Alabama, offers an excellent, comprehensive array of activities and materials that promote positive social interaction, especially focused on reducing racism and group prejudice. Its "Mixing It Up" materials provide grade-appropriate tools and resources that promote "mixing it up" among children of different ethnic and cultural groups.

http://www.esrnational.org. The website of Educators for Social Responsibility (ESR) is a national organization whose focus is developing social skills, caring classroom climates, and effective educational responses to local, national, and international crises. ESR offers curriculum units for all grade levels as well as teacher workshops and school presentations.

http://www.responsiveclassroom.org. The Northeast Foundation for Children in Greenfield, Massachusetts, offers a classroom-tested approach called "The Responsive Classroom." Schools adopting the RC approach commit to a set of practices that range from physical furniture arrangements and structured classroom meetings to discovery learning and communication with families, all directed at maintaining a climate that fosters responsibility, support, self-control, self-motivation, independence, and a sense of community. RC offers workshops and a regular newsletter.

http://pbskids.org/itsmylife/friends/bullies/index.html. Created by PBSKids, this website offers children definitions of bullying and ways to combat it, including how to handle the role of innocent bystander and how to create bully-free zones. Teachers can find lesson plans to support a feeling of community and safety in their classrooms.

http://www.rethinkingschools.org/. Rethinking Schools is an organization of educators dedicated to teaching for social justice and curriculum reform. It publishes a journal and book of articles describing classroom strategies undertaken by teachers working for social change. The website offers online articles, resources, and links to related associations of researchers, activists, and practitioners.

http://www.mainepbs.org/hometsom/program8.html. Maine Public Broadcasting System's series of programs on Maine history includes "People of the Dawn," the story of the state's native tribes (Wabanaki) and their contemporary issues. Includes sample lessons for teachers and background information.

CRITICAL READINGS

Building Classroom Relationships

BY ROXANN KRIETE

Every morning at 8:30 A.M., 5th grade teacher Ms. London rings an old-fashioned school bell, the signal in her classroom for everyone to stop and listen. "Morning meeting time," she announces. Students finish hanging up backpacks, return papers and books to cubbies, place art supplies and games on shelves, and in a practiced, quiet choreography, bring chairs from throughout the room to the meeting area to form a circle. Meanwhile, from a kindergarten classroom below, a simple melody drifts down the hallway: "It's time, it's time, it's time for morning meeting now." Begun by the teacher and picked up by the students as they scurry to put away lunches and coats, the song ends when all 25 students are seated in a circle on the rug, facing one another and ready to begin their morning meeting.

In elementary and middle schools across the United States, students and teachers launch their school day with a half-hour daily ritual that builds community and expresses important beliefs about the value of relationships in the classroom. Developed as part of the Responsive Classroom approach of the Northeast Foundation for Children, this routine works in kindergarten through 8th grade, in schools urban and rural, in classrooms large and small. During these morning meetings, students and teachers gather in a circle to greet one another, to listen and respond to one another's news, to practice academic and social skills, and to look forward to the day's events. The meetings have four sequential components: greeting, sharing, group activity, and news and announcements. Embedded in each are opportunities to practice the skills of being a caring community.

The meeting begins with students and teachers greeting one another by name. Varying the greetings keeps students interested. Some greetings are simple and straightforward. Amanda might start by turning to the classmate on her left with a "Good morning, Steven Michael," a smile, and a handshake. Steven Michael, who this year does not like being just Steven, and even more dislikes Steve or Stevie, responds, "Good morning, Amanda," and turns to his neighbor—"Good morning, Chandra." Other greetings are more complex. For example, children might name themselves, then say their nickname, and then choose another designation, such as "soccer player" or "big sister" or "reader." Simple or fanciful, all greetings help children learn one another's names and ensure that each child receives the warmth of a peer's greeting. These greetings provide practice in the verbal and nonverbal communication skills central to relationship building, in and out of school.

Each day, a few students share information about themselves with the class, concluding their statements with an invitation: "I'm ready for questions and comments." The responses show interest in the subject and the sharer. Being a sharer offers children practice at taking turns, orally expressing ideas, and shaping their presentation for a particular audience. The information that students share extends their knowledge of one another, and the respectful reception of their news builds students' sense of significance. "My grandma is in the hospital." "My soccer team won Saturday." "We're getting a dog from the animal shelter this weekend." Children often spot common ground for further conversations at lunch or other times, which enlarges each student's circle of friends. Sometimes the teacher assigns a topic, perhaps tying it to the current classroom curriculum. For example, one week the topic for sharing might be "an interesting fact you learned in the biography you are reading." Responding to classmates' sharing helps students develop a repertoire of responses appropriate to different kinds of information. Good questions show a genuine interest in the sharer and his or her news. Offering comments requires students to see events from someone else's perspective. "I'll bet you're excited to be getting a dog." "You must be sad that your grandma is so sick." Empathy, a cornerstone of caring, informs these comments.

Next, the whole class does a short activity together, building class cohesion. The activities are short and often fast-paced, involving everyone in the class. Some have clear academic skill-building components, such as math exercises or vocabulary building; others appear to be just for fun, although they may also offer practice in such crucial skills as following directions or exercising self-control. Group activities build a class's common collection of songs, games, chants, and poems, thereby nurturing the sense of familiarity and comfort that makes for a feeling of belonging. By knowing the shared words, the common tunes, and the familiar dance steps, each student possesses a valuable currency in the community.

During the final component of the morning meeting, students learn about events in the day ahead and develop language skills by reading and discussing the messages that their teacher has prepared and posted on a chart before the meeting. Even before the meeting begins, the chart's words welcome students, orient them, and get them excited about their day. The words on the chart also provide opportunities for quick, warm-up skill builders. For example, the chart's message may ask students to find and circle the ten punctuation mistakes that the teacher has deliberately inserted. It may acknowledge individual students' accomplishments; sometimes it may refer to past group events. The assumption of shared interest and identity that informs the teacher's construction of the chart—even the salutation—reinforces a sense of group identity. "Dear Upper Primes," one chart might begin. Or "Greetings, super scientists" to a group that spent the day before in an outdoor classroom, studying insects. Or "Welcome, soggy students" on the morning of a torrential rain. Teacher reading, choral reading, echo reading, or individual student reading of assigned sentences vary the pace, followed by short, related activities or brief conversations that may focus on academic skills or anticipate the day ahead.

When students and teachers come together on the first day of school, they are a group, but not yet a community. Developing community and the sense of belonging that defines it takes time. Members of a community must first know one another, starting with learning one another's names and how to pronounce them. Then they gradually learn about one another—favorite foods, hobbies, pets, families, hopes, strengths, and struggles. They also share a common vocabulary and culture, know the same words to songs, the same rules to games. They laugh about the same silly shared moments and lament the same shared losses.

Transforming a classroom group into a caring community of learners requires many ingredients. The teacher's purpose and set of expectations are essential beginning ingredients, but alone they are not enough. The teacher also needs time, patience, and good tools for turning intention and expectation into action and behavior. Done well, morning meetings can transform classroom groups into caring communities by offering daily instruction and practice in building a community. Over time, this daily practice weaves a web that binds a class together in community.

The way that teachers begin each day in the classroom sets the tone for learning and speaks volumes about what and whom they value, about their expectations for the way people will treat one another, and about the way they believe learning occurs. Children's learning about what school is like begins the moment they walk in the doors of the building. It matters whether adults and peers greet them warmly or overlook them, whether the classroom feels chaotic and unpredictable or ordered and comforting. A child who says, "My cat got hit by a car last night but it's gonna be all right," may find an interested, supportive audience or one that turns away. Every detail of students' experience informs them about their classroom and their place in it. Teachers who start the day with everyone together, face to face, welcoming one another, sharing news, listening to individual voices, and communicating as a caring group, are sharing the message that every person matters and that individual and group interactions matter. They foster a classroom culture that is friendly, thoughtful, courteous, warm, and safe.

To learn, individuals must take risks, perhaps offering up a tentative answer that they are far from sure is right or trying out a new part in the choir when they are not sure whether they can hit the notes. People can take these risks only when they know that others will respect and value them, no matter the outcome. Students must trust in order to risk, and morning meetings help create a climate of trust.

Humans strive to fulfill their needs in whatever way they can, whether those ways are positive or negative. The child whose friendly contributions are not recognized will seek recognition through trouble making. Having fun is also a universal human need. Being fully engaged in what we are doing—being playful and lighthearted even when the activity is hard and the challenge great—fosters the joy of learning. And when our classrooms don't provide constructive ways to meet our students' universal need for fun, students will devise their own, often not-so-constructive ways. Morning meetings offer opportunities for every class member to have fun and feel a sense of significance and belonging. The cumulative effect of morning meetings can be quite powerful, as the following story shows.

Pete was a 4th grade boy who struggled with anger and bullying tendencies at school. One day, while the principal was talking with Pete about his challenges and progress, the subject of morning meetings came up. "I hate morning meetings!" Pete blurted out.

This reaction startled the principal. "Most kids really like morning meetings. What do you hate about them?" Pete had his reasons:

"Well, you get to know kids, and you listen to them, and you do stuff together, and sometimes you like them, and then it makes it so you don't want to beat them up on the playground."

Morning meetings were putting Pete in considerable inner conflict. It's a lot easier to take a swing, verbal or physical, at someone whose name you don't know, whose voice you haven't heard, and whose story you don't have a clue about. Or to frame it more positively, when children know and feel connected to others, they treat one another better.

The daily ritual of "doing stuff together"—learning and using names, sharing stories, building a common repertoire of songs and experiences—is perhaps the greatest contribution of these morning gatherings. The sense of belonging, caring, and trust developed during morning meetings is a foundation for handling every lesson, every transition time, every lining-up, every upset and conflict, all day and all year. The morning meeting is a microcosm of the way we wish our schools to be—communities that are filled with learning and caring, classrooms that are safe and respectful and challenging for all.

Source: Educational Leadership, September 2003, Volume 61, Number 1, pp. 68–70.

A Closer Look at the Issues

1. How important are rituals in creating classroom communities?
2. The author says that children figure out what school is like the moment they walk in the doors of the building. What can teachers and administrators do to make the school appear welcoming?
3. What should a teacher do when a student is unwilling to share feelings or personal stories?

Creating a Literate and Compassionate Community

BY TRACY WAGNER

I knew that after the last week of classes in Period 3, English 10, I would never see some of my students again. Michael* was leaving to live with his mom in Milwaukee; D.J. might be moving back to Chicago, and might be taking classes at an area technical college; Janet was opting to leave "regular" high school classes for a work-to-learn program.

Teaching is a strange way to mark the passing of time: students arrive at the same time every day and, together, we figure each other out. Throughout the year, I felt these students becoming a physical part of my identity. . . . I also felt my heart widening with more anger and love and concern than I have ever felt before. At the end, I found myself wondering: What will happen when these students are gone?

While I had enjoyed a spectrum of emotions in all of my English classes during my first year of teaching, my Period 3 class was the hardest for me to let go. Within my high school's tracking system, this class rested at the "regular" level—under the TAG (Talented and Gifted) and ACAMO (Academically Motivated) tracks, but above self-contained special education. The students in that class were an array of ethnicities; all came from middle-class to lower-income homes, and some were labeled as "at-risk." Many students received special education services.

www.

On the last day of class, as the students chatted, I laid my own poem on one of the desks in the circle. Earlier in the week, armed with the "Remember Me" lesson plan from Linda Christensen's *Reading, Writing, and Rising Up: Teaching About Social Justice and the Power of the Written Word* (2000), I had placed students' names and mine in a hat. After choosing a name, students were to write a poem, praising what they remembered about this person in our class. The word had spread fast—not a small feat in a large urban school—and students had been able to explain the lesson before I even opened my mouth.

I wondered if the poems would live up to my expectations. I wanted them to be *gifts,* something that the recipients could take to remember our classroom community and their place in it. As I helped students brainstorm, a small part of me feared that I had not created the community that I had worked for since day one. Listening to their questions—"What if I got the name of someone I don't like?" "What if I've never talked to this person?" "What if there's really nothing good to say?"—I thought back on the year's activities and wondered if I had been overly optimistic.

Connecting Students and the World

Throughout the year, I designed, collaborated on, and discovered hands-on units that use literature to help students explore their lives and connect to the larger community and world. I wanted student to become more "literate," which, to me, meant not only working on basic reading and writing skills, but becoming compassionate members of society, capable of being agents of change. With this in mind, I started the year with a poetry unit inspired by Janice Mirikitani's poem "Who Is Singing This Song." Mirikitani explains the need to honor our ancestors' work by changing the injustices of the present. She writes: "Who is singing this song?/I am./ pulled by hands of history not to sit/ in these times, complacently,/ walkmans plugged to our ears,/ computers, soap operas lulling our passions to sleep." She then lists specific issues that have moved her and her ancestors to create change. In the end, she dares her readers "to love, to dream" enough to continue their quests. My students seemed to connect to the poem—to the richness of its language, the urgency of its message, and its rap-like flow.

After reading the poem in class, students brainstormed for their own "Who Is Singing This Song" poem by drawing a line down the middle of a sheet of paper. On one side, they named the issues important to their lives. On the other, they listed personal experiences that shaped these concerns. As this is difficult for some students, I supplied examples—racial profiling, the environment, fair treatment of people with disabilities—and told them to talk through why a person might care about each, and then write their own. On the back of the sheet, students listed the books, songs, movies, and role models that represented their beliefs. On the bottom, students filled in the sentence "I am." Responses ranged from "a student athlete" to "a dark poet," from "rebellious" to "macaroni and cheese." In the following days, students learned literary terms and then began the process of pre-writing, then writing a rough draft, soliciting a peer edit, and reworking it into a final poem. On the last day of the unit, students participated in a "read-around" as described in *Reading, Writing, and Rising Up,* listening to each poem and writing positive comments, then passing the comments to each author at the end of class.

I learned many facts about the students through this unit. I learned that I had to deal with the derogatory behavior and assumptions students had created about themselves through the reinforcement of prior classroom experiences. I learned that students could arrive in and disappear from my classes without warning. I learned that many students had not retained "the basics"—sentence structure, how to write a standardized test-ready essay, literary terms—that they would need to move ahead in their academic educations.

So, backed by a selection of 10th grade books that often felt like choosing the better of many evils, I set out to combine what already existed with resources from the library, my own books, and the collections of other English department teachers. For example, after focusing on the role of conflict in *The Lord of the Flies,* students watched Anna Deveare Smith's video *Twilight: Los Angeles,* based on interviews Smith conducted after the 1992 Rodney King beating. After conducting their own interviews about Rodney King with family members and school personnel and watching the video, my students wrote narratives about conflicts in their lives, from their perspective. Then students chose the point of view of another agent of conflict in the narrative—a person, nature, fate, society—and inserted that agent's view. Throughout, I sought to help students use writing and literature to feel compassion for people involved in conflicts in the larger world and in their lives.

Next I wanted students to see a connection between literature, writing, and others in their community. Built on a unit designed by Esmé Schwall and Tara Affolter, teachers who were also new to East High School's English department that year, my English 10 students read Sandra Cisneros's *The House on Mango Street* in thematic parts, then responded by writing a personal vignette that shared each theme. At the end, students edited and designed their own books, each with cover, illustrations, and author biography. I delivered the books to Lori Nelson, whose eighth graders had also read *The House on Mango Street.* The middle school kids packed the high schooler's books with letters and poems responding to what they had written. I remember the silence as the 10th graders read the responses that thanked them for sharing their stories, being brave, and being role models. Martellious, whose book featured stories of losing friends and family to violence in Chicago, told me it was one of the proudest days of his life. I knew he understood how writing about the struggles in his life could help him connect with others. While I couldn't verbalize it at the time, I now realize that giving the students opportunities to read and write for a larger audience validated them as literate, compassionate members of society.

Throughout the year, I created opportunities for students to experience literacy outside of the classroom. I wanted to take away the mystique of college, and to show them that their lives fit into an academic world. Mid-year, I coordinated with graduate student Nikola Hobbel to take a group of my ninth graders to the University of Wisconsin–Madison to be part of her teacher education young adult literature class's discussion on controversies of teaching Harper Lee's *To Kill A Mockingbird.* Bolstered by this experience, I took a carload of Period 3 students to hear Angie Cardamone, a pre-service teacher who spent time each week working in my classroom, give a presentation at the university about the effects of tracking in East's English 10 classes. As Michael, Janet, and Charlie listened to Angie, they recognized their voices in her recommendations. I remember Michael, a lower-income, African-American student sitting on the side of the room, surrounded by young, white, female pre-service teachers. When he participated in a discussion about how white teachers could increase "minority student achievement," I knew his confidence to speak in an academic community showed that he saw himself as a literate member of the discussion.

Near the end of the year, I wanted students to find connections between their lives and a seemingly unrelated text. So, to preface the reading of Chinua Achebe's novel *Things Fall Apart,* students studied Nigerian folktales and performed them for our class. Then I asked an African storytelling professor from UW–Madison to speak to the students. Angie Cardamone agreed to pick the professor up on campus; a student volunteered to videotape the presentation; I organized volunteers to set up the room. When I got sick I arranged for a sub I knew to cover the class, and trusted that my students could hold the event together. Sure enough, the students raved and the professor praised the attention and maturity they showed. And though they complained about the difficulty of the reading, the tediousness of text coding (a reading strategy described in Cris Tovani's excellent book *I Read It, but I Don't Get It: Comprehension Strategies for Adolescent Readers* (2000)), and the very idea of a "literary analysis" essay, my Period 3 students held on. As I look back on this unit, I realize that the students had gained enough confidence in themselves to tackle—and maybe even enjoy—a difficult read.

Sure, only a few students would routinely do work outside of class, and a lack of computer access caused many projects to be late. Sure, I had to wait for the kids to stop talking at the beginning of every class. Sometimes yelling helped, sometimes walking out, shutting the door behind me, and then walking back in with exaggerated gestures of "Good morning!" did the trick. Things were rarely easy, but by the end of the school year, I witnessed something remarkable that made it all worth the pain.

Conclusions

On the last day of class, I asked the students to read the poems they had written about each other. One by one, the students read loudly and slowly. When Brittany, a quiet, white, middleclass girl who loved the ballet, finished reading her poem about Janet, an extroverted African-American girl from a low-income family who loved Tupac Shakur, Janet gave her a hug. The students began a pattern of reading and walking the poems over to the classmates they'd written about, often wrapping their arms around each other. And when their poems were read, I was surprised to see my toughest boys cry.

After the reading, I started to stand but was shushed down by Michael. "Wait, Ms. Wagner," he said, rising, "I've got something to say." Student by student, Michael trailed his finger around the circle, saying one good thing about every one in it. Sometimes I didn't get the jokes, but it was clear that the students understood. He finished, and another student picked up the routine, often walking to the student in the spotlight, hugging, smiling, or hitting a shoulder with a fist. I remember what the students said to each other, and what they said to me.

In the last minutes of Period 3, I sat back and watched the class function as a community of caring individuals. I marveled that I didn't have to say a word.

---

*All students' names have been changed, unless permission was given.

Source: Rethinking Schools, Winter/Spring 2003, Vol. 17 (2).

A Closer Look at the Issues

1. How does Tracy Wagner's article demonstrate that a caring classroom is also an academically rich classroom?
2. In what ways do her teaching strategies reflect her commitment to the concept of personalized learning described in this chapter?
3. We introduced this chapter by describing two notions of community in schools. Describe these two notions as they appear in this selection.

REFERENCES

Aust, B. (2003). The power of voice in schools. *Classroom Leadership 7* (2).

Benard, B. (1995). Fostering resiliency in urban schools. In B. Williams, ed., *Closing the achievement gap: A vision to guide change in beliefs and practice.* Oak Brook, IL: Research for Better Schools and North Central Regional Educational Laboratory.

Bigelow, B. (1998). The human lives behind the labels: The global sweatshop, Nike, and the race to the bottom. In W. Ayres, J. Hunt, and T. Quinn, eds. *Teaching for social justice: A democracy and education reader.* New York: Teachers College Press.

Bloom, B., M. Englehart, E. Furst, W. Hill, and D. Krathwohl (1956). *Taxonomy of educational objectives: The classification of educational goals. Handbook I: Cognitive domain.* New York, Toronto: Longmans, Green. *Taxonomy of educational objectives: The classification of educational goals. Handbook I: Cognitive domain.* New York, Toronto: Longmans, Green.

Breitborde, M.-L. (1996). Creating community in the classroom: Modeling "new basic skills" in teacher education. *Journal of Teacher Education,* 47 (5), pp. 367–374.

Breitborde, M.-L. (2003). One-room schools of Illinois in the twentieth century: An oral history. Unpublished research. Available from author.

Brett, Jan (1989). *The mitten: A Ukrainian folktale.* Boston: Putnam.

Carter, S. (2002). *The impact of parent/family involvement on student outcomes: An annotated bibliography of research from the past decade.* Eugene, OR: Consortium for Appropriate Dispute Resolution Special Education.

Christenson, S. L., and S. M. Sheridan (2001). *Schools and families: Creating essential connections for learning.* New York: Guilford Press.

Cruickshank, D., D. Bainer, and K. Metcalf (1999). *The act of teaching,* 2nd ed. Boston: McGraw-Hill College.

de los Angeles-Bautista, F. (2000). Community-based ECCD: Living and learning with Aeta families in the Philippines. *Education Update* (UNICEF), *3* (3), October, pp. 16–18.

Epstein, J. L. (1995). School/family/community partnerships: Caring for the children we share. *Phi Delta Kappan 76* (9), May, pp. 701–712.

Fogleman, L. S. (2003). Baylor receives 3M Foundation Vision Grant award. *News & Events.* May 20. Waco, TX: Baylor University, http://pr.baylor.edu/story.php?id=4308. Retrieved September 19, 2004.

Gay, G. (2000). *Culturally responsive teaching: Theory, research, and practice.* New York: Teachers College Press.

Haynes, N. M., C. L. Emmons, S. Gebreyesus, and M. Ben-Avie (1996). The school development program evaluation process. In *Rallying the whole village: The Comer process for reforming education* (pp. 123–144). New York: Teachers College, Columbia University.

Hyson, M. (2004). *The emotional development of young children: Building an emotion-centered curriculum.* New York: Teachers College Press.

Jacobs, H. (1997). *Mapping the big picture: Integrating curriculum and assessment.* Alexandria, VA: Association for Supervision and Curriculum Development.

Jenkins, J. M., and J. W. Keefe (2002). Two schools, two approaches to personalized learning. *Phi Delta Kappan.* 83 (6), pp. 449–456.

Johnson, D. W., and F. P. Johnson (2000). *Joining together: Group theory and group skills,* 7th ed. Boston: Allyn & Bacon.

Kassabaum, D., illus. (1981). *Good old house neighborhood.* Ann Arbor, MI: Educational Designs.

Kellogg, S. (2000). *Missing Mitten Mystery.* NY: Penguin Group.

Kreidler, W. J. (1984). *Creative conflict resolution.* Glenview, IL: Scott Foresman.

March, T. (1998). Why WebQuests: An introduction. http://www.ozline.com/webquests/intro.html. April 20, 1998. Retrieved July 17, 2004.

Maslow, A. (1970). *Motivation and personality,* 2nd ed. New York: Harper & Row.

Mattise, M. C. (2004). True blue. *Teaching tolerance,* 25, April 20, pp. 18–21.

McKenzie, J. (2000). *Beyond technology: Questioning, research, and the information literate school.* Bellingham, WA: FNO Press.

McKenzie, J. (2003). Questioning as technology. *From Now On: The Educational Technology Journal, 12* (8), April. http://www.fno.org/apr03/qtech.html. Retrieved July 15, 2004.

Meier, D. (2002a). *In schools we trust: Creating communities of learning in an era of testing and standardization.* Boston: Beacon Press.

Meier, D. (2002b). Just let us be: The genesis of a small public school. *Educational Leadership, 59* (5), pp. 76–79.

Meier, D. (1996). Supposing that. *Phi Delta Kappan, 78* (5), pp. 271–277.

Meier, D. (1995). *The power of their ideas: Lessons for America from a small school in Harlem.* Boston: Beacon Press.

Noddings, N. (1992). *The challenge to care in schools: An alternative approach to education.* New York: Teachers College Press.

Noddings, N. (1996). On community. *Educational Theory, 46,* pp. 254–267.

Pollock, Y., and T. Hill, illus. (1994). *The old man's mitten.* Greenvale, NY: Mondo Publishing.

Postman, N., and C. Weingartner (1969). *Teaching as a subversive activity.* New York: Dell.

Rimm-Kaufman, S. E., and B. E. Sawyer (2004). Primary-grade teachers' self-efficacy beliefs, attitudes toward teaching, and discipline and teaching practice priorities in relation to the *Responsive Classroom* approach. *Elementary School Journal,* 104 (4), pp. 321–341.

Schmuck, R., and P. Schmuck (2001). *Group processes in the classroom (8th edition).* Dubuque, Iowa: McGraw Hill.

Sergiovanni, T. J. (1999). *Building community in schools.* San Francisco: Jossey-Bass.

Shaeffer, S. (2000). Who owns the school? *Education Update* (UNICEF), 3 (3), October, pp. 2–3.

Sizer, T. (1999). No two are quite alike. *Educational Leadership,* 57 (1), September. http://www.ascd.org/readingroom/edlead/9909/sizer.html. Accessed January 12, 2004.

Stewart, J., and M. Thomas (1995). Dialogic listening: Sculpting mutual meanings. In J. Stewart, ed., *Bridges Not Walls,* 6th ed., pp. 184–201. New York: McGraw-Hill.

Sturges, P., and G. Laroche, illus. (2000). *Sacred places.* New York: G. P. Putnam's Sons.

Swiniarski, L. (1991). Toys: Universals for teaching global education. *Childhood Education,* Spring, pp. 161–163.

Swiniarski, L., and Breitborde, M. (2003). *Educating the global village: Including the child in the world,* 2nd ed. Upper Saddle River, NJ: Merrill Prentice Hall.

Terry, W. S., and J. S. Burns (2001). Anxiety and repression in attention and retention. *Journal of General Psychology,* October.

Tomlinson, C. A. (2003). *Fulfilling the promise of the differentiated classroom: Strategies and tools for responsive teaching.* Alexandria, VA: Association for Supervision & Curriculum Development.

Tomlinson, C. A. (1999). *The differentiated classroom: Responding to the needs of all learners.* Alexandria, VA: Association for Supervision and Curriculum Development.

Tompert, A. (1990). *Grandfather Tang's story.* New York: Crown Publishers, Inc.

Toner, M. (2004). Northwest passage. *Teacher Magazine. 16* (1), August, pp. 40–45.

Tonnies, F. ([1887] 1957). *Gemeinschaft und Gesellschaft.* C. P. Loomis, trans. Ann Arbor: Michigan State University Press.

Tresselt, A., and Yaroslava, illus. (1964). *The mitten.* NY: Lothrop, Lee & Shepard.

Twomey, C., and J. Schleicher (2004). Students as teachers: Helping administrators attain technology skills. *Classroom Leadership,* 7 (9).

United Nations Education, Scientific and Cultural Organization (UNESCO) (2003). The mother tongue dilemma. *Education Today,* No. 6, July–September, pp. 4–7. http://www.unesco.org/education/education_

today/ed_today6.pdf. Retrieved September 19, 2004.

Wabanaki Studies Commission (2003). Final Report of the Wabanaki Studies Commission. Augusta, ME: Maine Department of Education and Maine Indian Tribal State Commission.

Westheimer, J. (1998). Conceptions of community: Problems and possibilities for research on teachers' work. *Journal of Research in Education, 8* (1), pp. 9–15.

Zulu, H. (2000). Communities fight HIV/AIDS through education. *Education Update* (UNICEF), 3 (3), October, pp. 12–13.

Conclusion: Our Message to Future Teachers

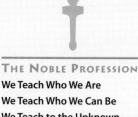

THE NOBLE PROFESSION

> Sometimes it gets frustrating. There's politics and there are pressures from outside to do things that I don't think are in the best interest of my kids. I'm not allowed to use my own judgment as much as I'd like to, my own professionalism. Yet I don't want anyone else to do it. I want to be there, every day, to be caring and to do the right thing in spite of whatever else is going on. It's about seeing them learn. It's when I hear one of my kids say, "I really like reading this year." The joy I get from them. The joy that's *in* them. You just can't beat that.
>
> —Mary Ann Grassia, first-grade teacher

We would like to end this book with some reflections on what the ideas we've presented in this book mean for you as a future teacher. How might you use this information? How will it help you teach in ways that speak to your own principles and your own promise as an educator of new generations of citizens of this nation and the world? How will the information in this book help you advocate for what you believe about education? How will it help you be heard?

We believe that principled teaching starts with knowing yourself. Then, remember that you and the students meet in the classroom to consider new possibilities—you are all there to learn. You won't know what your students, the next generation, will be like or what choices they'll have in life. But you can still guide them. Teachers can be leaders and reformers who know that change can happen and that the barriers to excellence and equality in education can be reduced. There are principled teachers and promising programs in schools right now that are achieving the goals of excellence and equity. In this message to you, we will take a closer look at the possibilities.

Teaching has always been challenging. The prairie schoolteacher in early Illinois had to contend with the physical problems of keeping the wood stove going and with the pedagogical problem of figuring out how to occupy a dozen children, ages five to fifteen, at different grade levels, in one room. The missionary teacher who went South during Reconstruction to teach former slaves to read was too often subject to the insults and violence of Southerners who were hostile to the cause. The big-city teacher at the turn of the twentieth century worked hard to prepare, with limited space and materials, some fifty pupils newly arrived from many different countries, most speaking no English, for their new American lives.

One might argue that teaching today is in many ways more challenging than it ever has been. Today's teachers teach everyone. The population of children in schools has grown in cultural and linguistic diversity, the children sometimes have vastly different learning needs, and they are increasingly exposed to mass media images and information not always intended for their eyes and ears. Today's children bring more richness and variety into classroom life than ever before; at the same time, they bring more complications. And in the background, looking over teachers' shoulders, are the administrators, policymakers, and politicians who hold them accountable for ensuring that all of these children reach the same performance standards, measured by scores on high-stakes, paper-and-pencil tests.

In the first chapter of this book, we claimed that *teaching is the noblest of professions and should be treated with the highest respect.* We believe that, since the *ultimate aim of public education is the improving of life on earth for all its people,* the work of teaching is crucial, and global in nature. Therefore, we agree with those who hold teachers to high intellectual, moral, and professional standards. In history and in today's classrooms there are thousands of examples of teachers who live up to the lofty goals and the day-to-day challenges of the work. They include the famous—Mary McLeod Bethune, Laura Towne, Elizabeth Peabody, Leonard Covello, Deborah Meier, Jonathan Kozol, Theodore Sizer—and the unsung heroes we have all been privileged to know. Among these unsung heroes are the teachers we all remember—the music teacher who gave disaffected high school students a reason to come to school, a place to "hang out" while they were there, and some free advice about their futures. We remember . . .

- The fourth-grade teacher who stayed after school for weeks to coach her whole class for a regional academic competition and then helped raise money so that the children, most of whose families had limited incomes, could go.
- The American government teacher who institutionalized a "Mock Town Meeting" every year for students whose research was often cited in actual town policy decisions.
- The elementary school principal who kept a school-phobic second grader by her side during the first three days of school.
- The math teacher who tutored our "math-phobic" friend after school, refusing to give up in the face of her own discouragement.

- And the gym teacher who took home a runaway for a few days and helped him make peace with his parents.

Given the importance of their work and the heroism with which they often carry it out, teachers' voices should be principled and loud. They should be participating actively in determining the standards of the profession and advocating for whatever is needed to help children learn and grow. They should be insisting on full support for free, public schools as institutions necessary to ensure the continuance of the democracy. In order to advocate for their profession and for those they serve, teachers first need to understand who they are as teachers and as human beings.

We Teach Who We Are

Parker Palmer (see Chapter 6) is the strongest voice reminding teachers that the reasons they teach, and how they teach, come from within. "We teach who we are," he says in *The Courage to Teach* (1998). Teaching is a vocation; those who love the work are "called" to it. Good teachers teach from a strong sense of identity and belief. They teach with integrity; that is, the "how" of their teaching matches the "who" of their essential identities. In your schooling, you had teachers who you thought were good because their lectures were interesting and substantive. You had other teachers who you thought were good because they led exciting class discussions. Others provided you with rich resources for your own exploration—simulations, field trips, excellent books to read. We loved one teacher for his sense of humor. We loved going to French class, because, along with learning the language, we could always count on one or two jokes (in French). Ms. Wells, on the other hand, was deadly serious, but excellent at explaining quadratic equations. No two teachers will teach well if they teach exactly the same way, for the art of teaching lies in the individuality of the teacher.

Good teachers understand the importance of listening to others' opinions about what should be taught and about how the evidence for learning should be collected. They pay attention to state curricula and learning standards. But they understand also that their success in helping students learn is a matter of their own connection with the subject matter and their ability to work with students to explore it together, as members of a learning community. They know that learning never ends, and that test scores, while important, are not the ultimate measures of students' learning experiences. Teachers whose voices are powerful in the classroom or the professional community are teachers whose voices are authentic expressions of their identities and their beliefs. Palmer urges teachers to hold onto that internal sense of being "right" and "true" as they confront the "culture of fear" that too often pervades public schools.

We Teach Who We Can Be

Teachers are intellectuals, says Henry Giroux (1988, 1997). Many are upset about the social and economic forces that distract or dissuade children from achieving. They worry that they spend their days "teaching to the test" rather than involving children in meaningful learning activities. You may find yourself in classrooms where you don't have enough of the materials you want to use. You may feel frustrated that you can't solve the problems your students may face in their home lives.

> leadership, the time frame for transforming culture, structure, belief, and practice is years (Evans, 1996, p. 299).

We Teach Toward the Possible

Article 28 of the United Nations Convention on the Rights of the Child (United Nations Children's Fund, 1989) says that every child has a right to an education, which should be free and available to all. Although the United States has not yet formally ratified the Convention (along with Somalia), the United States has an admirable history of providing mandatory, accessible, free public education to all children, through the secondary school level. From the time of Horace Mann, who took seriously Thomas Jefferson's admonition that the health of the democratic republic depended upon an educated populace, we have reaped the benefit of a strong system of public schools. The promise of public education is well expressed by Deborah Meier, a school reformer who has created new kinds of schools in difficult urban communities:

> There's a radical and wonderful new idea here—the idea that every citizen is capable of the kind of intellectual competence previously attained by only a small minority. . . . [I take] this vision of education and human possibility seriously (1995, p. 4).

Similarly, Jonathan Kozol, despite a long career exposing "savage inequalities" in and around public schools (Kozol, 1991), has never lost his faith in the institution itself: "The old and honored dream of public education as the common ground of an informed democracy . . . is a good dream," he says (quoted in Omara-Otunnu, 1999).

As a nation built on the principle of individual freedom, we allow alternatives for those parents who choose to school their children elsewhere—in parochial schools, other private schools, or at home, for instance. In a democracy, choice is healthy. But there is too much disparity in the quality of private schools, and too little oversight of them, to guarantee that other principle we espouse: the principle of equality. Horace Mann's dream of "common schools," where the child of a wealthy family would learn alongside the child of a poor one, has not yet been realized. Our most critical problem in education is social class. More than race or culture, social class differentiates the quality of the education children will receive and, thus, their future economic and social welfare (see Chapter 8). Race matters, of course. But for children of poverty and children of color, we've put Band-Aids on wounds, and without much sensitivity to how long the wounds have been there.

Social class in America is tied up with wealth and the acquisition of the material things that signify wealth. It hardly makes room for other measures of social class found in other parts of the world; for example, the amount of knowledge one has, one's competence, one's contributions to society, or good character. Too many American children see success as having enough money and power to get what they want and education as a necessary evil or unnecessary distraction. Too many teachers measure themselves against those standards and feel powerless as a result.

It can be argued that by academic and intellectual standards as well as the standard of equity, our public schools have not yet achieved their promise. We haven't done what Plato or John Dewey or Maxine Greene or Henry Giroux wanted; that is, taught our children to think critically, make informed judgments, question "taken-for-granted" reality. We may have left them in Plato's cave (see Chapter 2), more chained than ever to virtual reality, entertained by the shadows rather than the substance of things. Teachers who feel powerless against children's difficult life situations, against limited resources, against unfeeling policymakers, get caught up in the daily routines of teaching. When we only see ourselves as passing along some predetermined curriculum, we lose the "big picture"—our sense of purpose, our sense that we are "intellectuals." We become technicians, rather than teachers.

We trust that this book has convinced you that there is much that is positive in public schools and promising in the work of teaching. There exist many "promising practices": exciting developments in curriculum and instruction, in the way schools are organized, in the relationship of schools to their communities. We will mention just a few here:

- A commitment to high expectations for all students, a central tenet of the flawed but well-intentioned No Child Left Behind Act, communicates the message to students that they can all learn.
- The use of broad and engaging "essential questions" (see Chapter 11) allows teachers to depart from or extend strict, scripted, test-aligned curricula.
- Respect for cultural diversity and multiple intelligences leads teachers to offer a broader and richer curriculum using a variety of materials and approaches to instruction, which adds to the knowledge and experience of all students.
- Comprehensive programs such as the Responsive Classroom, which honor the connection between academic learning and a positive social climate, are contributing to the transformation of schools into learning communities.
- Full-service schools that open their doors to the community beyond and provide extended educational, social, and health services to support families and use the community as a resource for learning, reap significant benefits for the children and for teachers inside.

The greatest hope for the future of public schools lies in their greatest resource: teachers. Technology has brought many improvements to education: computers, multimedia, the Internet, the Web, email, distance learning, and online courses expand possibilities for teaching and learning. But technology is only a tool. It cannot replace the teacher. As Jonathan Kozol, who describes his one year of fourth-grade teaching in the Boston Public Schools as the most difficult job he ever had in his life, says about our work:

> Schools can survive without elaborate software if they have to, they can survive without a swimming pool or a gym. They can certainly survive without some of those lists of competencies. One thing schools cannot survive without are radiant and vital and well educated teachers (quoted in Omara-Otunnu, 1999).

Smart Is Something You Get

We urge you to understand the principles on which you base your work and your life. Be confident in those beliefs. Take something from each chapter that confirms your vision of the educated person and the purpose of schooling. Form alliances that reflect the best ideals and practices of the pioneers in education. Borrow from your colleagues. Raise your standards and expectations for your own work and for what your students know and can do. Remember that teaching is learning, so learn with your students and listen to their wisdom. As Jeff Howard said, "smart is something you get" (Blackman and Howard, 2000, p. 4).

Teaching remains a human endeavor with a proud tradition and a promising future. You carry the age-old heritage of teaching into a new generation. We encourage you to do so with the courage of your convictions, an honoring of multiple points of views, and a pride of membership in the profession.

Mary-Lou Breitborde

Louise Swiniarski

REFERENCES

Barth, R. (2001). Teacher leader. *Phi Delta Kappan* 82 (6), February, pp. 443–449.

Blackman, M., and J. Howard (2000). Proficiency for all: Can we ride the accountability wave to get there? *The Principal Advisor 1* (1), January, pp. 3–4.

Counts, G. S. (1969). *Dare the schools build a new social order?* New York: Random House.

Evans, R. (1996). *The human side of school change.* San Francisco: Jossey-Bass.

Giroux, H. A. (1988). *Teachers as intellectuals: Toward a critical pedagogy of learning.* Granby, Massachusetts: Bergin and Garvey.

Giroux, H. A. (1997). *Pedagogy and the politics of hope: Theory, culture, and schooling.* Boulder, Colorado: Westview Press.

Greene, M. (2003). Teaching as possibility: A light in dark times. http://www.lesley.edu/journals/jppp/1/jp3ii1.html. Accessed January 7, 2003.

Kozol, J. (1991). *Savage inequalities: Children in America's schools.* New York: Crown.

Meier, D. (1995). *The power of their ideas: Lessons for America from a small school in Harlem.* Boston: Beacon Press.

Omara-Otunnu, E. (1999,). Education advocate warns of dangers to public schooling. *Advocate,* October 4. Storrs, CT: University of Connecticut. http://www.advance.uconn.edu/10049902.htm. Accessed February 27, 2004.

Palmer, P. (1998). *The courage to teach.* San Francisco: Jossey-Bass.

United Nations Children's Fund (UNICEF) (1989). *Convention on the Rights of the Child.* http://www.unicef.org/crc/crc.htm. Accessed February 27, 2004.

Credits

Chapter 1 p. 26: E. D. Hirsch, from *Cultural Literacy: What Every American Needs to Know.* Copyright © 1988 by Houghton Mifflin Company. Used by permission. p. 28: *Literacy for What?* by Maxine Greene, Phi Delta Kappan, January 1982, pp. 326–329. Reprinted by permission of the author.

Chapter 2 p. 50: From Plato, *The Republic, Book VII,* translated by B. Jowett (New York: Doubleday), 514a-c to 521a-e, pp. 105–108. Copyright © 1960. p. 71: From *Emile, or On Education* by Jean-Jacques Rousseau by Allan Bloom, translator. Copyright © 1979 by Basic Books, Inc. Reprinted by permission of Basic Books, a member of Perseus Books, L.L.C.

Chapter 3 p. 88: Waldorf Education . . . an Introduction by Henry Barnes, former Chairman of the Board, Educational Leadership, October 1991. Reprinted by Permission. The Association for Supervision and Curriculum Development is a worldwide community of educators advocating sound policies and sharing best practices to achieve the success of each learner. To learn more, visit ASCD at http://www.ascd.orgp. p. 103: Elaine Winter, *Polishing the Progressive Approach: Why an Endangered Educational Species Should Be Protected,* from http://www.lrei .org/index.html. Reprinted by permission of the author. p. 105: John Henry Newman, *The Idea of a University, Discourse VII* (New York: Doubleday), pp. 191–192. Copyright © 1959.

Chapter 4 p. 137: Swiniarski, Louise Boyle; Breitborde, Mary-Lou, *Educating the Global Village: Including the Child in the World,* 2nd edition, © 2003. Adapted by permission of Pearson Education, Inc., Upper Saddle River, NJ. p. 141: Deborah Meier, "Standards Yes, Standardization No," Rochester Democrat and Chronicle, May 23, 1999. Reprinted by permission of the *Rochester Democrat and Chronicle.* p. 142: Diane Ravitch, "On School Reform, Let's Stay the Course," *Hoover Digest* 2003, No. 2 Spring Issue. Reprinted by permission of *Hoover Digest* and the author.

Chapter 5 p. 177: Reprinted with permission from Shirley Veenema and Howard Gardner, "Multimedia and Multiple Intelligences," *The American Prospect,* Volume 7, Number 29: November 01, 1996. The American Prospect, 11 Beacon Street, Suite 1120, Boston, MA 02108. All rights reserved. p. 179: Lisa Delpit, "Skills and Other Dilemmas of a Progressive Black Educator," *Harvard Educational Review,* 56, 1986, pp. 379–385. Reprinted by permission of *Harvard Educational Review.*

Chapter 6 p. 213: Preface to the American Edition from The Montessori Method by Maria Montessori, translated by Anne George. Copyright © 1988. Reprinted by permission of Random House, Inc. p. 213: Roland Barth, Foreword for *Educators as Learners: Creating a Professional Learning Community in Your School* by P. Wald & M. Castleberry (eds.). Copyright © 2000. Used with Permission. The Association for Supervision and Curriculum Development is a worldwide community of educators advocating sound policies and sharing best practices to achieve the success of each learner. To learn more, visit ASCD at *www.ascd.org.*

Chapter 7 p. 246: David Sadker is a Professor at American University in Washington, DC. To find out more about David and Myra Sadker's work, visit *www.sadker.org.* p. 249: *www.carlisleindian-school.org.*

Chapter 8 p. 273: From Wayne E. Fuller, *One-Room Schools of the Middle West.* Copyright © 1994. Reprinted by permission of University Press of Kansas. p. 248: From Mary Antin, *The Promised Land,* 1912. p. 313: Reprinted by permission of the author.

Chapter 9 p. 361: Figure, "Mission Hill School Four Year Curriculum Cycle." Reprinted by permission. p. 367: An Indian Father's Plea by Robert Lake-Thom (Medicine Grizzly Bear), Teacher Magazine, Vol. 2 (1), 1990. Reprinted by permission of the author. p. 370: From Gloria Ladson-Billings, Crossing Over to Canaan. Copyright © 2001. Reprinted with permission of John Wiley & Sons, Inc. p. 252: "Silence" by Tu-Uyen Nguyen, *Teaching Tolerance,* Spring 2004, p. 34. Reprinted by permission.

Chapter 10 p. 394: Code of Ethics of the Education Profession. Reprinted by permission of the National Education Association. p. 418: Directly from the Source: Mary Anne Raywid and Libby Oshiyama, "Musings in the Wake of Columbine: What Can Schools Do?" Phi Delta Kappan, February 2000, Vol. 81 (6), pp. 444–449. Reprinted by permission of the authors. p. 428: Nel Noddings, "A Morally Defensible Mission for Schools in the 21st Century," Phi Delta Kappan, vol. 76, No. 5, January 1995. Reprinted by permission of Nel Noddings, Lee Jacks Professor of Education Emerita, Stanford University. p. 429: Copyright © 1997 by Alfie Kohn. Excerpted from Phi Delta Kappan with the author's permission. For more information: *www.ALFIEKOHN.org.*

Chapter 11 p. 463: Reprinted by permission of CES National. p. 470: From *Teach Your Own: A Hopeful Path for Education* by John Holt. Copyright © 1981 by John Holt. Reprinted by permission of Da Capo, a member of Perseus Books, L.L.C. p. 474: "Epilogue: The Here and Now" reprinted by permission of the publisher from the *Schoolhome: Rethinking Schools for Changing Families* by Jane Roland Martin, pp. 205–211, Cambridge, Mass.: Harvard University Press, Copyright © 1992 by Jane Roland Martin. p. 477: Reprinted by permission of the publisher from *Seeking Common Ground: Public Schools in a Diverse Society* by David Tyack, pp. 181–185, Cambridge, Mass.: Harvard University Press, Copyright © 2003 by the President and Fellows of Harvard College.

Chapter 12 p. 496: Melissa Correa-Connolly, "Welcoming All Families" from *Responsive Classroom,* Spring 2003, 15 (2). © Northeast Foundation for Children. 800-360-6332. *www.responsiveclassroom.org.* Reprinted by permission of the Northeast Foundation for Children. p. 533: Roxann Kriete, "Building Classroom Relationships," Educational Leadership, September 2003, Vol. 61, No. 1, pp. 68–70. Used with permission. The Association for Supervision and Curriculum Development is a worldwide community of educators advocating sound policies and sharing best practices to achieve the success of each learner. To learn more, visit ASCD at *www.ascd.org.* p. 535: Reprinted from *Rethinking Schools,* vol. 17, no. 2. www.rethinkingschools.org.

GLOSSARY

ability groups An organizational plan for instruction that groups students by presumed ability to learn the subject matter or skill. It is used as a way to make instruction understandable and efficient, but often has the result of labeling and limiting students.

accredited institution A university or college that has been reviewed and approved by the state or professional agency.

acculturation The acquisition of dominant cultural norms by members of a non-dominant group, which typically loses its own culture, language, and perhaps even religion, in the process.

achievement gap The difference in academic performance, usually measured by standardized tests, between groups of students of various cultures, genders or social classes. The most serious gaps occur between the scores of black and white children, Anglos and Latinos, and whites and Native Americans.

active listening A communication technique that includes posture, eye contact, and gestures to show that a listener is paying attention to and thinking about what the speaker is saying.

anger management Strategies for expressing or controlling angry feelings in healthy, positive ways. Anger management strategies can include reporting feelings, cognitive restructuring (thinking differently), learning alternative responses, and relaxation techniques.

***a priori* knowledge** A proposition that is objectively true apart from human experience, or prior to our ever encountering it, derived from reason and analysis.

***a posteriori* knowledge** A proposition that is true on the basis of human perception, existing after we have experienced it, derived from direct sensory awareness.

assimilation The process of absorbing minority or immigrant groups into the larger community so that they become similar to the dominant social group and take on their language, culture, and behavior.

aesthetics Addresses standards of beauty.

assistive technology Devices that help students who are physically challenged or learning impaired to perform a task.

authority Relying on ideas, information, and experience of experts.

axiology The branch of philosophy that asks the question, What is of value? It is divided into ethics, which is concerned with right conduct, and aesthetics, which addresses standards of beauty.

behaviorism A theory of learning based on the belief that who we become depends on the experiences we are exposed to, how we are nurtured, and what behaviors we are rewarded for.

bilingual education The instruction of children whose English is limited in both English and their native languages so that English language learners do not fall behind their native English-speaking peers in learning content information in the academic subjects.

Bloom's taxonomy A schematic listing of types of questions or learning objectives requiring concrete to abstract levels of thinking. The taxonomy ranges from simple recall questions to higher-level evaluation questions.

bullying The willful and repeated exercise of power over another with hostile or malicious intent. Bullying can be physical or verbal, direct or indirect, and includes behaviors such as ostracism or rumor-spreading.

character education A movement designed to counter the rising incidence of violence in the schools through moral education programs and a curriculum prescribed with ethical, behavioral outcomes.

charter schools Special public schools established and controlled by groups of parents and/or educators, funded with local monies, but exempt from many existing rules and regulations. The "charter" is granted based on an approach to education that is different from what the regular public schools offer.

classical conditioning A process of learning, explained by behaviorists as the pairing of a conditioned stimulus with an emotional or physiological state, so that over time, the person responds to the conditioned stimulus with the same feeling that he or she would have made to the unconditioned stimulus.

code of ethics Collections of rules that are either presumed to be based on universal moral principles or on positive social outcomes.

cognitive development The increasing ability to think and solve problems.

compensatory education Educational opportunities designed to give disadvantaged or disabled students, or students whose achievement is significantly low, supplementary learning support through special programs, remedial and tutorial services, or co-curricular activities.

common schools The first system of accessible, free, tax-supported elementary schools proposed by Horace Mann.

conflict resolution The ability to choose constructive, nonviolent responses to student–student or teacher–student conflict, based on the premise that conflicts are inevitable but solvable problems.

conflict theory The contention that schools socialize students to prepare for and accept the unequal power relations in the larger society and the workplace. The content of the curriculum, the teaching approaches teachers use, and the way schools and students are organized reflect the norms and behaviors expected of various social classes.

congruent curriculum A uniting of the cognitive, affective, and behavioral domains of learning. The idea that the subject matter content of the curriculum, the processes of learning, and the values taught in the classroom should work toward the same goals and be mutually reinforcing.

constructivism An approach to learning that considers the learning process as the active making, or constructing, of meaning from experiences and observations. Constructivist learning includes posing one's own questions and conducting investigations to discover answers.

core curriculum A program of study that includes basic skills, attitudes, and a body of knowledge that includes the sciences and professional and vocational skills, along with communication, literacy, math, and civic understandings—all subjects that are necessary for participatory citizenship in a democracy and competent membership in the global community.

crisis response team A school team composed of counselors, psychologists, nurses, administrators, and law enforcement officials to deal with potential or actual critical problems such as violent incidents.

critical pedagogy An approach to teaching that engages students in examining underlying social and political conditions of life as they learn literacy and mathematics skills and academic content. Its goal is personal and social liberation.

cultural aphasia An obsolete and limited assumption of what comprises culture. Teachers may assume that white Anglo-Saxon middle-class concepts of, for example, good poetry and good music, are the ideal and only concepts worthy of consideration.

cultural deprivation An outdated assumption that the home lives of minority and low-income children lack culture, and that they fail to stimulate their intellectual development or provide the social experiences and standards expected by middle-class schools.

cultural fit The match or mismatch between the cultural background of students—their knowledge, language patterns, culture-based learning styles, beliefs and values—and the culture of the school. The assumption is that schools must recognize and respect these differences and adapt the curriculum and instruction to make them meaningful and effective.

cultural literacy Familiarity with the stock of knowledge and literary traditions of a particular culture that enables its members to communicate with each other based on common information and understanding.

cultural reproduction An element of conflict theory that claims that schools reproduce and transmit the culture of the larger society in the values, norms, and information that they provide to students in classrooms.

culturally responsive teachers Teachers who draw on their students' rich backgrounds and use instructional strategies that honor culture-based forms of expression and styles of learning.

culture A dynamic, creative, and continuous process including behaviors, values, and substance learned and shared by people that guides them in their struggle for survival and gives meaning to their lives.

culture of poverty The idea that poor children come from families caught in a culture of poverty that will keep them poor for generations to come, without a break in the cycle of low expectations, low education, and destructive habits of behavior.

curriculum The subject matter of education, the designed course of study.

dame schools A form of basic schooling in early New England where women who were single, widowed, or whose children had grown taught basic reading, writing, and arithmetic in their homes.

deductive reasoning Reaching a conclusion based on an analysis of general rules, principles, or premises and then logically applying them to specific cases.

de facto segregation Separate schooling of blacks and white children in northern cities due to residential segregation. Blacks and whites lived in different neighborhoods, sometimes by choice, sometimes because blacks were kept from buying homes in certain areas, and often because they could not afford to do so; neighborhood schools were, therefore, segregated.

de jure segregation Segregation of schools and other facilities mandated by law; for example, by the Jim Crow laws of the southern states.

deschooling A movement to separate education from schooling, based on the belief that learning is more authentic, more personally meaningful, and more effective if children engage in experiences and activities outside of formal institutionalized schools. Deschooling alternatives include apprenticeships, internships, and independent study.

developmentalism An approach to learning based on the belief that children's physical, mental, and social functioning is qualitatively different from adults' and develops in age-related stages, as part of the natural process of maturation.

dialogic listening A communication technique that treats a conversation as a shared activity, where the participants are "fully present" to teach other, aware of each other's point of view, and engaged in creating meaning together.

didactic materials Self-teaching materials designed by Maria Montessori.

differentiated instruction A method of organizing instruction where teachers present a common set of concepts and skills but vary the materials, methods of instruction, and tasks with students' learning levels.

discipline An academic area, with its own body of knowledge and set of principles.

distance learning Education via the computer, television, and radio.

district schools Early public schools, usually one room, established by groups of families, funded by the sale of a portion of township land and overseen by elected directors. Teachers often boarded with local citizens, who contributed their labor to the construction and maintenance of the schools.

effective questions Questions posed by teachers to help students assimilate and process ideas and concepts or the skills required for learning.

empiricism Often using a scientific method and gathering data as a way of knowing.

epistemology The branch of philosophy that asks how we know what is real, the processes of knowing and learning.

essential questions Broad questions that develop deep understandings of the world we live in. They are interdisciplinary, have no one right answer and make students investigators into provocative and meaningful issues linked to their direct experiences.

Essential School The Essential School follows the Ten Common Principles that guide mastery of personalized learning experiences of a few essential subjects and skills.

ethical behavior Actions guided by particular values and moral standards.

extrinsic versus intrinsic rewards External rewards for learning or behavior, such as stars or stickers, which convey the message that learning is something you do to get something else, versus the message that it is motivated by a personal desire to learn or because the subject itself is interesting.

field independent learners versus field dependent learners Learners who can focus on a discrete phenomenon and not be distracted by its context, as contrasted with learners whose perception is strongly influenced by the field or conditions surrounding or linked to the phenomenon.

free schools Alternative schools that give children complete charge of their own learning by allowing them to choose what they learn and when. Students typically design their own program of study and evaluate their own learning.

full-service schools Schools that seek to improve education by empowering families, and typically provide after-school programs, medical services, social services, parenting courses, and counseling.

gemeinschaft Ferdinand Tonnies's term describing a community of personal relationships, offering a sense of kinship and belonging, a sense of shared place, and common goals.

gesellschaft Tonnies's term describing the impersonal aspect of society based on contractual rules and relationships, where people interact for specific purposes and are evaluated on the performance of skills.

hidden curriculum The knowledge, values, attitudes, norms of behavior, and beliefs that students acquire in schools that are not part of the formal written curriculum objectives; messages that have moral and social meaning.

higher-order questions Questions requiring students to think abstractly and make judgments; for example, to analyze, synthesize, or evaluate information.

high-stakes testing A system in which a state awards high school diplomas only to students who achieve a passing grade on the state's designated standardized test.

home schooling Education that takes place in the home with family members and/or tutors.

humanists Encourage students to actualize their unique human potential to seek lofty goals for the betterment of all by study of a classical body of knowledge that focuses on intellectual, moral, political, and social issues.

immersion An approach that teaches the curriculum in a language yet to be mastered.

inductive reasoning Reaching a conclusion based on gathering information from specific examples and generalizing from our observations.

informal leaders Those who influence others, make change happen, and dare to take on challenges.

intuition Using insight as a way of knowing.

involuntary immigrants versus voluntary immigrants Anthropologist John Ogbu's distinction between people who have come to the United States, or become part of the United States, not by choice but through slavery, conquest or colonization, and those who have immigrated of their own free will. Involuntary immigrants have internalized the effects of historical discrimination and cultural denigration and do not expect to be accepted into the dominant white society, while voluntary immigrants perceive the conditions of their lives as far better than the poorer conditions of their homelands, and temporary.

knowledge by acquaintance Understanding a phenomenon through direct sensory experience.

knowledge by description Understanding something through reading or hearing about it from a variety of authoritative sources.

land-grant colleges Higher education institutions established by the federal Morrill Act of 1862, with the proceeds of the sale of public lands, to offer a program of agricultural, mechanical, and technical studies. These grew into large state-funded universities, some of which incorporated teacher education.

learning styles The ways we process information and the conditions we need to be able to pay attention.

logic Thinking through the question and using reason, reflecting on and analyzing facts and ideas.

magnet schools Schools originally offered to counter race-based school segregation, can specialize in a curriculum area such as the arts, offer an intensified math/science program, or expand their mission to include an international perspective to education.

maturationist theory Philosophy of learning that holds that children's development is innate and grows naturally in stages to its full potential in an environment with optimal conditions.

mentor A seasoned teacher who guides, counsels, and advises new teachers through the early years of their careers.

metaphysics The branch of philosophy that asks whether reality ultimately inheres in organized physical matter—the physical world—or in logical and correct ideas.

methodology A set of procedures, an analysis of principles, a body of rules or suggested approaches.

MindStyles Gregorc's four types of learners, combining concrete or abstract styles of perception with sequential or random conception, resulting in concrete sequential, abstract sequential, concrete random, or abstract random information processors.

modeling Learning by witnessing other peoples' behavior and its consequences.

moral development approach This approach to moral education looks at students' increasing ability to make moral decisions based on growing sophistication in thinking. According to this approach, moral thinking depends on students' general cognitive capabilities, which teachers can enhance through discussions of moral questions.

multiple intelligences Howard Gardner's theory that there are many ways of being "smart," including linguistic, logical-mathematical, spatial, kinesthetic, musical, interpersonal, intrapersonal, and naturalistic.

multiple modalities Teaching using a range of auditory, visual, physical, and print materials to reach children with varied learning styles.

National Board for Professional Teaching Standards (NBPTS) A professional organization that provides a rigorous national certification process for experienced teachers.

National Council for Accreditation for Teacher Education (NCATE) A professional organization that determines competencies in the accreditation of professional education programs throughout the United States.

normal schools Early teacher preparation institutions funded by counties and, later, states that offered one or two years of study to prepare prospective teachers for county and state licensure exams. The length of study depended on whether teachers taught in rural district schools or larger cities, and whether they were elementary or secondary teachers.

null curriculum Topics and skills that educators decide not to include in the curriculum on the assumption that they are not important or valid.

object lesson Using a familiar physical object as an inductive tool for instruction; for example, examining the parts of an apple begins a lesson on seeds and propagation.

open classrooms Settings where children are free to explore and choose from a variety of activities organized in learning centers, using real materials, audio-visual aids, and educational games. Children learn independently, according to their interests and abilities.

operant conditioning A process of learning explained as an individual's responses to the environment with specific behaviors based on their having experienced the consequences of those behaviors; for example, rewards or punishments.

orality-based culture versus literacy-based culture Cultures wherein education is conveyed through stories, chants, and myths representing truths, as opposed to cultures where truth is conveyed through the written word and mastered through careful reading and study. Teachers can accommodate these differences by including both story-telling and book-centered approaches in instruction.

oratorical arts The ability to not only write well but to speak persuasively was the mark of the educated person according to some philosophies.

overt curriculum The stated or written curriculum—the subject matter and the skills to be taught that are usually listed in a teacher's grade-level curriculum guide.

pedagogy The art and science of teaching, including instructional methods and strategies.

personalized learning An approach to instruction based on a teacher's knowledge of an individual student's talents, interests, and needs, where the curriculum builds on students' experience and encourages their own questions and expression.

philosophy for children A curriculum developed by Matthew Lipman that teaches children principles of logic and ethics in simple language describing everyday events in their lives.

place-based education Curriculum is presented in context with the students' community, family, and culture.

politics The branch of philosophy that asks the question, What is just?

positive interdependence Relationships within a group in which the information, resources, or role of each member are essential in order for the group to complete its task.

primer Early readers used in colonial America whose aim was to advance literacy in the context of moral and religious lessons.

programmed instruction Use of instructional kits, teaching machines, or materials that provide systematic and sequential learning activities with immediate feedback to teach skills in all subject areas.

race A term used to describe physical differences among groups of people, mostly having to do with skin color or physical features. In common usage, it has been used to describe social and cultural differences having to do with a group's traditions, foods, or language and has been confused with religion and countries of origin.

racism An attitude that results in an action of actual discrimination against particular groups, which can include preference, exclusion, or restriction of human rights and freedoms in political, economic, social, or cultural life.

recall questions Simple questions requiring that students remember specific, discrete facts; for example, names and dates.

resistance theory The idea that individuals and minority groups can transcend, or resist, the social messages that the majority or dominant groups in society, through their institutions, attempt to convey. Therefore, what happens in schools does not perfectly correspond with or reproduce the culture and relationships in the larger society.

revelation Using faith as a way of knowing.

schoolmarm A woman who took on the tasks of teaching in the nineteenth century.

sensory experience Looking and listening, using the senses, as a way of knowing.

service learning Students work in the community as volunteers to improve living conditions and learn how governments and social agencies function.

sheltered immersion An approach to teaching limited English-speaking students, or program, which offers support to English language learners in regular classrooms.

social class A sociological term referring to a group of people with a shared economic and social status, which affects the amount of power and control they have in society and the degree to which they control the means of production of its goods and services. Social class includes wealth, education, lifestyle, and political power.

standards-based education An approach to identify the common body of knowledge and skills that need to be built into a uniform curriculum for kindergarten through grade 12.

structural functionalism The sociological theory that describes institutions such as schools as serving the purpose of providing predictable, organized social structures that allow society to function smoothly. Schools teach students the norms of behavior that contribute to maintaining social order.

syllogism A deductive form of argument based on logic.

tabula rasa Latin for "blank slate," refers to the idea that human nature is basically neutral, that what humans become depends on their environment, what experience "writes" on their slate.

teacher expectation effect A term coined by Rosenthal and Jacobson to describe the impact that teachers' differential expectations for varying groups of students may influence those students' own expectations and performance. Teacher expectations may be based on student characteristics that have nothing to do with their academic achievement.

tracking An organization plan for instruction that places middle or high school students into groups such as "honors" or "college preparatory" or "vocational" classes, resulting in sorting and selecting patterns that can limit their futures.

transmissive versus transformative functions of school The argument regarding whether the ultimate purpose of public schooling should be to transmit to a new generation what previous generations have known and been able to do, so that they can converse with each other and keep existing institutions functioning and productive, or to transform society, fostering social change and enlightening students to new possibilities for themselves, their country, and the world.

values Beliefs about what is right and important. Values guide people's choices and actions. Schools communicate values in everyday classroom life.

values clarification approach A curriculum program that helps children identify and feel proud of their own particular sets of values; based on the idea that values are individual and changing. It assumes that values are not commonly accepted absolutes, but a product of group, and even individual, experiences and orientations.

virtues approach An approach to moral education that promotes the direct teaching of a set of values that are presumed to be universal and commonly accepted. Teachers help children "do" the right thing and "be" moral.

voucher system A system of payment of tuition to a private-sector school for parents who choose the placement in lieu of a public school.

ways of knowing Epistemological approaches that define pathways to knowledge, including authority, sensory experience, empiricism, logic, intuition, and revelation.

zone of proximal development Vygotsky's concept wherein a child functioning at a cognitive level characteristic of his age can be induced to a higher level of cognitive functioning if he is exposed to reasoning that is at the next higher level but still accessible to his powers of understanding.

zero tolerance policy Strict enforcement by schools of rules against acts of violence and bringing weapons to school, without exception. Consequences may include expulsion and referral to the criminal or juvenile justice system.

INDEX